IISS

THE MILITARY BALANCE 1994-1995

Published by BRASSEY'S for

THE INTERNATIONAL INSTITUTE FOR STRATEGIC STUDIES
23 Tavistock Street
London WC2E 7NQ

THE MILITARY BALANCE 1994–1995

Published by Brassey's (UK) Ltd for
The International Institute for Strategic Studies
23 Tavistock Street, London WC2E 7NQ

This publication has been prepared by the Director of the Institute and his Staff, who accept full responsibility for its contents. These do not, and indeed cannot, represent a consensus of views among the worldwide membership of the Institute as a whole.

First published October 1994

ISBN 1 85753 115 9
ISSN 0459-7222

The Military Balance 1994–1995 (ISSN 0459 7222) is published by Brassey's (UK) Ltd, 33 John Street, London, WC1N 2AT. All orders accompanied with payment should be sent directly to Marston Book Services, PO Box 87, Oxford OX2 0DT, UK. 1994 single copy rate is UK and overseas £37.00. North America $59.00. Airfreight and mailing in the USA by Publications Expediting Inc, 200 Meacham Avenue, Elmont, New York 11003, USA.
USA POSTMASTER: send address changes to Military Balance, Publications Expediting Inc, 200 Meacham Avenue, Elmont, New York 11003, USA. Application to mail at second-class postage is pending at Jamaica, New York 11431. All other despatches outside the UK by Printflow Air within Europe and Printflow Airsaver outside Europe.

PRINTED IN THE UK by Halstan & Co. Ltd, Amersham, Bucks.

CONTENTS

The Military Balance normally includes tables providing information on nuclear delivery means and a comparison of the defence expenditure and military manpower of all the countries listed. There is also a list of the type, name/designation, maker and country of origin of all aircraft and helicopters mentioned in *The Military Balance*. This year, because of page length overrun, they have been omitted. The tables have, however, been prepared and any reader requiring one or more of these tables can obtain them by writing to the Editor at the IISS. Please send £1.00 or $1.50 to cover the cost of printing and postage. These tables and a greater number of maps than previously will be published in *The Military Balance* next year when a new printing contract comes into force.

THE MILITARY BALANCE 1994–1995
LAYOUT AND PRINCIPLES OF COMPILATION

The Military Balance is updated each year to provide a timely, quantitative assessment of the military forces and defence expenditures of over 160 countries. The current volume contains data as of 1 June 1994 (although any significant developments that occurred in June and July are also reported). This chapter explains how *The Military Balance* is structured and outlines the general principles followed. The format for country entries remains the same as in the 1993–94 edition.

The break-up of the Soviet Union necessitated a re-evaluation of the way in which *The Military Balance* divides the world into geographical sections. Russia is both a European and an Asian state and is given a separate section in the book. *The Military Balance* assumes that Russia has taken on all former USSR overseas deployments unless there is specific evidence to the contrary. All the strategic nuclear forces of the former Soviet Union are shown in the Russian section as there still appears to be an attempt at joint control under the aegis of the Commonwealth of Independent States (CIS), and those not located in Russia are due to be eliminated. Those forces located in other republics are listed again in the relevant country entry. The section on 'Non-NATO Europe' now includes the Baltic republics, Belarus, Ukraine, Moldova and the three Transcaucasian republics (Azerbaijan, Armenia and Georgia). The latter have been included in Europe as signatories of the Conventional Armed Forces in Europe (CFE) Treaty. Bosnia-Herzegovina, Croatia, Macedonia and Slovenia are listed as independent, while Serbia and Montenegro are shown in a single entry as the follow-on states to the Federal Republic of Yugoslavia. There are now two Asian sections. 'Central and Southern Asia' covers the five Central Asian republics of the former Soviet Union (Kazakhstan, Kyrgyzstan, Tajikistan, Turkmenistan and Uzbekistan), Afghanistan, Bangladesh, India, Myanmar (Burma), Nepal, Pakistan and Sri Lanka. The remaining Asian countries are in the 'East Asia and Australasia' section (with China no longer receiving individual-section status). In the 'Sub-Saharan Africa' and the 'Caribbean and Latin America' sections, countries are no longer set out in alphabetical order throughout the sections, but are now grouped in sub-sections: East Africa, Central Africa, Southern Africa, and so on.

GENERAL ARRANGEMENT

There are two parts to *The Military Balance*. The first comprises national entries grouped by region; the Index on p. 12 gives the page reference for each national entry. Regional groupings are preceded by a short introduction describing the strategic issues facing the region, and significant changes in the defence postures, economic status and military-aid arrangements of the countries concerned. Inclusion of a country or state in no way implies legal recognition or IISS approval of it.

The second section contains more general analysis and tables, and includes three descriptive essays. The first examines developments in the field of Weapons of Mass Destruction (WMD): progress towards implementing the Strategic Arms Reduction Talks (START I) Treaty; the assistance being provided for the elimination of the nuclear weapons of the former Soviet Union; the nuclear test moratorium; targetting; the future of the Nuclear Non-Proliferation Treaty (NPT); the possibility of a fissile material production ban; progress towards a Comprehensive Test Ban Treaty (CTBT); North Korea and proliferation; and developments in the Chemical Weapons Convention (CWC) and the Missile Technology Control Regime (MTCR). The second essay covers all other aspects of arms control including: the CFE Treaty two years after it came into force; the new United Nations (UN) Register of Conventional Weapons; and the Conference for Security and Cooperation in Europe (CSCE). The third describes how the

IISS estimates and interprets data on defence expenditure. There is also a summary of the composition of all United Nations and other peacekeeping forces, together with a short description of their missions. In the 1993–94 edition of *The Military Balance*, a 'Reader Reaction Questionnaire' was enclosed. The main recommendations of readers who returned the questionnaire are set out on p. 286 of this edition.

A list of all the abbreviations and symbols used is printed on a card which can be detached from the book for easier use. A loose wall-map is provided which covers the territory of the former Soviet Union; it shows the internal administrative and Military District borders of Russia, gives the locations of strategic nuclear weapons and illustrates the armament holdings of all former Soviet Union republics and, where relevant, the CFE limit.

ABBREVIATIONS AND DEFINITIONS

Space limitations necessitate the use of abbreviations. The abbreviation may have both singular or plural meanings, for example, 'elm' = 'element' or 'elements'. The qualification 'some' means *up to*, whilst 'about' means *the total could be higher than given*. In financial data, the $ sign refers to US dollars unless otherwise stated; the term billion (bn) signifies 1,000 million (m). Footnotes particular to a country entry or table are indicated by letters, while those which apply throughout the book are marked by symbols (i.e., * for training aircraft counted by the IISS as combat capable, and † where serviceability of equipment is in doubt).

NATIONAL ENTRIES

Information on each country is given in a format as standard as the available information permits: economic and demographic data; military data, including manpower, length of conscript service, outline organisation, number of formations and units; and an inventory of the major equipments of each service, followed where applicable by a description of their deployment. Details of national forces stationed abroad and of foreign stationed forces are also given.

GENERAL MILITARY DATA

Manpower

The 'Active' total comprises all servicemen and women on full-time duty (including conscripts and long-term assignments from the Reserves). Under the heading 'Terms of service', only the length of conscript service is shown; where service is voluntary, there is no entry.

In *The Military Balance* the term 'Reserve' is used to describe formations and units not fully manned or operational in peacetime, but which can be mobilised by recalling reservists in an emergency. Unless otherwise indicated, the 'Reserves' entry includes all reservists committed to rejoining the armed forces in an emergency, except when national reserve service obligations following conscription last almost a lifetime. *The Military Balance* estimates of effective reservist strengths are based on the numbers available within five years of completing full-time service, unless there is good evidence that obligations are enforced for longer. Some countries have more than one category of Reserves, often kept at varying degrees of readiness; where possible these differences are denoted using the national descriptive title, but always under the heading of 'Reserves' to distinguish them from full-time active forces.

Other Forces

Many countries maintain paramilitary forces whose training, organisation, equipment and control suggest they may be usable in support, or in lieu, of regular military forces. These are listed, and their roles described, after the military forces of each country; their manpower is not normally included in the Armed Forces totals at the start of each entry. Home Guard units are counted as paramilitary. Where paramilitary groups are not on full-time active duty, the suffix (R) is added after the title to indicate that they have reserve status. When internal opposition forces are armed and appear to pose a significant threat to the security of a state, their details are listed separately after national paramilitary forces.

Equipment

Numbers are shown by function and type and represent total holdings, including active and reserve operational and training units and 'in store' stocks. Inventory totals for missile systems (e.g., SSM, SAM, ATGW, etc.) relate to launchers and not to missiles.

Stocks of equipment held in reserve and not assigned to either active or reserve units are listed as 'in store'. However, aircraft in excess of unit establishment holdings, held for such purposes as to allow repair and modification or immediate replacement, are not shown 'in store'. This accounts for apparent disparities between unit strengths and aircraft inventory strength.

Operational Deployments

The Military Balance does not normally list short-term operational deployments, particularly where military operations are in progress. An exception to this rule is made in the case of peacekeeping operations. The contribution or deployment of forces on operations are normally covered in the text preceding each regional section.

GROUND FORCES

The national designation is normally used for army formations. The term 'regiment' can be misleading. In some cases it is essentially a brigade of all arms; in others, a grouping of battalions of a single arm; and lastly (the UK and French usage) a battalion-sized unit. The sense intended is indicated. Where there is no standard organisation the intermediate levels of command are shown as HQs, followed by the total numbers of units which could be allocated between them. Where a unit's title overstates its real capability, the title is in inverted commas, and an estimate of the comparable North Atlantic Treaty Organisation (NATO) unit size in parentheses: 'bde' (coy).

Equipment

The Military Balance uses the same definitions as those agreed to at the CFE negotiations. These are:

Battle Tank (MBT): An armoured tracked combat vehicle weighing at least 16.5 metric tonnes unladen, maybe armed with a 360° traverse gun of at least 75mm calibre. Any new wheeled combat vehicles entering service which meet these criteria will be considered battle tanks.

Armoured Personnel Carrier (APC): A lightly armoured combat vehicle designed and equipped to transport an infantry squad, armed with integral/organic weapons of less than 20mm calibre. Versions of APC converted for other uses (such as weapons platforms, command posts, communications terminals) which do not allow infantry to be transported are considered 'look-alikes' and are not regarded as treaty-limited equipment (TLE), but are subject to verification.

Armoured Infantry Fighting Vehicle (AIFV): An armoured combat vehicle designed and equipped to transport an infantry squad, armed with an integral/organic cannon of at least 20mm calibre. There are also AIFV 'look-alikes'.

Heavy Armoured Combat Vehicle (HACV): An armoured combat vehicle weighing more than six metric tonnes unladen, with an integral/organic direct-fire gun of at least 75mm (which does not fall within the definitions of APC, AIFV or MBT). *The Military Balance* does not list

HACV separately, but under their equipment type (light tank, recce or assault gun), and where appropriate annotates them as HACV.

Artillery: Systems with calibres of 100mm and above, capable of engaging ground targets by delivering primarily indirect fire, namely guns, howitzers, gun/howitzers, multiple-rocket launchers (MRL) and mortars.

Weapons with bores of less than 14.5mm are not listed, nor, for major armies, are hand-held ATK weapons.

Military Formation Strengths

The manpower strength, equipment holdings and organisation of formations such as brigades and divisions differ widely from state to state. Where possible, the normal composition of formations is given in parentheses. It should be noted that where divisions and brigades are listed, only separate brigades are counted and not those included in divisions. The table which showed the manpower and equipment strength of divisions has been discontinued as these are being restructured in most countries following the end of the Cold War.

NAVAL FORCES

Categorisation is based partly on operational role, partly on weapon fit and partly on displacement. Ship classes are identified by the name of the first ship of that class, except where a class is recognised by another name (e.g., *Krivak, Kotlin*, etc.). Where the class is based on a foreign design, the original class name is added in parentheses.

Each class of vessel is given an acronym designator based on the NATO system. All designators are included in the list of abbreviations on the perforated card inserted in the book.

The term 'ship' refers to vessels of over both 1,000 tonnes full-load displacement and 60 metres overall length; vessels of lesser displacement, but of 16m or more overall length, are termed 'craft'. Vessels of less than 16m overall length are not included.

The term 'commissioning' has different meanings in a number of navies. In *The Military Balance* the term is used to mean that a ship has completed fitting out, initial sea trials, and has a naval crew; operational training may not have been completed, but in all other respects the ship is available for service. 'Decommissioning' means that a ship has been removed from operational duty and the bulk of its naval crew transferred. De-storing and dismantling of weapons may not have started.

Classifications and Definitions

To aid comparison between fleets, naval entries have been subdivided into the following categories, which do not necessarily agree with national categorisation:

Submarines: Submarines with SLBM are listed separately under 'Strategic Nuclear Forces'.

Principal Surface Combatants: These include all surface ships with both 1,000 tonnes full-load displacement and a weapons system other than for self-protection. They comprise aircraft carriers (with a flight-deck extending beyond two-thirds of the vessel's length); battleships (armour-protected, over 30,000 tonnes, and with armour-protected guns of at least 250mm bore); cruisers (over 8,000 tonnes) and destroyers (less than 8,000 tonnes), both of which normally have an anti-air-warfare role and may also have an anti-submarine capability; and frigates (less than 8,000 tonnes) which normally have an anti-submarine role.

Patrol and Coastal Combatants: These are ships and craft whose primary role relates to the protection of the sea approaches and coastline of a state. Included are: corvettes (600–1,000 tonnes carrying weapons systems other than for self-protection); missile craft (with permanently fitted missile-launcher ramps and control equipment); and torpedo craft (with an anti-surface-ship capability). Ships and craft which fall outside these definitions are classified as 'patrol'.

Mine Warfare: This category covers surface vessels configured primarily for mine-laying or mine countermeasures, which can be minehunters, mine-sweepers or dual-capable vessels.

A further classification divides both coastal and patrol combatants and mine-warfare vessels into: offshore (over 600 tonnes); coastal (300–600 tonnes); and inshore (less than 300 tonnes).

Amphibious: Only ships specifically procured and employed to disembark troops and their equipment over unprepared beachheads have been listed. Vessels with an amphibious capability, but which are known not to be assigned to amphibious duties, are not included. Amphibious craft are listed at the end of each entry.

Support and Miscellaneous: This category of essentially non-military vessels provides some indication of the operational sustainability and outreach of the navy concerned.

Weapons Systems: Weapons are listed in the order in which they contribute to the ship's primary operational role. After the word 'plus' are added significant weapons relating to the ship's secondary role. Self-defence weapons are not listed. To merit inclusion, a SAM system must have an anti-missile range of 10km or more, and guns must be of 100mm bore or greater.

Aircraft: The CFE definition of combat aircraft does not cover maritime aircraft. All armed aircraft, including anti-submarine-warfare and some maritime reconnaissance aircraft, are included as combat aircraft in naval inventories.

Organisations: Naval groupings such as fleets and squadrons are often temporary and changeable; organisation is only shown where it is meaningful.

AIR FORCES

The following remarks refer to aviation units forming an integral part of ground forces, naval forces and (where applicable) marines, as well as to separate air forces.

The term 'combat aircraft' comprises aircraft normally equipped to deliver ordnance in air-to-air or air-to-surface combat. The 'combat' totals include aircraft in operational units (OCU) whose main role is weapons training, and training aircraft of the same type as those in front-line squadrons and assumed to be available for operations at short notice. (Training aircraft considered to be combat-capable are marked by an asterisk: *.) Where armed maritime aircraft are held by air forces, these are not included in combat aircraft totals.

Air force operational groupings are shown where known. Squadron aircraft strengths vary; attempts have been made to separate total holdings from reported establishment strength.

The number of categories of aircraft listed is kept to a minimum. 'Fighter' is used to denote aircraft with the capability (weapons, avionics, performance) for aerial combat. Dual-capable aircraft are shown as FGA, fighter and so on, according to the role in which they are deployed. Different countries often use the same basic aircraft in different roles; the key to determining these roles lies mainly in air-crew training. For bombers, 'long-range' means having an unrefuelled radius of action of over 5,000km, 'medium-range' 1,000–5,000km and 'short-range' less than 1,000km; light bombers are those with a payload of under 10,000kg (which is no greater than the payload of many FGA).

The CFE Treaty lists three types of helicopters: attack (equipped to employ anti-armour, air-to-ground or air-to-air guided weapons by means of an integrated fire control and aiming system); combat support (which may or may not be armed with self-defence or area-suppression weapons, but do not have a control and guidance system); and unarmed transport helicopters. *The Military Balance* uses the term 'attack' in the CFE sense, and the term 'assault' to describe armed helicopters used to deliver infantry or other troops on the battlefield. Except in the case of CFE signatories, *The Military Balance* continues to employ the term 'armed helicopters' to cover those equipped to deliver ordnance, including ASW ordnance.

ECONOMIC AND DEMOGRAPHIC DATA

Defence economic data are provided in the first section under individual country entries, and in the second section under Tables and Analyses. The intention is to give a concise measure wherever possible of the absolute and relative defence effort and military potential of a country expressed in terms of defence expenditure, economic performance and demography. A more detailed explanation of the IISS methodology is given on p. 278.

Defence expenditure

Where possible, the data shown under individual country entries include both past (expenditure) and planned (budgetary) figures denominated at current prices in both national currencies and US$ at average market or, as appropriate, official exchange rates. In a few clearly marked cases, a purchasing-power-parity (ppp) $ exchange rate has been used. Available data for the two most recent years (typically 1992 and 1993) and the latest defence budgetary data for the current year (as at 30 June 1994) are cited.

In the case of NATO member-states, both national and NATO accounts of defence spending are provided. NATO uses a standardised definition of defence expenditure which includes all spending on national military forces, including pensions, host-government expenses for other NATO forces stationed in the country, allocated NATO common funding costs covering the three separate military, civilian staff and infrastructure accounts, foreign military assistance, and expenditure on paramilitary forces where these have a military role.

Data on foreign military assistance (FMA) refer to the USA unless otherwise specified. US foreign military assistance covers grants and loans for equipment purchases – Foreign Military Financing (FMF) – International Military Education and Training (IMET) funds and economic aid with a military end-use. The terminology of US military aid will change in 1995, with FMF being termed Military Assistance (MA) and IMET becoming Direct Training (DT). Details of US support for narcotics (Narcs) interdiction and control are also provided. Financial data on military assistance from other nations are identified where these are available.

Economic performance

Each country entry includes the following economic performance indicators for the latest two years available: nominal GDP at current market prices denominated in both the national currency and US$; real GDP growth; annual inflation measured by the consumer price index; and either one of two measures of debt. In the case of Organisation for Economic Cooperation and Development (OECD) countries, the measure used is gross public debt as a proportion of GDP; and for other countries, including former communist economies in transition, it is gross public and private-sector foreign debt denominated in US$. Average annual market exchange rates of the national currency with the US$, or, where necessary, official exchange rates, are provided. In a few cases where currency exchange rate distortions result in a misleading figure, ppp measures have been calculated. Otherwise, the UN System of National Accounts has been used for the primary economic indicators. This year, for the first time, GDP *per capita* has been included as an additional economic performance indicator; and readers should note that this measure has been calculated according to purchasing-power parity, not market or official exchange rates, and often differs (in some cases substantially) from calculations derived from exchange rates. GDP *per capita* data for 1992 and 1993 have been extrapolated from calculations for years up to 1991.

Demography

Population aggregates are based on the most recent official census data. In the absence of recent official census information, the source for demographic data is *World Population Projections*.

Disaggregated demographic data for three age groups (13–17, 18–22 and 23–32) of both sexes are provided as an indication of the human capital stock potentially available for military service.

Sources

International Financial Statistics (IMF)
Government Financial Statistics Yearbook (IMF)
World Economic Outlook (IMF)
OECD Economic Outlook (OECD)
World Tables (World Bank)
World Debt Tables (World Bank)
World Development Report (World Bank)
World Population Projections (World Bank)
Penn World Table (Mark 5.5) (National Bureau of Economic Research)
Human Development Report (UN)
Economic Survey of Europe in 1993–94 (UN)
IMF Economic Reviews (IMF)
Economic Panorama of Latin America (UN)
Economic and Social Progress in Latin America (IDB)
Key Indicators (Asian Development Bank)
Asian Development Outlook (Asian Development Bank)
African Development Report (African Development Bank)
Les Etats d'Afrique, de l'océan Indien et des Caraïbes (Ministère de la Coopération, France)
World Military Expenditures and Arms Transfers 1991–92 (ACDA)
Military Expenditure Register (UN Centre for Disarmament Affairs)

WARNING

The Military Balance is a quantitative assessment of the personnel strengths and equipment holdings of the world's armed forces. It is in no way an assessment of their capabilities. It does not attempt to evaluate the quality of units or equipment, nor the impact of geography, doctrine, military technology, deployment, training, logistic support, morale, leadership, tactical or strategic initiative, terrain, weather, political will or support from alliance partners.

The Institute is in no position to evaluate and compare directly the performance of items of equipment. Those who wish to do so can use the data provided to construct their own force comparisons. As essays in many past editions of *The Military Balance* have made clear, however, such comparisons are replete with difficulties, and their validity and utility cannot but be suspect.

The Military Balance provides the actual numbers of nuclear and conventional forces and weapons based on the most accurate data available, or, failing that, on the best estimate that can be made with a reasonable degree of confidence – this is not the number that would be assumed for verification purposes in arms-control agreements, although it is attempted to provide this information as well.

The data presented each year in *The Military Balance* reflect judgments based on information available to the Director and Staff of the Institute at the time the book is compiled. Information may differ from previous editions for a variety of reasons, generally as a result of substantive changes in national forces, but in some cases as a result of IISS reassessment of the evidence supporting past entries. Inevitably, over the course of time it has become apparent that some information presented in earlier versions was erroneous, or insufficiently supported by reliable evidence. Hence, it is not always possible to construct valid time-series comparisons from information given in successive editions, although in the text which introduces each regional section an attempt is made to distinguish between new acquisitions and revised assessments.

CONCLUSION

The Institute owes no allegiance to any government, group of governments, or any political or other organisation. Its assessments are its own, based on the material available to it from a wide variety of sources. The cooperation of all governments has been sought and, in many cases, received. Not all countries have been equally cooperative, and some of the figures have necessarily been estimated. Pains are taken to ensure that these estimates are as professional and free from bias as possible. The Institute owes a considerable debt to a number of its own Members and consultants who have helped in compiling and checking material. The Director and Staff of the Institute assume full responsibility for the facts and judgments contained in this study. They welcome comments and suggestions on the data presented, since they seek to make them as accurate and comprehensive as possible.

Readers may use items of information from *The Military Balance* as required, without applying for permission from the Institute, on condition that the IISS and *The Military Balance* are cited as the source in any published work. However, reproduction of major portions of *The Military Balance* must be approved in writing by the Deputy Director of the Institute prior to publication.

October 1994

The Editor of *The Military Balance* is grateful to the following countries who have assisted in the compilation of this edition by either vetting and correcting the draft entry for their country or providing the Institute with copies of Treaty (CFE/CSCE) data exchange documents:

Albania, Argentina, Armenia, Australia, Austria, Azerbaijan, Bahamas, Belarus, Belgium, Brazil, Bulgaria, Cape Verde, Colombia, Czech Republic, Denmark, Finland, France, Germany, Greece, Guyana, Hungary, Iceland, Italy, Japan, Kazakhstan, Kyrgyzstan, Latvia, Malta, Moldova, Mongolia, Netherlands, New Zealand, Norway, Poland, ROC (Taipei), Romania, Russia, Singapore, Slovenia, Spain, Sri Lanka, Switzerland, Thailand, Turkey, United Kingdom, United States, Uruguay, Venezuela, Yugoslavia and Zimbabwe.

(Because of interpretation and definitional differences, and of information dates, *The Military Balance* does not always reflect exactly the data provided by countries.)

INDEX OF COUNTRIES

The United States

Defence Policy

The last 12 months have been a period of change and uncertainty for the US Armed Forces. In September 1993, the much-heralded *Bottom-Up Review: Forces for a New Era* was published by the then Secretary of Defense, Les Aspin. The *Review* announced cuts in all services, bar the US Marine Corps, to be effected by FY1999, further to those already required to reach the FY1995 Base Force. Even so, the *Bottom-Up Review* plans will cost some $13 billion above the Administration's (as opposed to the Defense Department's) planned defence budgets up to 1999, despite $107bn in savings that the *Review* secures compared with the Bush Administration's plans. A National Security Strategy Paper, allegedly demonstrating wide differences of opinion between the Defense Department and the State Department's perceptions of national security, has been drafted but not yet released. Both the Secretary of Defense and the Chairman of the Joint Chiefs of Staff have changed in the past year: Secretary Aspin was forced to resign, and General Colin Powell retired. Aspin was replaced, after one false start, by his former deputy, William Perry, one of the main formulators of the *Bottom-Up Review*. The Defense Budget is seriously threatened by cuts likely to be made by Congress and would have been even more threatened had the Balanced Budget Amendment become law. The Defense Authorization Act, approved by Congress in November 1993, authorised an independent one-year study, *The Commission on Roles and Missions of the Armed Forces*, as a number of Congressmen were severely critical of General Powell's report, *Roles, Missions and Functions of the Armed Services*, published in February 1993, which they had hoped would recommend far more substantial changes than it did.

Bottom-Up Review

The *Bottom-Up Review* was based on the assessment that the US must be capable of fighting and winning two nearly simultaneous major regional conflicts (MRC) (the scenarios envisaged were a repeat of *Operation Desert Storm* in the Gulf, but with Iraqi forces at their post-war strength, and another Korean war). The two-MRC basis for force structure was decided on, not because two such conflicts are expected to erupt simultaneously, but because should the US embark on one conflict, it must have sufficient force available to deter a second from breaking out. The major savings resulting from implementing the *Review* will be achieved by cutting two active and one reserve army division; three active and four reserve air force wings; 55 surface ships and submarines; one aircraft carrier; and one active and one reserve naval air wing. Procurement projects cancelled include the Advanced Fighter Experimental (A/FX), the Multi-Role Fighter, and the production of F-16 aircraft after FY1994 and F/A-18CD naval aircraft after FY1997. Emphasis and increased priority has been given to: prepositioning Army equipment (in the same way as the US Marine Corps prepositions equipment packs at sea); increasing the readiness of a proportion of the Army National Guard (ARNG); providing additional air- and sealift; improving precision-guided weapons and Command, Control, Communications and Intelligence (C^3I) assets; and, for the first time for several budget requests, the Defense Department recommends developing the V-22 *Osprey* tilt-wing tactical transport aircraft for the US Marine Corps (previously this project, not backed by the Defense Department, was reinstated each year into the Defense Budget by Congress).

Peacekeeping

US security policy is still ambiguous in the field of peacekeeping, despite the Clinton Administration's *Policy on Reforming Multilateral Peace Operations*, issued by the White House in May 1994. The ease with which the US-led, and predominantly US-manned, coalition defeated Iraq in *Operation Desert Storm*, thanks mainly to General Powell's policy of reliance on overwhelming force, completed the process of restoring the US armed forces' confidence and pride in their professionalism, and helped to bury the spectre of Vietnam. However, the policy of deploying massive force did not appear to work in Somalia where, although the delivery of humanitarian aid was successful, military operations in Mogadishu against General Aideed's faction were not. Some blame this lack of success on insufficient force, pointing to Secretary Aspin's refusal to allow the deployment of main battle tanks. The most likely reasons, however, were a lack of good intelligence and a failure to understand the principles of low-intensity warfare. The main thrust of those advocating restructuring the armed forces is to prevent duplication. The Army light divisions are seen as purely duplicating the capability of the US Marine Corps (without the amphibious aspects), whereas light divisions are ideal for low-intensity and, more importantly, peacekeeping operations. There is, however, a widely held opinion that the US Armed Forces are there purely to win wars and should not be diverted from training to retain this capability by indulging in peacekeeping. The muddled thinking is well illustrated by the Clinton Administration which, on the one hand, was keen to use air power in Bosnia (despite some in the military who doubted the wisdom of this) and is prepared to provide large-scale peacekeeping forces (as many as 25,000 perhaps), but only after a fully agreed peace settlement is reached; but, on the other hand, is unwilling to deploy relatively small-scale reinforcements for the UN Protection Forces in the former Yugoslavia (UNPROFOR) to guarantee that the various small windows of opportunity, such as the Sarajevo cease-fire and the Muslim–Croat armistice which urgently need troops to monitor them, remain open. However, the Army is preparing for seemingly inevitable deployments in peace operations. A tactical doctrine is being developed for peace operations in their widest context and training exercises and programmes prepared particularly for units in US Army Europe. European Command (EUCOM) will be responsible for mounting the two most likely contingencies: the 25,000-strong force earmarked for Bosnia following an overall agreement; and the 6,000-strong force notionally earmarked for deployment on the Golan Heights following an Israeli–Syrian peace treaty.

Counter-proliferation

The proliferation of weapons of mass destruction was identified in the *Bottom-Up Review* as a primary threat to the US. A new post of Assistant Secretary of Defense for Nuclear Security and Counterproliferation has been established in the Defense Department to oversee counter-proliferation programmes. The comprehensive policy is divided into two parts, prevention and protection. Prevention, an inter-agency responsibility, comprises: discussion, designed to convince states that their interests are best served by not acquiring weapons of mass destruction; denial, through export controls and other supply measures; arms control; and international pressure, including publicity, isolation and sanctions. The Defense Department has special responsibility for the second part – protection. This includes: defusing tension with confidence-building measures; assistance with weapon dismantlement, safety and security; deterrence; offence, by developing measures to penetrate underground structures, hunt mobile launchers and so on; and defence, with warning systems, theatre missile defence and vaccines and antidotes for chemical and biological weapons.

Nuclear Developments

No fresh nuclear arms-control measures have been instituted in the last 12 months. However, at the Moscow summit in January 1994, President Clinton agreed to purchase 500 tons of highly enriched uranium (HEU) from Russia once it had been removed from nuclear warheads and converted into low-enriched uranium (LEU). He also agreed that Russia should receive an advance payment of $60m, in return for which Russia would supply Ukraine with 100 tons of LEU while Ukraine would transfer to Russia 200 nuclear warheads and would remove all the warheads from its 46 SS-24 ICBM by November 1994. President Clinton has extended the US nuclear test moratorium by a further 12 months until the end of September 1995. Presidents Clinton and

Yeltsin also agreed that neither US nor Russian nuclear missiles would be targeted at each other. To ensure this, either the targeting data component would be removed, or the missile re-targeted towards the open sea.

Strategic Forces

Although neither the Strategic Arms Reduction Talks Treaty (START) I or II have yet come into force, the US has continued to eliminate significant numbers of its strategic nuclear weapons. No new SSBN have been commissioned, but the seventh *Ohio*-class armed with *Trident* D-5 SLBM is due to commission before the end of FY1994 and three more are at various stages of construction. During the last 12 months, six *Trident* C-4 armed SSBN have been decommissioned. However, under START elimination rules, the US is still counted as having 16 *Poseidon* C-3 and 112 *Trident* C-4 accountable launchers in eight non-operational SSBN. There has been no change to the US long-term (post-START II) plan to deploy 18 SSBN armed with *Trident* C-4 and D-5 SLBM with no more than the Treaty limit of 1,750 warheads.

The elimination of *Minuteman* II ICBM has continued apace. 135 have been taken from their silos in the last 12 months and the remaining 126 have had their guidance and warhead components removed and are thus non-operational. There are now 302 non-deployed, but START-accountable ICBM. However, there has been an increase in deployed *Minuteman* III: 529 compared to the 500 when START was signed in July 1991. Then there were 74 non-deployed *Minuteman* III missiles, but it is not known whether the US intends to deploy any more of these as *Minuteman* II silos become available. So far only two ICBM silos have been destroyed. *Minuteman* III ICBM are to be maintained in service until at least 2010, with the rocket motors for all three stages being refurbished. ICBM will be concentrated at three bases: Malmstrom, Montana; Minot, North Dakota; and Warren, Wyoming. Long-term, post-START II plans remain as the deployment of 500 single warhead *Minuteman* III. It is probable that Mark 21 warheads currently deployed on *Peacekeeper* ICBM will be installed in single-warhead *Minuteman* III. The Defense Department does not anticipate the development of a new ICBM for at least 15 years.

In the strategic bomber force, all B-52 G bombers have been retired and transferred to the conversion/elimination facility at Davis-Monthan Air Force Base where a total of 237 heavy bombers await disposal. During the last 12 months, a total of 127 B-52C/D/E/F bombers have been eliminated in accordance with START I rules. The first B-2A squadron is forming. So far it has only two aircraft, but the squadron is expected to be operational by 1997. The B-1B bomber will, as permitted by Article IV of START II, be reoriented for a conventional role by the end of 1997 when it is planned to have only 60 aircraft in squadron service. For the first time, the Reserves are being equipped with heavy bombers; two Air National Guard (ANG) squadrons will have B-1B, and one Air Force Reserve (AFR) squadron will have B-52H bombers.

As a follow-up to the *Bottom-Up Review*, a comprehensive study of US nuclear forces is being conducted. Until the study is completed and its recommendations accepted, and assuming both START I and START II are ratified and implemented, the long-term size and shape of US nuclear forces by the year 2003 is expected to be:

- 500 single-warhead *Minuteman* III ICBM;
- 18 *Trident* SSBN, each with 24 C-4 or D-5 missiles, but with no more than 1,750 warheads;
- 48 B-52H bombers equipped with ALCM-B and ACM (maximum load eight internal and 12 external missiles);
- 20 B-2 bombers carrying B-61 or B-83 gravity bombs (maximum load 16 bombs).

Ballistic Missile Defence (BMD)

The Ballistic Missile Defence Organisation (BMDO), which replaced the Strategic Defense Initiative Organisation (SDIO) in May 1993, has as its first priority the early fielding of a Theater Missile Defense (TMD) system. In his report to the President and Congress, the Secretary of

Defense argued for the deployment of TMD based on *Patriot* (PAC 3) and an upgraded *Aegis* Standard Missile Block NA for a seaborne capability. These are both point-defence systems, and area defence would be covered by the Theater High Altitude Area Defence (THAAD) system.

The change in emphasis from strategic to theatre defence has allowed all three services to pursue their own projects. The Army has recommended, and the Defense Department has accepted, that *Patriot* will give way to the more lethal Extended Range Interceptor (ERINT). The Air Force, in collaboration with the BMDO, is developing an air-launched anti-missile missile. The basic theory is to attack incoming missiles in the atmosphere during their ascent phase with a defensive missile armed with individually targetted kinetic energy interceptors. This will require an interception within 20–80 seconds of launch. For the Navy, US Atlantic Command has established a task force to develop and test how TMD can best be integrated into the Adaptive Joint Task Force concept (see below). There is no doubt that in some scenarios an afloat TMD capability will be simpler to introduce into the theatre than a ground-based one.

Conventional Forces

US Atlantic Command (USLANTCOM), originally a purely naval command, has been re-established as a Joint Service Command with a new acronym (USACOM) and with greatly increased responsibilities. USACOM is now responsible for training and deploying units of all services in the continental USA, and Air Combat Command, Army Forces Command and Marine Forces Atlantic will now report to USACOM for training and operational matters, and to their own Service Chief for personnel and logistic requirements. USACOM is taking the lead in developing a new concept, 'Adaptive Joint Force Package', which provides for tailored force packages from all required elements of the armed forces, under an already-established joint headquarters, to deploy for contingency operations either on a stand-alone basis, or to reinforce an overseas command.

Ground Forces

The Military Balance 1993–1994 prematurely recorded the disbanding of two US Army infantry divisions which were still, albeit at much reduced strength, in the order of battle in January 1994. They will finally disband during FY1994 and so are not listed in this edition. Apart from this, there have been no changes to the number of active or reserve divisions and independent brigades in the last 12 months in either the Army or Marine Corps, although Army manpower strength has been reduced. Active Army strength is 26,300 lower, and Marine Corps manpower is 9,000 less at 174,000. Two more Army divisions are to be disbanded by FY1999. However, in future, all divisions will field three active brigades and the 'roundout' practice of the reserves finding the third brigade in some divisions will cease. The main changes have been in the air-defence area. More *Patriot* batteries have been added, and only ten more are needed to complete the target of nine battalions each of six batteries. The active Army has disbanded its last *Hawk* battalions and has formed three battalions equipped with *Avenger* SAM (eight *Stinger* SAM mounted on a High Mobility Multipurpose Wheeled Vehicle (HMMWV)). The ANG has received its first *Patriot* to form one battalion of four batteries, a fourth *Hawk* battalion has been formed, as has the first to be equipped with *Avenger*. Marine Corps air-defence assets have also been improved with *Avenger* SAM and more improved *Hawk* for the Marine Reserves.

Considerable numbers of Army weapons have been disposed of. During 1993 the US exported over 2,000 tanks, of which the great majority were surplus to requirements and were passed to other North Atlantic Treaty Organisation (NATO) countries under the 'cascading' scheme. Tank numbers have dropped since June 1993 from 15,120 to 14,520. Tank holdings in Europe have dropped dramatically from 5,900 when the Conventional Armed Forces in Europe (CFE) Treaty came into force, to under 2,000 in 1994, well below the Treaty ceiling of 4,006. Some 200 AH-1S and nearly 400 UH-1 helicopters have been taken out of service. Equipment increases include 50 MLRS and 300 *Avenger* fire units. The Army has proposed developing an extended-range version which would double the ATACMS 100km range. This development may aggravate the disagreement between the Army and Air Force over the control of long-range missiles.

The US Army presence in Germany has also been further reduced, and manpower now totals 81,000 (down from 98,000). The Berlin Garrison, along with those of the other allies, will have been totally withdrawn by the end of September 1994. The Armoured Cavalry Regiment has been withdrawn and the third brigade of the infantry division is now located in the US. The US Army has withdrawn over 3,000 men from its garrison in Panama in the last 12 months and all US forces are due to have left by the end of 1999.

All United States forces had been withdrawn from Somalia by the end of March 1994. The US Army contribution to UNPROFOR in Macedonia was increased from some 300 to 500 in April 1994. In view of the increased threat from North Korea, US forces in South Korea were reinforced in April 1994 by *Patriot* units; the equivalent of a six-battery battalion with some 48 launchers was deployed, as was a unit of attack helicopters.

The Army has also established its first prepositioned stockpile afloat. Some 16 vessels have been loaded with the vehicles and equipment for an armoured brigade with its 'slice' of combat support and combat service support elements, a theatre support base, theatre opening equipment (port handling) and 30 days' supplies for the force. Initially the afloat reserve will be located at Diego Garcia and Saipan (Marianas); final siting is planned to be Diego Garcia and Thailand. Other prepositioning plans include storing two brigade sets (ashore) in the Persian Gulf region and one in South Korea.

There is to be no change to the force structure of the Marine Corps, indeed its manpower establishment is planned to be 174,000 active and 42,000 reserve, as opposed to the 170,000 (dropping to 159,000 by 1999) and 35,000 allowed for in the Base Force concept. One decision reached in General Powell's *Roles, Missions and Functions* report was that the Army would be responsible for providing, when required, additional tank and MLRS support for the Marine Corps.

A number of changes are in progress for the ground-force reserves: Army Reserve, Army National Guard and Marine Corps Reserve (MCR). The Army Reserve is to lose its manoeuvre brigades and, while retaining some combat support capability, its main responsibility will be to provide combat service support. The ARNG will man about 37 brigades (nine less then at present). Of these, 15 are to be designated enhanced readiness combat brigades. They will be associated with active divisions for training and will be organised, manned, equipped and trained so that they can be mobilised and deployed within 90 days of call-up. ARNG enhanced-readiness combat brigades will be capable of reinforcing active divisions or deploying as separate brigades.

Air Force

Under the *Bottom-Up Review*, the Air Force is due to reduce from 26.5 fighter wings to 20 (13 active and 7 reserve) general-purpose fighter wings. In the last 12 months, four active fighter squadrons have been de-activated. Over 200 more aircraft (F-4, F-11, F-15 and F-16 A/B) have been placed in store. Few new aircraft have been added to the inventory, but those that have include key aircraft: 16 F-16D multi-role fighters; nine strategic transport (six new aircraft and three from the test flight); one E-8A JSTARS radar surveillance aircraft (although the first two JSTARS aircraft played an important role in the Gulf War, they are still considered to be under development and will not become fully operational until FY1997); and three OC-135 (C-135 transports converted to carry out observation fights under the 'Open Skies' regime). The Air Force is planning to retire its F-4G *Wild Weasel* aircraft designed to locate and destroy radar-controlled air defences. These will be replaced by some modified F-15 and F-16 aircraft. In FY2000, F-15E aircraft will replace F-111F in the long-range attack role.

Naval aviation is also being restructured. While the Navy will lose two active and one reserve air wing, the Marine Corps will maintain its four air wings, although their composition will be changed. Both Naval and Marine Corps A-6 medium bomber squadrons will be deactivated.

Carrier air wings will in future contain 36 F/A-18 multi-role aircraft and the USMC will establish two more squadrons with F/A-18D. Marine Corps aviation is being more closely integrated with naval air, and three active and two reserve F/A-18 squadrons are to operate as part of Carrier Air Wings.

In addition to modernisation programmes for virtually all combat aircraft types, both the Advanced Medium-Range Air-to-Air Missile (AMRAAM) and the short-range *Sidewinder* missile are to be enhanced. New weapons to be introduced over the next five years include:

- Standoff Land Attack Missile (SLAM), an infra-red guided version of the *Harpoon* anti-ship missile;
- Sensor Fuzed Weapon (SFW), an anti-armour munitions dispenser (already in procurement);
- Joint Direct Attack Munitions (JDAM), the provision of autonomous navigation capability to existing free-fall bombs;
- Joint Standoff Weapon (JSOW), a longer-range, aerodynamically efficient, autonomously navigated munitions dispenser (procurement begins in FY1996);
- Tri-Service Standoff Attack Missile (TSSAM), a low-observable (Stealth) long-range missile (already in procurement).

JSOW, whose tests have already begun, has been given the designator AGM-154. JSOW will have a 72km stand-off range and deliver six sub-munitions, each with four anti-armour *Skeet* kinetic energy penetrators with infra-red sensors.

Improvements are also planned in the unmanned aircraft (UAV) field. Short-Range UAV (SRUAV), a follow-on to the *Pioneer*, is now in production for the Army, Navy and USMC. Development of Close-Range UAV (CRUAV) for use by lower-echelon ground units will begin in FY1999. Both SRUAV and CRUAV will provide real-time imagery. Other UAVs with greater endurance and with high-altitude capability are under consideration.

There have been a number of changes to US Air Force deployment overseas. In the UK, manpower strength has been reduced by about 2,000 while a squadron of F-15C/D has been added. The fighter group in the Netherlands has been withdrawn, as has the F-15 air-defence squadron in Iceland. In Italy, air force strength has risen by about 1,000 with the decision to station a fighter wing at Aviano. In Japan, the F-15E squadron has been withdrawn, but numbers of other types have been increased (F-15C/D from 36 to 54 and F-16 from 24 to 42). The US Air Force still deploys aircraft on rotation to a number of operations: *Operation Poised Hammer* enforcing the no-fly zone over northern Iraq; *Operation Southern Watch* enforcing the no-fly zone over southern Iraq; *Operation Deny Flight* which both enforces the no-fly zone over Bosnia-Herzegovina and provides close air support for UN forces there; as well as providing transport for a number of humanitarian missions around the world.

Naval Forces

The *Bottom-up-Review* requires further reductions in naval strength. The Navy is expected to comprise about 330 ships by FY1999, of which the key elements will be 12 aircraft carriers (including one reserve/training carrier) and 11 large-deck amphibious ships capable of embarking both VTOL aircraft and helicopters. The US Navy sees a main role for both carriers and amphibious forces in major regional conflicts and plans that four or five carrier battle groups and the same number of Marine Expeditionary Brigades could be needed for a single MRC.

A significant number of warships have been decommissioned during the last 12 months, but some new ships have joined the fleet. Naval manpower has been reduced by around 28,000 during this period. There has been no change to the aircraft-carrier fleet, and the seventh *Nimitz*-class is scheduled to be commissioned in FY1996.

Four improved *Los Angeles* SSGN have been commissioned, while five SSN (four *Sturgeon* and one *Permit*-class) have been retired and one *Los Angeles* SSN has been placed 'In Commission

In Reserve' (ICIR) status. A further five *Los Angeles* SSGN are planned, and the last will be delivered in FY1996. Two new *Seawolf*-class attack submarines have been funded for construction; although the programme is strongly criticised by Congress on account of its cost, it may add some funding for a third boat to the FY1996 budget.

The cruiser force has been reduced by 18 ships with 20 being retired (two *Virginia* CGN, eight *Belknap*, nine *Leahy* and, by mid-September 1994, one *Long Beach*). The last two *Ticonderoga*-class base-line 2/3, which can be armed with *Tomahawk* SLCM, have been commissioned. There has been an increase in the number of destroyers in service with four more *Arleigh Burke*, *Aegis*-equipped ships being commissioned, and only one, the last *Coontz*-class, being placed in ICIR status. Seven more *Spruance*-class destroyers have been modified to carry the Vertical Launch System (VLS). Eight *Knox*-class frigates have been decommissioned and the eight *Knox* training frigates will all have been retired by the end of FY1994. Some earlier retired *Knox*-class frigates have been transferred, on lease, one to ROC (Taipei) and four to Turkey. The transfer of a further 18 ships of this class to six navies (Brazil, Egypt, ROC (Taipei), Thailand, Turkey and Venezuela) has been proposed to Congress.

Six of the new *Cyclone*-class coastal patrol craft will be in service by mid-June 1994, and seven more are planned. In the mine warfare area, a second *Osprey*-class coastal mine hunter commissioned in August 1994 and three more *Avenger*-class off-shore mine countermeasures ships (the last in July 1994) have joined the fleet to complete the class of 14 ships. A total of 12 *Ospreys* are planned. The Naval Reserve is to assume more responsibility for mine warfare and is slated to crew 16 ships, including a command-and-control ship, by 1998.

Changes in the amphibious fleet include the commissioning of a third *Wasp*-class landing ship assault, and three more of this class are due to enter service by FY 1999. One *Iowa Jima*-class landing platform helicopter is being converted to a mine countermeasure support ship and a second paid off in June 1994. Five *Newport* landing ship tanks have been retired and they and others retired earlier were being offered to other navies. The transfer process had been halted by the Senate after a Marine Corps lobbyist raised doubts as to whether the Navy could still lift two and a half MEFs without them. The three remaining *Charleston* amphibious cargo ships have been transferred from the Naval Reserve Force to the Inactive Reserve. Future plans include four cargo landing ship docks and 12 of a new class of amphibious assault ship to lift Marine Corps units.

The US Navy has tested a *Trident* D-5 SLBM armed with non-nuclear warheads to evaluate the use of the Global Positioning System (GPS) to guide the warheads to their targets. The aim of the project is accurately to deliver penetrating munitions with a similar capability to the GBU-28 aircraft-delivered bomb, developed after the Gulf War, for the deep penetration needed to attack command post and similarly protected bunkers. GBU-28 is said to be capable of penetrating 20 feet of concrete on 100 feet of earth. The *Trident* warhead would be fitted with metal rods and would achieve its penetration by virtue of the speed of impact. Accuracy is, of course, vital.

Defence Spending

FY1994 Budget Authority

The Administration's national Defense Budget authorisation request for FY1994 was $263.4bn, which included funding for Department of Energy and NASA military activities. Subsequently US Congress cut this request by almost $2bn to $261.7bn. In real terms, therefore, the 1994 Defense Budget authorisation was some $21bn, or 8%, less than that for FY1993.

With the exception of military construction – which accounts for just 2% of the total – and Operations and Maintenance, all of the Defense Budget titles were cut in real terms. In line with the policy of maintaining force-readiness states, there was a marginal real increase (1%) for Operations and Maintenance ($89.5bn). Research, Development, Test and Evaluation (RDTE) was cut to $38.6bn (a 1% decline). Much larger cuts were made to Military Personnel ($70.1bn)

– a 9% reduction – and, in particular, Procurement ($45.5bn) – a 17% reduction.

Concerning major new weapons-system programmes, the Budget protected development of the F-22 tactical combat aircraft, the RAH-66 *Comanche* reconnaissance and attack helicopter, the *Centurion* attack submarine, and the *Milstar* and *Spacelifter* space systems. Further orders (six) were placed for the C-17 *Globemaster* III airlift. No orders were placed for the V-22 *Osprey*, but the programme was kept alive by further development funding which was reinstated by Congress. Series production continued of the F/A-18 *Hornet*, F-16 *Falcon*, the T-45 *Goshawk* jet trainer, UH-60 *Blackhawk* and derivatives, and the CH/MH-53 *Super Stallion* helicopter; as in 1993, there were no further orders for the F-15, AV-8B or AH-64 *Apache*, nor more orders for the B-2. Modernisation programmes continued for DDG-51 *Aegis*-equipped destroyers, F-14 *Tomcat*, the *Longbow Apache* update, and the M1 *Abrams* tank and *Bradley* AIFV upgrades.

The largest single cut was to the BMDO, whose funding declined by some $2.5bn from the $6.3bn proposed by the previous Administration to $3.8bn.

In the event, US Congress added some further cuts, of which the main ones were: some $1bn more from BMD; the Air Force bid for 24 F-16s was halved; about $200m was taken from C-17 funding; and some $170m from the F-22 programme.

FY1995 Budget Request

The FY1995 national Defense Budget request, which will not be finally approved by Congress until late 1994, is for $263.7bn (a decline in real terms of 2% from the FY1993 authorisation), with total defence spending planned at $1.23 trillion for the period FY1995–99 (a drop of some $107bn – or 8% – from the previous Administration's plan).

In his Annual Report to the President and the Congress, the then Secretary of Defense Les Aspin listed the following as the guidelines which drove programme and budgetary decisions: adjustment to the dangers of the new security era; maintenance of the quality and morale of the armed forces personnel; readiness with emphasis on training, operations and maintenance; superior weapons technology; ensuring that essential elements in the defence industry survive.

The priorities listed above are reflected in the changing proportion of the defence budget allotted to each area. Operations and Maintenance (readiness) receives a 5.6% real increase over 1994, notwithstanding 7% cuts to force structure, and $92.9bn. Depot Maintenance is increased by 20% to $6.3bn, and Research and Development (R and D), which bore the brunt of Congressional cuts in 1994, increases by 3.8% to $36.2bn. On the other hand, procurement has been cut by 2.7%, reflecting the earlier policy decision to maintain an R and D lead and postpone procurement of new equipments until replacement was really necessary. The Secretary of Defense has given notice that procurement expenditure, which for the FY1995 request is $43.3bn, represents a 7% cut in real terms and compares with a 1991 spending level of $91bn, will start to rise after 1996.

So far as the individual services are concerned, the Army's request, $61bn, is $100m above the FY1994 authority, but down in real terms by some 2%. Operations and Maintenance funding, despite the cuts in force size, is increased by $1.8bn, while R and D and procurement drop by $900m. The R and D budget still includes substantial funding for: the *Comanche* attack helicopter; the *Longbow Apache* helicopter, an upgrade which includes improved operability, much improved maintainability and provision of a target-acquisition and a fire-and-target engagement system; modernisation of armoured vehicles; and 'smart' anti-armour munitions. But all these programmes are being extended and so will suffer delay. The main procurement bids from the Army are for: 60 *Black Hawk* UH-60 helicopters; 270 *Javelin* man-portable anti-armour missile launchers; and upgrading programmes for *Abrams* M-1 MBT and *Bradley* AIFVs.

The US Navy budget request of $78bn is over $1bn more than that of FY1994, but is a cut of 1% in real terms. New ship building in the budget is one aircraft carrier ($2.4bn) and three *Aegis*-equipped DDG-51 destroyers ($2.9bn). The other main requests are for: 24 more F/A-18C/D attack aircraft; four more E-2C AEW aircraft; 18 *Trident* D-5 SLBM; and 217 more *Tomahawk* SLCM. R and D requests include $1.35bn for F/A-18E/F aircraft development; $507m for the

Centurion new class of attack submarine; and $497m for continued development of the V-22 *Osprey* tactical transport tilt-wing aircraft for the USMC. The A/F X fighter aircraft programme has been cancelled in favour of the Joint [Navy and Air Force] Advanced Strike Technology (JAST) programme which is to develop low-cost modular engine and avionics technologies for use in future aircraft and weapons systems.

The Air Force budget, $788m more than in FY1994, but roughly the same in real terms, is for $74.5bn. The Air Force is strongly advocating selling older weapons and equipment for export and using the funding gained for newer models and upgrading. The main items in the Air Force request are: $2.6bn for six C-17 strategic transport aircraft (including advance funding for eight more aircraft in FY1996); $2.4bn for continuing F-22 fighter R and D; and $546m for R and D for improved E-8B JSTARS (including advance funding for two aircraft in FY1996). F-16 FGA aircraft procurement continues until 1996, but is terminated thereafter. The Follow-on Early Warning System (FEWS) (a satellite-based ballistic-missile warning and tracking system) has been cancelled because it is unaffordable. However, the Defense Support Program still needs to be upgraded or supplemented to provide a capability for the detection of tactical ballistic missiles.

Other major components of the defence budget request are: BMD $3.25bn, roughly $500m less than requested in FY1994 (the five-year 1995–99 spending plan allocates some $17bn for BMD, making it the largest single R and D programme in the period); $2.18bn for environmental programmes, including $200m for clean-up activities at contaminated sites. The Department of Energy Defense Activities budget request is for $10.6bn, a 5% cut from FY1994. Defence-related areas within the International Affairs budget request include: $608m to support international peacekeeping in addition to a supplemented request for $670m due to the UN, but unpaid in FY1994 (the Defense Department request includes $300m for UN peacekeeping contingencies, an item likely to be struck out by Congress); $1.6bn for humanitarian aid (migration and refugees, disaster relief, food aid); and $3.2bn for security assistance, the bulk of which will support the Middle East peace process. In addition to Egypt and Israel which, since their peace treaty was reached, have received the largest shares, only Jordan, Greece and Turkey are to receive security assistance in FY1995.

The House of Representatives has adopted an amendment to the Defense Budget requiring the European allies to meet, in four years' time, 75% (rather than the current 5%) of the financial costs of US forces (other than salaries) in Europe. The amendment, which has yet to be approved by the Senate, would require 1,000 troops to be withdrawn for each percentage point below 75%. The estimated savings could amount to $5bn over five years.

US Defence Budgets
Explanatory Note:

Each year the US government presents its Defense Budget to Congress for the next two fiscal years, together with a long-term spending plan covering a further three years. Until approved by Congress, the Budget is referred to as the Budget Request, after approval it becomes the Budget Authority (BA), and authorises funds for immediate and future disbursement. The term Total Obligational Authority (TOA) represents the value of direct defence programmes for each fiscal year regardless of financing (i.e., from previous fiscal years and receipts from earned income or interest). The term 'outlay' represents actual expenditure; each year the government estimates what the outlay will be, the difference between this and the BA providing for contingencies. However, moneys authorised, particularly in the procurement and construction areas, are rarely all spent in the year of authorisation, although contracts are signed which commit the government to payment in future years.

Table I: Selected Budgets 1988–95 ($bn, current year)[a]

FY 1 Oct– 30 Sept	National Defense Function[b] (BA)	National Defense Function[b] (outlay)	Defense Department (BA)	Defense Department (outlay)	Atomic Energy Defense Activities (outlay)	International Security Assistance[c] (outlay)	Veterans Administration[c] (outlay)	Total Federal Exp (outlay)	Total Federal Budget Deficit (outlay)
1988	292.008	290.361	283.755	281.935	7.913	8.598	29.428	1,064.051	155.090
1989	299.567	303.559	290.837	294.880	8.119	7.666	30.066	1,144.064	153.400
1990	303.263	299.331	292.999	289.755	8.988	8.393	29.112	1,251.778	220.470
1991	303.574	273.292	290.904	262.389	10.004	9.061	31.349	1,323.011	268.746
1992	295.070	298.350	282.127	286.892	10.619	6.682	34.138	1,380.856	290.400
1993	276.100	292.400	262.400	280.100	11.000	5.475	35.720	1,408.205	254.700
1994ε	261.700	280.600	250.000	268.300	11.200	4.499	38.129	1,483.829	234.800
(budget request)									
1995ε	263.700	271.100	252.200	259.800	10.500	3.721	39.247	1,518.945	176.100

[a] Data are from *Budget of the United States Government* – Fiscal Year 1995.
[b] The national Defense Budget function includes DoD Military Activities, Department of Energy Atomic Energy Defense Activities, and smaller support agencies
[c] Not included in National Defense Function.

THE UNITED STATES

GDP	1992:	$6,038.5bn	(per capita $24,000)
	1993:	$6,374.0bn	(per capita $24,800)
Growth	1992:	2.6%	1993: 2.9%
Inflation	1992:	3.3%	1993: 1.1%
Publ debt	1992:	62.0%	1993: 63.9%
Def bdgt	1993:	BA $276.1bn, Outlay $292.4bn	
	1994:	BA $261.7bn, Outlay $280.6bn	
Request	1995:	BA $263.7bn, Outlay $271.1bn	
NATO defn	1992:	$305.1bn	1993: $297.3bn

Population: 259,533,000

	13–17	*18–22*	*23–32*
Men	8,983,000	8,988,000	20,360,000
Women	8,538,000	8,618,000	19,788,000

TOTAL ARMED FORCES:

ACTIVE: 1,650,500 (198,800 women) (excl Coast Guard).

RESERVES: 2,048,000 (total incl Standby and Retired Reserve).

READY RESERVE: 1,839,400 Selected Reserve and Individual Ready Reserve to augment active units and provide reserve formations and units.

NATIONAL GUARD: 520,600. Army (ARNG) 405,900; Air Force (ANG) 114,700.

RESERVE: 1,318,800. Army 701,900; Navy 302,400; Marines 110,400; Air Force 204,100.

STANDBY RESERVE: 26,200. Trained individuals for mob: Army 900; Navy 13,700; Marines 300; Air Force 11,300.

RETIRED RESERVE: 182,400. Trained individuals to augment support and training facilities: Army 92,000; Navy 28,800; Marines 7,200; Air Force 54,400.

US STRATEGIC COMMAND (US STRATCOM):

HQ Offutt Air Force Base, Nebraska (manpower incl in Navy and Air Force totals).

NAVY: 384 SLBM in 17 SSBN:
(Plus 16 *Poseidon*-C3 and 112 *Trident*-C4 START-accountable launchers in 8 non-operational SSBN.)

SSBN: 17:
14 *Ohio:*
 6 (SSBN-734) with 24 UGM-133A *Trident* D-5 (144 msl) (1 more will be commissioned in FY1994).
 8 (SSBN-726) (includes 1 in refit) with 24 UGM-93A *Trident* C-4 (192 msl).
2 *Franklin* (SSBN-726) with 16 *Trident* C-4 (32 msl).
1 *Madison* (SSBN-627) with 16 *Trident* C-4 (16 msl) (will decommission in FY 1994).

AIR FORCE:

ICBM (Air Force Space Command (AFSPC)): 705: 3 strategic msl wings, 2 gp (1 test wing with 13 test silo launchers):
 126 *Minuteman* II (LGM-30F) (without guidance or warheads).
 529 *Minuteman* III (LGM-30G).
 50 *Peacekeeper* (MX; LGM-118A); in mod *Minuteman* silos.

AIRCRAFT (Air Combat Command (ACC)): 200 hy bbr (426 START-countable):
OPERATIONAL: 14 bbr sqn (7 B-1B, 1 B-2A, 6 B-52):
7 sqn (2 ANG) with 93 B-1B.
6 sqn (1 AFR) with 94 B-52H (with AGM-86B ALCM).
1 sqn with 2 B-2A.
FLIGHT TEST CENTRE: 11: 3 B-52B/G/H, 2 B-1B, 6 B-2A (not START-countable).
AWAITING CONVERSION/ELIMINATION: 343 B-52; -C 15, -D 85; -E 43; -F 52; -G 148 (87 ALCM-capable).

STRATEGIC RECCE/INTELLIGENCE COLLECTION (SATELLITES):

IMAGERY: KH-11: 160–400 mile polar orbit, digital imagery (perhaps 3 operational). KH-12 (*Ikon*): 1 launched 1989. AFP-731: optical imaging satellite with sensors operating in several wavebands. 203km orbit, at approx 60° inclination; to replace KH-11. *Lacrosse* radar-imaging satellite.
OCEAN SURVEILLANCE (OSUS): 4 satellite-clusters to detect ships by infra-red and radar.
NAVIGATIONAL SATELLITE TIMING AND RANGING (NAVSTAR): 24 satellites, components of global positioning system.
ELINT/COMINT: 2 *Chalet (Vortex)*, 2 *Magnum*, 2 *Jumpseat*; 'Ferrets' (radar-monitoring satellites).
NUCLEAR DETONATION DETECTION SYSTEM: detects and evaluates nuclear detonations. Sensors to be deployed in NAVSTAR satellites.

STRATEGIC DEFENCES:

US Space Command: (HQ: Peterson AFB, Colorado).
North American Aerospace Defense Command (NORAD), a combined US–Canadian org: (HQ: Peterson AFB, Colorado).
US Strategic Command: (HQ: Offutt AFB, Nebraska).

EARLY WARNING:

DEFENSE SUPPORT PROGRAM (DSP): infra-red surveillance and warning system. Approved constellation: 3 operational satellites and 1 operational on-orbit spare.
BALLISTIC-MISSILE EARLY-WARNING SYSTEM (BMEWS): 3 stations: Clear (Alaska); Thule (Greenland); Fylingdales Moor (UK). Primary mission to track ICBM and SLBM. Also used to track satellites.
SPACETRACK: USAF radars Pirinçlik (Turkey), Eglin (Florida), Clear, Thule and Fylingdales, Beale AFB (California), Cape Cod (Massachusetts), Robins AFB (Georgia), Eldorado AFS (Texas); optical tracking systems in New Mexico, Choejong-San (S. Korea), San Vito (Italy), Maui (Hawaii), Diego Garcia (Indian Ocean).
USN SPACE SURVEILLANCE SYSTEM (NAVSPASUR): 3 transmitting, 6 receiving-site field stations in south-east US.
PERIMETER ACQUISITION RADAR ATTACK CHARACTERISATION SYSTEM (PARCS): 1 north-facing phased-array system at Cavalier AFS (N. Dakota); 2,800km range.
PAVE PAWS: phased-array radars in Massachusetts, Georgia, Texas, California; 5,500km range.
MISCELLANEOUS DETECTION AND TRACKING RADARS: US Army: Kwajalein Atoll (Pacific). USAF: Ascension Island (Atlantic), Antigua (Caribbean), Kaena Point (Hawaii), MIT Lincoln Laboratory (Massachusetts).
GROUND-BASED ELECTRO-OPTICAL DEEP SPACE SURVEILLANCE SYSTEM (GEODSS): Socorro (New Mexico), Taegu (S. Korea), Maui (Hawaii), Diego Garcia (Indian Ocean).

AIR DEFENCE:

RADARS:

OVER-THE-HORIZON-BACKSCATTER RADAR (OTH-B):
1 in Maine (limited operation, 40 hrs per week), 1 in Mount Home AFB, Montana (mothballed). Range 500nm (minimum) to 3,000nm.
NORTH WARNING SYSTEM: to replace DEW line. 15 automated long-range (200nm) radar stations now operational. 40 short-range (110–150km) stations due in service by October 1994.
DEW LINE: 31 radars: Alaska (7), Canada (20) and Greenland (4) roughly along the 70°N parallel from Point Lay, Alaska, to Greenland (system deactivated September 1993).

AIRCRAFT:

ACTIVE: 36: 2 sqn with 36 F-15C/D (Alaska).
ANG: 216: 12 sqn:
2 with 36 F-15A/B.
10 with 180 F-16A/B.
Augmentation: ac on call from Navy, Marine Corps and Air Force.
AAM: *Sidewinder*, *Sparrow*, AMRAAM.

ARMY: 559,900 (68,800 women).
5 Army HQ, 4 Corps HQ (1 AB).
3 armd div (3 bde HQ, 5 tk, 4 mech inf, 3 SP arty, 1 MLRS, 1 AD bn; 1 avn bde) (incl 1 ARNG bde in 1 div).
4 mech div (3 bde HQ, 4 tk, 5 mech inf, 3 SP arty; 1 MLRS, 1 AD bn; 1 avn bde) (incl 1 ARNG bde in 4 div).
1 inf div (3 bde HQ, 2 air aslt, 4 mech inf, 2tk, 4 arty, 1 MLRS, 1 AD bn; 1 avn bde) (incl 1 ARNG bde).
2 lt inf div (3 bde HQ, 9 inf, 3 arty, 1 AD bn; 1 avn bde) (incl 1 ARNG, 1 AR bde in 2 div).
1 air aslt div (3 bde HQ, 9 air aslt, 3 arty bn; avn bde (7 hel bn: 3 ATK, 2 aslt, 1 comd, 1 med tpt)).
1 AB div (3 bde HQ, 9 para, 1 lt tk, 3 arty, 1 AD, 1 cbt avn bn).
2 indep armd bde (2 tk, 1 mech inf, 1 SP arty bn) (2–3 ARNG bn).
2 inf (theatre def) bde (3 inf, 1 lt arty bn).
1 inf, 1 AB bn gp.
7 avn bde (1 army, 4 corps, 2 trg).
2 armd cav regt.
7 arty bde.
1 theatre AD comd.
9 *Patriot* SAM bn: 5 with 6 bty, 2 with 4 bty, 2 with 3 bty.
3 *Avenger* SAM bn.

READY RESERVE:
ARMY NATIONAL GUARD (ARNG): 405,900 (31,500 women): capable after mob of manning 8 div (3 armd, 1 mech, 3 inf (2 cadre), 1 lt inf); 20 indep bde (5 armd, 6 mech, 9 inf (3 lt)) incl 7 'Roundout' (1 inf, 1 armd, 4 mech, 1 lt inf) for Regular Army div; 1 armd cav regt; 1 inf gp (Arctic recce: 4 scout bn); 16 fd arty bde HQ. Indep bn: 4 tk, 2 mech, 48 arty, 21 AD (4 *HAWK*, 7 *Chaparral*, 1 *Patriot*, 1 *Avenger*, 8 *Stinger* SP (div)), 61 engr.
ARMY RESERVE (AR): 701,900 (123,000 women): 9 trg div, 2 trg bde (no cbt role). 1 lt inf ('Roundout') bde; 3 arty bde HQ, 60 indep bn.
(Of these 260,000 Standing Reservists receive regular training and have mobilisation assignment. The remainder receive no training, but as former active-duty soldiers could be recalled in an emergency.)

EQUIPMENT:
MBT: some 14,524: 890 M-48A5, 1,439 M-60/-60A1, 4,657 M-60A3, 7,538 M-1 *Abrams* (incl M-1A1 M-1A2).
LIGHT TANKS: 123 M-551 *Sheridan*.
RECCE: 55 *Fuchs*.
AIFV: 6,633 M-2/-3 *Bradley*.
APC: some 28,400, incl 4,737 M-577, 11,928 M-113 incl variant with A2/A3.
TOWED ARTY: 2,085:
105mm: 424 M-101, 522 M-102, 294 M-119;
155mm: 138 M-114, 707 M-198.
SP ARTY: 3,346:
155mm: 2,510 M-109A1/A2/A6; 203mm: 836 M-110A1/A2.
MRL: 227mm: 540 MLRS, incl some 430 ATACMS capable.
MORTARS: 107mm: 2,585 (incl some 1,900 SP); 120mm: 63.
ATGW: 16,294 *TOW* (incl 36 M-113, 5,776 *Hummer*, 3,195 M-901, 7,287 M-2/M-3 *Bradley*), 5,790 *Dragon* launchers.
RL: 84mm: AT-4.
RCL: 84 mm: 27 *Carl Gustav*.
AD GUNS: 20mm: 43 M-167 *Vulcan* towed, 197 M-163 SP.
SAM: FIM-92A *Stinger*, 415 *Avenger* (vehicle-mounted *Stinger*), 144 M-54 and M-48 SP *Chaparral*, 96 *Improved HAWK*, 472 *Patriot* launchers.
SURV: AN/TPQ-36 (arty), AN/TPQ-37 (arty), AN/TRQ-32 (COMINT), AN/TSQ-138 (COMINT), AN/TLQ-17A (EW).
AMPHIBIOUS: 40 ships:
5 *Frank Besson* LST: capacity 32 tk.
35 *Runnymede* LCU: capacity 7 tk.
Plus craft: some 124 LCM, 26 ACV.
UAV: R4E-40 *Skyeye*, *Pioneer*.
AVIATION: incl eqpt in store.
AIRCRAFT: some 386, incl 35 OV-1D, 42 RC-12D/G/H/K, 12 RU-21, 13 RV-1D, 121 C-12D, 24 C-23A/B, 10 C-26, 108 U-21, 6 UV-18A, 2 UV-20A, 2 P-27, 4 T-34, 2 O-2, 2 C-182, 3 D-HC7.
HELICOPTERS: some 7,430 (1,487 armed hel): 680 AH-1S, 754 AH-64A, 53 AH-6/MH-6, 2,206 UH-1 (being replaced), 3 EH-1H (ECM), 1,216 UH/MH-60A, 66 EH-60A (ECM), 455 CH/MH-47, 90 OH-6A, 1,543 OH-58A/C, 335 OH-58D, 29 TH-67 Creek.

NAVY (USN): 482,800 (55,100 women): 4 Fleets: 2nd (Atlantic), 3rd (Pacific), 6th (Mediterranean), 7th (W. Pacific), plus Military Sealift Command.
SUBMARINES: 104:
STRATEGIC SUBMARINES: 17: (see p. 22).
TACTICAL SUBMARINES: 85 (incl about 8 in refit).

SSGN: 25:
17 imp *Los Angeles* (SSN-751) with 12 x *Tomahawk* SLCM (VLS), 533mm TT (Mk 48 HWT, *Harpoon, Tomahawk*).
8 mod *Los Angeles* (SSN-719) with 12 x *Tomahawk* SLCM (VLS); plus 533mm TT (Mk 48 HWT, *Harpoon, Tomahawk*).
SSN: 60:
30 *Los Angeles* (SSN-688) with Mk 48 HWT, plus *Harpoon*, *Tomahawk* SLCM.
28 *Sturgeon* (SSN-637) with Mk 48 HWT; plus *Harpoon*, 21 with *Tomahawk* SLCM.
(Incl 10 capable of special ops.)
1 *Permit* (SSN-594) with Mk 48 HWT, plus *Harpoon.*
1 *Narwhal* (SSN-671) with Mk 48 HWT, *Harpoon*, *Tomahawk.*
SUBMARINES, OTHER ROLES: 2:
2 ex-SSBN (SSBN 642 and 645) (special ops).
PRINCIPAL SURFACE COMBATANTS: 137:
AIRCRAFT CARRIERS: 11 (excl 2 in long refit/refuel):
CVN: 6 (plus *Enterprise* in long refit/refuel):
6 *Nimitz* (CVN-68) (96/102,000t).
CV: 5 (plus *Kennedy* in long refit):
3 *Kitty Hawk* (CV-63) (81,000t).
2 *Forrestal* (CV-59) (79,250/81,100t).
AIR WING: 13 (11 active, 2 reserve). The average mix of type and numbers of ac assigned to an Air Wing is:
2 ftr sqn with 18 F-14A.
2 FGA/ftr sqn with 20 F/A-18, 1 med with 14 A-6E.
2 ASW sqn:
1 with 6 S-3B **ac**; 1 with 8 H-60 **hel**.
2 ECM sqn with 4 EA-6B, 2 ES-3.
1 AEW sqn with 4 E-2C.
2 ECM sqn, 1 sqn with 4 EA-6, 1 with 2 ES-3.
1 support sqn with C-2.
CRUISERS: 34:
CGN: 6:
2 *Virginia* (CGN-38) with 2 x 2 SM-2 MR SAM/*ASROC* SUGW; plus 2 x 4 *Tomahawk* SLCM, 2 x 4 *Harpoon*, SH-2F hel (Mk 46 LWT), 2 x 3 ASTT, 2 x 127mm guns (excludes CGN-38 non-op by 30 September 1994).
2 *California* (CGN-36) with 2 x SM-2 MR; plus 2 x 4 *Harpoon*, 1 x 8 *ASROC*, 2 x 3 ASTT, 2 x 127mm guns.
1 *Truxtun* (CGN-35) with 1 x 2 SM-2 ER SAM/*ASROC*; plus 2 x 3 ASTT, 1 x SH-2F hel, 1 x 127mm gun.
1 *Bainbridge* (CGN-25) with 2 x 2 SM-2 ER, plus 2 x 4 *Harpoon*, 1 x 8 *ASROC*, 2 x 3 ASTT.
(Plus *Long Beach* (CGN-9) with 2 x 2 SM-2 ER; plus 2 x 4 *Tomahawk*, 2 x 4 *Harpoon*, 1 x 8 *ASROC*, 2 x 3 ASTT, 2 x 127mm guns, ICIR status by 30 September 1994.)
CG: 28:
27 *Ticonderoga* (CG–47 *Aegis*):
5 Baseline 1 (CG-47–51) with 2 x 2 SM-2 MR/*ASROC*; plus 2 x 4 *Harpoon*, 2 x 1 127mm guns, 2 x 3 ASTT, 2 x SH-2F or SH-60B hel.
22 Baseline 2/3 (CG-52) with 2 x VLS Mk 41 (61 tubes each) for combination of SM-2 ER, and *Tomahawk*. Other weapons as Baseline 1.
1 *Belknap* (CG-26) with 1 x 2 SM-2 ER/*ASROC*; plus 2 x 3 ASTT, 2 x 4 *Harpoon*, 1 x 127mm gun, 1 x SH-2F hel.
(All *Leahy* (CG-16) with 2 x 2 SM-2 ER/*ASROC*; plus 2 x 3 ASTT, 2 x 4 *Harpoon* will have paid off by 30 September 1994.)
DESTROYERS: 41 (incl some 6 in refit):
DDG: 10:
6 *Arleigh Burke* (DDG-51 *Aegis*) with 2 x VLS Mk 41 (32 tubes fwd, 64 tubes aft) for combination of *Tomahawk*, SM-2 ER and *ASROC*; plus 2 x 4 *Harpoon*, 1 x 127mm gun, 2 x 3 ASTT, 1 x SH-60B hel.
4 *Kidd* (DDG-993) with 2 x 2 SM-2 MR/*ASROC*; plus 2 x 3 ASTT, 2 x SH-2F hel, 2 x 4 *Harpoon*, 2 x 127mm guns.
DD: 31: *Spruance* (DD-963) (ASW):
6 with 1 x 8 *ASROC*, 2 x 3 ASTT, 1 x SH-2F hel; plus 2 x 4 *Harpoon*, 2 x 127mm guns, 2 x 4 *Tomahawk.*
25 with 1 x VLS Mk 41 (*Tomahawk*), 2 x 3 ASTT, 1 x SH-60B hel; plus 2 x 127mm guns, 2 x 4 *Harpoon.*
FRIGATES: 51 (incl some 5 in refit):
FFG: 51:
51 *Oliver Hazard Perry* (FFG-7) (16 in NRF) all with 2 x 3 ASTT; 24 with 2 x SH-60B hel; 27 with 2 x SH-2F hel; all plus 1 x SM-1 MR/*Harpoon.*
ADDITIONAL IN STORE: 2 CV, 4 BB.
PATROL AND COASTAL COMBATANTS: 24:
Note: mainly responsibility of Coast Guard.
MISSILE CRAFT: 6 *Pegasus* PHM with 2 x 4 *Harpoon.*
PATROL, COASTAL: 6 *Cyclone* PFC with SEAL team.
PATROL, INSHORE: 12⟨.
MINE WARFARE: 16:
MINELAYERS: none dedicated, but mines can be laid from attack submarines, aircraft and surface ships (limited).
MINE COUNTERMEASURES: 16:
2 *Osprey* (MHC-51) MHC.
14 *Avenger* (MCM-1) MCO.

AMPHIBIOUS: 47:
COMMAND: 2 *Blue Ridge*: capacity 700 tps.
LHA: 8:
3 *Wasp*: capacity 1,892 tps, 60 tk; with 6 AV-8B ac, 12 CH-46E, 4 CH-53E, 4 UH-1N, 4 AH-1W hel; plus 3 LCAC.
5 *Tarawa*: capacity 1,713 tps, 100 tk, 4 LCU or 1 LCAC, 6 AV-8B ac, 12 CH-46E, 4 CH-53E, 4 UH-1N, 4 AH-1T/W hel.
LPH: 3 *Iwo Jima*: capacity 1,489 tps, 12 CH-46E, 4 CH-53E, 4 UH-1N hel, 4 AH-1T/W.
LPD: 11: *Austin:* capacity 788 tps, 4 tk.
LSD: 13:
8 *Whidbey Island* with 4 LCAC: capacity 450 tps, 40 tk.
5 *Anchorage* with 3 LCAC: capacity 302 tps, 38 tk.
LST: 10 *Newport*: capacity 347 tps, 10 tk.
CRAFT: about 108:
About 71 LCAC: capacity 1 MBT.
About 37 LCU-1610: capacity 3 MBT.
Numerous LCVP, LCU, LCM.
SUPPORT AND MISCELLANEOUS: 137:
(Total includes 58 USN ships, 76 ships of the Military Sealift Command, Fleet Auxiliary Force, and 3 AGOR owned by the USN, but operated by civil research institutes.)
UNDERWAY SUPPORT: 45:
AO: 22: 5 *Cimarron*, 4 *Wichita*, 13 *Henry Kaiser* (MSC).
AOE: 5: 1 *Supply*, 4 *Sacramento*.
AE: 11: 1 *Kilauea* (MSC), 7 *Butte*, 3 *Suribachi/ Nitro*.
AF: 7: 5 *Mars* (4 MSC), 2 *Sirius* (MSC).
MAINTENANCE AND LOGISTICS: 53:
6 AD, 9 AS, 10 AT (7 MSC), 14 AOT (MSC), 2 AH (MSC), 12 salvage/rescue.
SPECIAL PURPOSES: 7:
2 comd, 5 technical spt (4 MSC).
SURVEY AND RESEARCH: 32:
14 *Stalwart* AGOS (towed array) (MSC).
5 AGOR (2 MSC), 9 AGHS (MSC).
4 *Victorious* AGOS (SWATH) (MSC).

MILITARY SEALIFT:

Military Sealift Command operates and administers some 290 strategic sealift ships in addition to the 76 ships of the Fleet Auxiliary Force.
FLEET AUXILIARY FORCE: those ships deployed in direct support of the Fleet listed under Support and Miscellaneous.
ACTIVE FORCE: about 39:
17 dry cargo (incl 2 ro-ro veh and 4 ro-ro container) and 22 tankers.

STANDBY FORCE: 259:
AFLOAT PREPOSITIONING FORCE: 33:
13 maritime prepositioning ships in 3 sqn (MPS) (each to support a MEB).
20 prepositioned ships (incl 8 tempy activated RRF vessels): 14 cargo/ammo, 1 heavy lift, 2 hospital (for Army use).
FAST SEALIFT: 8:
1 fast sealift ship sqn of 8 ro-ro (30 knot) ships at 4 days' notice.
NATIONAL DEFENSE RESERVE FLEET (NDRF): 226:
READY RESERVE FORCE (RRF): 97 regularly maintained ships: 86 dry cargo (incl 2 aviation spt ships and 11 tankers), 30% at 5 days' reactivation notice, remainder at 10 to 20 days.
NAVAL INACTIVE FLEET: about 130: includes about 50 'mothballed' USN ships, incl 2 CV, 4 battleships plus about 25 dry cargo, 10 tankers and some 60 'Victory' WW II cargo. (60 to 90 days' reactivation notice, but many ships very old and of doubtful serviceability.)
AUXILIARY STRATEGIC SEALIFT:
about a further 247 US-flag and effectively US-controlled ships potentially available to augment these holdings.

RESERVES:

NAVAL RESERVE SURFACE FORCES: 16 FFG, incl in main Navy entry. Crewed by about 70% active USN and 30% NR.
COMBAT SUPPORT FORCES (provision of units for MCM, underwater ops, ashore construction, cargo handling).
AUGMENT FORCES (provision of additional manpower to regular org).

NAVAL AVIATION: ε86,000, incl 13 carrier air wings.

Aircrew average annual flying hours: 299 for F-14, 319 for F-18, 221 for A-6.
AIRCRAFT:
FIGHTER: 18 sqn: 11 with F-14A, 4 with F-14B, 3 with F-14D.
FGA/ATTACK: 31 sqn:
9 with A-6E.
2 with F/A-18A.
20 with F/A-18C/N.
ELINT: 4 sqn: 2 with EP-3, 2 with ES-3A.
ECM: 11 sqn with EA-6B.
MR: 16 land-based sqn: 5 with P-3CII, 11 with P-3CIII.
ASW: 11 sqn with S-3B.

AEW: 12 sqn with E-2C.
COMD: 2 sqn with E-6A (TACAMO).
OTHER: 5 sqn: 1 with C-130F, 1 with LC-130, 3 with C-2A.
TRAINING: 19 sqn:
5 'Aggressor' sqn with F-5E/F, A-4, F-16N.
14 trg sqn with T-2C, T-34C, T-44, T-45A.
HELICOPTERS:
ASW: 27 sqn:
10 with SH-60B (LAMPS Mk III).
4 (2 NR) with SH-2F (LAMPS Mk II).
13 with SH-60F/HH-60H.
MCM: 3 sqn with MH-53E/CH-53E.
MISC: 4 sqn with SH-3, 5 with CH-46, 2 with CH-53E.
TRG: 2 sqn with TH-57B/C.

RESERVES:
FIGHTER ATTACK: 4 sqn with F-18.
ATTACK: 2 sqn with A-6E.
FIGHTER: 4 sqn with F-14.
AEW: 2 sqn with E-2C.
ECM: 2 sqn with EA-6B.
MPA: 9 sqn with P-3B/C.
FLEET LOGISTICS SUPPORT: 1 wing with 11 sqn with C-9B/DC-9, 3 sqn with C-130T.
HELICOPTERS: 1 wing with 4 ASW sqn with SH-2F/G and SH-3H, 2 MCM sqn with MH-53E, 2 HCS sqn with HH-60H.
EQUIPMENT (incl NR): 1,676 cbt ac; 392 armed hel.
AIRCRAFT:
F-14: 417. **-A:** 291 (ftr, incl 48 NR) plus 58 in store; **-B plus:** 68 (ftr); **-D:** 58 (ftr).
F/A-18: 485. **-A:** 152 (FGA, incl 36 NR); **-B:** 22* (trg); **-C:** 270 (FGA); **-D:** 41* (trg).
F-5E/F: 25 (trg).
F-16: 25. **-N:** 21 (trg); **TF-16N:** 4 (trg).
A-4: 170* (trg). **-E/-F:** 18 (trg); **-M:** 12 (trg); **TA-:** 140; **4F/J:** (trg) (plus in store **-M:** 9; **E/F:** 12; **TA-F/J:** 58).
A-6: 339. **E:** 236* (FGA, incl 20 NR); **EA-6B:** 103 (ECM, incl 4 NR plus 25 in store).
E-2: 111. **-C:** 109 (AEW, incl 10 NR) (plus 7 in store); **TE-2C:** 2 (trg).
P-3: 302. **-C:** 246* (MR incl 72, NR); **EP-3:** 16 (ELINT); **RP-3A/D:** 11 (survey); **U/VP-3A:** 18 (VIP); **TP-3A:** 11 (trg) (plus 23 **P-3B** in store).
S-3 143. **-A:** 4* (ASW) (plus 17 in store); **-B:** 118* (ASW); **ES-3A:** 16 (ECM); **-US-3A:** 5 (tpt).
C-130: 26. **-F:** 3 (tpt); **-T:** 14 (tpt NR); **-LC-130F/R:** 7 (antarctic); **-TC-130G/Q:** 2 (tpt/trg) (plus 4 **EC-130Q** (CMD) and 1 **TC-130G/Q** in store).
CT-39: 7 (misc).
C-2A: 39 (tpt).
C-9B: 19 (tpt).
DC-9: 10 (tpt).
C-20: 4 (**-D:** 2 VIP, **-G:** 2 (tpt)).
UC-12: 85. **-B:** 65; **-F:** 10; **-M:** 10.
NU-1B: 1 (UTL).
U-6A: 3 (UTL).
T-2B/C: 146 (trg) (plus 31 in store).
T-39D/N: 17 (trg).
TA-7C: 5 (trg) (plus 10 in store).
T-44: 57 (trg).
T-45: 45 (trg).
T-34C: 273 (plus 43 in store).
TC-4C: 8 (trg).
HELICOPTERS:
HH-1N: 38 (utl) plus 6 in store.
CH-53E: 17 (tpt).
SH-60: 214. **-B:** 144 (ASW); **-F:** 70 (ASW).
HH-60H: 18 (cbt spt, incl 16 NR).
SH-2F/G: 76 (ASW, incl 16 NR) plus 23 in store.
SH-3G/H: 102 (ASW/SAR) plus 25 in store.
CH-46D: 28 (tpt, trg).
UH/HH-46D: 58 (utl).
TH-57: 129. **-B:** 47 (trg); **-C:** 82 (trg) (plus B-2, C-6 in store).
VH-3A: 4 (VIP).
MISSILES:
AAM: AIM-120 AMRAAM . AIM-7 *Sparrow*, AIM-54A/C *Phoenix*, AIM-9 *Sidewinder*.
ASM: AGM-45 *Shrike*, AGM-88A *HARM* (anti-radiation); AGM-84 *Harpoon*, AGM-119 *Penguin* Mk-3.

MARINE CORPS: 174,000 (7,600 women).
GROUND: 3 div:
1 with 3 inf regt (10bn), 1 tk, 2 lt armd recce (LAV-25), 1 aslt amph, 1 cbt engr bn, 1 arty regt (4 bn).
1 with 3 inf regt (8 bn), 1 tk, 1 lt armd recce (LAV-25, 1 aslt amph, 1 cbt engr bn, 1 arty regt (4 bn).
1 with 2 inf regt (6 bn), 1 arty regt (2 bn), 1 cbt engr, 1 recce coy.
3 Force Service Support Groups.
1 bn Marine Corps Security Force (Atlantic and Pacific).
Marine Security Guard bn (1 HQ, 7 region coy).
RESERVES (MCR):
1 div (3 inf (9 bn), 1 arty regt (5 bn); 2 tk, 1 lt armd inf (LAV-25), 1 aslt amph, 1 recce, 1 cbt engr bn).
1 Force Service Support Group.
EQUIPMENT:
MBT: 271 M-1A1 *Abrams,* 16 M-60A1 (plus 140 M-60A1 in store).
LAV: 401 LAV-25 (25mm gun), 239 LAV (variants, excl ATGW).

AAV: 1,322 AAV-7A1 (all roles).
TOWED ARTILLERY: 105mm: 335 M-101A1; 155mm: 584 M-198.
SP ARTILLERY: 155mm: 131 M-109A3.
MORTAR: 81mm: 656.
ATGW: 1,300 *TOW*, 1,978 *Dragon*, 95 LAV-*TOW*.
RL: 84mm: AT-4.
RCL: 83mm: 1,919.
SAM: 1,929 *Stinger,* some *Avenger*.
UAV: *Pioneer*.

AVIATION: 41,900 (2,200 women), 3 active air wings.
Average annual flying hours cbt aircrew: 231.
AIR WING (no standard org, but a notional wing is shown below): 166 fixed-wing aircraft, 155 hel: 48 F/A-18A/C, 36 F/A-18D, 60 AV-8B, 10 EA-6B, 12 KC-130 **ac**; 12 CH-53D, 32 CH-53E, 30 AH-1W, 21 UH-1N, 60 CH-46E **hel**.
AIRCRAFT:
FIGHTER/ATTACK: 10 sqn with F-18A/C.
FGA: 7 sqn with AV-8B.
ECM: 4 sqn with 20 EA-6B.
COMD: 6 sqn with 72 F/A-18D.
TANKER: 3 sqn with KC-130F/R.
TRAINING: 3 sqn.
HELICOPTERS: 30 sqn:
ARMED: 6 lt attack/utility sqn with 84 AH-1W and 66 UH-1N.
TRANSPORT: 18 **med** sqn with 80 CH-46E and 36 CH-53D; 6 **hy** sqn with 96 CH-532.
TRAINING: 3 sqn.
SAM:
1 bn (3 bty) with phase III *HAWK*.
2+ bn (5 bty) with *Avenger* and *Stinger*.

RESERVES 5,300 (300 women) (MCR): 1 air wing.
AIRCRAFT:
FIGHTER/ATTACK: 4 sqn with 48 F-18A.
FGA: 2 sqn with 24 A-4M.
TANKER: 2 tkr/tpt sqn with 24 KC-130T.
HELICOPTERS:
ARMED: 2 attack/utl sqn with 30 AH-1W, 18 UH-1N.
TRANSPORT: 4 sqn: 2 **med** with 24 CH-46E, 2 **hy** with 16 RH-53A.
SAM: 1 bn (3 bty) with *Hawk*, 1 bn (2 bty) with *Avenger* and *Stinger*.
EQUIPMENT (incl MCR): 495 cbt ac; 242 armed hel.
AIRCRAFT:
F-18A/-B/-C/-D: 262 (FGA incl 48 MCR, 34* trg).
AV-8B: 204. 172 (FGA), 17* (trg); **TAV-8B:** 15* (trg).
A-4M: 20 (MCR).
EA-6B: 25 (ECM).
OV-10A/D: 9* (MCR).
F-5E/F: 13 (trg, MCR).
KC-130: 68. **-F:** 30 (OCU); **-R:** 14; **-T:** 24 (tkr, MRC).
HELICOPTERS:
AH-1W: 140* incl 96 (armed, incl 30 MCR), 18 trg, (plus 43 in store).
UH-1N: 102* (incl 18 MCR, 12 trg).
CH-46D/E: 230 (tpt, incl 24 MCR, 6 HMX, 20 trg).
CH-53A/-D/-E: 159 (tpt, incl 20 trg), plus 17 in store.
RH-53D: 16 (MCR) plus 1 in store.
VH-60A: 8 (VIP tpt).
VH-3D: 11 (VIP tpt).
MISSILES:
SAM: 60 phase III *Improved HAWK* launcher, 235 *Avenger*, *Stinger*.
AAM: *Sparrow*, *Sidewinder*.
ASM: *Maverick*.

COAST GUARD (by law a branch of the Armed Forces; in peacetime operates under, and is funded by, the Department of Transportation. Budgets are not incl in the figures at p. 22):
Budget 1992: BA $3.6bn
1993: BA $3.7bn
1994: request $3.8bn
Strength: 38,100 (includes 3,150 women).
PATROL VESSELS: 135:
PATROL, OFFSHORE: 45:
12 *Hamilton* high-endurance with HH-65A LAMPS *Dolphin* hel, 2 x 3 ASTT, 4 with 1 x 76mm gun, 3 with *Harpoon* SSM (4 in refit).
13 *Bear* med-endurance with 1 x 76mm gun, HH-65A hel.
15 *Reliance* med-endurance with 1 x 3 inch gun, hel deck (excl 2 undergoing modernisation).
1 *Vindicator* (*USN Stalwart*) med-endurance cutter.
4 other med-endurance cutters.
PATROL, INSHORE: 90:
49 *Farallon*, 41 *Point Hope*(.
SUPPORT AND OTHER: 12:
2 icebreakers, 9 icebreaking tugs, 1 trg.
AVIATION: 77 ac, 152 hel:
FIXED WING: 25 HU-25A, 7 HU-25B, 9 HU-25C, 1 EC-130V, 30 HC-130H, 1 CA-21, 2 RG-8A, 1 VC-4A, 1 VC-11.
HELICOPTERS: 36 HH-3F (being replaced with HH-60J), 20 HH-60J, 96 HH-65A.

COAST GUARD RESERVE: 15,100.
Selected: 7,450; Ready and Standby: 7,600–7,800.

AIR FORCE: 433,800 (66,300 women).
Air Combat Command (ACC): 5 air force (incl 1 ICBM), 33 ac wing.
Air Mobility Command (AMC): 3 air force, 14 ac wing.
Aircrew average annual flying hours: fighter 236, bomber 216.
STRATEGIC: (see p. 23):
TACTICAL: 53 tac ftr sqn (sqn may be 18 or 24 ac):
14 with F-15.
7 with F-15E.
21 with F-16C/D (incl 3 AD).
3 (2 trg) with F-111.
5 with A-10.
1 *Wild Weasel* with F-4G.
2 with F-117.
SUPPORT:
RECCE: 3 sqn with U-2R and RC-135.
AEW: 1 Airborne Warning and Control wing; 7 sqn (incl 1 trg) with E-3.
EW: 2 sqn with EC-130, 1 sqn with EF-111.
FAC: 7 tac air control sqn:
7 mixed A-10A/OA-10A.
SPECIAL OPERATIONS (5,900): 1 wing plus 2 groups, 12 sqn (see p. 30).
TRAINING:
1 'Aggressor' sqn with F-16.
31 trg sqn with F-16, T-37, T-38, T-41, T-43, UV-18, Schweizer 2-37, C-5, C-12, C-130, C-141 **ac;** HH-3, HH-53, HH-60, U/TH-1 **hel**.
TRANSPORT: 45 sqn:
16 strategic: 5 with C-5, 11 with C-141.
10 tac airlift with C-130.
Units with C-135, VC-137, C-140, C-9, C-12, C-20, C-21.
TANKER: 29 sqn:
23 with KC-135, 6 with KC-10A.
SAR: 9 sqn (incl STRATCOM msl spt), HH-1, HH-3, HH-60 hel, HC -130AC.
MEDICAL: 3 medical evacuation sqn with C-9A.
WEATHER RECCE: WC-135.
TRIALS/weapons trg units with A-10, F-4, F-15, F-16, F-111, T-38, C-141 ac, UH-1 hel.

RESERVES:
AIR NATIONAL GUARD (ANG): 114,700 (15,700 women).
BOMBER: 1 sqn with B-1B.
24 wings, 100 sqn.
FIGHTER:
12 AD sqn (see p. 23).
FGA: 33 sqn:
1 with A-10, OA-10.
6 with A-7D/K.
2 with A-10.
20 with F-16.
4 with F-15A/B.
RECCE: 4 sqn with RF-4C.
EW: 1 sqn with EC-130E.
FAC: 1 sqn with OA-10.
TRANSPORT: 22 sqn:
19 tactical (1 trg) with C-130A/B/E/H.
3 strategic: 1 with C-5, 2 with C-141B.
TANKER: 17 sqn with KC-135E/R.
SAR: 3 sqn with HC-130 **ac**, MH-60G **hel**.
TRAINING: 7 sqn.
AIR FORCE RESERVE (AFR):
21 wings, 62 sqn (41 with ac).
BOMBER: 1 sqn with B-52H.
FGA: 12 sqn:
8 with F-16, 4 (incl 1 trg) with A-10.
TRANSPORT: 20 sqn:
13 tactical with C-130B/E/H.
1 weather recce with WC-130E/H.
6 strategic: 2 with C-5A, 4 with C-141B.
TANKER: 4 sqn with KC-135E/R.
SPECIAL OPERATIONS: 1 sqn (AFSOC) with AC-130A.
SAR: 3 sqn (AMC) with HC-130H **ac**, HH-60 **hel**.
ASSOCIATE: 21 sqn (personnel only):
4 sqn for C-5, 13 for C-141, 1 aero-medical for C-9.
3 sqn for KC-10.
EQUIPMENT:
LONG-RANGE STRIKE/ATTACK: 200 cbt ac (plus 343 in store).
B-52: 97. **-H:** 95 strike (with AGM-86 ALCM 1 test) (plus in store: 343; -C: 15, -D: 85; -E: 43; -F: 52; -G: 148); **-B/G** 2 test.
B-1B: 95 (strike, test).
B-2: 8 (strike, test).
RECCE: U-2R/RT: 15; **RC-135:** 19
COMMAND: E-3: 34. **E-4B:** 4. **EC-135:** 15.
TACTICAL: 3,329 cbt ac (incl ANG, AFR plus 1,701 in store); no armed hel:
F-4: 122. **-E:** 14 (FGA); **-G:** 60 (incl 6 ANG (*Wild Weasel*)); **RF-4C:** 48. Plus 865 in store (incl 201 RF-4C).
F-15: 774. **-A/B/C/D:** 458 (ftr incl 146 ANG); 121 (OCU, test); **-E:** 195 (FGA); plus 109 F-15A in store.
F-16: 1,848. **-A:** 446 (incl ftr 168 ANG, FGA; 68 AFR, 353 ANG); **-B:** 99 (incl ftr 12 ANG, FGA 12 AFR, 51 ANG); **-C:** 1,099 (incl 89 AFR, 433 ANG); **-D:** 204 (incl 13 AFR, 67 ANG); plus 130 F-16A/B in store.
F-111E/F: 100 (FGA) (incl 23 OCU); plus 202 in store.
EF-111A: 40 (ECM).

F-117: 54. 42 (FGA), 10* (trg), plus 2 test.
A-7: 0; plus 226 in store.
A-10A: 240 (FGA, incl 69 ANG, 41 AFR); plus 169 in store.
OA-10A: 163 (FAC incl 47 ANG, 27 AFR).
EC-18B/D: 6 (Advanced Range Instrumentation).
E-8A: 3 (JSTARS ac).
WC-135B: 2 (weather recce).
OC-135: 3 (Open Skies Treaty).
AC-130: 28. **-A**: 6* (special ops, AFR); **-H/U**: 22* (special ops, USAF). **HC-130N/P:** 58 (28 special ops; 30 SAR incl 11 ANG, 12 AFR); **EC-130E/H:** 27 (special ops incl 8 ANG); **MC-130E/H:** 37 (special ops); **WC-130E/H:** 12 (weather recce, AFR).
OA-37B: 2 (test, plus 19 in store).
TRANSPORT:
C-5: 126. **-A**: 76 (strategic tpt; incl 13 ANG, 30 AFR); **-B**: 50 (incl 7 OCU).
C-141B: 239 (167 strategic tpt, 14 OCU, 18 ANG, 40 AFR); plus 18 in store.
C-130: 529. 498 (tac tpt, incl 188 ANG, 110 AFR); 31 (trg, incl 9 ANG); plus 78 in store.
C-135A/B/C/E: 6.
VC-137B/C: 7 (VIP tpt).
C-9A/C: 23.
C-12: 75 (liaison).
C-17A: 13 (4 test, 9 strategic tpt).
C-20: 14. **-A:** 3, **-B:** 7, **-C:** 3. **-D:** 1.
C-21: 79.
C-22B: 4 (ANG).
C-23A: 3.
VC-25A: 2.
C-26A/B: 33 (ANG); **VC-26C:** 1.
C-27A: 10 (tpt).
T-43A: 2 (tpt ANG).
TANKERS:
KC-135: 553 (295 USAF, 201 ANG, 57 AFR); plus 73 in store.
KC-10A: 59 tkr/tpt.
TRAINING:
T-3A: 42. **T-37B:** 559 (plus 24 in store). **T-38:** 560 (plus 24 in store). **T-39:** 5. **T-41A/D:** 100. **T-43A:** 10. **TC-135S:** 1. **TC-135W:** 1. **UV-18B**: 2. **Schweizer 2-37:** 18. **T-1A:** 80, **TG-7A:** 9.
HELICOPTERS:
MH-53-J: 41 *Pave Low* (special ops).
HH-60G: 80 (incl 27 AFR, 17 ANG).
MH-60G: 31.
HH-1H: 22.
UH-1N: 66.
MISSILES:
AAM: AIM-9P/L/M *Sidewinder*, AIM-7E/F/M *Sparrow*, AIM 120, A/B AMRAAM.
ASM: 1,300 AGM-69A SRAM; 1,666 AGM-86B ALCM; 26,000+ AGM-65A/B/D/G *Maverick*; 5,904 AGM-88A/B *HARM*; AGM-84A *Harpoon*; AGM-86C ALCM; 84 AGM-142A/B/C/D *HAVE NAP*.
CIVIL RESERVE AIR FLEET (CRAF): 353 commercial ac (numbers fluctuate):
LONG-RANGE: 314:
154 passenger (Boeing 747, L-1011, DC-8/-10, B-757, B-767, A-310, MD-11).
160 cargo (Boeing 707, 747, DC-8/-10, MD-11).
SHORT-RANGE: 39 (Boeing 727, 737, 767, L-100, DC-9, MD-80) (30 passenger, 9 cargo).

SPECIAL OPERATIONS FORCES:

units only listed – manpower and eqpt shown in relevant single service section.
ARMY: (15,000):
5 SF gp (each 3 bn).
1 Ranger inf regt (3 bn).
1 special ops avn regt (3 bn).
1 Psychological Operations gp (5 bn).
1 Civil Affairs bn (4 coy).
1 sigs, 1 spt bn.
RESERVES: (1,600 ARNG, 9,400 AR):
2 ARNG SF gp (6 bn).
12 AR Civil Affairs HQ (3 comd, 9 bde).
24 AR Civil Affairs 'bn' (coy).
NAVY: (4,000):
2 Naval Special Warfare Command (incl 1 trg).
2 Naval Special Warfare gp.
5 Naval Special Warfare units.
6 Sea-Air-Land (SEAL) teams.
2 SEAL delivery veh teams.
3 Special Boat sqn.
6 Drydeck shelters (DDS).
RESERVES: (1,400):
6 Naval Special Warfare gp det.
2 Naval Special Warfare unit det.
5 SEAL team det.
2 Special Boat unit.
1 engr spt unit.
2 cbt spt special hel sqn.
AIR FORCE: (6,000):
1 air force HQ, 1 wing, 2 groups 12 sqn:
4 with MC-130.
1 with AC-130.
3 with HC-130.
3 with MH-53 hel.
1 with MH-60 hel.
RESERVES: (1,100):
1 wing, 1 group.

2 sqn (AFSOC):
1 with 9 AC-130A/H (AFR).
1 with 8 EC-130E (ANG).

DEPLOYMENT:

Commanders' NATO appointments also shown (e.g., COMEUCOM is also SACEUR).

EUROPEAN COMMAND (EUCOM): some 159,600, incl Mediterranean Sixth Fleet: HQ Stuttgart-Vaihingen (Commander is SACEUR).
ARMY: HQ US Army Europe (USAREUR), Heidelberg.
NAVY: HQ US Navy Europe (USNAVEUR), London (Commander is also CINCAFSOUTH).
AIR FORCE: HQ US Air Force Europe (USAFE), Ramstein (Commander is COMAIRCENT).
GERMANY:
ARMY: 81,000.
V Corps with 1 armd, 1 mech inf div, 1 arty, 1 AD (1 *Patriot* (6 bty), 1 *Avenger* bn), 1 engr, 2 avn bde.
Army AD Comd (1 bde with 2 bn *Patriot* (each 3 bty)).
Prepositioned equipment (POMCUS) for 4 armd/ mech bde. Approx 57% stored in Ge.
EQUIPMENT (incl POMCUS in Ge, Be and Nl): some 1,968 MBT, 1,269 AIFV, 1,891 APC, 1,373 arty/MRL/mor, 153 atk hel.
AIR FORCE: 22,200, 90 cbt ac.
2 air force HQ: USAFE and 17th Air Force.
1 tac ftr wings: 5 sqn (3 with 54 F-16C/D, 1 with 18 F-15C/D, 1 with 12 A-10 and 6 OA-10).
1 cbt spt wing, 1 air control wing.
1 tac airlift wing: incl 16 C-130E and 4 C-9A.
BELGIUM:
ARMY: 800. Approx 22% of POMCUS.
NAVY: 100.
AIR FORCE: 500.
GREECE:
ARMY: 60.
NAVY: 200. Base facilities Soudha Bay, Makri (Crete).
AIR FORCE: 300; 1 air base gp. Facilities at Iraklion (Crete).
ITALY:
ARMY: 2,600. HQ Vicenza. 1 inf bn gp, 1 arty bty. Equipment for Theatre Reserve Unit/Army Readiness Package South (TRU/ARPS) incl 133 MBT, 165 AIFV, 116 APC, 98 arty/MLRS/mor.
NAVY: 6,800. HQ Gaeta; bases at Naples, La Maddalena, 1 MR sqn with 9 P-3C at Sigonella.
AIR FORCE: 3,200; 1 ftr sqn, 17 F-16C, 1 F-16D.
LUXEMBOURG:
ARMY: 30. Approx 21% of POMCUS.
MEDITERRANEAN:
NAVY: some 17,000 (incl 2,000 Marines).
Sixth Fleet: typically 4 SSN, 1 CVBG (1 CV, 6 surface combatants, 2 fast support ships), 1 URG (4 support ships, 2 escorts).
(**MARINES:** some 2,000: 1 MEU (SOC) embarked aboard amph ready gp ships.)
NETHERLANDS:
ARMY: 500. Approx 7% of POMCUS.
AIR FORCE: 850.
NORWAY: prepositioning for 1 MEB (24 arty, no aviation assets).
PORTUGAL (for Azores, see Atlantic Command):
NAVY: 55.
AIR FORCE: 1,100.
SPAIN:
NAVY: 4,100; base at Rota.
1 MR sqn with 9 P-3C.
AIR FORCE: 400.
TURKEY:
ARMY: 200.
NAVY: spt facilities at Iskenderun and Yumurtalik.
AIR FORCE: 3,200, facilities at Incirlik.
1 tac gp, 2 air base gps (ac on det only).
Some 57 ac: F-15, F-16, F-111F, EF-111, F-4G.
Installations for SIGINT, space tracking and seismic monitoring.
UNITED KINGDOM:
NAVY: 2,100. HQ London, admin and spt facilities, 1 SEAL det.
AIR FORCE: 12,300:
1 air force HQ: 4 ftr wings, 1 air base gp: 63 cbt ac, 4 sqn with 45 F-15E, 1 sqn with 18 F-15C/D.
1 special ops gp with 3 sqns: 1 with 5 MH-53J, 1 with 6 HC-130, 1 with 6 MC-130H.
1 air refuelling wg with 9 KC-135.

PACIFIC COMMAND (USPACOM): HQ: Hawaii.
ALASKA:
ARMY: 9,400; 1 lt inf div (2 inf bde, 2 arty bn, 1 avn bde).
AIR FORCE: 10,750. 1 air force HQ; 4 sqn (2 with 36 F-15C/D, 1 with 18 F-15E, 1 with 18 F-16C/D).
HAWAII:
ARMY: 18,800. HQ US Army Pacific (USARPAC).
1 lt inf div.
1 ARNG inf bde.
AIR FORCE: 4,800. HQ Pacific Air Forces (PACAF).
1 air base wing, 1 tac ftr sqn with 18 F-15A/B (ANG), 1 comd/control sqn with 2 EC-135.

NAVY: 12,000. HQ US Pacific Fleet. Homeport for some 17 submarines, 16 PSC and 10 spt and misc ships.
MARINES: 8,200. HQ Marine Forces Pacific, 1 MEB.
SINGAPORE:
NAVY: about 100, log facilities.
AIR FORCE: 40 det spt sqn.
JAPAN:
ARMY: 1,900.
1 corps HQ, base and spt units.
AIR FORCE: 15,600. 1 air force HQ: 96 cbt ac.
2 wings (6 sqn) with 54 F-15C/D, 42 F-16, 7 C-12F, 2 C-21A ac, 3 UH-1N hel.
1 sqn with 3 E-3 AWACS.
1 tac tpt gp with 20 C-130 (ANG).
1 sqn with 15 KC-135 tkr (ANG).
1 SAR sqn with 6 HC-130, 3 MC-130 **ac**, 4 HH-60 **hel** (ANG).
NAVY: 7,300. Bases: Yokosuka (HQ 7th Fleet): homeport for 1 CV, 8 surface combatants; Sasebo: homeport for 3 submarines, 3 amph ships.
MARINES: 20,000; 1 MEF.
SOUTH KOREA:
ARMY: 26,500.
1 Army HQ (UN command).
1 inf div (2 bde, (6 bn)), 2 SP arty, 1 MLRS, 1 AD bn.
AIR FORCE: 9,750. 1 air force HQ: 2 wings, 84 cbt ac.
3 sqn with 72 F-16.
1 tac control sqn with 12 OA-10.
1 SAR sqn, 2 HH-60G, 5 MH-53J.
1 recce det with 3 U-2, 2 C-12.
GUAM:
AIR FORCE: 2,450. 1 air force HQ.
NAVY: 4,600, MPS-3 (4 ships with eqpt for 1 MEB). Naval air station, comms and spt facilities.
AUSTRALIA:
AIR FORCE: 270.
NAVY: some 100. Comms facility at NW Cape, SEWS/SIGINT station at Pine Gap, and SEWS station at Nurrungar.
DIEGO GARCIA:
NAVY: 900, MPS-2 (5 ships with eqpt for 1 MEB). Naval air station, spt facilities.
US WEST COAST:
MARINES: 1 MEF.
AT SEA:
PACIFIC FLEET: (HQ Pearl Harbor).
Main base: Pearl Harbor.
Other bases: Bangor (Washington); San Diego and Long Beach (California).
Submarines: 7 *Ohio* SSBN, 5 SSGN, 27 SSN.
Surface Combatants: 6 CV/CVN, 29 CG/CGN, 2 DDG, 15 DD, 12 FFG, 4 FF.
Amphibious: 1 comd, 3 LHA, 3 LPH, 7 LPD, 6 LSD, 6 LST, 2 LKA.
Surface Combatants divided between two fleets:
3rd Fleet (HQ San Diego): covers Eastern and Central Pacific, Aleutians, Bering Sea, etc. Typically 4 CVBG, 4 URG. Amph gp.
7th Fleet (HQ Yokosuka, Japan): covers Western Pacific, Japan, Philippines, ANZUS responsibilities, Indian Ocean. Typically 1 CVBG, 1 URG, amph ready gp (1 MEU embarked).
INDIAN OCEAN: (det from 7th/2nd Fleets).

CENTRAL COMMAND (USCENTCOM): takes command of deployed forces in its region.
HQ USCENTCOM: MacDill AFB, Florida.
AT SEA:
Joint Task Force Middle East.
Average Composition of US Naval Forces deployed in Persian Gulf/North Arabian Sea: 1 CVBG (1 CV/CVN, 2 CG/CGN, 2 FFG, 1 AO/AOE/AE, 2 SSN). (Forces provided from Atlantic and Pacific.)
KUWAIT:
ARMY: prepositioned eqpt for 1 tk, 1 mech bn, 1 arty bty incl 58 MBT, 72 AIFV, 8 arty, 1 *Patriot* bn.
SAUDI ARABIA:
AIR FORCE: units on rotational detachment, numbers vary (incl: F-4G, F-15, F-16, F-117, C-130, KC-135, U-2, J-STARS).

SOUTHERN COMMAND (USSOUTHCOM):
HQ USSOUTHCOM: Quarry Heights, Panama.
PANAMA:
ARMY: HQ US Army South, Fort Clayton, Panama: 3,800.
1 inf bde (1 inf bn), 1 avn bde.
NAVY: HQ US Naval Forces Southern Command, Fort Amador, Panama: 700.
Special boat unit, fleet support.
MARINES: 200.
AIR FORCE: 2,400.
1 air div: 2 C-130, 1 C-21, 9 C-27, 1 CT-43.
HONDURAS:
ARMY: 300.
AIR FORCE: 50.

ATLANTIC COMMAND (USACOM):
HQ: Norfolk, Virginia (CINC has op control of all CONUS-based army and air forces).
US EAST COAST:
MARINES:
1 MEF.

NAVY:
MPS-1 (4 ships with eqpt for 1 MEB).

BERMUDA:
NAVY: 800.

CUBA:
NAVY: 1,900 (Guantánamo).
MARINES: 340 (Guantánamo).

ICELAND:
NAVY: 1,800. 1 MR sqn with 9 P-3.
AIR FORCE: 400.
1 SAR sqn with 4 HH-60G.
MARINES: 80.

PORTUGAL (AZORES):
NAVY: 10.
Limited facilities at Lajes.
AIR FORCE: 1,150.
1 SAR det.

UK:
NAVY: 150.
Comms and int facilities, Edzell, Thurso.

AT SEA:
ATLANTIC FLEET: (HQ: Norfolk, Virginia).
Other main bases: Groton (Connecticut); Charleston (S. Carolina); King's Bay (Georgia); Mayport (Florida). Submarines: 7 *Ohio*, 3 other SSBN, 16 SSGN, 35 SSN. Surface Combatants: 6 CV/CVN, 23 CG/CGN, 5 DDG, 16 DD, 23 FFG, 4 FF. Amphibious: 1 LCC, 2 LHA, 4 LPH, 6 LPD, 5 LSD, 6 LST, 1 LKA.
Surface Forces divided into two fleets:
2nd Fleet (HQ: Norfolk): covers Atlantic. Typically 4–5 CVBG, amph gp, 4 URG.
6th Fleet (HQ: Gaeta, Italy): Mediterranean. Under op comd of EUCOM. See EUCOM entry for typical force levels.

CONTINENTAL UNITED STATES

(CONUS): major units/formations only listed.
ARMY (USACOM): 222,700 provides general reserve of cbt-ready ground forces for other comd.
Active: 4 Army HQ, 3 Corps HQ (1 AB), 2 armd, 3 mech, 1 lt inf, 1 AB, 1 air aslt div; 2 armd, 6 arty bde; 2 armd cav regt, 8 AD bn (2 *Avenger*, 6 *Patriot*).
Reserve: ARNG: 3 armd, 1 mech, 3 inf, 1 lt inf div; 20 indep bde, 1 armd cav regt. AR: 1 lt inf bde.
US STRATEGIC COMMAND (USSTRATCOM): see entry on p. 22.
AIR COMBAT COMMAND (ACC): responsible for provision of strategic AD units and of cbt-ready Air Force units for rapid deployment.
US SPECIAL OPERATIONS COMMAND (USSOCOM): HQ MacDill AFB, Florida. Comd all active, reserve and National Guard special ops forces of all services based in CONUS. See p. 30.
US TRANSPORTATION COMMAND (USTRANSCOM): responsible for providing all common-user airlift, sealift and land transportation to deploy and maintain US forces on a global basis.
AIR MOBILITY COMMAND (AMC): responsible for providing strategic, tac and special op airlift, aero-medical evacuation, SAR and weather recce.
MILITARY SEALIFT COMMAND: see entry on p. 26.

FORCES ABROAD:

UN AND PEACEKEEPING:

CROATIA (UNPROFOR II): 322; field hospital.
EGYPT (MFO): 500; 1 inf bn.
GERMANY (*Provide Promise*): 4 C-141, 25 C-130.
IRAQ/KUWAIT (UNIKOM): 15 Observers.
ITALY (*Deny Flight*): USAF: 2,600: 8 F-15E, 12 F-16C, 12 O/A-10, 3 AC-130, 3 EC-130, 10 KC-135. USMC: 8 F/A-18D. USN: 1 CV/CVN 18 F/A-18C.
ADRIATIC (*Sharp Guard*): 1 CVBG plus 1 amph rdy gp (with MEU embarked): 1 CV/CVN, 2 CG/CGN, 2 FFG, 3AO/AOE/AE, plus 1 LPH/LHA/LHD, 1 LPD, 1 LSD, 1 LST, 12 F-14/F/A-18, 6 A-6E, KC-135, P-3C.
MACEDONIA: 500; inf bn, incl 3 UH-60 hel.
MIDDLE EAST(UNTSO): 16 Observers.
MOZAMBIQUE: (ONUMOZ): 5.
RWANDA (*Support Hope*): 225 engr, cargo handling at Kigale and Goma (Zaire); 985 elsewhere in Africa.
WESTERN SAHARA (MINURSO): 30 Observers.
SAUDI ARABIA (*Southern Watch*): USAF units on rotation, numbers vary (incl F-4G, F-15, F-16, F-117, C-130, KC-135, U-2, JSTARS).
TURKEY (*Provide Comfort*): 1,900. Army (600); Air Force (1,300). 1 tac, 1 Air Base GP with some 57 ac (F-15E, F-16, EF-111, F-4G).

PARAMILITARY:

CIVIL AIR PATROL (CAP): 68,000 (27,500 cadets); HQ, 8 geographical regions, 52 wings, 1,881 units, 579 CAP ac, plus 8,465 private ac.

NATO

Partnership for Peace

In late 1991, after the Cold War ended, the North Atlantic Treaty Organisation (NATO) formed the North Atlantic Cooperation Council (NACC) to improve its relations with the countries of East and Central Europe. All former members of the Warsaw Pact and republics of the former Soviet Union, including the Baltic states, automatically became members. Albania joined NACC on 5 June 1992. However, a number of countries still hoped for full NATO membership, while NATO considered it too early to expand the Alliance. On American initiative the Partnership for Peace (PFP) programme was developed to improve further military cooperation between NATO and other European states, including non-NACC members of the Conference on Security and Cooperation in Europe (CSCE) who wished to join. NATO's Partnership for Peace Invitation was issued at the summit meeting held on 10 January 1994 and the first application to join was made by Estonia on 3 February. By 13 July 22 countries, including Russia, had joined; only Armenia, Belarus and Tajikistan had not joined from NACC, and Finland, Sweden and Slovenia had joined from the CSCE.

Membership of Partnership for Peace requires two initial actions: first, the signing of the Framework Document which sets out the basic commitments of both NATO and participating partners; second each partner has to submit a Presentation Document setting out their programme for participation. Partners are committed to cooperating with NATO in the following areas:

- Facilitating transparency in national-defence planning and budgeting processes;
- Ensuring democratic control of defence forces;
- Maintaining the capability and readiness to contribute, subject to constitutional considerations, to operations under the authority of the UN and/or the responsibility of the CSCE;
- Developing cooperative military relations with NATO for joint planning, training and exercises to strengthen their ability to undertake missions in the fields of peacekeeping, search and rescue, humanitarian operations, and others as may subsequently be agreed;
- Developing, over the longer term, forces that are better able to operate with those of the members of the North Atlantic Alliance.

Each Presentation Document is specific to the country presenting it, but most contain items under the following headings:

Aerospace Research and Development
Air Defence
Arms Control and Disarmament
Civil Emergency Planning
Crisis Management
Defence Budgeting
Defence Policy
Defence Procurement
Democratic Control
Environmental Protection
Exercises (of all types)
Infrastructure
Interoperability (command and control)
Interoperability (troops)
Logistics
Peacekeeping
Personnel Management
Public Relations
Standardisation
Training

With the expansion of cooperative activities NATO has established a Partnership Coordination Cell at Mons in Belgium and is preparing accommodation at NATO headquarters for partners to maintain a permanent liaison presence there.

A key element in PFP is to develop forces in partner countries better able to operate with those of NATO, particularly in peacekeeping and humanitarian relief operations. NATO has reaffirmed that membership is open to other European states; Partnership for Peace is a qualifying step towards admission. In January 1994, President Clinton told European leaders in Prague that 'the question is no longer whether NATO will take on new members, but when and how we will do it'.

Until then NATO had committed itself to 'consulting any partner that perceives a direct threat to its territorial integrity, political independence or security'.

Peacekeeping

NATO continues to play an important role in support of the UN's peacekeeping operations in Bosnia-Herzegovina. The air exclusion zone and the naval blockade continue. A new element was added in August 1993 when NATO deployed ground-attack aircraft to Italy to provide air support for UN troops should this be necessary. The composition of NATO's forces operating in the region is listed in the Peacekeeping section at p. 268. NATO reaffirmed, both at the December 1993 summit and at the North Atlantic Council meeting in June 1994, its determination to contribute to the implementation of an agreed peace settlement. The Allied Rapid Reaction Corps headquarters and elements of the Corps are standing by should NATO peackeeping forces be requested. In addition to the deployed naval and air forces there are over 20,000 NATO troops on peacekeeping duties in Croatia, Bosnia-Herzegovina and Macedonia.

NATO Reorganisation

In July 1994 Allied Forces Northern Europe was disbanded and replaced by Allied Forces North-West Europe (AF NORTHWEST) with its headquarters at High Wycombe (UK). Its Principal Subordinate Commands (PSCs) are Allied Air Forces North-West Europe (AIR NORTHWEST), also headquartered at High Wycombe, Allied Naval Forces North-West Europe (NAVNORTHWEST), with its headquarters at Northwood (UK), and Allied Forces North Europe (HQ NORTH) located at Stavanger (Norway). The headquarters of the Allied Rapid Reaction Corps has now moved from Bielefeld to Rheindahlen (previously the headquarters of the Northern Army Group and 2 ATAF) where the headquarters of the Multi-National Division (Central) (NATO's air-mobile division) is also located. Allied Command Channel has been eliminated as planned, but neither Allied Land Forces South-Central Europe nor 7th Allied Tactical Air Force have been established.

Combined Joint Task Forces

Following the US initiative to develop the 'Adaptive Joint Force Package', NATO has adopted a programme to develop Combined Joint Task Forces (CJTF). 'Combined' because forces from more than one country would participate, and 'Joint' because elements from more than one service would take part. The key to a successful CJTF is fielding a practised, deployable joint force headquarters which can be expanded by adding staff officers from those countries contributing to the force, but which are not already represented at the headquarters. At present there is no such headquarters permanently established.

European Pillar

Western European Union (WEU)

Membership of the WEU now includes Greece which ratified its accession on 12 January 1994. However, not all members have yet ratified the decision on associate status. Nevertheless, the WEU decided at the Council of Ministers meeting in May 1994 that future associate members (Iceland, Norway and Turkey) may nominate officers to the Planning Cell and would be connected to the WEU communications network as soon as possible.

The WEU has also developed its own partnership scheme. On 9 May 1994 the WEU Council of Ministers and the Foreign and Defence Ministers of Bulgaria, the Czech Republic, Estonia, Hungary, Latvia, Lithuania, Poland, Romania and Slovakia agreed that the nine countries should become Associate Partners of the WEU. Associate Partners may participate in meetings of the WEU Council, may have a liaison arrangement with the Planning Cell, may participate in the implementation of humanitarian and rescue tasks, peacekeeping, crisis management and in related exercises. They will also be able to offer forces for specific operations.

A WEU report on the Planning Cell, which has now been established for over a year, commented that it had to work in a political vacuum as there was no common European defence policy on which to base its activity. The WEU Council of Ministers has tasked the Permanent Council to begin work on the formulation of a policy with a view to presenting their preliminary conclusions at the next ministerial meeting in November 1994.

Eurocorps

Three more countries have assigned troops to the Eurocorps. Spain's contribution is a mechanised brigade which will be expanded to a division by 1988; Luxembourg will assign its infantry battalion on 1 January 1995; and Belgium its mechanised division. The Corps is due to be fully operational in 1995.

German Constitution

On 12 July 1994 the German Constitutional Court ruled that the Constitution did not bar German forces from taking part in military operations outside the NATO area, including those requiring the use of force. However, each operation must be authorised by a simple majority of the Bundestag. On 22 July the Bundestag gave its approval for German participation in *Operation Deny Flight* and *Operation Sharp Guard*. For some time Germany has provided air crew for NATO AWACS monitoring the air exclusion zone over Bosnia, and a frigate as part of the naval force enforcing UN sanctions.

Turkey's Kurdish Problem

Turkey has been conducting operations against a Kurdish guerrilla movement headed by the Kurdistan Worker's Party (PKK) since 1984. Significantly large casualty figures for both Kurds and Turkish armed forces are announced virtually every week. The Interior Ministry has stated that 'more than 1,500 terrorists were killed in the first three months' of 1994. In 1993 over 4,000, including civilians, Turkish soldiers and PKK fighters, were killed compared to some 2,600 in 1992. Some 160,000 troops are said to be deployed in south-east Turkey compared to the normal figure of about 90,000. The guerrilla war is affecting the rate of desertion and 'draft dodging'. Some 250,000 men are said not to have reported for compulsory service, but over how long a period is not known. On two occasions the German government has temporarily halted delivery of armaments after reports that they were being used in counter-terrorist operations. In July 1994 the US Senate's Appropriations Committee added a requirement to the foreign military aid bill that the sale of any military equipment to Turkey 'shall expressly state that it will not be used for internal security purposes'. In April 1994 parliament voted to remove parliamentary immunity from six Kurdish MPs who are now on trial accused of treason.

Nuclear Weapons Developments

In November 1993 the **United Kingdom** Minister of Defence announced that when *Trident* SLBM armed submarines are deployed they will not carry more than 96 warheads per boat and on occasion a much lower number than this. In February 1994, Prime Minister John Major, during a visit to Moscow, announced that British strategic missiles would no longer be targeted at Russia. The second *Vanguard*-class SSBN was rolled out in September 1993 and will start sea trials late in 1994. HMS *Vanguard*, the first of the class, carried out test-firing of *Trident* SLBM in April 1994 and should be fully operational shortly. It is understood that the UK has procured 44 *Trident* missiles, including presumably the two that were test-fired. The government has dropped its plans to replace the WE-177 nuclear bomb with a stand-off weapon, and is considering the use of a single-warhead *Trident* missile in the sub-strategic role.

There has been no change to the **French** nuclear situation. In May 1994, President Mitterrand said that France had around 500 nuclear warheads, 384 of them for the M-4 SLBM. The first of the new class of SSBN, *Le Triomphant*, is expected to be in service in 1996. The third boat in this class was ordered in mid-1993.

Conventional Military Developments and Plans

In **Belgium** good progress has been made towards reducing the size of the armed forces to 40,000 by 1997. No more conscripts are being called up. During the last 12 months the Army has reduced by 6,000, there are 10,000 conscripts less and 4,000 volunteers added to the regular strength. The Air Force has reduced by 5,000 and now has no conscripts, and the Navy, down by 1,500, has only 300 conscripts remaining. The Army has been reorganised: the active tank brigade has been converted to a mechanised brigade; the amount of combat support has been reduced; and the reserve brigades disbanded. Surplus equipment is to be either sold or scrapped, including 200 MBT, 160 APC, 100 artillery and mortars. Air defence will be based solely on M-167 *Vulcan* guns and *Mistral* SAM (54 have been added during the year and 42 more are still to be delivered) with *Improved Hawk* SAM and *Gepard* SP AA guns being sold. Only *Milan* ATGW will remain in service with *Swingfire* SP ATGW and JPK 90mm SP guns being retired. It was announced in May 1994 that the Belgian and Netherlands navies were planning to integrate their operations. However, Netherlands submarines will not be integrated. The active Belgian ground forces under the Intervention Force Headquarters, but less the Para-Commando brigade which forms part of NATO's multinational air-mobile division, have been assigned to the Eurocorps. The Belgian Defence White Paper published in July included the commitment to make available two army battalions, one squadron of F-16s, one frigate, one command and logistic ship and three minesweepers for operations if needed by the UN, the CSCE, NATO or the WEU/EU.

The **Canadian** Navy will have commissioned three more *Halifax*-class frigates by the end of July 1994. One *Restigouche*-class and the last two *Mackenzie*-class frigates have been retired. The first defence budget set by the new government has cut spending by $US1.2bn, not counting the $US1.2bn saved by the cancellation of the EH-101 helicopter programme. Most savings will be achieved by base-closures and the reduction of 8,000 uniformed and 8,400 civilian personnel.

In **Denmark** the Army has replaced its *Redeye* SAM with *Stinger*. The Navy has commissioned three more *Flyvefisken* (standard Flex) coastal patrol craft, and three more are due by the end of 1995. One *Alssund*-class mine-countermeasures vessel has been retired and one *Flyvefisken*-class mine-hunter commissioned. The Air Force has disbanded its reconnaissance squadron which had eight RF-35 *Draken* aircraft.

The **French** Minister of Defence has clearly stated that conscription will not be discontinued. The French Army has resubordinated the mountain division from the Force Action Rapide to the 3rd Corps and two reserve light armoured divisions which had been based on the infantry and armoured schools have been disbanded. By the year 2,000 there are planned to be eight army divisions, one less than now; four will be 'heavy' and four 'light' divisions. The deployment of Foreign Legion and Marines units is better depicted this year. In France these units form part of the Army's divisions while overseas they are garrison troops. The Army has taken delivery of 36 more *Leclerc* tanks. Eventually 310 will be produced which will equip one-and-a-half divisions. A further 148 VBL M-11 armoured reconnaissance vehicles have been acquired, as have 50 more *Mistral* SAM. The Navy has retired one *Daphné*-class submarine and commissioned two more *Floréal*-class frigates. The *Charles de Gaulle* nuclear-powered aircraft carrier was launched in May 1994 and is expected to enter service in 1999. It will embark *Rafale* fighters and *Hawkeye* AWACS aircraft. At the launch ceremony, the Minister of Defence stated his intention to acquire a second of the class by 2003. The first of the new class of frigates, *La Fayette*, is expected to commission in 1995 with one more each in 1996, 1997, 1998, 2000 and 2001. The Air Force commands have been renamed, and the main changes are that the air-defence command is now entitled Commandement Air des Systèmes de Surveillance d'Information et de Communications (CASSIC), and the tactical air force is now Commandement des Forces Aériennes de Combat (CFAC). Two fighter squadrons with *Mirage* F1 CR have been disbanded. Two FGA squadrons have been disbanded and three re-equipped.

The reorganisation of the **German** Army is complete. There are still three Corps headquarters but one has now become a joint German/Netherlands headquarters. The number of divisions has been reduced to eight, and their headquarters also have the dual role of Military District Command (MDC). The Army's tank inventory is much reduced from 4,778 to 2,855. 1,276 *Leopard*-1 and 649 M-48 have been or will be disposed of and over 400 former East German tanks have been destroyed. All in-service *Leopard*-1 tanks are now upgraded to 1A5, and 34 more *Leopard*-2 have been acquired. All M-110 203mm SP artillery have been transferred to Greece and Turkey and over 600 BMP-1 (former East German Army) AIFV have been transferred to other countries. In the last 12 months, over 3,000 items of equipment from the former East German Army have been destroyed in accordance with the CFE Treaty, including 400 MBT, 700 APC, 1,200 armoured reconnaissance vehicles and 370 artillery pieces. Army manpower strength has been reduced by some 33,000. The Navy has retired two *Hamburg*-class destroyers and commissioned two more *Frankenthal*-class coastal minehunters. The Navy hopes to place a contract for four Type-212 submarines in 1995, but budgetary approval has not yet been obtained. 39 *Tornado* aircraft have been transferred to the Air Force which has retired its force of F-4F and *Alpha Jet* FGA aircraft. Some *Alpha Jet* are still kept in a training role, and 50 are to be transferred to Portugal. *Tornado* has now replaced RF-4E in the reconnaissance role and an Electronic Combat and Reconnaissance (ECR) wing with *Tornado* aircraft has been formed. Some 130 aircraft of the former East German Air Force have been destroyed. The governing coalition is debating whether to reduce the period of compulsory service from 12 to 10 months, while the 1994 White Paper confirmed that conscription would continue. Of the 210,000 volunteers in the armed forces only 38,000 were not officers or under-officers. The number of conscripts claiming to be conscientious objectors in 1993 rose to 111,000 from the 1990 total of 60,000. In July 1994 the Constitutional Court ruled that the Constitution did not preclude out-of-area operations, including those requiring the use of force, provided parliamentary approval had been given.

The **Greek** Army has acquired significant quantities of second-hand weapons and equipment during the last 12 months, mostly under NATO's cascading scheme. 80 US M-60 tanks have been delivered and 75 German *Leopard*-1 are due to be transferred. Greek M-47 tanks have been placed in store. ACV transfers include 200 German M-113 APC, 60 M-106A1 mortar carriers from the Netherlands and 500 former East German BMP-1 AIFV. 72 M-110 SP guns have been acquired from Germany, 150 RM-70 MRL and 20 MLRS will be delivered in 1994. The Army now has its first attack helicopters. Nine AH-1P *Cobra* have been delivered with a further eight still due. It has been reported that 24 AH-64 *Apache* will be delivered in 1995. The Navy has retired two *Katsonis* (US *Guppy*-class) submarines and two *Themistocles* (US *Gearing*-class) destroyers. A fourth *Elli* (Netherlands *Kortenaer*) frigate has been commissioned, as have two *I Votis*-class (German *Tiger*-class) fast patrol craft armed with Exocet SSM, and two Greek built *Pirpolitis*-class coastal patrol craft.

The **Italian** Navy has commissioned its third *Pelosi*-class submarine and its third *San Giorgio*-class amphibious ship (LPD). The last two *Albatross*-class corvettes have been retired. The first three AV-8B II *Harriers* for the aircraft carrier *G. Garibaldi* have been delivered.

The **Netherlands** Army is due to be reorganised during the second half of 1994. After reorganisation the ground forces will comprise one division consisting of an active light, an active mechanised and two reserve mechanised brigades which is to form part of the German/Netherlands Corps, and an active air-mobile brigade which forms part of the Multi-National Air-mobile Division (MND (C)). The Netherlands also provides a signals battalion for MND (C). Army aviation has been transferred to the Air Force which will provide the helicopters for the air-mobile brigade. The Navy has commissioned the fourth *Zeeleeuw*-class submarine and two more *Karel Doorman*-class frigates. A further *Kortenaer*-class frigate has been transferred to Greece and nine mine warfare vessels have been decommissioned but not yet disposed of. The Air Force has disbanded one F-16 FGA squadron and taken delivery of its first C-130H transport plane, a second is due in 1995.

The **Norwegian** Army has disposed of 117 tanks (M-48 and M-24/90). Future procurement plans for the Navy have been released. Up to eight fast patrol boats will be ordered first and, probably in 1998, six frigates are expected to be ordered to replace the *Oslo*-class which now number four following the loss of the *Oslo* in January 1994. Building of the new *Oksøy/Alta*-class of mine-warfare vessels is behind schedule and the first will not commission until August 1994. Three more *Oksøy*-class (mine-hunters) will be commissioned in 1994 and 1995 and five *Alta*-class (minesweepers) in 1996 and 1997.

The **Spanish** Army has disposed of 100 M-47 tanks and has transferred 16 M-60 A3 tanks to the Marines to replace their M-48. 72 *Mistral* SAM have been acquired. The Navy has commissioned one more *Santa Maria* (US *Perry*-class) frigate with the sixth expected to enter service by the end of 1994. *The Military Balance* has, in the past, incorrectly assessed the run-down of manpower in the Spanish armed forces. Numbers are therefore higher than those published in 1993.

Army operations against the Kurdish rebels of the PKK in eastern **Turkey** have caused the length of conscript service to be increased by five months, and in July 1994 it was announced that the discharge of certain intakes would be postponed for between four and five months depending on rank. Older M-47 tanks are being destroyed as the Army receives newer models under NATO's 'cascading' programme; during the last 12 months 226 M-60 and 85 *Leopard*-1 tanks have been delivered. The numbers of Army helicopters have been revised and result in substantially fewer being listed. Orders have been placed for 19 Mi-17, 45 UH-60 *Black Hawk* and 20 SA-365 *Cougar* helicopters. The Navy has commissioned eight US *Knox*-class destroyers. The Air Force has retired its F-104 fighters and FGA and RF-5A reconnaissance aircraft. 12 more F-16 FGA have been delivered from domestic production and 16 more F-4 from Germany. Better information has allowed a revision of Air Force squadron roles; there are now 14 FGA squadrons (previously 19 were listed), six fighter (two) and two reconnaissance (nil).

The force cuts required by the **United Kingdom**'s 'Options for Change' programme will have been completed when the last amalgamation of infantry battalions takes place in September 1994. The Armed Forces manpower strength in June 1994 was 254,000 compared with 306,000 in 1990 when the programme was announced. While the Army's manpower has reduced by some 30,000, its weaponry has been much improved: MLRS has been introduced; AS-90 155mm SP artillery has replaced the 105mm *Abbot*; numbers of *Warrior* AIFV have doubled; and *Starstreak* High Velocity Missile (HVM) is about to enter service. In the last 12 months 120 AS-90 and 80 *Warrior* have been delivered. The first *Challenger* 2 tank, of which 127 were ordered in 1992, has been delivered. An order for a further 259 tanks was placed in July 1994 to allow all armoured regiments to be equipped with the same tank, thus avoiding a costly up-grade to *Challenger* 1. The Royal Navy has commissioned three more *Norfolk*-class Type 23 frigates and a fifth *Sandown*-class mine-hunter. The remaining five *Amazon*-class, the last two in July 1994, and the last *Leander*-class frigates have been retired and will be sold. The last *Oberon*-class submarine has been retired; two *Upholder* class submarines have paid-off and the other two will by the end of 1994. It is hoped that all four will be sold. Five *Waveney*-class off-shore minesweepers have been retired and the remaining five re-classed as patrol craft. 18 *Sea Harrier* attack aircraft were ordered in January 1994. The Air Force inventory lists 561 combat aircraft with a further 71 in store; the total published in *The Military Balance 1993–1994* was incorrect and should have read 552 plus 118 in store. Four RAF squadrons have been disbanded and *Buccaneer* and *Victor* tankers taken out of service; *Tornado* GR-1B have taken on the *Buccaneer* maritime attack role. The Minister of Defence announced in February 1994 that he had commissioned studies to consider the UK's requirement for cruise missiles and anti-tactical ballistic missiles. On July 1994 the government announced the decisions resulting from the Defence Costs Study, known also as 'Front Line First', as a commitment had been given not to reduce further fighting capability. However, manpower will be further reduced: the Army by 2,200; the Navy by 1,900; and the Air Force by 7,500. Some 7,100 civil service jobs will also be lost. Reserve forces manpower is not affected except that the

Territorial Army's training pool of 4,500 posts, which was only introduced in 1992 will be abolished. The measures to be adopted to achieve the savings of £750m annually required by the Treasury mainly involve: headquarters staffs; medical services; repair and stores units; stores-holding policy; and some base closures. Some positive measures were also announced. Joint-service working will be improved by merging the three single-service staff colleges. A Joint Headquarters is to be established at the Naval Headquarters at Northwood to control all overseas operations (until now this has been delegated to the most appropriate service headquarters for the operation (RAF for *Desert Storm*, Army for support of UNPROFOR in former Yugoslavia)). A smaller deployable Joint Headquarters is to be formed as part of NATO's Joint Force concept. This will take command of whatever forces from all three services are committed to an operation, but will not command them normally. A number of equipment orders, some long-mooted, were confirmed. In addition to the order for *Challenger* 2 tanks, seven more *Sandown*-class minehunters, a mid-life upgrade for 142 *Tornado* GR-1 FGA aircraft, a number of *Paveway* III laser-guided bombs, and more thermal-imaging and laser-designator pods to equip *Jaguar* and *Harrier* as well as *Tornado* GR-1 aircraft have been ordered. Tenders for replacement amphibious ships and a follow-on class of *Trafalgar* attack submarine have been invited; the number ordered will depend on their price. The US is being asked to quote the cost of *Tomahawk* SLCM which would be deployed on submarines. The UK does not consider that such a buy would breach the Missile Technology Control Regime (MTCR) and has made it plain that SLCM would only be conventionally armed. Still awaited are decisions on further frigate buys and the choice of attack helicopter for the Army.

Weapons and Equipment Cooperation

Eurofighter 2000

The first flight of Eurofighter took place in Germany on 24 March 1994. A second development model flew in the UK in April. Germany has reduced the size of its initial order from 250 to 140 aircraft. Italy and Spain have also reduced their requirements. As the work-share programme between the four nations was originally based on the size of the aircraft order, there is likely to be wrangling over altering work-shares.

Future Large Aircraft

The multi-national FLA project is designed to produce a replacement transport aircraft for C-130 and C-160 aircraft. Global sales are estimated at up to 1,000 aircraft. The governments of France, Germany, Italy, Portugal, Spain and Turkey are supporting the project, whereas British Aerospace is privately funding the feasibility study. Present plans are for a first test flight in December 2000 with delivery of operational aircraft starting in mid-2002.

Other cooperative projects include: NH-90 Helicopter, EH-101 Helicopter, Eurocopter, *Project Horizon* Frigate and the Standard Hull Project.

BELGIUM

GDP 1992: fr 7,032.4bn ($218.7bn):
per capita $18,200
1993: fr 7,182.4bn ($221.5bn):
per capita $18,400

Growth 1991: 0.8% 1993: -1.3%

Inflation 1992: 2.4% 1993: 2.7%

Publ debt 1992: 135.2% 1993: 141.6%

Def exp 1992: fr 125.4bn ($3.9bn)
1993: fr 130.0bn ($4.0bn)

Def bdgt 1992: fr 101.7bn ($3.2bn)
1993: fr 97.2bn ($2.9bn)
1994: fr 100.6bn ($2.6bn)

NATO defn 1992: fr 132.8bn ($4.1bn)
1993: fr 130.0bn ($3.8bn)

$1 = fr 1992: 32.2 1993: 34.6
1994: 35.0

fr = Belgian franc

Population: 10,059,000

	13–17	18–22	23–32
Men	315,520	338,560	765,000
Women	301,560	324,400	738,920

TOTAL ARMED FORCES:

ACTIVE: 63,000 (incl 2,000 Medical Service, 3,000 women, 13,300 conscripts).
Terms of service: 8 months in Belgium, or 6 months in Germany. Conscription ended after 1993 intake.
RESERVES: 228,800: Army 139,100; Medical Service 36,800; Navy 12,400; Air Force 40,500. With service in past 3 years: ε146,000.

ARMY: 48,000 (13,000 conscripts). Both figures incl Medical Service.
1 Intervention Force HQ.
3 mech inf bde (each 1 tk, 2 mech inf, 1 SP arty bn).
1 para-cdo regt (3 para-cdo bn, 1 armd recce bn, 1 arty, 1 AD bty).
1 indep recce bn; 1 indep recce sqn.
1 SP arty bn.
1 AD bn.
1 engr bn.
1 lt avn gp (3 bn incl 2 ATK).
RESERVES:
territorial defence: 11 lt inf regt, 4 lt inf bn.
EQUIPMENT:
MBT: 334 *Leopard* (202 in store).
LIGHT TANKS: 133 *Scorpion* (all in store).
RECCE: 153 *Scimitar*.
AIFV: 236 AIFV-B (514 incl variants).
APC: 190 M-113 (509 incl variants), 198 *Spartan* (266 incl variants with 164 in store), 5 M-75/43 BDX (in store).
TOTAL ARTY: 358:
TOWED ARTY: 105mm: 21 M-101 (8 in store).
SP ARTY: 207: 105mm: 28 M-108; 155mm: 42 M-109A3 (all in store), 126 M-109A2; 203mm: 11 M-110 (in store).
MORTARS: 107mm: 130 M-30 (incl some SP; 40 in store); plus 81mm: 285.
SSM: 5 *Lance* launchers (in store).
ATGW: 420 *Milan* (325 veh-mounted).
AD GUNS: 100 M-167 *Vulcan*; 35mm: 54 *Gepard* SP (in store).
SAM: 39 *Improved HAWK* (in store), 118 *Mistral*.
AIRCRAFT: 10 BN-2A *Islander*.
HELICOPTERS: 38 SA-318, 46 A-109.
UAV: *Epervier*.

NAVY: 2,900 (300 conscripts).
(Belgium and the Netherlands have announced their intention to create an integrated operational command for the Belgian and Netherlands navies (except for submarines).)
BASES: Ostend, Zeebrugge.
FRIGATES: 2 *Wielingen* with 2 x ASTT (Fr L-5 LWT), 1 x 6 ASW mor; plus 4 x MM-38 *Exocet* SSM, 1 x 100mm gun and 1 x 8 *Sea Sparrow* SAM.
MINE WARFARE: 7 MCMV:
2 *Van Haverbeke* (US *Aggressive* MSO) (incl 1 used for trials).
5 *Aster* (tripartite) MHC.
SUPPORT AND MISCELLANEOUS: 3:
1 log spt/comd with hel deck, 1 research/survey, 1 aster MHC ammo tpt.
ADDITIONAL IN STORE: 1 FF, 2 MSO, 1 MHC and 1 log spt.
HELICOPTERS: 3 SA-318.

AIR FORCE: 12,100 (1,000 women).
Average annual flying hours for combat pilots: 165.
FGA: 4 sqn with F-16A/B.
FIGHTER: 2 sqn with F-16A/B.
TRANSPORT: 2 sqn: 1 with 12 C-130H; 1 with 2 Boeing 727QC, 3 HS-748, 5 *Merlin IIIA*, 2 *Falcon 20*.
TRAINING: 5 sqn: 3 with *Alpha Jet*; 1 with SF-260; 1 with CM-170.
SAR: 1 sqn with *Sea King* Mk 48.
EQUIPMENT: 133 cbt ac (plus 95 in store), no armed hel.
AIRCRAFT:
***Mirage* 5:** 62 in store (37 -BA, 15 -BR 10 -BD).
F-16: 133: **-A:** 113; **-B:** 20; plus 33 in store.
C-130: 12 (tpt).
Boeing 727QC: 2 (tpt). **HS-748:** 3 (tpt). ***Falcon 20*:** 2 (vip), SW 111. ***Merlin*:** 5 (vip, Photo, cal). **CM-170:** 11 (trg, liaison). **SF-260:** 36 (trg). ***Alpha Jet*:** 31 (trg).
HELICOPTERS:
***Sea King*:** 5 (SAR).
MISSILES:
AAM: AIM-9 *Sidewinder*.

FORCES ABROAD:

GERMANY: 10,300; 1 Force HQ, 1 mech bde, 2 hel bn.
UN AND PEACEKEEPING:
ADRIATIC (*Sharp Guard*): 1 FF.
BOSNIA (UNPROFOR BH): 422; Be/Fr inf bn, 1 tpt coy.
CROATIA (UNPROFOR I): 613; 1 inf bn, plus 6 Observers.

INDIA/PAKISTAN (UNMOGIP): 2 Observers.
MIDDLE EAST (UNTSO): 6 Observers.
WESTERN SAHARA (MINURSO): 1 Observer.

FOREIGN FORCES:

NATO: HQ NATO Brussels; HQ SHAPE Mons.
WEU: Military Planning Cell.
US: some 1,400: Army 800; Navy 100+; Air Force 500.

CANADA

GDP	1992: $C 688.5bn ($569.7bn): per capita $19,700	
	1993: $C 710.7bn ($598.5bn): per capita $20,500	
Growth	1992: 0.3%	1993: 2.4%
Inflation	1992: 0.7%	1993: 3.2%
Publ debt	1992: 83.0%	1993: 88.3%
Def exp	1992: $C 11.9bn ($9.8bn)	
Def bdgt	1992: $C 12.5bn ($10.3bn)	
	1993: $C 12.0bn ($9.6bn)	
	1994: $C 11.6bn ($9.0bn)	
NATO defn	1992: $C 13.7bn ($11.4bn)	
	1993: $C 13.2bn ($10.6bn)	
$ 1 = $C	1992: 1.21	1993: 1.29
	1994: 1.38	

$C = Canadian dollar

Population: 28,125,400

	13–17	*18–22*	*23–32*
Men	944,400	955,400	2,214,400
Women	901,800	919,400	2,170,800

Canadian Armed Forces are unified and organised in functional commands. Mobile Command commands land combat forces, and Maritime Command all naval forces. Air Command commands all air forces, but Maritime Command has operational control of maritime air forces. Mobile Command has operational control of Tactical Air Group.
This entry is set out in the traditional single service manner.

TOTAL ARMED FORCES:

ACTIVE: 78,100 (8,700 women); of the total strength some 25,000 are not identified by service.
RESERVES: primary 37,200: Army (Militia) (incl comms) 28,400; Navy 6,500; Air Force 2,300. Supplementary 39,000.

ARMY (Land Forces): 20,000.

1 Task Force HQ.
3 mech inf bde gp, each with 1 armd regt, 3 mech inf bn, 1 arty, 1 engr regt, 1 AD bty.
1 AB bn gp.
1 indep AD bty.
1 indep engr spt regt.
RESERVES: Militia: 28,400; 18 armd, 18 arty, 52 inf, 11 engr, 20 spt bn level units, 12 med coy.
Canadian Rangers: 3,100; 109 patrols.
EQUIPMENT:
MBT: 114 *Leopard* C-1.
RECCE: 174 *Lynx*, 195 *Cougar*.
APC: 1,404: 881 M-113 A2 (136 in store), 55 M-577, 269 *Grizzly*, 199 *Bison*.
TOWED ARTY: 258: 105mm: 12 Model 44 (L-5) pack, 189 C1 (M-101); 155mm: 57 M-114 (in store).
SP ARTY: 155mm: 76 M-109.
MORTARS: 81mm: 150.
ATGW: 150 *TOW* (incl 64 M-113 SP).
RL: *Eryx*.
RCL: 84mm: 780 *Carl Gustav;* 106mm: 111 M-40.
AD GUNS: 35mm: 20 GDF-005; 40mm: 57 L40/60.
SAM: 36 ADATS, 111 *Blowpipe*, 110 *Javelin, Starburst*.
UAV: CL-89 (AN/USD-501).

NAVY (Maritime Forces): 12,500.

SUBMARINES: 3 *Ojibwa* (UK *Oberon*) SS with Mk 48 HWT (equipped for, but not with, *Harpoon* USGW).
PRINCIPAL SURFACE COMBATANTS: 15:
DESTROYERS: 4:
DDG: 4 *Iroquois* ex-FFH (incl 1 in conversion refit) with 1 x Mk-41 VLS for 29 SM-2 MR, 2 CH-124 *Sea King* ASW hel (Mk 46 LWT), 2 x 3 ASTT, plus 1 x 76mm gun.
FRIGATES: 11:
FFH: 8:
6 *Halifax* with 1 CH-124A *Sea King* ASW hel (Mk 46 LWT), 2 x 2 ASTT; plus 2 x 4 *Harpoon* and 2 x 8 *Sea Sparrow* SAM (incl 2 commissioning mid-1994, 7 by end 1994).
2 *Annapolis* with 1 *Sea King* hel, 2 x 3 ASTT, 1 x 3 ASW mot; plus 2 x 76mm gun.
FF: 3:
3 improved *Restigouche* with 1 x 8 *ASROC*, 2 x 3 ASTT, 1 x 3 ASW mor, plus 2 x 76mm gun.
PATROL AND COASTAL COMBATANTS: 12:
6 *Fundy* (ex MSC) PCC (trg).
5 *Porte St Jean* PCC, 1 PCI⟨ (reserve trg).

MINE WARFARE: 2:
2 *Anticosti* MSO (converted offshore spt vessels) (reserve trg).
SUPPORT AND MISCELLANEOUS: 8:
2 *Protecteur* AO with 3 *Sea King*, 1 *Provider* AO with 2 *Sea King*, 1 AOT, 2 AGOR, 1 diving spt, 1 *Riverton* spt.

DEPLOYMENT AND BASES:

ATLANTIC: Halifax (HQ) (Maritime Commander is also COMCANLANT): 2 SS, 3 DDG, 6 FFH, 2 AO, 1 AGOR; 2 MR plus 1 MR (trg) sqn with CP-140 and 3 CP-140A, 1 ASW and 1 ASW (trg) hel sqn with 26 CH-125 hel.
PACIFIC: Esquimalt (HQ): 1 SS, 3 FFH, 3 FF, 6 PCC, 1 AO, 1 AGOR; 1 MR sqn with 4 CP-140 and 1 ASW hel sqn with 6 CH-124 hel.
RESERVES: 6,500 in 24 divisions: patrol craft, MCM, Naval Control of Shipping, augmentation of regular units.

AIR FORCE: 20,600.

FIGHTER GROUP:

FIGHTER: 5 sqn (1 trg) with CF-18.
1 sqn with CF-5.
EW: 2 sqn with CE-144 (CL-601), CT-133.
EARLY WARNING: Canadian NORAD Regional Headquarters at North Bay. 47 North Warning radar sites: 11 long-range, 36 short-range; Region Operational Control Centre (ROCC) (2 Sector Operational Control Centres (SOCC)).
4 Coastal Radars and 2 Transportable Radars.

MARITIME AIR GROUP:

MR: 4 sqn (1 trg) with CP-140 *Aurora*.
ASW: 3 hel sqn (1 trg) with CH-124, *Sea King*.

TACTICAL AIR GROUP (TAG):

HELICOPTERS: 11 sqn: 3 with CH-135, 2 with CH-135 and CH-136, 5 reserve sqn with CH-136,1 test with CH-135 and CH-136.

AIR TRANSPORT GROUP:

TRANSPORT: 6 sqn:
4 (1 trg) with CC-130E/H *Hercules*.
1 with CC-137 (Boeing 707), CC-150 (AIRBUS A-310).
1 with CC-109, CC-144.
SAR: 4 tpt/SAR sqn (1 with twinned reserve sqn) with CC-115, CC-130, CC-138 **ac**; CH-113/-113A **hel**.
LIAISON: 3 base hel flt with CH-118, CH-135.

TRAINING (reports direct to HQ Air Comd):

2 flying schools with CT-114 **ac**; CH-139 **hel**.
1 demonstration sqn with CT-114.

EQUIPMENT: 198 (incl 18 MR) cbt **ac** (plus 62 in store); 128 armed **hel**.
AIRCRAFT:
CF-18: 123: **-A:** 84; **-B:** 39 (plus **-A:** 2 in store).
CF-5: 57: **-A:** 26; **-D:** 31 (plus **-A:** 55, **-D:** 5 in store).
CP-140: 18 (MR).
CP-140A: 3 (environmental patrol).
CC-130E/H: 30 (25 tpt, 5 AAR/tpt).
CC-137: 5 (3 tpt, 2 tkr/ tpt).
CC-150: 5.
CC-109: 7 (tpt).
CC/E-144: 16 (6 EW trg, 3 coastal patrol, 7 VIP/tpt).
CC-138: 7 (SAR/tpt).
CC-115: 10 (SAR/tpt).
CT-133: 51 (EW trg/tpt plus 9 in store).
CT-114: 108 (trg).
CC/T-142: 6 (2 tpt, 4 trg).
HELICOPTERS:
CH-124: 31 (ASW, afloat); plus 3 in store.
CH-135: 43 (36 tac, 7 SAR/liaison).
CH-136: 63 (61 tac, 2 test/trg).
CH-113: 14 (SAR/tpt).
CH-118: 9 (liaison).
CH-139: 14 (trg).

FORCES ABROAD:

NORWAY: prepositioned TLE: 6 arty, 14 ACV.

UN AND PEACEKEEPING:

ADRIATIC *(Sharp Guard):* IFF.
BOSNIA (UNPROFOR BH): 789; 1 inf bn gp, 1 engr sqn, 14 Observers.
CROATIA (UNPROFOR I): 1,658; 1 inf bn, 2 log bn, 45 civ pol.
CYPRUS (UNFICYP): 9.
EGYPT (MFO): 27.
EL SALVADOR (ONUSAL): 2 Observers.
IRAQ/KUWAIT (UNIKOM): 5 Observers.
MIDDLE EAST (UNTSO): 15 Observers.
MOZAMBIQUE (ONUMOZ): 15 Observers.
RWANDA (UNAMIR): 11.
SOMALIA (UNOSOM): 5.
SYRIA/ISRAEL (UNDOF): 213; log unit.
WESTERN SAHARA (MINURSO): 30, incl 16 Observers.

PARAMILITARY:

COAST GUARD: 5,950 (civilian-manned); some 78 vessels including: 1 cable ship, 1 heavy, 5 medium and 11 light icebreakers; 13 large SAR cutters/tenders; 4 hovercraft; plus 1 DC-3 **ac**; 1 S-61, 5 Bell 212, 5 Bell 206L, 2 Bell 206L-1, 16 Bo 105 **hel**.

DENMARK

GDP	1992: kr 854.0bn ($141.5bn): per capita $18,700	
	1993: kr 892.8bn ($145.5bn): per capita $19,100	
Growth	1992: 1.3%	1993: 0.3%
Inflation	1992: 1.9%	1993: 1.3 %
Publ debt	1992: 62.4%	1993: 66.2%
Def exp	1990: kr 16.1bn ($2.6bn)	
Def bdgt	1992: kr 16.9bn ($2.8bn)	
	1993: kr 17.6bn ($2.7bn)	
	1994: kr 17.1bn ($2.6bn)	
NATO defn	1992: kr 16.8bn ($2.8bn)	
	1993: kr 17.5bn ($2.7bn)	
$1 = kr	1992: 6.0	1993: 6.5
	1994: 6.7	

kr = Danish kroner

Population: 5,196,600

	13–17	*18–22*	*23–32*
Men	157,000	180,800	401,200
Women	150,500	174,000	385,800

TOTAL ARMED FORCES:

ACTIVE: 27,000 (8,500 conscripts, 1,000 women).
Terms of service: 5–12 months (up to 24 months in certain ranks).
RESERVES: 70,000: Army 54,000; Navy 5,000; Air Force 11,000. Home Guard (*Hjemmevaernet*) (volunteers to age 50): Army 55,000; Naval 4,500; Air Force 9,400.

ARMY: some 16,300 (7,100 conscripts, 400 women).

2 Force HQ.
1 op comd, 1 land comd (east).
1 mech inf div (recce bn, 3 mech inf bde, div arty (reserve)).
2 mech inf bde each 2 mech/mot inf, 1 tk, 1 arty bn.
5 regt cbt gp (incl mot inf, arty bn).
1 recce bn.
Army avn.
RESERVES:
7 mil region (1–2 inf bn).
EQUIPMENT:
MBT: 452: 220 *Leopard* 1A3/4, 179 *Centurion* (51 in store), 53 M-41DK-1.
APC: 583 M-113 (incl variants).
TOTAL ARTY: 553:
TOWED ARTY: 317: 105mm: 184 M-101; 155mm: 24 M-59, 97 M-114/39; 203mm: 12 M-115.
SP ARTY: 155mm: 76 M-109.
MORTARS: 120mm: 160 Brandt; plus 81mm: 388 (incl 55 SP).
ATGW: 140 *TOW* (incl 56 SP).
RCL: 84mm: 1,096 *Carl Gustav*; 106mm: 158 M-40.
AD GUNS: 40mm: 36 L/60.
SAM: *Stinger*.
SURV: *Green Archer*.
AIRCRAFT: 8 SAAB T-17.
HELICOPTERS: 13 Hughes 500M/OH-6, 12 AS-550C2.

NAVY: 4,600 (incl 700 conscripts, 200 women).

BASES: Korsør, Frederikshavn.
SUBMARINES: 5:
3 *Tumleren* (mod No *Kobben*) SSC with Sw FFV Type 61 HWT.
2 *Narhvalen*, SSC with FFV Type 61 HWT.
FRIGATES: 3:
3 *Niels Juel* with 2 x 4 *Harpoon* SSM.
PATROL AND COASTAL COMBATANTS: 35:
MISSILE CRAFT: 10 *Willemoes* PFM with 2 x 4 *Harpoon*.
PATROL: 27:
OFFSHORE: 5:
1 *Beskytteren*, 4 *Thetis* PCO all with 1 *Lynx* hel.
COASTAL: 13:
10 *Flyvefisken* (Stanflex 300) PFC.
3 *Agdlek* PCC.
INSHORE: 9 *Barsø*.
MINE WARFARE: 9:
MINELAYERS: 6: 4 *Falster* (400 mines), 2 *Lindormen* (50 mines).
MINE COUNTERMEASURES: 3: 2 *Alssund* (US MSC-128) MSC, 1 *Flyvefisken* (SF300) MHC.
SUPPORT AND MISCELLANEOUS: 7:
2 AOT (small), 4 icebreakers (civilian-manned), 1 Royal Yacht.
HELICOPTERS: 8 *Lynx* (up to 4 embarked).

COAST DEFENCE: 1 coastal fortress; 150mm guns; 40mm AA guns. Coastal radar.
2 mobile coastal missile batteries: 2 x 4 *Harpoon* (not fully op until 1995).
RESERVES (Home Guard): 37 inshore patrol craft.

AIR FORCE: 6,100 (700 conscripts, 400 women).

Average annual flying hours for F-16 pilots: 180.

TACTICAL AIR COMMAND:

FGA/FIGHTER: 4 sqn with F-16A/B.
TRANSPORT: 1 sqn with C-130H, *Gulfstream III*.
SAR: 1 sqn with S-61A hel.

TRAINING: 1 flying school with T-17.

AIR DEFENCE GROUP:

AD: 2 SAM bn: 8 bty with 36 *Improved HAWK*, 160 40 mm L/60, 32 40 mm/L70.

CONTROL/REPORTING GROUP: 5 radar stations.

EQUIPMENT: 63 cbt ac, no armed hel.

AIRCRAFT:

F-16A/B: 63 (FGA/ftr).

C-130H: 3 (tpt). ***Gulfstream III*:** 3 (tpt). **SAAB T-17:** 29 (6 liaison, 23 trg).

HELICOPTERS:

S-61: 8 (SAR).

MISSILES:

ASM: AGM-12 *Bullpup*.

AAM: AIM-9 *Sidewinder*.

SAM: 36 improved *Hawk*.

FORCES ABROAD:

UN AND PEACEKEEPING:

ADRIATIC SEA (*Sharp Guard*): 98; 1 FF.

BOSNIA (UNPROFOR BH): 305; elm Nordic bn incl 1 tk sqn (10 Leopard MBT), HQ Coy. Aircrew with NATO E-3A operations. Air Force personnel in tactical air control parties (TACP).

CROATIA (UNPROFOR I): 942; 1 inf bn, 44 civ pol.

CYPRUS (UNFICYP): 1.

GEORGIA (UNOMIG): 4 Observers.

INDIA/PAKISTAN (UNMOGIP): 7 Observers.

IRAQ/KUWAIT (UNIKOM): 51; spt tps, 6 Observers.

MACEDONIA (UNPROFOR M): 34, incl 28 Observers.

MIDDLE EAST (UNTSO): 12 Observers.

TAJIKISTAN (UNMOT): 1 Observer.

FOREIGN FORCES:

NATO: HQ Allied Forces Baltic Approaches (BALTAP).

FRANCE

GDP	1992:	fr 6,998.9bn ($1,323bn): per capita $19,200		
	1993:	fr 7,094.1bn ($1,348bn): per capita $19,500		
Growth	1992:	1.4%	1993:	-0.7%
Inflation	1992:	2.4%	1993:	2.1%
Publ debt	1992:	51.6%	1993:	57.1%
Def exp	1992:	fr 197.9bn ($37.4bn)		
	1993:	fr 197.7bn ($37.2bn)		
Def bdgt	1993:	fr 197.9bn ($35.8bn)		
	1994:	fr 199.3bn ($35.6bn)		
Def exp	1993:	fr 192.4bn ($34.4bn)		
NATO defn	1992:	fr 241.4bn ($43.1bn)		
	1993:	fr 242.8bn ($43.4bn)		
$1 = fr	1992:	5.3	1993:	5.7
	1994:	5.8		

fr = franc

Population: 57,842,400

	13–17	*18–22*	*23–32*
Men	1,946,400	2,079,000	4,334,600
Women	1,856,200	1,983,600	4,223,200

TOTAL ARMED FORCES:

ACTIVE: some 409,600 (16,400 women, 189,200 conscripts; 5,200 Central Staff, 8,600 (2,300 conscripts) Service de santé, 400 Service des essences not listed below).

Terms of service: 10 months (can be voluntarily extended to 12–24 months).

RESERVES: earmarked for mob: 339,800; Army 240,000, Navy 29,800, Air Force 70,000. Potential: 1,353,700; Army 915,000, Navy 259,200, Air Force 179,500.

STRATEGIC NUCLEAR FORCES:

(17,000; some 1,700 Army; 5,000 Navy; 9,700 Air Force; 600 Gendarmerie).

NAVY: 80 SLBM in 5 SSBN.

SSBN: 5:

5 mod *Le Redoutable* with 16 M-4/TN-70 or -71; plus SM-39 *Exocet* USGW and 4 x 533mm HWT (F17.2).

AIR FORCE:

IRBM: 18 SSBS S-3D/TN-61 msl in 2 sqn.

BOMBERS: 2 sqn with 15 *Mirage* IVP (*ASMP*: *Air-Sol, Moyenne-Portée* nuclear ASM), plus 13 in store; 3 sqn with 45 *Mirage* 2000N (ASMP).

TRAINING: 5 *Mirage IIIB*, 1 *Mystère-Falcon 20P*, 1 *Alpha Jet*.

TANKERS: 1 wing:

2 sqn with 11 C-135FR.

COMMUNICATIONS: 4 C-160 *ASTARTE*.

RECCE: 3 *Mirage IVP*.

'PRE-STRATEGIC' NUCLEAR FORCES:

ARMY: 15 *Hadès* SSM launchers (in store).

NAVY: (190); 38 *Super Etendard* strike ac (*ASMP* nuc ASM); plus 19 in store.

Eqpt also listed with Service sections.

ARMY: 241,400 (8,600 women, 136,800 conscripts).
Note: regiments are normally of bn size.
1 Int and EW bde.
1 corps with 3 armd, 1 mtn inf div (55,100).
Summary of div cbt units:

7 armd regt.	8 arty regt.
6 mech inf regt.	4 recce sqn.
4 mot inf regt.	3 ATK sqn.

Corps units: 1 armd recce, 1 mot inf, 1 arty bde (1 MLRS, 2 *Roland* SAM (each of 4 bty), 1 *HAWK* SAM regt), 2 cbt hel regt (94 hel: 26 SA-330, 48 SA-342 *HOT* ATK, 20 SA-341 gunships), 1 engr bde (4 regt).
1 armd div (in Eurocorps): 3 armd, 2 mech inf, 2 arty, 1 *Roland* SAM, 1 engr regt.
1 Fr/Ge bde (2,100: Fr units incl 1 lt armd, 1 mot inf regt; 1 recce sqn).
Rapid Action Force (FAR: 42,500):
1 para div: 6 para inf, 1 armd cavalry, 1 arty, 1 engr regt.
1 air portable marine div: 2 inf, 2 lt armd, 1 arty, 1 engr regt.
1 lt armd div: 2 armd cavalry, 2 APC inf, 1 arty, 1 engr regt.
1 air-mobile div: 1 inf, 3 cbt, 1 spt hel regt (total 234 hel: 62 SA-330, 90 SA-342/*HOT*, 20 AS-532, 62 SA-341 (20 gun, 42 recce/liaison).)
Corps units: 1 arty bde (1 MLRS, 1 *Roland* SAM, 1 *HAWK* SAM regt), 1 engr regt.
Territorial def forces incl spt of UN missions: 7 regt.
FOREIGN LEGION: (8,500); 1 armd, 1 para, 6 inf, 1 engr regt (incl in units listed above).
MARINES: (31,000, incl 13,000 conscripts, mainly overseas enlisted): 1 div (see FAR above), 4 regt in France (see div cbt units above), 11 regt overseas.
Special Operations Forces (units see also above): 1 Marine inf regt (para), 1 AB regt, 2 hel units (EW, special ops).
RESERVES:
Individual reinforcements for 1 corps (incl Eurocorps) and FAR (92,000).
Territorial def forces: 65 regt.
EQUIPMENT:
MBT: 998 AMX-30 (658 -B2), 49 *Leclerc*.
RECCE: 325 AMX-10RC, 192 ERC-90F4 *Sagaie*, 570 AML-60/-90 (perhaps 300 in store), 694 VBL M-11.
AIFV: 713 AMX-10P/PC.
APC: 3,975 VAB (incl variants).
TOTAL ARTY: 1,546:
TOWED ARTY: 454: 105mm: 149 HM-2; 155mm: 200 BF-50, 105 TR-F-1.
SP ARTY: 431: 105mm: 55 AU-50; 155mm: 253 AU-F-1, 123 F-3.
MRL: 380mm: 41 MLRS.
MORTARS: 620: 120mm: 370 RT-F1, 250 M-51.
ATGW: 100 *Eryx*, 1,455 *Milan*, *HOT* (incl 135 VAB SP).
RL: 89mm: 11,200; 112mm: 10,800 *APILAS*.
AD GUNS: 1,176: 20mm: 19 53T1, 795 53T2; 30mm: 362 towed.
SAM: 453: 69 *HAWK*, 181 *Roland* I/II, 203 *Mistral*.
SURV: STENTOR (veh), RASIT-B/-E (veh, arty), RATAC (veh, arty).
HELICOPTERS 661: 22 AS-532, 109 SA-313/-318, 10 AS-555, 47 SA-316, 132 SA-330, 157 SA-341F/M (16 with *HOT*, 67 gun-armed, 74 utility), 184 SA-342M (154 with *HOT*, 30 utility).
AIRCRAFT: 2 Cessna *Caravan II* , 5 PC-6.
UAV: CL-89 (AN/USD-501), CL-289 (AN/USD-502).

NAVY: 64,200 (incl 8,818 Naval Air Force, 3,000 Marines, 2,400 women, 18,600 conscripts).
COMMANDS: 1 strategic sub (ALFOST), 2 home (CECLANT, CECMED); 2 overseas: Indian Ocean (ALINDIEN), Pacific Ocean (ALPACI).
BASES: *France:* Cherbourg, Brest (HQ), Lorient, Toulon (HQ). *Overseas:* Papeete (HQ) (Tahiti); La Réunion; Nouméa (New Caledonia); Fort de France (Martinique).
SUBMARINES: 18:
STRATEGIC SUBMARINES: 5 SSBN (see above).
TACTICAL SUBMARINES: 13:
SSN: 6 *Rubis* ASW/ASUW with F-17 HWT, L-5 LWT and SM-39 *Exocet* USGW.
SS: 7:
4 *Agosta* with F-17 HWT and L-5 LWT; plus *Exocet* USGW.
3 *Daphné*, with E-15 HWT and L-5 LWT (plus 5 in store).
PRINCIPAL SURFACE COMBATANTS: 43:
CARRIERS: 2:
2 *Clémenceau* CVS (33,300t), capacity 40 ac (typically 2 flt with 16 *Super Etendard*, 1 with 6 *Alizé*; 1 det with 2 *Etendard* IVP, 2 *Super Frelon*, 2 *Dauphin* hel).
CRUISERS: 1:
1 *Jeanne d'Arc* CCH (trg/ASW) with 6 MM-38 *Exocet* SSM, 2 x 2 100mm guns, capacity 8 x *Lynx* hel.
DESTROYERS: 4 DDG:
2 *Cassard* with 1 x 1 *Standard* SM-1 MR; plus 8 x MM-40 *Exocet*, 1 x 100mm gun, 2 x ASTT, 1 *Lynx* hel (ASW/OTHT).

2 *Suffren* with 1 x 2 *Masurca* SAM; plus 1 *Malafon* SUGW, 4 ASTT, 4 MM-38 *Exocet*, 2 x 100mm guns.
FRIGATES: 36:
6 *Floréal* with 2 MM-38 *Exocet*, 1 AS-365 hel and 1 x 100mm gun.
7 *Georges Leygues* with 2 *Lynx* hel (Mk 46 LWT), 2 x ASTT; plus 5 with 8 MM-40, 2 with 4 MM-38 *Exocet*, all with 1 x 100mm gun.
3 *Tourville* with 2 x *Lynx* hel, 1 *Malafon* SUGW, 2 x ASTT; plus 6 x MM-38 *Exocet*, 2 x 100mm guns.
1 *Aconit* with *Malafon*, 2 x ASTT; plus 8 MM-38 *Exocet*, 2 x 100mm guns.
2 *Commandant Rivière* with 2 x 3 ASTT, 1 x 12 ASW mor; plus 3 with 4 x MM-38 *Exocet*, all with 2 x 100mm guns.
17 *D'Estienne d'Orves* with 4 x ASTT, 1 x 6 ASW mor; plus 6 with 2 x MM-38, 6 with 4 x MM-40 *Exocet*, all with 1 x 100mm gun.
PATROL AND COASTAL COMBATANTS: 23:
PATROL, OFFSHORE: 1 *Albatross* PCO (Public Service Force).
COASTAL: 20:
10 *L'Audacieuse*.
8 *Léopard* PCC (trg).
1 *Sterne*, 1 *Grebe* PCC (Public Service Force).
INSHORE: 2 *Athos* PCI.
Plus 4 *Patra* PCI, 1 *La Combattante* PCI, 5 PCI⟨ (manned by Gendarmarie Maritime).
MINE WARFARE: 20:
MINELAYERS: nil, but submarines and *Thetis* (trials ship) have capability.
MINE COUNTERMEASURES: 20:
9 *Eridan* tripartite MHC.
5 *Circé* MHC.
1 *Ouistreham* (US *Aggressive*) MSO.
4 *Vulcain* MCM diver spt.
1 *Antares* (route survey/trg).
AMPHIBIOUS: 9:
1 *Foudre* LPD, capacity 450 tps, 30 tk, 4 *Super Puma* hel, 2 CDIC LCT or 10 LCM.
2 *Ouragan* LPD: capacity 350 tps, 25 tk, 2 *Super Frelon* hel.
1 *Bougainville* LSD: capacity 500 tps, 6 tk, 2 AS-332 hel (assigned to spt DIRCEN nuclear test centre South Pacific).
5 *Champlain* LSM (*BATRAL*): capacity 140 tps, tk.
Plus craft: 6 LCT, 24 LCM.
SUPPORT AND MISCELLANEOUS: 39:
UNDERWAY SUPPORT: 5:
5 *Durance* AO.
MAINTENANCE/LOGISTIC: 21:
1 AOT, 1 *Jules Verne* AR with 2 SA-319 hel, 4 *Rhin* depot/spt, 1 *Rance* med and trg spt, all with hel; 8 tpt, 6 ocean tugs (3 civil charter).
SPECIAL PURPOSES: 7:
2 msl trials, 1 electronics trials, 1 *Thetis* mine warfare trials, 1 div trials, 2 *Glycine* trg.
SURVEY/RESEARCH: 6: 5 AGHS, 1 AGOR.

NAVAL AIR FORCE: (8,818, incl 600 women, 530 conscripts).

Average annual flying time for *Etendard* and *Crusader* aircrew: 180.
NUCLEAR STRIKE: 2 flt with *Super Etendard* (ASMP nuc ASM).
FIGHTER: 1 flt with F-8E (FN) *Crusader*.
ASW: 2 flt with *Alizé*.
MR: 6 flt: 4 with *Atlantic*, 2 with *Gardian*.
RECCE: 1 flt, with *Etendard* IVP.
OCU: *Alizé*, *Zéphyr*.
TRAINING: 5 units with N-262 *Frégate*, EMB-121 *Xingu*, MS-760 *Paris*, *Falcon* 10MER, *Rallye* 880, CAP 10, *Zéphyr*.
MISCELLANEOUS: 4 comms/liaison units (1 VIP) with *Falcon* 10MER, *Alizé*, N-262, EMB 121, *Xingu*.
1 trial unit with *Atlantique* 2, MS-760 *Paris*.
2 lt ac units with 12 *Rallye* 880, 6 CAP-10.
ASW: 2 sqn with *Lynx*.
COMMANDO: 2 aslt sqn with SA-321.
TRAINING: SA-316.
MISCELLANEOUS: 2 comms/SAR units with SE-3130, SA-316, 1 trials unit with SE-3130, SA-319, *Lynx*, SA-321.
EQUIPMENT: 107 cbt ac (plus 43 in store); 40 armed hel (plus 14 in store).
AIRCRAFT:
***Super Etendard*:** 38 (strike); plus 19 in store. Total of 48 to be mod for *ASMP*.
***Etendard*:** IVP: 8 (recce); plus 7 in store.
***Crusader*:** 12 (ftr); plus 7 in store. 18 of these are undergoing modification to extend in-service life.
***Alizé*:** 19 (18 ASW, 1 trg); plus 6 in store.
***Atlantic*:** 16 (MR); plus 12 in store.
***Atlantique*:** 9 (MR).
***Gardian*:** 5 (MR).
***Zéphyr*:** 12 (trg). **Nord 262:** 23 (13 MR trg, 10 misc).
***Navajo*:** 6 (2 trg, 4 misc). ***Xingu*:** 17 (10 trg, 7 misc).
***Rallye* 880:** 14 (4 trg, 10 misc). **CAP-10:** 8 (misc).
MS-760: 7 (trg). ***Falcon* 10MER:** 5 (3 trg, 2 misc).
HELICOPTERS:
***Lynx*:** 28 (ASW); **SA-321:** 12 (12 ASW); plus 5 in store. **SA-313:** 8 (2 trg, 6 misc). **SA-316/-319:** 29 (6 trg, 23 misc). **AS-365:** 6 (SAR).

MISSILES:
ASM: AS-12/-20/-30, *Martel* AS-37, *Exocet* AM-39.
AAM: R-530, R-550 *Magic*, AIM-9 *Sidewinder*.
MARINES: (3,000).
COMMANDO UNITS: (460).
4 assault gp.
1 attack swimmer unit.
NAVAL BASE PROTECTION: (2,430).
FUSILIERS-MARIN: (1,290).

PUBLIC SERVICE FORCE: naval personnel, performing general coast guard, fishery, SAR, anti-pollution and traffic surveillance duties: 1 *Albatros*, 1 *Sterne*, 1 *Grebe* PCC, 4 N-262 **ac**, 3 SA-365 **hel** (ships incl in naval patrol and coastal totals). Command exercised through 'Maritime Prefectures' (Premar): Manche (Cherbourg), Atlantique (Brest), Mediterranée (Toulon).

AIR FORCE: 89,800 (6,000 women, 33,800 conscripts, incl strategic and pre-strategic forces).

AIR DEFENCE COMMAND (CASSIC):
CONTROL: automatic *STRIDA* II, 10 radar stations, 1 wing with 4 E3F.
SAM: 12 sqn (1 trg) with 24 *Crotale* bty (48 fire, 24 radar units).
4 sqn *Mistral*.
AA GUNS: 300 bty (20mm).

TACTICAL AIR FORCE (CFAC):
Average annual flying hours for Fighter/FGA pilots: 180.
9 wings, 25 sqn.
FIGHTER: 4 wings, 9 sqn:
2 with *Mirage* F-IC; 7 with *Mirage* 2000C/B.
FGA: 9 sqn:
1 with *Mirage* 2000N.
2 with *Mirage* 2000D.
4 with *Jaguar* A.
2 with *Mirage* F1-CT.
RECCE: 1 wing, 2 sqn with *Mirage* F-1CR.
TRAINING: 1 OCU sqn with *Jaguar* A/E.
1 OCU sqn with F1-C/B,
1 OCU sqn with *Mirage* 2000/BC.
EW: 2 sqn: 1 with C-160 ELINT/ESM **ac**, AS-330 **hel**; 1 with DC-8 ELINT.
HELICOPTERS: 1 sqn with SA-313, SA-319.

AIR TRANSPORT COMMAND (CFAP):
TRANSPORT: 20 sqn:
1 hy with DC-8F, A310-300.
5 tac with C-160/-160NG/C-130H.
14 lt tpt/trg/SAR with C-160, DH-6, EMB-121, CN235, *Falcon* 20, *Falcon* 50, *Falcon* 900, MS-760, TBM-700, N-262.
TRAINING: 1 OCU with N-262, C-160.
HELICOPTERS: 5 sqn with AS-332, AS-355, SA-313/-316/-319, SA-365.
TRAINING: 1 OCU with SA-313/-316, SA-330.

TRAINING COMMAND (CEAA): (5,000).
TRAINING: *Alpha Jet*, CAP-10B/-20, CM-170, EMB-121, TB-30.
EQUIPMENT: 761 cbt ac, no armed hel.
AIRCRAFT:
***Mirage*:** 470: **F-1B:** 18 (OCU); **F-1C:** 70 (ftr); **F-1CT:** 37 (FGA); **F-1CR:** 51 (recce); **IIIE:** 23 (FGA); **IIIB/BE:** 7* (trg); **-5F:** 17 (FGA); **IVP:** 18 (bbr); **-2000B/C:** 136 (112 -C, 24 -B); **-2000N:** 72; **-2000D:** 21.
Jaguar: 134: **-A:** 101 (strike, FGA, trg); **-E:** 33* (trg).
Alpha Jet: 157* (trg).
E-3F: 4 (AEW).
A 310-300: 2.
DC-8: 4.
C-130: 12: **-H:** 3 (tpt); **-H-30**: 9 (tpt).
C-135F/FR: 11 (tkr).
C-160: 76 (2 *Gabriel* ELINT/ESM, 4 *Astarte* comms, 40 tac tpt, 9 OCU, 21 -NG tac tpt/tkr).
CN-235M: 8 (tpt).
N-262: 24 (21 lt tpt, 2 trg, 1 trials).
Falcon*:** 19: **-20:** 13 (7 tpt, 6 misc); **-50:** 4 (tpt); **-900:** 2 (tpt). **MS-760:** 37 (misc). **DHC-6:** 10 (tpt). **EMB-121:** 25 (4 tpt, 21 trg). **TB-30**: 148 (trg). **CAP-10B/230:** 51 (trg). **TBM-700:** 8 (trg) ***Tucano: 2 (trg).
HELICOPTERS:
SA-313: 14 (incl 7 OCU) (*Alouette* II).
SA-319: 25 (*Alouette* III).
SA-330: 29 (25 tpt, 3 OCU) (*Puma*).
SA-365: 3 (tpt) (*Cougar*).
AS-332: 7 (tpt) (*Super Puma*).
AS-350: 6 (*Ecureuil*).
AS-355: 43 (tpt) (*Fennec*).
MISSILES:
ASM: AS-30/-30L, *Martel* AS-37.
AAM: *Super* 530F/D, R-550 *Magic* 1/II.

DEPLOYMENT:
NAVY:
Atlantic Fleet: (HQ, Brest): 5 SSBN, 6 SS, 1 CCH, 16 FF, 1 MSC, 11 MHC, 2AO.
Channel Flotilla: (HQ, Cherbourg): 1 patrol combatant.
Mediterranean Fleet: (HQ, Toulon): 6 SSN, 1 SS, 2 CV, 4 DDG, 12 FF, 3 MCMV, 3 amph, 2 AO.

FORCES ABROAD:
GERMANY: 15,000; Eurocorps with 1 armd div; Gendarmerie (260).
ANTILLES (HQ Fort de France): 5,000; 3 marine inf (incl 2 SMA), 1 marine inf bn.

FRENCH GUIANA (HQ Cayenne): 3,600; 2 marine inf (incl 1 SMA), 1 Foreign Legion regt, 1 spt bn, 8 ships (incl 1 log spt and 1 amph), 1 *Atlantic* ac (Dakar, Senegal), 1 air tpt unit (2 C-160 ac); Gendarmerie (1,400).
INDIAN OCEAN (Mayotte, La Réunion): 4,000; 2 marine inf (incl 1 SMA) regt, 1 spt bn, 1 Foreign Legion coy, 1 air tpt unit (2 C-160 **ac**, 2 SA-355 **hel**); Gendarmerie (700).
NAVY: Indian Ocean Squadron, Comd ALINDIEN (HQ afloat): (1,400); 4 FF, 2 patrol combatants, 2 amph, 3 spt (1 comd), 1 *Atlantic* ac.
NEW CALEDONIA (HQ Nouméa): 3,900; 1 marine inf regt; some 14 AML recce, 5 105mm arty; 1 air tpt unit, det (2 C-160, 1 *Gardian* MR **ac**, 2 SA-319, 7 SA-330 **hel**); Navy: 2 P-400 PCC; Gendarmerie (1,100).
POLYNESIA (HQ Papeete): 3,800 (incl Centre d'Expérimentations du Pacifique); 1 marine, 1 Foreign Legion regt, 1 air tpt unit (3 SE-210, 1 *Gardian* **ac**; 3 AS-332, 3 SA-319 **hel**); Gendarmerie (350).
PACIFIC NAVAL SQUADRON (comd, ALPACI, HQ Papeete): (500); 3 FF, 5 patrol and coastal, 3 amph, 1 AOT, 2 survey, 5 *Gardian* MR ac.
CENTRAL AFRICAN REPUBLIC: 1,300; GARRISON: 1bn gp incl 1 motor coy; 1 pl AML armd cars (6); spt coy with O-1E lt ac, 120mm mor, *Milan* ATGW.
FROM FRANCE: 1 AML armd car sqn and 1 tp (12 AML), 2 inf coy, 1 arty bty (105mm), 1 avn det (4 SA-330 **hel**); air elm with 5 *Jaguar*, 3 C-160 **ac**.
CHAD: 800; 2 inf coy, 1 AML sqn (-); 2 C-160 ac.
COTE D'IVOIRE: 700; 1 marine inf regt (14 AML-60/-90); 1 AS-355 hel.
DJIBOUTI: 3,900; 1 marine inf(-), 1 Foreign Legion regt(-); 36 ERC-90 recce, 5 155mm arty, 16 AA arty; 3 amph craft, 1 sqn with 10 *Mirage* F-1C, 1 C-160 **ac**, 3 SA-319, 2 AS-355 **hel**.
GABON: 600; 1 marine inf bn (9 AML-60); 1 C-160, 1 *Atlantic* **ac**, 1 SA-355 **hel**.
SENEGAL: 1,500; 1 marine inf bn (14 AML-60/-90); Atlantic MR **ac**; 1 air tpt unit (1 C-160 tpt ac; 1 SA-319 **hel**).

UN AND PEACEKEEPING:
ADRIATIC: 3,200 (all services); on average 2 FF and 1 naval air squadron to NATO/WEU (*Sharp Guard*).
BOSNIA (UNPROFOR BH): 4,872; 4 inf, Fr/Be inf, 1 engr bn, 1 hel sqn (5 AS-332, 4 SA-316); Gendarmerie (20).
CROATIA (UNPROFOR I): 826; 1 log bn; 1 ALAT det; Gendarmerie (21), 1 C-130 ac, plus 12 Observers.
EGYPT (MFO): 40; incl 1 DHC-6.
EL SALVADOR (ONUSAL): 18 Gendarmerie.
FORMER YUGOSLAVIA (*Provide Promise*): 3 C-130.
IRAQ/KUWAIT (UNIKOM): 15 Observers.
ITALY (*Deny Flight*): 10 *Mirage* 2000C, 5 *Mirage* F1-CR, 4 *Mirage* 2000D, FI-CR, 5 *Mirage* F1CT, 1 DHC6, 4 *Jaguar*, 1 C-135, 1 E-3F, 1 N-262, 2 SA-330.
LEBANON (UNIFIL): 441; 1 log bn; Gendarmerie (11).
MIDDLE EAST (UNTSO): 13 Observers.
SAUDI ARABIA (*Southern Watch*): 170; 9 *Mirage* 2000C, 1 C-135, 1 N-262.
TURKEY (*Provide Comfort*): 150; 4 *Mirage* F1-CR, 8 *Jaguar*, 1 C-135.
WESTERN SAHARA (MINURSO): 30 Observers (Gendarmerie).

PARAMILITARY:

GENDARMERIE: 91,800 (2,600 women, 11,700 conscripts, plus 1,200 civilians); incl: *Territorial* (54,000); *Mobile* (17,000); *Schools* (5,700); *Republican Guard* (3,200); *Overseas* (3,400); *Maritime* (1,200); *Air* (1,100); *Air Tpt* (1,200); *Arsenals* (400); *Administration* (4,600). *Reserves* (139,000).
EQUIPMENT: 121 AML, 28 VBC-90 armd cars; 33 AMX-VTT, 155 VBRG-170 APC; 278 81mm mor; 10 PCIs (listed under Navy), plus 11 other patrol craft and 4 tugs. 6 Cessna 206C **ac**, 3 SA-316, 9 SA-319, 29 AS-350 **hel**.

GERMANY

GDP	1992 DM 2,794.2bn ($1,791.9bn): per capita $20,600	
	1993: DM 2,832.0bn ($1,807.0bn): per capita $20,800	
Growth	1992: 2.1%	1993: -1.2%
Inflation	1992: 4.9%	1993: 4.7%
Publ debt	1992: 43.2%	1993: 46.2%
Def exp	1992: DM 54.9bn ($35.2bn)	
Def bdgt	1992: DM 52.1bn ($33.4bn)	
	1993: DM 49.6bn ($31.8bn)	
	1994: DM 47.2bn ($28.6bn)	
NATO defn	1992: DM 66.1bn ($42.4bn)	
	1993: DM 60.6bn ($36.7bn)	
	1994: DM 58.3bn ($35.3bn)	
$1 = DM	1992: 1.56	1993: 1.65
	1994: 1.70	

DM = Deutschmark

Population 80,974,600

	13–17	*18–22*	*23–32*
Men	2,142,300	2,520,200	7,220,500
Women	2,022,100	2,400,300	6,907,900

TOTAL ARMED FORCES:

ACTIVE: 367,300 (154,100 conscripts; 1,000 active Reserve trg posts, all Services).
Terms of service: 12 months.

RESERVES: 442,700 (men to age 45, officers/NCO to 60): Army 358,800, Navy 10,900, Air 73,000.

ARMY: 254,300 (122,800 conscripts; incl 4,300 staff not listed below).

(Military District Command = MDC).

ARMY FORCES COMMAND:

1 airmobile force (div) HQ with 3 AB bde.
1 army avn bde (156 UH-1D, 94 CH-53, 96 BO-105 hel).
1 SIGINT/ELINT bde.
1 spt bde.

CORPS COMMANDS:

I Ge/Nl Corps:
2 MDC/armd div.
1 MDC/armd inf div (for LANDJUT).
II Corps: 2 MDC/armd div; 1 MDC/mtn div.
IV Corps: 2 MDC/armd inf div.
(The 8 MDC/div command and control 6 armd, 1 Military Region Command (MRC)/armd, 6 armd inf, 6 MRC/armd inf, 1 mtn bde and the Ge elements of the Ge/Fr bde, of which 7 plus the Ge/Fr bde are fully manned, the remainder being mixed active and reserve units, all train their own recruits. The MDC divs also command and control 39 MRC. One armed div has been earmarked for the EUROCORPS.)
(For cbt spt a total of 8 recce bn, 6 arty rgt (each 24 FH-70, 8 110mm MRL, 18 MRLS), 2 arty rgt (each 24 M-109, 8 110mm MRL, 18 MRLS), and 7 AD regt (each 42 Gepard) are available.)
Corps Units: 2 armd recce bn, 3 AD regt (each 42 *Roland*), 3 ATGW hel regt (each 60 BO-105 hel).

EQUIPMENT:

MBT: 2,855: 731 *Leopard* 1A5, 2,124 *Leopard* 2 (225 to be upgraded) (plus some 1,400 *Leopard* A11 and M-48 in store awaiting disposal).
RECCE: 514: 408 SPz-2 *Luchs*, 106 TPz-1 *Fuchs* (NBC).
AIFV: 2,443: 2,100 *Marder* A3, 343 *Wiesel* (210-TOW, 133-20mm gun).
APC: 4,037: 913 TPz-1 *Fuchs* (incl 102 EW variant), 2,900 M-113 (incl 427 arty obs), 224 M-577.
TOTAL ARTY: 2,090:
TOWED ARTY: 378: 105mm: 19 M-56, 143 M-101; 155mm: 216 FH-70.
SP ARTY: 155mm: 577 M-109A3G.
MRL: 228: 110mm: 74 *LARS*; 227mm: 154 MLRS.
MORTARS: 907: 120mm: 368 Brandt, 102 Tampella, 437 Tampella on M-113.
ATGW: 2,513: 1,964 *Milan*, 98 *TOW*, 316 RJPz-(*HOT*) *Jaguar* 1, 135 RJPz-(*TOW*) SP.
AD GUNS: 2,347: 20mm: 1,977 Rh 202 towed; 35mm: 370 *Gepard* SP.
SAM: 1,511: 142 *Roland* SP, 233 *Stinger*, 1,100 *Strela*, 36 *Igla*.
SURV: *Green Archer* (mor), RASIT (veh, arty), RATAC (veh, arty).
HELICOPTERS: 205 PAH-1 (Bo-105 with *HOT*), 137 UH-1D, 110 CH-53G, 96 Bo-105M, 74 *Alouette*.
MARINE (River Engineers): 24 LCM, 24 PCI (river).
EQUIPMENT OF FORMER GDR ARMY (in store):
MBT: 815: 6 T-54, 623 T-55, 186 T-72M.
LIGHT TANKS: 140 PT-76.
AIFV: 823: 813 BMP-1, 8 BRM-1K, 2 BMP-2.
APC: 1,970: 47 BTR-40, 107 BTR-50, 726 BTR-60, 1,090 BTR-70.
TOWED ARTY: 187: 122mm: 5 D-30, 5 M-1938 (M-30); 130mm: 172 M-46; 152mm: 5 D-20.
SP ARTY: 246: 122mm: 231 2S1; 152mm: 15 2S3.
MRL: 103: 122mm: 61 Cz RM-70, 42 BM-21.
MORTARS: 17: 120mm: 9 M-120, 8 2B11.
HELICOPTERS: 45 Mi-24.
UAV: CL-89 (AN/USD-501), CL-289 (AN/USD-502).

NAVY: 30,100 (incl 4,230 Naval Air, 6,700 conscripts and 280 women).

Fleet Command organised into 7 type commands: Frigate; Patrol Boat; MCMV; Submarine; Support Flotillas; Naval Air; Naval Comms and Electronics Commands.

BASES: Glücksburg (Maritime HQ) and four main bases: Wilhelmshaven, Kiel, Olpenitz and Warnemünde. Other bases with limited support facilities: Baltic: Eckernförde, Flensburg, Neustadt; North Sea: Emden.

SUBMARINES: 20:
TACTICAL SUBMARINES: 20:
18 Type 206/206A SSC with *Seeaal* DM2 533mm HWT (12 conversions to T-206A complete).
2 Type 205 SSC with DM3 HWT.
PRINCIPAL SURFACE COMBATANTS: 12:
DESTROYERS: 4:
DDG: 3 *Lütjens* (mod US *Adams*) with 1 x 1 SM-1 MR SAM/*Harpoon* SSM launcher, 2 x 127mm guns; plus 1 x 8 *ASROC* (Mk 46 LWT), 2 x 3 ASTT.

DD: 1 *Hamburg* (ASUW) with 2 x 2 MM-38 *Exocet*, 4 x 533mm TT (SUT), 3 x 100mm guns.
FRIGATES: 8:
8 *Bremen* with 2 *Lynx* hel (ASW/OTHT), 2 x 2 ASTT; plus 2 x 4 *Harpoon*.
PATROL AND COASTAL COMBATANTS: 38:
MISSILE CRAFT: 38:
10 *Albatros* (Type 143) PFM with 2 x 2 *Exocet*, and 2 x 533mm TT.
10 *Gepard* (T-143A) PFM with 2 x 2 *Exocet*.
18 *Tiger* (Type 148) PFM with 2 x 2 *Exocet*.
MINE WARFARE: 42:
MINELAYERS: 1 *Sachsenwald* (600+ mines) mine transport, but can be used for minelaying.
MINE COUNTERMEASURES: 41:
10 *Hameln* (T-343) comb ML/MCC.
6 *Lindau Troika* MSC control and guidance, each with 3 unmanned sweep craft.
10 converted *Lindau* (T-331) MHC.
5 *Frankenthal* (T-332) MHC.
9 *Frauenlob* MSI.
1 MCM diver spt ship.
AMPHIBIOUS: craft only: some 11 LCU/LCM.
SUPPORT AND MISCELLANEOUS: 40:
UNDERWAY SUPPORT: 2:
2 *Spessart* AO.
MAINTENANCE/LOGISTIC: 25:
1 *Rhein* SS/MCMV spt, 5 *Elbe* spt, 4 small (2,000t) AOT, 3 *Lüneburg* log spt, 2 AE, 8 tugs, 2 icebreakers (civil).
SPECIAL PURPOSE: 9:
3 AGI, 2 trials, 3 multi-purpose (T-748), 1 trg.
RESEARCH AND SURVEY: 4:
1 AGOR, 3 AGHS (civil-manned for Ministry of Transport).

NAVAL AIR ARM: (4,230).

Average annual flying hours for *Tornado* aircrew: 180.
3 wings, 7 sqn, 1 transport gp.
1 wing with *Tornado*.
1 MR/ASW wing with *Atlantic*, *Lynx*.
1 SAR/liaison wing with Do-28, *Sea King*.
1 transport gp with 1 sqn Mi-8.
FGA/RECCE: 2 sqn with *Tornado*.
TRAINING: 1 sqn with *Tornado*.
MR/ELINT: 1 sqn with *Atlantic*.
LIAISON: 1 sqn with Do-28/Do-228.
ASW: 1 sqn with *Sea Lynx* Mk 88 hel.
SAR: 1 sqn with *Sea King* Mk 41 hel.
TRANSPORT: 1 sqn with Mi-8.
EQUIPMENT: 64 cbt ac, 17 armed hel.
AIRCRAFT:
***Tornado*:** 64.
***Atlantic*:** 18 (14 MR, 4 ELINT).
Do-28: 2.
Do-228: LM: 1 (environmental monitoring).
HELICOPTERS:
***Sea Lynx* Mk 88:** 17 (ASW).
***Mi-8*:** 17 (tpt).
***Sea King Mk 41*:** 22 (SAR).
MISSILES:
ASM: *Kormoran, Sea Skua*.
AAM: AIM-9 *Sidewinder*.

AIR FORCE: 82,900 (24,600 conscripts).

Average annual flying hours for *Tornado* aircrews: 150.

TACTICAL COMMAND (GAFTAC): 4 air div.

FGA: 4 wings with *Tornado*; 8 sqn.
FIGHTER: 4 wings with F-4F (6 sqn); 1 sqn with MiG-29.
RECCE: 1 wing with *Tornado*.
ECR: 1 wing with *Tornado*.
SAM: 6 groups (each 6 sqn) *Patriot*; 6 groups (each 6 sqn) *HAWK*; 14 sqn *Roland*.
RADAR: 1 tac Air Control Command, 2 tac Air Control regts.
7 sites; 6 remote radar posts.
2 sites; 6 remote radar posts in eastern division.

TRANSPORT COMMAND (GAFTC):

TRANSPORT: 3 wings: 4 sqn with Transall C-160, incl 1 (OCU) with C-160, 1 sqn (incl 1 OCU) with Bell UH-1D, 1 special air mission wing with Boeing 707-320C, Tu-154, Airbus A-310, VFW-614, CL-601, L-410S (VIP); UH-1D hel (VIP), Mi-8S (VIP).
HELICOPTERS: 1 wing: 3 sqn; plus 1 det with UH-1D (liaison/SAR).

TRAINING:

FGA: OCU 1 det (Cottesmore, UK) with 17 *Tornado*.
FIGHTER: OCU (Holoman AFB, New Mexico) with 24 F-4E (17 F-4E leased from USAF).
TRAINING: NATO joint pilot trg (Sheppard AFB, Texas) with 35 T-37B, 41 T-38A; primary trg sqn with Beech *Bonanza*.
EQUIPMENT: 454 cbt ac (24 trg (overseas)); no attack hel.
AIRCRAFT:
F-4: 157: **-F:** 150 (FGA, ftr); **-E:** 7 (OCU, in US).
***Tornado*:** 273 (193 FGA, 35* ECR, 28* OCU, 17* in tri-national trg sqn (in UK)).
MiG-29: 24: 20 (ftr), **-UB:** 4 *(trg).
***Alpha Jet*:** 34 (trg); plus 76 in store.
Transall C-160: 85 (tpt, trg).
Boeing 707: 4 (VIP). **A-310:** 3 (VIP, tpt). **CL-601:** 7 (VIP). **HFB-320:** 3 (tpt). **L-410-S:** 4 (VIP). **T-37B:** 35. **T-38A:** 41. **Tu-154:** 2 (tpt). **VFW-614:** 3 (VIP). **An -26:** 1.

HELICOPTERS:
UH-1D: 108 (104 SAR, tpt, liaison; 4 VIP).
Mi-8T: 16 (SAR tpt).
Mi-8S: 6 (VIP).
MISSILES:
ASM: AGM-65 *Maverick,* AGM-88 HARM.
AAM: AIM-9 *Sidewinder*, AA-11 *Archer* (for MiG-29).
SAM: 216 *Hawk* launchers; 95 *Roland* launchers. 288 *Patriot* launchers.
AIRCRAFT OF FORMER GDR AIR FORCE (not being operated):
FIGHTER: 79 MiG-21; 24 MiG-23; 24 Su-22 (all TLE will be disposed of in accordance with CFE).
TRAINING: 26 L-39.
HELICOPTERS: 11 Mi-2, 30 Mi-8.

FORCES ABROAD:

NAVY:
1 MCMV with STANAVFORCHAN.
3 MPA in ELMAS/Sardinia.
AIR FORCE: United States: 450 flying training at Sheppard and Holman Air Force bases; United Kingdom: OCU at RAF Cottesmore.
UN AND PEACEKEEPING:
ADRIATIC (*Sharp Guard*): 1 FF each with STANAVFORLANT and STANAVFORMED,
GEORGIA (UNOMIG): 2 Observers.
IRAQ (UNSCOM): 44; **ac:** 2 C-160; **hel:** 3 CH-53.
FORMER YUGOSLAVIA (*Provide Promise*): 3 C-160 (Frankfurt), 1 C-160 (Falconara, Italy).
WESTERN SAHARA (MINURSO): civ pol.

PARAMILITARY:

FEDERAL BORDER GUARD (Ministry of Interior): 24,100; 5 cmd (constitutionally has no cbt status). Eqpt: 297 MOWAG SW-3/-4 APC (to be 100 by end of 1994); hel: 32 SA-318C, 13 UH-1D, 8 Bell 212, 22 SA-330, 3 SA-332L.
COAST GUARD: 550; some 14 PCI, 1 inshore tug, plus boats.

FOREIGN FORCES:

NATO:
HQ Allied Land Forces Central Europe (LANDCENT).
HQ Allied Air Forces Central Europe (AIRCENT).
HQ Allied Land Forces Jutland and Schleswig-Holstein (LANDJUT).
HQ Allied Rapid Reaction Corps (ARRC).
Allied Rapid Reaction Force Air Staff.
HQ Multi-National Division (Central) (MND(C)).
HQ Allied Command Europe Mobile Force (AMF).
Airborne Early Warning Force: 18 E-3A *Sentry.*
BELGIUM: 10,300; 1 Force HQ, 1 mech bde, 2 hel bn.
FRANCE: 15,000; 1 armd div (Eurocorps).
NETHERLANDS: 3,000; 1 lt bde.
RUSSIA: 18,000; all to have withdrawn by 31 August 1994.
UNITED KINGDOM: 38,200; 1 corps HQ (multinational), 1 armd div, 2 armd recce, 1 MLRS, 1 engr regt. Air Force Group HQ (6,000); 2 air bases, 6 ac sqn, 1 hel sqn; **ac:** 52 *Tornado* GR1, 26 *Harrier*; **hel:** 5 *Chinook*, 5 *Puma*.
US: 103,200; 1 army HQ, 1 corps HQ; 1 armd, 1 mech div; 2 air force HQ; 1 tac ftr wing with 5 sqn FGA/ftr, 1 cbt spt wing, 1 air control wing, 1 tac airlift wing. 54 F-16C/D, 18F-15C/D, 12 A-10, 6 OA-10, 16 C-130E, 4 C-9A.

GREECE

GDP	1992: dr 14,846.9bn ($77.9bn): per capita $8,000	
	1993: dr 16,923.6bn ($79.9bn): per capita $8,000	
Growth	1992: 0.9%	1993: 0%
Inflation	1992: 15.8%	1993: 14.4%
Publ debt	1992: 104.1%	1993: 109.7%
Def exp	1992: dr 623.1bn ($3.3bn)	
	1993: dr 692.4bn ($3.3bn)	
Def bdgt	1993: dr 615.6bn ($3.3bn)	
	1994: dr 753.4bn ($3.3bn)	
NATO defn	1992: dr 809.4bn ($4.2bn)	
	1993: dr 934.0bn ($4.1bn)	
FMA	1993: $315.3m (FMF, IMET)	
	1994: $283.6m (FMF, IMET)	
	1995: $317.0m (FMF, IMET)	
$1 = dr	1992: 190.6	1993: 229.3
	1994: 249.1	

dr = drachma

Population: 10,569,500 (Albanian 2%)

	13–17	*18–22*	*23–32*
Men	361,100	370,400	770,200
Women	338,000	348,500	726,100

TOTAL ARMED FORCES:

ACTIVE: 159,300 (122,300 conscripts, 5,900 women).
Terms of service: Army up to 19 months, Navy up to 23 months, Air Force up to 21 months.

RESERVES: some 406,000 (to age 50): Army some 350,000 (Field Army 230,000, Territorial Army/National Guard 120,000); Navy about 24,000; Air Force about 32,000.

ARMY: 113,000 (100,000 conscripts, 2,200 women).

FIELD ARMY: (82,000); 3 Military Regions.

1 Army, 4 corps HQ.

2 div HQ (1 armd, 1 mech).

9 inf div (3 inf, 1 arty regt, 1 armd bn) 2 Cat A, 3 Cat B, 4 Cat C.

5 indep armd bde (each 2 armd, 1 mech inf, 1 SP arty bn) Cat A.

1 indep mech bde (2 mech, 1 armd, 1 SP arty bn), Cat A.

2 inf bde.

1 marine bde (3 inf, 1 lt arty bn, 1 armd sqn) Cat A.

1 cdo, 1 raider regt.

4 recce bn. 2 army avn bn.

10 fd arty bn. 1 indep avn coy.

6 AD arty bn.

2 SAM bn with *Improved HAWK*.

Units are manned at 3 different levels: Cat A 85% fully ready; Cat B 60% ready in 24 hours; Cat C 20% ready in 48 hours.

TERRITORIAL DEFENCE: (31,000).

Higher Mil Comd of Interior and Islands HQ.

4 Mil Comd HQ (incl Athens).

1 inf div. 4 AD arty bn.

1 para regt. 1 army avn bn.

8 fd arty bn.

RESERVES (National Guard): 34,000; role: internal security.

EQUIPMENT:

MBT: 2,722: 396 M-47 (in store), 1,220 M-48 (299, 110 A2, 212 A3, 599 A5), 671 M-60 (359 A1, 312 A3), 156 AMX-30 (in store), 279 *Leopard* (170 1A4, 109 1A3).

LIGHT TANKS: 67 M-24.

RECCE: 48 M-8.

AIFV: 96 AMX-10P, 500 BMP-1.

APC: 2,365 (517 in store): 130 *Leonidas*, 114 M-2, 403 M-3 half-track, 372 M-59, 1,346 M-113.

TOTAL ARTY: 2,019:

TOWED ARTY: 875: 105mm: 18 M-56, 469 M-101; 140mm: 32 5.5-in; 155mm: 271 M-114; 203mm: 85 M-115.

SP ARTY: 371: 105mm: 76 M-52; 155mm: 48 M-44A1, 51 M-109A1, 84 M-109A2; 175mm: 12 M-107; 203mm: 100 M-110A2.

MORTARS: 107mm: 773 M-30 (incl 132 SP); plus 81mm: 690.

ATGW: 394: *Milan, TOW* (incl 36 SP).

RL: 64mm: RPG-18.

RCL: 90mm: 1,057 EM-67; 106mm: 763 M-40A1.

AD GUNS: 20mm: 101 Rh-202 twin; 23mm: 300 ZU-23-2; 40mm: 227 M-1, 95 M-42A twin SP.

SAM: 42 *Improved HAWK, Redeye*.

SURV: AN/TPQ-36 (arty, mor).

AIRCRAFT: 2 *Aero Commander*, 2 *Super King Air*, 20 U-17A.

HELICOPTERS: 10 CH-47C1 (1 in store), 85 UH-1D/H/AB-205, 9 AH-1P, 1 AB-212, 15 AB-206, 10 Bell 47G, 30 Hughes 300C.

NAVY: 19,500 (7,900 conscripts, 2,600 women).

BASES: Salamis, Patras, Soudha Bay.

SUBMARINES: 8:

8 *Glavkos* (Ge T-209/1100) with 533mm TT (1 with *Harpoon* USGW).

PRINCIPAL SURFACE COMBATANTS: 14:

DESTROYERS: 6:

4 *Kimon* (US *Adams*) (US lease) with 1 x SM-1; plus 1 x 8 *ASROC*, 2 x 3 ASTT, 2 x 127mm guns, 4 *Harpoon* SSM.

2 *Themistocles* (US *Gearing*) (ASW) with 1 x 8 *ASROC*, 2 x 3 ASTT, 2 x 4 *Harpoon* SSM; plus 3 x 2 127mm guns.

FRIGATES: 8:

1 *Hydra* (MEKO 200) with 2 x 3 ASTT; plus 2 x 4 *Harpoon* SSM and 1 x 127mm gun (1 SH-60 hel, 1 DC).

4 *Elli* (Nl *Kortenaer*) with 2 AB-212 hel, 2 x 3 ASTT; plus 2 x 4 *Harpoon.*

3 *Makedonia* (ex-US *Knox*) (US lease) with 1 x 8 *ASROC*, 4 x ASTT; plus *Harpoon* (from *ASROC* launcher), 1 x 127mm gun.

PATROL AND COASTAL COMBATANTS: 42:

CORVETTES: 5:

5 *Niki* (ex-Ge *Thetis*) (ASW) with 1 x 4 ASW RL, 4 x 533mm TT.

MISSILE CRAFT: 18:

14 *Laskos* (Fr *La Combattante* II/III) PFM, 8 with 4 x MM-38 *Exocet*, 6 with 6 *Penguin* 2 SSM, all with 2 x 533mm TT.

2 *I. Votis* (Fr *La Combattante* IIA) PFM with 2 x 2 MM-38 *Exocet*.

2 *Stamou*, with 4 x SS-12 SSM.

TORPEDO CRAFT: 10:

6 *Hesperos* (Ge *Jaguar*) PFT with 4 x 533mm TT.

4 No *'Nasty'* PFT with 4 x 533mm TT.

PATROL: 9:

COASTAL: 4: 2 *Armatolos* (Dk *Osprey*) PCC, 2 *Pirpolitis* PCC.

INSHORE: 5: 2 *Tolmi*, 3 PCI .

MINE WARFARE: 16:
MINELAYERS: 2 *Aktion* (US LSM-1) (100–130 mines).
MINE COUNTERMEASURES: 14:
9 *Alkyon* (US MSC-294) MSC.
5 *Atalanti* (US *Adjutant*) MSC.
AMPHIBIOUS: 10:
1 *Samos* LST with hel deck: capacity 300 tps, 16 tk.
1 *Nafkratoussa* (US *Cabildo*) LSD: capacity 200 tps, 18 tk, 1 hel.
2 *Inouse* (US *County*) LST: capacity 400 tps, 18 tk.
4 *Ikaria* (US LST-510): capacity 200 tps, 16 tk.
2 *Ipopliarhos Grigoropoulos* (US LSM-1) LSM, capacity 50 tps, 4 tk.
Plus about 65 craft: 2 LCT, 8 LCU, 13 LCM, some 42 LCVP.
SUPPORT AND MISCELLANEOUS: 14:
2 AOT, 4 AOT (small), 1 *Axios* (ex-Ge *Lüneburg*) log spt, 1 AE, 5 AGHS, 1 trg.

NAVAL AIR: 12 armed hel.
ASW: 1 hel div: 2 sqn 2 with 9 AB-212 (ASW), 2 AB-212 (EW), 2 SA-319 (with ASM).

AIR FORCE: 26,800 (14,400 conscripts, 1,100 women).

TACTICAL AIR FORCE: 8 cbt wings, 1 tpt wing.
FGA: 6 sqn:
2 with A-7H. 1 with F-16.
2 with A-7E. 1 with F-4E.
FIGHTER: 10 sqn:
2 with *Mirage* F-1CG. 2 with F-5A/B.
1 with NF-5A/B, RF-5A. 1 with F-16 C/D.
2 with *Mirage* 2000 EG/BG. 2 with F-4E.
RECCE: 1 sqn with RF-4E.
MR: 1 sqn with HU-16B.
TRANSPORT: 3 sqn with C-130H/B, YS-11, C-47, Do-28, *Gulfstream*.
LIAISON: 4 T-33A.
HELICOPTERS: 2 sqn with AB-205A, Bell 47G, AB-212.
AD: 1 bn with *Nike Hercules* SAM (36 launchers). 12 bty with *Skyguard/Sparrow* SAM, twin 35mm guns.
AIR TRAINING COMMAND:
TRAINING: 4 sqn:
1 with T-41A; 1 with T-37B/C; 2 with T-2E.

EQUIPMENT: 355 cbt ac, incl 2 MR (plus 98 in store), no armed hel.
AIRCRAFT:
A-7: 92: **-H:** 38 (FGA) (plus 5 in store); **TA-7H:** 7 (FGA); **A-7E:** 40 (plus 15 in store); **A-7K:** 7.
F-5: 90: **-A:** 64 (plus 10 in store); **-B:** 8, plus 1 in store; **NF-5A:** 11; **NF-5B:** 1; **RF-5A:** 6 (plus 3 in store).
F-4: 74: **-E:** 54, plus 19 in store; **RF-4E:** 20 (recce), plus 7 in store.
F-16: 35: **-C:** 29 (FGA/ftr), plus 3 in store; **-D:** 6.
***Mirage F-1:* CG:** 26 (ftr), plus 3 in store.
Mirage 2000: 36: **-EG:** 32, plus 2 in store (ftr); **BG:** 4* (trg).
F104G: 20 in store; **RF-104G:** 6 in store; **TF-104G:** 4 in store.
HU-16B: 2 (MR), plus 3 in store. **C-47:** 4 (tpt). **C-130H:** 10 (tpt). **C-130B:** 5 (tpt). **CL-215:** 11 (tpt, fire-fighting). **Do-28**: 12 (lt tpt). ***Gulfstream I*:** 1 (VIP tpt). **T-2:** 36* (trg). **T-33A:** 30 (liaison). **T-37B/C:** 29 (trg). **T-41D:** 19 (trg). **YS-11-200:** 6 (tpt).
HELICOPTERS:
AB-205A: 14 (tpt). **AB-212:** 3 (VIP, tpt). **Bell 47G:** 5 (liaison).
MISSILES:
ASM: AGM-12 *Bullpup*, AGM-65 *Maverick*.
AAM: AIM-7 *Sparrow*, AIM-9 *Sidewinder*, R-550 *Magic*.
SAM: 36 *Nike Hercules*, 40 *Sparrow*.

FORCES ABROAD:

CYPRUS: 2,250; 2 inf bn and officers/NCO seconded to Greek-Cypriot forces.

UN AND PEACEKEEPING:

ADRIATIC (*Sharp Guard*): 1 FF.
IRAQ/KUWAIT (UNIKOM): 7 Observers.
WESTERN SAHARA (MINURSO): 1 Observer.

PARAMILITARY:

GENDARMERIE: 26,500; MOWAG *Roland*, 15 UR-416 APC, 6 NH-300 hel.
COAST GUARD AND CUSTOMS: 4,000; some 100 patrol craft, 2 Cessna *Cutlass*, 2 TB-20 *Trinidad* ac.

FOREIGN FORCES:

US: 760: Army (60); Navy (200), facilities at Soudha Bay; Air Force (500), 2 air base gp.

ICELAND

GDP	1992: K 383.3bn ($6.6bn): per capita $16,400	
	1993: K 397.4bn ($6.8bn): per capita $16,900	
Growth	1992: -3.4%	1993: 0.7%
Inflation	1992: 3.7%	1993: 4.1%
Debt	1992: $2.1bn	1993: $2.2bn
$1 = K	1992: 57.6	1993: 67.6
	1994: 72.0	

K = kronur

Population: 266,200

	13–17	*18–22*	*23–32*
Men	11,000	11,000	22,000
Women	10,300	10,100	21,600

ARMED FORCES: none.

PARAMILITARY: 130.
COAST GUARD: 130.
BASE: Reykjavik.
PATROL CRAFT: 4:
3 PCO: 2 *Aegir* with hel, 1 *Odinn* with hel deck.
1 PCI(.
AVIATION: 1 F-27 ac, 1 SA-360.

FOREIGN FORCES:
NATO: Island Commander Iceland (ISCOMICE, responsible to CINCEASTLANT).
US: 2,200.
NAVY: 1,800: **MR:** 1 sqn with 9 P-3C.
AIR FORCE: 400: 4 F-15C/D, 1 HH-130, 5 HH-60G.
NETHERLANDS:
NAVY: 30: 1 P-3C.

ITALY

GDP	1992: L 1,507,200bn ($1,223bn): per capita $17,700	
	1993: L 1,619,800bn ($1,246bn): per capita $18,000	
Growth	1992: 0.7%	1993: -0.7%
Inflation	1992: 5.2%	1993: 4.3%
Publ debt	1992: 108.1%	1993: 114.0%
Def bdgt	1992: L 24,517bn ($19.9bn)	
	1993: L 26,560bn ($16.5bn)	
	1994: L 26,167bn ($16.1bn)	
NATO defn	1992: L 30,813bn ($25.0bn)	
	1993: L 38,462bn ($24.4bn)	
$1 = L	1992: 1,232	1993: 1,574
	1994: 1,627	

L = lira

Population: 58,134,600

	13–17	*18–22*	*23–32*
Men	1,810,600	2,141,100	4,690,900
Women	1,721,200	2,047,400	4,557,800

TOTAL ARMED FORCES:
ACTIVE: 322,300 (197,100 conscripts).
Terms of service: all services 12 months.
RESERVES: 584,000. Army 520,000 (obligation to age 45), immediate mob 240,000; Navy 36,000 (to age 39 for men, variable for officers to 73); Air Force 28,000 (to age 25 or 45 (specialists)).

ARMY: 205,000 (154,000 conscripts).
FIELD ARMY:
(Note: regt are normally of bn size.)
3 Corps HQ (1 mtn):
1 with 1 mech, 1 armd bde, 1 armd cav regt, 1 arty, 1 AA regt, 1 avn regt.
1 with 2 mech, 1 armd, 1 armd cav bde, 1 amph, 4 arty, 1 avn regt.
1 with 4 mtn bde, 1 avn, 1 armd cav, 2 hy arty, 1 AA regt.
1 AD comd: 4 *HAWK* SAM, 3 AA regt.
1 avn gp (1 sqn AB-412, 2 sqn CH-47, 1 flt Do-228).
TERRITORIAL DEFENCE:
7 Military Regions.
8 indep mech, 1 AB bde (incl 1 SF bn, 1 avn sqn).
Rapid Intervention Force (*FIR*) formed from 1 mech, 1 AB bde (see above), plus 1 Marine bn (see Navy), 1 hel unit (Army), 1 air tpt unit (Air Force).
5 armd cav regt.
1 inf regt.
4 engr regt.
5 avn units.
RESERVES: on mob: 1 armd, 1 mech, 1 mtn bde.
EQUIPMENT:
MBT: 1,210: 300 M-60A1 (in store), 910 *Leopard*.
RECCE: 190 *Centauro* B-1.
APC: 2,831: 1,149 M-113, 1,613 VCC1/-2, 44 Fiat 6614, 25 LVTP-7.
TOTAL ARTY: 2,004:
TOWED ARTY: 938: 105mm: 357 Model 56 pack (233 in store); 155mm: 158 FH-70, 423 M-114 (in store).

SP ARTY: 274: 155mm: 256 M-109G/-L; 203mm: 18 M-110A2.
MRL: 227mm: 18 MLRS.
MORTARS: 120mm: 774 (389 in store); plus 81mm: 1,205 (381 in store).
ATGW: 326 *TOW* (incl 270 SP), 804 *Milan*.
RL: 1,000 *APILAS*.
RCL: 80mm: 720 *Folgore*.
AD GUNS: 25mm: 176 SIDAM SP; 40mm: 234.
SAM: 126 *HAWK*, 145 *Stinger*.
AIRCRAFT: 33: 30 SM-1019, 3 Do-228.
HELICOPTERS: 25 A-109, 17 A-129, 91 AB-205A, 116 AB-206 (observation), 14 AB-212, 23 AB-412, 34 CH-47C.
UAV: CL-89 (AN/USD-501), *Mirach* 20/-100/-150.

NAVY: 44,000 (incl 1,560 Naval Air, 1,500 Marines and 17,600 conscripts).

Commands: 1 Fleet Commander CINCNAV (also NATO COMEDCENT); 6 Area Commands: Upper Tyrrhenian; Adriatic; Lower Tyrrhenian; Ionian and Strait of Otranto; Sicily; and Sardinia.
BASES: La Spezia (HQ), Taranto (HQ), Ancona (HQ), Brindisi, Augusta, Messina (HQ), La Maddalena (HQ), Cagliari, Naples (HQ), Venice (HQ).
SUBMARINES: 9:
3 *Pelosi* (imp *Sauro*) with Type 184 HWT (4 by September 1994).
4 *Sauro* with Type 184 HWT (includes 2 non-op, undergoing modernisation).
2 *Toti* SSC with Type 184 HWT.
PRINCIPAL SURFACE COMBATANTS: 29:
CARRIER: 1:
1 *G. Garibaldi* CVV with 16 SH-3 *Sea King* hel, 3 AV-8B (plus 2 trg) V/STOL ac, 4 *Teseo* SSM, 2 x 3 ASTT.
CRUISERS: 1:
1 *Vittorio Veneto* CGH with 1 x 2 SM-1 ER SAM, 6 AB-212 ASW hel (Mk 46 LWT); plus 4 *Teseo* SSM, 2 x 3 ASTT.
DESTROYERS: 4:
2 *Luigi Durand de la Penne* (ex-*Animoso*) DDGH with 1 x SM-1 MR SAM, 2 x 4 *Teseo* SSM, plus 2 x AB-312 hel, 1 x 127mm gun, 2 x 3 ASTT .
2 *Audace* DDGH, with 1 x SM-1 MR SAM, 4 *Teseo* SSM, plus 2 x AB-212 hel, 1 x 127mm gun, 2 x 3 ASTT.
FRIGATES: 23:
8 *Maestrale* FFH with 2 AB-212 hel, 2 x 533mm DP TT; plus 4 *Teseo* SSM, 1 x 127mm gun.
4 *Lupo* FFH with 1 AB-212 hel, 2 x 3 ASTT; plus 8 *Teseo* SSM, 1 x 127mm gun (plus 4 *Lupo* FF built for Iraq to be taken into service during 1994–96).
1 *Alpino* FFH with 1 AB-212 hel, 2 x 3 ASTT, 1 x ASW mor.
8 *Minerva* FF with 2 x 3 ASTT.
2 *De Cristofaro* FF with 2 x 3 ASTT, 1 ASW mor (incl 1 paying off August 1994).
PATROL AND COASTAL COMBATANTS: 16:
MISSILE CRAFT: 6 *Sparviero* PHM with 2 *Teseo* SSM.
PATROL, OFFSHORE: 6:
4 *Cassiopea* with 1 AB-212 hel.
2 *Storione* (US *Aggressive*) ex-MSO.
COASTAL: 4 *Bambu* (ex-MSC) PCC assigned MFO.
MINE WARFARE: 13:
MINE COUNTERMEASURES: 13:
10 *Lerici* MHC.
3 *Castagno* (US *Adjutant*) MHC.
AMPHIBIOUS: 3:
3 *San Giorgio* LPD: capacity 350 tps, 30 trucks, 2 SH-3D or CH-47 hel, 7 craft.
Plus some 30 craft: about 3 LCU, 10 LCM and 20 LCVP.
SUPPORT AND MISCELLANEOUS: 42:
2 *Stromboli* AO, 8 tugs, 9 coastal tugs, 6 water tankers, 4 trials, 2 trg, 3 AGOR, 6 tpt, 2 salvage.
SPECIAL FORCES (Special Forces Command – COMSUBIN):
3 gp; 1 underwater ops; 1 school; 1 research.

MARINES (San Marco gp): (1,500).

1 bn gp.
1 trg gp.
1 log gp.
EQUIPMENT: 30 VCC-1, 10 LVTP-7 APC, 16 81mm mor, 8 106mm RCL, 6 *Milan* ATGW.

NAVAL AIR ARM: (1,560); 5 cbt ac, 30 armed hel.

FGA: 3 AV-8B II, plus 2* TAV-8B.
ASW: 5 hel sqn with 30 SH-3D, 54 AB-212.
ASM: *Marte* Mk 2.

AIR FORCE: 73,300 (25,500 conscripts).

FGA: 8 F FGA:
4 with *Tornado*.
1 with G-91Y.
3 with AMX.
CAS: 1 sqn:
1 lt attack with MB-339.
FIGHTER: 7 sqn with F-104 ASA.
RECCE: 2 sqn with AMX.
MR: 2 sqn with *Atlantic* (Navy-assigned).
EW: 1 ECM/recce sqn with G-222VS, PD-808.
CALIBRATION: 1 navigation-aid calibration sqn with G-222RM, PD-808, MB-339.

TRANSPORT: 3 sqn: 2 with G-222; 1 with C-130H.
TANKER: 1 sqn with 707-320.
LIAISON: 2 sqn with *Gulfstream III*, *Falcon* 50, DC-9 ac; SH-3D hel.
TRAINING: 1 OCU with TF-104G; 1 det (Cottesmore, UK) with *Tornado*;5 sqn with G-91T, MB-339A, SF-260M **ac**, NH-500 **hel**.
SAR: 1 sqn and 3 det with HH-3F.
6 det with AB-212.
AD: 8 SAM gp with *Nike Hercules*.
12 SAM sqn with *Spada*.
EQUIPMENT: 363 cbt ac (plus 87 in store), no armed hel.
AIRCRAFT:
***Tornado*:** 70 (66 FGA, 4* in tri-national sqn), plus 21 in store.
F-104: 112: **-ASA:** 99, plus 41 in store; **TF104G:** 13, plus 9 in store.
AMX: 67: 65 (FGA); **-T:** 2* (trg).
G-91: 51: **-Y:** 15; **-T:** 36* (trg); plus 7 in store.
MB-339: 78 (13 tac, 60 (incl 50*) trg, 5 calibration), plus 9 in store.
Atlantic: 18 (MR).
Boeing-707-320: 2 (tkr/tpt). **C-130H:** 12 (tpt). **G-222:** 42 (38 tpt, 4 calibration), plus **-GE:** 1 (ECM). **DC9-32:** 2 (VIP). ***Gulfstream III*:** 2 (VIP). ***Falcon* 50:** 4 (VIP). **P-166:** 14 (**-M:** 8; **-DL3:** 6 liaison and trg). **PD-808:** 18 (ECM, calibration, VIP tpt); **SF-260M:** 39 (trg). **SIAI-208:** 36 (liaison).
HELICOPTERS:
HH-3F: 28 (SAR). **SH-3D:** 2 (liaison).
AB-212: 36 (SAR). **AB-47G:** 6 (trg).
NH-500D: 50 (trg).
MISSILES:
ASM: AGM-88 HARM.
AAM: AIM-7E *Sparrow*, AIM-9B/L *Sidewinder*, *Aspide*.
SAM: 96 *Nike Hercules*, 7 bty *Spada,* ASPIDE.

FORCES ABROAD:
GERMANY: 93; Air Force, NAEW Force.
MALTA: 16; Air Force with 1 AB-212.
UNITED KINGDOM: 21; tri-national *Tornado* sqn.
UNITED STATES: 26 flying training.
UN AND PEACEKEEPING:
ADRIATIC (*Sharp Guard*): an average 3 DD/FF.
EGYPT (MFO): 82; 3 PCC.
EL SALVADOR (ONUSAL): 9 civ pol.
INDIA/PAKISTAN (UNMOGIP): 5 Observers.
IRAQ (UNSCOM): 1 Observer.
IRAQ/KUWAIT (UNIKOM): 7 Observers.
LEBANON (UNIFIL): 42; hel unit.
MIDDLE EAST (UNTSO): 7 Observers.
MOZAMBIQUE (ONUMOZ): 222.
SOMALIA (UNOSOM): 5 civ pol.
WESTERN SAHARA (MINURSO): 6 Observers.

PARAMILITARY:
CARABINIERI (Ministry of Defence): 111,800: Territorial: 5 bde, 17 regt, 96 gp; Trg: 1 bde; Mobile def: 2 bde, 1 cav regt, 1 special ops gp, 13 mobile bn, 1 AB bn, avn and naval units.
EQUIPMENT: 48 Fiat 6616 armd cars; 40 VCC2, 91 M-113 APC; 24 A-109, 4 AB-205, 40 AB-206, 17 AB-412 hel.
PUBLIC SECURITY GUARD (Ministry of Interior): 80,400: 11 mobile units; 40 Fiat 6614 APC, 3 P-64B, 5 P-68 ac; 12 A-109, 20 AB-206, 9 AB-212 hel.
FINANCE GUARDS (Treasury Department): 64,100; 14 Zones, 20 Legions, 128 Gps; 15 A-109, 66 Breda-Nardi NH-500M/MC/MD hel; 5 P-166-DL3 ac; 3 PCI, 65; plus about 300 boats.
HARBOUR CONTROL (*Capitanerie di Porto*) (subordinated to Navy in emergencies): some 12 PCI, 130+ boats.

FOREIGN FORCES:
NATO:
HQ Allied Forces Southern Europe (AFSOUTH).
HQ 5 Allied Tactical Air Force (5 ATAF).
US: 12,600: Army (2,600); 1 AB bn gp; Navy (6,800); Air Force (3,200); 1 ftr sqn with 17 F-16C, 1 F-16D.
***OPERATION DENY FLIGHT*:** France (10 *Mirage* 2000C, 4 *Mirage* F1-CR, 4 *Mirage* F-1CT, 7 *Mirage* 2000D, 6 *Etendard*, 8 *Jaguar*, 1 E-3F, 1 C-135), Netherlands (18 F-16), Spain (1 CASA 212 (spt ac)), Turkey (18 F-16), UK (6 *Tornado* F-3, 12 *Jaguar*, 6 *Sea Harrier*, 2 K-1 *Tristar* (tkr), 3 E-3D *Sentry*, 2 *Nimrod* MPA ac), US (8 F/A-18C, 12 F-16C, 8 F-15E, 12 O/A-10, 6 USN F/A-18C on A-6E, 3 AC-130, 3 EC-130, 10 KC-135).
***OPERATION SHARP GUARD*:** Canada (frigate), Denmark (frigate), France (frigate and destroyer), Germany (frigate and destroyer), Italy (two frigates, one corvette), Netherlands (two frigates), Spain (two frigates, Turkey (frigate), UK (destroyer, frigate, support tanker), US (cruiser and frigate). Maritime aircraft from France (*Atlantic* ac), Germany (*Atlantic* ac), Italy (*Atlantic* ac), Netherlands (P-3C ac), Portugal (P-3P ac), Spain (P-3B ac), UK (*Nimrod* ac), US (P-3C ac).

LUXEMBOURG

GDP	1992: fr 380.9bn ($11.9bn): per capita $20,200	
	1993: fr 394.1bn ($12.4bn): per capita $20,900	
Growth	1992: 2.8%	1993: 1.9%
Inflation	1992: 3.1%	1993: 3.6%
Publ debt	1992: 2.8%	1993: 2.8%
Def exp	1991: fr 3.1bn ($92.0m)	
Def bdgt	1992: fr 3.1bn ($95.9m)	
	1993: fr 3.4bn ($98.9m)	
	1994: fr 3.7bn ($106.1m)	
NATO defn	1992: fr 3.9bn ($120.8m)	
	1993: fr 4.0bn ($116.5m)	
	1994: fr 4.5bn ($127.3m)	
$1 = fr	1992: 32.2	1993: 34.6
	1994: 35.0	

fr = Luxembourg franc

Population: 395,200 (119,700 foreign citizens)

	13–17	*18–22*	*23–32*
Men	11,000	12,500	33,900
Women	10,400	11,800	32,400

TOTAL ARMED FORCES:

ACTIVE: 800.

ARMY: 800.

1 lt inf bn.

EQUIPMENT:

APC: 5 *Commando*.

MORTARS: 81mm: 6.

ATGW: *TOW* some 6 SP (*Hummer*).

RL: *LAW*.

AIR FORCE: (none, but for legal purposes NATO's E-3A AEW ac have Luxembourg registration).

1 sqn with 18 E-3A *Sentry* (NATO Standard), 2 Boeing 707 (trg).

PARAMILITARY:

GENDARMERIE: 560.

NETHERLANDS

GDP	1992: gld 563.2bn ($320.0bn): per capita $17,600	
	1993: gld 582.7bn ($329.3bn): per capita $18,000	
Growth	1992: 1.4%	1993: 0.3%
Inflation	1992: 3.1%	1993: 1.5%
Publ debt	1992: 78.0%	1993: 80.6%
Def exp	1992: gld 14.2bn ($8.0bn)	
Def bdgt	1992: gld 14.1bn ($8.0bn)	
	1993: gld 13.6bn ($7.3bn)	
	1994: gld 13.5bn ($7.2bn)	
	1995: gld 13.6bn ($7.1bn)	
NATO defn	1992: gld 14.6bn ($8.3bn)	
	1993: gld 13.1bn ($7.1bn)	
$1 = gld	1992: 1.76	1993: 1.86
	1994: 1.91	

gld = guilder

Population: 15,335,000

	13–17	*18–22*	*23–32*
Men	454,400	525,500	1,276,000
Women	434,900	502,200	1,215,800

TOTAL ARMED FORCES:

ACTIVE: 70,900 (incl 3,600 Royal Military Constabulary, 800 Inter-Service Organisation, 2,600 women, 29,500 conscripts).

Terms of service: 9 months.

RESERVES: 130,600 (men to age 35, NCO to 40, officers to 45): Army 111,600 (some – at the end of their conscription period – on short leave, immediate recall); Navy some 9,000 (7,000 on immediate recall); Air Force 10,000 (immediate recall).

ARMY: 43,200 (24,700 conscripts).

1 Corps HQ, 2 mech div HQ.

4 mech inf bde.

1 lt bde.

1 airmobile bde (3 inf bn (incl 1 forming).

2 fd arty, 1 AD gp.

1 eng gp.

Summary of combat arm units:

11 armd inf bn.	12 arty bn.
3 air mobile bn.	2 AD bn.
8 tk bn.	2 MLRS bty.
4 recce bn.	

RESERVES: (cadre bde and corps tps completed by call-up of reservists).

Territorial Command: 3 inf, 1 SF, 2 engr bn spt units, could be mob for territorial defence.

Home Guard: 3 sectors; lt inf weapons.

EQUIPMENT:
MBT: 740: 296 *Leopard* 1A4(in store), 444 *Leopard* 2.
AIFV: 717 YPR-765.
APC: 142 M-113, 1,055 YPR-765, 61 YP-408 (in store).
TOTAL ARTY: 581:
TOWED ARTY: 116: 105mm: 9 M-101 (in store); 155mm: 107 M-114 (incl 77 -114/39).
SP ARTY: 284: 155mm: 221 M-109A3; 203mm: 63 M-110 (in store).
MRL: 227mm: 22 MLRS.
MORTARS: 179: 107mm: 21 M-30 (in store); 120mm: 138 (incl 65 in store).
ATGW: 753 (incl 135 in store): 427 *Dragon*, 326 (incl 304 YPR-765) *TOW*.
RL: 84mm: *Carl Gustav*.
RCL: 106mm: 185 M-40 (in store).
AD GUNS: 35mm: 95 *Gepard* SP; 40mm: 131 L/70 towed.
SAM: 324 *Stinger*.
SURV: AN/TPQ-36 (arty, mor).
MARINE: 1 tk tpt, 3 coastal, 3 river patrol boats.

NAVY: 14,300 (incl 1,140 Naval Air, 2,930 Marines, 1,000 conscripts and 950 women).

(Belgium and the Netherlands have announced their intention to create an integrated operational command for the Belgian and Netherlands navies (except for submarines).)
BASES: Netherlands: Den Helder (HQ); Vlissingen. Overseas: Willemstad (Curaçao), Oranjestad (Aruba).
SUBMARINES: 6:
4 *Zeeleeuw* with Mk 48 HWT; plus *Harpoon* USGW.
2 *Zwaardvis* with Mk 37 HWT.
PRINCIPAL SURFACE COMBATANTS: 17:
DESTROYERS: 4 DDG (Nl desig = FFG):
2 *Tromp* with 1 SM-1 MR SAM; plus 2 x 4 *Harpoon* SSM, 1 x 2 120mm guns, 1 *Lynx* hel (ASW/OTHT), 2 x 3 ASTT (Mk 46 LWT).
2 *Van Heemskerck* with 1 SM-1 MR SAM; plus 2 x 4 *Harpoon*, 2 x 2 ASTT.
FRIGATES: 14:
6 *Karel Doorman* FF with 2 x 4 *Harpoon* SSM, plus 2 x 2 ASTT; 1 *Lynx* (ASW/OTHT) hel.
8 *Kortenaer* FF with 2 *Lynx* (ASW/OTHT) hel, 2 x 2 ASTT; plus 2 x 4 *Harpoon*.
MINE WARFARE: 21:
MINELAYERS: none, but *Mercuur*, listed under spt and misc, has capability.
MINE COUNTERMEASURES: 12:
10 *Alkmaar* (tripartite) MHC (plus 5 in reserve).
2 *Dokkum* MSC (plus 4 in reserve).
AMPHIBIOUS: craft only: about 12 LCA.
SUPPORT AND MISCELLANEOUS: 12:
1 *Poolster* AOR (1–3 *Lynx* hel), 3 survey, 1 *Mercuur* torpedo tender, 2 trg, 1 aux, 4 *Cerberus* div spt.

NAVAL AIR ARM: (1,140).

MR: 1 sqn with F-27M (see Air Force).
MR/ASW: 2 sqn with P-3C.
ASW/SAR: 2 sqn with *Lynx* hel.
EQUIPMENT: 13 cbt ac, 22 armed hel.
AIRCRAFT:
P-3C: 13 (MR).
HELICOPTERS:
***Lynx*:** 22 (ASW, SAR).

MARINES: (2,930).

3 marine bn (1 cadre); 1 spt bn.
RESERVE: 1 marine bn.
EQUIPMENT:
MORTARS: 120mm: 14 (2 in store).
ATGW: *Dragon*.
SAM: *Stinger*.

AIR FORCE: 9,000 (3,300 conscripts).

FIGHTER\FGA: 7 sqn with F-16A/B (1 sqn is tactical trg, evaluation and standardisation sqn).
FIGHTER/RECCE: 1 sqn with F-16A.
MR: 2 F-27M (assigned to Navy).
TRANSPORT: 1 sqn with F-27, C-130H-30.
TRAINING: 1 sqn with PC-7.
HELICOPTERS: 3 sqn.
SAR: 1 flt with SA-316.
AD: 8 bty with *HAWK* SAM (4 in Ge).
4 bty with *Patriot* SAM (in Ge).
EQUIPMENT: 183 cbt ac, no armed hel.
AIRCRAFT:
F-16: 183: **-A:** 148 (121 FGA/ftr, 19 recce, 8* trg); **-B:** 35.
F-27: 14 (12 tpt, 2 MR).
C-130: 1.
PC-7: 10 (trg).
HELICOPTERS:
AB-412 SP: 3 (SAR).
SA-316: 24.
BO-105: 27.
MISSILES:
AAM: AIM-9/L/N *Sidewinder*.
SAM: 48 *HAWK*, 20 *Patriot*, 100 *Stinger*.
AD: GUNS: 25 VL 4/41 *Flycatcher* radar, 75 L/70 40mm systems.

FORCES ABROAD:

GERMANY: 3,000; 1 lt bde (1 armd inf, 1 tk bn), plus spt elms.
ICELAND: Navy: 30; 1 P-3C.
NETHERLANDS ANTILLES: Navy: 20; 1 frigate, 1 amph cbt det, 1 MR det with 2 F-27MPA ac, 1 P-3C.
UN AND PEACEKEEPING:
ADRIATIC (*Sharp Guard*): 1 FF.
ANGOLA (UNAVEM II): 2 Observers, plus 2 civ pol.
BOSNIA (UNPROFOR BH): 1,676; elm 1 air mob bde, 1 tpt bn.
CROATIA (UNPROFOR I): 253; 1 sigs bn, 50 Observers, plus 10 civ pol.
EGYPT (MFO): 22.
ITALY: 360: *Deny Flight*: 18 F-16; *Sharp Guard*: 1 P-3C ac. Aircrew in NATO E-3 Force.
MIDDLE EAST (UNTSO): 16 Observers.
MOZAMBIQUE (ONUMOZ): 11.
SOMALIA (UNOSOM): 7 civ pol.
UGANDA/RWANDA (UNOMUR): 9 Observers.

PARAMILITARY:

ROYAL MILITARY CONSTABULARY
(*Koninklijke Marechaussee*): 3,600 (500 conscripts); 3 'div' comprising 10 districts with 72 'bde'.

FOREIGN FORCES:

NATO: HQ Allied Forces Central Europe (AFCENT).
US: 1,350: Army (500); Air (850).

NORWAY

GDP	1992:	kr 701.7bn ($113.0bn):		
		per capita $18,000		
	1993:	kr 733.6bn ($118.0bn):		
		per capita $18.700		
Growth	1992:	3.3%	1993:	1.8%
Inflation	1992:	2.3%	1993:	2.3%
Publ debt	1992:	43.4%	1993:	47.2%
Def exp	1993:	kr 22.9bn ($3.2bn)		
Def bdgt	1993:	kr 22.7bn ($3.3bn)		
	1994:	kr 23.0bn ($3.2bn)		
NATO defn	1992:	kr 23.8bn ($3.8bn)		
	1993:	kr 23.0bn ($3.3bn)		
$1 = kr	1992:	6.2	1993:	7.1
	1994:	7.4		

kr = kroner

Population: 4,322,000

	13–17	*18–22*	*23–32*
Men	140,800	159,100	338,100
Women	132,800	150,200	318,700

TOTAL ARMED FORCES:

ACTIVE: 33,500 (incl recalled reservists, 400 Joint Services org, 600 Home Guard permanent staff, and 22,100 conscripts).
Terms of service: Army, Air Force, 12 months, plus 4–5 refresher trg periods; Navy 12 months (9 months for some categories of Navy Coast arty).
RESERVES: 282,000 mobilisable in 24–72 hours; obligation to 44 (conscripts remain with fd army units to age 35; officers to age 55; regulars: 60): Army 160,000; Navy 21,500; Air Force: 24,900; Home Guard: some 87,000.

ARMY: 18,000 (incl recalled reservists, 14,000 conscripts).

2 Commands, 5 district comd, 1 div HQ, 14 territorial comd.
North Norway:
1 bde gp: 1 inf, 1 tk, 1 SP arty, 1 engr bn, 1 AD bty, spt units.
2 inf bn (incl 1 border guard).
South Norway:
1 inf bn (Royal Guard).
Indep units.
RESERVES: cadre units for mob: 2 subordinate comd, 3 mech, 6 inf bde, 18 inf, 7 arty bn; 50–60 indep inf coy, tk sqn, arty bty, engr coy, sigs units.
LAND HOME GUARD: 79,000.
18 districts each divided into 2–6 sub-districts and some 470 sub-units (pl).
EQUIPMENT:
MBT: 170 *Leopard* (111 -1A5, 59 -1A1).
AIFV: 53 NM-135 (M-113/20mm).
APC: 170 M-113 (incl variants).
TOTAL ARTY: 402:
TOWED ARTY: 276: 105mm: 228 M-101; 155mm: 48 M-114.
SP ARTY: 155mm: 126 M-109A3GN SP.
MORTARS: 81mm: 456 (12 SP), 28 M-106A1 SP.
ATGW: 292 *TOW*-1/-2, 97 NM-142 (M-113/*TOW*-2).
RCL: 84mm: 2,380 *Carl Gustav*.
AD GUNS: 20mm: 278 Rh-202.
SAM: 300 RBS-70.
SURV: *Cymberline* (mor).

NAVY: 6,600 (incl 1,400 Coastal Artillery, 680 Coast Guard and 4,000 conscripts).
2 Operational Commands: COMNAVSONOR and COMNAVNON with 7 regional Naval districts.
BASES: Horten, Haakonsvern (Bergen), Ramsund, Olavsvern (Tromsø).
SUBMARINES: 12:
6 *Ula* SS with Ge *Seeal* DM2A3 HWT.
6 *Kobben* SSC (with Swe T-612) HWT.
FRIGATES: 4 *Oslo* with 2 x 3 ASTT, 1 x 6 *Terne* ASW RL; plus 6 x *Penguin* 2 SSM.
PATROL AND COASTAL COMBATANTS: 30:
MISSILE CRAFT: 30:
14 *Hauk* PFM with 6 x *Penguin* 2, 2 x 533mm TT.
10 *Storm* PFM with 6 x *Penguin* 2.
6 *Snøgg* PFM with 4 x *Penguin* 2, 4 x 533mm TT.
MINE WARFARE: 8:
MINELAYERS: 2:
2 *Vidar*, coastal (300–400 mines).
Note: amph craft also fitted for minelaying.
MINE COUNTERMEASURES: 6:
3 *Sauda* MSC, 1 *Tana* MHC.
2 diver spt.
AMPHIBIOUS: craft only: 5 LCT.
SUPPORT AND MISCELLANEOUS: 3:
1 *Horten* sub/patrol craft depot ship.
1 *Marjata* AGOR (civ manned).
1 Royal Yacht.
ADDITIONAL IN STORE: 1 *Sauda* MSC.

NAVAL HOME GUARD: 7,000; on mob assigned to 7 naval/coast defence comd.
Some 400 fishing craft.
COAST DEFENCE: 26 fortresses:
75mm; 105mm; 120mm; 127mm; 150mm guns.
7 cable mine and 4 torpedo bty.

COAST GUARD: (680):
PATROL OFFSHORE: 13:
3 *Nordkapp* with 1 x *Lynx* hel (SAR/recce), 2 x 3 ASTT, fitted for 6 *Penguin* Mk 2 SSM.
1 *Nornen*, 2 *Farm*, 7 chartered (partly civ manned).
AIRCRAFT: 2 P-3N *Orion* **ac**, 6 *Lynx* **hel** (Air Force-manned).

AIR FORCE: 7,900 (4,100 conscripts).
Average annual flying hours for F-16/F-5 pilots: 180.
FGA: 4 sqn with F-16A/B.
FIGHTER: 1 trg sqn with F-5A/B.
MR: 1 sqn with P-3C/N *Orion* (2 assigned to Coast Guard).
TRANSPORT: 2 sqn:
1 with C-130 and *Falcon* 20C.
1 with DHC-6 (tpt, CAL, ECM).
TRAINING: MFI-15.
SAR: 1 sqn with *Sea King* Mk 43.
TAC HEL: 2 sqn with Bell-412SP.
SAM: 4 bty *Noah* (Norwegian adapted *Hawk*), 2 bty NASAMS (Norwegian advanced Surface-to-Air Missile).
COAST GUARD: 1 sqn with 6 *Lynx* Mk 86.
EQUIPMENT: 79 cbt ac (incl 4 MR), no armed hel.
AIRCRAFT:
F-5A/B: 15 (ftr/trg).
F-16: 60; **-A:** 48 (FGA); **-B:** 12 (FGA).
P-3: 6: **-C:** 4 (MR); **-N:** 2 (Coast Guard).
C-130H: 6 (tpt).
***Falcon* 20C:** 3 (EW/tpt Cal).
DHC-6: 3 (tpt).
MFI-15: 18 (trg).
HELICOPTERS:
Bell 412 SP: 18 (tpt).
***Sea King* Mk 43:** 10 (SAR).
***Lynx* Mk 86:** 6 (Coast Guard).
MISSILES:
ASM: *Penguin* Mk-3.
AAM: AIM-9L/N *Sidewinder*.
AD GUNS: 12.7mm and 40mm: 64 L/70 and Manpad (RBS 70).
SAM: NOAH (Norwegian-adapted *HAWK*).

ANTI-AIRCRAFT HOME GUARD (on mob under comd of Air Force): 3,000; 2 bn (9 bty) lt AA; some Rh-202 20mm, 72 L/60 40mm guns (being replaced by Rh-202).

FORCES ABROAD:

UN AND PEACEKEEPING:
ADRIATIC (*Sharp Guard*): 1 FF.
ANGOLA (UNAVEM II): 4 Observers.
BOSNIA (UNPROFOR BH): some 393; Nordic bn, incl hel unit with 4 Bell-412SP, fd hospital.
CROATIA (UNPROFOR I): 102, plus movement control unit, 40 Observers, 30 civ pol.
EGYPT (MFO): 3 Staff Officers.
INDIA/PAKISTAN (UNMOGIP): 5 Observers.
IRAQ/KUWAIT (UNIKOM): 7 Observers.
LEBANON (UNIFIL): 843; 1 inf bn, 1 service coy, plus HQ personnel.
MACEDONIA (UNPROFOR M): 234 (reducing to 40).
MIDDLE EAST (UNTSO): 15 Observers.
MOZAMBIQUE (ONUMOZ): 9 civ pol.

FOREIGN FORCES:

US: prepositioned eqpt for 1 MEB.
CANADA: prepositioned 6 arty, 14 ACV.
NATO: HQ Allied Forces North Europe (HQ North).

PORTUGAL

GDP	1992: esc 11,364.5bn ($84.2bn): per capita $8,700	
	1993: esc 12,852.0bn ($85.7bn): per capita $8,800	
Growth	1992: 1.5%	1993: -0.8%
Inflation	1992: 8.9%	1993: 6.5%
Publ debt	1992: 62.6%	1993: 67.6%
Def exp	1992: esc 325.2bn ($2.4bn)	
Def bdgt	1992: esc 224.6bn ($1.7bn)	
	1993: esc 230.2bn ($1.5bn)	
	1994ε: esc 258.5bn ($1.5bn)	
NATO defn	1992: esc 325.7bn ($2.4bn)	
	1993: esc 360.1bn ($2.4bn)	
FMA	1993: $91.0m (FMF, IMET)	
	1994: $82.0m (FMF, IMET)	
$1 = esc	1992: 135.0	1993: 160.8
	1994: 173.5	

esc = escudo

Population: 10,512,400

	13–17	*18–22*	*23–32*
Men	404,500	434,400	869,200
Women	386,000	419,000	853,400

TOTAL ARMED FORCES:

ACTIVE: 50,700 (17,600 conscripts).

Terms of service: Army: 4–8 months; Navy and Air Force: 4–18 months.

RESERVES: 210,000 (all services) (obligation to age 35).

ARMY: 27,200 (15,000 conscripts).

5 Territorial Commands (1 mil governance, 2 mil regions, 2 mil zones).

1 composite bde (1 mech, 2 mot inf, 1 tk, 1 fd arty bn).

3 inf bde. 1 lt inf bde.

1 AB bde. 3 cav regt.

9 inf regt. 2 engr regt.

2 fd, 1 AD, 1 coast arty regt.

EQUIPMENT:

MBT: 209+: 43 M-47, 86 M-48A5, 80 M-60A3.

RECCE: 8 *Saladin*, 40 AML-60, 15 V-150, 21 EBR-75, 8 ULTRAV M-11, 30 *Ferret* Mk 4.

APC: 385: 276 M-113, 79 V-200 *Chaimite*, 2 EBR, 28 YP 408.

TOTAL ARTY: 305:

TOWED ARTY: 142: 105mm: 54 M-101, 24 M-56; 140mm: 24 5.5-in; 155mm: 40 M-114A1.

SP ARTY: 155mm: 6 M-109A2.

MORTARS: 157: 107mm: 57 M-30 (incl 14 SP); 120mm: 100 Tampella.

COAST ARTY: 27: 150mm: 15; 152mm: 6; 234mm: 6.

ATGW: 51 *TOW* (incl 18 M-113, 4 M-901), 65 *Milan* (incl 6 ULTRAV M-11).

RCL: 90mm: 112; 106mm: 128 M-40.

AD GUNS: 105, incl 20mm: M-163A1 *Vulcan* SP; 40mm: L/60.

SAM: 12 *Blowpipe*, 5 *Chaparral*.

DEPLOYMENT:

Azores and Madeira: 2,000; 3 inf regt, 2 coast arty bn, 2 AA bty.

NAVY: ε12,500 (incl 1,850 Marines and 800 conscripts).

1 Naval area Cmd, with 5 Subordinate zone Cmds (Azores, Madeira, North Continental, Centre Continental and South Continental).

BASES: Lisbon (Alfeite), Portimão (HQ Continental comd), Ponta Delgada (HQ Azores), Funchal (HQ Madeira).

SUBMARINES: 3:

3 *Albacora* (Fr *Daphné*) SS with EL-5 HWT.

FRIGATES: 11:

3 *Vasco Da Gama* (Meko 200) with 2 x 3 ASTT (US Mk-46), plus 2 x 4 *Harpoon* SSM, 1 x 8 *Sea Sparrow* SAM, 1 x 100mm gun (with 2 x *Super Lynx* hel in some).

4 *Commandante João Belo* (Fr *Cdt Rivière*) with 2 x 3 ASTT, 1 x 4 ASW mor; plus 3 x 100mm gun.

4 *Baptista de Andrade* with 2 x 3 ASTT; plus 1 x 100mm gun.

PATROL AND COASTAL COMBATANTS: 30:

PATROL, OFFSHORE: 6:

6 *João Coutinho* PCO, hel deck.

PATROL COASTAL: 10 *Cacine*.

INSHORE: 13: 5 *Argos*, 8〈.

RIVERINE: 1 *Rio Minho*〈.

AMPHIBIOUS: craft only: 3 LCU, about 7 LCM.

SUPPORT AND MISCELLANEOUS: 8:

1 Berrio (UK Green Rover) AO, 3 AGHS, 2 trg, 1 ocean trg, 1 div spt.

MARINES: (1,850).

3 bn (2 lt inf, 1 police), spt units.

EQUIPMENT: *Chaimite* APC, mor.

AIR FORCE: 11,000 (incl 1,700 AB tps listed with Army and 1,800 conscripts).

1 operational air command (COFA).

FGA: 4 sqn:

2 with A-7P.

2 with Alpha Jets.

SURVEY: 1 sqn with C-212.
MR: 1 sqn with P-3P.
TRANSPORT: 4 sqn:
1 with C-130.
1 with C-212.
1 with *Falcon* 20 and *Falcon* 50.
1 with SA-316 hel.
SAR: 2 sqn: 1 with SA-330 hel; 1 with SA-330 hel and C-212.
LIAISON: 1 sqn with Reims-Cessna FTB-337G.
TRAINING: 2 sqn:
1 with T-38.
1 with SOCATA TB-30 *Epsilon.*
EQUIPMENT: 77 cbt ac, plus 6 MR ac, no attack hel.
AIRCRAFT:
Alpha Jet: 40 (FGA trg), plus 10 in store.
A-7: 37: **-7P:** 31 (FGA); **TA-7P:** 6* (trg).
P-3P: 6 (MR).
C-130H: 6 (SAR, tpt).
C-212: 22: **-A:** 18 (12 tpt/SAR, 1 Nav trg, 2 ECM trg, 3 fisheries protection); **-B:** 4 (survey).
Cessna 337: 12 (liaison).
***Falcon* 20:** 1 (tpt, calibration).
***Falcon* 50:** 3 (tpt).
RF-10: 2 (trg). **T-37:** 23 (trg). **T-38:** 12 (trg). ***Epsilon:*** 16 (trg).
HELICOPTERS:
SA-330: 10 (SAR/tpt). **SA-316:** 21 (trg, utility).

FORCES ABROAD:
UN AND PEACEKEEPING:
ADRIATIC (*Sharp Guard*): 1 FF.
CROATIA (UNPROFOR I): 9, plus 12 Observers, 43 civ pol.
MOZAMBIQUE (ONUMOZ): 277, incl 1 Observer plus 7 civ pol.

PARAMILITARY:
NATIONAL REPUBLICAN GUARD: 20,900; *Commando* Mk III APC, 7 SA-313 hel .
PUBLIC SECURITY POLICE: 20,000.
BORDER SECURITY GUARD: 8,900.

FOREIGN FORCES:
NATO: HQ IBERLANT area at Lisbon (Oeiras).
US: 1,155: Navy (55); Air (1,100) (incl Azores).

SPAIN

GDP	1992: pts 58,677bn ($573bn): per capita $13,200		
	1993: pts 60,704bn ($582bn): per capita $13,400		
Growth	1992: 0.8%	1993: -1.0%	
Inflation	1992: 5.9%	1993: 4.6%	
Publ debt	1992: 51.4%	1993: 57.4%	
Def exp	1992: pts 927.8bn ($9.1bn)		
	1993: pts 895.1bn ($7.7bn)		
Def bdgt	1992: pts 785.9bn ($7.7bn)		
	1993: pts 757.7bn ($6.5bn)		
	1994: pts 805.5bn ($5.8bn)		
NATO defn	1992: pts 927.9bn ($9.1bn)		
	1993: pts 917.5bn ($7.9bn)		
FMA	1993: $0.3m (IMET)		
$1 = pts	1992: 102.4	1993: 127.3	
	1994: 138.1		

pts = peseta

Population: 39,736,600

	13–17	*18–22*	*23–32*
Men	1,508,800	1,656,600	3,292,700
Women	1,421,600	1,568,000	3,169,700

TOTAL ARMED FORCES:
ACTIVE: 206,500 133,200 conscripts (to be reduced), some 200 women).
Terms of service: 9 months.
RESERVES: 498,000 (all services to age 38); Immediate Reserve: 140,000: Army 122,000; Navy 10,000; Air Force 8,000.

ARMY: 145,000 (102,500 conscripts).
8 Regional Operational Commands incl 2 overseas:
1 armd div (1 armd inf, 1 mech bde, 1 arty, 1 lt armd cav, 1 engr regt).
1 mech div (2 mech bde, 1 arty, 1 lt armd cav, 1 engr regt).
1 mot div (2 mot, 1 mech bde, 1 arty, 1 lt armd cav, 1 engr regt).
2 mtn div (each 2 bde, 1 arty, 1 engr regt).
2 armd cav bde (each 1 armd, 2 lt armd cav, 1 arty regt).
1 air portable bde.
5 island garrison (bde).
6 special ops bn.
6 regional engr units.
General Reserve Force:
1 AB bde (3 bn).

1 AD comd (6 AD regt incl 1 *HAWK* SAM bn, 1 composite *Aspide* bn, 1 *Roland* bn).
1 fd arty comd (1 fd, 1 locating, 1 MRL regt).
1 engr comd (3 engr regt).
4 Spanish Legion regt: (6,400):
 2 with 1 mech, 1 mot bn, 1 ATK coy.
 1 with 2 lt inf bn.
 1 with 1 lt inf bn, 1 special ops bn.
Army Aviation (FAMET):
 1 attack hel bn.
 1 tpt bn (1 med, 1 hy coy).
 4 utility units.
1 Coast Arty Comd (6 mixed arty regt; 1 coast arty gp).

EQUIPMENT:
MBT: 1,012: 279 AMX-30 (60-EM2), 229 M-47E1, 46 M-47E2, 164 M-48A5E, 294 M-60 (50 -A1, 244 -A3).
RECCE: 340 BMR-VEC, 100 BMR-625.
APC: 1,992: 1,313 M-113 (incl variants), 679 BMR-600.
TOTAL ARTY: 1,377:
TOWED ARTY: 711: 105mm: 283 M-26, 182 M-56 pack; 122mm: 138 122/46; 155mm: 84 M-114; 203mm: 24 M-115.
SP ARTY: 186: 105mm: 48 M-108; 155mm: 102 M-109A1; 203mm: 36 M-110A2.
MRL: 140mm: 14 *Teruel.*
MORTARS: 120mm: 466 (incl 19 2SP); plus 81mm: 1,200 (incl 187 SP).
COAST ARTY: 130: 6-in: 97; 305mm: 16; 381mm: 17.
ATGW: 443 *Milan*, 28 *HOT.*
RCL: 106mm: 654.
AD GUNS: 20mm: 329 GAI-BO1; 35mm: 92 GDF-002 twin; 40mm: 274 L/70.
SAM: 24 *Improved HAWK*, 18 *Roland*, 13 *Skyguard/ Aspide, 72 Mistral.*
HELICOPTERS: 180 (28 attack): 3 HU-8, 51 HU-10B, 70 HA-15 (31 with 20mm guns, 28 with *HOT*, 9 trg), 6 HU-18, 14 HR-12B, 18 HT-21, 18 HT-17.
SURV: AN/TPQ-36 (arty, mor).

DEPLOYMENT:

CEUTA AND MELILLA: 10,000;
2 armd cav, 2 Spanish Legion, 2 mot inf, 2 arty regt; 2 lt AD bn, 2 engr, 1 coast arty gp.
BALEARIC ISLANDS: 2,500;
1 mot inf regt: 2 mot inf bn,1 mixed arty regt: 2 fd arty, 1 coast arty; 1 engr bn, 1 special ops coy.
CANARY ISLANDS: 6,500;
2 inf regt; 1 Spanish Legion, 2 mixed arty regt, 2 engr bn, 2 special ops coy.

NAVY: 33,100 (incl 1,250 Naval Air, 7,150 Marines and 18,600 conscripts).
5 Commands (Fleet, plus 4 Naval Zones: Cantabrian, Strait (of Gibraltar), Mediterranean and Canary (Islands)).
BASES: El Ferrol (La Coruña) (Cantabrian HQ), San Fernando (Cadiz) (Strait HQ), Rota (Cadiz) (Fleet HQ), Cartagena (Murcia) (Mediterranean HQ), Las Palmas (Canary Islands HQ), Palma de Mallorca and Mahón (Menorca).
SUBMARINES: 8:
4 *Galerna* (Fr *Agosta*) with F-17 and L-5 HWT, plus possibly *Exocet* USGW.
4 *Delfin* (Fr *Daphné*) with F-17 and L-5 HWT.
PRINCIPAL SURFACE COMBATANTS: 17:
CARRIERS: 1 (CVV):
1 *Príncipe de Asturias* (16,200t); air gp: typically 6 to 10 AV-8S/EAV-8B FGA, 4 to 6 SH-3D ASW hel, 2 SH-3D AEW hel, 2 utility hel.
FRIGATES: 16
FFG: 10 (AAW/ASW):
5 *Santa Maria* (US *Perry*) with 1 x 1 SM-1 MR SAM/*Harpoon* SSM launcher, 2 x SH-60B hel, 2 x 3 ASTT; plus 1 x 76mm gun.
5 *Baleares* with 1 x 1 SM-1 MR SAM, 1 x 8 *ASROC*, 4 x 324mm and 2 x 484mm ASTT; plus 2 x 4 *Harpoon*, 1 x 127mm gun.
FF: 6 *Descubierta* with 2 x 3 ASTT, 1 x 2 ASW RL; plus 2 x 2 *Harpoon* SSM.
PATROL AND COASTAL COMBATANTS: 31:
PATROL, OFFSHORE: 5: 4 *Serviola,* 1 *Chilreu.*
COASTAL: 10:
10 *Anaga* PCC.
INSHORE: 16:
6 *Barceló* PFI; 10 PCI(.
MINE WARFARE: 12:
MINE COUNTERMEASURES: 12:
4 *Guadalete* (US *Aggressive*) MSO.
8 *Júcar* (US *Adjutant*) MSC.
AMPHIBIOUS: 4:
2 *Castilla* (US *Paul Revere*) amph tpt, capacity: 1,600 tps; plus some 15 amph craft.
2 *Velasco* (US *Terrebonne Parish*) LST, capacity: 400 tps, 10 tk, or some 20 amph craft.
Plus 13 craft: 3 LCT, 2 LCU, 8 LCM.
SUPPORT AND MISCELLANEOUS: 32:
1 AO, 5 ocean tugs, 3 diver spt, 2 tpt/spt, 3 water carriers, 6 AGHS, 1 AGOR, 1 sub salvage, 1 AK, 5 trg craft, 4 sail trg.

NAVAL AIR: (1,250 (310 conscripts)).
FGA: 2 sqn:
1 with AV-8S *Matador* (*Harrier*), TAV-8S.
1 with AV-8B.

LIAISON: 1 sqn with 3 *Citation II*.
HELICOPTERS: 4 sqn:
ASW: 2 sqn:
1 with SH-3D/G *Sea King* (mod to SH-3H standard).
1 with SH-60B (LAMPS-III fit).
AEW: 1 flt with SH-3D (*Searchwater* radar).
COMMAND/TRANSPORT: 1 sqn with AB-212.
TRAINING: 1 sqn with Hughes 500.
EQUIPMENT: 20 cbt ac, 28 armed hel.
AIRCRAFT:
EAV-8B: 10; **AV-8S:** 8; **TAV-8S:** 2 (trg).
***Citation* II:** 3 (liaison).
HELICOPTERS:
AB-212: 10 (ASW/SAR).**SH-3D:** 12 (9 **-H** ASW, 3 **-D** AEW). **Hughes 500:** 10 (trg). **SH-60B:** 6 (ASW).

MARINES: (7,150 (3,550 conscripts)).

1 marine regt (3,500); 2 inf, 1 spt bn; 3 arty bty.
5 marine garrison gp.
EQUIPMENT:
MBT: 16 M-60A3.
AFV: 17 *Scorpion* lt tk, 19 LVTP-7 AAV, 28 BLR APC.
TOWED ARTY: 105mm: 12 Oto Melara M-56 pack.
SP ARTY: 155mm: 6 M-109A.
ATGW: 12 *TOW*, 18 *Dragon*.
RL: 90mm: C-90C.
RCL: 106mm: 54.
SAM: 12 *Mistral*.

AIR FORCE: 28,400 (12,100 conscripts).

Average annual flying hours for EF-18/*Mirage* F-1: 180; F-5: 165.

CENTRAL AIR COMMAND (MACEN): 4 wings.

FIGHTER: 3 sqn:
2 with EF-18 (F-18 *Hornet*), 1 with RF-4C.
TRANSPORT: 7 sqn:
2 with C-212. 1 with Boeing 707.
2 with CN-235. 1 with *Falcon* (20, 50, 900).
1 with AS-332 (tpt).
SUPPORT: 4 sqn:
1 with CL-215.
1 with C-212 (EW) and *Falcon* 20.
1 with C-212, AS-332 (SAR).
1 with C-212 and Cessna *Citation*.
TRAINING: 4 sqn:
1 with C-212. 1 with Beech (*Baron*).
1 with C-101. 1 with Beech (*Bonanza*).

EASTERN AIR COMMAND (MALEV): 2 wings.

FIGHTER: 3 sqn:
2 with EF-18 (F-18 *Hornet*), 1 with *Mirage* F1.
TRANSPORT: 2 sqn:
1 with C-130H, 1 tkr/tpt with KC-130H.
SUPPORT: 1 sqn with C-212 **ac** (SAR) AS-332 **hel** .

GIBRALTAR STRAIT AIR COMMAND

(MAEST): 5 wings.
FIGHTER: 2 sqn with *Mirage* F-1 CE/BE.
FGA: 3 sqn:
2 with F-5B; 1 with C-101.
MR: 1 sqn with P-3A/B.
TRAINING: 6 sqn:
2 hel sqn with AB-205, *Hughes* 300C, S-76C.
1 with C-212; 1 with E-26 (*Tamiz*); 1 with C-101; 1 with C-212 and *Bonanza*.

CANARY ISLANDS, AIR COMMAND

(MACAN): 1 wing.
FGA: 1 sqn with *Mirage* F-1EE.
TRANSPORT: 1 sqn with C-212.
SAR: 1 sqn with F-27 ac, AS-332 hel (SAR).

LOGISTIC SUPPORT COMMAND

(MALOG):
1 sqn.
1 trials sqn with C-101, C-212, E-26.
EQUIPMENT: 150 cbt ac, no armed hel.
AIRCRAFT:
EF-18 A/B: 70 (ftr, OCU).
F-5B: 22 (FGA).
***Mirage*: 50: F-1CE:** 30 (FGA); **F-1BE:** 3 (ftr); **F-1EE:** 17 (ftr).
RF-4C: 8 (recce).
P-3: 7: **-A:** 2 (MR); **-B:** 5 (MR).
Boeing 707: 3 (tkr/tpt).
C-130H: 12: 7 (tpt); **KC-130H:** 5 (tkr).
C-212: 76 (32 tpt, 9 SAR, 6 recce, 25 trg, 2 EW, 2 trials).
Cessna *Citation*: 2 (recce).
C-101: 81 (trg).
CL-215: 21 (spt).
***Falcon* 20:** 5 (3 VIP tpt , 2 EW); ***Falcon* 50:** 1 (VIP tpt); ***Falcon* 900:** 2 (VIP tpt).
F-27: 3 (SAR).
E-26: 39 (trg).
CN-235: 20 (18 tpt, 2 VIP tpt). **E-20** (*Baron*): 5 trg; **E-24** (*Bonanza*): 27 trg.
HELICOPTERS:
AB-205/UH-1H: 7 (trg). **SA-330:** 5 (trg), **AS-332:** 16 (10 SAR, 6 tpt), **Hughes 300C:** 15 (trg), **S-76C:** 8 (trg).
MISSILES:
AAM: AIM-7 *Sparrow*, AIM-9 *Sidewinder*.
ASM: *Maverick, Harpoon, HARM*.

FORCES ABROAD:

UN AND PEACEKEEPING:
ADRIATIC (*Sharp Guard*): 2 FF/FFG.
BOSNIA (UNPROFOR BH): 1,415; 1 inf bn gp, 19 Observers.
ITALY (*Deny Flight*): 1 CASA-212 (spt ac).
EL SALVADOR (ONUSAL): 11 Observers, 83 civ pol.
MOZAMBIQUE (ONUMOZ): 21 Observers, 14 civ pol.

PARAMILITARY:

GUARDIA CIVIL: 72,000 (2,200 conscripts); 9 regions, 19 inf *tercios* (regt) with 56 rural bn, 6 traffic security gp, 6 rural special ops gp, 1 special sy bn; 22 BLR APC, 16 Bo-105, 5 BK-117 hel.
GUARDIA CIVIL DEL MAR: (550); about 19 PCI and PCI‹.

FOREIGN FORCES:

US: 4,500: Navy (4,100); Air Force (400).

TURKEY

GDP	1992: TL 1,103,843bn ($160.3bn): per capita $4,500	
	1993: TL 1,908,705bn ($173.7bn): per capita $4,800	
Growth	1992: 5.9%	1993: 7.0%
Inflation	1992: 70.0%	1993: 71.0%
Publ debt	1992: $56.1bn	1993: $59.4bn
Def exp	1992: TL 43,319bn ($6.3bn)	
Def bdgt[a]	1992ε: TL 27,989bn ($4.1bn)	
	1993ε: TL 49,615bn ($4.5bn)	
	1994: TL 93,453bn ($4.6bn)	
NATO defn	1992: TL 42,320bn ($6.1bn)	
	1993: TL 77,703bn ($7.1bn)	
	1994: TL 129,462bn ($7.3bn)	
FMA	1993: $653.5m (FMF, IMET, Econ aid)	
	1994: $526.0m (FMF, IMET, Econ aid)	
	1995: $554.4m (FMF, IMET, Econ aid)	
$1 = TL	1992: 6,887	1993: 10,986
	1994: 29,968	

TL = Turkish lira

[a] Excl budget for Gendarmerie. An additional $3bn will accrue to the national defence fund agreed by Saudi Arabia, Kuwait, UAE and the US within the next four years. No disbursements from this fund to date.

Population: 60,641,200 (Kurds 17%)

	13–17	*18–22*	*23–32*
Men	3,625,100	3,017,200	5,358,300
Women	3,461,100	2,973,900	5,202,700

TOTAL ARMED FORCES:

ACTIVE: 503,800 (410,200 conscripts).
Terms of service: 15 months.
RESERVES: 952,300 to age 41 (all): Army 831,700; Navy 55,600; Air Force 65,000.

ARMY: 393,000 (345,000 conscripts).

4 army HQ: 9 corps HQ.
1 mech div (1 mech, 1 armd bde).
1 mech div HQ.
1 inf div.
14 armd bde (each 2 armd, 2 mech inf, 2 arty bn).
17 mech bde (each 1 armd, 2 mech inf, 1 arty bn, 1 recce sqn).
9 inf bde (each 4 inf, 1 arty bn).
4 cdo bde (each 3 cdo, 1 arty bn).
1 inf regt.
1 Presidential Guard regt.
5 border def regt.
26 border def bn.
RESERVES:
4 coastal def regt.
23 coastal def bn.
EQUIPMENT:
MBT: some 4,919: 586 M-47 (in store), 3,004 M-48 (incl 584-A2C, 183-T5, 1,369-A5T1, 751-A5T2), 932 M-60 (658 A3, 274 A1), 397 Leopard (170 -1A1, 227 -1A3).
AIFV: 75 AIFV.
APC: 3,285: 125 IAPC, 2,815 M-113/-A1/-A2, 345 AWC.
TOTAL ARTY: 4,275:
TOWED ARTY: 1,576: 105mm: 640 M-101A1; 150mm: 161 Skoda; 155mm: 442 M-114A1\A2, 171 M-59; 203mm: 162 M-115.
SP ARTY: 821: 105mm: 363 M-52A1, 26 M-108; 155mm: 4 M-44A1, 164 M-44T1; 175mm: 36 M-107; 203mm: 9 M-55, 219 M-110A2.
MRL: 35: 107mm: 23; 227mm: 12 MLRS.
MORTARS: 1,843: 107mm: 1,265 M-30 (some SP); 120mm: 578; plus 81mm: 3,175 incl SP.
ATGW: 943: 186 *Cobra*, 365 *TOW* SP, 392 *Milan*.
RL: M-72.
RCL: 57mm: 871 M-18; 75mm: 606; 106mm: 2,317 M-40A1.
AD GUNS: 1,497: 20mm: 440 GAI-DO1; 35mm: 120 GDF-003; 40mm: 635 L60/70, 40 T-1, 262 M-42A1.
SAM: 108 *Stinger*, 789 *Redeye*.

SURV: AN/TPQ-36 (arty, mor).
AIRCRAFT: 174: 3 Cessna 421, 34 *Citabria*, 6 Do-28D, 4 B-200, 4 T-42A, 98 U-17, 25 T-41.
HELICOPTERS: 262: 8 S-70A, 38 AH-1W/P, 14 AB-204, 64 AB-205, 2 AB-212, 28 H-269C, 3 OH-58, 96 UH-1H, 9 R-22.

NAVY: 54,000 (incl 3,000 Marines and 36,500 conscripts).

BASES: Ankara (Navy HQ and COMEDNOREAST), Gölcük (HQ Fleet), Istanbul (HQ Northern area and Bosphorus), Izmir (HQ Southern area and Aegean), Eregli (HQ Black Sea), Iskenderun, Aksaz Bay, Mersin (HQ Mediterranean).
SUBMARINES: 15 SS:
6 *Atilay* (Ge Type 209/1200) with SST-4 HWT.
7 *Canakkale/Burakreis*† (plus 2 non op) (US *Guppy*) with Mk 37 HWT.
2 *Hizirreis* (US *Tang*) with Mk 37 HWT.
PRINCIPAL SURFACE COMBATANTS: 21:
DESTROYERS: 5:
3 *Yücetepe* (US *Gearing*) (ASW/ASUW) with 2 x 3 ASTT (Mk 46 LWT); 1 with 1 x 8 *ASROC*, 2 with *Harpoon* SSM, all with 2 x 2 127mm guns.
2 *Alcitepe* (US *Carpenter*) with 1 x 8 *ASROC*, 2 x 3 ASTT, 1 x 2 127mm guns.
FRIGATES: 16:
4 *Yavuz* (Ge *MEKO* 200) with 1 x AB-212 hel (ASW/OTHT), 2 x 3 ASTT; plus 2 x 4 *Harpoon* SSM, 1 x 127mm gun.
2 *Gelibolu* (Ge T-120 *Köln*) with 4 x 533mm ASTT, 2 x 4 ASW mor; plus 2 x 100mm gun.
2 *Berk* with 2 x 3 ASTT, 2 Mk 11 *Hedgehog*.
8 *Muavenet* (US *Knox*-class) with 1 x 8 ASROC, 4 x ASTT; plus *Harpoon* (from *ASROC* launcher), 1 x 127mm gun.
PATROL AND COASTAL COMBATANTS: 45:
MISSILE CRAFT: 16:
8 *Dogan* (Ge Lürssen-57) PFM with 2 x 4 *Harpoon* SSM.
8 *Kartal* (Ge *Jaguar*) PFM with 4 x *Penguin* 2 SSM, 2 x 533mm TT.
PATROL: 27:
COASTAL: 10: 1 *Girne* PFC, 6 *Sultanhisar* PCC, 3 *Trabzon* PCC.
INSHORE: 17: 1 *Bora* (US *Asheville*) PFI, 12 AB-25 PCI, 4 AB-21.
MINE WARFARE: 23:
MINELAYERS: 2:
1 *Nusret* (400 mines).
1 *Mordogan* (US LSM) coastal (400 mines).
Note: *Gelibolu* FF, *Bayraktar*, *Sarucabey* and *Çakabey* LST have minelaying capability.
MINE COUNTERMEASURES: 21:
11 *Seymen* (US *Adjutant*) MSC.
6 *Karamürsel* (Ge *Vegesack*) MSC.
4 *Foça* (US *Cape*) MSI.
AMPHIBIOUS: 8 LST:
1 *Osman Gazi*: capacity 980 tps, 17 tk, 4 LCVP.
2 *Ertuğal* (US *Terrebonne Parish*): capacity 400 tps, 18 tk.
2 *Bayraktar* (US LST-512): capacity 200 tps, 16 tk.
2 *Sarucabey:* capacity 600 tps, 11 tk.
1 *Çakabey:* capacity 400 tps, 9 tk.
Plus about 59 craft: 35 LCT, 2 LCU, 22 LCM.
SUPPORT AND MISCELLANEOUS: 27:
1 *Akar* AO, 5 spt tankers, 2 Ge *Rhein* plus 3 other depot ships, 3 salvage/rescue, 2 survey, 3 tpt, 5 tugs, 2 repair, 1 div spt.

NAVAL AVIATION: 21 combat ac, 17 armed hel.

ASW: 1 sqn with 21 S-2A/E/TS-2A *Tracker* **ac** (Air Force aircraft, Air Force and Navy crews); 3 AB-204AS, 17* AB-212 ASW **hel**.

MARINES: (3,000); 1 regt.

HQ, 3 bn, 1 arty bn (18 guns), spt units.

AIR FORCE: 56,800 (28,700 conscripts).

2 tac air forces, 1 tpt, 1 air trg comd, 1 air logistics command.
FGA: 14 sqn:
1 OCU with F-5A/B.
6 (1 OCU) with F-4E.
7 (1 OCU) with F-16C/D.
FIGHTER: 6 sqn:
2 with F-5 A/B.
2 with F-4E.
2 with F-16C/D.
RECCE: 2 sqn with RF-4E.
ASW: 1 sqn with S-2A/E *Tracker* (see Navy).
TRANSPORT: 6 sqn:
1 sqn with C-130B/E.
1 sqn with C-160D.
2 sqns with CN-235.
2 sqns VIP tpt units with *Gulfstream, Citation* and CN 235.
LIAISON:
10 base flt with T-33 ac; UH-1H.
TRAINING: 3 sqn: 1 with T-41; 1 with SF-260D, 1 with T-37; trg schools with **ac** CN-235, **hel** UH-1H.
SAM: 8 sqn with *Nike Hercules*; 2 *Rapier* sqn.
EQUIPMENT: 555 cbt ac (plus 122 in store), no attack hel.

AIRCRAFT:
F-16C/D: 138: **-C:** 114; **-D:** 24.
F-5: 215: **-A:** 108 (FGA); **-B:** 27; **RF-5A:** 20 (recce); **NF-5A/B:** 60 (FGA); (plus some 44 in store).
F-4E: 178: 152 FGA (30 OCU); **RF-4E:** 26 (recce) (plus 13 in store).
F-104G/TF-104G/F104S: 24 (plus some 65 in store).
S-2A/E *Tracker*: 33.
C-130: 13 (tpt). **C-160D:** 19 (tpt). ***Citation*:** 4 (VIP):
CN-235: 10 (tpt). **SF-260D:** 39 (trg). **BN-2A:** 2 (obs).
T-33: 34 (trg). **T-37:** 63 trg. **T-38:** 70 (trg). **T-41:** 28 (trg).
HELICOPTERS:
UH-1H: 21 (tpt, liaison, base flt, trg schools).
SAM: 128 *Nike Hercules*, 24 *Rapier*.

FORCES ABROAD:

CYPRUS: 30,000; 1 corps; 235 M-48A5 MBT; 57 M-113, 50 M-59 APC; 126 105mm, 36 155mm, 8 203mm towed; 18 105mm, 6 155mm SP; 102 107mm mor; 84 40mm AA guns; 8 ac, 13 hel.
UN AND PEACEKEEPING:
ADRIATIC (*Sharp Guard*): 1 FF/DDG.
BOSNIA (UNPROFOR BH): 1,534; 1inf bn gp.
IRAQ/KUWAIT (UNIKOM): 7 Observers.
ITALY (*Deny Flight*): 18 F-16C/D.

PARAMILITARY:

GENDARMERIE/NATIONAL GUARD (Ministry of Interior, Ministry of Defence in war): 70,000 active, 50,000 reserve.
EQUIPMENT: 300 BTR-60, 110 BTR-80, 59 UR-416 APC; 0-1E **ac**; 20 Mi-8, S-70A, AB-206A **hel**.
COAST GUARD: 1,100; 28 PCI, 8 PCI‹, plus boats, 2 tpt.

OPPOSITION:

KURDISTAN WORKERS PARTY (PKK): ε11,000.

FOREIGN FORCES:

NATO:
HQ Allied Land Forces South Eastern Europe (LANDSOUTHEAST).
HQ 6 Allied Tactical Air Force (6 ATAF).
***OPERATION PROVIDE COMFORT*:**
FRANCE: Air (150); 4 *Mirage* F-1CR, 4 *Jaguar*, 1C-135.
UK: Air (260); 8 *Harrier*, 2 VC-10 (tkr).
US: 3,400; Army (200). Air (3,200); 1 tac, 1 air base gp with some 57 ac (F-15E, F-16, F-111F, EF-111, F-4G).

UNITED KINGDOM

GDP	1992: £596.8bn ($1,052.5bn): per capita $16,700	
	1993: £644.0bn ($1,100.4bn): per capita $17,300	
Growth	1992: -0.6%	1993: 1.9%
Inflation	1992: 4.7%	1993: 3.0%
Publ debt	1992: 40.5%	1993: 47.3%
Def exp	1991: £23.0bn ($40.7bn)	
	1992: £23.6bn ($41.7bn)	
Def bdgt	1992: £24.0bn ($42.3bn)	
	1993: £22.8bn ($34.2bn)	
	1994: £22.9bn ($34.0bn)	
	1995ε: £22.7bn ($33.6bn)	
NATO defn	1992: £23.8bn ($41.9bn)	
	1993: £23.4bn ($35.1bn)	
$1 = £1	1992: 0.57	1993: 0.67
	1994: 0.67	

£ = pound sterling

Population: 58,130,200 (Northern Ireland 1,600,000: Protestant 56%, Roman Catholic 41%).

	13–17	*18–22*	*23–32*
Men	1,810,700	1,953,800	4,561,800
Women	1,720,900	1,859,200	4,400,300

TOTAL ARMED FORCES:

ACTIVE: 254,300 (incl 17,650 women and some 7,200 enlisted outside the UK).
RESERVES:
Army: 263,400: Regular 192,500; Territorial Army (TA) 65,500; R Irish Regt (Home Service) 5,400 (2,900 full time).
Navy: 33,300: Regular 27,500; Volunteers and Auxiliary Service 5,800.
Marines: 3,900: Regular 2,700; Volunteers and Auxiliary Forces 1,200.
Air Force: 75,620: Regular 73,920; Volunteers and Auxiliary Forces 1,700.

STRATEGIC FORCES: (1,900).

SLBM: 48 msl in 3 SSBN:
3 *Resolution* SSBN each with 16 *Polaris* A-3TK SLBM.
(Plus 1 Vanguard SSBN with 16 *Trident* (D5) (max of 46 warheads) undergoing fleet trials; op late 1994–early 1995.)
EARLY WARNING:
Ballistic-Missile Early-Warning System (BMEWS) station at Fylingdales.

ARMY: 123,000 (incl 7,050 women and 7,000 enlisted outside the UK, of whom some 6,000 are Gurkhas).
(Note: regt are normally of bn size.)
6 Military Districts, 1 UK Spt Comd Germany (UKSCG).
1 armd div with 3 armd bde, 3 arty, 4 engr, 1 avn, 2 AD regt.
1 div with 2 mech (*Warrior/Saxon*), 1 AB bde, 4 arty, 3 engr, 1 avn, 2 AD regt.
UKSCG tps: 2 armd recce, 1 MLRS, 1 engr regt.
1 air mobile bde.
1 inf bde (Hong Kong (Gurkha)).
14 inf bde HQ (3 control ops in N. Ireland, remainder mixed regular and TA for trg/administrative purposes only).
3 engr bde HQ.
Summary of combat arm units:
9 armd regt (incl 1 trg regt).
3 armd recce regt.
9 mech inf bn (5 FV 432, 4 *Saxon*).
6 armd inf bn (*Warrior*).
26 inf bn (incl 3 Gurkha).
3 AB bn (2 only in para role).
1 SF (SAS) regt.
12 arty regt (3 MLRS, 5 SP, 3 fd (1 cdo, 1 AB, 1 air mobile), 1 trg).
4 AD regt (2 *Rapier*, 2 *Javelin*).
12 engr regt (incl 1 Gurkha, 1 amph, 5 armd).
5 avn regt (plus N. Ireland spt units).
6 Home Service inf bn (N. Ireland only, some part-time).

RESERVES:
Territorial Army: 1 armd recce, 4 lt recce regt, 36 inf bn, 2 SF (SAS), 3 fd, 3 AD, 9 engr regt, 1 avn sqn. Hong Kong Regiment. Gibraltar Regiment.

EQUIPMENT:
MBT: 921: 426 *Challenger*, some 495 *Chieftain*.
LIGHT TANKS: 29 *Scorpion*.
RECCE: some 314 *Scimitar*, 11 *Fuchs*.
AIFV: some 760 *Warrior* (incl variants), 11 AFV 432 *Rarden*.
APC: 3,416: some 2,000 AFV 432 (incl variants), some 592 FV 103 *Spartan*, 664 *Saxon*, 63 *Saracen*, 97 Humber.
TOTAL ARTY: 569:
TOWED ARTY: 286: 105mm: 210 L-118; 140mm: 5 5.5-in; 155mm: 71 FH-70.
SP ARTY: 220: 155mm: 91 M-109A1, 129 AS-90 (plus 21 105mm *Abbot* in store).
MRL: 227mm: some 63 MLRS.
MORTARS: 81mm: some 500 (incl 110 SP).
ATGW: ε1,100 *Milan* (incl 72 FV 103 *Spartan* SP), 88 *Swingfire* (FV 102 *Striker* SP), *TOW*.
RCL: 84mm: *Carl Gustav*.
SAM: 42 *Starstreak*, some 382 *Javelin* and *Starburst*; 74 *Rapier* (some 24 SP).
SURV: *Cymbeline* (mor).
AIRCRAFT: 7 BN-2, 21 *Chipmunk* trg.
HELICOPTERS: 69 *Scout*, 159 SA-341, 126 *Lynx* AH-1/-7/-9.
UAV: CL-89 (AN/USD-501).
LANDING CRAFT: 2 *Ardennes*, 9 *Arromanches* log; 4 *Avon*, LCVP ; 3 tugs, 28 other service vessels.

NAVY (RN): 55,600 (incl ε6,000 Fleet Air Arm, 7,300 Marines, 4,200 women and 275 enlisted outside the UK).
ROYAL FLEET AUXILIARY (RFA): (2,150 civilians) mans major spt vessels.
ROYAL MARITIME AUXILIARY SERVICE (RMAS): (400 civilians) provides harbour/coastal services.

RESERVES:
ROYAL FLEET RESERVE: (ε20,000); ex-regulars, no trg commitment.
ROYAL NAVAL RESERVE (RNR): (3,120); 5 HQ units, 13 Sea Trg Centres (STC).
BASES: UK: Northwood (HQ Fleet, CINCEASTLANT), Devonport (HQ), Faslane, Portland, Portsmouth, Rosyth (HQ). Overseas: Gibraltar, Hong Kong.
SUBMARINES: 17:
STRATEGIC SUBMARINES: 3 SSBN (see p. 68).
TACTICAL SUBMARINES: 14:
SSN: 12 (incl 2 in refit):
7 *Trafalgar*, 5 *Swiftsure* all with Mk 24 HWT and *Harpoon* USGW.
SS: 2:
2 *Upholder* with Mk 24 HWT and *Harpoon* (to pay off by end 1994).
PRINCIPAL SURFACE COMBATANTS: 38:
CARRIERS: 3 *Invincible* CVV each with **ac:** 8 *Sea Harrier* V/STOL; **hel:** 12 *Sea King*: up to 9 ASW, 3 AEW; plus 1 x 2 *Sea Dart* SAM.
DESTROYERS: 12 DDG (incl 3 in refit):
12 *Birmingham* with 1 x 2 *Sea Dart* SAM; plus 1 *Lynx* hel, 2 x 3 ASTT, 1 x 114mm gun.
FRIGATES: 23 (incl 2 in refit):
4 *Cornwall* (Type 22 Batch 3) with 1 *Sea King* or 2 *Lynx* hel (*Sting Ray* LWT), 2 x 3 ASTT; plus 2 x 4 *Harpoon* SSM, 1 x 114mm gun.
10 *Broadsword* (Type 22 Batch 1/2) with 2 *Lynx* hel (2 with 1 x *Sea King*), 2 x 3 ASTT; plus 4 x MM-38 *Exocet* SSM (4 Batch 1 trg).
9 *Norfolk* (Type 23) with 1 x *Lynx* hel, 2 x 2 ASTT, plus 2 x 4 *Harpoon* SSM, 1 x 114mm gun (incl 1 commissioning later in 1994).
(Excl 2 *Amazon* with 1 *Lynx* hel, 2 x 3 ASTT; plus 4 x MM-38 *Exocet*, 1 x 114mm gun (to pay off July 1994)).

EXTENDED READINESS: 1 *Leander* (Batch 3A) (in addition to above).
PATROL AND COASTAL COMBATANTS: 33:
OFFSHORE: 17 PCO: 1 *Endurance*, 2 *Castle*, 6 *Jersey*, 3 *Peacock*, 5 *River/Waveney* (ex MSO).
INSHORE: 16 PCI: 2 *Kingfisher*, 12 *Archer* (incl 4 trg), 2 *Ranger*.
MINE WARFARE: 18:
MINELAYER: no dedicated minelayer, but all submarines have limited minelaying capability.
MINE COUNTERMEASURES: 18:
13 *Brecon* MCO.
5 *Sandown* MHC.
AMPHIBIOUS: 6:
1 *Fearless* LPD (plus 1 in store) with 4 LCU, 4 LCVP; capacity 400 tps, 15 tk, 3 hel.
1 *Sir Galahad*, 4 *Sir Lancelot* LST: capacity 340 tps, 16 tk (*Sir G.* 18), 1 hel (RFA manned).
Plus 32 craft: 15 LCU, 17 LCVP.
Note: see Army for additional amph lift capability.
SUPPORT AND MISCELLANEOUS: 30:
UNDERWAY SUPPORT: 9:
2 *Fort Victoria* AOE (not fully op).
2 *Olwen*, 3 *Green Rover* AO, 2 *Fort Grange* AF.
MAINTENANCE/LOGISTIC: 10:
1 AR, 4 AO, 2 AE, 3 AT.
SPECIAL PURPOSE: 6:
1 AVT, 2 trg (1 *Wilton*, 1 chartered), 2 trials/research, 1 Royal Yacht.
SURVEY: 5: 2 *Hecla*, 2 *Bulldog*, 1 *Roebuck* AGHS.
(23 of above civilian-manned, either RFA or RMAS.)

FLEET AIR ARM: (ε6,000 (450 women)).

A typical CVS air group consists of 8 *Harrier*, 9 *Sea King* (ASW), 3 *Sea King* (AEW).
Average annual flying hours for *Sea Harrier* pilots: 180.
FIGHTER/ATTACK: 3 ac sqn with *Sea Harrier* FRS-1/2 (1 trg sqn).
ASW: 5 hel sqn with *Sea King* HAS-6.
ASW/ATTACK: 2 sqn with *Lynx* HAS-2/-3 (in indep flt).
AEW: 1 hel sqn with *Sea King* AEW-2.
COMMANDO SUPPORT: 3 hel sqn with *Sea King* HC-4.
SAR: 1 hel sqn with *Sea King* HC-4.
1 hel sqn with *Sea King* HAS-5.
TRAINING: 2 sqn: 1 with *Jetstream* **ac**; 1 with SA-341 *Gazelle* HT-2 **hel**.
FLEET SUPPORT: *Hunter* T-8, GA-11, *Hawk*, *Mystère-Falcon* 20 (civil registration), 1 Cessna *Conquest* (civil registration), 1 Beech *Baron* (civil registration) (operated under contract).
TRANSPORT: *Jetstream*.
EQUIPMENT: 25 cbt ac, 118 armed hel.
AIRCRAFT:
***Sea Harrier:* FRS-1/-2:** 20 plus 15 in store. **T-4N:** 5* (trg) plus 2 in store.
Hunter: 6 (spt), (plus 16 in store).
Hawk: 7 (spt). ***Mystère-Falcon* 20:** 13 (spt).
Jetstream: 17: **T-2:** 14 (trg); **T-3:** 3 (trg).
HELICOPTERS:
Sea King: 95. **HAS-6:** 60, plus 10 in store; **HC-4:** 33, plus 4 in store (cdo); **AEW-2:** 9, plus 1 in store.
***Lynx* HAS-3:** 58, plus 19 in store.
***Gazelle* HT-2/-3:** 20 (trg plus 4 in store).
MISSILES:
ASM: *Sea Skua, Sea Eagle.*
AAM: AIM-9 *Sidewinder*.

MARINES: (7,300).

1 cdo bde: 3 cdo; 1 cdo arty regt (Army) + 1 bty (TA); 2 cdo engr sqn (1 Army, 1 TA), 1 log regt (joint service); 1 lt hel sqn.
1 mtn and arctic warfare cadre.
Special Boat Service (SF): HQ: 5 sqn.
1 aslt sqn.
1 gp (*Commachio).*
EQUIPMENT:
MORTARS: 81mm.
ATGW: *Milan*.
SAM: *Javelin, Blowpipe*.
HELICOPTERS: 9 SA-341 (*Gazelle*); plus 3 in store, 6 *Lynx* AH-1.
AMPHIBIOUS: 16 RRC, 2 LCU, 4 LCVP, 4 LACV.

AIR FORCE (RAF): 75,700 (incl 6,400 women).

Average annual flying hours for FGA/fighter aircrew: 220.
FGA/BOMBER: 6 (nuclear-capable) sqn:
4 with *Tornado* GR-1.
2 with *Tornado* GR-1B (maritime attack).
FGA: 5 sqn:
3 with *Harrier*; GR-7.
2 with *Jaguar*.
FIGHTER: 6 sqn, plus 1 flt:
6 with *Tornado* F-3 (1 flt in the Falklands).
RECCE: 2 sqn with *Tornado* GR-1A; 1 photo-recce unit with *Canberra* PR-9; 1 sqn with *Jaguar*.
MR: 3 sqn with *Nimrod* MR-2.
AEW: 1 sqn with *Sentry* E-3D.
ECM/ELINT: 2 sqn: 1 ECM with *Canberra*; 1 ELINT with *Nimrod* R-1.
TANKER: 2 sqn: 1 with VC-10 K-2/-3; 1 with *Tristar* K-1/KC-1 (tkr/tpt).
TRANSPORT: 5 sqn:
1 strategic with VC-10 C-1/C-1K.
4 tac with *Hercules* C-1/-1K/-1P/-3P.

LIAISON: 1 comms sqn with HS-125, *Andover* **ac**; SA-341E **hel**.

Queen's Flt: 3 BAe -146-100, 2 *Wessex* hel.

CALIBRATION: 2 sqn: 1 with *Andover* E-3; 1 target facility with *Hawk*.

OCU: 7: *Tornado* GR-1, *Tornado* F-3, *Jaguar* GR-1A/T2A, *Harrier* GR-5/7, *Hercules*, SA-330/CH-47. 1 wpn conversion unit with *Tornado* GR-1.

TRAINING: *Hawk* T-1/-1A, *Jetstream* T-1, *Bulldog* T-1, *Chipmunk* T-10, HS-125 *Dominie* T-1, *Tucano* T-1.

TACTICAL HELICOPTERS: 6 sqn: 1 with CH-47; 1 with CH-47 and SA-330 (*Puma*); 2 with *Wessex* HC-2; 2 with SA-330 (*Puma*).

SAR: 2 hel sqn; 8 flt: 3 with *Wessex* HC-2; 5 with *Sea King* HAR-3.

TRAINING: *Wessex*, SA-341 *Sea King*.

EQUIPMENT: 561 cbt ac, incl 26 MR (plus 71 in store), no armed hel.

AIRCRAFT:

Tornado: 305: **GR-1:** 131; **GR-1A:** 28; **GR-1B:** 12; **F-3:** 134; plus 33 in store (13 F-2, 20 GR-1).

Jaguar: 69: **GR-1A:** 56; **T-2A:** 13 (plus 16 in store).

Harrier: 80: **GR-7:** 67; **T-4:** 11, **GR-5:** 2 (plus 18 in store).

Hawk: **T-1/1-A:** 137 (*81 (T1-A) tac weapons unit *Sidewinder*-capable, 56 trg).

Canberra: 18: **T-4:** 3 (trg); **PR-7:** 2 (trg); **PR-9:** 5 (recce); **T-17:** 8 (ECM).

Nimrod: 29: **R-1:** 3 (ECM); **MR-2:** 26* (MR); plus 4 in store.

Sentry (E-3D): 7 (AEW).

Tristar: 9: **K-1:** 2 (tkr/tpt); **KC-1:** 4 (tkr/cgo); **C-2:** 3 (tpt).

VC-10: 21: **C-1/C-1K:** 13 (strategic tpt to be mod to tkr/tpt); **K-2:** 3 (tkr); **K-3:** 4 (tkr); **K-4:** 1.

Hercules: 61: **C-1:** 26; **C-1K:** 5 (tkr); **C-3:** 29; **W-2:** 1.

Andover: 6.

HS-125: 27: **T-1:** 19 (trg); **CC-1/-2/-3:** 8 (liaison).

Islander **CC-MK2:** 1.

BAe-146: 3 (VIP tpt).

Tucano: 108 (trg), plus 21 in store.

Jetstream: 11 (trg).

Bulldog: 115 (trg).

Chipmunk: 67 (trg).

HELICOPTERS:

Wessex: 64.

CH-47: 32.

SA-330: 42.

Sea King: 19.

SA-341 (*Gazelle*): 29.

MISSILES:

ASM: *Martel*, AGM-84D-1 *Harpoon*, *Sea Eagle*.

AAM: AIM-9G *Sidewinder*, *Sky Flash*.

ARM: ALARM.

ROYAL AIR FORCE REGIMENT:

3 fd sqn (with 81mm mortars), 5 SAM sqn with 52 *Rapier*.

RESERVES (Royal Auxiliary Air Force Regiment): 5 fd def sqn.

DEPLOYMENT:

ARMY:

United Kingdom Land Forces (UKLF): (53,300).

Reinforcements for ARRC (declared to LANDCENT).

Active: 1 div, 1 air-mobile bde, 1 recce, 1 arty, 1 AD regt.

Reserve: 2 inf bde.

Additional TA units incl 18 inf bn, 2 SAS, 3 AD regt.

Allied Command Europe Mobile Force (*Land*) (AMF(L)): (some 2,300); UK contribution: 1 inf bn, 1 arty bty, 1 sigs sqn, 1 log bn.

HQ Northern Ireland (some 11,400, plus 5,400 Home Service); 3 inf bde HQ, up to 12 major units in inf role (6 resident, 6 roulement inf bn), 1 engr regt, 6 Home Service inf bn.

Remainder of Army regular and TA units for Home Defence.

NAVY:

FLEET (CinC is also CINCEASTLANT):

Regular Forces, with the exception of most Patrol and Coastal Combatants, Mine Warfare and Support Forces, are declared to EASTLANT.

MARINES: 1 cdo bde (declared to AFNORTH).

AIR FORCE:

STRIKE COMMAND: commands all combat air operations other than for Belize, Cyprus, Falklands and Hong Kong: 5 Groups: No. 1 (Strike, Attack), No. 2 (Strike, Attack; based in Germany), No. 11 (Air Defence), No. 18 (Maritime), No. 38 (Transport/AAR).

LOGISTICS COMMAND: supply and maint spt of other comds.

PERSONNEL AND TRAINING COMMAND: flying and ground training.

OVERSEAS:

ANTARCTICA: 1 ice patrol ship (in summer).

ASCENSION ISLAND: RAF.

BELIZE: Army: some 600; 1 engr sqn, 1 hel flt (3 *Gazelle* AH-1) (force to be withdrawn in 1994).

BRUNEI: Army: some 900; 1 Gurkha inf bn, 1 hel flt (3 hel).

CANADA: Army: trg and liaison unit; RAF: 100; routine training deployment of *Tornado* GR1.

CYPRUS: 3,900.

Army: 2,400; 2 inf bn, 1 engr spt sqn, 1 hel flt.
Navy: 2 PCI.
RAF: 1,500; 1 hel sqn (*Wessex*), routine training deployment of *Tornado* ac, 1 sqn RAF regt.
FALKLAND ISLANDS: some 1,700. Army: 1 inf coy gp, 1 engr sqn (fd, plant); RN: 1 DD/FF, 1 PCO, 1 AO, 1 AR; RAF: 1 *Tornado* F-3 flt, 2 *Hercules* C-1K, 2 *Sea King* HAR-3, 2 CH-47 hel, 1 sqn RAF regt (*Rapier* SAM), 1 field sqn.
GERMANY: 38,200: Army (UKSCG): 32,200; 1 armd div, 2 armd recce, 1 MLRS, 1 engr regt (declared to LANDCENT); RAF (No. 2 GP RAF): 6,000; 6 ac sqn, 4 *Tornado*, 2 *Harrier*, 1 hel sqn (SA-330/CH-47 (tpt)), RAF regt; 2 *Rapier* SAM sqn, 1 fd sqn (declared to AIRCENT).
GIBRALTAR: 750: Army: 100; Gibraltar regt (400); Navy/Marines: 400; 2 PCI, Marine det, 2 twin *Exocet* launchers (coast defence), base unit; RAF: 250; periodic *Jaguar* ac det.
MEDITERRANEAN: 1 FF/DD STANAVFORMED (redeployed to op *Sharp Guard*).
HONG KONG: 1,900. Army: 1,400; Gurkha inf bde with 1 Gurkha inf bn, 1 Gurkha engr regt, 3 small landing craft, 3 other vessels; Navy/Marines: 250 (plus 275 locally enlisted); 3 *Peacock* PCC (12 patrol boats in local service); RAF: 250; 1 *Wessex* hel sqn (6 HC-2) (until 1997). Reserves: Hong Kong regt (1,200).
INDIAN OCEAN (*Armilla Patrol*): 2 DD/FF, 1 spt ship. Diego Garcia: 1 naval party, 1 Marine det.
NEPAL: Army: 1,200 (Gurkha trg org).
WEST INDIES (see also Belize): 1 DD/FF.
MILITARY ADVISERS: 455 in 30 countries.

UN AND PEACEKEEPING:
ADRIATIC (*Sharp Guard*): 1 CVV, 2–3 DD/FF, 3–4 spt ships; RAF: 32; 2 *Nimrod* MPA ac.
BOSNIA (UNPROFOR BH): 3,688; 1 armd inf, 1 mech inf bn gp, 2 armd recce sqn, 1 arty loc bty, 19 Observers; 1 engr sqn, 4 Royal Naval *Sea King* H-C4 hel.
CYPRUS (UNFICYP): 400; 1 inf bn(-), 1 hel flt, engr spt (incl spt for UNIFIL).
FORMER YUGOSLAVIA (*Provide Promise*): 41; 1 C-130 ac.
IRAQ/KUWAIT (UNIKOM): 15 Observers.
ITALY (*Deny Flight*): 580; 8 *Tornado* F3, 2 K-1 *Tristar* (tkr), 2 E-3D *Sentry*; 12 *Jaguar,* 6 *Sea Harrier*.
SAUDI ARABIA *(Southern Watch):* 310; 6 *Tornado* GR-IA, 1 VC-10 (tkr).
TURKEY (*Provide Comfort*): 310; 8 *Harrier* GR-7, 2 VC-10 tkr.

FOREIGN FORCES:
US: 14,400: Navy (2,100); Air (12,300): 1 Air Force HQ, 63 cbt ac, 4 sqn with 45 F-15E, 1 sqn with 18 F-15C/D. 1 Special Ops Gp, 3 sqn with 5 MH-53J, 6 HC-130, MC-130H, 1 air refuelling wg with 9 KC-135.
GERMANY/ITALY: tri-national *Tornado* trg sqn.
HQ Eastern Atlantic Area (EASTLANT).
NATO: HQ Allied Forces North-west Europe (AFNORTHWEST).
HQ Allied Naval Forces North-west Europe (NAV NORTHWEST).
HQ Allied Air Forces North-west Europe (AIR NORTHWEST).

Non-NATO Europe

Regional Problems

Europe has continued to suffer the consequences of the wars in Croatia and Bosnia-Herzegovina which have proceeded over the last 12 months at varying levels of intensity. Conflict in Georgia and over Nagorno-Karabakh have persisted, but cease-fires in these cases have held more firmly and solutions are perhaps closer to being found. There has been no resolution of the problems in Cyprus, Estonia or Moldova, and relations between Russia and Ukraine remain awkward, particularly given their failure to agree on a division of the Black Sea Fleet.

Former Yugoslavia

Croatia

The basic situation has not changed over the last 12 months. Forces of the breakaway Serbian Krajina still control large areas of Croatia and the UN has been unable to achieve its original mandate. Fighting has erupted on a number of occasions and several cease-fires have been agreed and later broken. The most recent cease-fire was reached on 30 March 1994 and came into effect on 4 April. Under its terms, all troops were to withdraw one kilometre and heavy weapons were to be pulled back 20km. UN troops were interposed between the two sides. Both sides agreed to hold talks on economic matters and on the political status of Krajina, however neither side has changed its position and no progress towards breaking the deadlock has been made. The renewal of the UN Protection Forces (UNPROFOR) mandate, due in September 1994, was by no means certain in late summer.

Bosnia-Herzegovina

The following does not pretend to be an analysis of the war, but only a summary of the principal military activity and its consequences. Two major events took place on 9 February 1994, following the outrage engendered by the mortar attack which killed 68 civilians in the Sarajevo market-place on 5 February. The North Atlantic Treaty Organisation (NATO), following a request from the UN Secretary-General, issued an ultimatum to the Bosnian Serbs. All heavy weapons had either to be withdrawn from a circular area around Sarajevo with a radius of 20km or, if left within the circle, placed under UN control. Any uncontrolled weapons found in the area after midnight on 20 February or any elsewhere which fired on Sarajevo would be subject to air attack. Earlier in the day, as a 'carrot' to balance NATO's 'stick', General Rose, Commander of UNPROFOR BH, successfully negotiated a cease-fire around Sarajevo. This agreement also included the withdrawal or control of heavy weapons on both sides and UN troops were to be deployed where the two sides faced each other across the streets in the suburbs of Sarajevo. It is impossible to judge the relative value of the contribution made by NATO's ultimatum, General Rose's cease-fire and the diplomatic activity of the Russian Special Envoy, Vitaly Churkin, but the siege of Sarajevo was over. The cease-fire has been remarkably successful despite frequent minor violations, but it was at some risk when a number of UN monitors at heavy-weapon sites were held hostage for some days as part of the Serb retaliation for the air strikes at Goradze. The Serbs decided on 26 July to close the roads into Sarajevo to Bosnian traffic, and the next day they fired on a UN convoy. However, early on 5 August heavy weapons were taken from one site and a UN helicopter monitoring their movement was fired on. Later that day NATO planes attacked and destroyed a selected Bosnian-Serb heavy weapon after one hour's warning had been given to avoid casualties. The heavy weapons removed have now been returned to UN control.

Aircraft taking part in *Operation Deny Flight* on 28 February 1994 shot down four Bosnian-Serb *Galeb* aircraft which had been engaged in a bombing raid against a Bosnian ammunition factory.

Throughout the siege of Sarajevo, another far more bloody siege was taking place, without the benefit of a Western media presence, at Mostar, where Bosnian-Croat forces had cut off the Muslim population in the east-bank half of the city. But on 18 March, as a result of US diplomacy, agreement was reached between the Bosnian-Croats and Muslims and a cease-fire came into effect. The accords signed in Washington created a Federation in which both Croats and Muslims had equal rights. A new Constitution was agreed and the responsibilities of the federal government and cantonal governments were delineated. Most importantly, the accord stated that a Confederation with Croatia should be established and that Croatia would lease to Bosnia an area of the port of Ploce and guarantee access to it both from the sea and from Bosnia-Herzegovina.

In March 1994 the Bosnian Serbs renewed their attack on the UN-declared safe area of Goradze, giving as their reasons: the eviction of Serbs from villages close to Goradze; the attacks launched from Goradze on the bypass road they were building east of the town; and the concern that Bosnian forces there were being reinforced in preparation for an offensive. It was hoped after the success of the threat of air strikes at Sarajevo that they would have the same effect at Goradze, but they did not, and when UN observers came under fire close air strikes were called on 10 and 11 April against Serb tanks. Serb attacks continued, but at a lower intensity and a short-lived cease-fire was arranged by the Russian envoy, Vitaly Churkin. Close air support was called for again on 15 April. Although an attack was prevented by bad weather, one UK *Harrier* was shot down. On 22 April NATO issued an ultimatum demanding the immediate cessation of attacks on Goradze, the 3km withdrawal of all troops, and that UN convoys be allowed unimpeded entry to Goradze. If these terms were not met by midnight on 23 April then NATO would attack Serb heavy weapons and other military targets within 20km of Goradze. UN troops reached Goradze on 23 April, and a 20km heavy-weapon exclusion zone was established around the town. No further air strikes were ordered in the period up to August 1994.

The UN Special Representative, Yashushi Akashi, brokered a cease-fire agreement in Belgrade to cover the whole of Bosnia from 10 June. Although it had been broken frequently, Mr Akashi managed to renew it for a second month on 12 July.

On 26 April a 'contact group' was established by the US, Russia, France, UK and Germany to take over the leading role in devising a peace plan for Bosnia. On 6 July the group presented to the parties their plan which, while maintaining a federal state within its present borders, would partition the country between the Serbs and the Muslim–Croat Federation. The Serbs, who currently occupy some 70% of the country, were offered 49% (while they claim legal ownership of around 67%). After two years the Serbs would have the option of holding a referendum to decide whether they would secede. The parties were given until 19 July to agree to the plan or suffer serious consequences.

The Bosnian government reluctantly accepted the peace plan, while the Serb reply was interpreted as a rejection. A referendum is to be held at the end of August. The contact group met on 30 July and decided on measures to increase the scope of sanctions against the Serbs, to improve enforcement of the sanctions, and to strengthen the protection of the safe areas which did not benefit from the heavy-weapons exclusion zones. By 5 August, the UN Security Council had not passed a new sanctions resolution.

In early August the Serbian President, Slobodan Milosevic, announced that Yugoslavia would cut its political and economic links with the Bosnian-Serbs. The border would be closed to all goods except food, medical supplies and clothing. How effective the measures will be remains to be seen. However, should the combination of a Serbian blockade and intensified UN sanctions fail to achieve Bosnian-Serb acceptance of the peace plan, then the lifting of the arms embargo, to allow the arming of the Bosnian government, will be difficult to avoid despite the reservations held by a number of UN troop-contributors. A body of opinion considers that the effect of lifting the arms embargo will be to intensify and spread the war and would lead to the withdrawal of UN peacekeeping troops.

Macedonia

There has been no progress towards resolving the question of the name of the Former Yugoslav Republic of Macedonia, as it is now called. In February 1994, Greece imposed a blockade on Macedonia trade through the Greek port of Thessalonika. The European Union worked to have the embargo lifted, and took Greece to the European Court of Justice which refused the European Commission's request for an emergency interim order for Greece to lift the blockade. It is reported that the Court's decision was based on the argument that European Union trade with Macedonia had not been damaged by the embargo. Meanwhile the Macedonian border with Serbia is the scene of large-scale violations of the UN-imposed trade sanctions against Serbia.

Ukraine

The division of the Black Sea Fleet between Russia and Ukraine has still not been resolved, although there is agreement in principle that it should be shared equally between the two countries, possibly with some ships going to Georgia. A number of incidents have inflamed the situation, but fortunately none have led to a permanent rift. In April, the Russians sailed a survey ship, loaded with some $10m-worth of navigation aid and equipment, from Odessa. The Ukrainian Coast Guard attempted unsuccessfully to stop the ship leaving. Later in April, the Ukrainians unilaterally converted a Black Sea Fleet unit (responsible for ships in preservation) into a Ukrainian naval brigade. Other incidents involved the arrest of Russian naval officers and the movement by both sides of troops in the Crimea. The main disagreement remains the question of shore facilities. The Russian proposal is that they should lease all naval facilities in the Crimea and that the Ukrainian Navy should vacate the peninsula. Ukraine is insisting that Sevastapol remains under its jurisdiction and that the two fleets use different harbours in the port.

The problem of the Black Sea Fleet was not eased by the differences arising between the Verkhovna Rada in Kiev and the Crimean parliament, the Pentagon. On 20 May 1994, the Pentagon voted to restore the May 1992 Constitution which the Ukrainian government had forced Crimea to rescind and which it considers to be a statement of independence. On 3 June the two assemblies agreed a joint statement which, while not resolving the problem, allowed the Rada to refrain from imposing the measures threatened earlier. The election of Leonid Kuchma as President of Ukraine may ease tensions between Ukraine and Russia, but the Crimean problem will remain a difficulty.

There are still considerable fears of another disaster at the Chernobyl nuclear power station complex. An inspection by the International Atomic Energy Agency (IAEA) and other international safety specialists concluded that international levels of safety were not being met in the operating units. Further, it was reported that the shelter enclosing the destroyed reactor is deteriorating and may collapse. Ukraine claims it cannot afford alternative sources of power and has estimated that some $6bn would be needed to close Chernobyl. Of this $2.5bn is needed for safety and dismantlement costs, $1.5bn to build new reactors and $2bn for other energy sources until a new reactor is completed. The Group of 7 at its Naples summit agreed to provide $1.8bn to close Chernobyl and to upgrade safety standards at three reactors still under construction.

Transcaucasus

Armenia/Azerbaijan

Both the Conference on Security and Cooperation in Europe (CSCE) and Russia have been working to achieve a settlement over the long-standing war between **Armenia** and **Azerbaijan** over the Armenian-populated Nagorno-Karabakh region of Azerbaijan. After a cease-fire agreed to on 12 May 1994 failed to last more than a few hours, a second cease-fire accord was reached on 16 May which included provision for establishing observer posts manned jointly by Armenian, Azerbaijani and Russian troops. The Commonwealth of Independent States (CIS) was to provide a 1,800-strong peacekeeping force. The cease-fire was extended by 90 days on 27 July. During its first two months there were some minor violations, but overall it has been kept. The CSCE observer group prepared for monitoring an Azeri–Armenian cease-fire had not deployed by the beginning of August.

Georgia

The situation in **Georgia** is much improved and an end to all three separate conflicts of the last few years is in sight. Former President Zviad Gamsakhurdia died, in Chechen, in December 1993. In Abkhazia a cease-fire was agreed on 14 May 1994. A 3,000-strong Russian peacekeeping force has been deployed with the agreement of the UN Security Council who have sent UN observers to work with the Russian troops.

Russian Bases

Russia has successfully negotiated the retention of a number of military bases in two of three Transcaucasian republics. It also wants a base in Azerbaijan, where an ABM phased-array radar is located at Lyaki, which Azerbaijan claims is its property but which it is prepared to lease to Russia. There will be three bases in Georgia at Batumi, Vaziani (near Tbilisi) and Akhalkalaki on the Turkish border. In January 1994 under-strength motor rifle divisions were located at Batumi and Akhalkalaki, Vaizani had housed elements of a training division earlier. Two bases will be maintained in Armenia at Yerevan and Gyumri, where a motor rifle division is now based.

Baltic States

Agreement has been reached by **Latvia** and Russia for all Russian troops to withdraw by the end of August 1994. In return Latvia has agreed that Russia can operate the early-warning radar at Skrunda until August 1998 when the Russians will have 18 months in which to dismantle the station. It had been thought that Russia had reached agreement with **Estonia** when an announcement was made on 26 July 1994 that Russian troops would withdraw by 31 August, but this was retracted the next day. However, agreement has been reached over the decommissioning of the nuclear reactors (for training submarine crews) installed at the Paldiski naval base. The Russians are still not satisfied with the status of the 400,000 Russian minority population. Meanwhile, some Russian military withdrawal continues. **Lithuania** and Russia have nearly completed their negotiations over military transit through Lithuania to Kaliningrad.

Nuclear Force Developments

Belarus ratified its accession to the Nuclear Non-Proliferation Treaty (NPT) in July 1993. Only mobile SS-25 ICBM are deployed in Belarus and these are being transferred to Russia where they will remain in service. It appears that there were 81 SS-25 in Belarus as opposed to the 80 listed in *The Military Balance 1993–1994*. Contradictory announcements have been made regarding the progress of the withdrawal programme. Certainly one, maybe more, regiment, each with nine launchers, redeployed in 1993. By June 1994 a total of three regiments with 27 launchers had left Lida, the northern of the two SS-25 bases in Belarus. There is no confirmed information as to the new location of these ICBM. One suggestion is the SS-17 site at Vypolzozo, north of Moscow, as SS-17 may be eliminated. Another is that some may be redeployed to the Transbaykal where there are three SS-11 sites which are most likely to be eliminated. Two more regiments are due to leave Belarus in 1994 and the remaining regiments in 1995.

The **Ukrainian** Rada removed the conditions attached to its ratification of the Strategic Arms Reduction Talks (START I) Treaty on 3 February 1994. However, Ukraine has still not ratified its accession to the NPT, although it did participate in the trilateral agreement with Russia and the US reached at the January 1994 Moscow summit on the transfer of nuclear warheads (see p 256 for details). Meanwhile the elimination of strategic nuclear weapons in Ukraine has proceeded. A number of ICBM have been deactivated by removing their nuclear warheads and 180 of these have been transferred to Russia. The Commander-in-Chief of Russia's Strategic Rocket Forces, who still has a degree of control over Ukraine's ICBM, has said that all 46 SS-24 in Ukraine have been deactivated as have 20 SS-19 missiles whose service life had expired (but ten of these may be the ten which it was announced in July 1993 were being dismantled). US Secretary of Defense, William Perry, when visiting the Pervomaisk SS-24 site said that 120 warheads from there were included in those transferred to Russia. Strategic nuclear bombers in Ukraine are under Ukrainian control, although the cruise missiles with which they would be armed are probably under Russian control. The Tu-160 *Blackjack* bombers are no longer considered by the Russians as operational because of the lack of spares, maintenance and aircrew. Ukraine is negotiating with Russia to exchange its 42 strategic bombers for the guaranteed maintenance of other aircraft types and supplies of spare parts for various weapon systems. In May 1994, at a meeting between the US Vice-President and Ukrainian Deputy-Prime Minister, Ukraine committed itself to complying with the criteria and standards of the Missile Technology Control Regime. As SS-18 ICBM were produced at the Uzhmash factory at Dnepropetrovsk this is an important commitment.

Conventional Force Developments

Baltic Republics

Estonia has acquired some 40 APCs (BTR series) and seven more patrol craft for its Maritime Border Guard, including two German *Kondor*-class and two Russian *Zhuk*-class. The strength of **Latvian** armed forces has increased by 1,500 during the year, of which 600 are in the Navy which has acquired two German *Kondor*-class and three Russian *Osa*-class patrol craft. Aircraft and helicopter numbers are now known. The **Lithuanian** Air Force has acquired some AN-2 transport aircraft and Mi-8 helicopters.

Former Warsaw Pact Countries

As Conventional Armed Forces in Europe (CFE) Treaty signatories, all countries have reduced their weapons holdings by destroying equipment above their treaty-limited equipment (TLE) quotas. Few have acquired any new equipment. The **Czech** Army has converted one mechanised division into a mechanised brigade, and the infantry division has been disbanded. Further reorganisation to a brigade basis is planned. The rapid-reaction battalion will be expanded to a brigade and a number of territorial defence brigades formed. In the Air Force, the two helicopter regiments have both attack and transport helicopters, as opposed to the previous situation of one attack and one assault transport helicopter regiment. The Air Force is to be divided into a tactical corps and an air-defence corps. In **Hungary** helicopter units have been transferred from the Air Force to the Army. *The Military Balance 1993–1994* gave an incorrect figure for the holding of D-20 howitzers, although this edition lists 320. There has not been a dramatic increase in numbers. The Air Force has taken delivery of 28 MiG-29 fighters as part of an arrangement to pay off Russia's inherited debt to Hungary. Conscription is to be reduced in length from 12 to ten months after the induction of the August 1994 intake. In **Poland**, conscription is to be reduced from 18 months to one year in 1995. The Army has disbanded one mechanised division, converted another to an armoured cavalry division and is establishing a new formation, the 25th Air Cavalry Division, which contains airborne troops and an Air Force helicopter regiment. Eventually the division will be equipped with the Polish-built PZL *Huzar* multi-role helicopter. The Air Force has retired its 50 plus Su-22 trainers and replaced these with further TS-11 *Iskra* aircraft.

Transcaucasus Republics

Both **Armenia** and **Azerbaijan** have expanded their armed forces. Manpower strengths have increased and a number of additional units have been formed. The number of weapons held has not increased appreciably, although Azerbaijan has acquired a further 200 MT-LB and more information is available on the detailed holdings of treaty-limited equipment. Little change in the organisation and strength of the **Georgian** armed forces has been noted; if anything equipment holdings are reduced in all categories.

Belarus and Ukraine

In **Belarus** the Army has been further reorganised. There are no Army headquarters, but there are three Corps headquarters. The four remaining divisions are all under Ministry of Defence direct command. The artillery division is a reserve formation while the airborne and motor rifle divisions are manned at just above 50%. Two of the Corps comprise an SSM brigade, an artillery regiment, an MRL regiment and a number of mechanised brigades. The third Corps appears to consist of mobilisable units only. Under its command are two weapons and equipment stores which hold a range of equipment similar to that of a mechanised brigade, while another could be a store for an artillery regiment. There are three other potential mechanised brigade mobilisation stores in the other two Corps. The Air Force also appears to be reorganising. Few Air Force units (regiments, squadrons) are listed and combat aircraft and helicopters are shown by air base. MiG-25 (reconnaissance and fighters), MiG-27 (FGA) and small numbers of other types are located at the reduction air base at Baranovichi, presumably prior to elimination or disposal. The armed forces have introduced a new type of engagement for those who have completed their compulsory service and are under the age of 35. They may enlist for two years, after which they can extend their contract for a further three or six years.

The **Ukrainian** armed forces are suffering a shortage of manpower mainly due to the very high numbers being granted deferment from compulsory service. The length of the period of compulsory service has therefore been extended from 18 months to two years. Both Ukraine and Russia are including certain naval air and coastal defence forces in their data returns to the CFE Treaty. The reorganisation of the Army has continued with the three military districts being replaced by two operational commands, Western and Southern. Each has three corps. The artillery corps has been disbanded, four motor rifle divisions have been converted to mechanised divisions, two have been given reserve status and four disbanded. Two more mechanised brigades have been created and the formation of the air-mobile division, which comprises one airborne and one air mobile brigade and one artillery regiment, has been completed. It is planned to reduce the manpower strength of the armed forces to some 450,000 by the end of 1995.

Neutral and Non-Aligned States

The **Albanian** Army has been reorganised on a divisional basis. There are nine divisions each with between 3,000 and 5,500 men, replacing some 15 brigades and regiments. There has been no change to the number of weapons, but *The Military Balance* now has more accurate information on the numbers held, particularly regarding artillery. The **Cypriot** National Guard is to be expanded and will be less dependent on conscripts. Some 3,000–4,000 men will be recruited on five-year contracts. The **Finnish** parliament approved in December 1993 the government's proposal to buy 64 F/A-18 aircraft, but as yet no firm orders have been placed. **Sweden** is to purchase 120 *Leopard*-2 tanks, and up to 800 MT-LB tracked carriers from the former East German Army stockpile. **Swiss** Army tank holdings have been revised. There are now 80 more *Leopard*-2 tanks than listed last year and the numbers of other types have been amended. The overall change, however, is only an increase of seven. There are rather less AIFV than listed in 1993–1994 and an equivalent number more APCs. The Air Force has started to retire its *Hunter* FGA aircraft.

Former Yugoslavia

Although the civil wars continue, more information is becoming available on the organisations and manpower and weapon strengths of the various forces and parties. In general, most forces show increases in manpower and in the number of units. There have been no dramatic increases in weapons holdings. *The Military Balance* is now able to differentiate between the active and reserve units of the Federal Republic of **Yugoslavia** Army (JA). Some JA weapon holdings have been reduced. For example, there are 25 MRL, 300 plus towed artillery pieces, 300 120mm mortars, 150 *Sagger* ATGW less than listed in *The Military Balance 1993–1994*. Previous *Military Balance* assessments could have overstated these holdings, but if they did not, then some of these weapons may have found their way to the Serb forces in Croatia and Bosnia-Herzegovina. The forces of Serbian Krajina have acquired 12 *Galeb* combat aircraft, possibly those listed as reconnaissance aircraft in the Yugoslav entry in 1993–94 and not listed by Yugoslavia in its Vienna Document data. In **Bosnia-Herzegovina** a sixth corps has been formed to control operations centred on Travnik.

ALBANIA

GDP[a]	1992ε: leke 59.4bn ($2.4bn): per capita $2,500	
	1993ε: leke 96.7bn ($2.7bn): per capita $2,800	
Growth	1992: -15.4%	1993: 11.0%
Inflation	1992: 236.6%	1993: 30.9%
Debt	1992: $625m	1993: $800m
Def bdgt[a]	1992: leke 2.6bn ($105.0m)	
	1993: leke 3.4bn ($95.5m)	
	1994: leke 4.4bn ($97.5m)	
FMA	1993: $0.2m (IMET)	
	1994: $0.1m (IMET)	
	1995: $0.2m (IMET)	
$1 = leke	1992: 75	1993: 103
	1994: 104	

[a] ppp est.

Population: 3,417,000 (Greek 8%)

	13–17	*18–22*	*23–32*
Men	173,200	162,500	303,400
Women	167,600	155,600	286,200

TOTAL ARMED FORCES:

ACTIVE: 73,000 (22,800 conscripts).
Terms of service: 15 months.
RESERVES: 155,000 (to age 56): Army 150,000; Navy/Air Force 5,000.

ARMY: 60,000 (incl reserves, 20,000 conscripts).

9 inf div.[b]
EQUIPMENT:
MBT: 138 T-34, 721 T-59.
LIGHT TANKS: 30 Type-62.
RECCE: 15 BRDM-1.
APC: 103 Ch Type-531.
TOWED ARTY: 122mm: 425 M-1931/37, M-30, 208 Ch Type-60; 130mm: 100 Ch Type-59-1; 152mm: 90 Ch Type-66.
MRL: 107mm: 270 Ch Type-63.
MORTARS: 82mm: 259; 120mm: 550 M-120; 160mm: 100 M-160.
RCL: 82mm: T-21.
ATK GUNS: 45mm: M-1942; 57mm: M-1943; 85mm: 61 D-44, Ch Type-56; 100mm: 50 Type-86.
AD GUNS: 23mm: 12 ZU-23-2/ZPU-1; 37mm: 100 M-1939; 57mm: 82 S-60; 85mm: 30 KS-12; 100mm: 56.

[b] Inf div strengths vary from 3,000 to 5,500.

NAVY: ε3,000 (incl 350 Coastal Defence and ε1,000 conscripts).

BASES: Durrës, Himarë, Sarandë, Sazan Island, Shëngjin and Vlorë.
SUBMARINES:† 2 Sov *Whiskey* with 533mm TT (plus 1 trg, unserviceable).
PATROL AND COASTAL COMBATANTS: † 35:
TORPEDO CRAFT: 24 Ch *Huchuan* PHT with 2 x 533mm TT.
PATROL: 11:
2 Sov *Kronshtadt* PCO; 6 Ch *Shanghai*-II; some 3 Sov PO-2 PFI.
MINE WARFARE:† 5: 1 Sov T-43 (in reserve), 4 Sov T-301 MSI.
SUPPORT: 4: 2 Sov *Khobi* harbour tankers, 2 Sov *Shalanda* AK.

AIR FORCE: 10,000 (1,800 conscripts); 99 cbt ac†, no armed hel.

Average annual flying hours for FGA/Fighter aircrew: 80.
FGA: 2 sqn with 10 J-2 (MiG-15), 15 J-6 (MiG-17), 23 J-6 (MiG-19).
FIGHTER: 2 sqn:
1 with 20 J-6 (MiG-19), 10 J-7 (MiG-21).
1 with 21 J-6 (MiG-19).
TRANSPORT: 1 sqn with 10 C-5 (An-2), 3 Il-14M, 6 Li-2 (C-47).
HELICOPTERS: 2 sqn with 15 Ch Z-5 (Mi-4).
TRAINING: 8 CJ-5, 15 MiG-15UTI, 6 Yak-11
SAM:† some 4 SA-2 sites, 22 launchers.

PARAMILITARY: 13,500.

INTERNAL SECURITY FORCE: (5,000).

PEOPLE'S MILITIA: (3,500).
BORDER POLICE (Ministry of Public Order): (ε5,000).

ARMENIA

GDP	1992ε: $2.1bn: per capita $2,500	
	1993ε: $1.9bn: per capita $2,300	
Growth	1992ε: -46.0%	1993ε: -9.9%
Inflation	1992ε: 729.0%	1993ε: 2,260.0%
Debt[a]	1992: $10.0m	1993: $11.0m
Def exp[b]	1992: $75.0m	
Def bdgt[b]	1993: $69.0m	
	1994: $71.0m	
$1 = d[c]	1992: n.k.	1993: n.k.
	1994: 77	

d = dram

[a] External debt in convertible currencies.
[b] ppp est.
[c] The dram was introduced in November 1993 at a floating exchange rate with convertible currencies.

Population: 3,421,000 (Azeri 3%, Kurd 2%, Russian 2%)

	13–17	*18–22*	*23–32*
Men	163,500	143,000	253,600
Women	154,800	134,800	245,500

TOTAL ARMED FORCES: some 32,700.

Terms of service: conscription, 18 months.
RESERVES: some mobilisation reported, possibly 300,000 with military service within 15 years.

ARMY: some 32,700.

1 Army HQ.
5 MR bde; 2 indep MRR.
1 arty bde; 1 arty regt.
1 MRL regt.
1 ATK regt.
1 tk trg sqn.
1 indep hel sqn.
EQUIPMENT:
MBT: 120 T-72.
AIFV: some 225 BMP-1/-2 (incl variants).
APC: some 108 BTR-60/-70/-80, 75 MT-LB.
TOTAL ARTY: 225:
TOWED ARTY: 122mm: 60 D-30; 152mm: 4 D-1, 31 D-20, 20 2A36.
SP ARTY: 122mm: 10 2S1; 152mm: 32 2S3.
MRL: 122mm: 50 BM-21.
MORTARS: 120mm: 18 M-120.
ATK GUNS: 95: 85mm: D-44; 100mm: T-12.
ATGW: 18 AT-3 *Sagger*, 27 AT-6 *Spiral.*
SAM: SA-2/-3, 54 SA-4, 20 SA-8.
AIRCRAFT: 6 cbt, 5 Su-25, 1 MiG-25.
HELICOPTERS: 8 Mi-2, 2 Mi-9, 7 Mi-8, 13 Mi-24.

PARAMILITARY:

Ministry of Interior: ε1,000; 4 bn: some BMP-1, BTR-70, BTR-152 AFV.

FOREIGN FORCES:

RUSSIA (Group of Russian Forces in the Transcaucasus):
Army: 5,000; 1 MRD, 80 MBT, 190 APC, 100 arty.

AUSTRIA

GDP	1992: OS 2,035.6bn ($185.2bn): per capita $18,400	
	1993: OS 2,109.7bn ($189.4bn): per capita $18,800	
Growth	1992: 1.5%	1993: -0.3%
Inflation	1992: 4.1%	1993: 3.6%
Publ Debt	1992: 55.8%	1993: 57.0%
Def exp	1992: OS 20.1bn ($1.8bn)	
Def bdgt	1992: OS 18.3bn ($1.7bn)	
	1993: OS 19.0bn ($1.6bn)	
	1994ε: OS 18.7bn ($1.6bn)	
$1 = OS	1992: 11.0	1993: 11.6
	1994: 11.7	

OS = Austrian schilling

Population: 7,959,000

	13–17	*18–22*	*23–32*
Men	233,600	257,600	640,800
Women	222,400	246,100	622,600

TOTAL ARMED FORCES (Air Service forms part of the Army):

ACTIVE: some 51,250 (ε20–30,000 conscripts; some 66,000 reservists a year undergo refresher training, a proportion at a time).
Terms of service: 6 months recruit trg, 60 days reservist refresher trg during 15 years (or 8 months trg, no refresher); 60–90 days additional for officers, NCO and specialists.

RESERVES: 119,000 ready (72 hrs) reserves; 960,000 with reserve trg, but no commitment. All ranks to age 50.

ARMY: 44,000 (19,500 conscripts).

3 Corps:

2 each with 1 engr bn, 1 recce, 1 arty regt, 3 Provincial mil comd; 17 inf regt (total).

1 with 3 mech inf bde (1 tk, 1 mech inf, 1 SP arty bn), 1 engr, 1 recce bn, 1 arty regt, 2 Provincial mil comd, 7 inf regt.

1 Provincial mil comd with 1 inf regt; on mob Provincial mil comd convert to bde.

EQUIPMENT:

MBT: 169 M-60A3.

APC: 447 Saurer 4K4E/F (incl variants).

TOWED ARTY: 105mm: 108 IFH (M-2A1); 155mm: 24 M-114.

SP ARTY: 155mm: 56 M-109/-A2.

FORTRESS ARTY: 155mm: 24 SFK M-2.

MRL: 128mm: 18 M-51.

MORTARS: 81mm: 700; 107mm: 100 M-2/M-30; 120mm: 245 M-43.

ATGW: 118 RBS-56 *Bill.*

RCL: 74mm: *Miniman*; 84mm: *Carl Gustav*; 106mm: 446 M-40A1.

ATK GUNS:

SP: 105mm: 234 *Kuerassier* JPz SK.

TOWED: 85mm: 220 M-52/-55.

STATIC: 90mm: some 60 M-47 tk turrets; 105mm: some 200 L7A1 (*Centurion* tk).

AD GUNS: 20mm: 560; 35mm: 74 GDF-002 twin towed; 40mm: 38 M-42A1 twin SP.

MARINE WING (under School of Military Engineering): 2 river patrol craft⟨; 10 unarmed boats.

AIR FORCE: 7,250 (2,400 conscripts); 54 cbt ac, no armed hel.

1 air div HQ; 3 air regt; 3 AD bn.

FGA: 1 regt with 30 SAAB 105Oe.

FIGHTER: 1 regt with 24 J-35Oe.

HELICOPTERS:

RECCE: 11 OH-58B, 12 AB-206A.

TRANSPORT: med: 23 AB-212; **lt**: 8 AB-204 (9 in store).

SAR: 24 A-316 B *Alouette*.

LIAISON: 1 sqn with 2 *Skyvan* 3M, 15 O-1 (10 -A, 5 -E), 11 PC-6B.

TRAINING: 16 PC-7.

AD: 3 bn with 36 20mm, 18 M-65 twin 35mm AA guns; *Super-Bat* and *Skyguard* AD, *Goldhaube*, Selenia MR(S-403) 3-D radar systems.

FORCES ABROAD:

UN AND PEACEKEEPING:

CYPRUS (UNFICYP): 347; 1 inf bn, plus 4 Observers.

EL SALVADOR (ONUSAL): 2 civ pol.

IRAQ/KUWAIT (UNIKOM): 17, incl 6 Observers.

LIBERIA (UNOMIL): 11 Observers.

MIDDLE EAST (UNTSO): 13 Observers.

RWANDA (UNAMIR): 15 Observers.

SYRIA (UNDOF): 461; 1 inf bn.

WESTERN SAHARA (MINURSO): 1 Observer, plus 6 civ pol.

AZERBAIJAN

GDP	1992ε: $4.9bn: per capita $2,700	
	1993ε: $4.4bn: per capita $2,400	
Growth	1992ε: -28.1%	1993ε: -13.3%
Inflation	1992ε: 1,063.0%	1993ε: 920.0%
Debt[a]	1992: $0.0m	1993: $82.0m
Def exp[b]	1992: $125.0m	
Def bdgt[b]	1993: $128.0m	
	1994: $132.0m	
$ = m[c]	1992: n.k.	1993: n.k.
	1994: 393.0	

m = manat

[a] External debt in convertible currencies.
[b] ppp est.
[c] The manat was introduced in August 1992 as a parallel currency to the rouble and made sole legal tender in January 1994.

Population: 7,462,000 (Russian 6%, Armenian 6%, Daghestan 3%)

	13–17	*18–22*	*23–32*
Men	367,100	328,600	608,900
Women	315,200	309,200	596,000

TOTAL ARMED FORCES:

ACTIVE: 56,000 (incl 2,000 MOD staff and centrally controlled units).

Terms of service: 17 months, but can be extended for ground forces.

RESERVES: some mob 560,000 with military service within 15 years.

ARMY: 49,000.

1 tk bde.

10 MR bde (2 with inf units only).

2 MR trg bde.

1 air aslt bde.
3 indep MRR.
2 mtn inf regt.
2 arty bde, 1 MRL, 1 Atk regt.
EQUIPMENT:
MBT: 279: T-72, T-55.
AIFV: 320 BMP-1/-2, BMD.
APC: 70 BTR-60/-70/-80, 410 MT-LB, 22 BTR-D.
TOTAL ARTY: 350:
TOWED ARTY: 122mm: 150 D-30; 152mm: 36 D-20, 24 2A36.
SP ARTY: 122mm: 14 2S1.
COMBINED GUN/MORTAR: 120mm: 36 2S9.
MRL: 122mm: 70 BM-21.
MORTARS: 120mm: 20 PM-38.
SAM: SA-4/-8/-13.

NAVY: ε3,000.
BASE: Baku.
As a member of the CIS, Azerbaijan's naval forces operate under CIS (Russian) control.
About 16 naval units from ex-Sov Caspian Flotilla and Border Guards, incl 1 *Petya-II* FF, 1 *Osa*-II, 2 *Stenka* PFI, 1 *Zhuk* PCI, 3 *Sonya* MSC, 2 *Yevgenya* MSI and about 4 *Polnochny* LSM.

AIR FORCE: 2,000; 48 cbt ac.
AIRCRAFT: 4 sqn with 30 MiG-25, 7 Su-24, 2 Su-17, 3 Su-25, 6 MiG-21, 52 L-29 (trg).
HELICOPTERS: 1 sqn with 7 Mi-2, 10 Mi-8, 6 Mi-24.

PARAMILITARY:
MILITIA (Ministry of Internal Affairs): 20,000+.
POPULAR FRONT (Karabakh People's Defence): ε20,000.

OPPOSITION:
Armed forces of Nagorno-Karabakh: ε20,000 (incl ε8,000 volunteers from Armenia). Eqpt reported incl MBT, APC, arty.

BELARUS

GDP	1992ε: $17.3bn: per capita $6,800	
	1993ε: $16.0bn: per capita $6,300	
Growth	1992ε: -10.6%	1993ε: -10.0%
Inflation	1992ε: 1,016.0%	1993ε: 666.4%
Debt[a]	1992: $181.2m	1993: $1.3bn
Def exp[b]	1992: $944.0m	
Def bdgt[b]	1993: r 51.8bn ($520.0m)	
	1994: r 686.6bn ($430.0m)	
FMA[c,d]	1993: $0.1m (IMET)	
	1994: $0.1m (IMET)	
	1995: $0.1m (IMET)	
$1 = r[e]	1992: n.k.	1993: 6,990
	1994: 9,150	

r = rubel

[a] External debt in convertible currencies.
[b] ppp est.
[c] Excl allocations 1992–94 by the US ($3.4m) and Japan to support nuclear dismantlement under START I.
[d] Costs of Russian Forces in Belarus are included in Russian def exp.
[e] The rubel was introduced in May 1992 as a parallel currency to the Russian rouble.

Population: 10,491,600 (Russian 12%, Polish 4%, Ukrainian 3%)

	13–17	*18–22*	*23–32*
Men	393,500	368,600	698,300
Women	381,000	360,900	704,200

TOTAL ARMED FORCES:
ACTIVE: 92,500 (reducing to 90,000 by 1995) incl about 1,300 MoD staff and 11,100 in centrally controlled units.
Terms of service: 18 months.
RESERVES: some 289,500 with military service within 5 years.

STRATEGIC NUCLEAR FORCES (Russian-controlled forces on Belarus territory):
ICBM: 54:
SS-25 *Sickle* (RS-12m): 54 (mobile, single-warhead msl; 2 bases with regt of 9).

ARMY: 52,500.
MOD tps: 2 MRD (1 trg), 1 ABD, 1 indep AB bde, 1 arty div, 2 arty, 2 MRL regt.
1 rear defence div (reserve inf units only).
1 SSM bde, 1 ATK bde, 1 *Spetsnaz* bde, 2 SAM bde.
3 Corps:
1 with 3 mech, 1 SSM, 1 SAM bde, 1 arty, 1 MRL regt.
1 with 1 mech, 1 SSM, 1 SAM bde, 1 arty, 1 MRL regt.
1 with no manned cbt units.
EQUIPMENT:
MBT: 3,108: 79 T-54, 639 T-55, 291 T-62, 299 T-64, 1,800 T-72.

LIGHT TANKS: 8 PT-76.

AIFV: 2,386: 796 BMP-1, 1,300 BMP-2, 161 BRM, 129 BMD-1.

APC: 1,020: 224 BTR-60, 418 BTR-70, 189 BTR-80, 117 BTR-D, 72 MT-LB.

TOTAL ARTY: 1,584:

TOWED ARTY: 440: 122mm: 190 D-30; 152mm: 6 M-1943 (D-1), 58 D-20, 136 2A65, 50 2A36.

SP ARTY: 588: 122mm: 239 2S1; 152mm: 168 2S3, 120 2S5; 152mm: 13 2S19; 203mm: 48 2S7.

COMBINED GUN/MORTAR: 120mm: 54 2S9.

MRL: 419: 122mm: 275 BM-21, 11 9P138; 130mm: 1 BM-13; 220mm: 84 9P140; 300mm: 48 9A52.

MORTARS: 83: 120mm: 78 2S12, 5 PM-38.

ATGW: 480: AT-4 *Spigot*, AT-5 *Spandrel* (some SP), AT-6 *Spiral* (some SP), AT-7 *Saxhorn.*

SSM: 60 *Scud*, 36 *FROG*/SS-21.

SAM: 350: SA-8/-11/-12/-13.

SURV: SNAR-10.

AIR FORCE: 15,800; 1 air army, 354 cbt ac, 78 attack hel. Average annual flying hours for ftr/FGA aircrew: about 40.

FGA/BOMBERS: 4 Su-17, 42 Su-24, 5 MiG-27.

FGA: 99 Su-25.

FIGHTER: 52 MiG-23, 43 MiG-25, 84 MiG-29, 25 Su-27.

RECCE: 19 MiG-25, 42 Su-24, 5 Yak-28.

HELICOPTER: 4 regt, 4 sqn: 26 Mi-2, 35 Mi-6, 140 Mi-8, 78* Mi-24, 14 Mi-26.

TRANSPORT: 29 Il-76, 6 An-12, 7 An-24, 1 An-26, 1 Tu-134.

AIR DEFENCE: 11,800.

SAM: 200 SA-2/-3/-5/-10.

PARAMILITARY:

BORDER GUARDS (Ministry of Interior): 8,000.

FOREIGN FORCES:

RUSSIA: Air Force; 130 cbt ac, 1 air div.

1 regt with 30 Su-24.

1 hy bbr div; 4 regt with 15 Tu-22M, 50 Tu-22.

1 regt with 20 Tu-22M, 15 Tu-16.

BOSNIA-HERZEGOVINA

GDP[a]	1992ε: $1.8bn: per capita $4,500
Debt	1992: $2.0bn
	1993: $2.9bn
Def exp	1992ε: $850.0m
	1993ε: $876.0m

[a] The civil war in Bosnia has resulted in a war economy. Consequently the standard presentation of economic data is not applicable.

Population: 4,300,000 (Muslim 44%, Serb 31%, Croat 17%)

	13–17	*18–22*	*23–32*
Men	126,800	126,200	247,000
Women	119,600	119,400	234,600

TOTAL ARMED FORCES:

ACTIVE: some 110,000.

RESERVES: some 100,000.

ARMY (BiH): 110,000.

1 'Army' HQ.

6 'Corps' HQ.

Some 78 inf 'bde'.

Some 13 mtn 'bde'.

1 recce bde.

2 arty 'bde'.

9 mot 'bde'.

1 SF 'bde'.

5 territorial def 'bde'.

Some 2 AD regt.

EQUIPMENT:

MBT: ε40 incl T-34, T-55.

APC: ε30.

ARTY: some, incl a few 130mm, 203mm.

MRL: 40+.

MORTARS: 300: 82mm; 120mm.

ATGW: 100 AT-3 *Sagger*, Ch *Red Arrow* (TF-8) reported.

AD GUNS: 20mm, 30mm.

DEPLOYMENT (manpower incl some reserves).

1 Corps: Sarajevo (incl Goradze, Srebenica, Zepa and Mt Igman): up to 40,000 and up to 21 inf, 8 mot, 7 mtn, 1 HVO, 2 arty bde.

2 Corps: Tuzla: up to 10,000 and up to 26 inf, 1 mot, 3 mtn, 2 HVO, 1 engr bde.

3 Corps: Zenica: up to 30,000 and up to 16 inf, 1 armd bde.

4 Corps: Mostar/Konjic: 5,000 plus and up to 5 inf, 1 mtn.

5 Corps: Bihac: up to 20,000 and up to 8 inf (1 HVO), 1 SF bde.

7 Corps: Travnik: 5 inf, 2 mtn bde.
Abdic Faction (Bihac): 2 defected BiH bde, expanded to 6 bde.

OTHER FORCES:

CROAT (Croatian Defence Council (HVO)): ε50,000.
4 op zone (Mostar, Tomislavgrad, Vitez, Orasge).
Some 36 'bde'.
1 mixed arty 'div'.
1 MRL 'div'.
3 'extremist bde'.
1 SF 'bde'.
EQUIPMENT:
MBT: ε75, incl T-34, T-55.
ARTY: ε200.
SAM: SA-7/-14/-16.
HELICOPTERS: 6: Mi-8, *Hughes* MD-500.
SERB (Army of the Serbian Republic of Bosnia and Herzegovina) (SRB: BH): up to 80,000.
7 'Corps' HQ.
8 armd 'bde'.
1 armd regt.
Some 62 inf 'bde'.
1 mech inf 'bde'.
1 mot inf 'bde'.
4 mtn 'bde'.
1 SF 'bde'.
1 arty 'bde'; 1 arty regt.
1 Atk, 1 AD regt.
EQUIPMENT:
MBT: ε330, incl T-34, T-55, M-84, T-72.
APC: 400.
TOWED ARTY: 800: 122mm: D-30, M-1938 (M-30); 130mm: M-46; 152mm: D-20.
SP ARTY: 122mm: 30 2S1.
MRL: 128mm: 70 M-63; 262mm: 6 M-87 *Orkan*.
MORTARS: 120mm.
SSM: *Frog* 7.
AD GUNS: incl 20mm, 23mm incl ZSU 23-4; 30mm: M53/59SP; 57mm: ZSU-57-2; 90mm.
SAM: 18 SA-2, some SA-3/-6/-7b/-8/-9/-14.
AIRCRAFT: some 40 *Jastreb*, G-4 *Super Galeb* and *Orao*, UTVA, An-2, *Kraguj*, *Cessna*.
HELICOPTERS: 12 Mi-8, 18 SA-341 *Gazela*.

DEPLOYMENT:

1 Krajina Corps: Banja Luka: up to 13 inf, 2 armd 'bde'; 1 Atk, 1 AD regt.
2 Krajina Corps: Bihak: 6 inf 'bde'.
3 Krajina Corps: Doboj: up to 13 inf, 2 armd, 1 SF 'bde'.
Tuzla Corps: Bijeljina: up to 8 inf, 1 armd 'bde'.
Drina Corps: 7 inf, 4 mtn, 2 armd 'bde'.
Sarajevo Corps: up to 8 inf, 1 mech, 1 mot, 1 arty 'bde'; 1 arty regt.
Herzegovina Corps: 7 inf, 1 armd 'bde'; 1 armd regt.

FOREIGN FORCES:

UNITED NATIONS (UNPROFOR BH): some 5,000, incl 6 inf bn for Sarajevo. Some 16,300 incl 11 inf bn (some armd recce and engr spt) for aid distribution and 'safe area' protection. See p. 275 for full details.

BULGARIA

GDP[a]	1992:	leva 214.0bn ($20.8bn): per capita $5,100		
	1993:	leva 286.0bn ($20.6bn): per capita $5,000		
Growth	1992:	-5.4%	1993:	-3.5%
Inflation	1992:	79.4%	1993:	63.9%
Debt	1992:	$13.0bn	1993:	$13.2bn
Def exp[a]	1992:	leva 5.8bn ($563.1m)		
	1993:	leva 8.2bn ($589.9m)		
Def bdgt[a]	1993:	leva 8.7bn ($625.9m)		
	1994:	leva 12.9bn ($586.4m)		
FMA	1993:	$0.3m (IMET)		
	1994:	$0.2m (IMET)		
	1995:	$0.5m (IMET)		
$1 = leva	1992:	23.6	1993:	26.0
	1994:	27.0		

[a] ppp est.

Population: 8,435,000 (Turk 8%, Romany 3%, Macedonian 3%)

	13–17	*18–22*	*23–32*
Men	312,100	318,000	578,300
Women	296,500	299,000	545,700

TOTAL ARMED FORCES:

ACTIVE: 101,900 (incl ε51,300 conscripts, about 22,300 centrally controlled, 3,400 MOD staff, but excl some 10,000 construction tps).
Terms of service: 18 months.
RESERVES: 303,000: Army 250,500; Navy (to age 55, officers 60 or 65) 7,500; Air Force (to age 60) 45,000.

ARMY: 51,600 (ε33,300 conscripts).
3 Military Districts/Army HQ.
1 with 1 tk bde.
1 with 1 MRD, 1 Regional Training Centre (RTC), 1 tk bde.
1 with 2 MRD, 2 RTC, 2 tk bde.
Army tps: 4 *Scud*, 1 SS-23, 1 SAM bde, 3 arty, 3 AD arty, 1 SAM regt.
1 AB regt.

EQUIPMENT:
MBT: 1,967: 358 T-34, 1,276 T-55, 333 T-72.
ASSAULT GUN: 124 SU-100.
RECCE: 60 BRDM-1/-2.
AIFV: 114 BMP-23, BMP-30.
APC: 780 BTR-60, 1,085 MT-LB.
TOTAL ARTY: 2,053:
TOWED: 731: 100mm: 16 M-1944 (BS-3); 122mm: 380 M-30, 25 M-1931/37 (A-19); 130mm: 72 M-46; 152mm: 32 M-1937 (ML-20), 206 D-20.
SP: 122mm: 656 2S1.
MRL: 122mm: 222 BM-21.
MORTARS: 444: 120mm: 6 M-38,18 2B11, 61 B-24, 359 *Tundzha* SP.
SSM launchers: 28 *FROG*-7, 36 *Scud*, 8 SS-23.
ATGW: 200 AT-3 *Sagger*.
ATK GUNS: 85mm: 150 D-44; 100mm: 200 T-12.
AD GUNS: 400: 23mm: ZU-23, ZSU-23-4 SP; 57mm: S-60; 85mm: KS-12; 100mm: KS-19.
SAM: 20 SA-3, 27 SA-4, 20 SA-6.

NAVY: ε3,000 (ε2,000 conscripts).
BASES: coastal: Varna (HQ), Atiya, Sozopol, Balchik. Danube: Vidin (HQ).
SUBMARINES: 2 *Pobeda* (Sov *Romeo*)-class with 533mm TT.
FRIGATES: 1 *Smeli* (Sov *Koni*) with 1 x 2 SA-N-4 SAM, 2 x 12 ASW RL; plus 2 x 2 76mm guns.
PATROL AND COASTAL COMBATANTS: 21:
CORVETTES: 7:
4 *Poti* ASW with 2 x ASW RL, 4 x ASTT.
1 *Tarantul II* ASUW with 2 x 2 SS-N-2C *Styx*, 2 x 4 SA-N-5 *Grail* SAM; plus 1 x 76mm gun.
2 *Pauk I* with 1 SA-N-5 SAM, 2 x 5 ASW RL; plus 4 x 406mm TT.
MISSILE CRAFT: 6 *Osa* PFM with 4 x SS-N-2A/B *Styx* SSM.
PATROL, INSHORE: about 8 *Zhuk* PFI.
MINE WARFARE: 28:
MINELAYERS: 10 *Vydra*.
MINE COUNTERMEASURES: 18:
4 *Sonya* MSC.
14 MSI: 4 *Vanya*, 4 *Yevgenya*, 6 *Olya*.
AMPHIBIOUS: 2:
2 Sov *Polnocny* LSM, capacity 150 tps, 6 tk.
SUPPORT AND MISCELLANEOUS: 7:
2 AOT, 2 AGHS, 1 AGI, 1 trg, 1 AT.
NAVAL AVIATION: 10 armed hel.
HELICOPTERS: 1 SAR/ASW sqn with 9 Mi-14 (ASW), 1 Ka-25.

COASTAL ARTY:
2 regt, 20 bty.
GUNS: 100mm: ε150; 130mm: 4 SM-4-1.
SSM: SS-C-1b *Sepal*, SSC-3 *Styx*.

NAVAL GUARD: 3 coy.

AIR FORCE: 21,600 (16,000 conscripts); 294 cbt ac, 44 attack hel. 2 air div, 1 mixed air corps.
FGA: 1 regt with 39 Su-25.
2 regt with 84 MiG-21.
1 regt with 37 MiG-23.
FIGHTER: 4 regt with some 41 MiG-23, 24 MiG-21, 22 MiG-29.
RECCE: 1 regt with 26 MiG-21, 21 Su-22.
TRANSPORT: 1 regt with 2 Tu-134, 3 An-24, 4 An-26, 5 L-410, 3 Yak-40 (VIP).
SURVEY: 1 An-30.
HELICOPTERS: 2 regt with 14 Mi-2, 7 Mi-8, 25 Mi-17, 44 Mi-24 (attack).
TRAINING: 3 trg regt with 74 L-29, 35 L-39.
MISSILES:
ASM: AS-7 *Kerry*.
AAM: AA-2 *Atoll*, AA-7 *Apex*, AA-8 *Aphid*.
SAM: SA-2/-3/-5/-10 (20 sites, some 110 launchers).

PARAMILITARY:
BORDER GUARDS (Ministry of Interior): 12,000; 12 regt, some 50 craft including about 12 Sov PO2 PCI‹.
SECURITY POLICE: 4,000.
RAILWAY AND CONSTRUCTION TROOPS: 18,000.

CROATIA

GDP	1992ε: $18.0bn:	
	per capita $5,200	
	1993: $10.7bn:	
	per capita $4,300	
Growth	1992ε: -20.0%	1993: -42.0%
Inflation	1992ε: 850.0%	1993ε: 1,900.0%
Debt[a]	1992: $3.3bn	1993: $3.8bn
Def bdgt	1993: $975.0m	
	1994ε: $1.0bn	
$1 = kuna	1992: n.k.	1993: n.k.
	1994: 9.0	

k = kuna[b]

[a] External debt in convertible currencies.

[b] The kuna was introduced in May 1994 to replace the Croatian dinar.

Population: 4,754,400 (Serb 12%, Muslim 1%, Slovene 1%)

	13–17	*18–22*	*23–32*
Men	167,000	164,600	334,800
Women	157,400	156,400	322,000

TOTAL ARMED FORCES:

ACTIVE: ε105,000 (65,000 conscripts).
Terms of Service: 10 months.
RESERVES: Army: 180,000; Home Defence: 10,000.

ARMY: ε99,600 (ε65,000 conscripts).

4 op zone (OZ) (Zagreb, Split, Osijek, Gospic).
26 inf 'bde'.
5 mech bde.
1 mixed arty div.
1 AD bde.
1 SF bde (2 SF, 1 mtn, 1 amph, 1 AB bn).
1 engr bn; 3 indep engr coy.
RESERVES: 10 inf bde, 14 Home Def regt.
EQUIPMENT:
MBT: 173: 2 T-34, 150 T-55, 21 M-84.
LIGHT TANKS: 5 PT-76.
RECCE: BRDM-2.
AIFV: 83 M-80.
APC: BTR-40/-50, 9 M-60.
TOTAL ARTY: some 900, incl:
TOWED ARTY: 76mm: ZIS-3; 85mm;105mm: 15 M-56, 58 M-2A1; 122mm: 28 M-1938, 10 D-30; 130mm: 22 M-46; 152mm: 17 D-20, 63 M-84.
SP ARTY: 122mm: 2 2S1.
MRL: 122mm: 5 BM-21; 128mm: 2 M-63; 262mm: M-87 *Orkan* reported.
MORTARS: 82mm; 120mm: 600 M-74/-75, 60 UBM-120.
ATGW: AT-3 *Sagger*, AT-4 *Spigot*.
ATK GUNS: 100mm: 77 T-12.
RL: 90mm: M-79.
AD GUNS: 600+: 14.5mm: ZPU-2/-4; 20mm: BOV-1 SP, M-55; 30mm: M-53/59, BOV-3SP.
SAM: SA-7, SA-9, SA-13, SA-14.

NAVY: 1,100.

BASES: Split, Pula, Sibenik, Ploce.
Minor facilities: Lastovo, Vis.
SUBMARINES: 1 *Una* SSI for SF ops.
PATROL AND COASTAL COMBATANTS: 9:
CORVETTES: 2 Krajl-class with 2 or 4 x2 Saab RBS SSM.
MISSILE CRAFT: 3:
2 *Rade Koncar* PFM with 2 x SS-N-2B *Styx*.
1 *Mitar Acev* (Sov *Osa-I*) PFM with 4 x SS-N-2A.
TORPEDO CRAFT: 2:
2 *Topcider* (Sov *Shershen*) with 4 x 533mm TT.
PATROL: 2:
INSHORE: 2 *Mirna*.
MINE WARFARE: 3:
MINELAYERS: 1: *Cetina* (*Silba*-class), 94 mines. D-3 and D-501 LCT can also lay 100 mines – see amph forces.
MCM: 2:
1 *Vukov Klanac* MHC.
1 UK *Ham* MSI.
AMPHIBIOUS: craft only: 5 D-3/D-501 LCT, 4 LCM and about 3 LCU.
SUPPORT AND MISCELLANEOUS: 5:
1 *Spasilac* salvage, 1 Sov *Moma* survey, 1 AE, 2 tugs.
MARINES: 7 indep inf coy.
COAST DEFENCE: some 16 coast arty bty.

AIR FORCE: ε300; 20 cbt ac, 2 armed hel.

FGA/FIGHTER: 13 MiG-21, 6 Galeb, 1 Orao.
TRANSPORT: 2 An-2, 2 An-26, 5 UTVA.
HELICOPTERS: 15 Mi-8, 2* Mi-24, 1 UH-1.

AIR DEFENCE: 4,000.

No details available.

PARAMILITARY:

POLICE: 40,000 armed.
HOS (military wing of Croatian Party of Rights (HSP)): up to 5,000 reported (deployed in Bosnia).

OTHER FORCES:

ARMY OF THE REPUBLIC OF SERB KRAJINA: 40–50,000.
6 'Corps' HQ (North Dalmatia, Lika, Kordun, Banija, Baranja/East Slavonia, West Slavonia).
Some 27 'bde'.
3 mech bde.
1 arty bde.
1 ATK regt.
1 SF bde.
Irregular Units: Capt Dragan, Arkan's Tiger, White Eagle, Chetniks.
EQUIPMENT:
MBT: ε240: T-34, T-55, M-84.
AIFV: M-80.
APC: ε100, incl M-60P.
TOTAL ARTY: ε500.
ARTY: 76mm: Z1S-3; 105mm: M-56; 122mm: D-30,

M-1931/37 (A-19); 130mm: M-46; 155mm: M-65.
MRL: 14 incl 128mm: M-63.
MORTARS: 81mm; 82mm; 120mm: UBM-52.
ATGW: AT-3 *Sagger* incl SP (BOV-1).
RCL: 82mm: M-60; 105mm: M-65.
ATK GUNS: 100mm: 30 T-12.
AD GUNS: 20mm: M-55/-75; 30mm: M-53/-59; 57mm: ZSU-57-2 SP.
AIRCRAFT: 12 *Galeb*.
HELICOPTERS: 5 SA-341 *Gazella*, 1 Mi-8.

FOREIGN FORCES:

UN (UNPROFOR I): 17,900; 13 inf bn, plus spt units from 15 countries. See p. 275 for full details.

CYPRUS

GDP	1992: £C 3.0bn ($6.7bn): per capita $9,400	
	1993ε: £C 3.3bn ($6.9bn): per capita $9,600	
Growth	1992: 8.5%	1993ε: 0%
Inflation	1992: 6.6%	1993: 4.8%
Publ Debt	1992: 52.5%	1993: 53.0%
Def exp	1993: £C 244.6m ($489.0m)	
Def bdgt	1992: £C 214.8m ($477.1m)	
	1993: £C 249.0m ($518.8m)	
	1994ε: £C 260.4m ($511.0m)	
FMA	1993: $15m (Econ aid)	
	1994: $15m (Econ aid)	
	1995: $15m (Econ aid)	
$1 = £C	1992: 0.5	1993: 0.5
	1994: 0.5	

£C = Cypriot pound

Population: 725,200 (Turkish 18%)

	13–17	*18–22*	*23–32*
Men	28,800	26,600	57,800
Women	26,900	25,100	54,200

TOTAL ARMED FORCES:

ACTIVE: 10,000 (8,700 conscripts; 445 women).
Terms of service: conscription, 26 months, then reserve to age 50 (officers 65).
RESERVES: 88,000: 45,000 first-line (age 20–34); 43,000 second-line (age 35–50).

NATIONAL GUARD: 10,000 (8,700 conscripts).

1 Army, 2 div HQ.
2 bde HQ.
1 armd bde (-).
2 lt inf regt.
1 SF bn.
1 ATK bn.
7 arty bn.

EQUIPMENT:
MBT: 52 AMX-30B-2.
RECCE: 124 EE-9 *Cascavel*, ε36 EE-3 *Jararaca*.
AIFV: 27 VAB-VCI.
APC: 92 *Leonidas*, 116 VAB (incl variants).
TOWED ARTY: 196: 75mm: 4 M-116A1 pack; 76mm: 54 M-42; 88mm: 18 25-pdr; 100mm: 36 M-1944; 105mm: 72 incl M-101, M-56; 155mm: 12 TR F1.
SP: 155mm: 12 F3.
MRL: 128mm: 24 Yug M-63 (YMRL-32).
MORTARS: 278: 81mm: 72 incl SP; 82mm: 80 M-41/-43 some SP; 107mm: 12 M-2; 120mm: 116 RT61.
ATGW: *Milan* (15 on EE-3 *Jararaca*), *HOT* (18 on VAB).
RL: 89mm: 450 M-20.
RCL: 360: 57mm: 216 M-18; 106mm: 144 M-40A1.
AD GUNS: 155: 20mm: M-55; 35mm: 8 GDF-005 with *Skyguard*; 40mm; 94mm: 3.7-in.
SAM: 24 SA-7, 18 *Mistral*.
MARINE: 1 *Salamis* PFI .
AIRCRAFT: 1 BN-2A *Maritime Defender*, 2 PC-9, 1 PA-22.
HELICOPTERS: 2 Bell 206, 2 MD-500, 4 SA-342 *Gazelle* (with *HOT*).

PARAMILITARY:

ARMED POLICE: 3,700; Shorland armd cars.
MARITIME POLICE: 320; 3 PFI: 2 *Evagoras* and 1 *Kinon* PFI .

FOREIGN FORCES:

GREECE: 950 (ELDYK) (Army); 2 inf bn, plus ε1,300 officers/NCO seconded to Greek-Cypriot National Guard.
UNITED KINGDOM (in Sovereign Base Areas): 3,900; Army: 2 inf bn, 1 armd recce sqn; Air Force: 1 hel sqn, plus ac on det.
UNITED NATIONS:
UNFICYP: some 1,200; 3 inf bn (Argentina, Austria, UK).

'TURKISH REPUBLIC OF NORTHERN CYPRUS'

Data presented here represent the *de facto* situation on the island. This in no way implies recognition, or IISS approval.

Def bdgt	1987ε: TL 5.2bn ($6.1m)	
	1988: TL 8.0bn ($5.6m)	
$1 = TL	(1987): 857	(1988): 1,422

TL = Turkish lira

TOTAL ARMED FORCES:

ACTIVE: some 4,000.
Terms of service: conscription, 24 months, then reserve to age 50.
RESERVES: 11,000 first-line; 10,000 second-line; 5,000 third-line.

ARMY:

7 inf bn.
MARITIME: 3 patrol boats.

FOREIGN FORCES:

TURKEY: 30,000; 1 corps, 235 M-48A5 MBT; 57 M-113, 50 M-59 APC; 126 105mm, 36 155mm, 8 203mm towed; 18 105mm, 6 155mm SP; 102 107mm mor, 84 40mm AA guns; 8 ac, 13 hel.

THE CZECH REPUBLIC

GDP	1992ε: Kcs 717.1bn ($25.4bn): per capita $7,200	
	1993ε: Kc 732.7bn ($26.0bn): per capita $7,400	
Growth	1992ε: -7.1%	1993ε: -0.3%
Inflation	1992: 11.1%	1993: 20.8%
Debt	1992: $7.5bn	1993: $8.7bn
Def exp	1993: Kc 22.8bn ($808.5m)	
Def bdgt[a]	1992: [Kcs 27.0bn ($954.0m)]	
	1993: Kc 21.6bn ($765.3m)	
	1994: Kc 22.8bn ($770.3m)	
FMA	1993: $0.5m (IMET)	
	1994: $0.4m (IMET)	
	1995: $0.5m (IMET)	
$1 = Kc, Kcs	1992: 28.3	1993: 28.2
	1994: 29.6	

Kcs = Czechoslovak koruna
Kc = Czech koruna

[a] Data in [ ] refer to former Czechoslovakia.

Population: 10,365,400 (Slovak 4%)

	13–17	*18–22*	*23–32*
Men	416,000	419,200	727,000
Women	403,600	405,100	703,200

TOTAL ARMED FORCES:

ACTIVE: 92,900 (incl 40,400 conscripts, about 6,800 MOD and 23,700 centrally controlled formations/units).
Terms of service: 12 months.

ARMY: 37,400 (21,400 conscripts).

2 Corps HQ.
2 armd div (each 2 tk, 1 mech regt).
2 mech div (each 2 mech, 1 tk regt).
1 mot inf div.
1 mech bde (4 mech bn).
2 arty bde.
2 AD bde.
1 SSM regt.
3 engr bde (incl 1 pontoon).
2 ATK,
1 rapid reaction bn.

EQUIPMENT:
MBT: 1,433: T-54/-55, T-72M.
RECCE: some 182 BRDM, OT-65.
AIFV: 822 BVP-1, BMP-2, BRM-1K.
APC: 837 OT-62A/B, OT-64A/C, OT-90, OT-810.
TOTAL ARTY: 1,418:
TOWED: 753: 100mm: 276 M-53; 122mm: 299 M-1938, 152 D-30, 11 M-1931/37; 130mm: 3 M-46; 152mm: 12 M-1937 (ML-20).
SP: 377: 122mm: 98 2S1; 152mm: 274 *Dana* (M-77); 203mm: 5 2S7.
MRL: 122mm: 168 RM-70.
MORTARS: 120mm: 118; 240mm: 2 2S4.
SSM: 10–14: *FROG*-7, SS-21, *Scud*, SS-23.
ATGW: AT-3 *Sagger*, AT-5 *Spandrel.*
AD GUNS: 30mm: M-53/-59, *Strop* SP; 57mm: S-60.
SAM: SA-7, SA-9/-13.

AIR FORCE: 25,000 (incl AD and 3,900 conscripts); 208 cbt ac (plus 32 MiG-21 in store), 36 attack hel.

Average annual flying hours for FGA/fighter pilots: 50.
FGA: 3 regt: 1 with 35 Su-22; 1 with 31 MiG-23 BN, 27 MiG-21; 1 with 25 Su-25.
FIGHTER: 1 regt, 1 sqn: 1 regt with 32 MiG-23, 10 MiG-29; 1 sqn with 26 MiG-21.
TRANSPORT: 2 regt with **ac**: 8 L-410, 4 An-24, 1 Tu-134, 1 Tu-154; **hel:** 2 Mi-2, 8 Mi-8, 1 Mi-9, 6 Mi-17.
1 regt with **ac:** 10 L-410, 1 Il-14, 1 An-30, 1 An-12, 4 An-26; **hel:** 2 Mi-17.
HELICOPTERS: 2 regt (assault/tpt/attack).
1 regt with 8 Mi-2, 2 Mi-8, 11 Mi-17, 19* Mi-24.
1 regt with 7 Mi-2, 13 Mi-17, 17* Mi-24.
TRAINING: 1 regt with *22 MiG-21 U/MF, 10 L-29, 13 L-39C, 3 L-59 (L-39MS).
AAM: AA-2 *Atoll*, AA-7 *Apex*, AA-8 *Aphid*, AA-10

Alamo, AA-11 *Archer*.
AD: 2 AD div (7 AD units), SA-2, SA-3, SA-5, SA-6.

FORCES ABROAD:
UN AND PEACEKEEPING:
CROATIA (UNPROFOR I): 918; 1 inf bn, 23 Observers.
LIBERIA (UNOMIL): 15 Observers.
MOZAMBIQUE (ONUMOZ): 20 Observers.

PARAMILITARY:
BORDER GUARDS: 4,000 (1,000 conscripts).
INTERNAL SECURITY FORCES: 1,600 (1,500 conscripts).
CIVIL DEFENCE TROOPS: 5,800 (3,500 conscripts).

ESTONIA

GDP	1992ε: kn 21.3bn ($1.7bn): per capita $6,300	
	1993ε: kn 22.4bn ($1.7bn): per capita $6,300	
Growth	1992ε: -14.4%	1993ε: -2.0%
Inflation	1992ε: 969.0%	1993: 87.6%
Debt[a]	1992: $51.2m	1993: $100.0m
Def exp	1992ε: kn 413.0m ($33.0m)	
	1993ε: kn 1,016.4m ($77.0m)	
Def bdgt	1993ε: kn 124.4m ($10.0m)	
	1994ε: kn 264.8m ($19.9m)	
	1995ε: kn 1.0bn ($75.8m)	
FMA[b]	1993: $0.1m (IMET)	
	1994: $0.1m (IMET)	
	1995: $0.2m (IMET)	
$1 = kn[c]	1992: 12.5	1993: 13.2
	1994: 13.2	

kn = kroon

[a] External debt in convertible currencies.
[b] FMA also received 1992–94 from Germany, Finland, Sweden.
[c] Estonia introduced the kroon in June 1992 to replace the Russian rouble at a fixed exchange rate of 8kn = 1 DM.

Population: 1,623,000 (Russian 30%, Ukrainian 3%)

	13–17	*18–22*	*23–32*
Men	59,600	57,800	114,900
Women	57,600	56,000	110,100

TOTAL ARMED FORCES:
ACTIVE: 2,500.
Terms of service: 12 months.
RESERVES: some 6,000 militia.

ARMY: 2,500.
3 inf, 1 guard, 1 AD bn.
RESERVES:
Militia: 16 Territorial Defence League units.
EQUIPMENT: incl 3 BRDM-2 recce, 41 BTR-60/-70/-80 APC.

PARAMILITARY:
BORDER GUARD (Ministry of Interior): 2,000 (1,200 conscripts); 1 regt.
MARITIME BORDER GUARD: also fulfils task of Coast Guard.
BASE: Tallinn.
PATROL CRAFT: some 12:
2 *Kondor*-I and 1 Finnish PCC.
1 Dk *Maagen* PCI.
2 Sov *Zhuk*, 3 Finnish *Koskelo*-Class and 3 Sov Coast Guard PCI‹.
SUPPORT AND MISCELLANEOUS: 2: 1 tpt, 1 AGOR.

FOREIGN FORCES:
RUSSIA: ε2,000; Army: elm 1 MRD, (31 MBT, 240 ACV, 84 arty/MRL/mor).

FINLAND

GDP	1992: m 475.7bn ($106.2bn): per capita $16,000	
	1993: m 471.4bn ($106.2bn): per capita $16,000	
Growth	1992: -3.8%	1993: -2.6%
Inflation	1992: 2.6%	1993: 2.2%
Publ debt	1992: 44.0%	1993: 51.7%
Def exp	1992: m 10.2bn ($2.3bn)	
	1993: m 9.2bn ($2.1bn)	
Def bdgt	1993: m 9.0bn ($2.0bn)	
	1994: m 8.5bn ($1.6bn)	
$1 = m	1992: 4.48	1993: 5.71
	1994: 5.41	

m = markka

Population: 5,092,900

	13–17	18–22	23–32
Men	164,800	161,400	360,700
Women	156,100	153,100	344,500

TOTAL ARMED FORCES:

ACTIVE: 31,200 (23,900 conscripts).

Terms of service: 8–11 months (11 months for officers, NCOs and soldiers with special duties). Some 30,000 a year do conscript service.

RESERVES (all services): some 700,000; some 30,000 reservists a year do refresher trg: total obligation 40 days (75 for NCO, 100 for officers) between conscript service and age 50 (NCO and officers to age 60).

Total strength on mob some 500,000, with 300,000 in general forces (bde etc) and 200,000 in local defence forces (Army 460,000, Navy 12,000, Air Force 30,000), plus 200,000 unallocated as replacements etc.

ARMY: 25,700 (21,600 conscripts).

3 Military comd; 12 Military Provinces.
1 armd trg bde (1 armd, 1 mech inf, 1 ATK bn, 1 arty regt, 1 AA bty).
8 inf trg bde (each 3 inf bn; 3 with 1 arty regt, 1 with 1 arty bn).
2 indep inf bn.
1 arty bde.
Coast arty: 2 regt; 3 indep bn (1 mobile).
4 AD regt (incl 1 SAM bn with SAM-79).
2 engr bn.
(All units have a primary trg role.)

RESERVES:
2 armd bde (3 armd, 1 arty, 1 AA bn).
10 *Jaeger* bde (each 4 *Jaeger*, 2 arty, 1 AA bn).
14 inf bde (each 4 inf, 2 arty bn).
1 coast bde.
Some 50 indep bn.
200 local defence units.

EQUIPMENT:
MBT: 70 T-55M, 160 T-72.
AIFV: 110 BMP-1, 110 BMP-2.
APC: 110 BTR-60, 310 XA-180 *Sisu*, 220 MT-LB.
TOWED ARTY: 105mm: 252 H 61-37; 122mm: 276 H 63 (D-30); 152mm: 72 H 55 (D-20), 47 H 88-40, H 88-37 (ML-20), H 38 (M-10); 155mm: 36 M-74 (K-83).
SP ARTY: 122mm: 50 PsH 74 (2S1); 152mm: 18 *Telak* 91 (2S5).
COAST ARTY: 100mm: D-10T (tank turrets); 122mm: M-60; 130mm: 170 M-54; (static).
COAST SSM: 5 RBS-15.
MRL: 122mm: Rak H 76 (BM-21), Rak H 89 (RM-70).
MORTARS: 81mm: 880; 120mm: 614.
ATGW: 24 M-82 (AT-4 *Spigot*), 12 M-83 (BGM-71D *TOW* 2), M-82M (AT-5 *Spandrel*).
RL: 112mm: *APILAS*.
RCL: 55mm: M-55; 66mm: 66 KES, 75 (M-72A3); 95mm: 100 SM-58-61.
AD GUNS: 23mm: 100+ ZU-23; 30mm; 35mm: GDF-005, *Marksman* GDF-005 SP; 57mm: 12 S-60 towed, 12 ZSU-57-2 SP.
SAM: SAM-78 (SA-7), SAM-79 (SA-3), SAM-86 (SA-16), 20 SAM-90 (*Crotale* NG).

NAVY: 2,500 (1,000 conscripts).

BASES: Upinniemi (Helsinki), Turku.
4 functional sqn (missile, patrol, two mine warfare). Approx 50% of units kept fully manned; others are in short-notice storage, rotated regularly.

PATROL AND COASTAL COMBATANTS: 21:
CORVETTES: 2 *Turunmaa* with 1 x 120mm gun, 2 x 5 ASW RL.
MISSILE CRAFT: 10:
4 *Helsinki* PFM with 4 x 2 MTO-85 (Sw RBS-15SF) SSM.
2 *Tuima* (Sov *Osa-II*) with 4 MTO-66 (Sov SS-N-2B) SSM.
4 *Rauma* PFM with 2 x 2 and 2 x 1 MTO-85 (Sw RBS-15SF) SSM.
PATROL CRAFT, INSHORE: 9:
2 *Rihtniemi* with 2 ASW RL.
2 *Ruissalo* with 2 ASW RL.
5 *Nuoli* PFI .
MINE WARFARE: 12:
MINELAYERS: 6:
2 *Hämeenmaa*, 150–200 mines, plus 1 x 6 MATRA *Mistral* SAM.
1 *Pohjanmaa*, 100–150 mines; plus 1 x 120mm gun and 2 x 5 ASW RL
2 *Pansio* aux minelayer, 50 mines.
1 *Tuima* (ex-PFM), 20 mines.
MINE COUNTERMEASURES: 6 *Kuha* MSI (plus 7 *Kiiski*-class minesweeping boats).
AMPHIBIOUS: craft only: 3 *Kampela* LCU tpt, 3 *Kala* LCU.
SUPPORT AND MISCELLANEOUS: 14:
4 *Valas* coastal tpt (can be used for minelaying).
Plus about 10 civilian-manned ships:
1 *Aranda* AGOR (Ministry of Trade control).
9 icebreakers (Board of Navigation control).

AIR FORCE: 3,000 (1,300 conscripts); 110 cbt ac, no armed hel.

3 AD areas: 3 fighter wings.

FIGHTER: 3 wings:
1 with 15 MiG-21bis; 10 *Hawk* Mk 51 and 51A.
2 with 39 J-35, 20 *Hawk* Mk 51 and 51A.
OCU: 4* MiG-21U/UM, 5* SAAB SK-35C.
RECCE: some *Hawk* Mk 51 and MiG-21T (incl in ftr sqn).
SURVEY: 3 *Learjet* 35A (survey, ECM trg, target-towing).
TRANSPORT: 1 **ac** sqn with 3 F-27; 1 **hel** flt with 2 Hughes 500D, 7 Mi-8 (tpt/SAR).
TRAINING: 17 *Hawk** Mk 51, 28 L-70 *Vinka*.
LIAISON: 15 Piper (9 *Cherokee Arrow*, 6 *Chieftain*), 10 L-90 *Redigo*.
AAM: AA-2 *Atoll*, AA-8, AIM-9 *Sidewinder*, RB-27, RB-28 (*Falcon*).

FORCES ABROAD:

UN AND PEACEKEEPING:
CROATIA (UNPROFOR I): 44; guard unit.
CYPRUS (UNFICYP): 1.
INDIA/PAKISTAN (UNMOGIP): 7 Observers.
IRAQ/KUWAIT (UNIKOM): 6.
LEBANON (UNIFIL): 526; 1 inf bn.
MACEDONIA (UNPROFOR M): 222; elm inf bn 12 Observers.
MIDDLE EAST (UNTSO): 17 Observers.
MOZAMBIQUE (ONUMOZ): 5 civ pol.
SYRIA (UNDOF): 2.

PARAMILITARY:

FRONTIER GUARD (Ministry of Interior): 4,400 (on mob 24,000); 4 frontier, 3 Coast Guard districts, 1 air comd; 2 offshore, 3 coastal, 7 inshore patrol craft. **Hel:** 3 AS-332, 6 AB-206L, 3 AB-412; **ac:** 1 PA-NAVAJO.

GEORGIA

GDP	1992ε: $3.5bn:	
	per capita $2,500	
	1993ε: $2.3bn:	
	per capita $1,700	
Growth	1992ε: -43.4%	1993ε: -35.0%
Inflation	1992ε: 768.7%	1993ε: 1,294.3%
Debt[a]	1992: $84.8m	1993: $89.6m
Def exp[b]	1992: $85.0m	
Def bdgt[b]	1993: $87.0m	
	1994: $88.0m	
$1 = r[c]	1992: n.k.	1993: 98,819
	1994: 230,000	

r = Russian rouble

[a] External debt in convertible currencies.
[b] ppp est.
[c] A coupon currency was introduced in April 1993 and became sole legal tender in August 1993.

Population: 5,682,000 (Russian 6%, Armenian 8%, Ossetian 3%)

	13–17	*18–22*	*23–32*
Men	220,100	212,200	404,700
Women	212,000	204,100	397,600

TOTAL ARMED FORCES: not known.

Terms of service: conscription, 2 years.
RESERVES: possibly up to 250,000 with military service in last 15 years.

ARMY: up to 20,000 planned, 10,000 probable.

2 Corps HQ.
Some 5 bde (incl border guard, plus trg centre).
EQUIPMENT:
MBT: 50 T-55, T-72.
AIFV/APC: 70.
TOTAL ARTY: 60.
SAM: 45 SA-2/-3, 65 SA-4.

NAVY: it is understood that Georgia intends to establish its own Coast Guard in due course. Some units of the Black Sea Fleet have been allocated to Georgia, but have not yet been transferred.

BASE: Poti.

AIR FORCE: 200.

Annual flying hours for Su-25 pilots: 20–30.
Some 15 Su-25 ac, some 15 Mi-2, Mi-6, Mi-8 and Mi-24 hel.

OPPOSITION FORCES:

ABKHAZIA: 4,000; T-55 MBT, ACV, arty.
SOUTH OSSETIA: no details known.

FOREIGN FORCES:

RUSSIA (Transcaucasus Group of Forces): Army: 20,000: 2 MRD, (230 MBT, 300 ACV, 220 arty/MRL/mor. Air Force: 1 composite regt. Some 35 tpt ac and hel incl An-12, An-26 and Mi-8.
PEACEKEEPING: ε2,500; 1 AB regt, 2 MR bn (Russia).
UNITED NATIONS:
UNOMIG: some 21 military observers.

HUNGARY

GDP	1992ε: f 2,805.0bn ($35.5bn): per capita $6,000	
	1993ε: f 3,320.0bn ($35.7bn): per capita $6,100	
Growth	1992: -5.0%	1993ε: -2.0%
Inflation	1992: 23.0%	1993: 22.4%
Debt	1992: $21.4bn	1993: $24.6bn
Def exp	1992: f 64.5bn ($816.8m)	
	1993: f 64.5bn ($702.2m)	
Def bdgt	1993: f 56.9bn ($720.2m)	
	1994: f 58.5bn ($636.6m)	
FMA	1993: $1.0m (FMF, IMET)	
	1994: $0.6m (IMET)	
	1995: $0.7m (IMET)	
$1 = f	1992: 79.0	1993: 91.9
	1994: 103.0	

f = forint

Population: 10,434,000 (Romany 4%, German 3%, Slovak 1%, Romanian 1%)

	13–17	*18–22*	*23–32*
Men	379,700	395,300	683,100
Women	362,000	374,500	650,000

TOTAL ARMED FORCES:

ACTIVE: 74,500 (53,400 conscripts).
Terms of service: 12 months.
RESERVES: 195,000: Army 183,600; Air Force 11,400 (to age 50).

LAND FORCES: 56,500 (41,100 conscripts).

4 Military District Corps/HQ:
- 1 with 2 tk, 2 mech bde, 1 MRL, 1 ATK, 1 AD arty, 1 engr regt.
- 1 with 1 tk, 3 mech, 2 arty, 1 ATK bde, 1 ATK, 1 engr regt.
- 1 with 4 mech, 1 arty, 1 AD arty, 1 engr bde, 1 attack hel, 1engr regt, 1 air mobile bn (SF).
- 1 (Budapest) with 1 guard, 1 engr regt, 1 rivercraft unit.

RESERVES:
1 Home Defence bde.

EQUIPMENT:
MBT: 1,191: 5 T-34, 34 T-54, 1,014 T-55 (323 in store), 138 T-72.
RECCE: 161 FUG D-442.
AIFV: 502 BMP-1, BRM-1K.
APC: 1,143: 148 BTR-80, 965 PSZH D-944, 30 MT-LB (plus some 836 'look-alike' types).
TOTAL ARTY: 991:
TOWED: 566: 122mm: 230 M-1938 (M-30) (147 in store); 152mm: 34 M-1943 (D-1), 302 D-20.
SP: 151: 122mm: 151 2S1 (3 in store).
MRL: 122mm: 56 BM-21.
MORTARS: 218: 120mm: 2 2B11, 216 M-120.
ATGW: 329: 117 AT-3 *Sagger*, 30 AT-4 *Spigot* (incl BRDM-2 SP), 182 AT-5 *Spandrel.*
ATK GUNS: 85mm: 69 D-44; 100mm: 101 MT-12.
AD GUNS: 23mm: 14 ZSU-23-4 SP; 57mm: 144 S-60.
SAM: 240 SA-7, 54 SA-14.
HELICOPTERS:
ATTACK: 39 Mi-24.
SP: 33 Mi-2. 58 Mi-8/-17.
RIVERCRAFT:
MCMV: 6 *Nestin* MSI (riverine); some 45 mine disposal/patrol boats (about 20 in reserve).

AIR FORCE: 18,000 (12,300 conscripts).

AIR DEFENCE COMD: 171 cbt ac.
FIGHTER: 3 regt with 110 MiG-21bis/MF, 12 MiG-23MF, 28 MiG-29.
RECCE: 1 sqn with 14* Su-22.
TRANSPORT: 2 An-24, 9 An-26, 3 L-410.
TRAINING: 7 *MiG-21U, 20 L-39, 12 Lak-52.
AAM: AA-2 *Atoll.*
AD: some 16 sites, 1 bde, 2 regt with 82 SA-2/-3/-5, 18 SA-4, 40 SA-6, 28 SA-9, 4 SA-13.

FORCES ABROAD:

UN AND PEACEKEEPING:
ANGOLA (UNAVEM II): 4 Observers.
CYPRUS (UNFICYP): 4 Observers.
GEORGIA (UNOMIG): 5 Observers.
IRAQ/KUWAIT (UNIKOM): 6 Observers.
MOZAMBIQUE (ONUMOZ): 23 Observers, plus 20 civ pol.
UGANDA/RWANDA (UNOMUR): 4 Observers.

PARAMILITARY:

BORDER GUARDS (Ministry of Interior): 730; 24 APC.
INTERNAL SECURITY FORCES: 1,500.

IRELAND

GDP	1992: £I 29.4bn ($50.2bn): per capita $12,100	
	1993ε: £I 31.1bn ($52.9bn): per capita $12,600	
Growth	1992: 4.9%	1993: 2.7%
Inflation	1992: 3.1%	1993: 1.4%
Publ debt	1992: 93.8%	1993: 92.1%
Def exp	1992: £I 377.8m ($640.3m)	
Def bdgt	1992: £I 328.5m ($560.2m)	
	1993: £I 339.0m ($529.7m)	
	1994ε: £I 343.1m ($504.5m)	
$1 = £I	1992: 0.59	1993: 0.68
	1994: 0.79	

£I = Irish pound

Population: 3,539,000

	13–17	*18–22*	*23–32*
Men	166,000	165,600	279,600
Women	157,200	155,400	264,400

TOTAL ARMED FORCES:

ACTIVE: 13,000 (incl 100 women).
Terms of service: voluntary, 3-year terms to age 60, officers 56–65.
RESERVES: 16,150 (obligation to age 60, officers 57–65). Army: first-line 1,000, second-line 14,800; Navy: 350.

ARMY: 11,200.

4 Territorial Commands.
1 inf force (2 inf bn).
4 inf bde:
2 with 2 inf bn, 1 with 3, all with 1 fd arty regt, 1 cav recce sqn, 1 engr coy; 1 with 2 inf bn, 1 armd recce sqn, 1 fd arty bty.
Army tps: 1 lt tk sqn, 1 AD regt, 1 Ranger coy.
(Total units: 11 inf bn; 1 UNIFIL bn *ad hoc* with elm from other bn, 1 tk sqn, 4 recce sqn (1 armd), 3 fd arty regt (each of 2 bty); 1 indep bty, 1 AD regt (1 regular, 3 reserve bty), 3 fd engr coy, 1 Ranger coy.)
RESERVES:
4 Army Gp (garrisons), 18 inf bn, 6 fd arty regt, 3 cav sqn, 3 engr sqn, 3 AA bty.
EQUIPMENT:
LIGHT TANKS: 14 *Scorpion*.
RECCE: 19 AML-90, 32 AML-60.
APC: 60 Panhard VTT/M3, 10 *Timoney*, 2 A-180 *Sisu*.
TOWED ARTY: 88mm: 48 25-pdr; 105mm: 12 lt.
MORTARS: 81mm: 400; 120mm: 72.
ATGW: 21 *Milan*.
RCL: 84mm: 444 *Carl Gustav*; 90mm: 96 PV-1110.
AD GUNS: 40mm: 24 L/60, 2 L/70.
SAM: 7 RBS-70.

NAVY: 1,000.

BASE: Cork.
PATROL AND COASTAL COMBATANTS: 7:
7 PCO:
1 *Eithne* with 1 *Dauphin* hel.
3 *Emer*, 1 *Deirdre*.
2 *Orla* (UK *Peacock*).

AIR FORCE: 800; 16 cbt ac, 15 armed hel.

3 wings (1 trg).
COIN: 1 sqn with 5 CM-170-2 *Super Magister*.
COIN/TRAINING: 1 sqn with 7 SF-260WE, 1 SF-260 MC **ac**, 2 SA-342L trg **hel**.
MR: 2 *Super King Air* 200, 1 CN 235.
TRANSPORT: 1 HS-125, 1 *Super King Air* 200, 1 *Gulfstream* IV.
LIAISON: 1 sqn with 6 Reims Cessna F-172H, 1 F-172K.
HELICOPTERS: 3 sqn:
1 Army spt with 8 SA-316B (*Alouette*).
1 Navy spt with 2 SA-365 (*Dauphin*).
1 SAR with 3 SA-365.

FORCES ABROAD:

UN AND PEACEKEEPING:
ANGOLA (UNAVEM II): 2 Observers.
CROATIA (UNPROFOR I): 9 Observers, plus 20 civ pol.
CYPRUS (UNFICYP): 30, incl 4 Observers, plus 14 civ pol.
EL SALVADOR (ONUSAL): 2 Observers.
IRAQ/KUWAIT (UNIKOM): 6 Observers.
LEBANON (UNIFIL): 660; 1 bn; 4 AML-90 armd cars, 10 *Sisu* APC, 4 120mm mor.
MIDDLE EAST (UNTSO): 17 Observers.
MOZAMBIQUE (ONUMOZ): 20 civ pol.
SOMALIA (UNOSOM: 93, plus 5 civ pol.
WESTERN SAHARA (MINURSO): 5 Observers.

LATVIA

GDP	1992ε: $1.9bn:	
	per capita $4,700	
	1993ε: $1.6bn:	
	per capita $3,900	
Growth	1992ε: -33.8%	1993ε: -19.9%
Inflation	1992: 950.0%	1993: 109.0%
Debt[a]	1992: $60.6m	1993: $100.0m
Def exp	1992ε: $47.0m	
Def bdgt	1993ε: $48.0m	
	1994ε: $51.0m	
FMA[b]	1993: $0.1m (IMET)	
	1994: $0.1m (IMET)	
$1 = lats[c]	1992: n.k.	1993: 0.68
	1994: 0.59	

L = lats

[a] External debt in convertible currencies.
[b] FMA received from Germany, Denmark and other Nordic countries, 1992–94.
[c] Latvia introduced the Latvian rouble (Lr) in May 1992 as an interim measure until its currency, the lats, could be introduced. The lats was introduced in June 1993 ($1 = 0.68 lats) at a floating exchange rate with convertible currencies.

Population: 2,622,000 (Russian 34%, Belarussian 5%, Ukrainian 3%, Polish 2%).

	13–17	*18–22*	*23–32*
Men	99,000	92,700	192,200
Women	96,000	90,600	187,600

TOTAL ARMED FORCES:
ACTIVE: 6,850 (incl Border Guard).
Terms of service: 18 months.
RESERVES: 18,000 Home Guard.

ARMY: 1,500.
1 inf bn.
1 recce bn.
1 engr bn.
RESERVES: Home Guard: 5 bde each of 5–7 bn.
EQUIPMENT: incl 2 BRDM-2 recce, 13 M-42 APC.

NAVY: 900 (incl 350 coastal defence).
BASES: Liepaja, Riga.
PATROL CRAFT: some 14, incl 2 *Kondor*-II, 3 *Osa*-I, 5-Sw Coast Guard PCI⟨ and 4 converted fishing boats⟨.
1 coast def bn (350).

AIR FORCE: 150.
2 An-2, 2 L-410 **ac**; 5 Mi-2, Mi-8 **hel**.

PARAMILITARY:
BORDER GUARD: 4,300; 1 bde (9 bn).

FOREIGN FORCES:
RUSSIA: 9,000; Army: 1 MR bde, (51 MBT, 65 AIFV, 30 arty/MRL/mor); Air Force: 1 composite regt: **ac:** An-12, An-26; **hel:** Mi-8. All to have withdrawn by 31 August 1994.

LITHUANIA

GDP	1992ε: $3.4m:	
	per capita: $3,700	
	1993ε: $2.9m:	
	per capita: $3,200	
Growth	1992ε: -37.7%	1993ε: -17.0%
Inflation	1992ε: 1,020.0%	1993: 410.2%
Debt[a]	1992: $37.7m	1993: $100.0m
Def exp	1992ε: $55.2m	
Def bdgt	1993ε: L 336.7m ($86.3m)	
	1994ε: L 375.8m ($96.4m)	
FMA[b]	1993: $0.1m (IMET)	
	1994: $0.1m (IMET)	
$1 = L[c]	1992: n.k.	1993: 3.9
	1994: 4.0	

L = litas

[a] External debt in convertible currencies.
[b] FMA also received from Germany, Denmark and other Nordic countries.
[c] The litas was introduced in June1993 at a floating exchange rate with convertible currencies.

Population: 3,833,000 (Russian 9%, Polish 8%, Belarussian 2%)

	13–17	*18–22*	*23–32*
Men	140,600	138,100	293,600
Women	136,900	135,200	285,800

TOTAL ARMED FORCES:
ACTIVE: ε8,900 (incl Border Guard).
Terms of service: 12 months.
RESERVES: 12,000.

ARMY: 4,300 (incl conscripts).
Rapid reaction bde (7 bn).
EQUIPMENT:
APC: 15 BTR-60.
RESERVES:
Volunteer Home Guard Service.

NAVY: ε350.

Lithuania is currently creating a Coast Guard to be modelled on the US Coast Guard.
BASE: Klaipeda.
FRIGATES: 2 ex-Sov 2 *Grisha-III*, with 2 x 12 ASW RL, 4 x 533mm TT.
PATROL AND COASTAL COMBATANTS: about 7: 1 ex-Sw Coast Guard PCI, plus 2 ex-Sov *Turya* PHT (no TT), 1 ex-GDR *Kondor*-I and some converted civilian craft (some promised, but not yet delivered).

AIR FORCE: 250: no cbt ac.

4 L-39, 2 L-410,24 AN-2 **ac**; 3 Mi-8 **hel**.

PARAMILITARY:

BORDER GUARD: 4,000.

'Former Yugoslav Republic of': MACEDONIA

GDP	1992ε: $3.0bn:	
	per capita $4,000	
	1993ε: $1.9bn:	
	per capita $2,600	
Growth	1992ε: -140.0%	1993ε: -37.0%
Inflation	1992ε: 9,000%	1993: 349.8%
Debt	1992: $600.0m	1993: $665.0m
Def bdgt	1993: $30.0m	1994: $30.0m
$1 = denar	1992: n.k.	1993: n.k.
	1994: n.k.	

Population: 2,214,000 (Albanian 30%, Turkish 5%, Romany 2%, Serb 2%, Muslim 2%).

	13–17	*18–22*	*23–32*
Men	64,400	64,100	125,600
Women	60,800	60,700	119,200

TOTAL ARMED FORCES:

ACTIVE: 10,400 (8,000 conscripts).
RESERVES: 100,000 planned.

ARMY: 10,400.

3 Corps HQ (cadre).
3 indep bde (planned).
EQUIPMENT: some T-34 tks reported, former Territorial Defence Force: mor, RCL, AD guns, man-portable SAM.

AIR FORCE: 50; no ac, only hel planned.

PARAMILITARY:

POLICE: 7,500 (some 4,500 armed).

FOREIGN FORCES:

UN AND PEACEKEEPING:
USA: 500; 1 inf bn, 3 UH-60 hel.
FINLAND/NORWAY/SWEDEN: 438; 1 inf bn.

MALTA

GDP	1992: LM 872.1m ($2.7bn):	
	per capita: $6,500	
	1993ε: LM 1,102.9m ($2.9bn):	
	per capita $6,900	
Growth	1992: 4.3%	1993ε: 3.8%
Inflation	1992: 1.6%	1993: 4.1%
Debt	1992: $603.3m	1993: $637.6m
Def exp	1992: LM 8.6m ($27.0m)	
Def bdgt	1992: LM 9.6m ($30.2m)	
	1993: LM 8.8m ($23.2m)	
	1994: LM 10.3m ($25.8m)	
$1 = LM	1992: 0.32	1993: 0.38
	1994: 0.40	

LM = Maltese lira

Population: 367,000

	13–17	*18–22*	*23–32*
Men	14,300	12,700	27,500
Women	13,400	11,900	26,300

TOTAL ARMED FORCES:

ACTIVE: 1,850.

'ARMED FORCES OF MALTA': 1,850.
Comd HQ, spt tps.
No. 1 Regt (inf bn) with 3 rifle, 1 spt coy.
No. 2 Regt (composite regt):
- 1 air sqn with 3 SA-316B, 2 NH-369M Hughes, 1 AB-206A, 4 AB-47G2 **hel** and 5 O–1 (*Bird Dog*) **ac**.
- 1 maritime sqn (200) with 2 ex-GDR *Kondor-II* PCC, 4 PCI⟨, plus boats.
- 1 AD bty; 14.5mm: 50 ZPU-4; 40mm: 40 Bofors.

No. 3 Regt (Depot Regt) with:
- 1 engr sqn.
- 1 workshop, 1 ordnance, 1 airport coy.

FOREIGN FORCES:

ITALY: 16; Air Force, hel 1 AB-212.

MOLDOVA

GDP	1992ε: $4.2bn:	
	per capita $3,900	
	1993ε: $4.1bn:	
	per capita $3,800	
Growth	1992ε: -21.3%	1993ε: -4.0%
Inflation	1992ε: 941.0%	1993ε: 1,576.3%
Debt[a]	1992: $37.5m	1993: $200.0m
Def exp[b]	1992: $45.0m	
Def bdgt[b]	1993: $48.0m	
	1994: $51.0m	
FMA	1994: $0.1m (IMET)	
	1995: $0.1m (IMET	
$1 = L[c]	1992: n.k.	1993: 3.64
	1994: 3.95	

L = leu

[a] External debt in convertible currencies.
[b] ppp est.
[c] The Moldovan leu was introduced in November 1993 in place of the coupon. The Trans-Dniestr region continues to use the pre-1993 Russian rouble and coupon.

Population: 4,472,000 (Ukrainian 14%, Russian 13%, Gaguaz 4%, Bulgarian 2%, Jewish 2%)

	13–17	*18–22*	*23–32*
Men	195,700	177,500	295,000
Women	217,100	157,100	268,800

TOTAL ARMED FORCES: 11,100.
Terms of service: up to 18 months.
RESERVES: some 100,000 with military service within last 5 years.

ARMY: 9,800.
3 MR bde. 1 arty bde.
1 recce/assault bn.
EQUIPMENT:
AIFV: 56 BMD.
APC: 11 BTR-80, 11 BTR-D, 2 BTR-60PB, 23 TAB-71, 30 MT-LB plus 67 'look-alikes'.
TOWED ARTY: 122mm: 18 M-30; 152mm: 32 D-20, 21 2A36.
COMBINED GUN/MORTAR: 120mm: 9 2S9.
MRL: 220mm: 28 9P140 *Uragan.*
MORTARS: 82mm: 54; 120mm: 30 M-120.
ATGW: 70 AT-4 *Spigot*, 19 AT-5 *Spandral*, 27 AT-6 *Spiral.*
RCL: 73mm: SPG-9.
ATK GUNS: 100mm: 45 MT-12.
AD GUNS: 23mm: 30 ZU-23; 57mm: 12 S-60.

AIR FORCE: 1,300 (incl AD).
1 ftr regt with 31 MiG-29. 1 hel sqn with 8 Mi-8.
5 tpt ac incl An-72.
SAM: 1 bde with 25 SA-3/-5.

PARAMILITARY:
INTERNAL TROOPS (Ministry of Interior): 2,500.
OPON (riot police) (Ministry of Interior): 900.

OPPOSITION FORCES:
Dniestr: 5,000; incl Republican Guard (Dniestr bn), Delta bn, ε1,000 Cossacks.

FOREIGN FORCES:
RUSSIA (14th Army): ε9,200. 1 army HQ, 1 MRD, 1 tk bn, 1 arty regt, 1 AA bde (120 MBT, 180 ACV, 130 arty/MRL/mors) (in Dniestr).
PEACEKEEPING: 6 AB bn (Russia), 3 inf bn (Moldova), 3 bn (Dniestr).

POLAND

GDP	1992: z 1,138,508.0bn ($83.1bn):	
	per capita $4,900	
	1993: z 1,556,000.0bn ($89.2bn):	
	per capita $5,200	
Growth	1992: 1.5%	1993: 4.0%
Inflation	1992: 45.3%	1993: 36.9%
Debt	1992: $47.1bn	1993: $46.8bn
Def exp	1992: z 26,236.0bn ($1.9bn)	
	1993: z 39,803.0bn ($2.2bn)	
Def bdgt	1992: z 25,643.5bn ($1.9bn)	
	1993: z 38,465.0bn ($2.1bn)	
	1994: z 47,856.0bn ($2.2bn)	
FMA	1993: $0.6m (IMET)	
	1994: $0.7m (IMET)	
	1995: $0.7m (IMET)	
$1 = z	1992: 13,626	1993: 18,115
	1994: 22,488	

z = zloty

Population: 38,814,400 (German 1.0%, Ukrainian 1.0%, Belarussian 1.0%)

	13–17	*18–22*	*23–32*
Men	1,658,200	1,474,600	2,678,400
Women	1,587,100	1,413,000	2,554,200

TOTAL ARMED FORCES:
ACTIVE: 283,600 (160,000 conscripts).

Terms of service: all services 18 months.
RESERVES: 465,500: Army 375,000; Navy 20,500 (to age 50); Air Force 70,000 (to age 60).

ARMY: 185,900 (incl 105,000 conscripts, 2,250 centrally controlled staffs, 26,800 trg, 20,500 log units and 3,100 Coast Defence).

4 Military Districts/Army HQ:
1 (Pomerania) with 2 mech div, 1 coast def, 1 arty, 1 engr bde, 1 *Scud,* 1 SA-6 regt.
1 (Silesia) with 3 mech div, 1 armed cav div, 2 arty, 2 engr, 1 SA-4 bde, 2 *Scud,* 1 SA-6 regt.
1 (Warsaw) with 3 mech div, 1 arty, 1 engr bde.
1 (Krakow) with 1 mech div, 1 armd, 1 air aslt, 1 podhale rifle bde, 1 mech regt.
Div tps: 8 SA-6/-8 regt.
RESERVES: 1 mob mech div.
EQUIPMENT:
MBT: 2,110: 1,330 T-55, 780 T-72.
RECCE: 510 BRDM-2.
AIFV: 1,406 BMP-1, 62 BMP-2.
APC: 130 OT-64 plus some 693 'look-alike' types.
TOTAL ARTY: 1,880:
TOWED: 566: 122mm: 406 M-1938 (M-30); 152mm: 160 D-20.
SP: 635: 122mm: 516 2S1; 152mm: 111 *Dana* (M-77); 203mm: 8 2S7.
MRL: 261: 122mm: 231 BM-21, 30 RM-70.
MORTARS: 120mm: 418 M-120.
SSM: launchers: 40 *FROG.*
ATGW: 404: 264 AT-3 *Sagger,* 115 AT-4 *Spigot,* 18 AT-5 *Spandrel,* 7 AT-6 *Spiral.*
ATK GUNS: 85mm: 711 D-44.
AD GUNS: 978: 23mm: ZU-23-2, ZSU-23-4 SP; 57mm: S-60.
SAM: 1,280: SA-6/-7/-8/-9/-13.

NAVY: 19,000 (incl 3,000 Naval Aviation, 10,300 conscripts).

BASES: Gdynia, Hel, Swinoujscie; Kolobrzeg (border/coast guard).
SUBMARINES: 3:
1 *Orzel* SS (Sov *Kilo*) with 533mm TT.
2 *Wilk* (Sov *Foxtrot*) with 533mm TT.
PRINCIPAL SURFACE COMBATANTS: 2:
DESTROYERS: 1 *Warszawa* DDG (Sov mod *Kashin*) with 2 x 2 SA-N-1 *Goa* SAM, 4 x SS-N-2C *Styx* SSM, 5 x 533mm TT, 2 x ASW RL.
FRIGATES: 1 *Kaszub* with 2 x ASW RL, 4 x 533mm TT, 76mm gun.
PATROL AND COASTAL COMBATANTS: 32:
CORVETTES: 4 *Gornik* (Sov *Tarantul I*) with 2 x 2 SS-N-2C *Styx* SSM.
MISSILE CRAFT: 7 Sov *Osa*-I PFM with 4 SS-N-2A SSM.
PATROL: 21:
COASTAL: 2 *Sassnitz.*
INSHORE: 8 *Obluze* PCI, 11 *Pilica* PCI(.
MINE WARFARE: 24:
MINELAYERS: none, but submarines, *Krogulec* MSC and *Lublin* LSM have capability.
MINE COUNTERMEASURES: 24:
6 *Krogulec* MSC.
15 *Goplo* (*Notec*) MSI.
1 *Mamry* (*Notec*) MHI.
2 *Leniwka* MSI.
AMPHIBIOUS: 5:
5 *Lublin* LSM, capacity 135 tps, 9 tk.
Plus craft: 3 *Deba* LCU.
(None of the above are employed in amph role.)
SUPPORT AND MISCELLANEOUS: 17:
1 cmd ship, 2 AGI, 4 spt tankers, 3 survey, 3 trg, 2 research, 2 salvage.

NAVAL AVIATION: (3,000).

35 cbt ac, 11 armed hel.
2 regt, 2 sqn.
FIGHTER: 1 regt, 35 MiG-21 BIS/U.
1 special naval regt with 14 TS-11, 7 An-2.
1 ASW/SAR sqn with 5 Mi-2, 11 Mi-14 (ASW), 3 Mi-14 (SAR).
1 sqn SAR/liaison sqn: 2 An-28, 6 W-3 Sokol.

COAST DEFENCE: (3,100, incl in Army total).

6 arty bn with M-1937 152mm.
3 SSM bn with SS-C-2B.

AIR FORCE: 78,700 (incl AD tps, 44,700 conscripts); 398 cbt ac (plus 49 in store for sale), 30 attack hel.

2 air div:
FGA: 4 regt with 15 Su-20, 103 Su-22.
FIGHTER: 3 Air Defence Corps: 7 regt with 207 MiG-21/U; 37 MiG-23MF; 12 MiG-29U.
RECCE: 24 MiG-21R/U.
TRANSPORT: 2 regt with **ac:** 10 An-2, 1 An-12, 10 An-26, 10 Yak-40, 1 Tu-154, 2 Il-14; **hel:** 4 Mi-8, 3 Mi-17, 7 W-3.
HELICOPTERS: 2 attack regt: 30 Mi-24 (attack), 40 Mi-2URP, 1 tpt hel regt with 35 Mi-8, 3 Mi-17, 5 W-3.
TRAINING: 205 TS-11 *Iskra,* 5 PZL I-22 *Iryda,* 20 PZL-130 *Orlik.*
IN STORE: 6 MiG-17, 40 MiG-21, 3 Su-20.
AAM: AA-2 *Atoll,* AA-8 *Aphid.*

ASM: AS-7 *Kerry*.
SAM: 4 bde; 1 indep regt with 50 sites with about 232 SA-2/-3/-5.

FORCES ABROAD:

UN AND PEACEKEEPING:
CROATIA (UNPROFOR I): 1,035; 1 inf bn, 20 Observers, plus 29 civ pol.
FORMER YUGOSLAVIA: 2 Observers (CSCE, EC).
GEORGIA (UNOMIG): 2 Observers (incl 1 CSCE).
IRAQ/KUWAIT (UNIKOM): 6 Observers.
KOREA (NNSC): staff.
LEBANON (UNIFIL): 567; 1 inf bn, mil hospital.
RWANDA (UNAMIR): 4 Observers.
SYRIA (UNDOF): 357; 1 inf bn.
WESTERN SAHARA (MINURSO): 2 Observers.

PARAMILITARY:

BORDER GUARDS (Ministry of Interior): 16,000; 14 Provincial Comd: 14 units.
MARITIME BORDER GUARD: about 28 patrol craft: 2 PCC, 9 PCI and 17 PCI‹.
PREVENTION UNITS OF POLICE (OPP): 7,400 (1,400 conscripts).

ROMANIA

GDP	1992:	lei 5,982.3bn ($38.8bn): per capita $2,800		
	1993:	lei 18,835.2bn ($39.8bn): per capita $2,900		
Growth	1992:	-13.6%	1993:	0%
Inflation	1992:	198.5%	1993:	295.0%
Debt	1992:	$3.4bn	1993:	$3.5bn
Def exp	1992:	lei 262.3bn ($1.7bn)		
Def bdgt	1993:	lei 474.2bn ($1.0bn)		
	1994:	lei 1,260.3bn ($1.1bn)		
FMA	1994:	$0.3m (IMET)		
	1995:	$0.2m (IMET)		
$1 = lei	1992:	308.0	1993:	760.1
	1994:	1,657.2		

Population: 23,177,000 (Hungarian 9%)

	13–17	*18–22*	*23–32*
Men	922,800	941,500	1,689,600
Women	881,200	900,200	1,624,400

TOTAL ARMED FORCES:

ACTIVE: 230,500 (incl 125,000 conscripts, 15,300 MOD staff and 8,300 centrally controlled units).
Terms of service: Army, Air Force: 12 months; Navy: 18 months.
RESERVES: 427,000: Army 400,000; Navy 6,000; Air Force 21,000.

ARMY: 160,500 (105,000 conscripts).

4 Army Areas:
- 1 with 1 TD, 1 mech div, 1 mtn bde.
- 1 with 2 mech div, 2 mtn, 1 AD bde, 1 arty, 1 ATK regt.
- 1 with 2 mech bde, 1 tk, 1 mtn, 1 AD bde, 2 arty, 1 ATK regt.
- 1 with 1 TD, 2 mech div, 2 mtn, 1 mech, 1 AD bde, 1 arty, 1 ATK regt.

MOD tps: 3 AB bde (Air Force) 1 gd bde.
Land Force tps: 2 *Scud*, 2 arty bde; 2 AA regt.

EQUIPMENT:
MBT: 2,395: 686 T-34, 822 T-55, 30 T-72, 632 TR-85, 225 TR-580.
ASSAULT GUN: 251: 185 SU-76, 66 SU-100.
RECCE: 139 BRDM-2, 8 TAB-80.
AIFV: 178 MLI-84.
APC: 2,272: 168 TAB-77, 422 TABC-79, 1,597 TAB-71, 85 MLVM, plus 980 'look-alikes'.
TOTAL ARTY: 3,138:
TOWED: 1,412: 100mm: 133 Skoda (various models); 105mm: 74 Schneider; 122mm: 440 M-1938 (M-30), 12 M-1931/37 (A-19); 130mm: 110 Gun 82; 150mm: 127 Skoda (Model 1934), 6 Ceh (Model 1937); 152mm: 84 D-20, 89 Gun-How 85, 60 Model 1938, 277 Model 81.
SP: 48: 122mm: 6 2S1, 42 Model 89.
MRL: 384: 122mm: 116 APR-21, 268 APR-40.
MORTARS: 1,294: 120mm: 672 M-120, 622 Model 1982.
SSM: launchers: 13 *Scud*, 12 *FROG*.
ATGW: 534: AT-1 *Snapper*, AT-3 *Sagger* (incl BRDM-2).
ATK GUNS: 1,450: 57mm: M-1943; 85mm: D-44; 100mm: 829 Gun 77, 75 Gun 75.
AD GUNS: 1,118: 30mm; 37mm; 57mm; 85mm; 100mm.
SAM: 62 SA-6/-7.

NAVY: ε19,000 (incl 8,000 Naval Infantry and ε10,000 conscripts).

1 maritime div, 1 patrol boat bde, 1 river bde, 1 maritime/river bde.
BASES: Coastal: Mangalia, Constanţa; Danube: Braila, Giurgiu, Tulcea.
SUBMARINE: 1 Sov *Kilo* SS with 533mm TT.
PRINCIPAL SURFACE COMBATANTS: 6:

DESTROYER: 1 *Marasesti* (ex-*Muntenia*) DDG with 4 x 2 SS-N-2C *Styx* SSM, plus SA-N-5 *Grail* SAM, 2 IAR-316 hel, 2 x 3 533mm TT.
FRIGATES: 5: 4 *Tetal* with 2 x ASW RL, 4 x ASTT, 1 improved *Tetal* with 2 x ASW RL, 4 x ASTT, plus 1 SA-316 hel.
PATROL AND COASTAL COMBATANTS: 82:
CORVETTES: 6:
3 Sov *Poti* ASW with 2 x ASW RL, 3 x 533mm TT.
3 *Tarantul I* with 2 x 2 SS-N-2C *Styx*, 1 x 4 SA-N-5 *Grail* SAM; plus 1 x 76mm gun.
MISSILE CRAFT: 6 Sov *Osa*-I PFM with 4 x SS-N-2A *Styx*.
TORPEDO: 34:
12 *Epitrop* PFT with 4 x 533mm TT.
22 Ch *Huchuan* PHT with 2 x 533mm TT.
PATROL: 36:
OFFSHORE: 4 *Democratia* (GDR M-40) PCO.
INSHORE: 8: 4 Ch *Shanghai* PFI, 4 Ch *Huchuan*.
RIVERINE: 24: some 6 *Brutar* with 1 x 100mm gun, 18‹.
MINE WARFARE: 34:
MINELAYERS: 2 *Cosar*, capacity 100 mines.
MINE COUNTERMEASURES: 32:
4 *Musca* MSC.
3 T.301 MSI (plus some 9 non-op).
25 VD141 MSI‹.
SUPPORT AND MISCELLANEOUS: 10:
2 *Constanta* log spt with 1 *Alouette* hel, 3 spt tankers, 2 AGOR, 1 trg, 2 tugs.
HELICOPTERS: 2 1AR-316.

NAVAL INFANTRY (Marines): (8,000).
2 inf, 1 tk, 1 arty regt, 1 recce bn.
1 indep inf bn.
EQUIPMENT:
MBT: 173 TR-580.
ASSAULT GUN: 18 SU-76.
APC: 145 TAB-71, 25 TABC-79 plus 84 'look-alikes'.
TOTAL ARTY: 230:
TOWED ARTY: 100mm: 54 Gun 77; 122mm: 36 M-1938 (M-30); 152mm: 36 Model 81.
MRL: 122mm: 18 APR-21, 18 APR-40.
MORTARS: 120mm: 37 Model 1982, 31 M-120.

COASTAL DEFENCE (1,000): HQ Constanta
4 sectors:
4 coastal arty bty with 32 130mm.
10 AA arty bty: 3 with 18 30mm; 5 with 30 37mm; 2 with 12 57mm.

AIR FORCE: 27,400 (10,000 conscripts); 382 cbt ac, 37 armed hel.

Air Force comd, plus 2 air div: 7 cbt regt.
FGA: 3 regt with 10 MiG-17, 75 IAR-93, 14 IAR-99, 43 MiG-15, 47 MiG-21.
FIGHTER: 4 regt with 123 MiG-21, 40 MiG-23, 18 MiG-29.
RECCE: 2 sqn: 1 with 14 Il-28 (recce/ECM), 1 with 12* MiG-21.
TRANSPORT: 1 regt with 9 An-24, 14 An-26, 2 Il-18, 2 Boeing 707, 2 Rombac 1-11, 10 1AR-316B, 7 Mi-8.
SURVEY: 3 An-30.
HELICOPTERS: 5 regt plus 4 sqn with 74 IAR-316B, 79 IAR-330-H, 22 Mi-8, 4 SA-365N.
TRAINING: ac: 45 L-29, 12 L-39, 2 MiG-15, 2 MiG-17; **hel:** 28* IAR-316, 9* IAR-330, 3 Mi-8, 2 Mi-17.
AAM: AA-2 *Atoll*, AA-7 *Apex*.
AD: 1 div: 20 SAM sites with 120 SA-2.

FORCES ABROAD:

UN AND PEACEKEEPING:
KUWAIT (UNIKOM): 7 Observers.
SOMALIA (UNOSOM): 231.

PARAMILITARY:

BORDER GUARDS (Ministry of Interior): 23,800 (incl conscripts: 6 bde, 7 naval gp; 20 Ch *Shanghai* II PFI).
GENDARMERIE (Ministry of Interior): 10,000; 8 bde; some APC.
SECURITY GUARD (Ministry of Interior): 38,300.

SLOVAKIA

GDP	1992ε: Kcs 346.0 bn ($12.2bn): per capita $5,600	
	1993ε: Ks 359.0bn ($12.0bn): per capita $5,500	
Growth	1992ε: -7.0%	1993ε: -4.7%
Inflation	1992: 10.2%	1993: 23.1%
Debt	1992: $2.3bn	1993: $2.9bn
Def bdgt	1993: Ks 8.2bn ($284.3m)	
	1994: Ks 10.4bn ($315.2m)	
FMA	1993: $0.4m (IMET)	
	1994: $0.2m (IMET)	
	1995: $0.4m (IMET)	
$ = Kcs, Ks	1992: 28.3	1993: 30.0
	1994: 33.0	

Ks = Slovak koruna
Kcs = Czechoslovak koruna

Population: 5,520,000 (Hungarian 11%, Romany 5%, Czech 1%)

	13–17	*18–22*	*23–32*
Men	221,000	223,000	387,000
Women	215,000	216,000	374,000

TOTAL ARMED FORCES:

ACTIVE: 47,000.
Terms of service: 18 months.

ARMY: 33,000.

1 Command HQ. 1 mech inf div.
1 TD. 1 arty bde.

EQUIPMENT:
MBT: 912 T-72M, T-54/-55.
RECCE: 129 BRDM, 90 OT-65.
AIFV: 476: BVP-1, BMP-2, BPZV, BRM-1K.
APC: 567: OT-90, 476 OT-64A/C.
TOTAL ARTY: 808:
TOWED: 297: 100mm: M-53; 122mm: M-1931/37 (A-19), M-1938, D-30.
SP: 189: 122mm 2S1; 152mm: *Dana* (M-77).
MRL: 243: 122mm: RM-70; 130mm: RM-130 (M-51).
MORTARS: 79: 120mm; 240mm: 2S4.
SSM: 9 *FROG*-7, SS-21, *Scud*, SS-23.
ATGW: AT-3 *Sagger*, AT-5 *Spandrel*.
AD GUNS: 286: 30mm: M-53/-59, *Strop* SP; 57mm: S-60.
SAM: 437: SA-7, SA-9/-13.

AIR FORCE: 14,000; 146 cbt ac, 19 attack hel.

FGA: 41, incl Su-22, Su-25.
FIGHTER: 87 MiG-21, 10 MiG-29.
RECCE: 8 MiG-21 RF.
TRANSPORT: 16, incl An-12, Tu-134, Tu-154, An-24/-26, L410M.
HELICOPTERS:
ATTACK: 19 Mi-24.
ASSAULT TPT: 26, incl Mi-8, Mi-17.
TRAINING: some 15 L-29, 25 L-39, 4 MiG-21 U/MF.
IN STORE: about 30 incl MiG-21, Su-7.
AAM: AA-2 *Atoll*, AA-7 *Apex*, AA-8 *Aphid*.
AD: SA-2, SA-6.

FORCES ABROAD:

UN AND PEACEKEEPING:

ANGOLA (UNAVEM II): 5 Observers.
CROATIA (UNPROFOR I): 557; 1 engr bn.
LIBERIA (UNOMIL): 10 Observers.
UGANDA/RWANDA (UNOMUR): 5 Observers.

PARAMILITARY:

BORDER GUARDS: 600.
INTERNAL SECURITY FORCES: 250.
CIVIL DEFENCE TROOPS: 3,100.

SLOVENIA

GDP	1992ε: t 510.4bn ($11.6bn): per capita $6,200	
	1993ε: t 1,435bn ($12.0bn): per capita $6,400	
Growth	1992ε: -6.0%	1993: 1.0%
Inflation:	1992: 150.0%	1993: 23.0%
Debt	1992: $1.2bn	1993: $1.8bn
Def exp	1992ε: t 15.0bn ($340.9m)	
Def bdgt	1993: t 21.2bn ($194.9m)	
	1994: t 24.6bn ($226.3m)	
FMA	1993: $0.1m (IMET)	
	1994: $0.1m (IMET)	
	1995: $0.1m (IMET)	
$1 = t	1992: 44.0	1993: 108.7
	1994: 123.2	

t = tolar

Population 1,988,300 (Croat 3%, Serb 2%, Muslim 1%)

	13–17	*18–22*	*23–32*
Men	77,100	74,900	146,100
Women	71,200	70,300	141,800

TOTAL ARMED FORCES:

ACTIVE: 8,100.
Terms of service: 7 months.
RESERVES: 70,000 (incl 47,000 first-line reserves).

ARMY: 8,000 (4,500 conscripts).

7 Military Districts; 27 Military Regions.
7 inf 'bde'.
1 SAM 'bde'.
1 hel 'bde'.
3 indep mech bn.
RESERVES: 1 special bde, 2 indep mech bn, 1 arty bty, 1 coast def det, 1 atk det.
EQUIPMENT:
MBT: 30 M-84, 27 T-55.
RECCE: 6 BRDM-2.
AIFV/APC: 45, incl 26 M-80.
MORTARS: 45.
SAM: 9 SA-9.
Plus arty, RCL, AD guns and manportable SAM.

AIR FORCE: 100; **hel:** 1 *Gazelle* (armed), 1 AB-109, 2 B-412; **ac:** 1 UTVA-66 (trg), 3 UTVA-75 (trg).
SAM: 50 *Strela.*

MARITIME ELEMENT: 35 (plus 460 reservists).
BASE: Koper.
2 PCI‹.

PARAMILITARY:

POLICE: 4,500 armed (plus 5,000 reserve); hel: 2 AB-206 Jet Ranger, 1 AB-109A, 1 AB-212, 1 AB-412.

SWEDEN

GDP	1992:	Skr 1,439.8bn ($240.0bn): per capita $17,600		
	1993:	Skr 1,449.5bn ($242.1bn): per capita $17,500		
Growth	1992:	-1.9%	1993:	-1.7%
Inflation	1992:	2.5%	1993:	4.5%
Publ Debt	1992:	52.9%	1993:	67.6%
Def exp	1992:	Skr 36.3bn ($6.2bn)		
Def bdgt	1992:	Skr 37.8bn ($6.5bn)		
	1993:	Skr 37.8bn ($5.2bn)		
	1994:	Skr 37.2bn ($4.8bn)		
$1 = Skr	1992:	5.8	1993:	7.8
	1994:	7.7		

Skr = Swedish kronor

Population: 8,781,000

	13–17	*18–22*	*23–32*
Men	253,000	283,700	619,200
Women	238,800	270,400	593,600

TOTAL ARMED FORCES:

ACTIVE: 64,000 (36,600 conscripts).
Terms of service: Army and Navy 7–15 months; Air Force 8–12 months.
RESERVES (obligation to age 47):[a] 729,000: Army (incl Local Defence and Home Guard) 586,000; Navy 66,000; Air Force 77,000.

[a] Each year some 100,000 reservists carry out refresher trg; length of trg depends on rank (officers up to 31 days, NCO and specialists, 24 days, others 17 days). Commitment is 5 exercises during reserve service period, plus mob call-outs.

ARMY: 43,500 (27,000 conscripts).
3 Military comd; 26 defence districts.

PEACE ESTABLISHMENT:
38 armd, cav, inf, arty, AA, engr, sig, spt trg units (local defence, cadre for mob, basic conscript plus refresher trg).
WAR ESTABLISHMENT: (630,000 on mob).
Field Army: (280,000).
3 armd bde.
2 mech bde (incl *Gotland* bde).
6 inf, 5 *Norrland* bde.
100 armd, inf, arty and AA arty bn.
1 avn bn.
6 arty avn pl.
Local Defence Units: (250,000).
60 bn, 400 indep coy.
Home Guard: (100,000), incl inf, arty, static arty, AD.
EQUIPMENT:
MBT: 338 *Centurion*, 289 Strv-103B.
LIGHT TANKS: 211 Ikv-91.
AIFV: 505 Pbv-302.
TOWED ARTY: 105mm: 489 Type-40; 155mm: 201 FH-77A.
SP ARTY: 155mm: 26 BK-1A.
MORTARS: 81mm: 1,000; 120mm: ε600.
ATGW: RB-55 (*TOW*, incl Pvrbv 551 SP), RB-56 *Bill.*
RL: 84mm: AT-4.
RCL: 84mm: *Carl Gustav*; 90mm: PV-1110.
AD GUNS: 40mm: 600.
SAM: RBS-70 (incl Lvrbv SP), RB-77 (*Improved HAWK*).
SURV: *Green Archer* (mor).
HELICOPTERS: 20 Hkp-9A ATK, 16 Hkp-3 tpt, 25 Hkp-5B trg, 19 Hkp-6A utility.

NAVY: ε9,000 (incl Coast Defence, 320 Naval Air and ε4,100 conscripts).
BASES: Muskö, Karlskrona, Härnösand, Göteborg (spt only).
SUBMARINES: 12:
4 *Västergötland* with TP-617 HWT and TP-613 and TP-43.
1 modernised *Näcken* (AIP) with TP-613 and TP-42, 2 *Näcken*, 5 *Sjöormen*, with TP-613 and TP-42.
PATROL AND COASTAL COMBATANTS: 41:
MISSILE CRAFT: 34 PFM:
4 *Göteborg* with 4 x 2 RBS-15 SSM; plus 4 x 400mm TT, 4 x ASW mor.
2 *Stockholm* with 4 x 2 RBS-15 SSM (or up to 4 additional 533 TT); plus 2 x 533mm, 4 x 400mm TT, 4 x ASW mor.
16 *Hugin* with 6 RB-12 (No *Penguin*) SSM; plus 4 ASW mor.
12 *Norrköping* with 4 x 2 RBS-15 SSM or up to 6 x 533mm TT.

PATROL: 7:
1 PCI, 6 PCI‹.
MINE WARFARE: 29:
MINELAYERS: 3:
1 *Carlskrona* (200 mines), trg.
2 *Älvsborg* (200 mines).
(Mines can be laid by all SS classes.)
MINE COUNTERMEASURES: 26:
1 *Utö* MCMV spt.
7 *Landsort* MCC.
3 *Arkö* MSC.
10 MSI, 5 MSI‹.
AMPHIBIOUS: craft only: 12 LCM.
SUPPORT AND MISCELLANEOUS: 12:
1 AGI, 1 sub rescue/salvage ship, 1 survey, 6 icebreakers, 2 tugs, 1 SES PCI (trials).

COAST DEFENCE:
6 coast arty bde: 12 mobile, 53 static units, incl 2 amph defence bn, arty, barrier bn, minelayer sqn.
EQUIPMENT:
GUNS: 40mm, incl L/70 AA, 75mm, 120mm incl CD-80 *Karin* (mobile); 75mm, 120mm *Ersta* (static).
MORTARS: 81mm.
SSM: RBS-17 *Hellfire*, RBS-08A, RBS-15KA, RB-52.
MINELAYERS: 9 inshore, 16 inshore‹.
PATROL CRAFT: 18 PCI .
AMPHIBIOUS: 10 LCM, 80 LCU, about 60 LCA.

NAVAL AIR: (320); 1 cbt ac, 10 armed hel.
ASW: 1 C-212 ac.
HELICOPTERS: 3 sqn with 10 Hkp-4B/C (ASW), 10 Hkp-6 liaison.

AIR FORCE: 11,500 (5,500 conscripts); 390 cbt ac (plus 91 in store), no armed hel.
1 attack staff.
3 Air Commands.
FGA: 4 sqn:
4 with 74 SAAB AJ-37 (plus 13 in store); incl 1 (OCU) with 15 SAAB SK-37 (plus 15 in store).
FIGHTER: 10 sqn:
2 with 44 SAAB J-35 (plus 21 in store), 10 SAAB SK-35C.
8 with 137 SAAB JA-37 (plus 42 in store).
RECCE: 2 sqn with *50 SAAB SH/SF-37.
ECM: 2 *Caravelle*, 13 SAAB 32E.
TRANSPORT: 1 sqn with 8 C-130E/H, 3 *King Air* 200, 2 *Metro* III (VIP), 13 SK-60D/E, 1 SAAB 340B.
TRAINING: 25 SAAB J-32B/D/E (13 -E ECM trg; 5 -D target-towing 7 -B), 60 *SK-60B/C (also have lt attack/recce role), 71 SK-61.
SAR: 10 Hkp, 10 *Super Puma*.
3 Hkp 9B (Bo-105 CBS).
UTILITY: 7 Hkp-3.
AAM: RB-24 (AIM-9B/3 *Sidewinder*), RB-27 (*Improved Falcon*), RB-28 (*Falcon*), RB-71 (*Skyflash*), RB-74 AIM 9L (*Sidewinder*).
ASM: RB-04E, RB-05A, RB-15F, RB-75 (*Maverick*).
AD: semi-automatic control and surveillance system, *Stril* 60, coordinates all AD components.

FORCES ABROAD:
UN AND PEACEKEEPING:
ANGOLA (UNAVEM II): 3 Observers.
BOSNIA (UNPROFOR BH): 1,150; 1 armd inf bn.
CROATIA (UNPROFOR I): 114; HQ coy, plus 5 Observers, 6 mil police, 35 civ pol.
EL SALVADOR (ONUSAL): 2 Observers, 1 civ pol.
GEORGIA (UNMOGIP): 3 Observers.
INDIA/PAKISTAN (UNMOGIP): 3 Observers.
IRAQ/KUWAIT (UNIKOM): 6 Observers.
KOREA (NNSC): 6 Staff.
LEBANON (UNIFIL): 495; 1 log bn.
MACEDONIA (UNPROFOR M): 121; elm Nordic bn.
MIDDLE EAST (UNTSO): 17 Observers.
MOZAMBIQUE (ONUMOZ): 19 Observers, plus 45 civ pol.
SOMALIA (UNOSOM): 3 civ pol.

PARAMILITARY:
COAST GUARD: (600); 1 *Gotland* PCO and 1 KBV-171 PCC (fishery protection), some 65 PCI; Air Arm: 3 C-212 MR, 1 Cessna 337G, 1 402C ac.
CIVIL DEFENCE: shelters for 6,300,000. All between age 16–25 liable for civil defence duty.
VOLUNTARY AUXILIARY ORGANISATIONS: some 35,000 volunteers from ten voluntary auxiliary organisations are provided for army units.

SWITZERLAND

GDP	1992:	fr 339.5bn ($241.4bn): per capita $22,100		
	1993:	fr 346.1bn ($246.0bn): per capita $22,300		
Growth	1992:	-0.1%	1993:	-0.7%
Inflation	1992:	4.1%	1993:	3.4%
Publ Debt	1992:	16.3%	1993:	18.8%
Def bdgt	1992:	fr 5.2bn ($3.7bn)		
	1993:	fr 5.6bn ($3.8bn)		
	1994:	fr 6.2bn ($4.2bn)		

$1 = fr	1992: 1.41	1993: 1.48
	1994: 1.41	

fr = Swiss franc

Population: 7,045,000

	13–17	18–22	23–32
Men	191,000	212,800	516,800
Women	181,500	203,600	502,200

TOTAL ARMED FORCES (Air Corps forms part of the Army):

ACTIVE: about 1,800 regular, plus recruits (2 intakes (1 of 11,000, 1 of 17,000) each for 17 weeks only).

Terms of service: 17 weeks compulsory recruit trg at age 19–20, followed by 8 refresher trg courses of 3 weeks over a 12-year period between ages 20–32 for *Auszug* (call-out), 39 days over a 10-year period (33–42) for *Landwehr* (militia). Some 390,000 attend trg each year.

RESERVES (all services): 625,000.

ARMY: 565,000 on mob.

3 fd corps, each 1 mech, 2 inf div, 1 territorial zone, 2–3 border bde.

1 mtn corps with 3 mtn div (each 3 inf, 1 arty regt), 6 fortress, 3 redoubt bde.

Corps tps:

Each corps with 1 inf, 1 cyclist, 1 engr regt, some arty (fd), indep inf (mtn), 1 hel sqn.

Army tps:

1 inf, 3 engr regt, 2 sigs (EW) bn.

EQUIPMENT:

MBT: 812: 117 Pz-61, 186 Pz-68, 39 Pz-68/75, 90 Pz-68/88, 380 Pz-87 (*Leopard* 2).

AIFV: 192 M-63/-73, 252 M-63/-89 (all M-113 with 20mm).

APC: 805 M-63/-73 (M-113) incl variants, some *Piranha*.

TOWED ARTY: 105mm: 216 Model-35, 341 Model-46.

SP ARTY: 155mm: 540 PzHb-66/-74 (M-109U).

MORTARS: 81mm: 2,750 M-33, M-72; 120mm: 324 M-87, 120 M-64 (M-113).

ATGW: 310 TOW-2 SP (MOWAG *Piranha*).

RL: 83mm: 20,000 M-80.

ATK GUNS: 90mm: 850 Model-50/-57.

AD GUNS: 20mm: 1,700.

SAM: 56 B/L-84 (*Rapier*).

SURV: *Green Archer* (mor).

UAV: *Scout*.

HELICOPTERS: 72 *Alouette* III.

MARINE: 11 *Aquarius* patrol boats.

AIR CORPS: 60,000 on mob (incl military airfield guard units); 216 cbt ac, no armed hel.

The Air Corps is an integral part of the Army, structured in 1 Air Force bde, 1 AD, 1 Air-base bde and 1 Comd-and-Control bde.

FGA: 6 sqn with 54 *Hunter* F-58, 7 T-68.

FIGHTER: 9 sqn:

7 with 91 *Tiger* II/F-5E, 12 *Tiger* II/F-5F.

2 with 30 *Mirage* IIIS, 4 -III DS.

RECCE: 1 sqn with 18 *Mirage* IIIRS.

LIAISON/SAR: 1 sqn with 18 PC-6, 2 *Learjet* 36.

HELICOPTERS: 3 sqn with 15 AS-332 M-1, 12 SA-316.

TRAINING: 19 *Hawk* Mk 66, 28 P-3, 39 PC-7, 8 PC-9.

ASM: AGM-65A/B *Maverick*.

AAM: AIM-9 *Sidewinder*, AIM-26 *Falcon*.

AIR DEFENCE:

1 air-base bde: 3 regt x 4 bn, each with 4 bty of 20mm and twin 35mm guns with *Skyguard* fire-control radar.

1 AD bde: 1 SAM regt (2 bn, each of 3 bty; 60 *Bloodhound*); 7 AD arty regt (each with 2 bn of 3 bty; 35mm guns, *Skyguard* fire control).

FORCES ABROAD:

UN AND PEACEKEEPING:

CROATIA (UNPROFOR I): 8 Observers, plus 6 civ pol.

GEORGIA (UNOMIG): 2 Observers.

KOREA (NNSC): 6 Staff.

MIDDLE EAST (UNTSO): 8 Observers.

MOZAMBIQUE (ONUMOZ): 3 civ pol.

WESTERN SAHARA (MINURSO): 39; medical unit, 1 Observer.

PARAMILITARY:

CIVIL DEFENCE: 480,000 (300,000 trained).

UKRAINE

GDP	1992ε: $62.9bn:	
	per capita $5,000	
	1993ε: $54.2bn:	
	per capita $4,300	
Growth	1992ε: -16%	1993ε: -16%
Inflation	1992ε: 1,240%	1993: 4,474%
Debt[a]	1992: $415.3m	1993: $1.6bn
Def exp[b]	1992: $5.3bn	
Def bdgt[b]	1992: r 116.0bn ($4.3bn)	
	1993: Kar 2,750.0bn ($3.9bn)	
	1994: Kar 16,823.0bn ($3.1bn)	

FMA[c]	1993:	$0.4m (IMET)	
	1994:	$0.5m (IMET)	
	1995:	$0.6m (IMET)	
$1 = r, kar[d]	1992:	n.k.	1993: 12,610
	1994:	35,000	

r = Russian rouble
Kar = karbovanets

[a] External debt in convertible currencies.
[b] ppp est.
[c] Excl obligations 1992–94 by the US ($277m) and Japan ($16m) to support nuclear dismantlement under START I.
[d] Ukraine introduced its coupon currency in January 1992 to circulate in parallel, and valued on a par, with the Russian rouble. The rouble alignment was abandoned in November 1993 with the introduction of a national currency, the karbovanets.

Population: 51,852,000 (Russian 22%, Polish 4%, Jewish 1%)

	13–17	*18–22*	*23–32*
Men	1,869,800	1,819,900	3,496,300
Women	1,809,900	1,776,300	3,461,000

TOTAL ARMED FORCES:

ACTIVE: 517,000 (excl Strategic Nuclear Forces and Black Sea Fleet; incl 47,000 in central staffs and units not covered below).
Terms of service: 2 years.
RESERVES: some 1m with military service within 5 years.

STRATEGIC NUCLEAR FORCES

(ownership and control disputed):
ICBM:
SS-19 *Stiletto* (RS-18): 110 (at two sites).
SS-24 *Scalpel* (RS-22): 46 (silo-based, one site co-located with SS-19) (said to have been deactivated).
BOMBERS: 42: 23 Tu-95H (with AS-15 ALCM), 19 Tu-160 (with AS-15 ALCM) (under Ukrainian command).

GROUND FORCES: 308,000.

MOD tps: 1 TD (trg), 1 arty div (trg), 1 arty, 1 ATK, 3 engr bde.
Western Op Comd:
Comd tps: 1 arty div (1 arty, 1 MRL, 1 ATK bde), 1 TD (trg), 1 engr regt.
3 Corps:
1 with 2 MRD (1 reserve), 2 mech (1 reserve), 1 arty, 1 engr bde, 1 MRL, 1 ATK regt.
1 with 2 mech div, 1 mech, 1 arty bde, 1 ATK, 1 MRL regt (both reserve).
1 with 1 TD, 1 ATK regt.
Southern Op Comd:
Comd tps: 2 mech div (1 trg), 1 air-mobile div, 1 arty div, 2 arty bde (1 reserve).
3 Corps:
1 with 2 mech bde, 1 arty bde, 1 ATK, 1 MRL regt (last 3 reserve).
1 with 1 MRD (reserve), 1 mech div, 1 MRL, 1 ATK (reserve) regt.
1 with 1 TD, 2 mech div, 1 arty bde, 1 ATK, 1 MRL regt.
Other units (subordination not known) 2 SF (*Spetsnaz*), 7 SSM bde, 8 SAM bde/regt.
EQUIPMENT:
MBT: some 5,380 (incl some 1,400 in store): 1,030 T-54/-55, 285 T-62, 2,400 T-64, 1,320 T-72, 345 T-80.
LIGHT TANKS: 50 PT-76.
RECCE: some 2,000, incl 520 BRM.
AIFV: some 3,026: 1,450 BMP-1, 1,450 BMP-2, 6 BMP-3, 120 BMD.
APC: some 2,190: 400 BTR-60, 1,300 BTR-70, 450 BTR-80, 40 BTR-D; plus 1,100 MT-LB, 3,000 'look-alikes'.
TOTAL ARTY: 3,638:
TOWED ARTY: 1,050: 122mm: 400 D-30; 152mm: 200 D-20, 175 2A65, 275 2A36.
SP ARTY: 1,304: 122mm: 640 2S1; 152mm: 500 2S3, 24 2S5, 40 2S19, 203mm: 100 2S7.
COMBINED GUN/MORTAR: 120mm: 64 2S9.
MRL: 640: 122mm: 375 BM-21, 25 9P138; 132mm: 5 BM-13; 220mm: 140 9P140; 300mm: 95 9A52.
MORTARS: 580: 120mm: 330 2S12, 250 PM-38.
SSM: 132 *Scud*, 140 *FROG*/SS-21.
ATGW: AT-4 *Spigot*, AT-5 *Spandrel*, AT-6 *Spiral*.
SAM: SA-4/-6/-8/-11/-12A/-15.
SURV: SNAR-10 (*Big Fred*), *Small Fred* (arty).

AIR FORCE (incl Air Defence): 146,000; some 993 cbt ac, plus 440 in store (MiG-21, MiG-23, MiG-27, MiG-29), 307 attack hel.

3 air army, 1 PVO army (3 AD regions).
BOMBERS: 2 div HQ, 3 regt (1 trg) with 11 Tu-16, 33 Tu-22, 30 Tu-22M.
FGA/BOMBER: 2 div HQ, 5 regt with 161 Su-24.
FGA: 1 regt with 34 Su-25.
FIGHTER: 2 div (8 regt), 3 PVO div (8 regt) with 145 MiG-23, 79 MiG-25, 172 MiG-29, 59 Su-15, 67 Su-27.
RECCE: 4 regt with 38 Tu-16, 22 Tu-22, 41 Su-17, 36 Su-24, 15 MiG-25.
ECM: 1 regt with 22 Yak-28, 7 Su-24.
TRANSPORT: 174 Il-76, 100 others incl An-12.
TRAINING: 4 centres, 10 regts with 50 Su-24, 475 L-39/L-29.

HELICOPTERS:
ATTACK: 307 Mi-24.
SUPPORT: 58 Mi-6, 132 Mi-8, 20 Mi-26.
SAM: 825: SA-2/-3/-5/-10.

NAVY: ε16,000 (incl 7,000 Naval Aviation, 5,000 Coastal Defence) (planned total is probably 40,000).
BASES: Sevastopol, Odessa.
PRINCIPAL SURFACE COMBATANTS: 4: 2 *Krivak-III* PCO, 1 *Petya-II* FF, 1 *Grisha* V FF.
OTHER SURFACE SHIPS: 1 *Slavutich* (Sov *Kamchatka*) comd vessel, some 40 coastal, inshore and riverine patrol craft, incl *Grisha II, Zhuk, Pauk I, Stenka, Muravey* and *Shemel* classes, 1 or 2 small log spt vessels; 2 large *Pomornik* hovercraft (capacity 3 tkr or 10 APC, 300 tps).
BLACK SEA FLEET: (ε48,000) (HQ Sevastopol): since August 1992 the Black Sea Fleet has been controlled *de jure*, jointly by Russia and Ukraine. In practice, this has been *de facto* Russian control. Some, mainly minor, units of the Fleet have already been transferred to Ukraine (see above, and Border Guard below) and and promised to Georgia.

NAVAL AVIATION: (7,000): 7 regts with 68 MiG-29, 43 Su-17, 44 Su-25, 10 Tu-16, 39 Tu-22M (Tu-16, Tu-22M also listed by Russia in CFE data).

COASTAL DEFENCE TROOPS: (5,000) (listed by both Ukraine and Russia in CFE data).
1 Coast Defence div (Reserve).
2 marine inf regt.
EQUIPMENT:
MBT: 244 T-64.
AIFV: 140 BMP-1, 150 BMD.
APC: 20 BTR-60, 150 BTR-70, 200 BTR-70.
TOWED ARTY: 72 D-30.
SP ARTY: 23 2S1.
COMBINED GUN/MORTAR: 24 2S9.

FORCES ABROAD
UN AND PEACEKEEPING:
BOSNIA (UNPROFOR BH): 580; 1 inf bn, plus 9 civ pol.
CROATIA (UNPROFOR I): 547; 1 inf bn.

PARAMILITARY FORCES: 66,000.
NATIONAL GUARD: 23,000 (to be 30,000; former MVD eqpt in service).
BORDER GUARD (incl Coast Guard): 43,000; about 40 minor units ex-Black Sea Fleet and KGB.

'Federal Republic of Yugoslavia':
SERBIA/MONTENEGRO

GDP	1992ε: $13.5bn:	
	per capita $5,000	
	1993ε: $9.5bn:	
	per capita $3,600	
Growth	1992ε: -26%	1993ε: -30%
Inflation	1992: hyper-inflation	
	1993: hyper-inflation	
Debt	1992: $5.5bn	1993: $6.2bn
Def exp[a]	1992: ND 32, 315bn ($1.3bn)	
Def bdgt[a]	1993: ND 677,680.0bn ($1,008.3m)	
	1994: ND 1,199,830.0bn ($705.8m)	
$1 = ND[b]	1992: n.k.	1993: n.k.
	1994: n.k.	

ND = new dinar

[a] ppp est.
[b] The super dinar was introduced in January 1994 at which time it was fixed at parity with the DM.

Population: Serbia 9,893,000 (Serb 66%, Albanian 17%, Hungarian 4%, Muslim 2%).
Montenegro 643,000 (Montenegrin 62%, Muslim 15%, Serb 9%, Albanian 7%). A further 2,032,000 Serbs were living in the other Yugoslav republics before the civil war began.

	13–17	*18–22*	*23–32*
Men	308,000	306,600	600,600
Women	290,800	290,400	570,200

TOTAL ARMED FORCES:
ACTIVE: 126,500 (ε60,000 conscripts).
Terms of service: 12–15 months.
RESERVES: some 400,000.

ARMY (JA): some 90,000 (ε37,000 conscripts).
3 Army, 8 Corps (incl 1 mech).

3 tk bde.	1 SF bde.
8 mech bde.	6 arty bde.
7 mot inf bde.	1 ATK arty bde.
1 AB bde.	9 AD regt.
2 Task Force.	5 SAM-6 regt.

RESERVES:
1 Task Force, 1 inf bde gp (4 bde), 22 mot inf, 10 inf, 1 mtn, 2 arty, 2 ATK arty bde; 3 arty, 2 ATK regt.

EQUIPMENT:
MBT: 639: 407 T-54/-55, some 232 M-84 (T-74; mod T-72).
RECCE: 38 BRDM-2.
AIFV: 517 M-80.
APC: 112 M-60P, BOV-VP.
TOTAL ARTY: 1,499:
TOWED ARTY: 786: 105mm: 174 M-56; 122mm: 168 M-1931/37, M-1938, 132 D-30; 130mm: 180 M-46; 152mm: 48: M-1937, D-20, M-84; 155mm: 84: M-59, M-65.
SP ARTY: 105mm: M-7; 122mm: 75 2S1.
MRL: 72: 128mm: 48 M-63, 24 M-77.
MORTARS: 82mm: 1,700; 120mm: 566.
ATGW: 135 AT-3 *Sagger*, incl SP (BOV-1, BRDM-1/2).
RCL: 57mm: 1,550; 82mm: 1,000 M-60PB SP; 105mm: 650 M-65.
ATK GUNS: 76mm: 60; 90mm: 74 M-36B2 (incl SP); 100mm: 130 T-12.
AD GUNS: 20mm: 475 M-55/-75, 65 BOV-3 SP triple; 30mm: 350 M-53, M-53/-59, 8 BOV-30 SP; 57mm: 54 ZSU-57-2 SP.
SAM: 175: SA-6/-7/-9.

NAVY: ε7,500 (some conscripts).
BASE: Kotor, Tivat, Bar. (Most former Yugoslav bases are now in Croatian hands.)
SUBMARINES: 5:
2 *Sava* SS with 533mm TT.
3 *Heroj* SS with 533mm TT.
(Plus 5 *Una* SSI for SF ops.)
FRIGATES: 4:
2 *Kotor* with 4 x SS-N-2B *Styx* SSM, 2 x 12 ASW RL, 2 x 3 ASTT.
2 *Split* (Sov *Koni*) with 4 SS-N-2B *Styx* SSM, 2 x 12 ASW RL.
PATROL AND COASTAL COMBATANTS: 40:
MISSILE CRAFT: 9:
5 *Rade Koncar* PFM with 2 x SS-N-2B *Styx* (some †).
4 *Mitar Acev* (Sov *Osa-I*) PFM with 4 x SS-N-2A.
TORPEDO CRAFT: 4:
4 *Topcider* (Sov *Shershen*) with 4 x 533mm TT.
PATROL: 27:
INSHORE: 6 *Mirna*.
RIVERINE: about 21⟨ (some in reserve).
MINE WARFARE: 5:
MINELAYERS: 1 *Sibla*-class, 94 mines.
D-3 and D-501 LCTs can also lay 100 mines.
MINE COUNTERMEASURES: 4:
2 *Vukov Klanac* MHC.
2 UK *Ham* MSI.
(Plus some 12 riverine MSI⟨.)
AMPHIBIOUS: craft only: about 18: 4 D-3/D-501 LCT, about 14 LCM.
SUPPORT AND MISCELLANEOUS: 5:
1 PO-91 *Lubin* tpt, 1 trg, 1 river flagship, 2 harbour tankers.
MARINES: (900).
2 marine bde (2 regt each of 2 bn).

AIR FORCE: 29,000 (3,000 conscripts); 284 cbt ac, 115 armed hel.
4 air bde, 2 hel regt.
FGA: some 80 *Jastreb*, *Super Galeb*, *Orao* 2.
FIGHTER: 7 sqn with 88 MiG-21F/PF/M/bis, 10 MiG-21U, 16 MiG-29 (14 -A, 2 -UB).
RECCE: 2 sqn with some 20 *Orao*, MiG-21.
ARMED HEL: some 115 Mi-8 (aslt); *Gazela*.
ASW: 1 hel sqn with 4 Mi-14, 4 Ka-25, 2 Ka-27.
TRANSPORT: 2 An-12, 15 An-26, 4 CL-215 (SAR, fire-fighting), 2 *Falcon* 50 (VIP), 2 *Learjet* 25, 6 Yak-40.
LIAISON: 46 UTVA-66 ac, 14 *Partizan* hel.
TRAINING: ac: 70 **Super Galeb/Jastreb*, 100 UTVA; **hel:** 20 *Gazela*.
AAM: AA-2 *Atoll*, AA-8 *Aphid*, AA-10 *Alamo*, AA-11 *Archer*.
ASM: AGM-65 *Maverick*, AS-7 *Kerry*.
AD: 8 SAM bn, 8 sites with 24 SA-2, 16 SA-3.
15 regt AD arty.

Russia

General Overview

While the last six months of 1993 witnessed turbulent events, the first six months of 1994 have been quieter and the internal disarray in parliament has allowed the government to develop a more consistent foreign policy.

In September 1993, President Boris Yeltsin suspended his Vice-President Alexander Rutskoi, refused to pass the inflationary budget drawn up by parliament, and brought back Yegor Gaidar to take charge of the economy. On 21 September he announced the dissolution of parliament with parliamentary elections to be held on 12 December, to be followed shortly by presidential elections. Rutskoi and the Speaker, Ruslan Khasbulatov, remained with their parliamentary backers in the White House where they were reinforced by armed supporters who later attacked the Moscow mayoral building and the Ostankino TV centre. On 4 October the General Staff decided to back the President and tanks and special forces attacked the White House and arrested its defenders.

At the 12 December election, the new Constitution, which greatly increased the President's powers, was narrowly approved. The vote, even though Khasbulatov, Rutskoi and their supporters were unable to stand for election, produced a new parliament composed mainly of those opposed to President Yeltsin. Major gains were made by the Liberal Democratic Party whose leader, Vladimir Zhirinovsky, made a number of inflammatory speeches which caused concern to those in the West who view the possibility of a resurgent, expansionist Russia as a future major threat. The divisions within the Russian parliament mean that there is no strong opposition, and this has allowed the government to develop policies that might not have been possible a year earlier.

Considerable debate arose over the question of Russia's membership of the North Atlantic Treaty Organisation (NATO's) Partnership for Peace (PFP). The Russians used reluctance to join as a lever to gain more influence over NATO and also aimed to reduce NATO's influence by calling for the Conference on Security and Cooperation in Europe (CSCE) to become Europe's prime security forum. Next they sought to achieve a special relationship with NATO, one that might give Russia an automatic right to be consulted on NATO decisions which could lead to it having a right of veto. In the event, Russia signed the Partnership Framework Document on 22 June 1994 when Foreign Minister Andrei Kozyrev said that Russia 'had no fundamental objections' to NATO enlargement.

Originally Russian involvement in the Bosnian crisis was foreseen as likely to be unhelpful at best, whereas in fact it has been a positive factor. The Russian envoy, Vitaly Churkin, played a major role in the negotiations at the time of the Sarajevo cease-fire in February 1994, and the Russian involvement in the contact group helped to ensure that policies were better coordinated. Later Russian disenchantment with Bosnian-Serb intransigence no doubt affected President Milosevic's calculations when he announced in August the closure of the border with Bosnia-Herzegovina.

Commonwealth of Independent States (CIS)

The CIS held a Heads of State meeting in April 1994 at which new regulations for the CIS Council of Ministers of Defence were approved. Heads of nine states (Armenia, Azerbaijan, Belarus, Georgia, Kazakhstan, Kyrgyzstan, Russia, Tajikistan and Uzbekistan) signed the regulations. A number of decisions relating to peacekeeping in Tajikistan, Georgia–Abkhazia and Nagorno-Karabakh were also taken. A declaration on the 'Observance of Sovereignty, Territorial Integrity and Inviolability of the Borders of the Member States of the Commonwealth of Independent States' was also signed by the same nine states less Armenia, but also by Moldova, Turkmenistan and Ukraine.

Nuclear Developments

Russian strategic nuclear weapons are no longer targeted against the US or the UK. A number of strategic weapons have been redeployed: 27 mobile SS-25 ICBM from Belarus to Russia, and 40 Tu-95H bombers from Kazakhstan to Russia. 300 nuclear warheads removed from SS-24 and SS-19 ICBM in Ukraine have also been transferred to Russia for dismantlement.

Russia has continued to eliminate strategic weapons ahead of ratification of the START I Treaty. Two *Delta-1* and four *Yankee-1* SSBN have been retired, however all but two *Yankee-1* remain START-countable. These retirements reduce Russia's SLBM force by 88, leaving 700 SLBM deployed in 46 SSBN. A further 40 SS-11 ICBM have been eliminated (there are probably no SS-11 now at Svobodny in the Far East Military District (MD) as this site is being converted to a space-launch site), as have 22 SS-18 (ten in Russia, 12 in Kazakhstan). There are ten less SS-19 in Ukraine (where other ICBM still in their silos have had their warheads removed). No SS-13 are reported as having been eliminated, but some may have been as a regiment of nine SS-25 has been deployed to the only SS-13 site at Yoshkar-Ola in the Volga MD where SS-25s are already stationed. Three new regiments each with nine SS-25 have been formed; there are now 369 in service of which 54 remain in Ukraine. There are now a total of 1,161 (START-countable) ICBM (54 in Belarus, 92 in Kazakhstan and 156 in Ukraine), but not all of these are operational either because they are unserviceable or because their warheads have been removed. 158 strategic bombers remain START-countable of which 42 in Ukraine are considered to be non-operational because of unserviceability and lack of aircrew. During the past year Russia has eliminated 16 Tu-95B/G. The correct number of Tu-160 is 24, of which five are in Russia and 19 in Ukraine.

Russia is expected to flight test both new ICBM and SLBM before the end of the century. The ICBM is likely to be a follow-on to the mobile SS-25. The new missile would be both road-mobile and silo-launched, probably from the 90 SS-18 silos in which single-warhead missiles can be deployed under START II rules. The SLBM development is believed to be a follow on to SS-N-20 now deployed in *Typhoon*-class SSBN and could be ready by 1996. There is speculation that a new class of SSBN with a new SLBM is being planned.

Conventional Forces Developments

CFE Treaty Limited Equipment (TLE)

Large numbers of TLE were eliminated during 1993 (*The Military Balance* does not have accurate figures for the first six months of 1994). Whilst some 700 tanks were eliminated, the number of T-72 tanks (in the Treaty zone) rose by over 200 and the first T-90 was reported. Around 1,800 APC were eliminated with numbers of BTR-80 rising by 100, and 1,000 AIFV were also eliminated. The number of artillery pieces eliminated was about 1,000, while small increases in the number of 2A65 towed artillery, 2S19 SP guns, 9P138 and 9A52 MRL have been noted. The first 2S23, a wheeled version of the 2S9 combined gun/mortar system, was reported. These figures do not include the destruction of some 1,200 unspecified TLE east of the Urals. In the CFE flanks zone (V.1) where Russia is attempting to have its Treaty quota raised, there is still much more TLE than is allowed once the Treaty is fully implemented in July 1996:

	1 January 1994	CFE Limit
Tanks	2,158	1,300
ACV	4,550	1,380
Artillery	2,444	1,680

Withdrawal from the Groups of Forces

The final withdrawal of Russian forces in Germany is due to be completed by 31 August 1994, just after *The Military Balance* has gone to press. However, by the end of July all combat formations and units had been withdrawn and *The Military Balance* no longer lists the Western

Group of Forces. Most of the last units to leave have been transferred to the Moscow MD (one army HQ, two tank divisions and two artillery brigades) and the Volga MD (one army HQ, two tank divisions, one artillery and one SSM brigade) rather than being disbanded as had been the case with some earlier withdrawals. Russian troops will also have withdrawn from Latvia by 31 August, but the withdrawal from Estonia is still not settled. Once withdrawal from Estonia is complete the North-West Group of Forces will cease to exist. Troops in Kaliningrad are in the 11th Army which is now directly under the command of GHQ Land Forces; there have been some reports of Kaliningrad forming a Military District. The only withdrawal from the Transcaucasus Group of Forces has been the Corps HQ and one SAM brigade. The two SSM brigades with the 14th Army in Moldova have been disbanded.

Manpower

There have been many official reports on the shortage of manpower in the Russian armed forces. This has been caused by the very high percentage of those due for conscription who are automatically granted deferment. However, it is not always possible to identify published figures as actual strengths (as opposed to authorised strengths). In May 1994 the Commander-in-Chief, Land Forces, said that the Army would be reduced from 900,000 to 550,000 by January 1995, whereas *The Military Balance* calculates Land Forces strength to be about 780,000. When the Defence Minister, Marshal Pavel Grachev, said in April 1994 'at the moment we have 2,300,000' he was most probably referring to authorised strength as he was arguing in favour of maintaining the armed forces strength at 2,100,000. The concept of contract service is a success: 120,000 men were recruited in 1993 and a further 150,000 are authorised in 1994. The Land Forces have estimated that by 1995 contract soldiers will form up to one-third of its total manpower. Most contract recruits are opting for technical and logistic units which leaves combat units still short of men. *The Military Balance* estimates that no combat formations, including airborne and the divisions earmarked for peacekeeping, have more than 75% of their authorised strength and roughly 70% of divisions have less than 50%. On the other hand, in the past, many Soviet divisions were deliberately undermanned and depended very heavily on reservists on mobilisation. It is likely that once redeployment has been achieved priority will be given to strengthening airborne formations and motor rifle brigades while the remaining divisions will be put on the same basis as the old Soviet category 'C' divisions which only had some 20% of their wartime strength in peacetime. Further divisions may be disbanded, particularly east of the Urals.

Bases in the 'Near Abroad'

Russia is seeking to obtain military bases – facilities might be a more accurate description – in the republics of the former Soviet Union; the figure 28 has been mentioned. In the Transcaucasus, agreement has been reached with Georgia and Armenia, but not yet with Azerbaijan which claims ownership of the *Lyaki* early-warning radar and which would be prepared to lease it to Russia. Three bases have been agreed in Georgia at Tbilisi (headquarters of the Transcaucasus Group of Forces), Akhalkalaki and Batumi where motor rifle divisions are currently based. There are to be two bases in Armenia, Yerevan and Gyumri, currently the bases for one motor rifle division. Agreement has also been reached with Belarus for an air force regiment to remain at Zyabrouka (where a long-range reconnaissance regiment is based) until the year 2000. An agreement was reached on 10 August 1994 over the withdrawal of Russian forces from Moldova within three years.

Peacekeeping

Russia now provides two battalions to UN peacekeeping missions, one in Croatia and one in Bosnia-Herzegovina (originally deployed in January 1994 to Croatia, but sent to Sarajevo to assist in monitoring the cease-fire lines there). Russia has observers with six other missions. Two motor rifle divisions have been specifically nominated to provide peacekeeping contingents. Peacekeeping troops, without UN mandates but with the agreement of the parties and states concerned, are deployed in the Dniestr area of Moldova (four motor rifle battalions), and in Georgia in South Ossetia (one motor rifle battalion) and Abkhazia (two motor rifle battalions, one airborne regiment). Russian peacekeepers are volunteers, are paid more and normally do a six-month tour of duty.

Ground Forces

The reorganisation of the ground forces continues slowly as redeployment takes priority. In the Moscow MD a large number of combat support units are under MD command, a second army has been formed with its HQ provided by the 1st Guards Tank Army withdrawn from Germany. Each army includes one independent motor rifle brigade. The Volga MD has also inherited an army HQ from the Group of Forces in Germany together with two tank divisions and an SSM brigade. There has been little change in the Leningrad MD, although one corps HQ has been disbanded and there now are only three arms and equipment depots with divisional mobilisation packs. The greatest change has taken place in the North Caucasus MD where the artillery division and one motor rifle division have been disbanded. One motor rifle division, one attack helicopter regiment and one SAM regiment have been redeployed there from Germany and two motor rifle brigades have been formed, but as yet they have no tanks, artillery or ACVs. In Kaliningrad a tank division has been reorganised and retitled 'tank brigade'. In the Airborne Forces the training division which was based in Lithuania is reportedly being established in Siberia. The former KGB brigade, shown in 1993 as an independent army brigade in the Moscow MD, is now under the command of the Airborne Force HQ.

Some new equipment is coming into service, albeit very slowly. The T-90 main battle tank has a 125mm smoothbore gun which can fire a laser-beam riding missile probably armed with a tandem warhead. It also has explosive reactive armour. The 2S23 is a wheeled self-propelled combined gun/mortar. It comprises a 2S9 120mm gun turret mounted on a BTR-80 chasis. The only gun declared at 1 January 1994 was located at the artillery engineering college at Penza (Volga MD). Its ultimate deployment is most likely with airborne and other rapid-reaction forces.

Naval Forces

A number of naval ships have been retired in the last 12 months, and the operational serviceability of others must be in doubt. All told some 25 tactical submarines, nine surface combatants, 20 patrol craft and 20 mine countermeasure ships have been retired. Two more *Oscar*-class attack submarines have been commissioned as has one more *Akula*-class; all are nuclear powered. The first *Udaloy*-II class cruiser has been commissioned. Its main armament is eight four-tube SS-N-22 SSM. The cruiser can embark two helicopters. One more *Sovremennyy*-class destroyer has been commissioned. Naval Aviation aircraft strength has been reduced by 130 aircraft, mainly trainers and some 45 FGA aircraft. Although the Su-27K was reported as operational as a carrier-borne aircraft, only training models have been delivered so far.

Air Forces

There are no immediate plans to merge the Air Force with the Air Defence Forces (PVO), but in the long term it is probable that a single Space Force may be formed which would also include the Strategic Rocket Forces. There has been a reorganisation within the Air Force. Two additional headquarters have been formed: the Headquarters for Frontline Aviation (KFA) has taken over the command of the air armies, with the exception of the Long-Range Aviation Force which remains directly under Air Force Headquarters; the Headquarters for Reserve and Training (KPLK) controls all training units (other than those under Long-Range Aviation and the Flying Training Centre at Borisogllebsk which remains under KFA) and the aircraft reserve bases.

Aircraft development continues. The MiG-31M, an improved version of the MiG-31, is likely to enter service with the Russian Air Defence Force in 1995. A project to develop an anti-satellite missile for the MiG-31 has been cancelled. The Mikoyan project 701, originally to be an ultra-long-range high-altitude interceptor ultimately to replace the MiG-31, has been cancelled due to lack of development funds. Mikoyan's project 1-42, the Russian counterpart to the United States Air Force F-22, is progressing, but a lack of funding and problems with the engines has delayed the first flights of two prototypes that have been built. A Mikoyan design for a light-weight fighter with a likely designation of MiG-33 and based on the MiG-29M has probably been cancelled. Sukhoi have been carrying out developments on the Su-27 Flanker. The Su-27K, a fighter/ground-attack version for operations on naval aircraft carriers, has been developed from the tandem two-seat trainer version of the Su-27B. The Su-35, an advanced development of the Su-27 airframe, is a single-seat all-weather fighter and ground-attack aircraft. It may have a rearward facing inteception radar to provide guidance for over-the-shoulder radar-guided missiles. Su-35 may enter production in 1995. A variant development of the Su-27 is the Su-34, probably intended to replace the Su-24 bomber/FGA aircraft, it is very similar to the Su-35. Two differently configured prototypes have been built and test flights have taken place. Sukhoi are developing a close-support aircraft designated the Su-37 as a successor to the Su-25 *Frogfoot*. None of these aircraft have entered squadron service yet.

RUSSIA

GDP[a]	1992ε: r 15,250.0bn ($1,200.0bn): per capita $8,000	
	1993ε: r 162,667.0bn ($1,160.0bn): per capita $7,800	
Growth	1992ε: -18.5%	1993ε: -11.5%
Inflation	1992ε: 1,468%	1993ε: 911%
Debt[b]	1992: $80.8bn	1993: $85.0bn
Def exp[c]		
Def bdgt	1992: r 985.0bn ($74.6bn)	
	1993: r 10,795.0bn ($76.6bn)	
	1994: r 40,626.0bn ($79.0bn)	
FMA[d]	1993: $39.0m (USA)	
	1990–94: $5.0bn (Germany)	
$1 = r	1992: 180.0	1993: 836.0
	1994: 1,691.0	

r = rouble

[a] ppp est.
[b] External debt in convertible currencies.
[c] See note on Russian def exp on p. 281.
[d] Under the US Nunn–Lugar programme, $1.2bn expenditure in support of START I implementation in the FSU has been authorised for 1992–94. Russia's share is estimated at $800m. Actual obligations by mid-1993 were $39m.

Population: 148,920,000 (Tatar 4%, Ukrainian 3%, Belarussian 1%, Moldovian 1%, other 10%)

	13–17	*18–22*	*23–32*
Men	5,653,800	5,268,000	9,847,400
Women	5,491,900	5,143,000	9,612,500

TOTAL ARMED FORCES:

ACTIVE: ε1,714,000 (perhaps 950,000 conscripts; incl about 150,000 MOD staff, centrally controlled units for EW, trg, rear services, not incl elsewhere).
Terms of service: Army 18 months, Navy 2 years. Women with medical and other special skills may volunteer.

RESERVES: some 20,000,000: some 2,400,000 with service within last 5 years; Reserve obligation to age 50.

STRATEGIC NUCLEAR FORCES:

167,000 (incl 53,000 assigned from Air Force, Air Defence and Navy).

NAVY: (ε13,000).
700 msl in 46 SSBN.
SSBN: 46 (all based in Russian ports):
6 *Typhoon* with 20 SS-N-20 *Sturgeon* (120 msl).
7 *Delta-IV* with 16 SS-N-23 *Skiff* (112 msl).
14 *Delta-III* with 16 SS-N-18 *Stingray* (224 msl).
4 *Delta-II* with 16 SS-N-8 *Sawfly* (64 msl).
15 *Delta-I* with 12 SS-N-8 *Sawfly* (180 msl).
(A further 2 *Delta-1*, 2 *Yankee-1* remain START-countable with 56 msl.)

STRATEGIC ROCKET FORCES: (114,000, incl 70,000 conscripts).
5 rocket armies, org in div, regt, bn and bty, 126 launcher groups, normally 10 silos (6 for SS-18) and

one control centre; SS-25 units each 9 launchers; 12 SS-24 trains each 3 launchers.

ICBM: 1,161:

SS-11 *Sego*: 60 mod 2/3 (at 3 fields; all in Russia).

SS-13 *Savage* (RS-12): 40 (at 1 field; all in Russia).

SS-17 *Spanker* (RS-16): 40 (at 1 field; mod 3/4 MIRV; all in Russia).

SS-18 *Satan* (RS-20): 280 (at 6 fields; mostly mod 4/5, 10 MIRV; 188 in Russia, 92 in Kazakhstan).

SS-19 *Stiletto* (RS-18): 280 (at 4 fields; mostly mod 3, 6 MIRV; 170 in Russia, 110 in Ukraine).

SS-24 *Scalpel* (RS-22): 92 (deployment complete; 56 silo-based and 36 rail-mobile, 10 MIRV; 10 silo, 36 train in Russia, 46 silo in Ukraine).

SS-25 *Sickle* (RS-12M): 369+ (mobile, single-warhead msl; 10 bases with some 41 units of 9; 315+ in Russia, 54 in Belarus).

GROUND DEFENCE: some 1,700 APC, 140 Mi-8 hel declared under CFE (APC: Russia (West of Urals) 700, Ukraine 416, Belarus 585).

STRATEGIC AVIATION: (19,000).

Long-Range Forces (Moscow).

Western Russia: 1 air army (Smolensk).

Far East: 1 air army (Irkutsk).

BOMBERS: 158, plus 19 trg and test ac:

45 Tu-95B/G (with 1 and 2 AS-4 ASM).

27 Tu-95H6 (with AS-15 ALCM).

62 Tu-95H16 (with AS-15 ALCM) (23 in Ukraine).

11 Tu-95T (trg), plus 8 test ac.

24 Tu-160 (with AS-15 ALCM) (19 in Ukraine).

STRATEGIC DEFENCE: (21,000).

ABM: 100: 36 SH-11 (mod *Galosh*), 64 SH-08 *Gazelle* (Russia).

WARNING SYSTEMS:

SATELLITES: 9 with ICBM/SLBM launch detection capability. Others incl 2 photo-recce, 11 ELINT, 3 recce.

RADARS:

OVER-THE-HORIZON-BACKSCATTER (OTH-B): 3: 2 near Kiev and Komsomolsk (Ukraine), covering US and polar areas; 1 near Nikolayevsk-na-Amure, covering China (these sites are non-operational).

LONG-RANGE EARLY-WARNING:

ABM-ASSOCIATED:

6 long-range phased-array systems at Baranovichi (Belarus), Olnegorsk (Kola), Lyaki (Azerbaijan), Sary-Shagan (Kazakhstan), Pechora (Urals), Mishelevka (Irkutsk).

11 *Hen House*-series; range 6,000km, 6 locations covering approaches from the west and south-west, north-east and south-east and (partially) south. Engagement, guidance, battle management: 1 *Pillbox* phased-array at Pushkino (Moscow).

ARMY: 780,000 (about 450,000 conscripts, 80,000 on contract).

8 Military Districts (MD), 2 Groups of Forces.

15 Army HQ, 6 Corps HQ.

17 TD (incl 4 trg) (3 tk, 1 motor rifle, 1 arty, 1 SAM regt; 1 armd recce bn; spt units).

57 MRD (incl 6 trg) (3 motor rifle, 1 arty, 1 SAM regt; 1 indep tk, 1 ATK, 1 armd recce bn; spt units).

5 ABD (each 3 para, 1 arty regt; 1 AA bn) (plus 1 trg div, status and location unknown).

8 MG/arty div.

4 arty div incl 1 trg (no standard org: perhaps 4 bde (12 bn): 152mm SP, 152mm towed and MRL: some will have older eqpt).

Some 48 arty bde/regt; no standard org: perhaps 4 bn: 2 each of 24 152mm towed guns, 2 each of 24 152mm SP guns, Some only MRL.

4 hy arty bde (with 4 bn of 12 203mm 2S7 SP guns).

Some 7 AB bde (each 4 inf bn; arty, SAM, ATK; spt tps).

1 tk bde.

11 MR bde (more forming).

6 SF (*Spetsnaz*) bde.

28 SSM bde (incl 3 trg).

19 ATK bde/regt.

25 SAM bde/regt

21 attack hel regt.

4 aslt tpt hel regt.

6 hel trg regt.

Other Front and Army tps: engr, pontoon-bridge, pipe-line, signals, EW, CW def, tpt, supply bde/regt/bn.

EQUIPMENT (figures in parentheses are those reported to CFE on 15 December 1993):

MBT: about 19,500 (7,494), incl: T-54/-55 (1,031), T-62 (689), T-64A/-B (625), T-72L/-M (2,144) and T-80/-M 9 (3,004), T-90 (1), plus some 11,000 in store east of Urals (incl Kazakhstan, Uzbekistan).

LIGHT TANKS: 350 PT-76 (282).

RECCE: some 2,000 BRDM-2.

AIFV: about 19,000 (8,172), incl: BMP-1 (3,014), BMP-2 (3,169), BMP-3 (17), some 1,600 BMD-1/-2/-3 (AB) (1,383), BRM (589).

APC: over 16,000, incl: BTR-50P/-60P/-70/-80/-152, BTR-D (4,117); MT-LB (895), plus 'look-alikes'.

TOTAL ARTY: 21,300 (6,069), plus some 13,000, mainly obsolete types, in store east of the Urals.

TOWED ARTY: about 9,500 (1,456), incl 122mm: D-30, M-30 (780); 152mm: D-20 (281), *Giatsint-B* 2A36 (245), *MSTA-B* 2A65 (150); 203mm: B-4M.

SP ARTY: some 3,900 (2,719), incl 122mm: *Gvozdika* 2S1 (1,037); 152mm: *Acatsia* 2S3 (1,004), *Giatsint-S* 2S5 (399), *MSTA-S* 2S19 (173); 203mm *Pion* 2S7 (106).

COMBINED GUN/MORTAR: about 400 (370): 120mm: *Nona-S* 2S9 SP (332), *Nona-K* 2B16 (37), 2 S23 (1).
MRL: about 2,500 (908), incl: 122mm: BM-21 (494), 9P138 (27); 220mm: 800 (314) 9P140 *Uragan*; 300mm: 100 (71) *Smerch* 9A52.
MORTARS: about 5,000 (550), incl: 120mm: 2S12 (455), PM-38 (82); 160mm: M-160 (3); 240mm: M-240 (1), *Tulpan* 2S4 SP (9).
SSM (nuclear-capable): some 600 launchers, incl *FROG* (*Luna*)/SS-21 *Scarab* (*Tochka*), *Scud* B/-C mod (R-17).
ATGW: AT-2 *Swatter*, AT-3 *Sagger*, AT-4 *Spigot*, AT-5 *Spandrel*, AT-6 *Spiral*, AT-7 *Saxhorn*, AT-9, AT-10.
RL: 64mm: RPG-18; 73mm: RPG-7/-16/-22/-26; 105mm: RPG-27/-29.
RCL: 73mm: SPG-9; 82mm: B-10.
ATK GUNS: 57mm: ASU-57 SP; 76mm; 85mm: D-44/SD-44, ASU-85 SP; 100mm: T-12/-12A/M-55 towed.
AD GUNS: 23mm: ZU-23, ZSU-23-4 SP; 37mm; 57mm: S-60, ZSU-57-2 SP; 85mm: M-1939; 100mm: KS-19; 130mm: KS-30.
SAM: 500 SA-4 A/B *Ganef* (twin) (Army/Front weapon).
400 SA-6 *Gainful* (triple) (div weapon).
SA-7 *Grail* (man-portable).
400 SA-8 *Gecko* (2 triple) (div weapon).
275 SA-9 *Gaskin* (2 twin) (regt weapon).
200 SA-11 *Gadfly* (quad) (replacing SA-4/-6).
40 SA-12A *Gladiator* (replacing SA-4).
40 SA-12B *Giant*.
350 SA-13 *Gopher* (2 twin) (replacing SA-9).
SA-14 *Gremlin* (replacing SA-7).
100 SA-15 (replacing SA-6/SA-8).
SA-16 (replacing SA-7 and some SA-14).
SA-18 (replacing SA-7/SA-14).
SA-19 (2S6 SP) (8 SAM, plus twin 30mm gun).
HELICOPTERS: some 2,600:
ATTACK: 1,000 Mi-24 (880), Ka-50 *Hokum*.
TRANSPORT: some 1,300, Mi-6, Mi-8 (some armed), Mi-26 (hy).
EW/ECM: 100 Mi-8.
GENERAL PURPOSE: 200, incl Mi-2, Mi-8 (comms).

AIR FORCE: 170,000 (some 85,000 conscripts; incl 19,000 with Strategic Aviation) (see p. 112); some 2,150 cbt ac.

Four Commands: Long-Range Aviation, Frontal Aviation, Military Transport Aviation, Reserve and Training.
Force strengths vary, mostly org with div of 3 regt of 3 sqn (total 90–120 ac), indep regt (30–40 ac). Regt roles incl AD, interdiction, recce, tac air spt.

LONG-RANGE AVIATION COMMAND (DA):
2 air army, 4 div.
BOMBERS: about 220, incl 40 Tu-22, 170 Tu-26 (22M).
RECCE/ECM: some 30 Tu-22.
TANKERS: 40: 20 Mya-4, 20 Il-78.

FRONTAL AVIATION COMMAND (KFA):
6 air army.
FGA: some 775: incl 50 MiG-27/Su-17, 525 Su-24, 200 Su-25.
FIGHTER: some 625: incl 400 MiG-29, 140 Su-27.
RECCE: some 200: incl 50 MiG-25/Su-17, 150 Su-24.
ECM: some 75: incl 40 Yak-28.
TRAINING: 2 centres for operational conversion: 300 ac, incl 140 MiG-29, 50 Su-24, 30 Su-25, 20 Su-27, 50 MiG-25/Su-17.
AAM: AA-8 *Aphid*, AA-10 *Alamo*, AA-11 *Archer*.
ASM: AS-7 *Kerry*, AS-10 *Karen*, AS-11 *Kilter*, AS-12 *Kegler*, AS-13 *Kingbolt*, AS-14 *Kedge*, AS-16 *Kickback*, AS-17 *Krypton*.

MILITARY TRANSPORT AVIATION COMMAND (VTA):
3 div, each 3 regt, each 30 ac; some indep regt.
EQUIPMENT: some 350 ac, incl: An-12, Il-76M/MD *Candid* B (replacing An-12), An-22, An-124.
Additional long- and medium-range tpt ac in comd other than VTA: some 300: Tu-134, Tu-154, An-12 , An-72, Il-18, Il-62.
Civilian Aeroflot fleet: 1,700 medium- and long-range passenger ac, incl some 220 An-12 and Il-76.

RESERVE AND TRAINING COMMAND (KPLK):
TRAINING: 6 schools (incl 1 for foreign students): 1,500 ac, incl 1,000 L-39, 300 L-410/Tu-134, 85 MiG-29/Su-22/Su-24/Su-27.
RESERVES: 600 ac, incl MiG-23, MiG-27, Su-17, Su-22 plus 200 L-39 (probably awaiting elimination).

AIR DEFENCE TROOPS (VPVO): 205,000 (100,000 conscripts); 5 Air Defence Armies: air regt and indep sqn; AD regt.

AIRCRAFT (Aviation of Air Defence – APVO):
FIGHTER: some 1,200, incl (trg), 350 MiG-23 (6 AAM), 100 MiG-25 (4 AAM), 425 MiG-31 (4 AA-9), 325 Su-27 (plus some 50 cbt capable MiG-23 trg variants in regts).
TRAINING: 1 trg school: 75 MiG-23, 225 L-39.
RESERVES: 440 ac, inc MiG-21, MiG-23, Su-15, Tu-128 (probably awaiting elimination).
AEW AND CONTROL: 20 11-76.
AAM: AA-6 *Acrid*, AA-7 *Apex*, AA-8 *Aphid*, AA-9 *Amos*, AA-10 *Alamo*, AA-11 *Archer*.

SAM: some 3,500 launchers in some 450 sites:
SA-2 *Guideline*: 700 (being replaced by SA-10).
SA-3 *Goa*: 300 (2 or 4 launcher rails).
SA-5 *Gammon*: 1,000 launchers.
SA-10 *Grumble*: some 1,500 launchers quad.
COMBAT AIRCRAFT (CFE totals as at 15 December 1993 for all air forces less maritime):
Su-15: 189; Su-17: 242; Su-22: 67; Su-24: 366; Su-25: 202; Su-27: 367; MiG-21: 141; MiG-23: 911; MiG-25: 277; MiG-27: 261, MiG-29: 466; MiG-31: 196; Tu-22: 93; Tu-26: (-22M) 76; Tu-128: 67.

NAVY: ε295,000 (incl ε180,000 conscripts, ε13,000 Strategic Forces, ε45,000 Naval Aviation, ε29,500 Coastal Defence Forces).

SUBMARINES: 185:
STRATEGIC SUBMARINES: 46 (see p. 111).
TACTICAL SUBMARINES: 127:
SSGN: 19:
12 *Oscar* with 24 x SS-N-19 *Shipwreck* USGW (VLS); plus T-65 HWT.
2 *Charlie-I* with 8 x SS-N-7 *Starbright* USGW; plus T-53 HWT.
1 *Echo-II* with 8 SS-N-12 *Sandbox* SSM; plus T-53 HWT.
3 *Yankee 'Notch'* with 20+ SS-N-21 *Sampson* SLCM.
1 *Yankee* (trials) with ε12 SS-NX-24 SLCM.
SSN: 44:
11 *Akula* with T-65 HWT; plus SS-N-21.
3 *Sierra* with T-65 HWT; plus SS-N-21.
26 *Victor-III* with T-65 HWT; plus SS-N-15.
4 *Victor-I* with T-53 HWT.
SSG: 2 *Juliet* with 4 x SS-N-3A *Shaddock* SSM.
SS: 62 (all with T-53 HWT): 24 *Kilo*, 18 *Tango*, 20 *Foxtrot*.
OTHER ROLES: 12:
SSN: 4: 2 *Uniform*, 1 *Alfa*, 1 *Echo* II experimental/ trials.
SS: 8: 1 *Beluga*, 3 *Bravo* wpn targets, 1 *Lima*, 2 *India* rescue, 1 *X-Ray* trials.
IN STORE: probably some *Foxtrot*.
PRINCIPAL SURFACE COMBATANTS: 161:
CARRIERS: 2:
1 *Kuznetsov* CVV (65,000t) capacity 25–30 fixed wing ac (Su-27) and 8–10 ASW hel with 12 SS-N-19 *Shipwreck* SSM, 4 x 6 SA-N-9 SAM, 8 CADS-1, 2 RBU-12 (not fully op).
1 *Gorshkov* (ex-*Baku*) (CVV) (38,000t) capacity 15 V/STOL ac, 16 Ka-25/-27 hel (ASW with E-45/-75 LWT/AEW/OTHT/SAR); plus 6 x 2 SS-N-12 *Sandbox* SSM, 4 x 8 SA-N-6 *Grumble* SAM. 2 x 100mm guns.
CRUISERS: 25:
CGN: 3 *Admiral Ushakov* (ex-*Kirov*) (AAW/ASUW) with 12 x 8 SA-N-6 *Grumble*, 20 SS-N-19 *Shipwreck* SSM, 3 Ka-25/-27 hel for OTHT/AEW/ASW; plus 1 with 1 x 2 130mm guns, 1 with 1 x 2 SS-N-14 *Silex* SUGW (LWT or nuc payload), 10 x 533mm TT.
CG: 22:
1 *Moskva* (CGH) (ASW) with 18 Ka-25 hel (E45-75 LWT), 1 x 2 SUW-N-1; plus 2 x 2 SA-N-3 SAM.
3 *Slava* (AAW/ASUW) with 8 x 8 SA-N-6 *Grumble*, 8 x 2 SS-N-12 *Sandbox* SSM, 1 Ka-25/-27 hel (AEW/ASW); plus 8 x 533mm TT, 1 x 2 130mm guns.
11 *Udaloy* (ASW) with 2 x 4 SS-N-14 *Silex* SUGW, 2 x 12 ASW RL, 8 x 533mm TT, 2 Ka-27 hel; plus 2 x 100mm guns.
1 *Udaloy*-II with 8 x 4 SS-N-22, 8 x SA-N-9, 2 Cads-N-1, 8 SA-N-11, 10 x 533mm TT, 2 Ka-27 hel plus 2 x 100mm guns.
5 *Nikolayev (Kara)* (ASW) with 2 x 4 SS-N-14 *Silex* SUGW, 10 x 533mm TT, 1 Ka-25 hel; plus 2 x 2 SA-N-3 *Goblet* (1 (*Azov*) with 3 x 8 SA-N-6, only 1 x SA-N-3 and other differences).
1 *Admiral Zozulya (Kresta-I)* (ASUW/ASW) with 2 x 2 SS-N-3b *Shaddock* SSM, 1 Ka-25 hel (OTHT), 10 x 533mm TT.
DESTROYERS: 22:
DDG: 22:
AAW/ASUW: 19:
17 *Sovremennyy* with 2 x 4 SS-N-22 *Sunburn* SSM, 2 x 1 SA-N-7 *Gadfly* SAM, 2 x 2 130mm guns, 1 Ka-25 (B) hel (OTHT); plus 4 x 533mm TT.
1 *Grozny (Kynda)* (ASUW) with 2 x 4 SS-N-3b; plus 1 x 2 SA-N-1 *Goa* SAM, 6 x 533mm TT.
1 *Sderzhannyy* (mod *Kashin*) with 4 SS-N-2C *Styx* SSM, 2 x 2 SA-N-1 SAM; plus 5 x 533mm TT.
ASW: 3:
3 *Komsomolets Ukrainyy (Kashin)* with 2 x 12 ASW RL, 5 x 533mm TT; plus 2 x 2 SA-N-1 SAM (1 with trials fit 1 x SA-N-7).
FRIGATES: 112:
11 *Rezvyy (Krivak-II)* with 1 x 4 SS-N-14 *Silex* SUGW, 8 x 533mm TT, 2 x 12 ASW RL; plus 2 x 100mm guns.
19 *Bditelnyy (Krivak-I)* (weapons as *Rezvyy* but with 2 x twin 76mm guns).
1 *Neustrashimyy* with 2 x 12 ASW RL.
(Note: frigates listed below lie between 1,000 and 1,200 tonnes full-load displacement and are not counted in official releases.)
65 '*Grisha-I, -III, -V*', with 2 x 12 ASW RL, 4 x 533mm TT.
12 '*Parchim-II*' (ASW) with 2 x 12 ASW RL, 4 x 406mm ASTT.
4 '*Petya*' with ASW RL, 5 or 10 x 406mm ASTT.

PATROL AND COASTAL COMBATANTS: 145:
CORVETTES: about 77:
about 44 *Tarantul* (ASUW), 2 *-I*, 18–*II*, both with 2 x 2 SS-N-2C *Styx*; 24 *-III* with 2 x 2 SS-N-22 *Sunburn*.
33 *Nanuchka* (ASUW) *-I*, *-III* and *-IV* with 2 x 3 SS-N-9 *Siren*.
MISSILE CRAFT: 28:
15 *Osa* PFM with 4 x SS-N-2C.
13 *Matka* PHM with 2 x 1 SS-N-2C.
TORPEDO CRAFT: 27:
27 *Turya* PHT with 4 x 533mm TT.
PATROL CRAFT: about 13:
OFFSHORE: about 3 T-58/-43.
COASTAL: 10:
7 *Pauk* PFC (ASW) with 2 x ASW RL, 4 x ASTT.
1 *Babochka* PHT (ASW) with 8 x ASTT.
2 *Mukha* PHT (ASW) with 8 x ASTT.
MINE WARFARE: about 193:
MINELAYERS: 3 *Pripyat* (*Alesha*), capacity 300 mines.
(Note: most submarines and many surface combatants are equipped for minelaying.)
MINE COUNTERMEASURES: about 190:
OFFSHORE: 38:
2 *Gorya* MCO.
31 *Natya-I* and *-II* MSO.
5 T-43 MSO.
COASTAL: about 87:
15 *Yurka* MSC.
2 *Andryusha* MSC (trials).
About 70 *Sonya* MSC.
INSHORE: about 65:
15 *Vanya*, about 10 MSI and 40 MSI⟨.
AMPHIBIOUS: 69:
LPD: 3 *Ivan Rogov* with 4–5 Ka-27 hel: capacity 520 tps, 20 tk.
LST: 38:
28 *Ropucha*: capacity 225 tps, 9 tk.
10 *Alligator*: capacity 300 tps, 20 tk.
LSM: about 28 *Polnocny* (3 types): capacity 180 tps, 6 tk (some adapted for mine warfare, but retain amph primary role).
Plus CRAFT: about 80:
LCM: about 14 *Ondatra*.
LCAC AND SES: about 65: incl 9 *Pomornik*, 14 *Aist*, 9 *Tsaplya*, 16 *Lebed*, 2 *Utenok*, 6 *Gus*.
2 *Orlan* and 1 *Utka* 'wing-in-ground-effect' (WIG) experimental.
SUPPORT AND MISCELLANEOUS: about 600:
UNDERWAY SUPPORT: 27:
1 *Berezina*, 6 *Chilikin*, 20 other AO.
MAINTENANCE AND LOGISTICS: about 230: incl some 15 AS, 38 AR, 12 general maint/spt, 20 AOT, 18 missile spt/resupply, 70 tugs, 14 special liquid carriers, 13 water carriers, 30 AK.
SPECIAL PURPOSES: about 130: incl some 50 AGI (some armed), 5 msl range instrumentation, 8 trg, about 63 icebreakers (civil manned), 4 AH.
SURVEY/RESEARCH: about 210: incl some 35 naval, 50 civil AGOR; 80 naval, 35 civil AGHS; 10 space-associated ships (civil-manned).
MERCHANT FLEET (auxiliary/augmentation): about 2,800 ocean-going vessels (17 in Arctic service), incl 125 ramp-fitted and ro-ro, some with rails for rolling stock, 3 roll-on/float-off, 14 barge carriers, 48 passenger liners, 500 coastal and river ships.

NAVAL AVIATION: (ε45,000); some 783 cbt ac; 251 armed hel.

Four Fleet Air Forces; org in air div, each with 2–3 regt of HQ elm and 2 sqn of 9–10 ac each; recce, ASW, tpt/utility org in indep regt or sqn.
BOMBERS: some 188:
7 regt with some 140 Tu-26 (Tu-22M) (AS-4 ASM).
2 regt with some 33 Tu-16 (AS-5/-6 ASM), 15 Tu-22.
FGA: 280:
115 Su-17.
70 Su-24.
65 Su-25.
30 MiG-23/-27.
TRAINING: some 140: Tu-16*, Tu-26*, Tu-95*, Su-25*, Su-27*, MiG-29*.
ASW: 175 **ac**, 251 **hel**.
AIRCRAFT: 50 Tu-142, 36 Il-38, 89 Be-12.
HELICOPTERS: 63 Mi-14, 88 Ka-25, 100 Ka-27.
MR/EW: some 95 **ac**, 25 **hel**.
AIRCRAFT: incl 24 Tu-95, 35 Tu-16 MR/ECM, 6 Tu-22, 20 Su-24, 7 An-12, 3 Il-20.
HELICOPTERS: 25 Ka-25.
MCM: 25 Mi-14 hel.
CBT ASLT: 25 Ka-27 hel.
TANKERS: 6 Tu-16.
TRANSPORT:
AIRCRAFT: some 120 An-12, An-24, An-26.
HELICOPTERS: 80 Mi-6/-8.
ASM: AS-2 *Kipper*, AS-4 *Kitchen*, AS-5 *Kelt*, AS-6 *Kingfish*, AS-7 *Kerry*, AS-10 *Karen*, AS-11 *Kilter*, AS-12 *Kegler*, AS-13 *Kingbolt*, AS-14 *Kedge*.

COASTAL DEFENCE FORCES: ε29,500

(incl Naval Infantry, Coastal Artillery and Rocket Troops, Coastal Defence Troops).

NAVAL INFANTRY (Marines): (some 12,000).
1 inf div (7,000: 3 inf, 1 tk, 1 arty regt).
4 indep bde (1 reserve) (type: 3,000: 4 inf, 1 tk, 1 arty, 1 MRL, 1 ATK bn).
4 fleet SF bde: 2–3 underwater, 1 para bn, spt elm.

EQUIPMENT:
MBT: 260 T-55.
LIGHT TANKS: 120 PT-76.
RECCE: 60 BRDM-2/*Sagger* ATGW.
APC: some 900: BTR-60/-70/-80, 250 MT-LB.
SP ARTY: 122mm: 96 2S1; 152mm: 18 2S3.
MRL: 122mm: 96 9P138.
COMBINED GUN/MORTAR: 120mm: 168 2S9 SP, 11 2S23 SP.
ATGW: 72 AT-3/-5.
AD GUNS: 23mm: 60 ZSU-23-4 SP.
SAM: 250 SA-7, 20 SA-8, 50 SA-9/-13.

COASTAL ARTILLERY AND ROCKET TROOPS: (4,500).
1 coastal arty div (role: protects approaches to naval bases and major ports).
EQUIPMENT:
ARTY: incl SM-4-1 130mm.
SSM: 40 SS-C-1b *Sepal* (similar to SS-N-3), SS-C-3, *Styx*, SS-C-4 reported.

COASTAL DEFENCE TROOPS: (13,000).
3 Coast Defence div.
2 arty regt.
1 MG/arty bn.
EQUIPMENT:
MBT: 700 T-80.
AIFV: 450 BMP.
APC: 280 BTR-60/-70/-80, 790 MT-LB.
TOTAL ARTY: 600.
TOWED ARTY: 516: 122mm: 240 D-30; 152mm: 40 D-20, 186 2A65, 50 2A36.
SP ARTY: 152mm: 48 2S5.
MRL: 122mm: 36 BM-21.

NAVAL DEPLOYMENT:
NORTHERN FLEET (Arctic and Atlantic) (HQ Severomorsk):
BASES: Kola Inlet, Motovskiy Gulf, Gremikha, Polyarnyy, Litsa Gulf.
SUBMARINES: 104: strategic: 30 SSBN; tactical: 67: 15 SSGN, 30 SSN, 22 SS; 7 other roles.
PRINCIPAL SURFACE COMBATANTS: 48: incl 2 CVV, 8 cruisers, 8 destroyers, 30 frigates.
OTHER SURFACE SHIPS: about 10 patrol and coastal combatants, 40 mine warfare, 13 amph, some 180 spt and misc.
NAVAL AVIATION:
190 cbt ac; 69 armed hel.
BOMBERS: 70: 30 Tu-16, 40 Tu-26.
FIGHTER/FGA: 75: 30 MiG-27, 45 Su-24/-25.
ASW:
AIRCRAFT: 45: 5 Tu-142, 16 Il-38, 24 Be-12;
HELICOPTERS: 64 (afloat): 14 Ka-25, 50 Ka-27.
MR/EW:
AIRCRAFT: 37: 2 An-12, 20 Tu-16, 14 Tu-95, 1 Il-20.
HELICOPTERS: 5 Ka-25.
MCM: 8 Mi-14 hel.
CBT ASLT HEL: 10 Ka-27.
COMMUNICATIONS: 6 Tu-142.
TANKERS: 1 Tu-16.
NAVAL INFANTRY:
2 bde (80 MBT, 130 arty).
COASTAL DEFENCE:
1 Coast Defence div (267 T-80, 660 MT-LB, 150 arty), 1 arty regt (120 arty).

BALTIC FLEET (HQ Kaliningrad):
BASES: Kronshtadt, Baltiysk.
SUBMARINES: 10: strategic: nil; tactical: 9: 9 SS; other roles: 1 SS.
PRINCIPAL SURFACE COMBATANTS: 32: incl 3 cruisers, 3 destroyers, 26 frigates.
OTHER SURFACE SHIPS: about 60 patrol and coastal combatants, 50 mine warfare, 21 amph, some 100 spt and misc.
NAVAL AVIATION:
195 cbt ac, 35 armed hel.
FGA: 180: 5 regts: 80 Su-17, 100 Su-24.
ASW:
AIRCRAFT: 15: 15 Be-12.
HELICOPTERS: 35: 3 Ka-25, 22 Ka-27, 10 Mi-14.
MR/EW:
AIRCRAFT 7: 1 An-12, 6 Su-24.
HELICOPTERS: 5 Ka-25.
MCM: 5 Mi-14 hel.
CBT ASLT HEL: 5 Ka-29.
NAVAL INFANTRY:
1 bde, (26 MBT, 43 arty/MRL) (Kaliningrad).
COAST DEFENCE:
1 arty regt (120 arty).
1 SSM regt: some 8 SS-C-1b *Sepal*.

BLACK SEA FLEET: ε48,000 (incl Naval Air, Naval Infantry and Coastal Defence) (HQ Sevastopol) (Ukraine). Under joint Russian/Ukrainian command for 3–5 years, then to be divided between Russia and Ukraine.
BASES: Sevastopol, Odessa (Ukraine).
SUBMARINES: 20: tactical 17: 2 SSG, 15 SS; other roles: 3.
PRINCIPAL SURFACE COMBATANTS: 31: incl 1 CGH, 4 cruisers, 5 destroyers, 21 frigates.
OTHER SURFACE SHIPS: about 40 patrol and coastal combatants, 30 mine warfare, 16 amph, some 130 spt and misc.

NAVAL AVIATION: (7,600); some 241 cbt ac; 85 armed hel.
BOMBERS: 69: some 40 Tu-22M, 29 Tu-16.
FGA: 2 regt: 83: 40 Su-17, 43 Su-25.
FIGHTER: 2 regt: 66: 47 MiG-29, 5 Su-25, 14 Su-27.
ASW: 23* Be-12 **ac**; 31 Mi-14, 49 Ka-25, 5 Ka-27 **hel**.
MR/EW: 2 An-12, 12 Tu-16, 6 Tu-22, 1 Il-20 **ac**, 5 Ka-25 **hel**.
MCM: 5 Mi-14 hel.
NAVAL INFANTRY: (2,000).
1 bde (203 APC, 47 arty (2S1, 2S9)).
COASTAL DEFENCE: (1,900).
1 Coast Defence div (250 MBT (T-64), 320 AIFV (BMP-2), 72 arty (D-30)).

CASPIAN FLOTILLA:

BASES: Astrakan (Russia).
The Caspian Sea Flotilla has been divided between Azerbaijan (about 25%) and Russia, Kazakhstan and Turkmenistan which are operating a joint flotilla under Russian command and currently based at Astrakan.
PRINCIPAL SURFACE COMBATANTS: 2 frigates.
OTHER SURFACE SHIPS: 12 patrol and coastal combatants, 18 mine warfare, some 20 amph ships and craft, about 10 spt.

PACIFIC FLEET (Indian Ocean) (HQ Vladivostok):

BASES: Vladivostok, Petropavlovsk, Kamchatskiy, Magadan, Sovetskaya Gavan.
SUBMARINES: 51: strategic: 16 SSBN; tactical: 34: 4 SSGN, 14 SSN, 16 SS; other roles: 1 SS.
PRINCIPAL SURFACE COMBATANTS: 50: incl: 9 cruisers, 6 destroyers, 35 frigates.
OTHER SURFACE SHIPS: about 25 patrol and coastal combatants, 55 mine warfare, 19 amph, some 180 spt and misc.
NAVAL AIR (Pacific Fleet Air Force) (HQ Vladivostok): 170 cbt ac, 89 cbt hel.
BOMBERS: 60: 2 regt with 60 Tu-26.
FGA: 40: 1 regt with 40 Su-17, Su-24, Su-25.
ASW:
AIRCRAFT 70: 20 Tu-142, 20 Il-38, 30 Be-12.
HELICOPTERS: 89: afloat: 23 Ka-25, 38 Ka-27; ashore: 28 Mi-14.
MR/EW:
AIRCRAFT: some 20 An-12, Tu-95.
HELICOPTERS: 10 Ka-25.
MCM: 6 Mi-14 hel.
CBT ASLT HEL: 10 Ka-27.
COMMUNICATION: 7 Tu-142.
TANKERS: 2 Tu-16.
NAVAL INFANTRY:
1 div HQ, 3 inf, 1 tk and 1 arty regt:
COAST DEFENCE:
1 Coast Defence div.

DEPLOYMENT:

Determining the manning category of Russian div is difficult. The following assessment is based on the latest available information. Category A (above 75%): none reported; Category B (50–75%): possibly 5 TD, 13 MRD and 5 ABD. The remaining div are assessed as Category C (20–50%).

MILITARY DISTRICTS OF RUSSIA:

KALININGRAD:
GROUND: 38,000: 1 army HQ, 1 TD, 2 MRD, 1 tk, 1 arty, 3 SSM, 1 AB, 2 SAM bde, 2 MRL, 2 ATK, 1 attack hel regt, 1,100 MBT, 1,300 ACV, 600 arty/MRL/mors, 24 *Scud*, 16 SS-21, 48 attack hel.
AIR DEFENCE:
FIGHTER: 1 regt (35 Su-27).
SAM: 250.

LENINGRAD MD (HQ St Petersburg):
GROUND: 78,000: 1 army HQ, 1 corps HQ; 6 MRD (1 trg), 1 ABD; plus 1 arty (5 regt), 1 MG arty div, 4 arty bde, 3 SSM, 1 AB, 1 *Spetsnaz*, 4 SAM bde, 3 ATK, 2 attack hel, 1 aslt tpt hel regt, 1,100 MBT, 1,800 ACV, 1,400 arty/MRL/mors, 12 *Scud*, 36 SS-21, 70 attack hel.
AIR: 1 air army; 2 bbr regt (90: Su-24), 1 recce regt (35: MiG-25, Su-17), 1 ftr regt (35 Su-27, 60 MiG-29).
AIR DEFENCE: 8 regt: 30 MiG-23, 25 MiG-25, 125 MiG-31, 80 Su-27.
SAM: 400.

MOSCOW MD (HQ Moscow):
GROUND: 103,000: 2 Army HQ, 5 TD (1 trg), 1 MRD, 2 ABD, 11 arty bde/regt, 3 ATK, 4 SSM, 3 indep MR, 1 *Spetsnaz*, 3 SAM bde, 5 attack hel, 1 aslt tpt hel regt, 2,200 MBT, 2,200 ACV, 1,200 arty/MRL/mors, 24 *Scud*, 18 SS-21, 230 attack hel.
AIR: 1 air army: 1 bbr div (75 Su-24), 1 ftr div (35 Su-27, 85 MiG-29), 1 FGA regt (50 Su-25), 1 recce regt (25 Su-24/MiG-25), 2 trg regt: 200 L-39 plus 410 in store.
AIR DEFENCE: 7 regt: 70 MiG-23, 20 MiG-25, 70 MiG-31, 70 Su-27 plus 170 in store.
SAM: 1,000.

VOLGA MD (HQ Kuybyshev (Samarra)):
GROUND: 60,000: 1 Army HQ, 2 TD, 2 MRD (1 trg), 1 ABD plus 3 arty bde/regt, 2 SSM, 2 SAM bde, 1 ATK, 2 attack hel, 1 aslt tpt hel, 6 hel trg regt, 1,100 MBT, 2,000 ACV, 400 arty/MRL/mor, 24 *Scud*, 18 SS-21, 250 attack hel.

AIR: 2 ftr trg regt: 57 MiG-29, 24 Su-17, 10 Su-25, 180 cbt ac in store.
AIR DEFENCE: 270 cbt ac in store.
NORTH CAUCASUS MD (HQ Rostov):
GROUND: 38,000: 1 Army HQ, 2 corps HQ, 2 MRD, 1 ABD, 2 AB, 4 MR bde, 1 *Spetsnaz,* 5 arty bde, 3 SSM, 3 SAM bde, 3 ATK, 2 attack hel, 1 aslt tpt hel regt, 250 MBT, 815 ACV, 520 arty/MRL/mor, 24 *Scud,* 72 attack hel.
AIR: 1 Air Army: 1 bbr div (90 Su-24), 1 FGA div (90 Su-25), 1 ftr div (90 MiG-29), 1 recce regt (35 Su-24).
5 trg regt: 35 Su-22, 15 Su-24, 15 Su-27, 20 MiG-29, 70 L-39, plus 130 cbt ac in store.
AIR DEFENCE: 3 regt, 30 MiG-25, 65 Su-27; 2 trg centre: 175: MiG-21, MiG-23, Su-15 (half are trainer variants), 165 L-29/L-39.
SAM: 150.
URAL MD (HQ Yekaterinburg):
GROUND: 2 TD (1 trg), 2 MRD, 2 arty bde/regt, 1 ATK bde. 1,200 MBT, 1,200 ACV, 750 arty/MRL/mor.
AIR: bbr 30 Su-24.
AIR DEFENCE: 3 regt: 75 MiG-23, 40 MiG-25, plus in store 25 MiG-23, 110 Su-15.
SAM: 100.
SIBERIAN MD (HQ Novosibirsk):
GROUND: 1 Corps HQ, 7 MRD, 1 arty div, 2 MR bde, 3 arty bde/regt, 2 SSM, 2 SAM, 1 *Spetsnaz* bde, 1 ATK, 1 attack hel regt, 2,000 MBT, 3,500 ACV, 2,200 arty/MRL/mor, 24 *Scud,* 40 attack hel.
AIR: trg units, 275: L-29, L-39.
AIR DEFENCE: 4 regt: 140: MiG-23, MiG-31.
TRANSBAYKAL MD (HQ Chita):
GROUND: 3 army HQ, 4 TD (1 trg), 11 MRD (1 trg), plus 2 MG/arty div, 1 arty div, 5 arty bde/regt, 3 SSM, 1 AB, 1 *Spetsnaz,* 2 ATK, 3 SAM bde, 2 attack hel regt, 3,000 MBT, 4,000 ACV, 4,000 arty/MRL/mor, 24 *Scud,* 18-SS-21, 80 attack hel.
AIR: 1 air army, bbr: 80 Su-24, ftr 30 MiG-29; FGA 30 MiG-27; recce: 75 Su-17/24.
FAR EASTERN MD (HQ Khabarovsk):
GROUND: 4 army, 1 corps HQ, 3 TD (1 trg), 16 MRD (2 trg), plus 5 MG/arty div, 1 arty div, 11 arty bde/regt, 2 AB, 5 SSM, 6 SAM, 1 *Spetsnaz,* 3 ATK bde, 6 attack hel regt, 6,000 MBT, 8,700 ACV, 5,800 arty/MRL/mor, 60 *Scud,* 200 attack hel.
AIR: bbr: 120 Su-24; FGA: 100: Su-17, Su-25; ftr div, 85: MiG-29, Su-27; recce 60: Su-17, Su-24.
AIR DEFENCE (Transbaykal and Far Eastern MD): 350 MiG-23, MiG-31, Su-27.
SAM: 570.
GROUPS OF FORCES:
NORTH-WESTERN GROUP OF FORCES (HQ Riga): (11,000).
ESTONIA: (2,000).
GROUND: elm 1 MRD, 31 MBT, 240 ACV, 84 arty/MRL/mor.
LATVIA: (9,000): all to have withdrawn by 31 August 1994.
GROUND: 1 MR bde, 51 MBT, 65 ACV, 30 arty/MRL/mor.
AIR: 1 composite regt: **ac:** An-12, An-26; **hel:** Mi-8.
TRANSCAUCASUS GROUP OF FORCES (HQ Georgia): (ε25,000) (excl peacekeeping forces).
ARMENIA:
GROUND: (ε5,000): 1 MRD, 80 MBT, 190 ACV, 100 arty/MRL/mors.
GEORGIA:
GROUND: (20,000): 2 MRD, 230 MBT, 300 ACV, 220 arty/MRL/mors.
AIR: 1 composite regt: with some 35 **ac:** An-12, An-26; **hel:** Mi-8.

FORCES IN OTHER FORMER SOVIET REPUBLICS:

BELARUS:
AIR: 1 regt, 30 Su-24; 1 regt with 20 Tu-22M, 15 Tu-16; 1 hy bbr div with 15 Tu-22M; 50 Tu-22; 1 recce regt with 20 Tu-22.
MOLDOVA (Dniestr) (14th Army): (9,200): 1 army HQ, 1 MRD, 120 MBT, 180 ACV, 130 arty/MRL/mor.
SAM: 25: SA-3, SA-5.
TAJIKISTAN:
GROUND: (12,000): 1 MRD, 180 MBT, 340 ACV, 180 arty/MRL/mors.
AIR DEFENCE:
SAM: 10: SA-2, SA-3.
TURKMENISTAN:
JOINT TURKMENISTAN/RUSSIAN FORCES:
GROUND: (28,000): 1 Corps HQ, 3 MRD (1 trg), 3 arty bde, 900 MBT, 1,800 ACV, 900 arty/MRL/mor.
AIR: 1 FGA regt 60 Su-17, 1 regt, 3 Su-7B, 3 MiG-21, 2 L-39, 8 Yak-28, 3 An-12, 1 (trg) unit with **ac:** 16 MiG-29, 16 Su-27; **hel:** 3 Mi-8.
AIR DEFENCE: 2 regt: 38 MiG-23, 30 MiG-25.
SAM: 75: SA-2, SA-3, SA-5.

FORCES ABROAD (other than in the republics of the former USSR or in Groups of Forces):
VIETNAM: (500); naval base; 1 Tu-142, 8 Tu-16 MR ac on det; AA, SAM, electronic monitoring station.
OTHER: Algeria 100; Angola 50; Cambodia 500; Congo 20; Cuba some 800 SIGINT and ε10 mil advisers; India 500; Libya 1,000; Mali 20; Mongolia: ε500 SIGINT; Mozambique 25; Peru 10; Syria 500; Yemen 300; Africa (remainder) 100.

UN AND PEACEKEEPING:

ANGOLA (UNAVEM): 15 Observers.
BOSNIA (UNPROFOR BH): 575; 1 inf bn.
CROATIA (UNPROFOR I): 879; 1 AB bn, 12 Observers.
GEORGIA/ABKHAZIA: ε3,000; 1 AB regt, 2 MR bn.
GEORGIA/SOUTH OSSETIA: 1 inf bn.
IRAQ/KUWAIT (UNIKOM): 15 Observers.
MIDDLE EAST (UNTSO): 12 Observers.
MOLDOVA/DNIESTR: 4 inf bn.
MOZAMBIQUE (ONUMOZ): 19 Observers.
RWANDA (UNAMIR): 15 Observers.
WESTERN SAHARA (MINURSO): 29 Observers.

PARAMILITARY: 280,000.

FRONTIER FORCES (directly subordinate to the President): 100,000, 6 frontier districts, Arctic, Kaliningrad, Moscow units.
EQUIPMENT:
1,500 ACV (incl BMP, BTR).
90 arty (incl 2S1, 2S9, 2S12).
AIR: ac: some 70: An-2, An-26; **hel:** some 200+: Mi-8, Mi-24, Mi-26, Ka-17.
PATROL AND COASTAL COMBATANTS: about 212:
OFFSHORE PATROL: about 25:
7 *Krivak-III* with 1 x Ka-27 hel, 1 x 100mm gun.
12 *Grisha-II*, 6 *Grisha-III*.
COASTAL PATROL: about 32: 25 *Pauk*, 7 *Svetlyak*.
INSHORE PATROL: about 155: 110 *Stenka*, 15 *Muravey*, 30 *Zhuk*.
RIVERINE MONITORS: about 126: 19 *Yaz*, 10 *Piyavka*, 7 *Vosh*, 90 *Shmel*.
SUPPORT AND MISCELLANEOUS: about 26:
8 *Ivan Susanin* armed icebreakers, 18 *Sorum* armed ocean tugs.
MVD (*Ministerstvo Vnutrennikh Del*): internal security tps: 180,000; 1 div, some indep regt (30,000); special motorised units (40,000); guards and escorts (some 110,000). Eqpt incl 1,200 ACV, 20 D-30.

The Middle East and North Africa

Political and Security Developments

Twelve months ago this section began, 'not a great deal has changed in the last 12 months'. This year, however, has witnessed a new Middle East war, distinct progress towards an Arab–Israeli peace settlement and the establishment of a Palestinian autonomous entity in Gaza and Jericho.

The Yemen Civil War

The civil war in Yemen which broke out at the end of April 1994 was the result of rivalry between the southern Yemini Vice-President, Ali Salim al-Bid, and the northern President Ali Abdullah Saleh. Northern authorities, believing that al-Bid was plotting to overthrow President Saleh, identified arms caches in San'a and launched a pre-emptive attack on southern troops garrisoned in the north. The escalation from pre-emptive action to full-scale war between the two former Yemeni states was made easier by the fact that the two armies had never been properly integrated after unification. Only a token exchange of garrisons had taken place with a southern brigade being located at Amran some 40km north of San'a and a northern brigade at Zinjibar 50km north-east of Aden. The northern forces were stronger in all respects, particularly manpower, although the south had longer-range, but less accurate, SSM (*Scud* missiles were fired at San'a on two or three occasions).

Northern troops rapidly advanced towards Aden and southern forces were unable to block the advance in the mountainous area south of the border. Northern forces spent some time overcoming the garrison of the southern Russian-built base at Al-Anad, 40km north of Aden, before the open desert surrounding Aden was reached. The south announced its secession from the unified Yemen state on 21 May 1994, but although some Middle East states supported the south's cause, none recognised its secession. On 7 July Aden fell, as did the eastern city of Mukallah, and to all intents and purposes the war was over. The southern leadership has fled the country and may attempt to organise a guerrilla movement to oppose the government. There have been few reports of the scale of casualties suffered in the war; on 5 June 1994 the government admitted to 613 dead, 2,030 wounded with 2,100 missing or prisoners of war (these last presumably from the Zinjibar brigade). Total northern casualties are likely to be around double these figures (less the missing), while the south will certainly have suffered even more.

Arab–Israeli Peace Process

A major step forward was taken towards an overall Middle East peace settlement when it was revealed at the end of August 1993 that Israel and the PLO, during secret talks held in Oslo, had agreed formally to recognise each other. The revelation was followed in September by an exchange of letters between Chairman Arafat and Prime Minister Rabin, and on 13 September by the signing in Washington DC of the 'Declaration of Principles on Interim Self-Government Arrangements'. The key element to the agreement was that Israel would withdraw its troops and hand over administrative responsibility to a Palestinian authority in the West Bank city of Jericho and in the Gaza strip. Also agreed were:

- A timetable for detailed talks on, and implementation of, Israeli withdrawal.
- A redeployment of Israeli troops elsewhere in the West Bank to avoid major centres of Arab population.
- An election throughout the West Bank and Gaza before 13 July 1994 to elect a Council.
- Responsibility for education, health, social welfare, taxation and tourism to be Palestinian.
- The formation of a Palestinian police force.
- Negotiations regarding the permanent status of the territories to start no later than the third year of the five-year transitional period.

Agreement over Jerusalem, settlements, refugees, security and borders would be left to the permanent-status talks.

A serious interruption to the peace process was threatened when, on 25 February 1994, an Israeli resident of Kiryat Arba opened fire with an automatic weapon on Palestinians praying at Abraham's tomb in Hebron, killing some 30 people. A high level of civil disturbance ensued throughout the West Bank and Gaza to which not only the Army and police, but militant settlers reacted. The Israeli Prime Minister, and many others, promptly condemned the massacre. There were calls (including from Israeli government ministers) for the removal of 400 Israeli settlers from Hebron whose protection the Army said would require 1,000–1,500 soldiers. The Israeli government outlawed two extremist anti-Arab groups, Kahane Chai and Kach, and eventually agreed to the deployment of a small group of international observers in Hebron. The peace process was not derailed, but the Muslim extremist group – Hamas – swore to commit five acts of revenge; by the end of July 1994 two had taken place, both involving bombs on buses.

In the event none of the originally agreed deadlines were met, but control of Jericho was handed over on 15 May 1994 and of Gaza the next day. Chairman Arafat visited Gaza in early July 1994 and on 5 July the Palestine National Authority was sworn in at Jericho. At a meeting in Rome, Arafat and Rabin agreed to set up committees to settle outstanding issues in Gaza and Jericho, the expansion of civil administration in the West Bank and the problem of Palestinian refugees in the diaspora. Jordan and Egypt were to be represented at these talks. On 7 July 1994, Arafat announced that the Palestinian National Council would convene in Gaza to amend the PLO Charter.

No substantive agreement has been reached over a peace treaty with Syria, but the process continues. Prime Minister Rabin has indicated that Israel would withdraw totally from the Golan and that the settlers there would be relocated, assuming acceptable military arrangements could be made and that a truly comprehensive peace is achieved. The Syrians have still not clarified what they mean by full peace which continues to hamper the process, but it is understood that they may well accept the principles of a phased withdrawal, the deployment of an international peacekeeping force, and even the possibility of Syrian forces redeploying back from their present front-line positions.

The most recent developments in the peace process concern Israel and Jordan. Although a common agenda for peace talks had been signed in September 1993, no progress was made until June 1994 when it was revealed that Prime Minister Rabin and King Hussein had held secret talks. Jordan and Israel agreed to set up commissions to settle the questions of sharing water resources, environmental concerns, demarcation of borders, security including combatting terrorism and subversion, trade and economic cooperation. The first meeting took place on 18 July and King Hussein and Rabin met for their first open face-to-face talks in Washington DC on 25 July 1994 when they signed a declaration that the state of war was over and pleded to forge economic links. However, Jordan is unlikely to sign a formal peace treaty with Israel until an Israeli treaty with Syria is agreed.

Successful progress towards an overall peace settlement has not inhibited Israeli military action either against Hamas and other terrorists in the West Bank, or against Hizbollah in Lebanon. There have been frequent air-raids on the latter's locations, and in May 1994 a commando raid kidnapped a Shi'ite leader, Mustafa Dirani, on the grounds that he could be involved in the imprisonment of the Israeli pilot held since 1986.

Other Political Matters

Muslim extremist terrorists continue their campaigns in **Egypt** and **Algeria,** targeting foreigners as much as the security forces. There has also been little progress in the problem of the **Western Sahara**. The latest setback to the United Nations planned referendum was the Moroccan objection to observers from the Organisation of African Unity (which recognises the Saharawi Arab Democratic Republic which the Polisario Front has been fighting to establish since 1976)

at the identification and registration of voters due to start in June 1994. UN-imposed sanctions on **Libya** are still in force as it will not hand over two men suspected of causing the crash of the Pan-Am flight over Lockerbie in 1988.

Weapons of Mass Destruction

The United Nations Special Commission (UNSCOM) has reported that the last quantity of plutonium in **Iraq** was transferred to Russia on 12 February 1994. The UNSCOM Chemical Destruction Group completed its task in June 1994; in all, 480,000 litres of chemical agent and 28,000 munitions were destroyed. The **UAE** has acquired six *Scud B* launchers. Iranian SSM now include 20 Chinese CSS-8, considered to have a range of 150km with a 190kg warhead. Iran is the first country to field CSS-8.

Conventional Force Developments

In **Algeria** the number of Russian military advisers has been drastically reduced (there are probably now less than 100) following the murder of two advisers in October 1993. The Army has ten more 2S3 152mm SP guns and 15 more Mi-8/-17 helicopters (five attack, ten transport models). During 1992, 53 APCs were imported from Egypt. **Libyan** helicopter holdings have been reassessed; there are now 65 attack helicopters (five more Mi-24 and 15 more Mi-35) and 19 more transport helicopters (nine more Mi8/-17 and ten more Mi-2). The **Moroccan** Army has taken delivery of 240 US M-60A3 tanks. The two Italian-built frigates, originally destined for Iraq, have not yet been delivered.

The **Egyptian** Army has received 67 more, locally fabricated, M-1A1 *Abrams* tanks and has acquired 112 *Commando Scout* armoured reconnaissance vehicles from the US. Improved information has allowed a revision of artillery holdings; the main changes are that there are 96 (as opposed to 75) 122mm BM-11 MRL, and 1,800 (as opposed to 900) 120mm mortars. ATGW numbers have increased considerably; there are a total of 5,220 *TOW* launchers including 2,900 improved *TOW* (incorporating an improved warhead) and 520 *TOW*-2A aimed to defeat reactive armour. The first of four Chinese-built *Romeo*-class submarines has returned after modernisation in the US; it is now armed with *Harpoon* SSM and US Mk-37 torpedoes. Two US *Knox*-class frigates will join the fleet on lease before the end of 1994. Patrol craft numbers have been revised and there are five more than previously listed. The Air Force has taken delivery of its first two Turkish-assembled F-16 aircraft; 44 have been ordered to be delivered by the end of 1995. **Egypt** is hoping to obtain a number of surplus US weapons at little or no cost; the shopping list is said to include 1,500 M-113 APCs, over 800 M60-A3 tanks, *Hawk* Phase III SAM, *Stinger* shoulder-launched SAM, C-130 transport aircraft and KC-135 tankers.

The **Lebanese** Army strength has been increased by some 3,000. Equipment holdings have been reassessed and show increases of 15 AMX-13 light tanks, ten AML-90 armoured reconnaissance vehicles and 100 M-113 and 60 AMX-VC1 APCs over the previous listing. This year *The Military Balance* lists the Palestinian entity of **Gaza and Jericho** for the first time. There are no armed forces, but a police force which will have small arms, machine guns and some APCs is being established mainly from Palestinian Liberation Army (PLA) units which have formed part of a number of Arab armies for some years. PLA units are no longer listed. The police has an agreed authorised strength of 9,000 men.

The **Israeli** Army has taken delivery of 60 more *Merkava* III tanks, and a new heavy APC, the *Achzarit*, which is based on a T-55 tank chassis, is being introduced (this is the IDF's second heavy APC, the other being the *Nagmashot* based on a *Centurion* tank chassis). Experience has shown that if infantry are to work closely or ahead of tanks they need better protection than that offered by normal APC armour; it is, however, an expensive option and no other army has introduced heavy APCs. The Army is also purchasing a number of MLRS from the US. The Navy has commissioned the first of three *Eilat*-class corvettes; the *Eilat* are Sa'ar 5 and are being built in the US, but with weapons systems installed in Israel. They are armed with *Harpoon* and

Gabriel SSM and *Barak* SAM and can embark a helicopter. In February 1994 the *Kidon* missile craft, a Sa'ar 4.5, was relaunched. Sa'ar 4.5 models are rebuilt and improved *Reshef*-class missile boats and will also be armed with *Harpoon*, *Gabriel* and *Barak*. The Air Force listing has been substantially revised. The conversion of two squadrons from F-4E to *Phantom* 2000 has been completed. Additional numbers of *Kfir*, F-4E and A-4 aircraft have been taken out of squadron service and are now shown in store; some may well be refurbished and offered for export. The Air Force has increased its attack helicopter capability by adding 24 more AH-64A *Apache* helicopters. It is to purchase some 20 F-15I, costing about $100m each, and there are plans to replace the remaining *Kfir* and A-4 aircraft with 50 second-hand F-16 from surplus US Air Force stocks. Delivery is expected to begin in August 1994.

Following the report of a commission, the length of conscript service is to be shortened by four months. The first soldiers to benefit from this cut will be those inducted into the Army in February 1993. Women's service is to be reduced to 21 months. Prime Minister Rabin has told the Knesset that the size of the reserve will be reduced by about half by 1996. In January 1994, Israeli industries unveiled a new missile warning device, *Piano*, which employs passive, electro-optic technology. Development of the ATBM *Arrow* continues, largely financed by the US, although *Arrow* is no longer a component of the US Ballistic Missile Defense programme. The most recent *Arrow* test was made in June 1994 when a target missile was successfully intercepted for the first time.

Jordan has many more anti-tank rocket-launchers than previously listed; there are some 2,000 LAW-80 launchers and 2,000 *Apilas*. **Syria** is reported to have ordered from Russia 14 Su-17, 30 Su-24 and 50 MiG-29 aircraft and a number of SA-10 SAM, which is claimed to have an anti-tactical ballistic-missile capability.

Iraq has formed an eighth Revolutionary Guard force division, but appears to have reduced the number of infantry divisions and special forces brigades. Improved information has allowed *The Military Balance* to give more details of **Iranian** Army weapons holdings. The number of tanks in service has been reassessed as 1,245, of which the most recent acquisitions have been some 260 Chinese Type-59 and 140 T-72 tanks. SP artillery and MRL increases have also been noted. The number of *Scud*-B SSM launchers is much lower than had previously been thought and it is now believed that Iran has acquired 20 Chinese CSS-8 SSM launchers. More detail is also available on helicopter holdings which are larger than had been thought and include additional types. The Air Force has incorporated some Iraqi aircraft (which had flown out to Iran as the coalition air attacks on Iraq began in 1991); it now has 30 Su-24 FGA and 50 MiG-29 fighters in service. The Navy expects the third *Kilo*-class submarine to reach Iranian waters before the end of 1994.

Kuwait has completed the 207km-long ditch, sand-wall and barbed-wire fence demarcating the border with Iraq. Work is under way to build a patrol road along the border and the next stage will be the installation of observation posts and monitoring sensors. The Army has added a further 1,000 men to its strength and has formed a commando battalion. No ground-forces heavy weapons have been delivered during the last 12 months, but the first of 218 M1A2 *Abrams* ordered in late 1991 have been delivered. Also on order are 254 British-made *Warrior* AIFVs. The Army has still not finalised its plans for artillery, but both MRL and SP guns are expected to be acquired, possibly some from Russia. Kuwait appears to be giving priority to air defence and will acquire both US and Russian systems. An order for five batteries-worth of *Patriot* SAM has been placed, and the Russian order is for SA-12 SAM, but the extent of the order is not known. Kuwait currently fields four *Hawk* batteries with six Phase III launchers each, and six batteries each with a *Sky Guard* radar, two *Aspede* SAM and two twin 30mm *Oerlikon* guns. The Air Force's A-4 FGA and *Mirage* F-1 fighters are no longer in service. The Navy has commissioned two more Australian 31.5 metre inshore patrol craft. In **Bahrain,** the Army has been reorganised to form two tank, two mechanised and one motor infantry battalions. Artillery holdings have been increased by nine MLRS, making this the first Arab army to be equipped with such a weapon, and 13 203mm M-110 SP guns. 14 AH-1E *Cobra* attack helicopters have been purchased, but not yet delivered. The **UAE** Army strength has been increased by 4,000 and 85 more BMP-3 have been acquired. An order for 436 *Leclerc* tanks was placed in June 1994 with delivery to start in 1995. The Air Force has formed a third FGA squadron, this one equipped with 18 *Hawk* 102 aircraft. In **Saudi Arabia**, the Army has taken delivery of 40 more M60A3 tanks and the first 30 M-1A2 *Abrams* out of an order for 315. Plans to buy another 150 have been shelved. *The Military Balance* incorrectly listed 400 M-2 *Bradley* AIFVs last year. Only 200 have been delivered, but more are on order. Orders for military equipment worth more than $20bn are in hand, but low oil prices have led to a cash-flow crisis for Saudi Arabia which has had to prolong a number of orders and to arrange for a number of payments to be rescheduled, although this will mean higher costs as a result of interest charges incurred by the supplying countries. The **Oman** Air Force is retiring its elderly *Hunters* and is replacing them with *Hawk* 203, four of an order for 12 have been delivered so far. The Army has ordered 18 British *Challenger* II tanks and 80 MOWAG *Piranha* ACV (without a chain gun) to be made in the UK under Swiss licence. The Army is said to be about to place an order for South African G-6 SP guns. This would be the first order to be placed after the lifting of the UN embargo on arms trading with South Africa.

MIDDLE EAST

BAHRAIN

GDP	1992: D 1.6bn ($4.2bn):		
	per capita $7,900		
	1993ε: D1.7bn ($4.4bn):		
	per capita $8,000		
Growth	1992: 2.5%	1993: 1.5%	
Inflation	1992: -0.2%	1993: 1.0%	
Debt	1992: $2.4bn	1993: $2.6bn	
Def exp	1991: D 89.2m ($237.0m)		
	1992: D 94.6m ($252.0m)		
Def bdgt[a]	1993: D 92.0m ($244.1m)		
	1994: D 93.3m ($248.1m)		
FMA	1993: $0.6m (FMF, IMET)		
	1994: $0.1m (IMET)		
	1995: $0.1m (IMET)		
$1 = D	1992–94: 0.38		
D = dinar			

[a] Excl a subsidy from the Gulf Cooperation Council (GCC) of $1.8bn (1984–94) shared between Bahrain and Oman.

Population: 560,000 (Nationals 68%, other Arab 10%, Asian 13%, Iranian 8%, European 1%)

	13–17	*18–22*	*23–32*
Men	23,900	21,000	42,800
Women	24,000	20,900	37,600

TOTAL ARMED FORCES:

ACTIVE: 8,100.

ARMY: 6,800.

1 bde: 2 mech inf, 1 mot inf, 2 tk bn.

EQUIPMENT:

MBT: 80 M-60A3.

RECCE: 22 AML-90, 8 *Saladin*, 8 *Ferret*, 8 *Shorland*.

APC: some 10 AT-105 *Saxon*, 110 Panhard M-3, 115 M-113A2.

TOWED ARTY: 105mm: 8lt; 155mm: 20 M-198.

SP ARTY: 203mm: 13 M-110.

MRL: 227mm: 9 MLRS.

MORTARS: 81mm: 9; 120mm: 9.

ATGW: 15 BGM-71A *TOW*.

RCL: 106mm: 30 M-40A1; 120mm: 6 MOBAT.

SAM: 40+ RBS-70, 18 *Stinger*, 7 *Crotale*.

NAVY: 600.

BASE: Mina Sulman.

PATROL AND COASTAL COMBATANTS: 10:

CORVETTES: 2 *Al Manama* (Ge Lürssen 62-m) with 2 x 2 MM-40 *Exocet* SSM, hel deck.

MISSILE CRAFT: 4 *Ahmad el Fateh* (Ge Lürssen 45-m) with 2 x 2 MM-40 *Exocet*.

PATROL: 4:

2 *Al Riffa* (Ge Lürssen 38-m) PFI.

2 PFI< .

SUPPORT AND MISCELLANEOUS: 4 *Ajeera* LCU-type spt.

AIR FORCE: 700; 24 cbt ac, 10 armed hel.

FGA: 1 sqn with 8 F-5E, 4 F-5F.

FIGHTER: 1 sqn with 8 F-16C, 4 -D.

TRANSPORT: 2 *Gulfstream* (1 -II, 1 -III; VIP), 1 Boeing 727.

HELICOPTERS: 1 sqn with 12 AB-212 (10 armed), 4 Bo-105, 1 UH-60L (VIP).
MISSILES:
ASM: AS-12, AGM-65 *Maverick*.
AAM: AIM-9P *Sidewinder*, AIM-7F *Sparrow*.

PARAMILITARY:

COAST GUARD (Ministry of Interior): ε250; 1 PCI, some 20 PCI‹, 2 spt/landing craft, 1 hovercraft.
POLICE (Ministry of Interior): 9,000; 2 Hughes 500, 2 Bell 412, 1 Bell 205 hel.

EGYPT

GDP	1992: £E 139.1bn ($41.8bn): per capita $4,000	
	1993ε: £E 145.9bn ($43.3bn): per capita $4,050	
Growth	1992: 4.4%	1993ε: 1.0%
Inflation	1992: 13.7%	1993: 12.0%
Debt	1992: $40.4bn	1993: $36.0bn
Def exp	1992ε: £E 6.9bn ($2.1bn)	
Def bdgt	1992: £E 4.6bn ($1.4bn)	
	1993: £E 5.4bn ($1.6bn)	
	1994ε: £E 6.2bn ($1.8bn)	
FMA	1993: $2.1bn (FMF, IMET, Econ aid)	
	1994: $2.1bn (FMF, IMET, Econ aid)	
	1995: $2.1bn (FMF, IMET, Econ aid)	
$1 = £E	1992: 3.33	1993: 3.37
	1994: 3.38	

£E = Egyptian pound

Population: 60,776,700

	13–17	*18–22*	*23–32*
Men	3,137,600	2,666,200	4,517,200
Women	2,964,000	2,502,000	4,247,000

TOTAL ARMED FORCES:

ACTIVE: 440,000 (some 272,000 conscripts).
Terms of service: 3 years (selective).
RESERVES: 254,000: Army 150,000; Navy 14,000; Air Force 20,000; AD 70,000.

ARMY: 310,000 (perhaps 200,000 conscripts).

4 Military Districts, 2 Army HQ:
4 armd div (each with 2 armd, 1 mech bde).
8 mech inf div (each with 2 mech, 1 armd bde).
1 Republican Guard armd bde.
2 indep armd bde. 2 air-mobile bde.
3 indep inf bde. 1 para bde.
4 indep mech bde. 7 cdo gp.
15 indep arty bde. 2 hy mor bde.
2 SSM bde (1 with *FROG-7*, 1 with *Scud* B).
EQUIPMENT:[a]
MBT: 3,234: 840 T-54/-55, 200+ *Ramses II* (mod T-54/55), 500 T-62, 1,547 M-60 (700A1, 847A3), 147 M1A1 *Abrams*.
RECCE: 300 BRDM-2, 112 *Commando Scout*.
AIFV: some 470: 220 BMP-1, some 250 BMR-600P.
APC: 3,619: 650 *Walid*, 165 *Fahd*, 1,075 BTR-50/OT-62, 1,685 M-113A2, 44 M-577.
TOWED ARTY: 971: 122mm: 36 M-31/37, 359 M-1938, 156 D-30M; 130mm: 420 M-46.
SP ARTY: 155mm: 200 M-109A2.
MRL: 122mm: 96 BM-11, 200 BM-21/*as-Saqr*-10/-18/-36.
MORTARS: 82mm (some 50 SP); 107mm: some M-30 SP; 120mm: 1,800 M-43; 160mm: 60 M-160.
SSM launchers: 12 *FROG-7*, *Saqr*-80 (trials), 9 *Scud* B.
ATGW: 1,400 AT-3 *Sagger* (incl BRDM-2); 220 *Milan*; 200 *Swingfire*; 520 *TOW* (incl I-*TOW*, *TOW*-2A (with 52 on M-901 SP)).
RCL: 107mm: B-11.
AD GUNS: 14.5mm: 475 ZPU-2/-4; 23mm: 550 ZU-23-2, 117 ZSU-23-4 SP, 45 *Sinai*; 37mm: 150 M-1939; 57mm: 300 S-60, 40 ZSU-57-2 SP.
SAM: 2,000 SA-7/*'Ayn as-Saqr*, 20 SA-9, 26 M-54 SP *Chaparral*.
SURV: AN/TPQ-37 (arty/mor), RASIT (veh, arty).
UAV: R4E-50 *Skyeye*.

[a] Most Soviet eqpt now in store, incl MBT and some cbt ac.

NAVY: ε20,000 (incl ε2,000 Coast Guards and ε12,000 conscripts).

BASES: Alexandria (HQ, Mediterranean), Port Said, Mersa Matruh, Safaqa, Port Tewfig; Hurghada (HQ, Red Sea).
SUBMARINES: 3:
2 Sov *Romeo* with 533mm TT (plus 2 non-op).
1 Ch Romeo with Sub *Harpoon* and 533mm TT (plus 3 undergoing modernisation).
PRINCIPAL SURFACE COMBATANTS: 5:
DESTROYER: 1 *El Fateh* (UK 'Z') (trg) with 4 x 114mm guns, 5 x 533mm TT.
FRIGATES: 4:
2 *El Suez* (Sp *Descubierta*) with 2 x 3 ASTT, 1 x 2 ASW RL; plus 2 x 4 *Harpoon* SSM.
2 *Al Zaffir* (Ch *Jianghu*-I) with 2 x ASW RL; plus 2 x CSS-N-2 (HY-2) SSM.
(Plus 2 US *Knox*-class to be leased from mid-1994.)

PATROL AND COASTAL COMBATANTS: 44:
MISSILE CRAFT: 26:
6 *Ramadan* with 4 *Otomat* SSM.
6 Sov *Osa-I* with 4 x SS-N-2A *Styx* SSM.
6 *6th October* with 2 *Otomat* SSM.
2 Sov *Komar* with 2 x SSN-2A *Styx*.
6 Ch *Hegu* (*Komar*-type) with 2 HY-2 SSM.
PATROL: 18:
8 Ch *Hainan* PFC with 4 x ASW RL.
6 Sov *Shershen* PFI; 2 with 4 x 533mm TT and BM-21 (8-tube) 122mm MRL; 4 with SA-N-5 and 1 BM-24 (12-tube) 240mm MRL.
4 Ch *Shanghai* II PFI.
MINE WARFARE: 8:
MINE COUNTERMEASURES: 8:
4 *Aswan* (Sov *Yurka*) MSC.
4 *Assiout* (Sov T-43 class) MSC.
AMPHIBIOUS: 3 Sov *Polnocny* LSM, capacity 100 tps, 5 tk, plus 11 LCU (some in reserve).
SUPPORT AND MISCELLANEOUS: 20:
7 AOT (small), 5 trg, 6 tugs, 1 diving spt, 1 *Tariq* (ex-UK FF) trg.

NAVAL AVIATION: 14 armed Air Force hel: 5 *Sea King* Mk 47 (ASW, anti-ship); 9 SA-342 (anti-ship).

COASTAL DEFENCE (Army tps, Navy control):
GUNS: 130mm: SM-4-1.
SSM: *Otomat*.

AIR FORCE: 30,000 (10,000 conscripts);[a] 551 cbt ac, 79 armed hel.
FGA: 7 sqn:
2 with 40 *Alpha Jet*.
2 with 40 Ch J-6.
2 with 25 F-4E.
1 with 16 *Mirage* 5E2.
FIGHTER: 16 sqn:
2 with 30 F-16A.
5 with 100 MiG-21.
2 with 80 F-16C.
3 with 54 *Mirage* 5D/E.
3 with 60 Ch J-7.
1 with 16 *Mirage* 2000C.
RECCE: 2 sqn with 6 *Mirage* 5SDR, 14 MiG-21.
EW: 2 C-130H (ELINT), 4 Beech 1900 (ELINT) **ac**; 4 *Commando* 2E **hel** (ECM).
AEW: 5 E-2C.
ASW: 9 SA-342L, 5 *Sea King* 47 (with Navy).
MR: 2 Beech 1900C surveillance ac.
TRANSPORT: 19 C-130H, 5 DHC-5D, 1 *Super King Air*, 3 *Gulfstream III*, 1 *Gulfstream IV*, 3 *Falcon 20*.
HELICOPTERS: 15 sqn:
ATTACK: 4 sqn with 65 SA-342K (44 with *HOT*, 30 with 20mm gun).
TACTICAL TRANSPORT: hy: 14 CH-47C; **med**: 40 Mi-8, 25 *Commando* (5 -1 tpt, 17 -2 tpt, 3 -2B VIP), 2 S-70 (VIP); **lt**: 12 Mi-4, 17 UH-12E (trg), 2 UH-60A, 3 AS-61.
TRAINING: incl 4 DHC-5, 54 EMB-312, 15* F-16B, 6* F-16D, 36 *Gumhuria*, 16* JJ-6, 40 L-29, 48 L-39, 25* L-59E, MiG-21U, 5* *Mirage* 5SDD, 3* *Mirage* 2000B.
MISSILES:
ASM: AGM-65 *Maverick*, *Exocet* AM-39, AS-12, AS-30, AS-30L *HOT*.
ARM: *Armat*.
AAM: AA-2 *Atoll*, AIM-7E/F/M *Sparrow*, AIM-9F/L/P *Sidewinder*, R-530, R-550 *Magic*.
RPV: 20 R4E-50 *Skyeye*, 27 Teledyne-Ryan 324.

AIR DEFENCE COMMAND: 80,000 (50,000 conscripts).
5 div: regional bde.
100 AD arty bn.
40 SA-2, 53 SA-3, 14 SA-6 bn.
12 bty *Improved HAWK*.
12 bty *Chaparral*.
14 bty *Crotale*.
EQUIPMENT:
AD GUNS: some 2,000: 20mm, 23mm, 37mm, 57mm, 85mm, 100mm.
SAM: some 738: some 360 SA-2, 210 SA-3, 60 SA-6, 72 *Improved HAWK*, 36 *Crotale*.
AD SYSTEMS: some 18 *Amoun* (*Skyguard*/RIM-7F *Sparrow*, some 36 twin 35mm guns, some 36 quad SAM); *Sinai*-23 short-range AD (Dassault 6SD-20S radar, 23mm guns, *'Ayn as-Saqr* SAM).

FORCES ABROAD: advisers in Oman, Saudi Arabia, Zaire.
UN AND PEACEKEEPING:
BOSNIA (UNPROFOR BH): 418; 1 inf bn.
CROATIA (UNPROFOR I): 11 Observers, 10 civ pol.
LIBERIA (UNOMIL): 15 Observers.
MOZAMBIQUE (ONUMOZ): 20 Observers, 52 civ pol.
RWANDA (UNAMIR): 10 Observers.
SOMALIA (UNOSOM): 1,683; 1 inf bde, 6 civ pol.
WESTERN SAHARA (MINURSO): 9 Observers.

PARAMILITARY:
COAST GUARD: ε2,000 (incl in Naval entry).
PATROL, INSHORE: 34:
13 *Timsah* PCI, 10 *Swiftships*, 5 *Nisr*†, 6 *Crestitalia* PFI⟨, plus some 60 boats.
CENTRAL SECURITY FORCES: 300,000; 110 *Hotspur Hussar* APC.

NATIONAL GUARD: 60,000; *Walid* APC.
BORDER GUARD FORCES: 12,000; 18 Border Guard Regt.

FOREIGN FORCES:

PEACEKEEPING (MFO Sinai): some 2,600; contingents from Canada, Colombia, Fiji, France, Italy, Netherlands, New Zealand, Norway, Uruguay and US.

GAZA AND JERICHO

GDP	1993ε: $3.3bn: per capita $1,700
Gaza:	$817.7m: per capita $1,200
West Bank:	$2.5bn: per capita $2,000
Sy bdgt	1994ε: $84m
$1 = n.k.	

Population:[a] Total for West Bank and Gaza: 1,913,600 (Israeli 7%);
Gaza and Jericho only: 808,000 (Israeli 5%).

	13–17	*18–22*	*23–32*
Men	64,400	56,900	37,600
Women	60,500	53,100	43,200

[a] 500,000 Palestinian refugees are living in camps in Lebanon. A further 250,000 have non-permanent status in Jordan.

PARAMILITARY:

ARMED POLICE: up to 9,000 authorised (still forming); small arms, 45 APCs allowed.

PALESTINIAN GROUPS:

All significant Palestinian factions are listed here irrespective of the countr(ies) in which they are based. The faction leader is given after the full title. Strengths are estimates of the number of active 'fighters'; these could be doubled perhaps to give an all-told figure. In 1991, the Lebanon Armed Forces (LAF), backed by the Syrians, entered refugee camps in southern Lebanon to disarm many Palestinian groups of their heavier weapons, such as tanks, artillery and armoured personnel carriers. The LAF conducted further disarming operations against Fatah Revolutionary Council (FRC) refugee camps in spring 1994.

PLO (Palestine Liberation Organisation; Leader: Yasser Arafat):
FATAH: Political wing of the PLO.
PNLA (Palestine National Liberation Army): 8,000. Based in Algeria, Egypt, Lebanon, Libya, Jordan, Iraq, Sudan and Yemen. The PNLA is effectively the military wing of the PLO. Its units in various Middle East countries are closely monitored by host nations' armed forces.
PLF (Palestine Liberation Front; Leader: Al-Abas): ε300–400. Based in Iraq.
DFLP (Democratic Front for the Liberation of Palestine; Leader: Hawatmah): ε500–600. Based in Syria, Lebanon, elsewhere.
FATAH DISSIDENTS (Abu Musa gp): ε1,000. Based in Syria and Lebanon.
PFLP (Popular Front for the Liberation of Palestine; Leader: Habash): ε800. Based in Syria, Lebanon, Occupied Territories.
PFLP (GC) (Popular Front for the Liberation of Palestine (General Command); Leader: Jibril): ε600. Based in Syria, Lebanon, elsewhere.
PSF (Popular Struggle Front; Leader: Samir Ghansha): ε600–700. Based in Syria.
SAIQA (Leader: al-Khadi): ε1,000. Based in Syria.

GROUPS OPPOSED TO THE PLO:
FRC (Fatah Revolutionary Council, Abu Nidal Group): ε300. Based in Lebanon, Syria, Iraq, elsewhere.
HAMAS: ε300. Based in Occupied Territories.
PIJ (Palestine Islamic Jihad): ε350 all factions. Based in Occupied Territories.
PLA (Palestine Liberation Army): ε4,500. Based in Syria.
ARAB LIBERATION FRONT: ε500. Based in Lebanon and Iraq.

IRAN

GDP[a]	1992: r 67,811bn ($54.2bn): per capita $4,800	
	1993ε: r 73,333bn ($57.8bn): per capita $4,900	
Growth	1992: 6.0%	1993ε: 4.0%
Inflation	1992: 23.0%	1993: 20.3%
Debt	1992: $18.8bn	1993: $18.7bn
Def exp[a, b]	1990ε: r 217.0bn ($3.2bn)	
	1991ε: r 391.0bn ($5.8bn)	
	1992ε: r 527.7bn ($2.3bn)	
Def bdgt[a, b]	1992: r 413.0bn ($1.8bn)	
	1993: r 368.0bn ($2.0bn)	
	1994: r 4,020.0bn ($2.3bn)	

$1 = r	1992: 65.6	1993: 1,268
	1994: 1,748.0	

r = rial

[a] ppp est.
[b] The 1992 and 1993 def bdgt represent official bdgt figures and do not incl arms purchases.

Population: 65,581,000 (Azeri 25%, Kurdish 9%, Gilaki/Mazandarani 8%, Sunni 4%)

	13–17	*18–22*	*23–32*
Men	3,487,000	3,026,000	4,860,800
Women	3,272,700	2,841,700	4,651,400

TOTAL ARMED FORCES:

ACTIVE: 513,000.
Terms of service: 24 months.
RESERVES: Army: 350,000, ex-service volunteers.

ARMY: 345,000 (perhaps 250,000 conscripts).

ε3 Army HQ.
4 armd div. 1 AB bde.
7 inf div. 1 SF div (4 bde)
Some indep armd, inf, cdo bde.
5 arty gps.
EQUIPMENT:†
MBT: ε1,245, incl: ε190 T-54/-55, ε260 Ch T-59, ε150 T-62, ε150 T-72, *Chieftain* Mk 3/5, ε135 M-47/-48, ε135 M-60A1.
LIGHT TANKS: 80 *Scorpion.*
RECCE: 25 EE-9 *Cascavel.*
AIFV: 200 BMP-1.
APC: 700: BTR-50/-60, M-113.
TOTAL ARTY: 2,320 (excl mor):
TOWED: 1,820: 105mm: 130 M-101A1, 50 M-56; 122mm: 400 D-30, 150 Ch Type-54; 130mm: 800 M-46/Type-59; 152mm: 30 D-20; 155mm: 50 WA-021, 50 M-114; ε130 GHN-45; 203mm: some 30 M-115.
SP: 275: 122mm: 50 2S1; 155mm: 180 M-109; 175mm: 15 M-1978, 20 M-107; 203mm: 10 M-110.
MRL: 225: 107mm: 90 Ch Type-63; 122mm: 40 *Hadid/Arash/Noor*, 90 BM-21, 5 BM-11; 240mm: BM-24; 320mm: *Oghab*; 333mm: *Shahin* 1/-2; 355mm: *Nazeat*; *Iran*-130 reported.
MORTARS: 3,500, incl: 60mm; 81mm; 82mm; 107mm: 4.2-in M-30; 120mm.
SSM: 6+ *Scud* B/-C, 20 CSS-8, local manufacture msl reported under development.
ATGW: *Dragon*, *TOW*, AT-3 *Sagger* (some SP), AT-4 *Spigot.*
RCL: 106mm: M-40.
AD GUNS: 1,500: 23mm: ZU-23 towed, ZSU-23-4 SP; 35mm; 57mm: ZSU-57-2 SP; 100mm: KS-19.
SAM: SA-7, some HN-5.
AIRCRAFT: incl 40+ Cessna (185, 310, O-2A), 2 F-27, 2 *Falcon* 20, 15 PC-6, 5 *Shrike Commander.*
HELICOPTERS: 100 AH-1J (attack); 40 CH-47C (hy tpt); 170 Bell 214A; 40 AB-205A; 90 AB-206; 12 AB-212; 30 Bell 204; 5 Hughes 300C; 5 RH-53D; 10 SH-53D, 10 SA-319; 40 UH-1H.

REVOLUTIONARY GUARD CORPS

(*Pasdaran Inqilab*): some 120,000.
GROUND FORCES: some 100,000; loosely org in bn of no fixed size, grouped into perhaps 15–20 inf, 2–4 armd div and many indep bde, incl inf, armd, para, SF, arty (incl SSM), engr, AD and border defence units, serve indep or with Army; limited numbers of tks, APC and arty; controls *Basij* (see Paramilitary) when mob.
NAVAL FORCES: some 20,000; five island bases (Al Farsiyah, Halul (oil platform), Sirri, Abu Musa, Larak); some 40 Swedish Boghammar Marin boats armed with ATGW, RCL, machine guns. Controls coast-defence elm incl arty and CSS-N-2 (HY-2) *Silkworm* SSM bty. Now under joint command with Navy.
MARINES: 3 bde reported.

NAVY: 18,000 (incl 2,000 Naval Air and Marines).

BASES: Bandar Abbas (HQ), Bushehr, Kharg, Bandar-e-Anzelli, Bandar-e-Khomeini, Chah Bahar.
SUBMARINES: 2:
2 Sov *Kilo* SS with 6 x 533mm TT (probably not fully op).
(Plus some 2 SS1s.)
PRINCIPAL SURFACE COMBATANTS: 5:
DESTROYERS: 2:
2 *Babr* (US *Sumner*) with 4 x 2 SM-1 SSM (boxed), 2 x 2 127mm guns; plus 2 x 3 ASTT.
FRIGATES: 3:
3 *Alvand* (UK Vosper Mk 5) with 1 x 5 *Sea Killer* SSM, 1 x 3 AS mor, 1 x 114mm gun.
PATROL AND COASTAL COMBATANTS: 45:
CORVETTES: 2 Bayandor (US PF-103).
MISSILE CRAFT: 10 *Kaman* (Fr *Combattante* II) PFM, some fitted for 4 *Harpoon* SSM.
PATROL INSHORE: 33:
3 *Kaivan*, 3 *Parvin* PCI, 1 ex-Iraqi *Bogomol* PFI, 3 N. Korean *Chaho* PFI⟨, some 10 other PFI⟨, plus some 13 hovercraft⟨ (not all op).
MINE WARFARE: 4:
2 *Shahrokh* MSC (excl 1 in Caspian Sea trg), 2 *Riazi*

(US *Cape*) MSI.
(1 *Iran Ajr* LST used for mine-laying.)
AMPHIBIOUS: 8:
4 *Hengam* LST, capacity 225 tps, 9 tk, 1 hel.
3 *Iran Hormuz 24* (S. Korean) LST, capacity 140 tps, 8 tk.
1 *Iran Ajr* LST (plus 1 non-op).
Plus craft: 3 LCT.
SUPPORT AND MISCELLANEOUS: 23:
1 *Kharg* AOE with 2 hel, 2 *Bandar Abbas* AOR with 1 hel, 1 repair, 4 water tankers, 7 *Delva* and about 6 *Hendijan* spt vessels, 1 AT, 1 *Shahrokh* msc trg.

MARINES: 3 bn.

NAVAL AIR: 9 armed hel.
ASW: 1 hel sqn with ε3 SH-3D, 6 AB-212 ASW.
MCM: 1 hel sqn with 2 RH-53D.
TRANSPORT: 1 sqn with 4 *Commander*, 4 F-27, 1 *Falcon* 20 ac; AB-205, AB-206 hel.

AIR FORCE: 30,000 (incl 12,000 Air Defence); some 295 cbt ac (probably less than 50% of US ac types serviceable); no armed hel.

FGA: 9 sqn:
4 with some 60 F-4D/E. 4 with some 60 F-5E/F.
1 with 30 Su-24 (including former Iraqi ac).
FIGHTER: 7 sqn:
4 with 60 F-14. 1 with 25 F-7.
2 with 30 MiG-29 (incl former Iraqi ac).
MR: 5 P-3F, 1 RC-130.
RECCE: 1 sqn (det) with some 8 RF-4E.
TANKER/TRANSPORT: 1 sqn with 4 Boeing 707.
TRANSPORT: 5 sqn with 9 Boeing 747F, 11 Boeing 707, 1 Boeing 727, 19 C-130E/H, 3 *Commander* 690, 15 F-27, 5 *Falcon* 20.
HELICOPTERS: 2 AB-206A, 39 Bell 214C, 5 CH-47.
TRAINING: incl 26 Beech F-33A/C, 10 EMB-312, 45 PC-7, 7 T-33, 5* MiG-29B, 5* FT-7, 20* F-5B.
MISSILES:
ASM: AGM-65A *Maverick*, AS-10, AS-11, AS-14.
AAM: AIM-7 *Sparrow*, AIM-9 *Sidewinder*, AIM-54 *Phoenix*, probably AA-8, AA-10, AA-11 for MiG-29, PL-7.
SAM: 12 bn with 150 *Improved HAWK*, 5 sqn with 30 *Rapier*, 15 *Tigercat*, 45 HQ-2J (Ch version of SA-2). Probable SA-5, FM-80 (Ch version of *Crotale*).

FORCES ABROAD:

LEBANON: ε500 Revolutionary Guard.
SUDAN: military advisers.

PARAMILITARY:

BASIJ ('Popular Mobilisation Army'): volunteers, mostly youths; strength has been as high as 1 million during periods of offensive operations. Small arms only. Not currently embodied for mil ops.
GENDARMERIE: 45,000, incl border-guard elm; Cessna 185/310 lt **ac**, AB-205/-206 **hel**, patrol boats: about 90 inshore, 40 harbour craft.

OPPOSITION:

KURDISH COMMUNIST PARTY OF IRAN (KOMALA): strength unknown.
KURDISH DEMOCRATIC PARTY OF IRAN (KDP–Iran): ε8,000.
NATIONAL LIBERATION ARMY (NLA): some 15,000 reported, org in bde, armed with captured eqpt. Perhaps 160+ T-54/-55 tanks. BMP-1 AIFV, D-30 122mm arty, BM-21 122mm MRL, Mi-8 hel. Iraq-based.

IRAQ

GDP	1989ε: $35.0bn		
	1991ε: $15.0bn		
	1992ε: $17.0bn		
	1993ε: $17.0bn		
Growth	1992ε: 10.0%	1993ε:	0%
Inflation	1992ε: 34.0%	1993ε:	170.0%
Debt[a]	1992: $83.0bn	1993:	$86.0bn
Def exp[b]	1989: $11.0bn		
	1992: $2.5bn		
	1993: $2.6bn		
$1 = D[c]	1992–1994: 0.31		
D = dinar			

[a] Exl liabilities up to $80bn for Gulf War reparations.
[b] ppp est.
[c] Informal market rates in 1994 value $1 at 500 dinars.

Population: 19,877,000 (Kurdish 17%, other Arab 5%)

	13–17	*18–22*	*23–32*
Men	1,305,400	1,068,400	1,570,600
Women	1,246,400	1,025,300	1,516,900

TOTAL ARMED FORCES:

ACTIVE: perhaps 382,000.
Terms of service: 18–24 months.
RESERVES: ε650,000.

ARMY: ε350,000 (incl ε100,000 recalled reserves).

6 corps HQ.
19 armd/mech/inf div.
8 Republican Guard Force div (4 armd/mech, 4 inf).
Presidential Guard/Special Security Force.
10 SF/cdo bde.

EQUIPMENT:

MBT: perhaps 2,200, incl T-54/-55/M-77, Ch T-59/-69, T-62, T-72, *Chieftain* Mk 3/5, M-60, M-47.
RECCE: perhaps 1,500, incl BRDM-2, AML-60/-90, EE-9 *Cascavel*, EE-3 *Jararaca*.
AIFV: perhaps 700 BMP-1/-2.
APC: perhaps 2,000, incl BTR-50/-60/-152, OT-62/-64, MTLB, YW-531, M-113A1/A2, Panhard M-3, EE-11 *Urutu*.
TOWED ARTY: perhaps 1,500, incl 105mm: incl M-56 pack; 122mm: D-74, D-30, M-1938; 130mm: incl M-46, Type 59-1; 155mm: some G-5, GHN-45, M-114.
SP ARTY: 230, incl 122mm: 2S1; 152mm: 2S3; 155mm: M-109A1/A2, AUF-1 (GCT).
MRL: perhaps 250, incl 107mm; 122mm: BM-21; 127mm: *ASTROS* II; 132mm: BM-13/-16, 262mm: *Ababeel*.
MORTARS: 81mm; 120mm; 160mm: M-1943; 240mm.
ATGW: AT-3 *Sagger* (incl BRDM-2), AT-4 *Spigot* reported, SS-11, *Milan*, *HOT* (incl 100 VC-TH).
RCL: 73mm: SPG-9; 82mm: B-10; 107mm.
ATK GUNS: 85mm; 100mm towed.
HELICOPTERS: ε500 (120 armed), incl:
ATTACK: ε120 Bo-105 with AS-11/*HOT*, Mi-24, SA-316 with AS-12, SA-321 (some with *Exocet*), SA-342.
TRANSPORT: ε350 **hy:** Mi-6; **med:** AS-61, Bell 214 ST, Mi-4, Mi-8/-17, SA-330; **lt:** AB-212, BK-117 (SAR), Hughes 300C, Hughes 500D, Hughes 530F.
AD GUNS: ε5,500: 23mm: ZSU-23-4 SP; 37mm: M-1939 and twin; 57mm: incl ZSU-57-2 SP; 85mm; 100mm; 130mm.
SAM: SA-2/-3/-6/-7/-8/-9/-13/-14/-16, *Roland*.
SURV: RASIT (veh, arty), *Cymbeline* (mor).

NAVY: ε2,000.

BASES: Basra (limited facilities), Az Zubayr, Umm Qasr (currently closed).
FRIGATES: 1 *Ibn Marjid* (ex-*Khaldoum*) (trg) with 2 x ASTT.
PATROL AND COASTAL COMBATANTS: 11:
MISSILE CRAFT: 1 Sov *Osa*-I with 4 SS-N-2A *Styx*.
PATROL INSHORE: 10:
1 Sov *Bogomol* PFI, 5 PFI⟨, 1 PCI⟨, 3 SRN-6 hovercraft, plus boats.
MINE WARFARE: 5:
2 Sov *Yevgenya*.
3 Yug *Nestin* MSI⟨.
SUPPORT AND MISCELLANEOUS: 2:
1 *Aka* (Yug *Spasilac*-class) AR.
1 Yacht with hel deck.
(Plus 1 *Agnadeen* (It *Stromboli*) AOR laid-up in Alexandria. 3 *Al Zahraa* ro-ro AK with hel deck. Capacity 16 tk, 250 tps. Inactive in foreign ports.)

AIR FORCE: 30,000 (incl 15,000 AD personnel).

The serviceability of fixed-wing aircraft is probably good, whereas the serviceability of the helicopters is poor.

BOMBERS: ε6, incl: H-6D, Tu-22.
FGA: ε130, incl J-6, MiG-23BN, MiG-27, *Mirage* F1EQ5, Su-7, Su-20, Su-25.
FIGHTER: ε180, incl F-7, MiG-21, MiG-25, *Mirage* F-1EQ, MiG-29.
RECCE: incl MiG-25.
AEW: incl Il-76 *Adnan*.
TKR: incl 2 Il-76.
TRANSPORT: incl An-2, An-12, An-24, An-26, Il-76.
TRAINING: incl AS-202, EMB-312, some 40 L-29, some 40 L-39, MB-233, *Mirage* F-1BQ, 25 PC-7, 30 PC-9.
MISSILES:
ASM: AM-39, AS-4, AS-5, AS-11, AS-9, AS-12, AS-30L, C-601.
AAM: AA-2/-6/-7/-8/-10, R-530, R-550.

PARAMILITARY:

FRONTIER GUARDS: ε20,000.
SECURITY TROOPS: 4,800.

OPPOSITION:

KURDISH DEMOCRATIC PARTY (KDP): 25,000 (30,000 more in militia); small arms, some Iranian lt arty, MRL, mor, SAM-7.
PATRIOTIC UNION OF KURDISTAN (PUK): ε12,000 cbt (plus 6,000 spt); some T-54/-55 MBT; 450 mor (60mm, 82mm, 120mm); 106mm RCL; some 200 12.5mm AA guns; SA-7 SAM.
SOCIALIST PARTY OF KURDISTAN: ε500.
SUPREME ASSEMBLY OF THE ISLAMIC REVOLUTION (SAIRI): ε1 'bde'; Iran-based; Iraqi dissidents, ex-prisoners of war.

FOREIGN FORCES:

UN (UNIKOM): some 895 tps and 252 military observers from 33 countries.

ISRAEL

GDP	1992: NS 161.3bn ($65.6bn): per capita $14,100	
	1993: NS 197.0bn ($69.6bn): per capita $15,000	
Growth	1992: 6.4%	1993: 3.5%
Inflation	1992: 11.8%	1993: 11.3%
Debt	1992: $25.0bn	1993: $25.7bn
Def exp	1991: NS 11.4bn ($5.0bn)	
	1992: NS 16.9bn ($6.9bn)	
Def bdgt[a]	1992: NS 18.1bn ($7.4bn)	
	1993: NS 17.8bn ($6.8bn)	
	1994: NS 20.2bn ($7.2bn)	
FMA	1993: $3bn (FMF, Econ aid)	
	1994: $3bn (FMF, Econ aid)	
	1995: $3bn (FMF, Econ aid)	
$1 = NS	1992: 2.46	1993: 2.83
	1994: 2.97	

NS = new sheqalim

[a] The defence budget excludes several items of military-related expenditure which are charged to other government accounts, including defence industry structural funds (estimated at $800m for 1992–94), civil defence funds ($510m), civilian administration expenses in the Occupied Territories, and the maintenance of emergency inventories. In addition, the social security account reimburses reservists for wages lost while on military service.

Population:[b] 5,100,000 (Jewish 82%, Arab 14%, Christian 2.0%, Druze 2.0%).

	13–17	*18–22*	*23–32*
Men	266,100	263,900	499,600
Women	253,000	254,600	471,100

[b] Incl Jewish settlers in East Jerusalem, Golan, Gaza and Jericho.

TOTAL ARMED FORCES:

ACTIVE: ε172,000 (ε138,500 conscripts).
Terms of service: officers 48 months, men 36 months, women 21 months (Jews and Druze only; Christians, Circassians and Muslims may volunteer). Annual trg as cbt reservists to age 45 (some specialists to age 54) for men, 24 (or marriage) for women.
RESERVES: 430,000: Army 365,000; Navy 10,000; Air Force 55,000. Male commitment until 54 in reserve op units may be followed by voluntary service in the Civil Guard or Civil Defence.

STRATEGIC FORCES:

It is widely believed that Israel has a nuclear capability with up to 100 warheads. Delivery means could include ac, *Jericho* 1 SSM (range up to 500km), *Jericho* 2 (tested 1987–89, range ε1,500km) and *Lance*.

ARMY: 134,000 (114,700 conscripts, male and female); some 598,000 on mob.

3 territorial, 1 home front comd.
3 corps HQ.
3 armd div (2 armd, 1 arty bde, plus 1 armd, 1 mech inf bde on mob).
2 div HQ (op control of anti-*intifada* units).
3 regional inf div HQ (border def).
4 mech inf bde (incl 1 para trained).
1 *Lance* SSM bn.
3 arty bn with 203mm M-110 SP.

RESERVES:
9 armd div (2 or 3 armd, 1 affiliated mech inf, 1 arty bde).
1 airmobile/mech inf div (3 bde manned by para trained reservists).
10 regional inf bde (each with own border sector).
4 arty bde.

EQUIPMENT:
MBT: 3,895: 1,080 *Centurion*, 325 M-48A5, 500 M-60/A1, 750 M-60A3, 150 *Magach* 7, 50 T-54/-55, 110 T-62, 930 *Merkava* I/II/III.
RECCE: about 400, incl RAMTA RBY, M-2/-3, BRDM-2, ε8 *Fuchs*.
APC: ε6,000 M-113A1/A2, ε80 *Nagmashot*, some *Achzarit*, BTR-50P, ε3,000 M-2/-3 half track.
TOWED ARTY: ε400, incl: 105mm: 60 M-101; 122mm: 70 D-30; 130mm: 80 M-46; 155mm: 40 Soltam M-68/-71, M-839P/-845P.
SP ARTY: 1,284: 105mm: 34 M-7; 155mm: 200 L-33, 100 M-50, 530 M-109A1/A2; 175mm: 200 M-107; 203mm: 220 M-110.
MRL: 100+: 122mm: 40 BM-21; 160mm: LAR-160; 240mm: 30 BM-24; 290mm: MAR-290.
MORTARS: 2,740: 81mm: 1,600; 120mm: 900; 160mm: 240 (some SP).
SSM: 20 *Lance*, some *Jericho* 1/2.
ATGW: 200 *TOW* (incl *Ramta* (M-113) SP), 780 *Dragon*, AT-3 *Sagger*, 25 *Mapats*.
RL: 82mm: B-300.
RCL: 84mm: *Carl Gustav*; 106mm: 250 M-40A1.
AD GUNS: 20mm: 850: incl TCM-20, M-167 *Vulcan*, 35 M-163 *Vulcan*/M-48 *Chaparral* gun/msl systems; 23mm: 100 ZU-23 and 60 ZSU-23-4 SP; 37mm: M-39; 40mm: L-70.
SAM: *Stinger*, 900 *Redeye*, 45 *Chaparral*.

SURV: EL/M-2140 (veh), AN/TPQ-37 (arty), AN/PPS-15 (arty).
UAV: *Impact, Mastiff III, Scout, Pioneer, Searcher.*

NAVY: ε6,000–7,000 (2,000–3,000 conscripts), 10,000–12,000 on mob.
BASES: Haifa, Ashdod, Eilat.
SUBMARINES: 3 *Gal* (UK Vickers) SSC with Mk 37 HWT, *Harpoon* USGW.
PATROL AND COASTAL COMBATANTS: 55:
CORVETTE: 1:
1 *Eilat* (Sa'ar 5) with 8 *Harpoon*, 8 *Gabriel*-II SSM, 2 *Barak* VLS SAM (2 x 32 mls), 6 x 324mm ASTT plus 1 SA-366G hel.
MISSILE CRAFT: 19 PFM:
2 *Aliya* with 4 *Harpoon*, 4 *Gabriel* SSM, 1 SA-366G *Dauphin* hel (OTHT).
2 *Romat* with 8 *Harpoon*, 8 *Gabriel.*
1 *Hetz* (ex-*Nirit*) with 8 *Harpoon*, 6 *Gabriel* and *Barak* VLS.
8 *Reshef* with 2–4 *Harpoon*, 4–6 *Gabriel.*
6 *Mivtach/Sa'ar* with 2–4 *Harpoon*, 3–5 *Gabriel.*
PATROL, INSHORE: 35:
about 35 *Super Dvora/Dvora/Dabur* PFI⟨, some with 2 x 324mm TT.
AMPHIBIOUS: 1:
1 *Bat Sheva* LST type tpt.
Plus craft: 3 *Ashdod* LCT, 1 US type LCM.

MARINES: naval cdo: 300.

AIR FORCE: 32,000 (21,800 conscripts, mainly in AD), 37,000 on mob; 478 cbt ac (plus perhaps 250 stored), 117 armed hel.
FGA/FIGHTER: 13 sqn:
2 with 50 F-4E.
2 with 50 Phantom 2000.
2 with 63 F-15 (36 -A, 2 -B, 18 -C, 7 -D).
6 with 209 F-16 (57 -A, 7 -B, 89 -C, 56 -D).
1 with 20 *Kfir* C2/C7 (plus 120 in store).
FGA: 2 sqn with 50 A-4N, plus 130 in store.
RECCE: 14 RF-4E, 6 *Kfir* RC-2, 2 F-15D.
AEW: 4 E-2C.
EW: 6 Boeing 707 (ELINT/ECM), 4 RC-12D, 3 IAI-200, 15 Do-28.
MR: 3 IAI-1124 *Seascan.*
TANKER: 3 Boeing-707, 5 KC-130H.
TRANSPORT: 1 wing: incl 4 Boeing 707, 12 C-47, 24 C-130H, 10 IAI-201, 4 IAI-200.
LIAISON: 2 *Islander,* 20 Cessna U-206, 8 *Queen Air* 80, 4 *King Air* 200.
TRAINING: 80 CM-170 *Tzukit*, 10 *Kfir* TC2/7, 30 *Super Cub*, 10* TA-4H, 4* TA-4J, 4 *Queen Air* 80.
HELICOPTERS:
ATTACK: 40 AH-1F, 35 Hughes 500MD, 42 AH-64A.
SAR: 2 HH-65A.
TRANSPORT: hy: 42 CH-53D; **med:** 30 UH-1D, 10 UH-60; **lt:** 54 Bell 212, 39 Bell 206.
MISSILES:
ASM: AGM-45 *Shrike*, AGM-62A *Walleye*, AGM-65 *Maverick*, AGM-78D *Standard, Luz, Gabriel* III (mod), *Hellfire,* TOW.
AAM: AIM-7 *Sparrow*, AIM-9 *Sidewinder*, R-530, *Shafrir*, *Python* III, IV.
SAM: 17 bty with MIM-23 *Improved HAWK*, 3 bty *Patriot,* 8 bty *Chapparal.*

FORCES ABROAD
RWANDA: 80; field medical unit.

PARAMILITARY:
BORDER POLICE: 6,000; 600 *Walid* 1, BTR-152 APC.
COAST GUARD: ε50; 1 US PBR, 3 other patrol craft.

JORDAN

GDP	1992: D 3.3bn ($4.8bn):	
	per capita $5,300	
	1993ε: D 3.6bn ($5.2bn):	
	per capita $5,600	
Growth	1992: 11.2%	1993ε: 5.8%
Inflation	1992: 4.0%	1993: 4.8%
Debt	1992: $8.0bn	1993: $6.9bn
Def exp	1991: D 282.2m ($414.5m)	
Def bdgt	1992ε: D 357.0m ($525.2m)	
	1993ε: D 298.0m ($431.6m)	
	1994ε: D 288.0m ($411.1m)	
FMA	1993: $9.5m (FMF, IMET)	
	1994: $9.8m (FMF, IMET)	
	1995: $17.1m (FMF, IMET, Econ aid)	
$1 = D	1992: 0.68	1993: 0.69
	1994: 0.70	
D = dinar		

Population:[a] 3,960,100 (Palestinian est 50%)

	13–17	*18–22*	*23–32*
Men	219,800	201,700	335,600
Women	210,000	191,100	307,200

[a] Population data do not include Palestinian refugees whose number is estimated to be at least 250,000.

TOTAL ARMED FORCES:

ACTIVE: 98,600.
RESERVES: 35,000 (all services): Army 30,000 (obligation to age 40).

ARMY: 90,000.

2 armd div (each 2 tk, 1 mech inf, 1 arty, 1 AD bde).
2 mech inf div (each 2 mech inf, 1 tk, 1 arty, 1 AD bde).
1 indep Royal Guard bde.
1 SF bde (3 AB bn).
1 fd arty bde (4 bn).
EQUIPMENT:
MBT: some 1,141: 270 M-47/-48A5 (in store), 218 M-60A1/A3, 360 *Khalid/Chieftain*, 293 *Tariq* (*Centurion*).
LIGHT TANKS: 19 *Scorpion*.
RECCE: 150 *Ferret*.
AIFV: some 35 BMP-2.
APC: 1,100 M-113.
TOWED ARTY: 123: 105mm: 50 M-102; 155mm: 38 M-114 towed, 10 M-59/M-1; 203mm: 25 M-115 towed (in store).
SP ARTY: 370, incl: 105mm: 30 M-52; 155mm: 20 M-44, 220 M-109A1/A2; 203mm: 100 M-110.
MORTARS: 81mm: 450 (incl 130 SP); 107mm: 50 M-30; 120mm: 300 *Brandt*.
ATGW: 330 *TOW* (incl 70 SP), 310 *Dragon*.
RL: 94mm: 2,000 LAW-80; 112mm: 2,000 *APILAS*.
RCL: 106mm: 330 M-40A1.
AD GUNS: 360: 20mm: 100 M-163 *Vulcan* SP; 23mm: 44 ZSU-23-4 SP; 40mm: 216 M-42 SP.
SAM: SA-7B2, 50 SA-8, 50 SA-13, 300 SA-14, 240 SA-16, 250 *Redeye*.
SURV: AN-TPQ-36/-37 (arty, mor).

NAVY ε600.

BASE: Aqaba.
PATROL: 5:
3 *Al Hussein* (Vosper 30-m) PFI, 2 Ge *Bremse* PCI⟨ (ex-GDR). Plus 3 Rotork craft (capacity 30 tps) and other armed boats.

AIR FORCE: 8,000 (incl 2,000 AD); 102 cbt ac, 24 armed hel.

FGA: 4 sqn with 58 F-5 (48 -E, 10 -F).
FIGHTER: 2 sqn with 30 *Mirage* F-1 (14 -CJ, 16 -EJ).
TRANSPORT: 1 sqn with 6 C-130 (2 -B, 4 -H), 3 C-212A.
VIP: 1 sqn with **ac**: 2 *Gulfstream III*, IL-1011; **hel**: 4 S-76, 3 S-70, SA-319.
HELICOPTERS: 4 sqn:
ATTACK: 3 sqn with 24 AH-1S (with *TOW* ASM).
TRANSPORT: 1 sqn with 9 AS-332M.
TRAINING: 16 *Bulldog*, 15 C-101, 12 PA-28-161, 6 PA-34-200, *12 F-5A/B, 2* *Mirage* F-1B hel, 8 Hughes 500D.
AD: 2 bde: 14 bty with 80 *Improved HAWK*.
MISSILES:
ASM: *TOW*.
AAM: AIM-9 *Sidewinder*, R-530, R-550 *Magic*.

FORCES ABROAD:

UN AND PEACEKEEPING:

ANGOLA (UNAVEM II): 2 Observers.
BOSNIA (UNPROFOR BH): 94; arty loc unit.
CROATIA (UNPROFOR I): 3,244; 3inf bn, 46 Observers, 71 civ pol.
LIBERIA (UNOMIL): 40 Observers.
MOZAMBIQUE (ONUMOZ): 45 civ pol.

PARAMILITARY:

PUBLIC SECURITY DIRECTORATE (Ministry of Interior): ε10,000; some *Scorpion* lt tk, 25 EE-11 *Urutu*, 30 *Saracen* APC.
CIVIL MILITIA 'PEOPLE'S ARMY': ε200,000; men 16–65, women 16–45.

KUWAIT

GDP	1992: D 6.4bn ($21.7bn): per capita $14,800		
	1993: D 7.3bn ($24.0bn): per capita $15,400		
Growth	1992: 93.8%	1993: 8.0%	
Inflation	1992: 10.0%	1993: 8.0%	
Debt	1992: $9.8bn	1993: $10.0bn	
Def exp[a]	1991: D 4.5bn ($15.5bn)		
	1992: D 869.0m ($2.9bn)		
Def bdgt[b, c]	1992: D 2.6bn ($9.3bn)		
	1993: D 534.0m ($1.8bn)		
	1994:[c] D 500.0m ($1.7bn)		
$1 = D	1992: 0.29	1993: 0.30	
	1994: 0.30		
D = dinar			

[a] 1991 exp data incl $7.5bn in off-bdgt payments for *Operation Desert Storm*. Total war-related expenses are est to reach $10.3bn in addition to the $9.3bn def bdgt in FY1991. 1992 exp data excl off-bdgt payments for the Gulf War.
[b] 1992 incl supplementary bdgt for arms procurement.
[c] 1994 def bdgt excl D3.5bn ($11.8bn) of supplementary bdgt for arms procurement over a 12-year period.

Population: 1,650,000 (Nationals 39%, other Arab 35%, South Asian 9%, Iranian 4%).

	13–17	*18–22*	*23–32*
Men	114,500	97,400	191,100
Women	109,700	85,300	137,200

TOTAL ARMED FORCES:

ACTIVE: 16,600 (some conscripts; incl 1,000 central staff and 600 Amiri Guard).
Terms of service: voluntary, conscripts 2 years.
RESERVES: 23,700: obligation to age 40 years; 1 month annual trg.

ARMY: ε10,000.

1 mech bde (-).
3 armd bde (-).
1 cdo bn.
1 reserve bde (-)
1 arty bde (-).

EQUIPMENT:
MBT: 150 M-84, 14 M-1A2
AIFV: 41 BMP-2.
APC: 44 M-113, 6 M-577, 40 *Fahd.*
SP ARTY: 155mm: 3 M-109A2, 18 GCT (in store).
MORTARS: 81mm: 6 SP; 107mm: 6 M-30 SP.
ATGW: *TOW/Improved TOW* (8 M-901 SP).
(Captured eqpt returned by Iraq incl 68 *Chieftain* MBT, 20 M-109 155mm SP how, 15 AMX-13 155mm SP how, 12 120mm mor which may be refurbished and added to the inventory.)

NAVY: ε2,500 (incl Coast Guard).

BASE: Ras al Qalaya.
PATROL AND COASTAL COMBATANTS: 6:
MISSILE CRAFT: 2:
1 *Istiqlal* (Ge Lürssen FPB-57) PFM with 2 x 2 MM-40 *Exocet* SSM.
1 *Al Sanbouk* (Ge Lürssen TNC-45) with 2 x 2 MM-40 *Exocet.*
PATROL CRAFT: 4:
INSHORE: 4:
4 *Inttisar* (Aust 31.5m) PFI.
Plus some 55 armed boats.

AIR FORCE: ε2,500; 83 cbt ac, 16 armed hel.

FIGHTER/FGA: 40 F/A-18 (-C 32, -D 8).
FIGHTER: 15 *Mirage* F1CK/BK.
COIN/TRAINING: 1 sqn with 12 *Hawk* 64, 16 Shorts *Tucano.*
TRANSPORT: 3 L-100-30, 1 DC-9.
HELICOPTERS: 3 sqn.
TRANSPORT: 3 AS-332 (tpt/SAR/attack), 8 SA-330.
TRAINING/ATTACK: 16 SA-342 (with *HOT*).
AIR DEFENCE: 4 *Hawk* Phase III bty with 24 launchers. 6 bty *Amoun* (each bty, 1 *Skyguard* radar, 2 *Aspede* launchers, 2 twin 35mm *Oerliken).*

PARAMILITARY:

NATIONAL GUARD: 5,000.

FOREIGN FORCES:

UN (UNIKOM): some 895 tps and 252 Observers from 33 countries.
US: prepositioned eqpt for 6 coy (3 tk, 3 mech), 1 arty bty, incl 44 MBT, 44 AIFV, 8 arty.

LEBANON

GDP	1992: LP 9,796.0bn ($5.7bn): per capita $3,500	
	1993ε: LP 10,933.5bn ($6.3bn): per capita $3,700	
Growth	1992: 4.0%	1993ε: 7.0%
Inflation	1991: 45%	1992: 90%
Debt	1992: $1.8bn	1993: $1.9bn
Def exp	1992: LP 400bn ($233m)	
	1993: LP 479bn ($275m)	
Def bdgt	1994: LP 520bn ($307m)	
FMA	1993: $19.6m (IMET, Econ aid)	
	1994: $8.3m (IMET, Econ aid)	
	1995: $4.4m (IMET, Econ aid)	
$1 = LP	1992: 1,713	1993: 1,741
	1994: 1,692	

LP = Lebanese pound

Population: 3,616,000 (Christian 30%, Druze 6%, Armenian 4%)

	13–17	*18–22*	*23–32*
Men	148,700	146,500	219,000
Women	145,900	144,800	245,200

NATIONAL ARMED FORCES:

ACTIVE: 44,300.
Terms of Service: 1 year.

ARMY: some 43,000.

11 inf bde (-).
1 Presidential Guard bde.
1 cdo/Ranger, 3 SF regt.
2 arty regt.
1 air aslt regt.
EQUIPMENT:
MBT: some 100 M-48A1/A5, 200 T-54/-55.

LIGHT TANKS: 30 AMX-13.
RECCE: 40 *Saladin*, 5 *Ferret*, 70 AML-90, 30 *Staghound*.
APC: 550 M-113, 20 *Saracen*, 60 VAB-VCI, 25 VAB-VTT, 70 AMX-VCI, 15 *Panhard* M3/VTT.
TOWED ARTY: 105mm: 15 M-101A1, 10 M-102; 122mm: 30 M-1938, 10 D-30; 130mm: 25 M-46; 155mm: 60, incl some Model 50, 15 M-114A1, 35 M-198.
MRL: 122mm: 5 BM-11, 25 BM-21.
MORTARS: 81mm: 150; 120mm: 130.
ATGW: *ENTAC*, *Milan*, 20 BGM-71A *TOW*.
RL: 85mm: RPG-7; 89mm: M-65.
RCL: 106mm: M-40A1.
AD GUNS: 20mm; 23mm: ZU-23; 40mm: 10 M-42A1.

NAVY: 500.

BASES: Juniye, Beirut, Tripoli.
PATROL CRAFT: inshore: 9 PCI‹, 5 UK *Attacker* and 4 UK *Tracker* PCI‹, plus armed boats.
AMPHIBIOUS: craft only: 2 *Sour* (Fr *Edic*) LCT.

AIR FORCE: some 800; 3† cbt ac; 4† armed hel.

EQUIPMENT:
FIGHTERS: 3 *Hunter* (2 F-70, 1 T-66).
HELICOPTERS:
ATTACK: 4 SA-342 with AS-11/-12 ASM.
TRANSPORT: (med)†: 4 AB-212, 6 SA-330; 2 SA-318, 2 SA-319.
TRAINING: 3 *Bulldog*, 3 CM-170.
TRANSPORT: 1 *Dove*, 1 *Turbo-Commander* 690A.

PARAMILITARY:

INTERNAL SECURITY FORCE (Ministry of Interior): ε13,000 (incl Regional and Beirut Gendarmerie coy plus Judicial Police); 30 *Chaimite* APC.
CUSTOMS: 5 armed boats.

MILITIAS: most militias, except *Hizbollah* and the SLA, have been substantially disbanded and hy wpns handed over to the National Army.

HIZBOLLAH ('Party of God'; Shi'i, fundamentalist, pro-Iranian): ε3,000 (-) active; total spt unknown.
EQUIPMENT: incl APC, arty, RL, RCL, ATGW, (AT-3 *Sagger*) AA guns.

SOUTH LEBANESE ARMY (SLA): ε2,500 active (mainly Christian, some Shi'i and Druze, trained, equipped and supported by Israel, occupies the 'Security Zone' between Israeli border and area controlled by UNIFIL).
EQUIPMENT:
MBT: 30 T-54/-55.
APC: M-113, BTR-50.
TOWED ARTY: 122mm: D-30; 130mm: M-46; 155mm: M-1950.

FOREIGN FORCES:

UNITED NATIONS (UNIFIL): some 5,200; 6 inf bns: 1 each from Fiji, Finland, Ghana, Ireland, Nepal, Norway, plus spt units from France, Italy, Norway, Poland.
SYRIA: 30,000.
BEIRUT: 1 SF div HQ, elm 1 armd bde, elm 5 SF regt.
METN: elm 1 mech bde.
BEKAA: 1 mech div HQ, elm 2 mech inf bde.
TRIPOLI: 2 SF regt.

OMAN

GDP	1992: R 4.4bn ($11.5bn): per capita $10,100	
	1993: R 4.6bn ($12.0bn): per capita $10,200	
Growth	1992: 10.0%	1993: 2.0%
Inflation	1992: 3.5%	1993: 0.9%
Debt	1992: $2.9bn	1993: $3.1bn
Def exp	1992: R 679.5m ($1.8bn)	
	1993ε: R 702.8m ($1.8bn)	
Def bdgt[a]	1993: R 630.0m ($1.6bn)	
	1994: R 612.0m ($1.6bn)	
FMA	1993: $6.1m (FMF, IMET, Econ aid)	
	1994: $1.1m (IMET, Econ aid)	
	1995: $0.4m (IMET, Econ aid)	
$1 = R	1992–94: 0.39	
R = rial		

[a] Excl $1.8bn military subsidy from GCC between 1984 and 1994, shared with Bahrain.

Population: 2,018,000 (expatriates 27%)

	13–17	*18–22*	*23–32*
Men	98,800	78,200	126,800
Women	94,800	73,800	110,000

TOTAL ARMED FORCES:

ACTIVE: 42,900 (incl Royal Household tps, and some 3,700 foreign personnel).

ARMY: 25,000 (regt are of bn size).
1 div HQ.
2 bde HQ.
2 armd regt (3 tk sqn).
1 armd recce regt (3 armd car sqn).
4 arty (2 fd, 1 med (2 bty), 1 AD (2 bty)) regt.
8 inf regt (incl 3 Baluch).
1 inf recce regt (3 recce coy), 2 indep recce coy.
1 fd engr regt (3 sqn).
1 AB regt.
Musandam Security Force (indep rifle coy).
EQUIPMENT:
MBT: 6 M-60A1, 43 M-60A3, 24 *Qayid al-Ardh* (*Chieftain* Mk 7/-15).
LIGHT TANKS: 37 *Scorpion*, 6 VBC-90.
APC: 6 *Spartan*, 13 *Sultan*.
TOWED ARTY: 96: 105mm: 42 ROF lt; 122mm: 30 D-30; 130mm: 12 M-46, 12 Type 59-1.
MORTARS: 81mm: 54; 107mm: 20 4.2-in M-30.
ATGW: 18 *TOW*, 32 *Milan* (incl 2 VCAC).
AD GUNS: 20mm (incl 2 VAB VD); 23mm: 4 ZU-23-2; 40mm: 12 *Bofors* L/60.
SAM: *Blowpipe*, 28 *Javelin*, 34 SA-7.

NAVY: 4,200.
BASES: Seeb (HQ), Wudam (main base), Raysut, Ghanam Island, Alwi.
PATROL AND COASTAL COMBATANTS: 12:
MISSILE CRAFT: 4 *Dhofar*, 1 with 2 x 3 MM-40, 3 with 2 x 4 MM-40 *Exocet* SSM.
PATROL: 8:
4 *Al Wafi* (Brooke-Marine 37-m) PCI, 4 *Seeb* (Vosper 25-m) PCI⟨.
AMPHIBIOUS: 2:
1 *Nasr el Bahr* LST†, capacity 240 tps, 7 tk, hel deck (effectively in reserve).
1 *Al Munassir* LST, capacity 200 tps, 8 tk, hel deck (non-op, harbour trg).
Plus craft: 3 LCM, 1 LCU.
SUPPORT: 2: 1 spt, 1 *Al Mabrukah* trg with hel deck (also used in offshore patrol role).

AIR FORCE: 3,500; 48 cbt ac (plus 10 in store), no armed hel.
FGA: 2 sqn with 15 *Jaguar* S(O) Mk 1, 1 GR1, 4 T-2 (plus 10 in store).
FGA/RECCE: 1 sqn with 5 *Hunter* FGA-73, 2 T-67, 1 FR-10, 1 T-66A, 4 *Hawk* 203.
COIN/TRAINING: 1 sqn with 11* BAC-167 Mk 82, 7 BN-2 *Defender,* 4* Hawk 108.
TRANSPORT: 3 sqn:
1 with 3 BAC-111; 2 with 15 *Skyvan* 3M (7 radar-equipped, for MR), 3 C-130H.
HELICOPTERS: 2 med tpt sqn with 20 AB-205, 3 AB-206, 3 AB-212, 5 AB-214.
TRAINING: 4 AS-202-18.
AD: 2 sqn with 28 *Rapier* SAM, *Martello* radar.
MISSILES:
ASM: *Exocet* AM-39.
AAM: AIM-9P *Sidewinder*.

ROYAL HOUSEHOLD: 6,500 (incl HQ staff).
Royal Guard bde: (4,500).
2 SF regt: (800).
Royal Yacht Squadron (based Muscat): (150);
 1 Royal Yacht, 3,800t with hel deck.
 1 *Fulk Al Salamah* tps and veh tpt with up to 2 AS-332C *Puma* hel.
Royal Flight: (250): **ac**: 2 Boeing-747 SP, 1 DC-8-73CF, 2 *Gulfstream* IV; **hel**: 3 AS-330, 2 AS-332C, 1 AS-332L.

PARAMILITARY:
TRIBAL HOME GUARD (*Firqat*): 3,500.
POLICE COAST GUARD: 400; 15 AT-105 APC, some 16 inshore patrol craft.
POLICE AIR WING: 1 DHC-5D, 1 Do-228, 2 CN 235M, 1 *Gulfstream* GII, 1 BN-2T Islander **ac**; 3 Bell 205A, 6 Bell 214ST **hel**.

QATAR

GDP	1992: R 25.8bn ($7.1bn):	
	per capita $15,600	
	1993ε: R 27.6bn ($7.3bn):	
	per capita $16,000	
Growth	1992: 4.0%	1993ε: 0.0%
Inflation	1992: 2.0%	1993: 4.2%
Debt	1992: $1.9bn	1993: $1.7bn
Def bdgt	1992ε: R 1.3bn ($350m)	
	1993ε: R 1.2bn ($324m)	
	1994ε: R 1.1bn ($299m)	
$1 =R	1992–94: 3.64	
R = rial		

Population: 590,000 (nationals 25%, expatriates 75%, of which Pakistani 18%, Indian 18%, Iranian 10%)

	13–17	*18–22*	*23–32*
Men	22,000	18,500	42,400
Women	20,100	16,100	26,900

TOTAL ARMED FORCES:
ACTIVE: 10,100.

ARMY: 8,500.

1 Royal Guard regt.
1 tk bn.
4 mech inf bn.
1 SF 'bn' (coy).
1 fd arty regt.

EQUIPMENT:
MBT: 24 AMX-30.
RECCE: 6 VBL.
AIFV: 40 AMX-10P.
APC: 160 VAB, 22 *Saracen*.
TOWED ARTY: 155mm: 12 G5.
SP ARTY: 155mm: 28 AMX Mk F-3.
MRL: 4 *ASTROS* II.
MORTARS: 81mm (some SP); 120mm: 15.
ATGW: 100 *Milan*, *HOT* (incl 24 VAB SP).
RCL: 84mm: *Carl Gustav*.
SAM: *Blowpipe*, 12 *Stinger*.

NAVY: ε800 (incl Marine Police).

BASE: Doha.
PATROL AND COASTAL COMBATANTS: 9:
MISSILE CRAFT: 3 *Damsah* (Fr *Combattante* III) with 2 x 4 MM-40 *Exocet* SSM.
PATROL, INSHORE: 6:
6 *Barzan* (UK 33-m) PCI.
Plus some 44 small craft operated by Marine Police.
AMPHIBIOUS: craft only: 1 LCT.
COAST DEFENCE: 4 x 4 MM-40 *Exocet* bty.

AIR FORCE: 800; 17 cbt ac, 20 armed hel.

FGA: tac spt unit with 6 *Alpha Jet*.
FIGHTER: 1 AD sqn with 11 *Mirage* F1 (10 -E, 1 -B).
TRANSPORT: 1 sqn with 2 Boeing 707, 2 Boeing 727.
HELICOPTERS:
ATTACK: 12 SA-342L (with *HOT*), 8 *Commando* Mk 3 (*Exocet*).
TRANSPORT: 4 *Commando* (3 Mk 2A tpt, 1 Mk 2C VIP).
LIAISON: 2 SA-341G.
MISSILES:
ASM: *Exocet* AM-39, *HOT*.
SAM: 9 *Roland*.

SAUDI ARABIA

GDP	1992: R 453.5bn ($121.1bn): per capita $10,100	
	1993ε: R 470.0bn ($125.5bn): per capita $10,200	
Growth	1992: 4.5%	1993ε: 1.0%
Inflation	1992: -0.5%	1993: 1.8%
Debt	1992ε: $12.0bn	1993ε: $15.0bn
Def exp	1990ε: R 86.8bn ($23.2bn)	
	1991ε: R 133.0bn ($35.5bn)	
Def bdgt	1992: R 54.3bn ($14.5bn)	
	1993: R 61.6bn ($16.5bn)	
	1994: R 48.1bn ($13.9bn)	
$1 = R	1992–94: 3.75	
R = rial		

Population: 18,196,000 (nationals 69%, of which Bedouin up to 10%, Shi'ite 6%; expatriates 31%, of which Asians 21%, Arabs 8%, Africans 2% and Europeans ⟨1%).

	13–17	*18–22*	*23–32*
Men	524,500	423,000	1,231,200
Women	524,500	402,700	1,071,300

TOTAL ARMED FORCES:

ACTIVE: 104,000 (plus 57,000 active National Guard).

ARMY: 70,000.

3 armd bde (each 3 tk, 1 mech, 1 fd arty, 1 recce, 1 AD, 1 ATK bn).
5 mech bde (each 3 mech, 1 tk, 1 fd arty, 1 AD, 1 spt bn).
1 AB bde (2 AB bn, 3 SF coy).
1 Royal Guard bde (3 bn).
8 arty bn.
1 army avn comd.

EQUIPMENT:
MBT: 770: 30 M-1A2 *Abrams*, 290 AMX-30 (in store), 450 M60A3.
RECCE: 235 AML-60/-90.
AIFV: 570+ AMX-10P, 200 M-2 *Bradley*.
APC: 1,700 M-113 (incl variants), 150 Panhard M-3.
TOWED ARTY: 105mm: 100 M-101/-102 (in store); 155mm: 40 FH-70 (in store), 90 M-198, M-114; 203mm: M-115 (in store).
SP ARTY: 170: 155mm: 110 M-109A1B/A2, 60 GCT.
MRL: 60 *ASTROS II*.
MORTARS: 400, incl: 107mm: 4.2-in M-30; 120mm: 175 Brandt.
SSM: some 10 Ch CSS-2 (40 msl).
ATGW: *TOW*-2 (incl 200 VCC-1 SP), M-47 *Dragon*, *HOT* (incl 90 AMX-10P SP).
RCL: 84mm: 300 *Carl Gustav*; 90mm: M-67; 106mm: M-40A1.
AVIATION:
HELICOPTERS: 12 AH-64, 11 S-70A-1, 10 UH-60

(tpt, 4 medevac), 6 SA-365N (medevac), 15 Bell 406CS.
SAM: *Crotale, Stinger*, 500 *Redeye*.
SURV: AN/TPQ-36/-37 (arty, mor).

NAVY: ε12,000 (incl 1,500 Marines).
BASES: Riyadh (HQ Naval Forces); Western Fleet: Jiddah (HQ), Yanbu; Eastern Fleet: Al-Jubayl (HQ), Ad-Dammam, Ras al Mishab, Ras al Ghar.
FRIGATES: 8:
4 *Madina* (Fr F.2000) with 4 x 533mm, 2 x 406mm ASTT, 1 x AS-365N hel (AS 15 ASM); plus 8 *Otomat-2* SSM, 1 x 100mm gun.
4 *Badr* (US Tacoma) (ASUW) with 2 x 4 *Harpoon* SSM, 2 x 3 ASTT (Mk 46 LWT).
PATROL AND COASTAL COMBATANTS: 29:
MISSILE CRAFT: 9 *Al Siddiq* (US 58-m) PFM with 2 x 2 *Harpoon*.
TORPEDO CRAFT: 3 *Dammam* (Ge *Jaguar*) with 4 x 533mm TT (trg, incl 1 in reserve).
PATROL CRAFT: 17 US Halter Marine PCI⟨ (some with Coast Guard).
MINE WARFARE: 6:
2 *Al Jawf* (UK *Sandown* MCC).
4 *Addriyah* (US MSC-322) MCC.
AMPHIBIOUS: craft only: 4 LCU, 4 LCM.
SUPPORT AND MISCELLANEOUS: 7:
2 *Boraida* (mod Fr *Durance*) AO with 1 or 2 hel, 3 ocean tugs, 1 salvage tug, 1 Royal Yacht with hel deck.

NAVAL AVIATION: 20 armed hel.
HELICOPTERS: 24 AS-365N (4 SAR, 20 with AS-15TT ASM), 12 AS 332B/F (6 tpt, 6 with AM-39 *Exocet*).

MARINES: (1,500).
1 inf regt (2 bn), with 140 BMR-600P.

AIR FORCE: 18,000+; 292 cbt ac, no armed hel.
FGA: 5 sqn:
3 with 51 F-5E, 2 with 44 *Tornado* IDS.
FIGHTER: 3 sqn with 78 F-15C, 20 F-15D.
2 with 24 *Tornado* ADV.
RECCE: 1 sqn with 10 RF-5E.
AEW: 1 sqn with 5 E-3A.
TANKER: 8 KE-3A (tkr/tpt), 8 KC-130H.
OCU: 2 with 14* F-5B, 21* F-5F.
TRANSPORT: 3 sqn with 41 C-130 (7 -E, 34 -H), 8 L-100-30HS (hospital ac).
HELICOPTERS: 2 sqn with 22 AB-205, 25 AB-206B, 27 AB-212, 20 KV-107 (SAR, tpt).
TRAINING: 36 BAC-167 Mk-80/80A, 30* *Hawk* Mk 65, 30 PC-9, 1 *Jetstream* 31.
ROYAL FLIGHT:
ac: 4 BAe 125-800, 2 C-140, 4 CN-235, 2 *Gulfstream III*, 2 *Learjet* 35, 6 VC-130H, 1 Cessna 310; **hel:** 3 AS-61, AB-212, 1 -S70.
MISSILES:
ASM: AGM-65 *Maverick*, AS-15, AS-30, *Sea Eagle*.
ARM: ALARM.
AAM: AIM-9J/L/P *Sidewinder*, AIM-7F *Sparrow*, *Skyflash*.

AIR DEFENCE FORCES: 4,000.
33 SAM bty:
16 with 128 *Improved HAWK*.
17 with 68 *Shahine* fire units and AMX-30SA 30mm SP AA guns.
73 *Shahine/Crotale* fire units as static defence.
EQUIPMENT:
AD GUNS: 20mm: 92 M-163 *Vulcan*; 30mm: 50 AMX-30SA; 35mm: 128; 40mm: 150 L/70 (in store).
SAM: 141 *Shahine*, 128 MIM-23B *Improved HAWK*, 40 *Crotale*.

NATIONAL GUARD (directly under Royal command): 77,000 (57,000 active, 20,000 tribal levies).
2 mech inf bde, each 4 all arms bn.
6 inf bde.
1 ceremonial cav sqn.
EQUIPMENT:
LAV: 262 LAV-25.
APC: 1,100 V-150 *Commando, 65 Piranha*.
TOWED ARTY: 105mm: 40 M-102; 155mm: 30 M-198.
RCL: 106mm: M-40A1.
ATGW: *TOW*.

PARAMILITARY:
FRONTIER FORCE: 10,500.
COAST GUARD: 4,500; 4 *Al Jouf* PFI, about 30 PCI⟨, about 20 hovercraft, 1 trg, 1 Royal Yacht (5,000t) with 1 Bell 206B hel, about 350 armed boats.
GENERAL CIVIL DEFENCE ADMINISTRATION UNITS: 10 KV-107 hel.
SPECIAL SECURITY FORCE: 500; UR-416 APC.

FOREIGN FORCES:
PENINSULAR SHIELD FORCE: ε7,000; 1 inf bde (elm from all GCC states).

FRANCE: 130; 9 *Mirage* 2000C, 1 C 135, 1 N-262.
US: Air Force units on rotational det, numbers vary (incl: F-4G, F-15, F-16, F-117, C-130, KC-135, U-2 JSTARS), 1 *Patriot* bn.
UK: 6 *Tornado* GR-1A, 2 VC-10 (tkr).

SYRIA

GDP	1992: £S 265.7bn ($23.7bn): per capita $5,500	
	1993: £S 299.8bn ($26.7bn): per capita $6,000	
Growth	1992: 9.7%	1993ε: 10.0%
Inflation	1992: 9.4%	1993: 11.8%
Debt[a]	1992: $16.5bn	1993: $16.9bn
Def exp	1991ε: £S 50.9bn ($4.5bn)	
	1992ε: £S 24.7bn ($2.2bn)	
Def bdgt[b]	1993: £S 6.7bn ($593.9m)	
	1994: £S 8.7bn ($778.0bn)	
$1 = £S	1992: 11.2	1993: 11.2
	1994: 11.2	

£S = Syrian pound

[a] Syria's reported debt to the FSU (Russia) for arms purchases is $7bn.
[b] Excl arms purchases.

Population: 14,360,000

	13–17	*18–22*	*23–32*
Men	852,500	689,200	1,045,900
Women	826,000	673,400	1,005,600

TOTAL ARMED FORCES:

ACTIVE: 408,000.
Terms of service: conscription, 30 months.
RESERVES (to age 45): 400,000. Army 300,000 active; Navy 8,000; Air Force 92,000.

ARMY: 300,000 (200,000 conscripts, 100,000 reservists).

2 corps HQ.
6 armd div (each 3 armd, 1 mech bde, 1 arty regt).
3 mech div (-) (each 2 armd, 2 mech bde, 1 arty regt).
1 Republican Guard div (3 armd, 1 mech bde, 1 arty regt).
1 SF div (3 SF regt).
3 indep inf bde. 1 Border Guard bde.
2 indep arty bde. 1 indep ATK bde.
7 indep SF regt. 1 indep tk regt.
3 SSM bde (each of 3 bn):
1 with *FROG*; 1 with *Scud*; 1 with SS-21.
1 coastal def SSM bde with SS-C-1B *Sepal* and SS-C-3 *Styx*.
RESERVES: 1 armd div HQ (cadre), 30 inf, arty regt.
EQUIPMENT:
MBT: 4,500: 2,100 T-54/-55, 1,000 T-62M/K, 1,400 T-72/-72M. (Total incl some 1,200 in static positions and in store.)
RECCE: 1,000 BRDM-2.
AIFV: 2,250 BMP-1, 50 BMP-2.
APC: 1,500 BTR-40/-50/-60/-152.
TOWED ARTY: some 1,630, incl: 122mm: 100 M-1931/-37 (in store), 150 M-1938, 500 D-30; 130mm: 800 M-46; 152mm: 20 D-20, 50 M-1937; 180mm: 10 S23.
SP ARTY: 122mm: 400 2S1; 152mm: 50 2S3.
MRL: 107mm: 200 Type-63; 122mm: 280 BM-21.
MORTARS: 82mm; 120mm: 350 M-1943; 160mm: 100 M-160; 240mm: ε8 M-240.
SSM launchers: 18 *FROG*-7, some 18 SS-21, 20 *Scud* B/-C; SS-C-1B *Sepal*, SS-C-3 coastal.
ATGW: 4,700 AT-3 *Sagger* (incl 4,000 SP), 150 AT-4 *Spigot* and 200 *Milan*.
AD GUNS: some 1,985: 23mm: 600 ZU-23-2 towed, 400 ZSU-23-4 SP; 37mm: 300 M-1939; 57mm: 675 S-60, 10 ZSU-57-2 SP; 100mm: some KS-19.
SAM: SA-7/-9, 20 SA-13.

NAVY: ε8,000.

BASES: Latakia, Tartus, Minet el-Baida.
SUBMARINES: 1 Sov *Romeo* † with 533mm TT (plus 2 more non-op).
FRIGATES: 2 Sov *Petya-II* with 4 x ASW RL, 5 x 533mm TT.
PATROL AND COASTAL COMBATANTS: 29:
MISSILE CRAFT: 18: 14 Sov *Osa-I* and *II* PFM with 4 SS-N-2 *Styx* SSM, 4 Sov *Komar*⟨ † with 2 SS-N-2 *Styx* SSM.
PATROL: 11:
8 Sov *Zhuk* PFI⟨ .
1 Sov *Natya* (ex-MSO).
About 2 *Hamelin* PFI⟨ (ex-PLF).
MINE COUNTERMEASURES: 7:
1 Sov T-43, 1 *Sonya* MSC.
5 *Yevgenya* MSI.
AMPHIBIOUS: 3 *Polnocny* LSM, capacity 100 tps, 5 tk.
SUPPORT AND MISCELLANEOUS: 3: 1 spt, 1 trg, 1div spt.

NAVAL AVIATION: 29 armed hel.
ASW: 20 Mi-14, 5 Ka-25, 4 Ka-28 (Air Force manpower).

AIR FORCE: 40,000; 591 cbt ac; 100 armed hel (some may be in store).

FGA: 10 sqn:
5 with 70 Su-22. 2 with 44 MiG-23 BN.
1 with 20 Su-20. 2 with 20 Su-24.
FIGHTERS: 18 sqn:
8 with 150 MiG-21. 2 with 30 MiG-25.
5 with 80 MiG-23. 3 with 20 MiG-29.
RECCE: 6 MiG-25R.
EW: 10 Mi-8 *Hip* J/K hel.
TRANSPORT: 4 An-24, civil-registered ac incl: 5 An-26, 2 *Falcon* 20, 4 Il-76, 7 Yak-40, 1 *Falcon* 900, 6 Tu-134.
HELICOPTERS:
ATTACK: 50 Mi-25, 50 SA-342L.
TRANSPORT: 10 Mi-2, 10 Mi-6, 90 Mi-8/-17.
TRAINING: incl 10 L-29, 80* L-39, 20 MBB-223, 50* MiG-21U, 16* MiG-23UM, 5* MiG-25U.
MISSILES:
ASM: AT-2 *Swatter*, AS-7 *Kerry*, AS-12, *HOT*.
AAM: AA-2 *Atoll*, AA-6 *Acrid*, AA-7 *Apex*, AA-8 *Aphid*, AA-10 *Alamo*.

AIR DEFENCE COMMAND: ε60,000.
22 AD bde (some 95 SAM bty):
11 (some 60 bty) with some 450 SA-2/-3.
11 (27 bty) with some 200 SA-6 and AD arty.
2 SAM regt (each 2 bn of 2 bty) with some 48 SA-5, 60 SA-8.

FORCES ABROAD:

LEBANON: 30,000; 1 mech div HQ, 1 SF div HQ, elm 1 armd, 3 mech bde, 7 SF, 2 arty regt.

PARAMILITARY:

GENDARMERIE (Ministry of Interior): 8,000.
BA'TH PARTY: Workers' Militia (People's Army).

FOREIGN FORCES:

UNITED NATIONS (UNDOF): some 1,033; contingents from Austria, Canada and Poland.

UNITED ARAB EMIRATES (UAE)

GDP	1992: Dh 128.4bn ($34.9bn): per capita $19,800	
	1993ε: Dh 135.2bn ($36.0bn): per capita $19,900	
Growth	1992: 2.7%	1993ε: 0.5%
Inflation	1992: 3.5%	1993: 2.3%
Debt	1992: $10.5bn	1993: $10.6bn
Def exp[a]	1991: Dh 18.0bn ($4.9bn)	
	1992: Dh 7.7bn ($2.1bn)	
Def bdgt	1993: Dh 6.5bn ($1.8bn)	
	1994: Dh 7.0bn ($1.9bn)	
$1 = Dh	1992–94: 3.67	
Dh = dirham		

[a] Includes police and sy exp.

Population: 2,415,000 (nationals 24%, expatriates 76%, of which Indian 30%, Pakistani 16%, other Asian 12%, other Arab 12%, European 1%)

	13–17	*18–22*	*23–32*
Men	78,600	66,900	143,700
Women	75,000	58,300	79,600

TOTAL ARMED FORCES:

The Union Defence Force and the armed forces of the UAE (Abu Dhabi, Dubai, Ras Al Khaimah and Sharjah) were formally merged in 1976. Abu Dhabi and Dubai still maintain a degree of independence.
ACTIVE: 61,500 (perhaps 30% expatriates).

ARMY: 57,000 (incl Dubai: 12,000) (being reorganised).

MoD (Dubai); GHQ (Abu Dhabi).
INTEGRATED:
1 Royal Guard 'bde'. 1 armd bde.
1 mech inf bde. 2 inf bde.
1 arty bde.
NOT INTEGRATED:
2 inf bde (Dubai).
EQUIPMENT:
MBT: 125: 95 AMX-30, 30 OF-40 Mk 2 (*Lion*).
LIGHT TANKS: 76 *Scorpion*.
RECCE: 90 AML-90, 50 *Saladin* (in store), 20 *Ferret* (in store).
AIFV: 15 AMX-10P, 240 BMP-3.
APC: 50 VCR (incl variants), 240 Panhard M-3, 60 EE-11 *Urutu*.
TOWED ARTY: 108: 105mm: 70 ROF lt, 18 M-56 pack; 130mm: 20.
SP ARTY: 155mm: 18 Mk F-3, 70 G-6.

MRL: 122mm: 40 *FIROS*-25.
MORTARS: 81mm: 80; 120mm: 21.
SSM: 6 *Scud* B.
ATGW: 230 *Milan, Vigilant*, 25 *TOW, HOT* (20 SP).
RCL: 84mm: *Carl Gustav*; 106mm: 30.
AD GUNS: 20mm: 48 M-3VDA SP; 30mm: 20 GCF-BM2.
SAM: 20+ *Blowpipe*, 10 SA-16.

NAVY: ε2,000.
BASES: Abu Dhabi (main base): Dalma, Mina Zayed, Ajman; Dubai: Mina Rashid, Mina Jabal, Al Fujairah; Ras al Khaimah: Mina Sakr; Sharjah: Taweela, Mina Khalid, Khor Fakkan.
PATROL AND COASTAL COMBATANTS: 19:
CORVETTES: 2 *Muray Jip* (Ge Lürssen 62-m) with 2 x 2 MM-40 *Exocet* SSM, plus 1 SA-316 hel.
MISSILE CRAFT: 8:
6 *Ban Yas* (Ge Lürssen TNC-45) with 2 x 2 MM-40 *Exocet* SSM.
2 *Mubarraz* (Ge Lürssen 45-m) with 2 x 2 MM-40 *Exocet* SSM, plus 1 x 6 *Sadral* SAM.
PATROL, INSHORE: 9: 6 *Ardhana* (UK Vosper 33-m) PFI, 3 *Kawkab* PCI‹.
AMPHIBIOUS: craft only: 3 *Al Feyi* LCT, 1 LCM.
SUPPORT AND MISCELLANEOUS: 3: 1 div spt, 1 log spt, 1 tug.

AIR FORCE (incl Police Air Wing): 2,500 (incl Dubai: 700); 97 cbt ac, 39 armed hel.
FGA: 3 sqn:
1 with 9 *Mirage* 2000E. 1 with 18 *Hawk* 102.
1 with 14 *Hawk* Mk 63A (FGA/trg).
FIGHTER: 1 sqn with 22 *Mirage* 2000 EAD.
COIN: 1 sqn with 6 MB-326 (4 -KD, 2 -LD), 5 MB-339A.
OCU: *7 *Hawk* Mk 61, *2 MB-339A, *6 *Mirage* 2000 DAD.
RECCE: 8 *Mirage* 2000 RAD.
TRANSPORT: incl 1 BN-2, 4 C-130H, 2 L-100-30, 1 G-222, 5 DHC-5, 4 C-212.
HELICOPTERS:
ATTACK: 2 AS-332F (anti-ship, with *Exocet* AM-39), 10 SA-342K (with *HOT*), 7 SA-316/-319 (with AS-11/-12), 20 AH-64A.
TRANSPORT: 8 AS-332 (2 VIP), 1 AS-350, 26 Bell (8 -205, 9 -206A, 5 -206L, 4 -214), 7 SA-319.
SAR: 3 Bo-105, 1 S-76.
TRAINING: 23 PC-7, 5 SF-260 (4 -TP, 1 -W).
MISSILES:
ASM: *HOT*, AS-11/-12, *Exocet* AM-39, *Hellfire*, Hydra-70.
AAM: R-550 *Magic*, AIM 9L.
AD:
1 AD bde (3 bn).
5 bty *Improved HAWK*.
12 *Rapier*, 9 *Crotale*, 13 RBS-70, 100 *Mistral* SAM.

PARAMILITARY:

COAST GUARD (Ministry of Interior): some 40 PCI‹, plus boats.

FOREIGN FORCES:

MOROCCO: some 2,000; army, gendarmerie and police.

REPUBLIC OF YEMEN

The Republic of Yemen was formed in May 1990 by the Yemen Arab Republic (north) and the People's Democratic Republic of Yemen (south). Civil war broke out between the forces of the two former states in May 1994 which ended in victory for the north in July. It is too early to assess accurately the scale of manpower and equipment casualties suffered by either side, but obviously the south will have lost more. To give some idea of the scale of the fighting the forces of the two sides have been listed as they were before unification took place, up-dated as far as possible by addition and retirement since 1990.

GDP[a]	1992: R121.1bn ($7.6bn): per capita $1,350	
	1993ε: R 126.9bn ($7.7bn): per capita $1,300	
Growth	1992: -1.5%	1993ε: -1%
Inflation	1991: 45%	1992ε: 70%
Debt	1992: $6.5bn	1993: $6.7bn
Def exp	1991ε: R12.7bn ($1.1bn)	
Def bdgt	1992ε: R 6.4bn ($400.0m)	
	1993ε: R 6.2bn ($375.0m)	
$1 = R	1992: 16.0	1993: 16.5
	1994: 17.9	

R = rial

[a] Prior to the unification of the Yemen Arab Republic and the People's Democratic Republic of Yemen in 1990, the GDP of the north comprised about 80% of the combined GDP.

NORTH YEMEN

Population:[b] 8,723,000

	13–17	18–22	23–32
Men	523,000	463,000	705,000
Women	522,000	458,000	710,000

[b] Since the end of the Gulf War, over 900,000 (out of 1,500) Yemenis returned to the Republic of Yemen from Saudi Arabia having been expelled following a change in Saudi immigration rules.

TOTAL ARMED FORCES:

ACTIVE: 38,500 (perhaps 25,000 conscripts).
Terms of service: conscription, 3 years.
RESERVES: Army: perhaps 40,000.

ARMY: 37,000 (perhaps 25,000 conscripts).

5 armd bde. 1 SF bde.
12 inf bde. 4 arty bde.
3 mech bde. 1 SSM bde.
2 AB/cdo bde. 1 central guard force.
3 AD arty bn.2 AD bn (1 with SA-2 SAM).

EQUIPMENT:
MBT: 475 T-54/-55, 100 T-62, 50 M-60A1.
RECCE: 60 AML-245, 125 AML-90.
AIFV: 120 BMP-1/-2.
APC: 370: 70 M-113, 300 BTR-40/-60/-152.
TOWED ARTY: 277: 76mm: 200 M-194; 105mm: 35 M-101; 122mm: 30 M-1931/37; 155mm 12 M-114.
ASSAULT GUNS: 100mm: 30 SU-100.
MRL: 122mm: 65 BM-21.
MORTARS: 81mm; 82mm; 120mm: 50 M-43.
SSM: 12 SS-21.
ATGW: 20 *Vigilant*, 12 *TOW*, 24 *Dragon*.
RL: 66mm: M72 *LAW*.
RCL: 75mm: M-20; 82mm.
AD GUNS: 20mm: 52 M-167, 20 M-163 *Vulcan* SP; 23mm: 30 ZU-23, ZSU-23-4; 37mm: 150 M-1939; 57mm: 120 S-60.
SAM: SA-7, SA-9.

NAVY: 500.

BASE: Hodeida.
PATROL CRAFT, INSHORE: 8:
3 *Sana'a* (US *Broadsword* 32-m) PFI.
5 Sov *Zhuk*(.
MINE COUNTERMEASURES: 3 Sov *Yevgenya* MSI.
AMPHIBIOUS: craft only: 2 Sov *Ondatra* LCU.

AIR FORCE: 1,000; 61 cbt ac (plus some 40 in store), no armed hel.

FGA: 11 F-5E, 15 Su-22.
FIGHTER: 23 MiG-21.
TRANSPORT: 1 An-12, 3 An-24, 4 An-26, 2 C-130H, 2 F-27, 2 *Skyvan* 3M.
HELICOPTERS: 2 AB-204, 4 AB-206, 1 AB-212, 3 AB-214, 20 Mi-8, 1 AB-47.
TRAINING: 2 F-5B*, 2 MiG-15*, 4 MiG-21U*, 4 Su-22U*.
AD: some SA-2, -3, -5, -6.
AAM: AA-2 *Atoll*, AIM-9 *Sidewinder*.

PARAMILITARY:

MINISTRY OF NATIONAL SECURITY FORCE: 10,000.
TRIBAL LEVIES: at least 20,000.

SOUTH YEMEN

Population: 2,319,000

	13–17	18–22	23–32
Men	139,000	123,000	187,000
Women	129,000	122,000	189,000

TOTAL ARMED FORCES:

ACTIVE: 27,500 (perhaps 18,000 conscripts).
Terms of service: 2 years.
RESERVES: Army: 45,000.

ARMY: 24,000 (perhaps 18,000 conscripts).

3 armd bde. 1 arty bde.
2 mech bde. 10 arty bn.
11 inf bde. 2 SSM bde.

EQUIPMENT:
MBT: 250 T-34, 250 T-54/-55, 15 T-62.
RECCE: 150 BRDM-2.
AIFV: some 180 BMP-1.
APC: 300 BTR-40/-60/-152.
TOWED ARTY: 122mm: 50 M-1938, 150 D-30; 90 M-46, 152mm: 10 D-20.
COAST ARTY: 130mm: 36 SM-4-1.
MRL: 155: 122mm: 140 BM-21; 140mm: 15 BM-14.
MORTARS: 82mm; 120mm: 50 M-43; 160mm.
SSM launchers: 12 *FROG-7*, 6 *Scud* B.
ATGW: AT-3 *Sagger* (incl 36 BRDM SP).
RCL: 82mm: 20 B-10; 107mm: B-11.
ATK GUNS: 70: 85mm: 30 D-44; 100mm: 40.
AD GUNS: 200: 23mm: ZU-23, ZSU-34-4 SP; 37mm: 30 M-1939; 57mm: S-60; 85mm: 20 KS-12.
SAM: SA-7/-9.

NAVY: 1,000.
BASES: Aden, Perim Island, Al Mukalla.
PATROL AND COASTAL COMBATANTS: 6:
MISSILE CRAFT: 6 Sov *Osa*-II with 4 x SSN-2B *Styx* SSM.
AMPHIBIOUS: 2 Sov *Polnocny* LSM, capacity 100 tps, 5 tk.

AIR FORCE: 2,500; 49 cbt ac, 12 armed hel.
FGA: 8 MiG-21, 20 SU-20.
FIGHTER: 16 MiG-21.
TRANSPORT: 1 An-12, 6 An-24, 2 An-26, 4 Il-14.
HELICOPTERS: 2 Ka-26, 4 Mi-4, 20 Mi-8, 12 Mi-24 (attack).
TRAINING: 3 MiG-15UTI*, 2 MiG-21U*.
AD: Some SA-2, -3, -6.
MISSILES:
AAM: AA-2 *Atoll.*

PARAMILITARY:
PEOPLE'S MILITIA: 15,000.
PUBLIC SECURITY FORCE: 30,000; 6 PFI(.

NORTH AFRICA

ALGERIA

GDP	1992: D 1,019.3bn ($46.7bn): per capita $5,900	
	1993ε: D 1,098.3bn ($47.0bn): per capita $5,800	
Growth	1992: 2.2%	1993ε: -1.8%
Inflation	1992: 31.7%	1993: 20.5%
Debt	1992: $26.4bn	1993: $26.0bn
Def exp	1990: D 17.0bn ($1.9bn)	
Def bdgt	1992: D 23.0bn ($1.1bn)	
	1993: D 29.8bn ($1.2bn)	
	1994ε: D 36.4bn ($1.1bn)	
FMA	1993: $0.1m (IMET)	
	1994: $0.1m (IMET)	
	1995: $0.2m (IMET)	
$1 = D	1992: 21.8	1993: 23.4
	1994: 37.6	

D = dinar

Population: 28,207,200

	13–17	*18–22*	*23–32*
Men	1,713,500	1,479,900	2,245,700
Women	1,593,600	1,379,800	2,087,400

TOTAL ARMED FORCES:
ACTIVE: 121,700 (90,000 conscripts).
Terms of service: Army 18 months (6 months basic, 1 year civil projects).
RESERVES: Army: some 150,000, to age 50.

ARMY: 105,000 (90,000 conscripts).
6 Military Regions. Reorganising into div structure. Numbers of indep bde, regt unclear.
2 armd div (each 3 tk, 1 mech regt).
2 mech div (each 3 mech, 1 tk regt).
5 mot inf bde (4 inf, 1 tk bn).
1 AB div.
7 indep arty, 5 AD bn.
EQUIPMENT:
MBT: some 960: 330 T-54/-55, 330 T-62, 300 T-72.
RECCE: 120 BRDM-2.
AIFV: 915: 690 BMP-1, 225 BMP-2.
APC: 460 BTR-50/-60.
TOWED ARTY: 405: 122mm: 25 D-74, 100 M-1931/37, 60 M-30 (M-1938), 190 D-30; 130mm: 10 M-46; 152mm: 20 ML-20 (M-1937).
SP ARTY: 185: 122mm: 150 2S1; 152mm: 35 2S3.
MRL: 126: 122mm: 48 BM-21; 140mm: 48 BM-14-16; 240mm: 30 BM-24.
MORTARS: 330: 82mm: 150 M-37; 120mm: 120 M-1943; 160mm: 60 M-1943.
RCL: 178: 82mm: 120 B-10; 107mm: 58 B-11.
ATK GUNS: 298: 57mm: 156 ZIS-2; 85mm: 80 D-44; 100mm: 12 T-12, 50 SU-100 SP.
AD GUNS: 895: 14.5mm: 80 ZPU-2/-4; 20mm: 100; 23mm: 100 ZU-23 towed, 210 ZSU-23-4 SP; 37mm: 150 M-1939; 57mm: 75 S-60; 85mm: 20 KS-12; 100mm: 150 KS-19; 130mm: 10 KS-30.
SAM: SA-7/-8/-9.

NAVY: ε6,700 (incl ε630 Coast Guard).
BASES: Mers el Kebir, Algiers, Annaba, Jijel.
SUBMARINES: 2:
2 Sov *Kilo* with 533mm TT (both refitting in Russia).
FRIGATES: 3 *Mourad Rais* (Sov *Koni*) with 2 x 12 ASW RL.
PATROL AND COASTAL COMBATANTS: 22:
CORVETTES: 3 *Rais Hamidou* (Sov *Nanuchka II*) with 4 x SS-N-2C *Styx* SSM.
MISSILE CRAFT: 11 *Osa* with 4 x SS-N-2 SSM.
PATROL: 8:
COASTAL: 2 *Djebel Chinoise.*
INSHORE: about 6 *El Yadekh* PCI.
MINE WARFARE: 1 Sov T-43 MSC.
AMPHIBIOUS: 3:
2 *Kalaat beni Hammad* LST: capacity 240 tps, 10 tk, hel deck.
1 *Polnocny* LSM: capacity 180 tps, 6 tk.

SUPPORT AND MISCELLANEOUS: 3:
1 *El Idrissi* AGHS, 1 div spt, 1 *Poluchat* torpedo recovery vessel.

COAST GUARD (under naval control): ε630.
Some 7 Ch *Chui-E* PCC, about 6 *El Yadekh* PCI, 16 PCI‹, 1 spt, plus boats.

AIR FORCE: 10,000; 193 cbt ac, 63 armed hel.
Average Annual Flying Hours: 100+.
FGA: 3 sqn:
1 with 10 Su-24. 2 with 40 MiG-23BN.
FIGHTER: 8 sqn:
1 with 14 MiG-25. 1 with 20 MiG-23B/E.
6 with 95 MiG-21MF/bis.
RECCE: 1 sqn with 3 MiG-25R.
MR: 1 sqn with 2 *Super King Air* B-200T.
TRANSPORT: 2 sqn with 6 An-12, 10 C-130H, 6 C-130H-30, 3 Il-76.
VIP: 2 *Falcon* 900, 3 *Gulfstream III*, 2 F-27.
HELICOPTERS: 5 sqn:
ATTACK HEL: 2 with 38 Mi-24, 1 with 25 Mi-8/-17.
TRANSPORT HEL: (hy): 1 with 25 Mi-8/-17; 1 with 12 Mi-4.
TRAINING: 3* MiG-21U, 5* MiG-23U, 3* MiG-25U, 6 T-34C, 30 L-39, plus 30 ZLIN-142.
AAM: AA-2, AA-6.
AD GUNS: 3 bde+: 85mm, 100mm, 130mm.
SAM: 3 regt: 1 with SA-3, SA-6, SA-8.

PARAMILITARY:

GENDARMERIE (Ministry of Interior): 24,000; 44 Panhard AML-60/M-3, 100 *Fahd* APC, 28 Mi-2 hel.
NATIONAL SECURITY FORCES (Ministry of Interior): 16,000; small arms.
REPUBLICAN GUARD BDE: 1,200; AML-60, M-3 recce.

LIBYA

GDP	1992ε: D 8.8bn ($29.2bn):	
	per capita $6,000	
	1993: D 9.8bn ($30.3bn):	
	per capita $6,000	
Growth	1992ε: -4.9%	1993ε: 1.0%
Inflation	1992ε: 10.0%	1993ε: 10.0%
Debt	1989: $5.4bn	
Def exp	1991ε: D 724m ($2.7bn)	
	1992ε: D 692m ($2.3bn)	
Def bdgt	1993ε: D 488m ($1.5bn)	
	1994ε: D 421m ($1.4bn)	
$1 = D	1992: 0.30	1993: 0.33
	1994: 0.30	

D = dinar

Population: 5,054,000

	13–17	*18–22*	*23–32*
Men	303,280	253,320	186,600
Women	292,240	243,560	174,000

TOTAL ARMED FORCES:

ACTIVE: 70,000.
Terms of service: selective conscription, 2 years.
RESERVES: People's Militia, some 40,000.

ARMY: 40,000 (ε25,000 conscripts).
6 Military Districts.
5 elite bde (regime sy force).
10 tk bn. 20–25 arty bn.
20–30 inf bn. 5–10 AD arty bn.
5–10 mech inf bn. 10–20 para/cdo bn.
5 SSM bde.
EQUIPMENT:
MBT: 2,350 (incl 1,200 in store): 1,700 T-54/-55, 350 T-62, 300 T-72.
RECCE: 250 BRDM-2, 380 EE-9 *Cascavel*.
AIFV: 1,000 BMP-1.
APC: 800 BTR-50/-60, 100 OT-62/-64, 40 M-113, 100 EE-11 *Urutu*.
TOWED ARTY: some 720: 105mm: some 60 M-101; 122mm: 270 D-30, 60 D-74; 130mm: 330 M-46.
SP ARTY: some 350: 122mm: 130 2S1; 152mm: 40 2S3, *DANA*; 155mm: 160 *Palmaria*, 20 M-109.
MRL: some 700: 107mm: Type 63; 122mm: BM-21/RM-70, BM-11.
MORTARS: 82mm; 120mm: M-43; 160mm.
SSM launchers: 40 *FROG-7*, 80 *Scud* B.
ATGW: 3,000: *Milan*, AT-3 *Sagger* (incl BRDM SP), AT-4 *Spigot*.
RCL: 106mm: 220 M-40A1.
AD GUNS: 600: 23mm: ZU-23, ZSU-23-4 SP; 30mm: M-53/59 SP; 57mm: S-60.
SAM: SA-7/-9/-13, 24 quad *Crotale*.
SURV: RASIT (veh, arty).

NAVY: 8,000 (incl Coast Guard).
BASES: Tripoli, Benghazi, Derna, Tobruk, Sidi Bilal, Al Khums.
SUBMARINES: 4 *Al Badr* † (Sov *Foxtrot*) with 533mm and 406mm TT.

FRIGATES: 2:
2 *Al Hani* (Sov *Koni*) with 4 x ASTT, 2 x ASW RL; plus 4 SS-N-2C SSM.
(Plus 1 *Dat Assawari* † (UK Vosper Mk 7) with 2 x 3 ASTT; plus 4 *Otomat* SSM, 1 x 114mm gun (non-op).)
PATROL AND COASTAL COMBATANTS: 36:
CORVETTES: 4:
1 *Assad al Bihar*† (It *Assad*) with 4 *Otomat* SSM; plus 2 x 3 ASTT (A244S LWT) (plus 3 more non-op).
3 *Ean al Gazala* (Sov *Nanuchka*-II) with 2 x 2 SS-N-2C *Styx* SSM.
MISSILE CRAFT: 24:
9 *Sharaba* (Fr *Combattante* II) with 4 *Otomat* SSM.
12 *Al Katum* (Sov *Osa* II) with 4 SS-N-2C SSM.
3 *Susa* with 8 SS-12M SSM.
PATROL CRAFT: 8:
INSHORE: 8: 4 *Garian*, 3 *Benina*, 1 Sov *Poluchat*.
MINE WARFARE: 8 *Ras al Gelais* (Sov *Natya* MSO).
(*El Temsah* and about 5 other ro-ro tpt have mine-laying capability.)
AMPHIBIOUS: 5:
2 *Ibn Ouf* LST, capacity 240 tps, 11 tk, 1 SA-316B hel.
3 Sov *Polnocny* LSM, capacity 180 tps, 6 tk.
Plus craft: 3 LCT.
SUPPORT AND MISCELLANEOUS: 10:
1 *Zeltin* log spt/dock, 1 *Tobruk* trg, 1 salvage, 1 diving spt, 1 *El Temsah* and about 5 other ro-ro tpt.

NAVAL AVIATION: 30 armed hel.
HELICOPTERS: 2 sqn:
1 with 25 Mi-14 (ASW), 1 with 5 SA-321.

AIR FORCE: 22,000 (incl Air Defence Command); 406 cbt ac, 65 armed hel (many ac in store, number n.k.).
BOMBERS: 1 sqn with 6 Tu-22.
FGA: 7 sqn with 40 MiG-23BN, 15 MiG-23U, 30 *Mirage* 5D/DE, 14 *Mirage* 5DD, 14 *Mirage* F-1AD, 6 Su-24, 45 Su-20/-22.
FIGHTER: 9 sqn with 50 MiG-21, 75 MiG-23, 60 MiG-25, 3 -25U, 12 *Mirage* F-1ED, 6 -BD.
COIN: 1 sqn with 30 J-1 *Jastreb*.
RECCE: 1 sqn with 5 *Mirage* 5DR, 7 MiG-25R.
TRANSPORT: 2 sqn with 15 An-26, 12 Lockheed (7 C-130H, 2 L-100-20, 3 L-100-30), 16 G-222, 20 Il-76, 15 L-410.
HELICOPTERS:
ATTACK: 40 Mi-24, 25 Mi-35.
TRANSPORT: hy: 18 CH-47C; **med:** 34 Mi-8/17; **lt:** 30 Mi-2, 11 SA-316, 5 AB-206.
TRAINING: 80 *Galeb* G-2 **ac**; 20 Mi-2 **hel**; other ac incl 1 Tu-22, 150 L-39ZO, 20 SF-260WL.
MISSILES:
ASM: AT-2 *Swatter* ATGW (hel-borne), AS-7, AS-9, AS-11.
AAM: AA-2 *Atoll*, AA-6 *Acrid*, AA-7 *Apex*, AA-8 *Aphid*, R-530, R-550 *Magic*.

AIR DEFENCE COMMAND:
'Senezh' AD comd and control system.
4 bde with SA-5A: each 2 bn of 6 launchers, some 4 AD arty gun bn; radar coy.
5 Regions: 5–6 bde each 18 SA-2; 2–3 bde each 12 twin SA-3; ε3 bde each 20–24 SA-6/-8.

PARAMILITARY:
CUSTOMS/COAST GUARD (Naval control): a few patrol craft incl in naval totals, plus armed boats.

MAURITANIA

GDP	1992: OM 104.2bn ($1.2bn): per capita $1,400	
	1993: OM 152.2bn ($1.3bn): per capita $1,450	
Growth	1992: 2.4%	1993ε: 2.5%
Inflation	1992: 10.9%	1993: 9.4%
Debt	1992: $2.3bn	1993: $2.4bn
Def exp	1991: OM 3.2bn ($39.6m)	
Def bdgt	1992ε: OM 3.2bn ($37.0m)	
	1993ε: OM 4.3bn ($36.0m)	
	1994ε: OM 4.5bn ($36.3m)	
$1 = OM	1992: 87.0	1993: 120.8
	1994: 123.4	

OM = Mauritanian ouguiya

Population: 2,195,400

	13–17	*18–22*	*23–32*
Men	120,500	105,600	156,100
Women	115,000	100,400	156,200

TOTAL ARMED FORCES:
ACTIVE: ε15,650:
Terms of service: conscription (2 years) authorised.

ARMY: 15,000.
6 Military Regions.
7 mot inf bn.
8 inf bn.
3 arty bn.
4 AD arty bty.

1 para/cdo bn. 1 Presidential sy bn.
2 Camel Corps bn. 1 engr coy.
1 armd recce sqn.

EQUIPMENT:

MBT: 35 T-54/-55.

RECCE: 60 AML (20 -60, 40 -90), 40 *Saladin*, 5 *Saracen*.

TOWED ARTY: 105mm: 35 M-101A1/HM-2; 122mm: 20 D-30, 20 D-74.

MORTARS: 81mm: 70; 120mm: 30.

ATGW: *Milan*.

RCL: 75mm: M-20; 106mm: M-40A1.

AD GUNS: 23mm: 20 ZU-23-2; 37mm: 15 M-1939; 57mm: S-60; 100mm: 12 KS-19.

SAM: SA-7.

NAVY: ε500.

BASES: Nouadhibou, Nouakchott.

PATROL CRAFT: 6:
1 *N'Madi* (UK *Jura*) PCO (fishery protection).
3 *El Vaiz* (Sp *Barcelo*) PFI† .
1 *El Nasr* (Fr *Patra*) PCI.
1 *Z'Bar* (Ge *Neustadt*) PFI.
Plus about 3 armed boats.

AIR FORCE: 150; 7 cbt ac, no armed hel.

COIN: 5 BN-2 *Defender*, 2 FTB-337 *Milirole*.

MR: 2 *Cheyenne* II.

TRANSPORT: 2 Cessna F-337, 1 DHC-5D, 1 *Gulfstream II*.

PARAMILITARY:

GENDARMERIE (Ministry of Interior): ε3,000; 6 regional coy.

NATIONAL GUARD (Ministry of Interior): 2,000, plus 1,000 auxiliaries.

MOROCCO

GDP	1992: D 245.6bn ($28.8bn): per capita $3,300	
	1993ε: D 277.1bn ($29.8bn): per capita $3,300	
Growth	1992: -2.9%	1993ε: 1.0%
Inflation	1992: 4.9%	1993: 4.7%
Debt	1992: $21.4bn	1993: $22.0bn
Def exp[a]	1990: D 12.2bn ($1.5bn)	
Def bdgt	1992: D 9.8bn ($1.1bn)	
	1993: D 10.1bn ($1.1bn)	
	1994ε: D 9.7bn ($1.0bn)	
FMA	1993: $41.2m (FMF, IMET)	
	1994: $0.5m (IMET)	
	1995: $2.1m (IMET, Econ aid)	
$1 = D	1992: 8.5	1993: 9.3
	1994: 9.5	

D = dirham

[a] Incl D4.37bn ($530m) border and internal security costs.

Population: 27,787,000

	13–17	*18–22*	*23–32*
Men	1,571,400	1,405,000	2,249,200
Women	1,514,700	1,353,000	2,226,200

TOTAL ARMED FORCES:

ACTIVE: 195,500.

Terms of service: conscription 18 months authorised; most enlisted personnel are volunteers.

RESERVES: Army 150,000: obligation to age 50.

ARMY: 175,000 (ε100,000 conscripts).

2 Comd (Northern Zone, Southern Zone).
3 mech inf bde. 1 lt sy bde.
2 para bde. 8 mech inf regt.
Independent units:
12 arty bn. 3 mot (camel corps) bn.
1 AD gp. 2 cav bn.
10 armd bn. 1 mtn bn.
37 inf bn. 7 engr bn.
4 cdo units. 2 AB bn.

ROYAL GUARD: 1,500; 1 bn, 1 cav sqn.

EQUIPMENT:

MBT: 224 M-48A5, 300 M-60 (60-A1, 240-A3).

LIGHT TANKS: 100 SK-105 *Kuerassier*.

RECCE: 16 EBR-75, 80 AMX-10RC, 190 AML-90, 38 AML-60-7, 20 M-113.

AIFV: 60 *Ratel* (30 -20, 30 -90), 45 VAB-VCI, 10 AMX-10P.

APC: 420 M-113, 320 VAB-VTT, some 45 OT-62/-64 may be op.

TOWED ARTY: 105mm: 35 lt (L-118), 20 M-101, 36 M-1950; 130mm: 18 M-46; 155mm: 20 M-114, 35 FH-70.

SP ARTY: 105mm: 5 Mk 61; 155mm: 98 F-3, 44 M-109, 20 M-44.

MRL: 122mm: 39 BM-21.

MORTARS: 81mm: 1,100; 120mm: 600 (incl 20 VAB SP).

ATGW: 440 *Dragon*, 80 *Milan*, 150 *TOW* (incl 42 SP), 50 AT-3 *Sagger*.

RL: 89mm: 150 3.5-in M-20.

RCL: 106mm: 350 M-40A1.

ATK GUNS: 90mm: 28 M-56; 100mm: 8 SU-100 SP.
AD GUNS: 14.5mm: 200 ZPU-2, 20 ZPU-4; 20mm: 40 M-167, 60 M-163 *Vulcan* SP; 23mm: 90 ZU-23-2; 100mm: 15 KS-19 towed.
SAM: 37 M-54 SP *Chaparral*, 70 SA-7.
SURV: RASIT (veh, arty).
UAV: R4E-50 *Skyeye*.

NAVY: 7,000 (incl 1,500 Marines).
BASES: Casablanca, Agadir, Al Hoceima, Dakhla, Tangier.
FRIGATE: 1 *Lt Col. Errhamani* (Sp *Descubierta*) with 2 x 3 ASTT (Mk 46 LWT), 1 x 2 375mm AS mor (fitted for 4 x MM-38 *Exocet* SSM).
PATROL AND COASTAL COMBATANTS: 27:
CORVETTES: 2:
2 It *Assad* (ex-Iraqi Navy) with 3 x 2 *Otomat* SSM; plus 2 x 3 ASTT (A244S LWT) (reported purchased, but not yet delivered).
MISSILE CRAFT: 4 *Cdt El Khattabi* (Sp *Lazaga* 58-m) PFM with 4 x MM-38 *Exocet* SSM.
PATROL: 23:
COASTAL: 13:
2 *Okba* (Fr PR-72) PFC.
6 *LV Rabhi* (Sp 58-m B-200D) PCC.
5 *El Hahiq* (Dk *Osprey* 55) PCC (incl 2 with customs).
INSHORE: 10 *El Wacil* (Fr P-32) PFI‹ (incl 4 with customs).
AMPHIBIOUS: 3 *Ben Aicha* (Fr *Champlain BATRAL*) LSM, capacity 140 tps, 7 tk.
Plus craft: 1 *Edic*-type LCU.
SUPPORT: 4: 2 log spt, 1 tpt, 1 AGOR (US lease).

MARINES: (1,500). 1 naval inf bn.

AIR FORCE: 13,500; 95 cbt ac, 24 armed hel.
Annual flying hours for F-5 and *Mirage*: over 100.
FGA: 2 sqn:
1 with 16 F-5E, 4 F-5F.
1 with 14 *Mirage* F-1EH.
FIGHTER: 1 sqn with 15 *Mirage* F-1CH.
COIN: 2 sqn:
1 with 23 *Alpha Jet*; 1 with 23 CM-170, 4 OV-10.
RECCE: 1 sqn with 2 C-130H (with side-looking radar).
EW: 2 C-130 (ELINT), 1 *Falcon* 20 (ELINT).
TANKER: 1 Boeing 707; 2 KC-130H (tpt/tanker).
TRANSPORT: 11 C-130H, 7 CN-235, 3 Do-28, 3 *Falcon 20*, 1 *Falcon 50* (VIP), 2 *Gulfstream II* (VIP), 5 *King Air 100*, 3 *King Air 200*.
HELICOPTERS:
ATTACK: 24 SA-342 (12 with *HOT*, 12 with cannon).
TRANSPORT: hy: 7 CH-47; **med**: 27 SA-330, 27 AB-205A; **lt**: 20 AB-206, 3 AB-212, 4 SA-319.
TRAINING: 10 AS-202, 2 CAP-10, 4 CAP-230, 12 T-34C.
LIAISON: 2 *King Air 200*, 2 UH-60 *Blackhawk*.
AAM: AIM-9B/D/J *Sidewinder*, R-530, R-550 *Magic*.
ASM: AGM-65B *Maverick* (for F-5E), *HOT*.

FORCES ABROAD:
UAE: some 2,000.
UN AND PEACEKEEPING:
ANGOLA (UNAVEM II): 2 Observers.

PARAMILITARY: 42,000.
GENDARMERIE ROYALE: 12,000; 1 bde, 4 mobile gp, 1 para sqn, air sqn, coast guard unit; 18 boats, 2 *Rallye* **ac**; 3 SA-315, 3 SA-316, 2 SA-318, 6 *Gazelle*, 6 SA-330, 2 SA-360 **hel**.
FORCE AUXILIAIRE: 30,000, incl 5,000 Mobile Intervention Corps.
CUSTOMS/COAST GUARD: 2 PCC, 4 PFI (included in Navy), plus boats.

OPPOSITION:
POLISARIO: Military Wing of Sahrawi People's Liberation Army: ε3–6,000, org in bn.
EQUIPMENT: 100 T-55, T-62 tk; 50+ BMP-1, 20–30 EE-9 *Cascavel* MICV; 25 D-30/M-30 122mm how; 15 BM-21 122mm MRL; 20 120mm, mor; AT-3 *Sagger* ATGW; 50 ZSU-23-2, ZSU-23-4 23mm SP AA guns; SA-6/-7/-8/-9 SAM. (Captured Moroccan eqpt incl AML-90, *Eland* armd recce, *Ratel* 20, Panhard APC, Steyr SK-105 *Kuerassier* lt tks.)

FOREIGN FORCES:
UN (MINURSO): some 54 tps, 230 military observers and 26 civpol in Western Sahara from 28 countries.

TUNISIA

GDP	1992: D 13.7bn ($15.5bn): per capita $5,100	
	1993: D 14.9bn ($16.4bn): per capita $5,200	
Growth	1992: 8.5%	1993: 2.6%
Inflation	1992: 5.5%	1993: 4.0%
Debt	1992: $8.5bn	1993: $8.7bn
Def exp[a]	1992: D 527.0m ($596.0m)	

Def bdgt	1993:	D 561.7m ($574.7m)
	1994ε:	D 563.2m ($547.3m)
FMA	1993:	$8.2m (IMET, Econ aid)
	1994:	$3.5m (IMET, Econ aid)
	1995:	$1.1m (IMET, Econ aid)
$1 = D	1992:	0.88 1993: 1.00
	1994:	1.03

D = dinar

[a] Incl D 290.3m ($328m) for police and sy exp.

Population: 8,740,000

	13–17	*18–22*	*23–32*
Men	492,600	444,700	766,800
Women	468,300	426,600	741,400

TOTAL ARMED FORCES:

ACTIVE: 35,500 (26,400 conscripts).
Terms of service: 12 months selective.

ARMY: 27,000 (25,000 conscripts).

3 mech bde (each with 1 armd, 2 mech inf, 1 arty, 1 AD regt).
1 Sahara bde. 1 SF bde.
1 engr regt.

EQUIPMENT:
MBT: 84: 54 M-60A3, 30 M-60A1.
LIGHT TANKS: 55 SK-105 *Kuerassier*.
RECCE: 24 *Saladin*, 35 AML-90.
APC: 268: 140 M-113A1/-A2, 18 EE-11 *Urutu*, 110 Fiat F-6614.
TOWED ARTY: 117: 105mm: 48 M-101A1/A2; 155mm: 12 M-114A1, 57 M-198.
MORTARS: 81mm: 95; 107mm: 40 4.2-in.
ATGW: 65 *TOW* (incl some SP), 500 *Milan*.
RL: 89mm: 300 LRAC-89, 300 3.5-in M-20.
RCL: 57mm: 140 M-18; 106mm: 70 M-40A1.
AD GUNS: 20mm: 100 M-55; 37mm: 15 Type-55/-65.
SAM: 48 RBS-70, 25 M-48 *Chaparral*.
SURV: RASIT (veh, arty).

NAVY: ε5,000 (ε700 conscripts).

BASES: Bizerte, Sfax, Kelibia.
PATROL AND COASTAL COMBATANTS: 20:
MISSILE CRAFT: 6:
3 *La Galite* (Fr *Combattante* III) PFM with 8 MM-40 *Exocet* SSM.
3 *Bizerte* (Fr P-48) with 8 x SS-12 SSM.
PATROL: 14:
INSHORE: 14: 2 *Gafsah* (Ch *Shanghai*) PFI, 2 *Tazarka* (UK Vosper 31-m) PCI, some 10 PCI⟨ .
SUPPORT AND MISCELLANEOUS: 2: 1 *Inkhad* (US *Savage*) FF trg, 1 *Salambo* (US *Conrad*) survey/trg.

AIR FORCE: 3,500 (700 conscripts); 32 cbt aircraft, 5 armed hel.

FGA: 15 F-5E/F.
COIN: 1 sqn with 3 MB-326K, 2 MB-326L.
TRANSPORT: 2 C-130H.
LIAISON: 2 S-208M.
TRAINING: 18 SF-260 (6-C, *12-W), 5 MB-326B.
HELICOPTERS:
ARMED: 5 SA-341 (attack).
TRANSPORT: 1 wing with 15 AB-205, 6 AS-350B, 1 AS-365, 6 SA-313, 3 SA-316, 2 UH-1H, 2 UH-1N.
AAM: AIM-9J *Sidewinder*.

FORCES ABROAD:

UN AND PEACEKEEPING:

CROATIA (UNPROFOR I): 10 civ pol.
RWANDA (UNAMIR): 40.
WESTERN SAHARA (MINURSO): 9 Observers.

PARAMILITARY:

NATIONAL POLICE: 13,000.
NATIONAL GUARD: 10,000; incl Coastal Patrol with 4 (ex-GDR) *Kondor-I*-class PCC, 5 (ex-GDR) *Bremse*-class PCI⟨, plus some 10 other PCI⟨ .

Central and Southern Asia

Central Asia

The civil war in **Afghanistan** continues unabated with the bulk of the fighting still centred around Kabul. General Abdul Rashid Dostum, the former commander of the Northern Corps (the only Army formation to maintain any sort of military cohesion), deserted Ahmed Shah Masud (the Minister of Defence) and joined forces with Gulbuddin Hekmatyar (the Prime Minister) in his fight against those backing Burhanuddin Rabbani (the President). This desertion of a strong force does not appear to have had any decisive effect; if anything, Rabbani's forces are gaining control over Kabul. In **Tajikistan**, the rebels who crossed into Afghanistan in 1993 continue to carry out small-scale attacks on border posts.

Southern Asia

India's internal situation has showed a marked improvement over the last 12 months. Despite the continuing strife in Kashmir, the Army's presence there has been reduced and the plan to increase the strength of the paramilitary *Rashtriya* or National Rifles, predominantly deployed in Kashmir, from five to 30 battalions will allow further Army withdrawals. India continues to accuse Pakistan of interfering in its internal affairs, particularly by supplying arms and funding foreign mercenaries in Kashmir; Pakistan denies the charges, but continues to advocate Kashmiri self-determination at international fora. In the Punjab, although the political situation is far from stable, violence has virtually ended. The threat of Hindu fundamentalism has receded and the Bharatiya Janata Party (BJP) suffered defeat in five crucial Hindi-speaking states to a new combination of lower-caste and Muslim parties in unusually peaceful elections. In the north-eastern region, while there has been some respite from the insurgency prevalent in Assam, Nagaland and Manipur, inter-tribal rivalries resulted in killings during the year.

The guerrilla war being waged against Tamil rebels in north-eastern **Sri Lanka** shows no sign of ending, with both sides continuing to suffer heavy casualties.

While **Myanmar** remains under military rule and Aung San Suu Kyi, whose National League for Democracy (NLD) won the 1990 election, remains under house arrest, the various insurgent campaigns which have plagued the country for 30 years appear to be on the wane. The most recent agreement to be reached, in October 1993, was with the Kachin Independence Army (KIA), probably the strongest of the ethnic insurgent groups. The main remaining insurgent groups are the northern-based Shan Mong Tai Army and the Karen and Mon groups in south-east Myanmar where the Karen National Liberation Army is the largest. The groups which once formed the Communist Party of Burma and which no longer have to battle with the government have turned their attention with great success to the drug trade.

Nuclear Developments

Kazakhstan acceded to the Nuclear Non-Proliferation Treaty (NPT) in February 1994 and is negotiating a full-scope safeguards agreement with the International Atomic Energy Agency (IAEA) for its civil nuclear facilities. The dismantlement of the ICBM force has begun and 12 SS-18 missiles have been returned to Russia for elimination. The nuclear warheads from these missiles are believed to be still stored in Kazakhstan, as are the ALCMs associated with the strategic Tu-95H bomber force which has been redeployed to Russia. There are a few older Tu-95G based in Kazakhstan, but it is not known whether they are under Russian or Kazakh control. The former, however, is the more likely. Nor is it known if there are any nuclear bombs left in Kazakhstan with which they could be armed. Kazakhstan is eligible for aid and assistance under the US Cooperative Threat Reduction initiative and the Nunn–Lugar programme, but no details are available. Japan has pledged $11.43m in disarmament aid for Kazakhstan. All nuclear warheads in Kazakhstan are expected to be transferred to Russia by mid-1995.

India maintains its implaccable opposition to any form of regional non-proliferation treaty, nor will it join the NPT until this is both universal and non-discriminatory. Prime Minister Rao has also made it clear that India will not halt its *Agni* missile development, asserting that it is not a weapons programme, but 'an experiment in re-entry technology'; that is not how it is viewed in Pakistan. The **Pakistani** Prime Minister, Benazir Bhutto, said in November 1993 that Pakistan had no bomb, but did have all the elements to make one. Pakistan is opposed to any non-proliferation agreement of which India is not a signatory, but has suggested to India several proposals to prevent the spread of nuclear weapons.

Conventional Military Developments

The provision of the Conference on Security and Cooperation in Europe (CSCE) Vienna Document data exchange returns to the IISS by certain Central Asian states has allowed a more detailed and comprehensive listing of the military forces there than in 1993. On the other hand, there is no reliable information available to allow any revision of weapons holdings in Afghanistan, other than to state the obvious that there are less. Nor is it possible to estimate how much weaponry is held by each of the various groups and factions.

India has carried out several more tests, the latest in June 1994, of production models of the *Privthi* 250km-range surface-to-surface missile. It is claimed that *Privthi*, which can carry a 1,000kg payload, has an error probability of less than 20m at 80km range. *Privthi* launchers were paraded in Delhi on Republic Day in January 1994, an SSM regiment is forming and up to 15 launchers are being produced. In addition to *Privthi* and *Agni* SSM, India is developing three other missiles. The *Trishul* SAM, a short-range weapon whose engagement range is 9km, is mounted on a tracked launcher for the Army and a wheeled launcher for the Air Force. The *Akash* SAM is said to be able to engage up to five aircraft with its multi-warheads at a range of 25km. It will be controlled by an Indian-developed phased array radar. The *Nag* ATGW is a 4km-range 'top-attack' missile which may come into service in 1996. India is moving towards developing a cruise-missile capability. An unmanned air vehicle (UAV) for use as an aerial target, the *Lakshya*, is about to enter series production. It will be followed by the *Nishant* UAV which will carry sensors and provide real-time information. The Indian Army has accepted the *Arjun* main battle tank for service, but no funds have been authorised for procurement. India now provides a brigade of nearly 5,000 men for the UN force in Somalia. Russia is to upgrade Indian MiG-21 aircraft and there are reports of a possible MiG-29 order for 30 aircraft and that Su-30 might be produced in India under licence.

There have been no reports during the last 12 months of further tests of **Pakistan's** *Hatf*-series SSM. *Hatf* 1, which can carry a 500kg payload up to 80km, entered service in 1992; *Hatf* 2 is believed to have a 500kg payload and a 300km range and could be in service in 1995. There have also been unconfirmed reports of a longer-range *Hatf* 3 SSM. Delivery of Chinese Type-85 tanks has begun, over 100 are now in service. The Pakistani Army has formed a seventh independent armoured brigade. It is now known that the eight air-defence brigades have a central command headquarters and are formed into three groups. The Pakistan Navy has returned four *Brooke* (*Badr*)-class and four *Garcia* (*Saif*)-class frigates to the US at the end of their five-year lease. The *Babur* (UK *Devonshire*) destroyer has been retired, while all three *Alamgir* (US *Gearing*) are now fully operational. A total of six *Amazon*-class frigates have been purchased from the UK for delivery by the end of 1994. The Navy has acquired six *Lynx* HAS MK3 helicopters for ASW. The Air Force has a fighter squadron with 30 *Mirage* 1110 aircraft which had previously been listed as in store.

The *rapprochement* between **Myanmar** and China has led to the Air Force acquiring significant numbers of Chinese aircraft. The Air Force inventory now includes two fighter squadrons with 20 F-7 and 4 FT-7 and two with 24 A-5M FGA aircraft. In 1992 **Nepal** acquired eight 105mm pack howitzers from Britain and 52 120mm mortars from India; this represents a 200% increase in its artillery capability. The **Bangladesh** Navy has taken into service one UK

Jersey-class offshore patrol craft. Bangladesh has contributed two more battalions to UN peacekeeping missions: one to UNIKOM in Kuwait; and one to UNOSOM in Somalia. One battalion remains with UNOMOZ in Mozambique and one has returned from Cambodia at the end of UNTAC's mandate. In **Sri Lanka**, the Army has formed three more infantry brigades and is forming one mechanised and one air-mobile brigade.

AFGHANISTAN

GDP	1989ε: Afs 152.0bn ($3.0bn): per capita $700	
Growth	1989: 0%	1993ε: 0%
Inflation	1991ε: 56.7%	1992: n.k.
Debt	1992: $2.3bn	1993ε: $2.5bn
Def exp	1990: Afs 22.0bn ($430.0m)	
Def bdgt	1992: n.k.	1993: n.k.
FMA:	1990ε: $3.5–4.5bn	
$1 = Afs	1992–94: 50.6	
Afs = afghani		

Population:[a] 16,060,000 (Pashtun 38%, Tajik 25%, Hazara 19%, Uzbek 6%, Aimaq 4%, Baluchi 0.5%)

	13–17	*18–22*	*23–32*
Men	1,240,300	1,049,000	1,625,000
Women	1,193,400	1,005,900	1,552,000

[a] Includes 3,751,000 refugees in Pakistan and 1,278,000 in Iran. More than half were reported to have returned to Afghanistan during 1993.

Following the fall of the Najibullah government in April 1992, the bulk of the armed forces broke up with only the Northern corps retaining its structure. The rest appear to have transferred their allegiance to their local *Mujaheddin* group.

EQUIPMENT:

It is not possible to show how ground forces equipment has been divided among the different factions. The list below represents weapons known to be in the country in April 1992.

MBT: 1,200: T-54/-55, T-62.
LIGHT TANKS: 60 PT-76.
RECCE: 250 BRDM-1/-2.
AIFV: 550 BMP-1/-2.
APC: 1,100 BTR-40/-60/-70/-80/-152.
TOWED ARTY: 1,000+: 76mm: M-1938, M-1942; 85mm: D-48; 100mm: M-1944; 122mm: M-30, D-30; 130mm: M-46; 152mm: D-1, D-20, M-1937 (ML-20).
MRL: 185: 122mm: BM-21; 140mm: BM-14; 220mm: BM-22.
MORTARS: 1,000+: 82mm: M-37; 107mm; 120mm: 100 M-43.
SSM: 30: *Scud*, *FROG*-7 launchers.
ATGW: AT-1 *Snapper*, AT-3 *Sagger*.
RCL: 73mm: SPG-9; 82mm: B-10.
AD GUNS: 600+: 14.5mm; 23mm: ZU-23, 20 ZSU-23-4 SP; 37mm: M-1939; 57mm: S-60; 85mm: KS-12; 100mm: KS-19.
SAM: SA-7/-13.

AIR FORCE:

Air Force organisation and loyalty following the fall of the government is uncertain. The majority are controlled either by the Defence Ministry or by General Dostum. The inventory shows aircraft in service in April 1992. Since then an unknown number of fixed-wing aircraft and helicopters have either been shot down or destroyed on the ground. The serviceability of the remainder is doubtful.

FGA: 30 MiG-23, 80 Su-7/-17/-22.
FIGHTER: 80 MiG-21F.
ARMED HELICOPTERS: 25 Mi-8, 35 Mi-17, 20 Mi-25.
TRANSPORT: ac: 2 Il-18D; 50 An-2, An-12, An-26, An-32; **hel:** 12 Mi-4.
TRAINING: 25 L-39*, 18 MiG-21*.
AIR DEFENCE:
SAM: 115 SA-2, 110 SA-3, 37mm, 85mm and 100mm guns.

MUJAHEDDIN GROUPS:

Afghan insurgency was a broad national movement, united only against the Najibullah government.

GROUPS ORIGINALLY BASED IN PESHAWAR:

TRADITIONALIST MODERATE:

NATIONAL LIBERATION FRONT (*Jabha't-Nija't-Milli'*): ε15,000. Leader: Sibghatullah Modjaddi. Area: enclaves in Kandahar, Zabol provinces, eastern Konar. Ethnic group: Pashtun.
NATIONAL ISLAMIC FRONT (*Mahaz-Millin Isla'mi*): ε15,000. Leader: Sayyed Amhad Gailani. Area: eastern Paktia, astride Vardak/Lowgar border. Ethnic group: Pashtun.

ISLAMIC REVOLUTIONARY MOVEMENT (*Haraka't-Inqila'b-Isla'mi*): ε25,000. Leader: Mohammed Nabi Mohammed. Area: Farah, Zabol, Paktika, southern Ghazni, eastern Lowgar, western Paktia, northern Nimruz, northern Helmand, northern Kandahar. Ethnic group: Pashtun.

ISLAMIC FUNDAMENTALIST:

ISLAMIC PARTY (*Hizbi-Isla'mi-Kha'lis*): ε40,000. Leader: Yu'nis Kha'lis. Area: central Paktia, Nangarhar, south-east Kabul. Ethnic group: Pashtun.

ISLAMIC PARTY (*Hizbi-Isla'mi-Gulbaddin*): ε50,000. Leader: Gulbuddin Hekmatyar. Area: north and southern Kabul, Parvan, eastern Laghman, northern Nangarhar, south-east Konar; large enclave junction Badghis/Ghowr/Jowzjan, western Baghlan; enclaves in Farah, Nimruz, Kandahar, Oruzgan and Zabol. Ethnic groups: Pashtun/Turkoman/Tajik.

ISLAMIC UNION (*Ittiha'd-Isla'mi Barai Azadi*): ε18,000. Leader: Abdul Rasul Sayyaf. Area: east of Kabul. Ethnic group: Pashtun.

ISLAMIC SOCIETY (*Jamia't Isla'mi*): ε60,000. Leader: Burhanuddin Rabbani. Area: eastern and northern Farah, Herat, Ghowr, Badghis, Faryab, northern Jowzjan, northern Balkh, northern Kondoz, Takhar, Baghlan, Kapisa, northern Laghman, Badakhshan. Ethnic groups: Turkoman/Uzbek/Tajik.

GROUPS ORIGINALLY BASED IN IRAN:

Shia groups have now formed an umbrella party known as the *Hezbi-Wahdat* (Unity Party).

Sazman-e-Nasr: some 50,000. Area: Bamian, northern Oruzgan, eastern Ghowr, southern Balkh, southern Samangan, south-west Baghlan, south-east Parvan, northern Vardak. Ethnic group: Hazara.

Harakat-e-Islami: 20,000. Area: west of Kabul; enclaves in Kandahar, Ghazni, Vardak, Samangan, Balkh. Ethnic groups: Pashtun/Tajik/Uzbek.

Pasdaran-e-Jehad: 8,000.

Hizbollah: 4,000.

Nehzat: 4,000.

Shura-Itifaq-Islami: some 30,000+. Area: Vardak, eastern Bamian. Ethnic group: Hazara.

NATIONAL ISLAMIC MOVEMENT (NIM):

Formed in March 1992 by Uzbek militia commander, Abdul Rashid Dostum, mainly from troops of former Northern Command of the Afghan Army. Predominantly Uzbek, Tajik, Turkomen, Ismaeli and Hazara Shia. Strength ε65,000 (120–150,000 in crisis). 2 Corps HQ, 5–7 inf div, some indep bde. Now supports Gulbuddin Hekmatyar.

BANGLADESH

GDP	1992: Tk 906.5bn ($23.3bn): per capita $1,200	
	1993: Tk 968.8bn ($24.5bn): per capita $1,250	
Growth	1992: 4.2%	1993: 4.3%
Inflation	1992: 4.3%	1993: 0%
Debt	1992: $13.2bn	1993: $13.9bn
Def exp	1992: Tk 13.8bn ($355.0m)	
Def bdgt	1993ε: Tk 14.8bn ($375.0m)	
	1994ε: Tk 16.2bn ($402.5m)	
FMA	1993: $0.46m (IMET)	
	1994: $0.18m (IMET)	
	1995: $0.18m (IMET)	
$1 = Tk	1992: 39.0	1993: 39.6
	1994: 40.2	

Tk = taka

Population: 124,867,000 (Hindu 16%)

	13–17	*18–22*	*23–32*
Men	7,243,800	6,289,400	9,624,600
Women	6,856,000	5,985,500	9,151,700

TOTAL ARMED FORCES:

ACTIVE: 115,500.

ARMY: 101,000.

7 inf div HQ.
16 inf bde (some 26 bn).
1 armd bde (2 armd regt).
1 armd regt.
3 arty bde (6 arty regt).
1 engr bde.

EQUIPMENT:†

MBT: some 80 Ch Type-59/-69, 60 T-54/-55.
LIGHT TANKS: some 40 Ch Type-62.
TOWED ARTY: 105mm: 30 Model 56 pack, 50 M-101; 122mm: 20 Ch Type-54; 130mm: 40+ Ch Type-59.
MRL: 122mm: reported.
MORTARS: 81mm; 82mm: Ch Type-53; 120mm: 50 Ch Type-53.
RCL: 106mm: 30 M-40A1.
ATK GUNS: 57mm: 18 6-pdr; 76mm: 50 Ch Type-54.
AD GUNS: 37mm: 16 Ch Type-55; 57mm: Ch Type-59.

NAVY:† ε8,000.

BASES: Chittagong (HQ), Dhaka, Khulna, Kaptai.
FRIGATES: 4:
1 *Osman* (Ch *Jianghu I*) with 2 x 5 ASW mor, plus 2 x 2 CSS-N-2 *Hai Ying*-2 (HY-2) SSM, 2 x 2 100mm guns.

1 *Umar Farooq* (UK *Salisbury*) with 1 x 3 *Squid* ASW mor, 1 x 2 114mm guns.
2 *Abu Bakr* (UK *Leopard*) with 2 x 2 114mm guns.
PATROL AND COASTAL COMBATANTS: 40:
MISSILE CRAFT: 8:
4 *Durdarsha* (Ch *Huangfeng*) with 4 x HY-2 SSM.
4 *Durbar* (Ch *Hegu*) PFM〈 with 2 x HY-2 SSM.
TORPEDO CRAFT: some 8 Ch *Huchuan* PFT〈 with 2 x 533mm TT.
PATROL, OFFSHORE: 1 *Shaeed Ruhul Amin* (ex-UK Jersey) PCO (trg).
PATROL, COASTAL: 5:
2 *Durjoy* (Ch *Hainan*) with 4 x 5 ASW RL.
2 *Meghna* fishery protection.
1 *Shahjalal.*
PATROL, INSHORE: 13:
8 *Shahead Daulat* (Ch *Shanghai II*) PFI.
2 *Karnaphuli*, 2 *Padma*, 1 *Bishkali* PCI.
RIVERINE: 5 *Pabna*〈.
AMPHIBIOUS: 1 *Shahamanat* LCU; plus craft: 4 LCM, 3 LCVP.
SUPPORT AND MISCELLANEOUS: 3:
1 coastal tanker, 1 repair, 1 ocean tug.

AIR FORCE:† 6,500; 69 cbt ac, no armed hel.

FGA: 3 sqn with 17 J-6/JJ-6 (F-6/FT-6), 13 Q-5 (A-5 *Fantan*), 12 Su-7BM (ex-Iraqi ac).
FIGHTER: 2 sqn with 17 J-7 (F-7M), 4 MiG-21MF, 2 MiG-21U.
TRANSPORT: 1 sqn with 1 An-24, 4 An-26, 1 DHC-3.
HELICOPTERS: 3 sqn with 2 Bell 206L, 10 Bell 212, 7 Mi-8, 4 Mi-17, 3 UH-1N.
TRAINING: 20 Ch CJ-6, 8 CM-170, 4* JJ-7 (FT-7), 4 MiG-15UTI, 3 Su-7U.

FORCES ABROAD:

UN AND PEACEKEEPING:
CROATIA (UNPROFOR I): 35 Observers, 29 civ pol.
GEORGIA (UNOMIG): 3 Observers.
IRAQ/KUWAIT (UNIKOM): 790; 1 mech inf bn, 9 Observers.
LIBERIA (UNOMIL): 118, incl 53 Observers.
MOZAMBIQUE (ONUMOZ): 1,209; 1 inf bn plus spt, 30 Observers, 25 civ pol.
RWANDA (UNAMIR): 37, incl 33 Observers.
UGANDA/RWANDA (UNOMUR): 20 Observers.
SOMALIA (UNOSOM): 975; 1 inf bn.
WESTERN SAHARA (MINURSO): 7 Observers.

PARAMILITARY:

BANGLADESH RIFLES: 30,000 (border guard); 37 bn.
ARMED POLICE: 5,000.
ANSARS (Security Guards): 20,000.

OPPOSITION:

SHANTI BAHINI (Peace Force): Chakma tribe, Chittagong Hills, ε5,000.

INDIA

GDP	1992: Rs 7,056.0bn ($272.2bn): per capita $1,200	
	1993ε: Rs 8,856.0bn ($290.4bn): per capita $1,250	
Growth	1992: 4.6%	1993ε: 4.0%
Inflation	1992: 11.8%	1993: 6.4%
Debt	1992: $77.0bn	1993: $79.0bn
Def exp	1992: Rs 174.1bn ($6.7bn)	
	1993: Rs 215.0bn ($7.0bn)	
Def bdgt	1993: Rs 191.2bn ($6.3bn)	
	1994: Rs 230.0bn ($7.3bn)	
FMA	1994: $0.2m (IMET)	
	1995: $0.2m (IMET)	
$1 = Rs	1992: 25.9	1993: 30.5
	1994: 31.4	

Rs = rupee

Population: 913,839,800 (Muslim 11%, Sikh 2%)

	13–17	*18–22*	*23–32*
Men	48,983,100	44,800,200	77,401,600
Women	45,676,000	41,300,100	70,565,100

TOTAL ARMED FORCES:

ACTIVE: 1,265,000 (incl 200 women).
RESERVES: Army 300,000 (first-line reserves within 5 years of full-time service; a further 650,000 have a commitment until the age of 50); Territorial Army (volunteers) 160,000; Air Force 140,000; Navy 55,000.

ARMY: 1,100,000.

HQ: 5 Regional Comd (= Fd Army), 12 Corps (incl 1 AD arty).
2 armd div (each 2/3 armd, 1 SP arty (2 SP fd, 1 med regt) bde).
1 mech div (each 3 mech (4/6 mech bn), 3 armd regt, 1 arty bde) 1 more reported forming.
22 inf div (each 2–5 inf, 1 arty bde; some have armd regt).

10 mtn div (each 3–4 bde, 1 or more arty regt).
14 indep bde: 5 armd, 7 inf, 1 mtn, 1 AB/cdo; 3 indep arty bde.
1 SSM regt (forming).
6 AD bde.
3 engr bde.
These formations comprise:
55 tk regt (bn).
355 inf bn (incl 25 mech, 9 AB/cdo).
290 arty regt (bn) reported: incl 1 hy, 2 MRL, 50 med (11 SP), 69 fd (3 SP), 39 mtn, 29 AD arty regt; perhaps 10 SAM gp (3–5 bty each).
Army Aviation:
14 hel sqn: 6 ATK, 8 air obs.

EQUIPMENT:

MBT: 3,400: some 800 T-55, 1,400 T-72/-M1, 1,200 *Vijayanta*, plus 339 in store.
RECCE: BRDM-2.
AIFV: 900 BMP-1/-2 (*Sarath*).
APC: 157 OT-62/-64.
TOWED ARTY: 3,325 incl: 75mm: 900 75/24 mtn, 215 Yug M-48; 105mm: some 1,200 IFG Mk I/II, 50 M-56; 122mm: D-30 reported; 130mm: 550 M-46; 155mm: 410 FH-77B.
SP ARTY: 105mm: 80 *Abbot*; 130mm: 100 mod M-46.
MRL: 122mm: 80 BM-21, LRAR.
MORTARS: 81mm: L16A1, E1; 120mm: 1,000 incl M-43, 500 *Brandt* AM-50, E1; 160mm: 200 M-160.
SSM: some 15 *Prithvi*.
ATGW: *Milan*, AT-3 *Sagger*, AT-4 *Spigot*, AT-5 *Spandrel*.
RCL: 57mm: M-18; 84mm: *Carl Gustav*; 106mm: 1,000+ M-40A1.
AD GUNS 2,468: 20mm: *Oerlikon* (reported); 23mm: 140 ZU 23-2, 75 ZSU-23-4 SP; 30mm: 8 2S6 SP (reported); 40mm: 1,245 L40/60, 1,000 L40/70.
SAM: 100 SA-6, 620 SA-7, 48 SA-8A/-B, 200 SA-9, 50 SA-11, 45 SA-13, 200 SA-16.
HELICOPTERS: 200 *Chetak*, *Cheetah*.
SURV: MUFAR (mor), *Green Archer* (mor).

RESERVES: Territorial Army: 25 inf bn, plus 31 'departmental' units.

DEPLOYMENT:

North: 2 Corps with 7 inf, 1 mtn div.
West: 3 Corps with 1 armd, 8 inf div.
Central: 1 Corps with 1 armd, 2 inf div, plus 1 inf, 1 mtn div.
East: 3 Corps with 8 mtn div.
South: 2 Corps with 1 mech, 3 inf div.

NAVY: 55,000 (incl 5,000 Naval Aviation and ε1,000 Marines).

PRINCIPAL COMMANDS: Western, Eastern, Southern.
Sub-Commands: Submarine, Naval Air.

BASES: Bombay (HQ Western Cmd), Goa (HQ Naval Air), Karwar (under construction); Cochin (HQ Southern Cmd), Visakhapatnam (HQ Eastern and Submarines), Calcutta, Madras, Port Blair (Andaman Is), Arakonam (Naval Air).

FLEETS: Western (based Bombay); Eastern (based Visakhapatnam).

SUBMARINES: 15:
SS: 15:
8 *Sindhughosh* (Sov *Kilo*) with 533mm TT.
4 *Shishumar* (Ge T-209/1500) with 533mm TT.
3 *Kursura* (Sov *Foxtrot*) with 533mm TT trg (plus 3 non-op reserve).

PRINCIPAL SURFACE COMBATANTS: 25:
CARRIERS: 2:
1 *Viraat* (UK *Hermes*) (29,000t) CVV.
1 *Vikrant* (UK *Glory*) (19,800t) CVV.
Air group typically: **ac:** 12 (*Viraat*) and 6 (*Vikrant*) *Sea Harrier* fighter/attack; **hel:** 7 (*Viraat*) and 9 (*Vikrant*) *Sea King* ASW/ASUW (*Sea Eagle* ASM).
DESTROYERS: 5:
5 *Rajput* (Sov *Kashin*) DDG with 2 x 2 SA-N-1 *Goa* SAM; plus 4 SS-N-2C *Styx* SSM, 5 x 533mm TT, 2 x ASW RL, 1 Ka-25 or 27 hel (ASW).
FRIGATES: 18:
3 *Godavari* FFH with 1 x *Sea King* hel, 2 x 3 324mm ASTT; plus 4 x SS-N-2C *Styx* SSM and 1 x 2 SA-N-4 SAM.
6 *Nilgiri* (UK *Leander*) with 2 x 3 ASTT, 4 with 1 x 3 *Limbo* ASW mor, 1 *Chetak* hel, 2 with 1 *Sea King*, 1 x 2 ASW RL; plus 2 x 114mm guns (all).
4 *Kamorta* (Sov *Petya*) with 4 ASW RL, 3 x 533mm TT.
5 *Khukri* (ASUW) with 2 or 4 SS-N-2C (*Styx*), hel deck.
Additional in store: some 2 ex-UK FF and 4 *Kamorta* FF.

PATROL AND COASTAL COMBATANTS: 40:
CORVETTES: 15:
3 *Vijay Durg* (Sov *Nanuchka* II) with 4 x SS-N-2B *Styx* SSM.
5 *Veer* (Sov *Tarantul*) with 4 x *Styx* SSM.
3 *Vibhuti* (similar to *Tarantul*) with 4 x *Styx* SSM.
4 *Abhay* (Sov *Pauk-II*) (ASW) with 4 x ASTT, 2 x ASW mor.
MISSILE CRAFT: 6 *Vidyut* (Sov *Osa* II) with 4 x *Styx*.
PATROL, OFFSHORE: 7 *Sukanya* PCO.
PATROL, INSHORE: 12 SDB Mk 2/3.

MINE WARFARE: 20:
MINELAYERS: none, but *Kamorta* FF and *Pondicherry* MSO have minelaying capability.

MINE COUNTERMEASURES: 20:
12 *Pondicherry* (Sov *Natya*) MSO.
2 *Bulsar* (UK *'Ham'*) MSI.
6 *Mahé* (Sov *Yevgenya*) MSI⟨.
AMPHIBIOUS: 9:
1 *Magar* LST, capacity 200 tps, 12 tk, 1 hel.
8 *Ghorpad* (Sov *Polnocny* C) LSM, capacity 140 tps, 6 tk (includes 2 in reserve).
Plus craft: 7 *Vasco da Gama* LCU.
SUPPORT AND MISCELLANEOUS: 22:
2 *Deepak* AO, 5 small AO, 1 *Amba* (Sov *Ugra*) sub spt, 1 div spt, 2 ocean tugs, 6 *Sandhayak* and 4 *Makar* AGHS, 1 *Tir* trg.

NAVAL AVIATION: (5,000); 65 cbt ac, 75 armed hel.

Annual flying hours for attack pilots: some 180.
ATTACK: 2 sqn with 23 *Sea Harrier* FRS Mk-51, 4 T-60 trg.
ASW: 6 hel sqn with 26 *Chetak*, 7 Ka-25, 10 Ka-28, 32 *Sea King* Mk 42A/B.
MR: 3 sqn: 5 Il-38, 10 Tu-142M *Bear* F, 10 Do-228, 13 BN-2 *Defender*.
COMMUNICATIONS: 1 sqn with 5 BN-2 *Islander*, 2 Do-228 **ac**; 3 *Chetak* **hel**.
SAR: 1 hel sqn with 6 *Sea King* Mk 42C.
TRAINING: 2 sqn: 6 HJT-16, 8 HPT-32 **ac**; 2 *Chetak*, 4 Hughes 300 **hel**.
MISSILES:
AAM: R-550 *Magic* I and II.
ASM: *Sea Eagle, Sea Skua*.

MARINES: (ε1,000).

1 regt (2nd forming).

AIR FORCE: 110,000; 799 cbt ac, 36 armed hel.

5 Air Comd.
Annual flying hours for FGA/fighter pilots: some 180.
FGA: 22 sqn:
3 with 54 MiG-23 BN/UM.
5 with 89 *Jaguar* IS.
5 with 120 Mig-27.
9 with 144 MiG-21 MF/PFMA.
FIGHTER: 20 sqn:
4 with 74 MiG-21 FL/U. 9 with 170 MiG-21 bis/U.
2 with 26 MiG-23 MF/UM. 3 with 59 MiG-29
2 with 35 *Mirage* 2000H/TH.
ECM: 5 *Canberra* B(I) 58.
AWAC: 4 HS-748.
MARITIME ATTACK: 8 *Jaguar* with *Sea Eagle*.
ATTACK HELICOPTERS: 2 sqn:
1 with 18 Mi-25. 1 with 18 Mi-35.
RECCE: 2 sqn:
1 with 8 *Canberra* (6 PR-57, 2 PR-67).
1 with 6 MiG-25R, 2 MiG-25U.
MR/SURVEY: 2 *Gulfstream* IV SRA, 2 *Learjet* 29.
TRANSPORT:
AIRCRAFT: 12 sqn:
6 with 105 An-32 *Sutlej*. 2 with 30 Do-228.
2 with 33 BAe-748. 2 with 24 Il-76 *Gajraj*.
HELICOPTERS: 11 sqn with 80 Mi-8, 50 Mi-17, 10 Mi-26 (hy tpt).
VIP: 1 HQ sqn with 2 Boeing 707-337C, 3 Boeing 737, 7 BAe-748.
LIAISON: flt and det: 16 BAe-748.
TRAINING: 28 BAe-748, 7 *Canberra* (2 T54, 5 TT18), 120 *Kiran* I, 56 *Kiran* II, 88 HPT-32, *Hunter* (20 F-56, 18 T-66), 15* *Jaguar* IB, 5* MiG-29UB, 44 TS-11 *Iskara* **ac**; 20 *Chetak*, 2 Mi-24, 2 Mi-35 **hel**.
MISSILES:
ASM: *Akash*, AS-7 *Kerry*, AS-11B (ATGW), AS-12, AS-30, *Sea Eagle*.
AAM: AA-2 *Atoll*, AA-7 *Apex*, AA-8 *Aphid*, AA-10 *Alamo*, AA-11 *Archer*, R-550 *Magic*, *Super* 530D.
SAM: 30 sqns: 280 *Divina* V75SM/VK (SA-2), SA-3, SA-5.

FORCES ABROAD:

UN AND PEACEKEEPING:

ANGOLA (UNAVEM II): 3 Observers.
IRAQ/KUWAIT (UNIKOM): 6 Observers.
LIBERIA (UNOMIL): 20 Observers.
MOZAMBIQUE (ONUMOZ): 910 (HQ coy, engr, log).
SOMALIA (UNOSOM): 4,975.

PARAMILITARY:

NATIONAL SECURITY GUARDS (Cabinet Secretariat): 7,500: anti-terrorism contingency deployment force. Comprises elements of the Armed Forces, CRPF and Border Security Force.
CENTRAL RESERVE POLICE FORCE (CRPF) (Ministry of Home Affairs): 120,000; 70 bn, internal security duties, only lightly armed, deployable throughout the country.
BORDER SECURITY FORCE (BSF) (Ministry of Home Affairs): 120,000; some 147 bn, small arms, some lt arty, tpt/liaison air spt.
ASSAM RIFLES (Ministry of Home Affairs): 35,000; 31 bn, security within north-eastern states mainly Army officered, better trained than BSF.
INDO-TIBETAN BORDER POLICE (Ministry of Home Affairs): 29,000; 28 bn, security on Tibetan border.

SPECIAL FRONTIER FORCE (Cabinet Secretariat): 10,000, mainly ethnic Tibetans.
NATIONAL RIFLES (Ministry of Home Affairs): 5,000; serves only in Kashmir; 6 bns, to become 30.
CENTRAL INDUSTRIAL SECURITY FORCE (Ministry of Home Affairs):[a] 50,000.
DEFENCE SECURITY CORPS:[a] 31,000; provides security at Defence Ministry Sites.
RAILWAY PROTECTION FORCES: 30,000.
HOME GUARD (R): 464,200; purely men on lists, no training.
COAST GUARD: ε5,000.
PATROL CRAFT: 43:
9 *Vikram* PCO, 11 *Tara Bai* PCC, 5 *Rajhans* PFI, 7 *Jija Bai* PCI, 11‹.
AVIATION: 3 air sqn with 20 Do-228, 2 Fokker F-27 **ac**, 13 *Chetak* **hel**.

[a] Lightly armed security guards only.

KAZAKHSTAN

GDP	1992ε: $20.2bn:	
	per capita $4,800	
	1993ε: $18.2bn:	
	per capita $4,300	
Growth	1992: -15.0%	1993ε: -12.0%
Inflation	1992: 1,380%	1993ε: 1,150%
Debt[a]	1992: $24.9m	1993: $2.0bn
Def exp[b]	1992: $1.5bn	
Def bdgt[b]	1992ε: $1.6bn	
	1993ε: $707.0m	
	1994: $450.0m	
FMA[c]	1993: $91.2m (IMET, econ aid)	
	1994: $85.1m (IMET, econ aid)	
	1995: $85.1m (IMET, econ aid)	
$1 = t	1992: n.k.	1993: n.k.
	1994: 15.8	
t = tenge[d]		

[a] External debt in convertible currencies.
[b] Purchasing-power-parity (PPP) est.
[c] Econ aid includes funds to support dismantlement of nuclear weapons under START I and excl allocations from Japan.
[d] The tenge was introduced in November 1993 to replace the old Russian rouble.

Population: 17,407,600 (Kazakh 42%, Russian 37%, Ukrainian 5%, German 5%, Uzbek 2%, Tatar 2%)

	13–17	*18–22*	*23–32*
Men	829,000	748,500	1,288,600
Women	810,000	731,500	1,250,500

TOTAL ARMED FORCES:
ACTIVE: 40,000.

STRATEGIC NUCLEAR FORCES
(Russian-controlled forces on Kazakhstan territory):
ICBM: 92:
SS-18 *Satan* (RS-20), 92 at 2 sites.
BOMBERS: ε6 Tu-95G (may not be nuclear-armed).

ARMY: ε25,000.
1 Corps HQ.
1 TD.
2 MRD (1 trg).
1 indep MRR.
1 arty bde; 1 arty regt.
1 MRL regt.
1 SSM regt.
1 AB bde.
EQUIPMENT:
MBT: 1,100 T-62, T-72.
RECCE: 140 BRDM:
ACV: 2,200 incl BMP-1/-2 AIFV, BTR-70/-80, MT-LB APC.
TOTAL ARTY: ε1,850:
TOWED ARTY: 1,000: 100mm: M-1944 (BS-3); 122mm: D-30, M-30; 130mm: M-46; 152mm: D-1, D-20, M-1937, 2A65, 2A36.
SP ARTY: 200: 122mm 2S1; 152mm: 2S3.
MRL: 350: 122mm: 122mm: BM-21; 220mm: 9P140 *Uragan*.
MORTARS: 300: 120mm: 2B11, M-120.
ATK GUNS: 100mm:125 T-12.
(In 1991 the former Soviet Union transferred some 2,680 tanks (T-64/-72), 2,428 ACV and 6,900 arty pieces to open storage bases in Kazakhstan. This eqpt is under Kazakh control, but has suffered considerable deterioration.)

NAVY:
none at present, although formation of maritime force has been announced. However, Caspian Sea Flotilla (see Russia) is operating as a joint Russian, Kazakhstan and Turkmenistan flotilla under Russian command and based at Astrakan.

AIR FORCE:
ε15,000; 1 Air Force div, 178 cbt ac, 48 attack hel.
Average annual flying hours for FTR/FGA: 25.
FIGHTER: 1 regt with 14 MiG-29, 9 MiG-29UB, 12 MiG-23, 4 MiG-23UB.
FGA: 3 regt: 1 with 34 MiG-27, 9 MiG-23UB; 1 with 7 MiG-27, 6 MiG-23UB; 1 with 24 Su-24.
RECCE: 1 regt with 12 Su-24*, 13 MiG-25 RB*, 2 MiG-25 RU*.
HELICOPTERS: 1 regt (ATK/armed) 48 Mi-24, 14 Mi-8, 1 regt (tpt), 42 Mi-8.

AIR DEFENCE:
FIGHTER: 32 MiG-31.
SAM: 85 SA-2, SA-3, SA-5.

PARAMILITARY:
REPUBLICAN GUARD: 2,500.
INTERNAL SECURITY TROOPS (Ministry of Interior): ε20,000.
BORDER GUARDS (National Security Committee): ε12,000.

KYRGYZSTAN

GDP	1992ε: $3.2bn:	
	per capita $2,800	
	1993ε: $2.9bn:	
	per capita $2,600	
Growth	1992ε: -19.0%	1993ε: -13.0%
Inflation	1992ε: 870%	1993ε: 1,150%
Debt[a]	1992: $0.0m	1993: n.k.
Def bdgt[b]	1992: $47.1m	
	1993: $50.7m	
	1994: $57.3m	
FMA	1994: $0.05m (IMET)	
	1995: $0.05m (IMET)	
$1 = r	1992: n.k.	1993: n.k.
	1994: n.k.	
s = som[c]		

[a] External debt in convertible currencies.
[b] ppp est.
[c] The som was introduced in May 1993 replacing the old Russian rouble at a conversion rate of 1 som = 200 roubles. Since then the som has floated against the rouble.

Population: 4,684,600 (Russian 21%, Uzbek 13%, other 14%)

	13–17	*18–22*	*23–32*
Men	247,360	212,400	344,680
Women	243,080	209,080	340,240

TOTAL ARMED FORCES:
ACTIVE: ε12,000+.
Terms of service: 18 months.

ARMY: 12,000.
1 MRD (3 MR, 1 tk, 1 arty, 1 AA regt).
1 indep MR bde (mtn).
EQUIPMENT:
MBT: 204 T-72.
RECCE: 42 BRDM-2.
AIFV: 277 BMP-1/-2.
APC: 74 BTR-70.
TOTAL ARTY: 216, incl:
TOWED ARTY: 100mm: 18 M-1944 (BS-3), 122mm: 50 D-30, 36 M-30; 152mm: 16 D-1.
COMBINED GUN/MORTAR: 120mm: 12 2S9.
MORTARS: 120mm: 6 2S12, 70 M-120.
AD GUNS: 57mm: 24 S-60.

AIR FORCE:
1 trg centre: 1 regt with 133 MiG-21, 1 regt with 66 L-39, 1 hel regt with 63 hel, incl Mi-8, Mi-17, Mi-24, Mi-25, Mi-35.
AIR DEFENCE:
SAM: 26 SA-2, SA-3.

MYANMAR (BURMA)

GDP	1992: K 69.5bn ($11.4bn):	
	per capita $730	
	1993ε: K 80.1bn ($13.0bn):	
	per capita $810	
Growth	1992: 11.3%	1993: 11.0%
Inflation	1992: 21.9%	1993: 31.8%
Debt	1992: $5.3bn	1993: $5.8bn
Def exp	1990: K 5.4bn ($858.0m)	
	1991: K 6.1bn ($971.0m)	
Def bdgt	1992ε: K 7.1bn ($1.2bn)	
	1993ε: K 8.5bn ($1.4bn)	
	1994ε: K 8.3bn ($1.4bn)	
$1 = K	1992: 6.1	1993: 6.2
	1994: 6.1	
K = kyat		

Population: 45,452,200 (Shan 9%, Karen 7%, Rakhine 4%, Chinese 3%)

	13–17	*18–22*	*23–32*
Men	2,456,600	2,306,800	3,801,600
Women	2,379,000	2,233,400	3,855,600

TOTAL ARMED FORCES:
ACTIVE: ε286,000.

ARMY: 265,000.
10 lt inf div (each 3 tac op comd (TOC)).
10 Regional Comd (8 with 3 TOC, 2 with 4 TOC).
32 TOC with 145 garrison inf bn.
Summary of cbt units:

223 inf bn.	7 arty bn.
3 armd bn.	1 AA arty bn.

EQUIPMENT:†
MBT: 26 *Comet*, 30 Ch T-69II.
LIGHT TANKS: 55 Type-63.
RECCE: 45 *Ferret*, 40 *Humber*, 30 *Mazda* (local manufacture).
APC: 20 *Hino* (local manufacture).
TOWED ARTY: 76mm: 100 M-1948; 88mm: 50 25-pdr; 105mm: 96 M-101; 140mm: 5.5-in.
MRL: 107mm: 30 Type-63.
MORTARS: 81mm; 82mm; 120mm: 80 Soltam.
RCL: 84mm: 500 *Carl Gustav*; 106mm: M40A1.
ATK GUNS: 60: 57mm: 6-pdr; 76.2mm: 17-pdr.
AD GUNS: 37mm: 24 Type-74; 40mm: 10 M-1; 57mm: 12 Type-80.

NAVY:† 12,000–15,000 (incl 800 Naval Infantry).

BASES: Bassein, Mergui, Moulmein, Seikky, Rangoon (Monkey Point), Sittwe.
PATROL AND COASTAL COMBATANTS: 56:
CORVETTES: 2:
1 *Yan Taing Aung* (US PCE-827).
1 *Yan Gyi Aung* (US *Admirable* MSF).
PATROL: 54:
COASTAL: 10 *Yan Sit Aung* (Ch *Hainan*).
INSHORE: 15: 12 US PGM-401/412, 3 Yug PB-90 PFI⟨.
RIVERINE: 29: 2 *Nawarat,* 2 imp Yug Y-301 and 10 Yug Y-301, about 15⟨, plus some 25 boats.
AMPHIBIOUS: 5:
5 LCU, plus craft: 10 LCM.
SUPPORT: 4: 1 coastal tpt, 2 AGHS, 1 PC/div spt.

NAVAL INFANTRY: (800): 1 bn.

AIR FORCE: 9,000; 91 cbt ac, 10 armed hel.

FIGHTERS: 3 sqn: 30 F-7, 6 FT-7.
FGA: 2 sqn: 24 A-5M.
COIN: 2 sqn: 15 PC-7, 4 PC-9, 12 *Super Galeb* G4.
TRANSPORT: 1 F-27, 4 FH-227, 5 PC-6A/-B, 2 Y-8D.
LIAISON: 6 Cessna 180, 1 Cessna 550.
HELICOPTERS: 4 sqn: 12 Bell 205, 6 Bell 206, 9 SA-316, 10 Mi-2 (armed), 12 PZL W-3 *Sokol*.

PARAMILITARY:

PEOPLE'S POLICE FORCE: 50,000.
PEOPLE'S MILITIA: 35,000.
PEOPLE'S PEARL AND FISHERY MINISTRY: ε250; 11 patrol boats (3 *Indaw* (Dk *Osprey*) PCC, 3 US *Swift* PGM PCI, 5 Aust *Carpentaria* PCI⟨).

OPPOSITION AND FORMER OPPOSITION:

GROUPS WITH CEASE-FIRE AGREEMENTS:

KACHIN INDEPENDENCE ARMY (KIA): some 8,000, northern Myanmar, incl Kuman range, the Triangle. Reached cease-fire agreement with government in October 1993.
NEW DEMOCRATIC ARMY (NDA): ε500, along Chinese border in Kachin state; was Communist Party of Burma (CPB).
MYANMAR NATIONAL DEMOCRATIC ALLIANCE ARMY (MNDAA): 2,000, north-east corner of Shan state.
PALAUNG STATE LIBERATION ARMY (PSLA): ε700, hill tribesmen north of Hsipaw.
UNITED WA STATE ARMY (UWSA): ε12,000, Wa hills between Salween river and Chinese border; was CPB.
SHAN STATE ARMY (SSA): ε3,000, Shan state west of Salween.
NATIONAL DEMOCRATIC ALLIANCE ARMY (NDAA): ε1,000, eastern corner of Shan state on Chinese/Laos border; was CPB.

GROUPS STILL IN OPPOSITION:

MONG TAI ARMY (MTA) (formerly Shan United Army): 10,000+, along Thai border and between Lashio and Chinese border.
KAREN NATIONAL LIBERATION ARMY (KNLA): ε4,000, on Thai border in Karen state.
KARENNI ARMY (KA): ⟩1,000, on Thai border in Kayah state.
MON NATIONAL LIBERATION ARMY (MNLA): ε1,000, on Thai border in Mon state.

NEPAL

GDP	1992:	NR 126.2bn ($3.0bn): per capita $1,100	
	1993ε:	NR 151.2bn ($3.1bn): per capita $1,120	
Growth	1992:	3.1%	1993ε: 2.9%
Inflation	1992:	21.0%	1993ε: 8.0%
Debt	1992:	$1.8bn	1993: $1.9bn
Def exp	1990:	NR 1,077m ($36.7m)	
	1991:	NR 1,114m ($29.9m)	
Def bdgt	1992ε:	NR 1.5bn ($35.1m)	
	1993ε:	NR 2.0bn ($40.1m)	
	1994:	NR 2.1bn ($42.3m)	
FMA	1994:	$0.1m (IMET)	
	1995:	$0.1m (IMET)	

$1 = NR	1992: 42.7	1993: 48.6
	1994: 49.2	

NR = Nepalese rupee

Population: 20,979,200

	13–17	18–22	23–32
Men	1,185,700	1,008,100	1,566,200
Women	1,118,000	940,000	1,466,200

TOTAL ARMED FORCES:

ACTIVE: 35,000 (to be 40,000).
RESERVES: none.

ARMY: 34,800.

1 Royal Guard bde: incl 1 cav sqn, 1 garrison bn.
5 inf bde (14 inf bn).
1 spt bde: incl AB bn, arty regt, engr bn, armd recce sqn.

EQUIPMENT:
RECCE: 25 *Ferret*.
TOWED ARTY: 75mm: 6 pack; 94mm: 5 3.7-in mtn; 105mm: 14 pack.
MORTARS: 81mm; 120mm: 70.
AD GUNS: 14.5mm: 30 Ch; 40mm: 2 L/60.

AIR FORCE: 200; no cbt ac, nor armed hel.

TRANSPORT: ac: 1 BAe-748, 2 *Skyvan*, 1 *Twin Otter*; **hel:** 2 AS-332 (Royal Flight), 1 Bell 206L, 3 SA-316B *Chetak*, 2 SA-330.

FORCES ABROAD:

UN AND PEACEKEEPING:
CROATIA (UNPROFOR 1): 900; 1 inf bn, plus 6 Observers, 50 civ pol.
LEBANON (UNIFIL): 722; 1 inf bn.
SOMALIA (UNOSOM): 314.

PARAMILITARY:

POLICE FORCE: 28,000.

PAKISTAN

GDP	1992: Rs 1,211.3bn ($48.3bn): per capita $2,100	
	1993: Rs 1,359.3bn ($50.8bn): per capita $2,150	
Growth	1992: 7.8%	1993: 2.6%
Inflation	1992: 8.9%	1993: 4.2%
Debt	1992: $24.1bn	1993: $26.0bn
Def exp	1992: Rs 89.1bn ($3.6bn)	
	1993: Rs 93.8bn ($3.3bn)	
Def bdgt	1993: Rs 94.0bn ($3.3bn)	
	1994: Rs 101.9bn ($3.4bn)	
FMA	1994: $2.5m (Narcs)	
	1995: $2.5m (Narcs)	
$1 = Rs	1992: 25.1	1993: 28.1
	1994: 30.3	

Rs = rupee

Population: 126,067,000 (less than 3% Hindu)

	13–17	18–22	23–32
Men	7,388,500	6,439,000	10,383,200
Women	6,696,800	5,720,600	9,238,700

TOTAL ARMED FORCES:

ACTIVE: 587,000.
RESERVES: 313,000; Army ε300,000: obligation to age 45 (men) or 50 (officers); active liability for 8 years after service; Navy 5,000; Air Force 8,000.

ARMY: 520,000.

9 Corps HQ.
2 armd div.
19 inf div.
1 area comd (div).
7 indep armd bde.
9 indep inf bde.
9 corps arty bde.
7 engr bde.
3 armd recce regt.
1 SF gp (3bn).
1 AD comd (3 AD gp: 8 bde).
Avn: 17 sqn: 7 ac, 8 hel, 1 VIP, 1 obs flt.

EQUIPMENT:
MBT: 1,950+: 120 M-47, 280 M-48A5, 50 T-54/-55, 1,200 Ch Type-59, 200 Ch Type-69, 100+ Ch Type-85.
APC: 820 M-113.
TOWED ARTY: 1,566: 85mm: 200 Ch Type-56; 105mm: 300 M-101, 50 M-56 pack; 122mm: 200 Ch Type-60, 400 Ch Type-54; 130mm: 200 Ch Type-59-1; 155mm: 30 M-59, 60 M-114, 100 M-198; 203mm: 26 M-115.
SP ARTY: 240: 105mm: 50 M-7; 155mm: 150 M-109A2; 203mm: 40 M-110A2.
MRL: 122mm: 45 *Azar*.
MORTARS: 81mm: 500; 120mm: 225 AM-50, M-61.
SSM: 18 *Hatf*-1, *Hatf*-2 (under development).
ATGW: 800: *Cobra*, *TOW* (incl 24 on M-901 SP), *Green Arrow* (Ch *Red Arrow*).
RL: 89mm: M-20 3.5-in.
RCL: 75mm: Type-52; 106mm: M-40A1.
AD GUNS: 2,000+ incl: 14.5mm; 35mm: 200 GDF-002; 37mm: Ch Type-55/-65; 40mm: M1, 100 L/60; 57mm: Ch Type-59.
SAM: 350 *Stinger*, *Redeye*, RBS-70, 500 *Anza*.
SURV: RASIT (veh, arty), AN/TPQ-36 (arty, mor).

AIRCRAFT:
SURVEY: 1 *Commander* 840.
LIAISON: 1 Cessna 421, 2 *Commander* 690, 80 *Mashshaq,* 1 F-27.
OBSERVATION: 40 O-1E, 50 *Mashshaq.*
HELICOPTERS:
ATTACK: 20 AH-1F (*TOW*).
TRANSPORT: 7 Bell 205, 10 Bell 206B, 16 Mi-8, 6 IAR/SA-315B, 23 IAR/SA-316, 35 SA-330, 5 UH-1H.

NAVY: 22,000 (incl Naval Air, ε1,200 Marines and ε2,000 Maritime Security Agency (see Paramilitary)).

BASE: Karachi (Fleet HQ).
SUBMARINES: 6:
2 *Hashmat* (Fr *Agosta*) with 533mm TT (F-17 HWT), *Harpoon* USGW.
4 *Hangor* (Fr *Daphné*) with 533mm TT (L-5 HWT), *Harpoon* USGW.
Plus 3 SX-756 SSI SF insertion craft.
PRINCIPAL SURFACE COMBATANTS: 9:
DESTROYERS: 3:
3 *Alamgir* (US *Gearing*) (ASW) with 1 x 8 *ASROC*; plus 2 x 3 ASTT, 2 x 2 127mm guns, 3 x 2 *Harpoon* SSM and hel deck (1 trg).
FRIGATES: 6:
FFG: 4:
4 *Tariq* (UK *Amazon*) with 1 *Lynx* hel, 2 x 3 ASTT; 1 x 114mm gun (plus 2 more by end of 1994).
FF: 2:
2 *Shamsher* (UK *Leander*) with SA-316 hel, 1 x 3 ASW mor, plus 2 x 114mm guns.
PATROL AND COASTAL COMBATANTS: 13:
MISSILE CRAFT: 8:
4 Ch *Huangfeng* with 4 x *Hai Ying 2* SSM.
4 Ch *Hegu*(with 2 x *Hai Ying 2*.
PATROL: 5:
COASTAL: 1 *Baluchistan* (Ch *Hainan*) PFC with 4 x ASW RL.
INSHORE: 4:
3 *Quetta* (Ch *Shanghai*) PFI.
1 *Rajshahi* PCI.
MINE WARFARE: 3: 1 *Munsif* (Fr *Eridan*) MHC, 2 *Mahmood* (US-MSC 268) MSC.
SUPPORT AND MISCELLANEOUS: 3:
1 *Nasr* (Ch *Fuqing*) AO, 1 *Dacca* AO, 1 AGOR.

NAVAL AIR:

4 cbt ac, 16 armed hel.
ASW/MR: 1 sqn with 4 *Atlantic* (operated by Air Force).
ASW/SAR: 2 hel sqn with 4 SA-316B (ASW), 6 *Sea King* Mk 45 (ASW), 6 *Lynx* HAS Mk-3.
COMMUNICATIONS: 3 Fokker F-27 ac (Air Force).
ASM: *Exocet* AM-39.

MARINES: (ε1,200); 1 cdo/SF gp.

AIR FORCE: 45,000; 430 cbt ac, no armed hel.

FGA: 7 sqn:
1 with 18 *Mirage* (15 IIIEP (some with AM-39 ASM), 3 IIIDP (trg)).
3 (1 OCU) with 58 *Mirage* 5 (54 -5PA/PA2, 4 -5DPA/DPA2).
3 with 50 Q-5 (A-5 *Fantan*).
FIGHTER: 10 sqn:
4 with 100 J-6/JJ-6, (F-6/FT-6).
3 (1 OCU) with 34 F-16A/B.
2 (1 OCU) with 80 J-7 (F-7P).
1 with 30 *Mirage* 1110.
RECCE: 1 sqn with 12 *Mirage* IIIRP*.
ASW/MR: 1 sqn with 4 *Atlantic*.
SAR: 1 hel sqn with 6 SA-319.
TRANSPORT: ac: 12 C-130 (5 -B, 7 -E), 1 L-100; 3 Boeing 707, 3 *Falcon 20*, 2 F-27-200 (1 with Navy), 2 Beech (1 *Travel Air*, 1 *Baron*); **hel**: 1 sqn with 12 SA-316, 4 SA-321, 12 SA-315B *Lama*.
TRAINING: 12 CJ-6A (PT-6A), 30 JJ-5 (FT-5), *45 MFI-17B *Mashshaq*, 6 MiG-15UTI, 10 T-33A, 44 T-37B/C, 2 K-8.
AD: 7 SAM bty:
6 each with 24 *Crotale*.
1 with 6 CSA-1 (SA-2).
MISSILES:
ASM: AM-39 *Exocet*.
AAM: AIM-7 *Sparrow*, AIM-9 *Sidewinder*, R-530, R-550 *Magic*.

FORCES ABROAD:

UN AND PEACEKEEPING:
BOSNIA (UNPROFOR BH): 677; elm 2 inf bn.
CROATIA (UNPROFOR I): 30 Observers.
IRAQ/KUWAIT (UNIKOM): 7 Observers.
LIBERIA (UNOMIL): 41 Observers.
MOZAMBIQUE (ONUMOZ): 22 civ pol.
SOMALIA (UNOSOM): 7,152; 2 inf bde.
WESTERN SAHARA (MINURSO): 4 Observers.

PARAMILITARY:

NATIONAL GUARD: 185,000; incl Janbaz Force; Mujahid Force; National Cadet Corps; Women Guards.
FRONTIER CORPS (Ministry of Interior): 65,000; 45 UR-416 APC.

PAKISTAN RANGERS (Ministry of Interior): 25,000.
MARITIME SECURITY AGENCY: (ε2,000); 1 *Alamgir* (US *Gearing* DD) (no *ASROC* or TT), 4 *Barakat* PCC, 4 (Ch *Shanghai*) PFI.
COAST GUARD: some 23 PFI, plus boats.

SRI LANKA

GDP	1992:	Rs 423.3bn ($9.7bn):		
		per capita $2,900		
	1993:	Rs 507.3bn ($10.5bn):		
		per capita $3,100		
Growth	1992:	4.3%	1993:	5.7%
Inflation	1992:	11.4%	1993:	11.7%
Debt	1992:	$6.4bn	1993:	$7.0bn
Def exp	1992:	Rs 23.9bn ($547.2m)		
Def bdgt	1993:	Rs 24.0bn ($496.7m)		
	1994:	Rs 24.1bn ($488.9m)		
FMA	1993:	$0.4m (IMET)		
	1994:	$0.1m (IMET)		
	1995:	$0.1m (IMET)		
$1 = Rs	1992:	43.8	1993:	48.3
	1994:	49.2		

Rs = rupee

Population: 17,788,400 (Tamil 18%, Moor 7%)

	13–17	*18–22*	*23–32*
Men	922,100	841,200	1,613,300
Women	884,600	814,600	1,520,400

TOTAL ARMED FORCES:

ACTIVE: some 126,000 (incl recalled reservists).
RESERVES: some 10,700; Army 1,100; Navy 1,100; Air Force 8,500. Obligation: 7 years post-regular service.

ARMY: 105,000 (incl 42,000 recalled reservists).

3 div, 3 task force HQ.
1 mech inf bde (to form).
1 air mobile bde (to form).
23 inf bde.
1 indep SF bde (1 cdo, 1 SF regt).
1 armd regt.
3 armd recce regt (bn).
4 fd arty (1 reserve), 4 fd engr regt (1 reserve).
EQUIPMENT:
MBT: 25 T-55.
RECCE: 26 *Saladin*, 29 *Ferret*, 12 Daimler *Dingo*.
APC: 35 Ch Type-85, 10 BTR-152, 31 *Buffel*, 57 *Unicorn*, 8 Shorland, 9 *Hotspur*, 35 *Saracen*.
TOWED ARTY: 76mm: 14 Yug M-48; 85mm: 12 Ch Type-56; 88mm: 26 25-pdr; 130mm: 12 Ch Type-59 -1.
MRL: 107mm: 1.
MORTARS: 81mm: 276; 82mm: 19; 120mm: 36 M-43.
RCL: 105mm: 15 M-65; 106mm: 34 M-40.
AD GUNS: 40mm: 7 L-40; 94mm: 3 3.7-in.

NAVY: 10,300 (incl 1,100 recalled reservists).

BASES: Colombo (HQ), Trincomalee (main base), Karainagar, Tangalle, Kalpitiya, Galle, Welisara.
PATROL AND COASTAL COMBATANTS: 43:
PATROL, COASTAL: 2 *Jayesagara* PCC.
PATROL, INSHORE: 41:
5 *Sooraya*, 3 *Rana* (Ch *Shanghai* II) PFI.
11 Is *Dvora* PFI⟨.
3 S. Korean PFI⟨.
19 PCI⟨, plus some 30 boats.
AMPHIBIOUS: craft only: 4 LCM (1 non-op), 2 fast personnel carrier.
SUPPORT AND MISCELLANEOUS: 3:
3 *Abheetha* spt/cmd.

AIR FORCE: 10,700; 27 cbt ac, 17 armed hel.

FGA: 4 F-7M.
COIN: 8 SF-260TP, 4 FMA IA58A *Pucará*.
ATTACK HELICOPTERS: 13 Bell 212, 4 Bell 412.
MR: 1 sqn with 6 Cessna 337 **ac**; 2 SA-365 **hel**.
TRANSPORT: 1 sqn with 5 BAe 748, 1 Cessna 421C, 1 *Super King Air*, 1 Ch Y-8, 9 Y-12.
HELICOPTERS: 7 Bell 206, 3 Mi-17.
TRAINING: incl 6 Cessna 150, 4 DHC-1, 2* FT-5, 1* FT-7, 8* SF-260 MB.
RESERVES: Air Force Regt, 3 sqn; Airfield Construction Regt, 1 sqn.

FORCES ABROAD:

UN AND PEACEKEEPING:

MOZAMBIQUE (ONUMOZ): 11 civ pol.

PARAMILITARY:

POLICE FORCE (Ministry of Defence): 40,000 active, incl 1,000 women (22,000 reserves, increase to 28,000 planned). Total incl Special Task Force: 3,000-man anti-guerrilla unit.
NATIONAL GUARD: ε15,000.
HOME GUARD: 15,200.

OPPOSITION:

LIBERATION TIGERS OF TAMIL EELAM (LTTE): Leader: Velupillai Prabhakaran; ε4,000 active, plus 3,000 spt and log.

TAJIKISTAN

GDP	1992ε: $2.9bn:	
	per capita $2,000	
	1993ε: $2.5bn:	
	per capita $1,700	
Growth	1992: -31.0%	1993ε: -15.0%
Inflation	1992ε: 910%	1993ε: 1,300%
Debt[a]	1992: $0.0m	1993: n.k.
Def bdgt[b]	1992ε: $107m	
	1993: $110m	
	1994: $115m	
$1 = r[c]	1994: 1,650	
r = rouble		

[a] excl debt in convertible currencies and NIS.
[b] ppp est.
[c] The old Russian rouble remains the official currency.

Population: 5,897,200 (Uzbek 25%, Russian 4%, Tatar 2%)

	13–17	*18–22*	*23–32*
Men	330,800	268,600	422,900
Women	323,000	262,800	425,300

TOTAL ARMED FORCES

ACTIVE: some 2–3,000.

Tajikistan has not yet been able to form any military units. A number of potential officers are under training at the Higher Army Officers and Engineers College in Dushanbe. It is planned to form an air force sqn and the intention to acquire Su-25 from Belarus has been expressed.

PARAMILITARY:

BORDER GUARDS (Ministry of Interior): ε6,000; 1 bde reported.

FOREIGN FORCES:

RUSSIA:

ARMY: 12,000+.
1 MRD.

EQUIPMENT:
MBT: 180 T-72.
AIFV: 340 BMP-1, BTR-60/-70/-80.
TOTAL ARTY: 185:
TOWED ARTY: 65: 122mm: D-30, M-1938.
SP ARTY: 50: 122mm: 2S1; 152mm: 2S3.
MRL: 122mm: 15 BM-21.
MORTARS: 120mm: 55 PM-38.

AIR DEFENCE:
SAM: 10: SA-2/-3.

TURKMENISTAN

GDP	1992ε: $3.9bn:	
	per capita $4,000	
	1993ε: $3.8bn:	
	per capita $3,900	
Growth	1992ε: -17.0%	1993ε: -5.0%
Inflation	1992ε: 470%	1993ε: 1,150%
Debt	1992: $9.7m	1993: n.k.
Def bdgt[a]	1992ε: $144.0m	
	1993: $143.0m	
	1994: $153.0m	
FMA	1994: $0.05m (IMET)	
	1995: $0.05m (IMET)	
$1 = m	1992: n.k.	1993: n.k.
	1994: 16.5	
m = manat[b]		

[a] ppp est.
[b] The manat was introduced in November 1993. The rate of exchange was fixed at 1 manat = 500 roubles.

Population: 3,987,400 (Russian 10%, Uzbek 9%, Kazakh 2%)

	13–17	*18–22*	*23–32*
Men	218,800	187,600	308,200
Women	214,700	184,100	305,700

FORCES UNDER JOINT CONTROL:

Turkmenistan/Russia:

ARMY: 28,000.
1 Corps HQ.
3 MRD (1 trg).
1 arty bde.
1 MRL regt.
1 atk regt.
3 engr regt.
1 indep hel sqn.

EQUIPMENT:
MBT: 570 T-72.
RECCE: BRDM.
AIFV: 288 BMP-1, 390 BMP-2.
APC: 348 BTR, 173 BTR-70, 6 BTR-80.
TOWED ARTY: 122mm: 250 D-30; 152mm: 76 D-1, 72 2A65.
SP ARTY: 152mm: 16 2S3.

COMBINED GUN/MORTAR: 120mm: 21 2S9.
MRL: 122mm: 42 BM-21, 18 9P138; 220mm: 54 9P140.
MORTARS: 120mm: 66.
ATGW: AT-2 *Swatter*, AT-3 *Sagger*, AT-4 *Spigot*, AT-5 *Spandrel*.
ATK GUNS: 85mm: 6 D-44; 100mm: 48 MT-12.
AD GUNS: 23mm: 32 ZSU-23-4 SP; 57mm: 22 S-60.

NAVY: none at present. Has announced intention to form a Navy/Coast Guard. However, Caspian Sea Flotilla (see Russia) is operating as a joint Russian, Kazakhstan and Turkmenistan flotilla under Russian command and based at Astrakan.

AIR FORCE: 174 cbt ac (plus 650 in storage).
FGA: 1 regt with 60 Su-17.
ASSAULT: 1 unit with 3 Su-7B, 3 MiG-21, 2 L-39, 8 Yak-28, 3 An-12.
TRAINING: 1 unit with 16 MiG-29, 16 Su-27, 3 Mi-8.

AIR DEFENCE:
FIGHTER: 2 regt: 38 MiG-23, 30 MiG-25.
SAM: 75: SA-2/-3/-5.
STORAGE: 490 MiG-23, 60 MiG-25, 100 Su-25, 18 Mi-8.

UZBEKISTAN

GDP	1992ε: $14.0bn: per capita $2,600	
	1993ε: $13.8bn: per capita $2,500	
Growth	1992ε: -19.0%	1993: -4.0%
Inflation	1992ε: 787%	1993: 750%
Debt[a]	1992: $15.5m	1993: n.k.
Def bdgt[b]	1992ε: $420.0m	
	1993ε: $390.0m	
	1994ε: $375.0m	
FMA	1995: $0.05m (IMET)	
$1 = s	1992: n.k.	1993: n.k.
	1994: 1,650	

s = sum [c]

[a] External debt in convertible currencies.
[b] ppp est.
[c] The sum coupon was introduced in November 1993 as a temporary measure to replace the old Russian rouble.

Population: 22,318,400 (Russian 8%, Tajik 5%, Kazakh 4%, Tatar 2%, Karakalpak 2%)

	13–17	*18–22*	*23–32*
Men	1,241,800	1,038,900	1,686,300
Women	1,215,800	1,022,300	1,693,600

TOTAL ARMED FORCES: 45,000 (incl MOD staff and centrally controlled units).
Terms of service: conscription, 18 months.

ARMY: some 35,000.
1 MRD. 1 ABD (cadre).
1 arty bde. 1 attack hel regt.
EQUIPMENT:
MBT: 125 T-62, T-72
ACV: 700: BMP-1/-2, BMD, BTR-60/-70.
TOWED ARTY: 375: 122mm: D-30, M-1938; 152mm: D-20, 2A36.
SP ARTY: 90: 122mm: 2S1; 152mm: 2S3.
COMBINED GUN/MORTAR: 120mm: 2S9.
MRL: 122mm: 15 BM-21.
MORTARS: 120mm: 50.
SSM: 4.
ATTACK HELICOPTERS: 50. Mi-24.
(In 1991 the former Soviet Union transferred some 2,000 tanks (T-64), 1,200 ACV and 750 arty pieces to open storage bases in Uzbekistan. This eqpt is under Uzbek control, but has suffered considerable deterioration.)

AIR FORCE: some 4,000; 142 cbt ac.
FGA: 70 Su-17, Su-24, Su-25.
FIGHTER: 40 MiG-29, 32 Su-27.
TRANSPORT: 20 An-2.
SAM: 45 SA-2/-3/-5.

PARAMILITARY: 8,000:
INTERNAL SECURITY TROOPS (Ministry of Interior).
NATIONAL GUARD: 700; 1 bde.

East Asia and Australasia

Political Developments

East Asian security in the short term has been dominated by the crisis in North Korea. In the medium and longer term there are worries about Chinese intentions, the risks of a regional arms race, and uncertainty about the implications of domestic developments in Japan. Attempts to develop a regional security dialogue, such as the Association of South-East Asian Nations (ASEAN) Regional Forum meeting in Bangkok in July 1994, have so far failed to develop into anything substantial.

North Korea's continued refusal fully to comply with International Atomic Energy Agency (IAEA) demands for full inspections of its suspect sites has meant that concern over the risk of conflict in North-east Asia is at its highest for many years. North Korea withdrew fuel rods from its reactor without allowing IAEA inspectors to observe the process. Efforts to impose sanctions on North Korea were halted when former American President Jimmy Carter brokered a pause to explore possibilities for a deal. Exploration of the options, as well as the prospects for an inter-Korean presidential summit, were in turn halted with the death of North Korea's President Kim Il Sung in July. A period of uncertainty in North Korean politics coincides with major international tension and an even more pressing domestic economic crisis. The Korean crisis also comes at a time of major shifts in the Japanese political landscape, with several governments in various permutations taking power only briefly.

North Korea's willingness to snub the IAEA may have been related to the sense of confusion in American policy towards East Asia, and towards China in particular. After issuing threats to **China** about the non-renewal of Most Favoured Nation (MFN) trading status if no improvement were made in China's human-rights policies, the Clinton Administration decided to renew MFN even without progress on human rights. The United States hoped for Chinese cooperation in dealing with North Korea, but China was not in a mood to be cooperative. Chinese leaders have expressed increased concern about the risks of domestic instability as the economy overheats. Rapid decentralisation of economic power to China's booming coastal regions, coupled with signs that Taipei was creeping towards greater independence, caused alarm in Beijing. Even in Hong Kong, Governor Chris Patten's democratic reforms were passed by the legislature, despite dire warnings from China.

China's behaviour in the South China Sea continued to ring alarm bells in South-east Asia. Oil companies from the United States, Europe and East Asia are now prospecting on behalf of China, the Philippines, Malaysia, Indonesia and Vietnam. Chinese naval vessels blocked attempts by companies working on behalf of Vietnam in July. China refuses to discuss sovereignty, and ASEAN states remain reluctant to organise regional efforts to deter China from extending its hold over disputed territory.

In **Cambodia**, after the elections of May 1993, the UN mandate came to an end on 26 September 1993 and all UN troops withdrew. At its height, the UN Transitional Authority in Cambodia (UNTAC) deployed 22,000 troops, police and civil administrators. The operation cost $1.7bn and the UN suffered 67 casualties, including 27 killed. The Khmer Rouge failed to fulfil its promises and resumed its policy of intimidation and violence, and in June 1994 its representatives in Phnom Penh were ordered home. On 3 July a coup was apparently attempted by Prince Norodom Chakrapong, but the Prince was swiftly deported by order of his father, King Sihanouk.

Armed resistance continues in **East Timor** where activists have appealed to ASEAN to mediate in their dispute with Indonesia. In **Papua New Guinea**, secessionists rejected yet another set of proposals from the government in July 1994. Rebels in the **Philippines** continue their terrorist attacks, although in the north communists suffered a major blow with the arrest of Felimon Lagman in Manilla in May 1994.

Weapons of Mass Destruction

While most attention has been directed at the long-drawn-out saga over North Korea's refusal to allow all its nuclear facilities to be inspected, fully detailed in the analysis at p. 256, several observers have reported on nuclear-weapon developments in China.

China has conducted two nuclear tests in the last 12 months, the only country to do so in that period. The first test on 5 October 1993 is estimated to have had a yield of between 50 and 100 kilotons (KT). The second took place on 10 June 1994, and early assessment put the yield at between 10 and 60 KT. Previously a megaton weapon had been tested in May 1992 and one of less than 10KT in September 1992. The differences in yields tested suggest that a number of new weapons are being developed. Two ballistic-missile systems are believed to be under development. The first is a dual-purpose missile for both submarine (JL-2) and ground (DF-31) launch, estimated to have a range of 8,000km. The second, designated DF-41, could have a 12,000km range. All three missiles will have solid-fuel propulsion, and DF-31 and DF-41 can be fired from mobile launchers. The DF-41 is expected to be in service before the end of the decade, but there have been no confirmed reports of the development of a new submarine from which to launch JL-2. There has also been an unconfirmed report of a variant of the DF-31, the DF-25, which would have a range of less than 2,000km and is expected to be operational, as is the DF-31, before the year 2000. There have been no reports of any Chinese plans to introduce multiple warheads, although this would be a natural development.

There is still no categorically confirmed information over **North Korean** possession of nuclear weapons. The Director of the CIA has estimated that, before the reactor closure of April 1994, North Korea had sufficient plutonium to build a nuclear device. US intelligence sources claim to have evidence of high-explosive tests indicative of the development of implosion devices and of the conversion of plutonium nitrate to metal, necessary for bomb manufacture. There is rather more evidence of North Korean ballistic-missile development. North Korea has probably produced the best modification of the Soviet *Scud* SSM believed to have a range of up to 600km with a payload of 6–700kg and with improved accuracy. In May 1993, two missile tests were attributed to be tests of the *No-Dong* missile, estimated to have a 1,000km range with maybe a 1,000kg payload. The Koreans are attempting to export both *Scud C* and *No-Dong*. Syria and Iran are both believed to have bought *Scud C* and there have been unconfirmed reports that the *No-Dong* will be tested in Iran before long. One report also claims that Iran will buy 150 missiles. CIA Director James Woolsey has stated publicly that North Korea is developing two more missiles, *Taepo Dong* 1 and *Taepo Dong* 2, but that no test launches have yet taken place. There has been no speculation so far as to the missiles' ranges and payloads.

Conventional Military Developments

In **Australia** the Navy has retired one *Oxley*-class (UK *Oberon*) submarine and the frigate *Derwent* is to be paid off in August 1994. One more *Adelaide* (US *Perry*)-class guided-weapons frigate has been commissioned and two US *Newport*-class LST were to have been acquired. However, the US Senate blocked the sale of all *Newport* LST (some six to eight were being disposed of abroad) after a Marine Corps lobbyist raised the question of whether the Navy could still deploy two-and-a-half MEF without them. The LSTs would be converted into helicopter training and support ships, each able to embark 450 troops and four helicopters. The first of eight *Collins*-class submarines was launched in August 1993. The second boat is scheduled to be launched in early 1995. **Fiji** has taken delivery of the *Kulu* inshore patrol craft, the first of three acquired by Fiji under the Pacific Forum programme. So far a total of 16 Pacific Forum PCIs have been delivered all, with the exception of Papua New Guinea which has four, to Pacific states not listed in *The Military Balance*: Tonga (3); Micronesia (2); Solomon Islands (2); Vanuatu (1); Eastern Samoa (1); Marshall Islands (1); and Cook Islands (1). These PCIs have a range of 2,500 miles at 12 knots.

New Zealand is, for the first time, supplying troops (as opposed to observers) for United Nations peacekeeping missions. 250 men in a reinforced company group will join the UN Protection Force (UNPROFOR) in Bosnia in August 1994.

The reorganisation of the People's Liberation Army (PLA) in **China** continues. The delivery of the first launchers for the Russian SA-10 have been confirmed. A number of Y-8 transport aircraft are being converted for use as in-flight refuelling tankers. The Navy continues to commission new and retire old ships. During the last 12 months three more improved *Ming*-class submarines, three more guided-missile frigates (one *Jiangwei* and two *Jianghu*) and two more *Houxin* missile craft have joined the fleet. Three *Jianguan*-class and one *Chengdu*-class frigate have been retired.

The **South Korean** Air Force has taken delivery of 20 *Hawk* trainers and eight more CN-235M transport aircraft. The Navy has commissioned a second *Chang Bogo* (Ge T-209/1400)-class submarine and seven more are planned. One US *Sumner*-class destroyer has been retired. During 1992, **North Korea** acquired 19 tanks from Belarus. What type these are is unconfirmed, but perhaps T-72 or T-80 (Belarus had declared having 5 T-80 tanks to the Conventional Armed Forces in Europe (CFE) Commission, but none were declared in January 1994), nor is it clear whether more are being acquired. Japan has ordered two more B-767 AWACS aircraft for delivery in early 1998.

The **Indonesian** Army's holding of AMX-13 light tanks has been revised by 150 to 275 tanks. The first of the ships of the former East German Navy, including five frigates and three LSTs, have been delivered, but are not yet in service. The **Malaysian** Air Force has taken delivery of ten Hawk 108 and six Hawk 208 FGA aircraft and a further 12 have still to be delivered. Malaysia has also ordered 18 MiG-29 fighters from Russia and eight F/A-18D multi-role aircraft from the US for delivery in 1996. The Navy has ordered two GEC 2000 frigates from UK. The Malaysian infantry battalion with UNPROFOR in Bosnia has been equipped with 42 South Korean KIFV infantry fighting vehicles. **Singapore** air defences have been improved by forming an additional battalion, equipped with the French *Mistral* SAM. The Air Force now has 18 F-16A/B FGA aircraft; 11 are still in the US where training is not restricted by Singapore's severe lack of air space. The decision to buy 18 more F-16C/D was announced in July 1994. Singapore's F-16s will be armed with the *Maverick* air-to-surface missile. Helicopter holdings have been increased by 16 UH-1HB *Iraquois*, and six AS-532 UL *Cougar*. The Navy has commissioned its first new mine warfare vessel, the *Bedok* coastal minehunter (Swedish *Landsort*-class). A total of four are being acquired, but the other three will be pre-fabricated in Sweden and then assembled in Singapore.

The **Republic of China (Taipei)** continues to modernise its forces. The first operational *Ching-Kuo*, a domestically produced FGA aircraft, has entered squadron service. Eight, of an order for 42, AH-1W *Cobra* attack helicopters and four, of 26, OH-58 Kiowa armed scout helicopters have been delivered to the Army, as have four more CH-47 *Chinook* transport helicopters. The Navy has commissioned a second *Cheng Kung*-class guided-missile frigate and taken delivery of a third US *Knox*-class frigate. Two *Tien Shan* (US *Lawrence/Crossley*)-class frigates have been retired. The **Thai** Air Force has acquired 36 L-39 armed trainers from the Czech Republic and *Python* 3 air-to-air missiles from Israel. Delivery of the L-39 will be completed in 1995. The Navy has postponed its plans to acquire a second helicopter carrier, and the acquisition of submarines is now unlikely. Two US-*Knox*-class frigates are due to be transferred. As yet there is no confirmation of the Navy's intentions to buy Spanish EAV8A *Harriers* for the helicopter carrier which will have a ski-jump and is being built in Spain, or US Navy A-7 *Corsair* attack aircraft. 12 *Sea Hawk* inshore patrol craft have been transferred from the South Korean Navy to the **Philippines.**

Defence Economics

Notwithstanding the continuing global recession, economic performance in the region was again significantly better than elsewhere in the world. In 1993, aggregate GDP grew by some 7% compared with less than 1% for the world as a whole. A significant exception was Japan, where an uninterrupted sequence of growth dating back to the Second World War ended. Efforts to generate closer economic cooperation within the region are largely symbolic, as the 15-member Asia-Pacific Economic Cooperation (APEC) summit in November 1993 demonstrated. Most East Asian economies are flourishing as a result of their comparative advantages in labour and production costs and to date regional competition rather than cooperation is the ruling economic imperative.

Last year's edition of *The Military Balance* included a statistical analysis of the rise in defence capability in Asia. Since then, there has been a growing awareness of the implications of increased military efforts for regional security – both within the region and externally. In 1993, defence expenditure increased again – albeit not at the rate of economic growth. East Asia and Australasia account for some 15% of global defence spending (as opposed to arms purchases) – the highest regional proportion apart from the North Atlantic Treaty Organisation (NATO). A significant emphasis on defence-industrial investment remains evident in the case of several East Asian countries, reflecting the sustained commitment to achieve a practical level of self-sufficiency in industrial capability across the range of conventional weapon systems. For this reason alone, defence expenditure is likely to remain at relatively high levels and is likely to increase further if and when political tensions escalate.

AUSTRALIA

GDP	1992: $A 395.3bn ($290.7bn): per capita $16,700	
	1993: $A 423.5bn ($310.2bn): per capita $17,600	
Growth	1992: 2.0%	1993: 4.0%
Inflation	1992: 1.7%	1993: 1.8%
Debt	1992: 29.6%	1993: 34.2%
Def exp	1992: $A 9.8bn ($7.2bn)	
	1993: $A 10.4bn ($7.3bn)	
	1994: $A 10.2bn ($7.3bn)	
Def bdgt	1993: $A 9.8bn ($7.2bn)	
Request	1994: $A 9.6bn ($6.9bn)	
$1 = $A	1992: 1.36	1993: 1.47
	1994: 1.40	

$A = Australian dollar

Population: 18,136,200

	13–17	*18–22*	*23–32*
Men	671,100	707,800	1,536,900
Women	630,600	675,500	1,480,900

TOTAL ARMED FORCES:

ACTIVE: 61,600 (incl 7,600 women).
RESERVES: 29,400: Army 26,200; Navy 1,600; Air Force 1,600.

ARMY: 28,600 (incl 3,000 women).

1 Land HQ, 1 northern comd.
1 inf div, 2 bde HQ.
1 armd regt (3 sqn: 1 active, 1 ready, 1 general reserve).
1 armd recce regt (2 sqn).
1 APC sqn.
4 inf bn (incl 1 AB, 1 mech).
2 arty regt (1 fd, 1 med (each 2 bty)).
1 AD regt (2 bty).
2 cbt engr regt.
1 SF regt (3 sqn).
2 avn regt.

RESERVES:
READY RESERVE: 1 bde HQ, 1 APC/recce regt, 3 inf bn, 1 fd arty regt, 1 engr regt.
GENERAL RESERVE: 1 div HQ, 7 bde HQ, 14 inf bn, 1 cdo (2 coy), 5 arty regt (4 fd, 1 med), 2 indep arty bty, 2 engr (1 fd, 1 construction) regt, 6 indep fd engr sqn, 3 regional surveillance units.

EQUIPMENT:
MBT: 103 *Leopard* 1A3.
AIFV: 47 M-113 with 76mm gun.
APC: 724 M-113 (incl variants, 119 in store), 15 LAV.
TOWED ARTY: 105mm: 216 M2A2/L5, 105 *Hamel*; 155mm: 34 M-198.
MORTARS: 81mm: 302.
ATGW: 10 *Milan*.
RCL: 84mm: 608 *Carl Gustav*; 106mm: 67 M-40A1.
SAM: 19 *Rapier*, 19 RBS-70.
AIRCRAFT: 22 GAF N-22B *Missionmaster*.
HELICOPTERS: 38 S-70 A-9 (Army/Air Force crews), 44 OH-58 *Kalkadoon*, 25 UH-1H (armed), 18 AS-350B.
MARINE: 15 LCM, 53 LARC-5 amph craft.
SURV: RASIT (veh, arty); AN-TPQ-36 (arty, mor).

NAVY: 14,800 (incl 870 Fleet Air Arm, 1,800 women).

Maritime Command, Support Command, 6 Naval Area comd.

BASES: Sydney, NSW (Maritime Command HQ). Base for: 4 SS, 3 DDG, 6 FF, 1 patrol, 1 LST, 1 AOR, 1 AGT, 2 LCT.
Cockburn Sound, WA. Base for: 2 SS, 3 FF, 3 patrol, 1 survey, 1 AOR.
Cairns, Qld: 5 patrol, 1 survey, 2 LCT.
Darwin, NT: 6 patrol, 1 LCT.
SUBMARINES: 4 *Oxley* (mod UK *Oberon*) (incl 1 in refit) with Mk 48 HWT and *Harpoon* SSM (plus 1 alongside trg).
PRINCIPAL SURFACE COMBATANTS: 12 (incl 2 at 14 days notice for ops):
DESTROYERS: 3 *Perth* (US *Adams*) DDG with 1 SM-1 MR SAM/*Harpoon* SSM launcher; plus 2 x 3 ASTT (Mk 46 LWT), 2 x 127mm guns.
FRIGATES: 9:
6 *Adelaide* (US *Perry*) FFG, with S-70B-2 *Sea Hawk*, 2 x 3 ASTT; plus 1 x SM-1 MR SAM/ *Harpoon* SSM launcher.
2 *Swan*, 1 *Paramatta* FF (pays off August 1994) with 2 x 3 ASTT; plus 2 x 114mm guns.
PATROL AND COASTAL COMBATANTS: 16:
INSHORE: 16:
15 *Fremantle* PFI.
1 *Banks* PCC (reserve trg).
MINE WARFARE: 6:
2 *Rushcutter* MHI.
2 *Bandicoot* and 2 *Brolga* auxiliary MSI.
AMPHIBIOUS: 1:
1 *Tobruk* LST, capacity 22 tk, 378 tps, hel deck.
Plus craft: 6 *Balikpapan* LCT, capacity 3 tk (incl 3 in store).
(Plus 2 ex-US *Newport*-class LST for trg/amph tasks expected to be transferred by end of 1994.)
SUPPORT AND MISCELLANEOUS: 9:
1 *Success* (mod Fr *Durance*), 1 *Westralia* AO, 1 *Protector* sub trials and safety, 2 AGHS, 4 small AGHS.

FLEET AIR ARM: (870); no cbt ac, 23 armed hel.
ASW: 1 hel sqn with 7 *Sea King* Mk 50/50A, 1 hel sqn with 16 S-70B-2.
UTILITY/SAR: 1 sqn with 6 AS-350B, 3 Bell 206B and 2 BAe-748 (EW trg).
SURVEY: 1 F-27.

AIR FORCE: 18,200 (incl 2,800 women); 155 cbt ac incl MR, no armed hel.

Average annual flying hours: F-111, 200; F/A-18, 175.
FGA/RECCE: 2 sqn with 17 F-111C, 13 F-111G, 4 RF-111C.
FIGHTER/FGA: 3 sqn with 52 F-18 (-A: 50; -B: 2).
TRAINING: 2 sqn with 32* MB-326H.
MR: 2 sqn with 19 P-3C.
OCU: 1 with 18* F-18B.
FAC: 1 flt with 4 PC-9.
TANKER: 4 Boeing 707-32OC.
TRANSPORT: 7 sqn:
2 with 24 C-130 (12 -E, 12 -H).
1 with 5 Boeing 707 (4 fitted for air-to-air refuelling).
2 with 16 DHC-4.
1 VIP with 5 *Falcon*-900.
1 with 10 HS-748 (8 for navigation trg, 2 for VIP tpt).
TRAINING: 61 PC-9.
SUPPORT: 4 *Dakota*, 2 *Nomad*.
MISSILES:
ASM: AGM-84A.
AAM: AIM-7 *Sparrow*, AIM-9M *Sidewinder*.
AD: *Jindalee* OTH radar: 1 experimental, 3 planned.
3 control and reporting units (1 mobile).

FORCES ABROAD:

MALAYSIA: Army: 1 inf coy (on 3-month rotational tours); Air Force: det with 2 P-3C ac.
PAPUA NEW GUINEA: 100; trg unit, 2 engr unit, 75 advisers.
Advisers in Fiji, Indonesia, Solomon Islands, Thailand, Vanuatu, Tonga, W. Samoa, Kiribati.

UN AND PEACEKEEPING:

CYPRUS (UNFICYP): 20 civ pol.
EGYPT (MFO): 10 Observers.
MIDDLE EAST (UNTSO): 13 Observers.
MOZAMBIQUE (ONUMOZ): 16 civ pol.
SOMALIA (UNOSOM): 66.

PARAMILITARY:

AUSTRALIAN CUSTOMS SERVICE: ac: 3 *Seascan*, 3 *Nomad*, 11 *Strike Aerocommander 500*; **hel**: 4 AS-350; about 6 boats.

FOREIGN FORCES:

US: 370. Air Force: 270; Navy: 100; joint facilities at NW Cape, Pine Gap and Nurrungar.
NEW ZEALAND: Air Force: 50; 4 A-4K/TA-4K (providing trg for Australian Navy).
SINGAPORE: (160) Flying Training School with 27 S-211 ac.

BRUNEI

GDP	1992: $B 7.5bn ($4.7bn): per capita $6,400	
	1993ε: $B 8.1bn ($5.0bn): per capita $6,600	
Growth	1992: 5.0%	1993ε: 4.0%
Inflation	1992: 1.5%	1993ε: 2.0%
Def bdgt	1992: $B 636.9m ($395.6m)	
	1993ε: $B 572.4m ($349.0m)	
	1994ε: $B 496.1m ($312.0m)	
$1 = $B	1992: 1.61	1993: 1.64
	1994: 1.59	

$B = Brunei dollar

Population: 288,800 (Chinese 20%)

	13–17	*18–22*	*23–32*
Men	13,600	12,500	28,100
Women	13,800	12,500	21,800

TOTAL ARMED FORCES (all services form part of the Army; Malays only eligible for service):
ACTIVE: 4,400 (incl 250 women).
RESERVES: Army: 700.

ARMY: 3,400.
3 inf bn.
1 armd recce sqn.
1 SAM bty: 2 tps with *Rapier*.
1 SF sqn.
1 engr sqn.
EQUIPMENT:
LIGHT TANKS: 16 *Scorpion*.
APC: 24 Sankey AT-104, 26 VAB.
MORTARS: 81mm: 24.
SAM: 12 *Rapier* (with *Blindfire*).
RESERVES: 1 bn (forming).

NAVY: ε700.
BASE: Muara.
PATROL AND COASTAL COMBATANTS: 6†:
MISSILE CRAFT: 3 *Waspada* PFM with 2 x MM-38 *Exocet* SSM.
PATROL: 3 *Perwira* PFI‹.
RIVERINE: boats only.
AMPHIBIOUS: craft only: 2 LCM‹.

AIR FORCE: 300; 2 cbt ac, 6 armed hel.
COIN: 1 sqn with 6 Bo-105 armed hel.
HELICOPTERS: 1 sqn with 10 Bell 212, 1 Bell 214 (SAR).
SULTAN'S FLIGHT: 1 A-320 *Airbus*, 2 A-340 *Airbus*. 1 B747-400, 1 B727-200, 2 *Gulfstream II*.
VIP tpt: 2 S-70 hel, 2 Bell 214ST.
TRAINING: *2 SF-260W (COIN, trg) **ac**; 2 Bell 206B **hel**.

PARAMILITARY:
GURKHA RESERVE UNIT: 2,300+; 2 bn.
ROYAL BRUNEI POLICE: 1,750; 3 PCI‹, boats.

FOREIGN FORCES:
UK: some 900 (Army): 1 Gurkha inf bn, 1 hel flt.
SINGAPORE: some 500: trg school incl hel det (5 UH-1).

CAMBODIA

GDP	1992: r 1,863bn ($2.2bn): per capita $500	
	1993ε: r 8,494bn ($2.4bn): per capita $520	
Growth	1992: 7.0%	1993ε: 5.7%
Inflation	1992: 112.5%	1993ε: 41.0%
Def exp	1992ε: r 49bn ($58m)	
Def bdgt	1993ε: r 185bn ($52m)	
	1994ε: r 164bn ($47m)	
FMA[a]	1994: $0.1m (IMET)	
	1995: $0.2m (IMET)	
$1 = r	1992: 847	1993: 3,560
	1994: 3,485	

r = riel

[a] The reported costs of the UNAMIC and UNTAC operations are $1.58bn for the period November 1991–December 1993 and $8.6m for 1994.

Population: 10,335,400 (Vietnamese 5%, Chinese 1%)

	13–17	*18–22*	*23–32*
Men	331,200	323,100	837,500
Women	333,800	324,800	815,500

TOTAL ARMED FORCES:
ACTIVE: some 88,500 (incl Provincial Forces).
Terms of service: conscription, 5 years; ages 18 to 35. Militia serve 3 to 6 months with Regulars.

ARMY: some 36,000.
6 Military Regions.
7 inf div.[a]
3 indep inf bde.
9 indep inf regt.
3 armd regt.
Some indep recce, arty, AD bn.
EQUIPMENT:
MBT: 150 T-54/-55/-59.
LIGHT TANKS: 10 PT-76.
APC: 210 BTR-60/-152, M-113.
TOWED ARTY: some 400: 76mm: M-1942; 122mm: M-1938, D-30; 130mm: Type 59.
MRL: 107mm: Type-63; 122mm: 8 BM-21; 132mm: BM-13-16; 140mm: 20 BM-14-16.
MORTARS: 82mm: M-37; 120mm: M-43; 160mm: M-160.
RCL: 82mm: B-10; 107mm: B-11.
AD GUNS: 14.5mm: ZPU 1/-2/-4; 37mm: M-1939; 57mm: S-60.
SAM: SA-7.

[a] Inf div strength est 5,000.

NAVY: ε2,000.
PATROL AND COASTAL COMBATANTS: 10:
2 Sov *Turya* PFI (no TT).
2 Sov *Stenka* PFI (no TT), about 2 Sov Zhuk PCI⟨ and about 4 Sov Shmel PCI⟨.
AMPHIBIOUS: craft only: 3 Sov LCVP.

AIR FORCE: 500; 21 cbt ac†; no armed hel.
FIGHTER: 21 MiG-21.
TRANSPORT: 3 An-24, Tu-134.
HELICOPTERS: 5 Mi-8/-17.

PROVINCIAL FORCES: some 50,000.
Reports of at least 1 inf regt per province, with varying number of inf bn with lt wpn.

PARAMILITARY:
MILITIA: some 220,000 local forces, org at village level for local defence: ε10–20 per village. Not all armed.

OPPOSITION:
KHMER ROUGE (National Army of Democratic Kampuchea): some 9,000 org in 25 'bde', plus 2 indep regt.

CHINA

GDP[a]	1992: Y 2,404bn ($436.3bn): per capita $1,900	
	1993: Y 3,000bn ($507.5bn): per capita $2,200	
Growth	1992: 12.8%	1993: 13.4%
Inflation	1992: 10.4%	1993: 13.5%
Debt	1992: $69.2bn	1993: $83.5bn
Def exp[b]	1992: $24.3bn	1993: $27.4bn
Def bdgt[c]	1992: Y 37.0bn ($6.7bn)	
	1993: Y 43.2bn ($7.4bn)	
	1994: Y 58.0bn ($6.7bn)	
$1 = Y	1992: 5.5	1993: 5.8
	1994: 8.7	

Y = yuan

[a] Calculations of GDP using ppp give a larger GDP. An IMF study est GDP at $1,413bn in 1991; other est for 1991 incl $1,931bn (World Bank) and $3,439bn (Penn World Table).
[b] ppp est.
[c] Def bdgt shows official figures.

Population: 1,201,248,000

	13–17	*18–22*	*23–32*
Men	50,381,700	58,958,300	120,113,300
Women	47,054,000	55,249,700	111,812,800

TOTAL ARMED FORCES:
ACTIVE: some 2,930,000 (perhaps 1,275,000 conscripts, some 136,000 women), being reduced.
Terms of service: selective conscription; Army, Marines 3 years; Navy, Air Force 4 years.
RESERVES: 1,200,000+ militia reserves being formed on a province-wide basis.

STRATEGIC MISSILE FORCES:
OFFENSIVE (Strategic Rocket Units): 90,000.
MISSILES: org in 6 bases (army level) with bde/regt incl 1 msl testing and trg regt; org varies by msl type.
ICBM: some 14:
4 CSS-4 (DF-5); mod tested with MIRV.
10+ CSS-3 (DF-4).
IRBM: 60+ CSS-2 (DF-3), some updated.
SUBMARINES: 1:
SSBN: 1 *Xia* with 12 CSS-N-3 (J-1).
DEFENSIVE:
Tracking stations: Xinjiang (covers Central Asia) and Shanxi (northern border).
Phased-array radar complex: ballistic-missile early-warning.

ARMY: 2,200,000 (incl Strategic Rocket Units, perhaps 1,075,000 conscripts) (reductions continue).
7 Military Regions, 28 Military Districts, 3 Garrison Comd.
24 Integrated Group Armies (GA, equivalent to Western corps), org varies, normally with 3 inf div, 1 tk, 1 arty, 1 AAA bde or 3 inf, 1 tk div, 1 arty, 1 AAA bde, cbt readiness category varies.
Summary of Combat units:
78 inf div (incl 2 mech 'all arms').
10 armd div (normally 3 regt, 323 MBT).
5 field arty div.
2 indep armd, 5 indep fd arty, 5 indep AA bde.
15 indep engr regt.
6 Rapid Deployment Force bn.
Avn: 3 group hel bn (2 more forming); some hel regt, 1 hel trg regt.
AB (manned by Air Force):
1 corps of 3 div.
Spt tps.

EQUIPMENT:
MBT: some 7,500–8,000: incl 700 T-34/85, some T-54, 6,000 Type-59, 200 T-69 (mod Type-59), some Type-79, Type-80, Type-85 IIM.
LIGHT TANKS: 1,200 Type-63 amph, 800 Type-62.
AIFV: WZ-501, YW-307/-309.
APC: 2,800 Type-531 C/-D/-E, YW-534, Type-85 (YW-531H), Type-55 (BTR-40), -56 (BTR-152), -63, Type-77-1/-2 (Sov BTR-50PK amph); Type-523.
TOWED ARTY: 14,500:
100mm: Type-59 (fd/ATK), Type-86; 122mm: 6,000 Type-54, Type-60, Type-83, D-30; 130mm: 1,000 Types-59/-59-1; 152mm: Type-54, 1,400 Type-66, Type-83; 155mm: ε30 WAC-21.
SP ARTY: 122mm: Type-54-1 (Type-531 chassis), Type-85; 152mm: Type-83.
MRL: 3,800: 107mm: Types-63 towed /-81 SP (being replaced by 122mm); 122mm: Type-81, Type-83; 130mm: Type-63, Type-70 SP, Type-82, Type-85; 140mm: BM-14-16; 273mm: Type-83; 284mm: Type-74 minelayer; 320mm: WS-1; 425mm: Type-762 mine clearance.
MORTARS: 82mm: Type-53 (incl SP); 120mm: Type-55 (incl SP); 160mm: Type-56.
SSM: M-9 (CSS-6/DF-15) (range 500km); M-11 (CSS-7/DF-11) (range 120–150km).
ATGW: HJ-73 (*Sagger*-type), HJ-8 (*TOW*/ Milan-type).
RCL: 75mm: Type-52, Type-56; 82mm: Type-65.
RL: 90mm: Type-51.
ATK GUNS: 57mm: Type-55; 76mm: Type-54; 100mm: Type-73, Type-86.
AD: GUNS: 15,000: incl 23mm: (ZSU-23 type); 37mm: Types-55/-65/-74, -63 twin SP; 57mm: Types-59, -80 SP; 85mm: Type-56; 100mm: Type-59.
SAM: HN-5, HN-5A/-C (SA-7 type); HQ-61 twin SP.
HELICOPTERS: 30 Z-9, 8 SA-342 (with *HOT*), 24 S-70.
SURV: Cheetah (arty), Type-378 (veh), RASIT (veh, arty).
RESERVES (undergoing major reorganisation on a provincial basis): perhaps 900,000; ε80 inf div.

NAVY: ε260,000 (incl 25,000 Coastal Regional Defence Forces, 25,000 Naval Air Force, some 5,000 Marines and some 40,000 conscripts).
SUBMARINES: 50:
STRATEGIC SUBMARINES: 1 SSBN.
TACTICAL SUBMARINES: 48:
SSN: 5 *Han* with 533mm TT, 2 with 12 x C801 SSM.
SSG: 1 modified *Romeo* (Type ES5G), with 6 C-801 (YJ-6, *Exocet* derivative) SSM; plus 533mm TT.
SS: 42:
9 *Improved Ming* (Type ES5E) with 533mm TT.
About 33 *Romeo* (Type ES3B)† with 533mm TT.
(Note: probably some 50 additional *Romeo*-class non-operational.)
OTHER ROLES: 1 *Golf* (SLBM trials).
PRINCIPAL SURFACE COMBATANTS: 55:
DESTROYERS: 18 DDG:
1 *Luhu* with 4 x 2 C-801 SSM, 1 x 2 100mm gun, 2 Z-9A (Fr *Dauphin*) hel, plus 2 x 3 ASTT, 1 x 8 *Crotale* SAM.
2 modified *Luda*, 1 with 2 x 3 CSS-N-2 *Hai Ying-2* (HY-2 *Styx* derivative) and 1 with 4 x 2 C-801 SSM, 1 x 2 130mm guns, 2 Z-9A (Fr *Dauphin*) hel (OTHT), 2 x 3 ASTT, 1 x 8 *Crotale* SAM.
15 *Luda* (Type-051) (ASUW) with 2 x 3 HY-2 SSM, 2 x 2 130mm guns; plus 2 x 12 ASW RL.
FRIGATES: 37:
FFG: 35:
3 *Jiangwei* with 2 x 3 C-801 SSM, 2 x 5 ASW RL, 1 x 2 100mm gun, 1 Z-9A (Fr *Dauphin*) hel.
About 29 *Jianghu*; 4 variants:
About 13 Type I, with 4 x 5 ASW RL, plus 2 x 2 HY-2 SSM, 2 x 100mm guns.
About 9 Type II, with 2 x 5 ASW RL, plus 2 x 2 HY-2, 2 x 2 100mm guns.
About 5 Type III, with 8 x C-801 SSM, 2 x 2 100mm guns; plus 4 x 5 ASW RL.
About 2 Type IV, with 1 Z-9A hel, 2 x 3 ASTT, 2 x 5 ASW RL, 2 x 2 HY-2 SSM, 1 x 100mm gun.
1 *Jiangdong* with 2 x 5 ASW RL, 2 x 2 CSA-NX-2 SAM, 2 x 2 100mm guns.

2 *Chengdu* with 1 x 2 HY-2 SSM, 3 x 100mm guns.
FF: 2:
2 *Jiangnan* with 2 x 5 ASW RL, 3 x 100mm guns.
PATROL AND COASTAL COMBATANTS: about 870:
MISSILE CRAFT: 217:
1 *Huang* with 6 x C-801 SSM.
6 *Houxin* with 4 x C-801 SSM.
Some 120 *Huangfeng/Hola* (Sov *Osa-I*-type) with 6 or 8 x C-801 SSM; some with 4 x HY-2.
About 90 *Hegu/Hema*⟨ (*Komar*-Type) with 2 x HY-2 or 4 x C-801 SSM.
TORPEDO CRAFT: about 160:
100 *Huchuan*, some 60 P-6, all ⟨ with 2 x 533mm TT.
PATROL: about 495:
COASTAL: about 100:
4 *Haijui* with 3 x 5 ASW RL.
About 96 *Hainan* with 4 x ASW RL.
INSHORE: about 350:
300 *Shanghai*, 5 *Huludao* PFI, about 45 *Shantou*⟨.
RIVERINE: about 45⟨.
(Note: some minor combatants have reportedly been assigned to paramilitary forces (People's Armed Police, border guards, the militia) to the Customs Service, or into store. Totals, therefore, may be high.)
MINE WARFARE: about 121:
MINELAYERS: 1 *Beleijan* reported. In addition *Luda, Anshan, Jiangnan, Chengdu*-class DD/FF, *Hainan, Shanghai* PC and T-43 MSO have minelaying capability.
MCM: about 120:
35 Sov T-43 MSO.
1 *Wosao* MSC.
About 80 *Lienyun* aux MSC.
3 *Wochang* and 1 *Shanghai II* MSI; plus about 60 drone MSI⟨.
AMPHIBIOUS: 51:
3 *Yukan* LST, capacity about 200 tps, 10 tk.
13 *Shan* (US LST-1) LST, capacity about 150 tps, 16 tk.
30 *Yuliang*, 1 *Yuling*, 4 *Yudao* LSM, capacity about 100 tps, 3 tk.
Plus about 400 craft: 320 LCU, 40 LCP, 10 LCT and some hovercraft.
SUPPORT AND MISCELLANEOUS: about 164: 2 *Fuqing* AO, 33 AOT, 14 AF, 10 submarine spt, 1 sub rescue, 2 repair, 9 *Qiong Sha* tps tpt, 30 tpt, 33 survey/research/experimental, 4 icebreakers, 25 ocean tugs, 1 trg.

COASTAL REGIONAL DEFENCE FORCES: (25,000).
ε35 indep arty and SSM regt deployed in 25 coastal defence regions to protect naval bases, offshore islands and other vulnerable points.
GUNS: 85mm, 100mm, 130mm.
SSM: CSS-C-2 (*Hai Ying 2* variant, *'Silkworm'*), some with *Hai Ying* 4/C-201.

MARINES (Naval Infantry): (some 5,000).
1 bde.
special recce units.
RESERVES: on mob to total 8 div (24 inf, 8 tk, 8 arty regt), 2 indep tk regt.
(3 Army div also have an amph role.)
EQUIPMENT:
MBT: T-59.
LIGHT TANKS: T-60/-63, PT-76.
APC: Type-531, LVT; some Type-77.
ARTY: how: 122mm: Type-54 (incl -54-1 SP).
MRL: Type-63.

NAVAL AIR FORCE: (25,000); 875 shore-based cbt ac, 68 armed hel.
Org in 3 bbr, 6 ftr div, incl:
BOMBERS: some 25 H-6, some H-6D reported with two C-601 anti-ship ALCM.
About 130 H-5 torpedo-carrying lt bbr.
FGA: some 100 Q-5.
FIGHTER: some 600, incl J-5/-6/-7/-8.
RECCE: H-5.
MR/ASW: 15 ex-Sov Be-6 *Madge*, 5 PS-5 (SH-5).
HELICOPTERS: ASW: 15 SA-321, 40 Z-5, 3 Z-8, 10 Z-9.
MISCELLANEOUS: some 60 lt tpt ac incl Y-8; JJ-5/-6 trg ac.
ALCM: FL-1/C-601.
Naval fighters are integrated into the national AD system.

DEPLOYMENT AND BASES:
NORTH SEA FLEET: coastal defence from Korean border (Yalu River) to south of Lianyungang (approx 35°10'N); equates to Shenyang, Beijing and Jinan Military Regions, and to seaward.
BASES: Qingdao (HQ), Dalian (Luda), Huludao, Weihai, Chengshan.
9 coastal defence districts.
FORCES: 2 submarine, 3 escort, 1 mine warfare, 1 amph sqn; plus Bohai Gulf trg flotillas. About 300 patrol and coastal combatants.
EAST SEA FLEET: coastal defence from south of Lianyungang to Dongshan (approx 35°10'N to 23°30'N); equates to Nanjing Military Region, and to seaward:

BASES: Shanghai (HQ), Wusong, Dinghai, Hangzhou.
7 coastal defence districts.
FORCES: 2 submarine, 2 escort, 1 mine warfare, 1 amph sqn. About 250 patrol and coastal combatants.
Marines: 1 cadre div.
Coastal Regional Defence Forces: Nanjing Coastal District.
SOUTH SEA FLEET: coastal defence from Dongshan (approx 23°30'N) to Vietnam border; equates to Guangzhou Military Region, and to seaward (including Paracel and Spratly Islands).
BASES: Zhanjiang (HQ), Shantou, Guangzhou, Haikou, Yulin, Beihai, Huangpu; plus outposts on Paracel and Spratly Islands.
9 coastal defence districts.
FORCES: 2 submarine, 2 escort, 1 mine warfare, 1 amph sqn. About 300 patrol and coastal combatants.
Marines: 1 bde.

AIR FORCE: 470,000 (incl strategic forces, 220,000 AD personnel and 160,000 conscripts); some 4,970 cbt ac, few armed hel.

7 Military Air Regions, HQ Beijing.
Combat elm org in armies of varying numbers of air div (each with 3 regt of 3 sqn of 3 flt of 4–5 ac, 1 maint unit, some tpt and trg ac); tpt ac in regt only.
BOMBERS:
MEDIUM: 120 H-6 (some may be nuclear-capable). Some carry C-601 ASM.
LIGHT: some 350 H-5 (some with C-801 ASM).
FGA: 500 Q-5.
FIGHTER: ε4,000, some 60 regt with about 400 J-5, 3,000 J-6/B/D/E, 500 J-7, 100 J-8, 20 Su-27, 4 Su-27B.
RECCE: ε40 HZ-5, 150 JZ-5, 100 JZ-6 ac.
TRANSPORT: some 600, incl 18 BAe *Trident* 1E/2E, 30 Il-14, 10 Il-18, 10 Il-76, 50 Li-2, 300 Y-5, 25 Y-7, 25 Y-8 (some tkr), 15 Y-11, 2 Y-12.
HELICOPTERS: some 400: incl 6 AS-332, 4 Bell 214, 28 Mi-17, 20 S-70C-2, 30 Mi-8, 250 Z-5, 100 Z-6, 15 Z-8, 50 Z-9.
TRAINING: incl CJ-5/-6, HJ-5, J-2, JJ-2, JJ-4/-5/-6.
MISSILES:
AAM: PL-2/-2A, PL-5B *Atoll*-type, PL-7, PL-8.
ASM: HOT: C-601 subsonic ALCM (anti-ship, perhaps HY-2 SSM derivative); C-801 surface skimmer.
AD ARTY:
16 div: 16,000 35mm, 57mm, 85mm and 100mm guns; 28 indep AD regts (100 SAM units with HQ-2/-2B, -2J (CSA-1), -61 SAM, SA-10).

FORCES ABROAD:

UN AND PEACEKEEPING:
MIDDLE EAST (UNTSO): 3 Observers.
LIBERIA (UNOMIL): 15 Observers.
IRAQ/KUWAIT(UNIKOM): 13 Observers.
MOZAMBIQUE (ONUMOZ): 10 Observers.
WESTERN SAHARA (MINURSO): 20 Observers.

PARAMILITARY:

PEOPLE'S ARMED POLICE (Ministry of Defence): 1,200,000: 60 div, duties incl border and internal security (returned to PLA control June 1993).

FIJI

GDP	1992: $F 2.3bn ($1.5bn): per capita $4,600	
	1993ε: $F 2.5bn ($1.6bn): per capita $4,800	
Growth	1992: 2.8%	1993ε: 3.0%
Inflation	1992: 4.9%	1993: 5.2%
Debt	1992: $337m	1993: $346m
Def exp	1991: $F 47.8m ($ 32.4m)	
	1993: $F 41.9m ($ 27.2m)	
Def bdgt	1992: $F 34.7m ($ 23.1m)	
	1993: $F 39.9m ($ 25.9m)	
	1994: $F 39.2m ($26.3m)	
FMA	1993: $0.4m (IMET)	
	1995: $0.2m (IMET)	
$1 = $F	1992: 1.50	1993: 1.54
	1994: 1.49	

$F = Fiji dollar

Population: 774,400

	13–17	*18–22*	*23–32*
Men	44,800	38,600	63,400
Women	42,800	36,800	63,400

TOTAL ARMED FORCES:

ACTIVE: 3,900 (incl recalled reserves).
RESERVES: some 5,000 (to age 45).

ARMY: ε3,600 (incl Reserves).

7 inf bn (incl 4 cadre).
1 engr bn.
EQUIPMENT:
MORTARS: 81mm: 12.

NAVY: 300.
BASE: Suva.
PATROL AND COASTAL COMBATANTS: 7:
1 *Kulu* (*Pacific Forum*) PCI.
4 *Vai* (Is *Dabur*) PCI‹.
2 *Levuka* PCI‹.
SUPPORT AND MISCELLANEOUS: 2:
1 *Kiro* (US *Redwing*-class) trg.
1 *Cagidonu* presidential yacht (trg).

AIR WING:
1 AS-350 F-2, 1 SA-365N.

FORCES ABROAD:
UN AND PEACEKEEPING:
EGYPT (MFO): 350; 1 inf bn(-).
IRAQ/KUWAIT (UNIKOM): 7 Observers.
LEBANON (UNIFIL): 643; 1 inf bn.
RWANDA (UNAMIR): 1 Observer.

INDONESIA

GDP	1992: Rp 256,508bn ($126.4bn): per capita $3,000	
	1993ε: Rp 288,152bn ($138.1bn): per capita $3,200	
Growth	1992: 5.7%	1993ε: 6.5%
Inflation	1992: 7.5%	1993: 9.7%
Debt	1992: $84bn	1993: $90bn
Def exp	1991: Rp 2,822.0bn ($1.5bn)	
	1992: Rp 3,742.0bn ($1.8bn)	
Def bdgt	1993: Rp 4,239.1bn ($2.0bn)	
	1994: Rp 5,008.1bn ($2.3bn)	
$1 = Rp	1992: 2,030	1993: 2,087
	1994: 2,148	

Rp = rupiah

Population: 197,287,000 (Sudanese 14%, Madurese 8%, Malay 8%)

	13–17	*18–22*	*23–32*
Men	10,912,600	9,614,100	15,274,400
Women	10,464,900	9,477,700	16,519,800

TOTAL ARMED FORCES:
ACTIVE: 276,000.
Terms of service: 2 years selective conscription authorised.
RESERVES: 400,000: Army: cadre units; numbers, strengths unknown, obligation to age 45 for officers.

ARMY: 214,000.
Strategic Reserve (KOSTRAD): (9,400).
2 inf div HQ.
3 inf bde (9 bn).
3 AB bde (9 bn).
2 fd arty regt (6 bn).
1 AD arty regt (2 bn).
2 engr bn.
10 Military Area Comd (KODAM): (195,000): (Provincial (KOREM) and District (KORIM) comd).
62 inf bn (incl 4 AB).
8 cav bn.
11 fd arty, 10 AD bn.
8 engr bn.
1 composite avn sqn, 1 hel sqn.
SF (KOPASSUS): (3,500): 2 SF gp (each 2 bn).
EQUIPMENT:
LIGHT TANKS: some 275 AMX-13, 30 PT-76.
RECCE: 60 *Saladin*, 45 *Ferret*.
APC: 200 AMX-VCI, 45 *Saracen*, 200 V-150 *Commando*, 22 *Commando Ranger*, 80 BTR-40, 100 BTR-50.
TOWED ARTY: 76mm: M48; 105mm: 170 M-101, 10 M-56.
MORTARS: 81mm: 800; 120mm: 75 Brandt.
RCL: 90mm: 90 M-67; 106mm: 45 M-40A1.
RL: 89mm: 700 LRAC.
AD GUNS 20mm: 125; 40mm: 90 L/70; 57mm: 200 S-60.
SAM: 51 *Rapier*, 42 RBS-70.
AIRCRAFT: 1 BN-2 *Islander*, 2 C-47, 4 NC-212, 2 Cessna 310, 2 *Commander* 680, 18 *Gelatik* (trg).
HELICOPTERS: 12 Bell 205, 15 Bo-105, 4 NB-412, 10 Hughes 300C (trg).

NAVY: ε42,000 (incl ε1,000 Naval Air and 12,000 Marines).
PRINCIPAL COMMANDS:
WESTERN FLEET (HQ Tanjung Priok (Jakarta)).
BASES: Jakarta, Belawan (Sumatra); Minor Facilities: Tanjung Pinang (Riau Is.), Sabang.
EASTERN FLEET (HQ Surabaya):
BASES: Surabaya, Ujung Pandang, Jayapura (Irian Jaya); Minor Facilities: Manado (Celebes), Ambon (Moluccas).
MILITARY SEALIFT COMMAND (KOLINLAMIL): controls some amph and tpt ships used for inter-island comms and log spt for Navy and Army (assets incl in Navy and Army listings).
SUBMARINES: 2 *Cakra* (Ge T-209/1300) with 533mm TT (Ge HWT).
FRIGATES: 13:
6 *Ahmad Yani* (Nl *Van Speijk*) with 1 *Wasp* hel (ASW) (Mk 44 LWT), 2 x 3 ASTT; plus 2 x 4 *Harpoon* SSM.

3 *Fatahillah* with 2 x 3 ASTT (not *Nala*), 1 x 2 ASW mor, 1 *Wasp* hel (*Nala* only); plus 2 x 2 MM-38 *Exocet*, 1 x 120mm gun.
3 *M.K. Tiyahahu* (UK *Ashanti*) with 1 *Wasp* hel, 1 x 3 *Limbo* ASW mor; plus 2 x 114mm guns.
1 *Hajar Dewantara* (Yug) (trg) with 2 x 533mm TT, 1 ASW mor; plus 2 x 2 MM-38 *Exocet*.
(Plus 4 *Samadikun* (US *Claud Jones*) with 2 x 3 ASTT (in store).)
PATROL AND COASTAL COMBATANTS: 42:
MISSILE CRAFT: 4 *Mandau* PFM with 4 x MM-38 *Exocet* SSM.
TORPEDO CRAFT: 2 *Singa* (Ge Lürssen 57-m (NAV I)) with 2 x 533mm TT and 1 x 57mm gun.
PATROL: 36:
COASTAL: 9:
2 *Pandrong* (Ge Lürssen 57-m (NAV II)) PFC, with 1 x 57mm gun.
3 *Barakuda* (Sov *Kronshtadt*)†.
4 *Kakap* (Ge Lürssen 57-m (NAV III)) PFC, with 40mm gun and hel deck.
INSHORE: 27:
8 *Sibarau* (Aust *Attack*) PCI, 1 *Bima Samudera* PHM, 18‹.
MINE WARFARE: 4:
2 *Pulau Rengat* (mod Nl *Tripartite*) MCC (mainly used for coastal patrol).
2 *Pulau Rani* (Sov T-43) MCC (mainly used for coastal patrol).
AMPHIBIOUS: 14:
6 *Teluk Semangka* LST, capacity about 200 tps, 17 tk, 4 with 3 hel (2 fitted as comd ships and 1 as hospital ship).
1 *Teluk Amboina* LST, capacity about 200 tps, 16 tk.
7 *Teluk Langsa* (US LST-512) and 2 *Teluk Banten* (mod US LST-512) LST, capacity: 200 tps, 16 tks).
(3 LST assigned to Military Sealift Command.)
Plus about 80 craft, incl 4 LCU, some 45 LCM.
SUPPORT AND MISCELLANEOUS: 17:
1 *Sorong* AO, 1 *Arun* AO (UK *Rover*), 2 Sov *Khobi* AOT, 1 cmd/spt/replenish, 1 repair, 4 tpt (Military Sea Lift Command), 1 ocean tug, 6 survey/research.
(The following ships have been purchased from Germany; some have been delivered, but none were operational as of 1 June 1994: 16 *Parchim* corvettes; 9 *Kondor-II* MCMV; 12 *Frosch I* LST; 2 *Frosch II* spt ships.)

NAVAL AIR: (ε1,000); 24 cbt ac, 23 armed hel.
ASW: 8 *Wasp* HAS-1 hel, 10 AS-332L.
MR: 12 N-22 *Searchmaster* B, 6 *Searchmaster* L, 6 CN-235-100 IPTN/CASA.
OTHER:
AIRCRAFT: incl 4 *Commander*, 4 NC-212; 2 *Bonanza* F33 (trg), 6 PA-38 (trg).
HELICOPTERS: 4 NAS-332F, *5 NBo-105.
MARINES: (12,000).
2 inf bde (6 bn).
1 SF bn(-).
1 cbt spt regt (arty, AD).
EQUIPMENT:
LIGHT TANKS: 80 PT-76†.
RECCE: 20 BRDM.
AIFV: 10 AMX-10 PAC-90.
APC: 25 AMX-10P, 75 BTR-50P.
TOWED ARTY: 105mm: some LG-1 Mk II; 122mm: 40 M-38.
MRL: 140mm: BM-14.
AD GUNS: 40mm, 57mm.

AIR FORCE: 20,000; 79 cbt ac, no armed hel.
2 Air Operations Areas.
FGA: 2 sqn with 28 A-4 (26 -E, 2 TA-4H).
1 with 11 F-16 (7 -A, 4 -B).
FIGHTER: 1 sqn with 14 F-5 (10 -E, 4 -F).
COIN: 2 sqn:
1 with 14 *Hawk* Mk 53 (COIN/trg).
1 with 12 OV-10F.
MR: 1 sqn with 3 Boeing 737-200, 1 C-130H-MP.
TANKER: 2 KC-130B.
TRANSPORT:
19 C-130 (9 -B, 3 -H, 7 -H-30), 7 L100-30.
1 Boeing 707, 5 Cessna 401, 2 Cessna 402, 7 F-27-400M, 1 F-28-1000, 10 NC-212, 1 *Skyvan* (survey), 30 CN-235M.
HELICOPTERS: 3 sqn:
1 with 12 S-58T.
2 with 2 Bell 204B, 2 Bell 206B, 10 Hughes 500, 12 Bo-105, 12 NSA-330, 3 SE-3160.
TRAINING: 4 sqn with 40 AS-202, 2 Cessna 172, 5 Cessna 207 (liaison), 23 T-34C, 10 T-41D.
AIRFIELD DEFENCE: 5 bn *Rapier*.

FORCES ABROAD:
UN AND PEACEKEEPING:
IRAQ/KUWAIT (UNIKOM): 6 Observers.
SOMALIA (UNOSOM): 4 Observers.

PARAMILITARY:
POLICE (POLRI): some 174,000: incl 6,000 Police 'Mobile bde' (BRIMOB) org in coy, incl Police COIN unit (GEGANA); 3 *Commander*, 1 Beech 18, 7 lt **ac**; 10 Bo-105, 3 Bell 206 **hel**.

MARINE: about 10 PCC, 9 PCI and 6 PCI⟨ (all armed).
KAMRA (People's Security): 1.5m: some 300,000 a year undergo 3 weeks' basic trg. Part-time police auxiliary.
WANRA (People's Resistance): part-time local military auxiliary force under comd of Regional Military Commands (KOREM).
CUSTOMS: about 72 PFI⟨, armed.
SEA COMMUNICATIONS AGENCY (responsible to Department of Transport): 5 *Kujang* PCI, 4 *Golok* PCI (SAR), plus boats.

OPPOSITION:

FRETILIN (Revolutionary Front for an Independent East Timor): FALINTIL mil wing with some 100 incl spt; small arms.
FREE PAPUA MOVEMENT (OPM): perhaps 200–300 (100 armed).
FREE ACEH MOVEMENT (Gerakan Aceh Merdeka): 100 armed reported.

JAPAN

GDP	1992: ¥463,850bn ($3,662.5bn): per capita $20,200	
	1993: ¥468,769bn ($3,761.5bn): per capita $20,700	
Growth	1992: 1.3%	1993: 0.1%
Inflation	1992: 1.7%	1993: 1.2%
Debt	1992: 67.3%	1993: 68.3%
Def exp[a]	1992: ¥7,418.8bn ($58.6bn)	
Def bdgt[a]	1992: ¥4,551.8bn ($35.9bn)	
	1993: ¥4,640.6bn ($39.7bn)	
	1994: ¥4,683.5bn ($42.1bn)	
$1 = ¥	1992: 126.7	1993: 111.2
	1994: 103.5	

¥ = yen

[a] Def bdgt excl military spending on pensions, space and the MSA.

Population: 125,271,800

	13–17	*18–22*	*23–32*
Men	4,276,200	4,810,800	8,927,200
Women	4,062,600	4,574,300	8,574,800

TOTAL ARMED FORCES:

ACTIVE: 237,700 (incl 160 Central Staffs (reducing), 8,000 women).
RESERVES: 47,900: Army 46,000; Navy 1,100; Air Force 800.

ARMY (Ground Self-Defense Force): some 150,000.
5 Army HQ (Regional Commands).
1 armd div.
12 inf div (6 at 7,000, 6 at 9,000 each).
2 composite bde.
1 AB bde.
1 arty bde; 2 arty gp.
2 AD bde; 4 AD gp.
4 trg bde; 2 trg regt.
5 engr bde.
1 hel bde.
5 ATK hel sqn, 1 more forming.
EQUIPMENT:
MBT: some 1,160: some 190 Type-61 (retiring), some 870 Type-74, some 100 Type-90.
RECCE: some 80 Type-87.
AIFV: some 50 Type-89.
APC: 400 Type-60, 300 Type-73, some 200 Type-82.
TOWED ARTY: 510: 105mm: 110 M-101; 155mm: 390 FH-70; 203mm: 10 M-115.
SP ARTY: 310: 105mm: 20 Type-74; 155mm: 200 Type-75; 203mm: 90 M-110A2.
MRL: 130mm: some 70 Type-75 SP.
MORTARS: some 1,260, incl 81mm: 770 (some SP); 107mm: 490 (some SP).
SSM: some 50 Type-88 coastal.
ATGW: 220 Type-64, 230 Type-79, 180 Type-87.
RL: 89mm: 70 3.5-in M-20.
RCL: 3,200: 84mm: 2,700 *Carl Gustav*; 106mm: 500 (incl Type 60 SP).
AD GUNS: 90: 35mm: 50 twin, Type-8 SP.
SAM: 330 *Stinger*, some 60 Type 81, 200 *Improved HAWK*.
AIRCRAFT: 20 LR-1.
HELICOPTERS:
ATTACK: 90 AH-1S.
TRANSPORT: 3 AS-332L (VIP), 30 CH-47J, 10 KV-107, 180 OH-6D/J, 150 UH-1B/H, some TH-55 (trg).
SURV: Type-92 (mor), J/MPQ-P7 (arty).

NAVY (Maritime Self-Defense Force): 43,000 (incl ε12,000 MSDF Air Arm and 2,900 women).
BASES: Yokosuka, Kure, Sasebo, Maizuru, Ominato.
Fleet: Surface units org into 4 escort flotillas, of 7–8 DD/FF each; 2 based at Yokosuka, 1 at Sasebo and 1 at Maizuru. Submarines org into 2 flotillas based at Kure and Yokosuka. Remainder assigned to 10 regional/district units.

SUBMARINES: 17:
TACTICAL SUBMARINES: 15:
5 *Harushio* with 533mm TT (Jap Type-89 HWT) with *Harpoon* USGW.
10 *Yuushio* with 533mm TT (Jap Type-89 HWT), 7 with *Harpoon* USGW.
OTHER ROLES: 2: 1 *Uzushio* (trg), 1 *Uzushio* (trials).
PRINCIPAL SURFACE COMBATANTS: 62:
DESTROYERS: 7 DDG:
1 *Kongo* with 2 x VLS for *Standard* SAM and *ASROC* SUGW (29 cells forward, 61 cells aft); plus 2 x 4 *Harpoon* SSM, 2 x 3 ASTT and hel deck.
2 *Hatakaze* with 1 x SM-1-MR Mk 13 SAM; plus 2 x 4 *Harpoon* SSM, 1 x 8 *ASROC* SUGW (Mk 46 LWT) 2 x 3 ASTT, 2 x 127mm guns.
3 *Tachikaze* with 1 x SM-1-MR; plus 1 x 8 *ASROC*, 2 x 3 ASTT, 8, 2 x 127mm guns.
1 *Amatsukaze* with 1 x SM-1-MR; plus 1 x 8 *ASROC*, 2 x 3 ASTT.
FRIGATES: 55 (incl 1 trg):
FFH: 24:
2 *Shirane* with 3 x SH-60J *Sea Hawk* ASW hel, 1 x 8 *ASROC*, 2 x 3 ASTT; plus 2 x 127mm guns.
2 *Haruna* with 3 x *SH-60J* hel, 1 x 8 *ASROC*, 2 x 3 ASTT; plus 2 x 127mm guns.
8 *Asagiri* with 1 *SH-60J* hel, 1 x 8 *ASROC*, 2 x 3 ASTT; plus 2 x 4 *Harpoon* SSM.
12 *Hatsuyuki* with 1 *SH-60J*, 1 x 8 *ASROC*, 2 x 3 ASTT; plus 2 x 4 *Harpoon* SSM.
FF: 31:
6 *Abukuma* with 1 x 8 *ASROC*, 2 x 3 ASTT; plus 2 x 4 *Harpoon* SSM.
4 *Takatsuki* with 1 x 8 *ASROC*, 2 x 3 ASTT, 1 x 4 ASW RL; plus 2 x 4 *Harpoon* SSM, 1 x 127mm gun.
3 *Yamagumo* with 1 x 8 *ASROC*, 2 x 3 ASTT, 1 x 4 ASW RL.
3 *Minegumo* with 1 x 8 *ASROC*, 2 x 3 ASTT, 1 x 4 ASW RL.
2 *Yubari* with 2 x 3 ASTT, 1 x 4 ASW RL; plus 2 x 4 *Harpoon* SSM
1 *Ishikari* with 2 x 3 ASTT, 1 x 4 ASW RL; plus 2 x 4 *Harpoon* SSM.
11 *Chikugo* with 1 x 8 *ASROC*, 2 x 3 ASTT.
1 *Katori* (trg) with 2 x 3 ASTT, 1 x ASW RL.
PATROL AND COASTAL COMBATANTS: 6:
MISSILE CRAFT: 3:
3 *Ichi-Go* type PHM with 4 SSM-1B.
PATROL: 3 *Jukyu-Go* PCI⟨.
MINE WARFARE: 39:
MINELAYERS: 1:
1 *Souya* (460 mines) plus hel deck, 2 x 3 ASTT, also MCM spt/comd.
MINE COUNTERMEASURES: 38:
1 *Hayase* MCM cmd with hel deck, 2 x 3 ASTT, plus minelaying capacity (116 mines).
22 *Hatsushima* MCC.
7 *Uwajima* MCC.
3 *Yaeyama* MSO.
4 *Nana-go* MSI⟨.
1 *Fukue* coastal MCM spt.
AMPHIBIOUS: 6:
3 *Miura* LST, capacity 200 tps, 10 tk.
3 *Atsumi* LST, capacity 130 tps, 5 tk.
Plus craft: 2 *Yura* and 2 *Ichi-Go* LCM.
SUPPORT AND MISCELLANEOUS: 19:
3 *Towada* AOE, 1 *Sagami* AOE (all with hel deck); 2 sub depot/rescue, 2 *Yamagumo* trg, 2 trg spt, 8 survey/experimental, 1 icebreaker.

MSDF AIR ARM: (ε12,000); 110 cbt ac (plus 15 in store), 100 armed hel. Average annual flying hours for P-3 aircrew: 500.
7 Air Groups.
MR: 10 sqn (1 trg) with 100 P-3C.
ASW: 6 hel sqn (1 trg) with 60 HSS-2B, 40 SH-60J.
MCM: 1hel sqn with 10 MH-53E.
EW: 1 sqn with 2 EP-3C.
TRANSPORT: 1 sqn with 4 YS-11M.
TEST: 1 sqn with 3 P-3C **ac**; 2 HSS-2B, 2 SH-60J **hel**.
SAR: 1 sqn with 10 US-1A.
3 rescue sqn with 10 S-61 hel, 10 UH-60J.
TRAINING: 5 sqn with 10 KM-2, 10* P-3C, 30 T-5, 30 *King Air* TC-90/UC-90, 10 YS-11T/M **ac**; 10 HSS-2B, 10 OH-6D/J **hel**.

AIR FORCE (Air Self-Defense Force): 44,500; 440 cbt ac, no armed hel.
7 cbt air wings; 1 cbt air unit; 1 recce gp; 1 AEW unit.
FGA: 3 sqn with 50 F-I.
FIGHTER: 10 sqn:
7 with 170 F-15J/DJ.
3 with 110 F-4EJ.
RECCE: 1 sqn with 20 RF-4E/EJ.
AEW: 1 sqn with 10 E-2C.
EW: 1 flt with 1 C-1, 4 YS-11 E.
AGGRESSOR TRAINING: 1 sqn with a few F-15.
TRANSPORT: 5 sqn:
3 with 20 C-1, 10 C-130H, 10 YS-11.
2 heavy-lift hel sqn with 10 CH-47J.
Plus 2 747-400 (VIP).
SAR: 1 wing (10 det) with 30 MU-2 **ac**; 20 KV-107, 10 CH-47J, 9 UH-60J **hel**.
CALIBRATION: 1 sqn with 1 YS-11, 2 U-125-800.
TRAINING: 5 wings: 10 sqn: 40* T-1A/B, 50* T-2, 40 T-3, 60 T-4.

LIAISON: U-65, 40T-33, 70 T-4.
TEST: 1 wing with F-15J, T-4.
MISSILES:
ASM: ASM-1.
AAM: AAM-1, AIM-7 *Sparrow*, AIM-9 *Sidewinder*.
AIR DEFENCE: ac control and warning: 4 wings; 28 radar sites.
SAM: 6 AD msl gp (24 sqn) with 120 *Patriot*.
Air Base Defense Gp with 20mm *Vulcan* AA guns, Type 81, Type 91, *Stinger* SAM.

FORCES ABROAD:

UN AND PEACEKEEPING:
MOZAMBIQUE (ONUMOZ): 56 (movement control).

PARAMILITARY:

MARITIME SAFETY AGENCY (Coast Guard) (Ministry of Transport, no cbt role): 12,000.
PATROL VESSELS: some 335:
OFFSHORE (over 1,000 tons): 48, incl 1 *Shikishima* with 2 *Super Puma* hel, 2 *Mizuho* with 2 Bell 212, 8 *Soya* with 1 Bell 212 hel, 2 *Izu,* 28 *Shiretoko* and 1 Kojima (trg).
COASTAL (under 1,000 tons): 36.
INSHORE: about 250 patrol craft most(.
MISCELLANEOUS: about 90 service, 80 tender/trg vessels.
AIRCRAFT: 5 NAMC YS-11A, 2 Short *Skyvan*, 16 *King Air*, 1 Cessna U-206G.
HELICOPTERS: 32 Bell 212, 4 Bell 206, 2 Hughes 369.

FOREIGN FORCES:

US: 44,800: Army (1,900): 1 Corps HQ; Navy (7,300) bases at Yokosuka (HQ 7th Fleet) and Sasebo; Marines (20,000): 1 MEF in Okinawa; Air Force (15,600): 1 Air HQ, 96 cbt **ac:** 54 F-15C/D, 42 F-16, 7 C-12F, 2 C-21A, 3 E-3 (AWACS), 20 C-130, 15 KC-135 (tkr), 6 HC-130, 3 MC-130; **hel:** 4 HH-60, 3 UH-1N.

KOREA: DEMOCRATIC PEOPLE'S REPUBLIC (NORTH)

GNP[a]	1992ε: won 45.9bn ($21.1bn): per capita $1,100	
	1993ε: won 44.4bn ($20.8bn): per capita: $1,000	
Growth	1992ε: -6.7%	1993ε: -4.3%
Inflation	1992ε: 3%	1993ε: 5%
Debt[b]	1992: $1.6bn	1993: $1.6bn
Def exp	1992ε: won 11.8bn ($5.5bn)	
	1993ε: won 11.3bn ($5.3bn)	
Def bdgt	1992: won 4.5bn ($2.1bn)	
	1993ε: won 4.7bn ($2.2bn)	
	1994ε: won 4.8bn ($2.3bn)	
$1 = won	1992: 2.13	1993: 2.13
	1994: 2.14	

[a] GNP shows an increase over GDP as a consequence of remitted earnings of N. Korean expatriates in Japan.
[b] External debt in convertible currencies.

Population: 23,112,000

	13–17	*18–22*	*23–32*
Men	1,013,500	1,222,600	2,486,100
Women	991,700	1,201,600	2,454,200

TOTAL ARMED FORCES:

ACTIVE: 1,128,000.
Terms of service: Army 5–8 years; Navy 5–10 years; Air Force 3–4 years, followed by compulsory part-time service in the Pacification Corps to age 40. Thereafter service in the Worker/Peasant Red Guard to age 60.
RESERVES: 540,000: Army 500,000, Navy 40,000.
Mob claimed in 12 hours: up to 6,000,000 have some Reserve/Militia commitment (see Paramilitary).

ARMY: 1,000,000.

16 Corps (1 armd, 4 mech, 8 inf, 1 arty, 1 capital defence, 1 Special Purpose).
26 inf/mot inf div.
14 armd bde.
23 mot/mech inf bde.
5 indep inf bde.
Special Purpose Corps: 3 cdo, 4 recce, 1 river-crossing regt, 3 amph, 3 AB bn, 22 lt inf bn.
'Bureau of Reconnaissance SF' (8 bn).
Army tps: 8 hy arty bde (incl MRL), 1 indep *Scud* SSM regt.
Corps tps: 14 bde incl 122mm, 152mm SP, MRL.
RESERVE: Pacification Corps: some 1.2m; 23 inf div, 6 inf bde.
EQUIPMENT:
MBT: some 3,700: T-34, T-54/-55, T-62, Type-59.
LIGHT TANKS: 500 PT-76, M-1985.
APC: 2,500 BTR-40/-50/-60/-152, Ch Type-531, N. Korean Type M-1973.

TOWED ARTY: 2,300: 122mm: M-1931/-37, D-74, D-30; 130mm: M-46; 152mm: M-1937, M-1938, M-1943.
SP ARTY: Some 4,500: 122mm: M-1977, M-1981, M-1985; 130mm: M-1975, M-1991; 152mm: M-1974, M-1977; 170mm: M-1978, M-1989.
MRL: 2,280: 107mm: Type-63; 122mm: BM-21, BM-11, M-1977/-1985/-1992/-1993; 240mm: M-1985/-1989/-1991.
MORTARS: 9,000: 82mm: M-37; 120mm: M-43; 160mm: M-43.
SSM: 54 *FROG*-3/-5/-7; some 30 *Scud* B/-C (Korean improved).
ATGW: AT-1 *Snapper*, AT-3 *Sagger*, AT-4 *Spigot*, AT-5 *Spandrel*.
RCL: 82mm: 1,500 B-10.
AD GUNS: 8,800: 14.5mm: ZPU-1/-2/-4 SP, M-1983 SP; 23mm: ZU-23, ZSU-23-4 SP; 37mm: M-1939; 57mm: S-60; 85mm: KS-12; 100mm: KS-19.
SAM: 10,000 SA-7/-16.

NAVY: ε46,000.

BASES: East Coast: Toejo (HQ), Changjon, Munchon, Songjon-pardo, Mugye-po, Mayang-do, Chaho Nodongjagu, Puam-Dong, Najin.
West Coast: Nampo (HQ), Pipa Got, Sagon-ni, Chodo-ri, Koampo, Tas-ri.
2 Fleet HQ.
SUBMARINES: 25:
21 Ch Type-031/Sov *Romeo* with 533mm TT.
4 Sov *Whiskey*† with 533mm and 406mm TT.
(Plus some 50 midget submarines mainly used for SF ops, but some with 2 x TT.)
FRIGATES: 3:
1 *Soho* with 4 x ASW RL, plus 4 x SS-N-2 *Styx* SSM, 1 x 100mm gun and hel deck.
2 *Najin* with 2 x 5 ASW RL, plus 2 SS-N-2 *Styx* SSM, 2 x 100mm guns.
PATROL AND COASTAL COMBATANTS: about 390:
CORVETTES: some 3 *Sariwon* with 1 x 100mm gun.
MISSILE CRAFT: 46:
15 *Soju*, 8 Sov *Osa*, 4 Ch *Huangfeng* PFM with 4 x SS-N-2 *Styx,*
9 *Sohung*, 10 Sov *Komar* PFM with 2 x SS-N-2.
TORPEDO CRAFT: 173:
3 Sov *Shershen* with 4 x 533mm TT.
Some 170 with 2 x 533mm TT.
PATROL: 166:
COASTAL: 18 PFC: 6 *Hainan* with 4 x ASW RL, 12 *Taechong* with 2 x ASW RL.
INSHORE: some 148:
13 SO-1, 12 *Shanghai* II, 3 *Chodo*, some 120⟨.
MINE WARFARE: about 25 MSI⟨.
AMPHIBIOUS: craft only: 24 LCM, 7 LCU, about 100 *Nampo* LCVP , plus about 100 hovercraft.
SUPPORT AND MISCELLANEOUS: 7: 2 ocean tugs, 1 AS, 1 ocean and 3 inshore survey.
COAST DEFENCE: SSM: 2 regt: *Silkworm* in 6 sites.
GUNS: 122mm: M-1931/-37; 130mm: SM-4-1; 152mm: M-1937.

AIR FORCE: 82,000; 770 cbt ac, 50 armed hel.

Average annual flying bonus for ftr/FGA pilots: some 30.
BOMBERS: 3 lt regt with 80 H-5.
FGA: 6 regt:
3 with 160 J-5 (MiG-17).
2 with 120 J-6 (MiG-19).
1 with 14 Su-7, 36 Su-25.
FIGHTER: 10 regt:
2 with 80 J-5 (MiG-17).
2 with 60 J-6 (MiG-19).
1 with 40 J-7 (MiG-21).
3 with 120 MiG-21.
1 with 46 MiG-23.
1 with 14 MiG-29.
ATTACK HELICOPTERS: 50 Mi-24.
TRANSPORT: ac: 162 An-2, 6 An-24, 5 Il-14, 2 Il-18, 4 Il-62M, 2 Tu-134, 4 Tu-154, 120 Y-5; **hel:** 1 Hughes 300C, 80 Hughes 500D, 6 Hughes 500E, 140 Mi-2, 15 Mi-8/-17, 48 Z-5.
TRAINING: incl 10 CJ-5, 170 CJ-6.
AAM: AA-2 *Atoll*, AA-7 *Apex*.
SAM: 240 SA-2, 36 SA-3, 24 SA-5.

FORCES ABROAD: advisers in some 12 African countries.

PARAMILITARY:

SECURITY TROOPS (Ministry of Public Security): 115,000, incl border guards.
WORKER/PEASANT RED GUARD: some 3.8m. Org on a provincial/town/village basis. Comd structure is bde – bn – coy – pl. Small arms with some mor and AD guns (but many units unarmed).

KOREA: REPUBLIC OF (SOUTH)

GDP	1992: won 231,727bn ($296.8bn): per capita $9,200	
	1993: won 265,548bn ($319.5bn): per capita $10,000	
Growth	1992: 4.8%	1993: 7.8%
Inflation	1992: 6.2%	1993: 4.8%
Debt	1992: $43.0bn	1993: $50.7bn
Def exp	1991: won 7,892bn ($10.8bn)	
	1992ε: won 8,924bn ($11.4bn)	
Def bdgt	1993: won 10,753bn ($13.4bn)	
	1994: won 11,339bn ($14.0bn)	
$1 = won	1992: 780.7	1993: 802.7
	1994: 808.6	

Population: 44,979,600

	13–17	*18–22*	*23–32*
Men	2,035,300	2,216,600	4,378,400
Women	1,882,100	2,054,400	4,079,500

TOTAL ARMED FORCES:

ACTIVE: 633,000.

Terms of service: conscription: Army 26 months; Navy and Air Force 30 months; then First Combat Forces (Mobilisation Reserve Forces) or Regional Combat Forces (Homeland Defence Forces) to age 33.

RESERVES: 4,500,000; being reorganised.

ARMY: 520,000 (140,000 conscripts).

HQ: 3 Army, 9 Corps.

3 mech inf div (each 3 bde: 3 mech inf, 3 tk, 1 recce, 1 engr bn; 1 fd arty bde).

19 inf div (each 3 inf regt, 1 recce, 1 tk, 1 engr bn; 1 arty regt (4 bn)).

2 indep inf bde.

7 SF bde.

3 counter-infiltration bde.

3 SSM bn with NHK-I/-II (*Honest John*).

3 AD arty bde.

3 *HAWK* bn (24 sites), 2 *Nike Hercules* bn (10 sites).

1 avn comd.

RESERVES: 1 Army HQ, 23 inf div.

EQUIPMENT:

MBT: 1,900: 550 Type 88, 400 M-47, 950 M-48.

APC: some 2,000, incl 1,500 KIFV, 300 M-113, 200 Fiat 6614/KM-900/-901.

TOWED ARTY: some 3,500: 105mm: 1,700 M-101, KH-178; 155mm: M-53, M-114, KH-179; 203mm: M-115.

SP ARTY: 900: 155mm: M-109A2; 175mm: M-107; 203mm: M-110.

MRL: 130mm: 140 *Kooryong* (36-tube).

MORTARS: 6,000: 81mm: KM-29; 107mm: M-30.

SSM: 12 NHK-I/-II.

ATGW: *TOW*.

RCL: 57mm, 75mm, 90mm: M67; 106mm: M40A2.

ATK GUNS: 76mm: 8 M-18; 90mm: 50 M-36 SP.

AD GUNS: 600: 20mm: incl KIFV (AD variant), 60 M-167 *Vulcan*; 30mm: 20 B1 HO SP; 35mm: 20 GDF-003; 40mm: 80 L60/70, M-1.

SAM: 350 *Javelin*, 60 *Redeye*, 130 *Stinger*, 170 *Mistral*, 110 *HAWK*, 200 *Nike Hercules*.

AIRCRAFT: 5 O-1A.

HELICOPTERS:

ATTACK: 65 AH-1F/-J, 68 Hughes 500 MD.

TRANSPORT: 15 CH-47D.

UTILITY: 195 Hughes 500, 125 UH-1H, 30 UH-23, 124 UH-60P.

SURV: RASIT (veh, arty).

NAVY: 60,000 (incl 25,000 Marines and ε19,000 conscripts).

BASES: Chinhae (HQ), Cheju, Inchon, Mokpo, Mukho, Pukpyong, Pohang, Pusan.

3 Fleet Commands.

SUBMARINES: 2:

2 *Chang Bogo* (Ge T-209/1400) with 8 x 533 TT.

Plus 3 KSS-1 *Dolgorae* SSI (175t) with 2 x 406mm TT.

PRINCIPAL SURFACE COMBATANTS: 40:

DESTROYERS: 8:

7 *Chung Buk* (US *Gearing*) with 2 or 3 x 2 127mm guns; plus 2 x 3 ASTT; 5 with 2 x 4 *Harpoon* SSM, 1 *Alouette* III hel (OTHT), 2 with 1 x 8 *ASROC*.

1 *Dae Gu* (US *Sumner*) with 3 x 2 127mm guns; plus 2 x 3 ASTT, 1 *Alouette III* hel.

FRIGATES: 32:

9 *Ulsan* with 2 x 3 ASTT (Mk 46 LWT); plus 2 x 4 *Harpoon* SSM.

23 *Po Hang* with 2 x 3 ASTT; some with 2 x 1 MM-38 *Exocet*.

PATROL AND COASTAL COMBATANTS: 122:

CORVETTES: 4 *Dong Hae* (ASW) with 2 x 3 ASTT.

MISSILE CRAFT: 11:

8 *Pae Ku*-52, 3 with 4 *Standard* (boxed) SSM, 5 with 2 x 2 *Harpoon* SSM.

1 *Pae Ku*-51 (US *Asheville*), with 2 x *Standard* SSM.

2 *Kilurki-71* (*Wildcat*) with 2 x MM-38 *Exocet* SSM.

PATROL, INSHORE: 107:

92 *Kilurki-11* ('*Sea Dolphin*') 37-m PFI.

15 *Chebi-51* (*'Sea Hawk'*) 26-m PFI⟨ (some with 2 x MM-38 *Exocet* SSM).
MINE WARFARE: 14:
6 *Kan Keong* (mod It *Lerici*) MHC.
8 *Kum San* (US MSC-268/289) MSC.
AMPHIBIOUS: 14:
7 *Un Bong* (US LST-511) LST, capacity 200 tps, 16 tk.
7 *Ko Mun* (US LSM-1) LSM, capacity 50 tps, 4 tk.
Plus about 36 craft; 6 LCT, 10 LCM, about 20 LCVP.
SUPPORT AND MISCELLANEOUS: 12:
2 AOE, 2 spt tankers, 2 ocean tugs, 2 salv/div spt, about 4 survey (civil-manned, Ministry of Transport-funded).

NAVAL AIR: 15 cbt ac; 47 armed hel.
ASW: 2 sqn:
1 **ac** with 15 S-2E; 1 **hel** with 25 Hughes 500MD (maritime patrol).
1 flt with 10 SA-316 hel (maritime patrol), 12 *Lynx* (ASW).

MARINES: (25,000).
2 div, 1 bde.
spt units.
EQUIPMENT:
MBT: 60 M-47.
APC: 60 LVTP-7.
TOWED ARTY: 105mm, 155mm.
SSM: *Harpoon* (truck-mounted).

AIR FORCE: 53,000; 447 cbt ac (plus 52 in store), no armed hel. 8 cbt, 2 tpt wings.
FGA: 8 sqn:
2 with 48 F-16 (36 -C, 12 -D).
6 with 190 F-5 (60 -A, 130 -E). Plus 16 in store.
FIGHTER: 4 sqn with 96 F-4D/E. Plus 36 in store.
COIN: 1 sqn with 23 A-37B.
FAC: 10 O-2A, 20 OA-37B.
RECCE: 1 sqn with 18 RF-4C, 10 RF-5A.
SAR: 1 hel sqn with 25 Bell UH-1B, 2 UH-1N, UH-60.
TRANSPORT:
AIRCRAFT: 2 BAe 748 (VIP), 1 Boeing 737-300 (VIP), 1 C-118, 15 C-123J/K, 10 C-130H, 3 *Commander,* 12 CN-235M.
HELICOPTERS: 7 Bell 212, 3 Bell 412, 5 UH-1D/H.
TRAINING: 25* F-5B, 35* F-5, 25 T-33A, 50 T-37, 20 T-41B, 20 Hawk Mk-67.
MISSILES:
ASM: AGM-65A *Maverick.*
AAM: AIM-7 *Sparrow*, AIM-9 *Sidewinder.*

FORCES ABROAD:
UN AND PEACEKEEPING:
SOMALIA (UNOSOM): 6, plus 2 civ pol.

PARAMILITARY:
CIVILIAN DEFENCE CORPS (to age 50): 3,500,000.
COAST GUARD: ε4,500.
PATROL CRAFT: 74:
OFFSHORE: 10:
3 *Mazinger* (HDP-1000) (1 CG flagship).
1 *Han Kang* (HDC-1150).
6 *Sea Dragon/Whale* (HDP-600).
COASTAL: 26:
22 *Sea Wolf/Shark.*
2 *Bukhansan,* 2 *Hyundai*-type.
INSHORE: 38: 18 *Seagull*; about 20⟨, plus numerous boats.
SUPPORT AND MISCELLANEOUS: 2 salvage.
HELICOPTERS: 9 Hughes 500.

FOREIGN FORCES:
US: 36,250. Army (26,500): 1 army HQ, 1 inf div; Air Force (9,750): 1 Air Force HQ: 2 wings: 84 cbt ac, 72 F-16, 12 0A-10 SAR 2 HH-60G, 5MH -53J, recce det with 3 U-2, 2 C-12.

LAOS

GDP	1992: kip 831bn ($1.2bn): per capita $1,900	
	1993ε: kip 916bn ($1.3bn): per capita $2,000	
Growth	1992: 7.1%	1993ε: 6.0%
Inflation	1992: 9.5%	1993ε: 9.0%
Debt	1992: $1.9bn	1993: $2.0bn
Def bdgt[a]	1992: kip 72.5bn ($102.2m)	
	1993: kip 75.5bn ($104.9m)	
$1 = kip	1992: 710	1993: 720
	1994: 720	

[a] Incl Public Security budget.

Population: 4,743,600 (Phoutheung 15%, Thai 20% Hmong 10%)

	13–17	*18–22*	*23–32*
Men	248,300	209,400	333,000
Women	244,500	207,300	331,600

TOTAL ARMED FORCES:

ACTIVE: 37,000.

Terms of service: conscription, 18 months minimum.

ARMY: 33,000.

4 Military Regions.
5 inf div.
7 indep inf regt.
5 arty, 9 AD arty bn.
3 engr (2 construction) regt.
65 indep inf coy.
1 lt ac liaison flt.

EQUIPMENT:

MBT: 30 T-54/-55, T-34/85.
LIGHT TANKS: 25 PT-76.
APC: 70 BTR-40/-60/-152.
TOWED ARTY: 75mm: M-116 pack; 105mm: 25 M-101; 122mm: 40 M-1938 and D-30; 130mm: 10 M-46; 155mm: M-114.
MORTARS: 81mm; 82mm; 107mm: M-2A1, M-1938; 120mm: M-43.
RCL: 57mm: M-18/A1; 75mm: M-20; 106mm: M-40; 107mm: B-11.
AD GUNS: 14.5mm: ZPU-1/-4; 23mm: ZU-23, ZSU-23-4 SP; 37mm: M-1939; 57mm: S-60.
SAM: SA-3, SA-7.

NAVY (Army Marine Section): ε500.

PATROL CRAFT, river: some 12 PCI‹, 4 LCM, plus about 40 boats.

AIR FORCE: 3,500; 31 cbt ac; no armed hel.

FGA: 1 regt with some 29 MiG-21.
TRANSPORT: 1 sqn with 5 An-24, 2 An-26, 2 Yak-40.
HELICOPTERS: 1 sqn with 2 Mi-6, 10 Mi-8.
TRAINING: *2 MiG-21U.
AAM: AA-2 *Atoll.*

PARAMILITARY:

MILITIA SELF-DEFENCE FORCES: 100,000+: village 'homeguard' org for local defence.

OPPOSITION:

Numerous factions/groups. Total armed strength ε2,000. Largest group United Lao National Liberation Front (ULNLF).

MALAYSIA

GDP	1992: $M 140.8bn ($55.3bn): per capita $7,800	
	1993: $M 157.4bn ($61.2bn): per capita $8,400	
Growth	1992: 8.5%	1993: 8.0%
Inflation	1992: 4.8%	1993: 3.4%
Debt	1992: $19.8bn	1993: $21.4bn
Def exp	1992ε: $M 6.2bn ($2.5bn)	
	1993ε: $M 6.8bn ($2.6bn)	
Def bdgt	1992: $M 5.6bn ($2.0bn)	
	1993: $M 6.3bn ($2.5bn)	
	1994ε: $M 7.1bn ($2.8bn)	
FMA:	1995: $0.5m (IMET)	
$1 = $M	1992: 2.55	1993: 2.57
	1994: 2.69	

$M = ringgit

Population: 19,678,600 (Chinese 32%, Indian 9%)

	13–17	*18–22*	*23–32*
Men	1,025,200	915,100	1,617,700
Women	975,800	879,800	1,601,200

TOTAL ARMED FORCES:

ACTIVE: 114,500.

RESERVES: 58,300: Army 55,000; Navy 2,700; Air Force 600.

ARMY: 90,000 (reducing to 85,000).

2 Military Regions.
1 corps, 5 div HQ.
10 inf bde, consisting of 36 inf bn (1 APC, 2 AB), 4 armd, 5 fd arty, 1 AD arty, 5 engr regt.
1 SF regt (3 bn).

RESERVES: 1 bde HQ; 12 inf regt; 4 highway sy bn.

EQUIPMENT:

LIGHT TANKS: 26 *Scorpion* (90mm).
RECCE: 156 SIBMAS, 140 AML-60/-90, 92 *Ferret* (60 mod).
AIFV: 42 KIFV (incl variants).
APC: 184 V-100/-150 *Commando*, 25 *Stormer*, 460 *Condor*, 32 M-3 *Panhard.*
TOWED ARTY: 105mm: 150 Model 56 pack, 40 M-102A1 († in store); 155mm: 12 FH-70.
MORTARS: 81mm: 300.
ATGW: SS-11.
RL: 89mm: M-20.
RCL: 84mm: *Carl Gustav*; 106mm: 150 M-40.
AD GUNS: 35mm: 16 Oerlikon; 40mm: 36 L40/70.

SAM: 48 *Javelin, Starburst*, 12 *Rapier*.
ASSAULT CRAFT: 165 Damen.

NAVY: 12,000 (incl 160 Naval Air).

2 Regional Commands: plus Fleet.
Area 1: Malayan Peninsula (west of 109°E).
Area 2: Borneo Area (east of 109°E).
BASES: Area 1: Lumut (Fleet HQ), Tanjong Gelang (Area HQ), Kuantan, Woodlands (Singapore), trg base.
Area 2: Labuan (Area HQ), Sungei Antu (Sarawak), Sandakan (Sabah).
FRIGATES: 4:
2 *Kasturi* (FS-1500) with 2 x 2 ASW mor, deck for *Wasp* hel; plus 2 x 2 MM-38 *Exocet* SSM, 1 x 100mm gun.
1 *Hang Tuah* (UK *Mermaid*) with 1 x 3 *Limbo* ASW mor, hel deck for *Wasp*; plus 1 x 2 102mm gun (trg).
1 *Rahmat* with 1 x 3 ASW mor, 1 x 114mm gun hel deck.
PATROL AND COASTAL COMBATANTS: 37:
MISSILE CRAFT: 8:
4 *Handalan* (Sw *Spica*) with 4 MM-38 *Exocet* SSM.
4 *Perdana* (Fr *Combattante* II) with 2 *Exocet* SSM.
PATROL: 29:
OFFSHORE: 2 *Musytari* with 1 x 100mm gun, hel deck.
INSHORE: 27: 6 *Jerong* PFI, 3 *Kedah*, 4 *Sabah*, 14 *Kris* PCI.
MINE WARFARE: 5:
4 *Mahamiru* (mod It *Lerici*) MCO.
1 diving tender (inshore).
AMPHIBIOUS: 2:
2 *Sri Banggi* (US LST-511) LST, capacity 200 tps, 16 tk (but usually employed as tenders to patrol craft).
Plus 33 craft: 5 LCM, 13 LCU, 15 LCP.
SUPPORT AND MISCELLANEOUS: 3:
2 log/fuel spt, 1 survey.

NAVAL AIR: (160); no cbt ac, 12 armed hel.

HELICOPTERS: 12 *Wasp* HAS-1.

AIR FORCE: 12,500; 92 cbt ac, no armed hel; 4 Comd.

Average annual flying hours for FGA/fighter pilots: 200.
FGA: 2 sqn: 1 with 35 A-4 (30 A-4PTM, 5 TA-4), 1 with 10 *Hawk* 108, 6 *Hawk* 208.
FIGHTER: 1 sqn with 13 F-5E.
RECCE: 1 recce/OCU sqn with 2 RF-5E, 3 F-5F.
MR: 1 sqn with 3 C-130HMP, 4 B200T.
TRANSPORT:
AIRCRAFT: 4 sqn:
1 with 6 C-130H.
2 with 14 DHC-4.
1 with 2 BAe-125 (VIP), 1 *Falcon*-900 (VIP), 15 Cessna 402B ac.
HELICOPTERS: 4 sqn with 33 S-61A, 20 SA-316A/B (liaison).
TRAINING: ac: 11* MB-339, 39 PC-7 (12* wpn trg); **hel:** 8 SA-316, 6 Bell 47G, 4 S-61.
AAM: AIM-9 *Sidewinder*.
AIRFIELD DEFENCE TROOPS: 1 sqn.

FORCES ABROAD:

UN AND PEACEKEEPING:
ANGOLA (UNAVEM II): 1 Observer, 3 civ pol.
BOSNIA (UNPROFOR BH): 1,504; 1 inf bn gp, plus 19 Observers.
IRAQ/KUWAIT (UNIKOM): 6 Observers.
LIBERIA (UNOMIL): 25 Observers.
MOZAMBIQUE (ONUMOZ): 24 Observers, 35 civ pol.
SOMALIA: (UNOSOM II): 1,089; 1 inf bn, 5 hel, 5 civ pol.
WESTERN SAHARA (MINURSO): 6 Observers, 5 civ pol.

PARAMILITARY:

POLICE FIELD FORCE: 18,000; 4 bde HQ: 21 bn (incl 2 Aboriginal, 1 cdo), 4 indep coy; *Shorland* armd cars, 140 AT-105 *Saxon*, SB-301 APC.
MARINE POLICE: about 2,100; 48 inshore patrol craft:
15 *Lang Hitam* (38-m) PFI.
6 *Sangitan* (29-m) PFI.
27 PCI〈, plus boats.
POLICE AIR WING: 4 Cessna 206, 7 PC-6 **ac**, 1 Bell 206L3, 2 AS-355F2 **hel**.
AUXILIARY POLICE FIELD FORCE (Area Security Units): 3,500 in 89 units.
BORDER SCOUTS (in Sabah, Sarawak): 1,200.
PEOPLE'S VOLUNTEER CORPS (RELA): 168,000.
CUSTOMS SERVICE: 56 patrol craft: 6 *Perak* (Vosper 32-m) armed PFI, about 50 craft〈.

FOREIGN FORCES:

AUSTRALIA: Army: 1 inf coy; Air Force: det with 2 P-3C ac.

MONGOLIA

GDP	1992:	t 42.9bn ($357.3m)		
	1993:	t 133.9bn ($339.1m)		
Growth	1992:	-7.6%	1993:	-8.1%
Inflation	1992:	196%	1993:	380%
Debt	1992:	$9.1m	1993:	$38.1m
Def exp	1992:	t 3.1bn ($25.8m)		
Def bdgt	1992:	t 3.5bn ($29.2m)		
	1993:	t 9.2bn ($23.3m)		
	1994ε:	t 7.2bn ($18.2m)		
FMA	1993:	$0.1m (IMET)		
	1994:	$0.1m (IMET)		
	1995:	$0.1m (IMET)		
$1 = t	1992:	120.0	1993:	395.0
	1994:	408.6		

t = tugrik

Population: 2,210,000 (Kazakh 4%, Russian 2%, Chinese 2%)

	13–17	*18–22*	*23–32*
Men	131,640	117,000	189,400
Women	126,640	112,700	187,300

TOTAL ARMED FORCES:

ACTIVE: 21,250 (perhaps 12,350 conscripts).

Terms of service: conscription: males 18–28 years, 1 year.

RESERVES: Army 140,000.

ARMY: 20,000 (perhaps 12,000 conscripts).

4 MRD (3 understrength, 1 cadre).
1 arty bde.
1 AD bde.
2 indep inf bn.
1 AB bn.

EQUIPMENT:
MBT: 650 T-54/-55/-62.
RECCE: 135 BRDM-2.
AIFV: 420 BMP-1.
APC: 300 BTR-40/-60/-152.
TOWED ARTY: 300: 122mm: M-1938/D-30; 130mm: M-46; 152mm: M-1937.
MRL: 122mm: 135+ BM-21.
MORTARS: 140: 82mm, 120mm, 160mm.
ATK GUNS: 100mm: T-12.
AD GUNS: 100: 14.5mm: ZPU-4; 37mm: M-1939; 57mm: S-60.
SAM: 300 SA-7.

AIR FORCE: 1,250 (350 conscripts); 15 cbt ac; 12 armed hel.

FIGHTER: 1 sqn with 12 MiG-21.
ATTACK HELICOPTERS: 12 Mi-24.
TRANSPORT: at least 2 sqn with 15 An-2, 18 An-24, 3 An-26, 1 Tu-154.
HELICOPTERS: 1 sqn with 10 Mi-4, 4 Mi-8.
TRAINING: 2 MiG-15U, 3* MiG-21U, 3 PZL-104, 6 Yak-11, Yak-18.

PARAMILITARY:

MILITIA (Ministry of Public Security): 10,000: internal security troops, frontier guards; BTR-60/-152 APC.

FOREIGN FORCES:

RUSSIA: ε500 (SIGINT station).

NEW ZEALAND

GDP	1992:	$NZ 77.1bn ($41.5bn): per capita $14,300		
	1993:	$NZ 81.6bn ($44.1bn): per capita $15,200		
Growth	1992:	0.5%	1993:	3.6%
Inflation	1992:	1.0%	1993:	1.5%
Publ debt	1992:	54.3%	1993:	50.1%
Def exp	1992:	$NZ 1.1bn ($607.5m)		
	1993:	$NZ 1.3bn ($681.1m)		
Def bdgt	1993:	$1.3bn ($681.1m)		
	1994:	$1.3bn ($727.3m)		
$1 = $NZ	1992:	1.86	1993:	1.85
	1994:	1.76		

$NZ = New Zealand dollar

Population: 3,535,400

	13–17	*18–22*	*23–32*
Men	132,400	144,000	294,300
Women	123,900	135,100	279,100

TOTAL ARMED FORCES:

ACTIVE: 10,000 (incl 1,150 women).

RESERVES: 7,850. *Regular* 2,650: Army 1,400, Navy 1,050, Air Force 200. *Territorial* 5,200: Army 4,600, Navy 450, Air Force 150.

ARMY: 4,500 (incl 400 women).

2 Land Force Gp HQ.
1 APC/Recce regt (-).

2 inf bn.
1 arty regt (2 fd bty).
1 engr regt (-).
2 SF sqn (incl reserves).
RESERVES: Territorial Army: 6 inf bn, 4 fd arty bty, 2 armd sqn (incl 1 lt recce).
EQUIPMENT:
LIGHT TANKS: 26 *Scorpion* (18 in store).
APC: 78 M-113 (incl variants).
TOWED ARTY: 105mm: 20 M-101A1 (8 in store), 24 *Hamel.*
MORTARS: 81mm: 72.
RL: *LAW.*
RCL: 84mm: 61 *Carl Gustav.*
SURV: *Cymbeline* (mor).

NAVY: 2,200 (incl 250 women).
BASE: Auckland (Fleet HQ).
FRIGATES: 4 *Waikato* (UK *Leander*) with 1 *Wasp* hel, 2 x 3 ASTT and 3 with 2 x 114mm guns.
PATROL AND COASTAL COMBATANTS: 4:
4 *Moa* PCI (reserve trg).
SUPPORT AND MISCELLANEOUS: 4:
1 *Endeavour* AO, 1 *Monowai* AGHS, 1 *Tui* AGOR, 1 diving spt.

NAVAL AIR:
no cbt ac, 5 armed hel.
HELICOPTERS: 5 *Wasp* (see Air Force).

AIR FORCE: 3,300 (incl 500 women); 37 cbt ac, no armed hel.
Annual flying hours for A-4 pilots: 180.
OPERATIONAL GROUP:
FGA: 2 sqn with 15 A-4K, 5 TA-4K.
MR: 1 sqn with 6 P-3K *Orion.*
LIGHT ATTACK/TRG: 1 sqn for *ab initio* and ftr lead-in trg with 17 MB-339C.
ASW: 5 *Wasp* HAS-1 (Navy-assigned) (plus 2 in store and 1 being rebuilt).
TRANSPORT: 3 sqn:
AIRCRAFT: 2 sqn:
1 with 5 C-130H, 2 Boeing 727.
1 with 9 *Andover.*
HELICOPTERS: 1 sqn with 14 UH-1H, 5 Bell 47G.
SUPPORT GROUP:
TRAINING: 1 wing with 18 CT-4 ac.
MISSILES:
ASM: AGM-65B/G *Maverick.*
AAM: AIM-9L *Sidewinder.*

FORCES ABROAD:
AUSTRALIA: 50: 4 A-4*K*/TA-4K, navigation trg.
SINGAPORE: 20: spt unit.
UN AND PEACEKEEPING:
ANGOLA (UNAVEM II): 3 Observers.
BOSNIA (UNPROFOR II): 250; 1 inf coy + (deploys August 1994).
CROATIA (UNPROFOR I): 9 Observers.
EGYPT (MFO): 25.
MIDDLE EAST (UNTSO): 9 Observers.
MOZAMBIQUE (ONUMOZ): 2 Observers.
SOMALIA (UNOSOM II): 50.

PAPUA NEW GUINEA

GDP	1992:	K 4.1bn ($4.3bn): per capita $1,900	
	1993ε:	K 4.9bn ($5.0bn): per capita $2,200	
Growth	1992:	8.9%	1993ε: 14.4%
Inflation	1992:	4.7%	1993: 4.9%
Debt	1992:	$3.7bn	1993: $3.8bn
Def exp	1992:	K 56.5m	($58.9m)
	1993:	K 85.0m	($86.7m)
Def bdgt	1992:	K 56.5m	($58.9m)
	1993:	K 54.5m	($55.6m)
	1994ε:	K 54.4m	($55.5m)
$1 = K	1992:	0.96	1993: 0.98
	1994:	1.04	

K = kina

Population: 4,326,200

	13–17	*18–22*	*23–32*
Men	245,500	222,800	362,800
Women	228,900	203,800	316,000

TOTAL ARMED FORCES:
ACTIVE: about 3,800.

ARMY: 3,200.
2 inf bn.
1 engr bn.

NAVY: 500.
BASES: Port Moresby (HQ and landing-craft sqn base), Lombrum (Manus Island) (patrol boat sqn base). Forward bases at Kieta and Alotau.
PATROL AND COASTAL COMBATANTS: 4:
4 *Tarangau* (Aust *Pacific Forum* 32-m) PCI.
AMPHIBIOUS: craft only: 2 *Salamaua* (Aust

Balikpapan) LCT plus 6 other landing craft (4 civilian-manned and operated by Department of Defence).

AIR FORCE: 100; 2 cbt ac, no armed hel.

MR: 2 N-22B *Searchmaster* B.
TRANSPORT: 2 N-22B *Missionmaster*, 2 CN-235, 3 IAI-201 *Arava*.
HELICOPTERS: 4 UH-1H.

OPPOSITION:

Bougainville Revolutionary Army: 2,000+.

FOREIGN FORCES:

AUSTRALIA: 100; 2 engr unit, 75 advisers.

PHILIPPINES

GDP	1992: P 1,346.3bn ($52.8bn): per capita $2,500		
	1993: P 1,458.0bn ($55.0bn): per capita $2,600		
Growth	1992: 0.1%	1993: 1.7%	
Inflation	1992: 8.9%	1993: 7.6%	
Debt	1992: $32.6bn	1993: $33.4bn	
Def exp	1992: P 26.3bn ($1.1bn)		
Def bdgt	1992: P 29.1bn ($1.1bn)		
	1993: P 33.0bn ($1.2bn)		
	1994ε: P 34.4bn ($1.3bn)		
FMA	1993: $57.5m (Econ aid, IMET, FMF)		
	1994: $0.9m (IMET)		
	1995: $1.2m (IMET)		
$1 = P	1992: 25.5	1993: 27.1	
	1994: 27.5		

P = peso

Population: 66,501,600 (Muslim Malay 4%, Chinese 2%)

	13–17	*18–22*	*23–32*
Men:	3,889,100	3,399,900	5,516,500
Women:	3,673,800	3,205,500	5,421,800

TOTAL ARMED FORCES:

ACTIVE: 106,500.
RESERVES: 131,000: Army 100,000 (some 75,000 more have commitments); Navy 15,000; Air Force 16,000 (to age 49).

ARMY: 68,000.

5 Area Unified Comd (joint service).
8 inf div (each with 3 inf bde).
1 lt armd bde ('regt').
1 scout ranger regt.
3 engr bde; 1 construction bn.
8 arty bn.
1 SF regt.
1 Presidential Security Group.
EQUIPMENT:
LIGHT TANKS: 41 *Scorpion*.
AIFV: 85 YPR-765 PRI.
APC: 100 M-113, 20 *Chaimite*, 165 V-150, some 10 *Simba*.
TOWED ARTY: 105mm: 230 M-101, M-102, M-26 and M-56; 155mm: 12 M-114 and M-68.
MORTARS: 81mm: M-29; 107mm: 40 M-30.
RCL: 75mm: M-20; 90mm: M-67; 106mm: M-40 A1.

NAVY:† ε23,000 (incl 8,500 Marines). 6 Naval Districts.

BASES: Sangley Point/Cavite, Zamboanga, Cebu.
FRIGATES: 1:
1 *Datu Siratuna* (US *Cannon*) with ASW mor.
PATROL AND COASTAL COMBATANTS: 44:
PATROL, OFFSHORE: 9:
1 *Rizal* (US *Auk*) with hel deck.
7 *Miguel Malvar* (US PCE-827).
1 *Magat Salamat* (US-MSF).
INSHORE: 35:
2 *Aguinaldo*, 3 *Kagitingan*, 12 *Sea Hawk* PCI⟨ and about 18 other PCI⟨.
AMPHIBIOUS: 8:
2 US *F.S. Beeson*-class LST, capacity 32 tk plus 150 tps, hel deck.
Some 6 *Agusan del Sur* (US LST-1/511/542) LST, capacity: either 16tk or 10tk plus 200 tps.
Plus about 39 craft: 30 LCM, 3 LCU, some 6 LCVP.
SUPPORT AND MISCELLANEOUS: 11:
2 AOT (small), 1 repair ships, 3 survey/research, 3 spt, 2 water tankers.

NAVAL AVIATION: 8 cbt ac, no armed hel.

MR/SAR: 8 BN-2A *Defender*, 1 *Islander;* hel: 11 Bo-105 (SAR).

MARINES: (8,500).

4 bde (10 bn).
EQUIPMENT:
APC: 30 LVTP-5, 55 LVTP-7.
TOWED ARTY: 105mm: 150 M-101.
MORTARS: 4.2-in (107mm): M-30.

AIR FORCE: 15,500; 43 cbt ac, some 104 armed hel.
FIGHTER: 1 sqn with 7 F-5 (5 -A, 2 -B).
COIN: 4 sqn:
AIRCRAFT: 1 sqn with 23 OV-10 *Broncos*.
HELICOPTERS: 3 sqn with 62 Bell UH-1H/M, 16 AUH-76 (S-76 gunship conversion), 26 Hughes 500/520MD.
MR: 2 F-27M.
RECCE: 6 RT-33A.
SAR: 4 HU-16 **ac**, 10 Bo-105C **hel**.
PRESIDENTIAL AIRCRAFT WING:
AIRCRAFT: 1 F-27, 1 F-28.
HELICOPTERS: 2 Bell 212, 2 S-70A, 2 SA-330.
TRANSPORT: 3 sqn:
AIRCRAFT:
1 with 3 C-130H, 3 L-100-20, 5 C-47, 7 F-27.
2 with 22 BN-2 *Islander*, 14 N-22B *Nomad Missionmaster*.
HELICOPTERS: 2 sqn with 55 Bell 205, 17 UH-1H.
LIAISON: 7 Cessna 180, 2 Cessna 210, 1 Cessna 310, 5 DHC-2, 12 U-17A/B.
TRAINING: 4 sqn:
1 with 6 T-33A.
1 with 10 T-41D.
1 with 16 SF-260TP.
1 with 13* S-211.
AAM: AIM-9B *Sidewinder*.

PARAMILITARY:

PHILIPPINE NATIONAL POLICE (Department of Interior and Local Government): 40,500; 62,000 active auxiliary; 12 Regional, 73 Provincial Comd.
COAST GUARD: 2,000 (no longer part of Navy).
EQUIPMENT:
1 *Kalinga* PCO, 4 *Basilan* (US PGM-39/42 PCI, 2 *Tirad Pass* PCI (SAR), 4 ex-US Army spt ships, plus some 50 patrol boats, 2 lt ac.
CITIZEN ARMED FORCE GEOGRAPHICAL UNITS (CAFGU): Militia: 60,000, 56 bn. Part-time units which can be called up for extended periods.

OPPOSITION:

NEW PEOPLE'S ARMY (NPA; communist): ε8,000.
BANGSA MORO ARMY (armed wing of Moro National Liberation Front (MNLF); Muslim): ε3,300.
MORO ISLAMIC LIBERATION FRONT (breakaway from MNLF; Muslim): 3,400.
MORO ISLAMIC REFORMIST GROUP (breakaway from MNLF; Muslim): 900.

SINGAPORE

GDP	1992:	S75.0bn ($46.0bn): per capita $16,800		
	1993:	S84.0bn ($51.9bn): per capita $18,700		
Growth	1992:	5.8%	1993:	9.8%
Inflation	1992:	2.2%	1993:	2.4%
Debt	1990:	$4.2bn	1993:[a]	$0.0
Def exp	1992:	S4.1bn ($2.5bn)		
Def bdgt	1992:	S4.1bn ($2.5bn)		
	1993:	S4.3bn ($2.7bn)		
	1994:	S4.7bn ($3.0bn)		
FMA	1993:	$0.02m (IMET)		
	1995:	$0.02m (IMET)		
$1 = S	1992:	1.63	1993:	1.62
	1994:	1.56		

S = Singapore dollar

[a] Singapore is a net creditor state.

Population: 2,860,000 (Malay 15%, Indian 6%)

	13–17	*18–22*	*23–32*
Men	115,000	122,700	291,400
Women	107,600	116,500	281,000

TOTAL ARMED FORCES:

ACTIVE: 54,000 (33,800 conscripts).
Terms of service: conscription 24–30 months.
RESERVES: ε262,000: Army 250,000: annual trg to age 40 for men, 50 for officers; Navy ε4,500; Air Force ε7,500.

ARMY:

45,000 (30,000 conscripts).
3 combined arms div: 1 with 2 inf bde (each 3 inf bn), 1 mech bde, 1 recce, 2 arty, 1 AD, 1 engr bn (mixed active/reserve units, see also Reserves).
1 cdo bn.
1 arty, 1 SP mor bn.
1 engr bn.
RESERVES:
2 op reserve div, 1 mech, 6 inf bde HQ; 18 inf, 1 cdo, 10 arty, 2 AD arty, 3 engr bn.
People's Defence Force: some 30,000; org in 2 comd, 7 bde gp, ε21 bn.
EQUIPMENT:
LIGHT TANKS: ε350 AMX-13SM1.
RECCE: 22 AMX-10 PAC 90.
AIFV: 25 AMX-10P.
APC: 720 M-113, 30 V-100, 250 V-150/-200 *Commando*.
TOWED ARTY: 105mm: 36 LG1; 155mm: 38 Soltam

M-71, 16 M-114A1 (may be in store), M-68 (may be in store), 52 FH88.
MORTARS: 81mm (some SP); 120mm: 50 (some SP in M-113); 160mm: 12 Tampella.
ATGW: 30 *Milan*.
RL: *Armbrust*; 89mm: 3.5-in M-20.
RCL: 84mm: *Carl Gustav*; 106mm: 90 M-40A1 (in store).
AD GUNS: 20mm: 30 GAI-CO1 (some SP).
SAM: RBS-70 (some SP in V-200), some *Mistral*.
SURV: AN/TPQ-37 (arty, mor).
UAV: *Scout*.

NAVY: ε3,000 (800 conscripts); 3 Commands:

Fleet (1st and 3rd Flotillas), Coastal Command and Naval Logistic Command.
BASES: Pulau Brani, Tuas (Jurong).
PATROL AND COASTAL COMBATANTS: 26:
CORVETTES: 6 *Victory* (Ge Lürssen 62-m) with 8 x *Harpoon* SSM, 2 x 3 ASTT.
MISSILE CRAFT: 6 *Sea Wolf* (Ge Lürssen 45-m) PFM with 2 x 2 *Harpoon*, 2 x *Gabriel* SSM.
PATROL, INSHORE: 14:
6 *Independence/Sovereignty* (33-m).
8 *Swift*⟨, plus boats.
MINE WARFARE: 1: 1 *Bedok* (SW *Landsort*) MHC. (*Jupiter* has mine-hunting capability.)
AMPHIBIOUS: 5:
1 *Perseverance* (UK *Sir Lancelot*) LST capacity: 340 tps, 16 tk, hel deck.
4 *Endurance* (US LST-511) LST, capacity 200 tps, 16 tk, hel deck.
Plus craft: 10 LCM, 1 hovercraft and boats.
SUPPORT AND MISCELLANEOUS: 2: 1 *Jupiter* div spt and salvage, 1 trg.

AIR FORCE: 6,000 (3,000 conscripts); 155 cbt ac, 20 armed hel.

FGA: 4 sqn:
3 with 62 A-4S/SI, 13 TA-4S/SI.
1 with 7 F-16 (3 -A, 4 -B) (with a further 11 F-16A/B in USA).
FIGHTER: 2 sqn with 29 F-5E, 9 F-5F.
RECCE: 1 sqn with 8 RF-5E.
MR: 4 *Fokker* 50 *Enforcer*.
AEW: 1 sqn with 4 E-2C.
ARMED HELICOPTERS: 1 sqn with 20 AS 550A2/C2.
TRANSPORT: 5 sqn:
AIRCRAFT: 2 sqn:
1 with 4 C-130B (tkr/tpt), 6 C-130H/H-30.
1 with 6 *Skyvan* 3M (tpt/SAR).
HELICOPTERS: 3 sqn:
1 with 4 Bell 205A; 16 UH1H/B.
1 with 20 AS-332M (incl 3 SAR).
1 with 6 AS-532UL (*Cougar*).
TRAINING: 3 sqn:
2 with 27* SIAI S-211.
1 with 22 SF-260 (12 -MS, 10 -WS).
AD: 4 bn: 3 SAM, 1 arty:
1 with 10 *Rapier* (with *Blindfire*).
1 with 12 *Improved HAWK*.
1 with *Mistral*.
1 with 35mm Oerlikon (towed) guns.
AIRFIELD DEFENCE: 1 field defence sqn (reservists).
AAM: AIM-9 J/P *Sidewinder*.
ASM: AGM-65B *Maverick*.

FORCES ABROAD:

AUSTRALIA: (250); flying trg school with 27 S-211 ac.
BRUNEI: (500); trg school, incl hel det (with 5 UH-1).
TAIWAN: 4 trg camps.
UNITED STATES: 100; 11 F-16A/B leased from USAF at Luke AFB.

UN AND PEACEKEEPING:

IRAQ/KUWAIT (UNIKOM): 7 Observers.

PARAMILITARY:

POLICE/MARINE POLICE: 11,600; incl some 750 Gurkhas, 4 Swift PCI⟨, some 4 PCI and about 80 boats.
CIVIL DEFENCE FORCE: ε100,000 (incl regulars, conscripts, ε34,000 former army reservists); 1 construction bde (2,500 conscripts).

FOREIGN FORCES:

NEW ZEALAND: 20: spt unit.
US: 140: Navy (100); Air Force (40).

REPUBLIC OF CHINA (TAIPEI)

GNP	1992: $NT 5,204bn ($204.1bn): per capita $9,900	
	1993: $NT 5,789bn ($220.1bn): per capita $10,700	
Growth	1992: 6.0%	1993: 5.3%
Inflation	1992: 4.5%	1993: 2.9%
Debt	1990: $18.6bn	1993:[a] $0.0
Def exp	1992: $NT 255.8bn ($10.0bn)	

Def bdgt	1992:	$NT 262.3bn ($10.3bn)
	1993[b]:	$NT 317.9bn ($12.1bn)
	1994[b]:	$NT 298.3bn ($11.3bn)
$1 = $NT	1992: 25.5	1993: 26.3
	1994: 26.4	

$NT = New Taipei dollar

[a] Taipei is a net creditor state.
[b] Incl special appropriations for F-16 and Mirage 2000 acquisition: 1993 $NT 46.9bn; 1994 $NT 39.9bn.

Population: 21,303,000 (mainland Chinese 14%)

	13–17	*18–22*	*23–32*
Men	1,003,100	934,900	1,890,200
Women	947,800	880,300	1,797,400

TOTAL ARMED FORCES:

ACTIVE: 425,000.
Terms of service: 2 years.
RESERVES: 1,657,500: Army 1,500,000 with some Reserve obligation to age 30; Navy 32,500; Marines 35,000; Air Force 90,000.

ARMY: 289,000 (incl mil police).

3 Army, 1 AB Special Ops HQ.
10 inf div.
2 mech inf div.
2 AB bde.
6 indep armd bde.
1 tk gp.
2AD SAM gp with 5 SAM bn: 2 with *Nike Hercules*, 3 with *HAWK*.
2 avn gp, 6 avn sqn.
RESERVES: 7 lt inf div.
EQUIPMENT:
MBT: 309 M-48A5, some M-48A3, 200+ M-48H.
LIGHT TANKS: 230 M-24 (90mm gun), 675 M-41/Type 64.
AIFV: 225 M-113 with 20/30mm cannon.
APC: 650 M-113, 300 V-150 *Commando*.
TOWED ARTY: 105mm: 650 M-101 (T-64); 155mm: M-44, 90 M-59, 250 M-114 (T-65); 203mm: 70 M-115.
SP ARTY: 105mm: 100 M-108; 155mm: 45 T-69, 110 M-109A2; 203mm: 60 M-110.
MRL: 117mm: KF VI; 126mm: KF III/IV towed and SP.
MORTARS: 81mm: M-29 (some SP); 107mm.
ATGW: 1,000: *TOW* (some SP).
RCL: 90mm: M-67; 106mm: 500 M-40A1/Type 51.
AD GUNS: 40mm: 400 (incl M-42 SP, Bofors).
SAM: 40 *Nike Hercules*, 100 *HAWK*, *Tien Kung* (*Sky Bow*)-1/-2, some *Chaparral*.
AVIATION: ac: 20 O-1; **hel**; 112 UH-1H, 8 AH-1W, 4 OH-58, 12 KH-4, 7 CH-47, Hughes 500.
DEPLOYMENT:
QUEMOY: 55,000.
MATSU: 18,000.

NAVY: 68,000 (incl 30,000 Marines).

3 Naval Districts.
BASES: Tsoying (HQ), Makung (Pescadores), Keelung.
SUBMARINES: 4:
2 *Hai Lung* (Nl mod *Zwaardvis*) with 533mm TT.
2 *Hai Shih* (US *Guppy* II) with 533mm TT (trg only).
PRINCIPAL SURFACE COMBATANTS: 33:
DESTROYERS: 22:
DDG: 7 *Chien Yang* (US *Gearing*) (*Wu Chin* III conversion) with 10 x SM-1 MR SAM (boxed), plus 1 x 8 *ASROC*, 2 x 3 ASTT, plus 1 *Hughes* MD-500 hel.
DD: 15:
7 *Fu Yang* (US *Gearing*) (ASW); 5 with 1 *Hughes* MD-500 hel, 1 with 1 x 8 *ASROC*, all with 2 x 3 ASTT; plus 1 or 2 x 2 127mm guns, 3 or 5 *Hsiung Feng-I (HF-1)* (Is *Gabriel*) SSM.
4 *Po Yang* (US *Sumner*)† with 1 or 2 x 2 127mm guns; plus 2 x 3 ASTT; 5 or 6 *HF-1* SSM, 2 with 1 *Hughes* MD-500 hel.
4 *Kun Yang* (US *Fletcher*) with 2 or 3 x 127mm guns; 1 x 76mm gun; plus 2 x 3 ASTT with 5 *HF-1* SSM.
FRIGATES: 11:
FFG: 2 *Cheng Kung* with 1 x SM-1 MR SAM, 1 S-70C hel, 2 x 3 ASTT plus 2 x 4 *Hsiung Feng-II*.
FF: 9:
5 *Tien Shan* (US *Lawrence/Crosley*), some with 2 x 3 ASTT; plus 2 x 127mm guns (fishing protection and transport 160 tps).
1 *Tai Yuan* (US *Rudderow*) with 2 x 3 ASTT; plus 2 x 127mm guns.
3 J1 *Yang* (ex-US *Knox)* with 1 x 8 *ASROC*, 1 x SH-2F hel, 4 x ASTT; plus *Harpoon* (from *ASROC* launchers), 1 x 127mm gun.
PATROL AND COASTAL COMBATANTS: 97:
MISSILE CRAFT: 52:
2 *Lung Chiang* PFM with 2 x *HF-1* SSM.
50 *Hai Ou* (mod Is *Dvora*)⟨ with 2 x *HF-1* SSM.
PATROL, INSHORE: 45 (operated by marine police):
22 Vosper-type 32-m PFI, 7 PCI and about 16 PCI⟨.
MINE WARFARE: 13:
MINELAYERS: nil, but *Tai Yuan* has capability.
MINE COUNTERMEASURES: 13:
9 *Yung Chou* (US *Adjutant*) MSC.
4 MSC converted from oil rig spt ships.

AMPHIBIOUS: 21:
1 *Kao Hsiung* (US LST 511) amph comd.
14 *Chung Hai* (US LST 511) LST, capacity 16 tk, 200 tps.
4 *Mei Lo* (US LSM-1) LSM, capacity about 4 tk.
1 *Cheng Hai* (US *Cabildo*) LSD, capacity 3 LCU or 18 LCM.
1 *Chung Cheng* (US Ashland) LSD, capacity 3 LCU or 18 LCM.
Plus about 400 craft: 22 LCU, some 260 LCM, 120 LCVP.
SUPPORT AND MISCELLANEOUS: 19:
3 spt tankers, 2 repair/salvage, 1 *Wu Yi* combat spt with hel deck, 2 *Yuen Feng* and 2 *Wu Kang* attack tpt with hel deck, 2 tpt, 7 ocean tugs.
COASTAL DEFENCE: 1 SSM coastal def bn with *Hsiung Feng* (*Gabriel* type).

NAVAL AIR: 32 cbt ac; 22 armed hel.
MR: 1 sqn with 32 S-2 (25 -E, 7 -G) (Air Force-operated).
HELICOPTERS: 1 sqn with 12 Hughes 500MD ASW *Defender*, 10 S-70C(M)-1.

MARINES: (30,000).
2 div, spt elm.
EQUIPMENT:
AAV: LVTP-4/-5.
TOWED ARTY: 105mm, 155mm.
RCL: 106mm.

AIR FORCE: 68,000; 459 cbt ac, no armed hel.
5 cbt wings.
Average anuual flying hours for F-5A, F-104 pilots: 180.
FGA/FIGHTER: 10 sqn with 277 F-5 (-B: 8, -E: 215, -F: 54).
4 sqn with 94 F-104 (models incl D/DJ, G, J and TF).
22 *Ching-Kuo* (10 testing).
RECCE: 1 sqn with 6 RF-104G.
SAR: 1 sqn with 14 S-70.
TRANSPORT: 8 sqn:
AIRCRAFT: 2 with 8 C-47, 1 C-118B, 1 DC-6B.
3 with 30 C-119G.
1 with 12 C-130H.
1 VIP with 4 -727-100, 12 Beech 1900.
HELICOPTERS: 5 CH-34, 1 S-62A (VIP), 14 S-70.
TRAINING: ac, incl 60* AT-3A/B, 20 T-38A, 42 T-34C.
MISSILES:
ASM: AGM-65A *Maverick*.
AAM: AIM-4D *Falcon*, AIM-9J/P *Sidewinder*, *Shafrir*.

PARAMILITARY:
SECURITY GROUPS: 25,000:
National Police Administration (Ministry of Interior); Bureau of Investigation (Ministry of Justice); Military Police (Ministry of Defence).
MARITIME POLICE: ε1,000 with about 38 armed patrol boats. They also man many of the patrol craft listed under Navy.
CUSTOMS SERVICE (Ministry of Finance): 650; 5 PCO, 2 PCC, 1 PCI, 5 PCI‹; most armed.

FOREIGN FORCES:
SINGAPORE: 4 trg camps.

THAILAND

GDP	1992: b 2,671bn ($105.2bn): per capita $5,700	
	1993: b 2,931bn ($115.8bn): per capita $6,200	
Growth	1992: 7.0%	1993: 7.3%
Inflation	1992: 4.1%	1993: 3.5%
Debt	1992: $39.4bn	1993: $41.4bn
Def exp	1992: b 73.2bn ($2.9bn)	
Def bdgt	1992: b 68.8bn ($2.7bn)	
	1993: b 78.9bn ($3.2bn)	
	1994ε: b 85.6bn ($3.5bn)	
FMA	1993: $6.3m (IMET, Narcs)	
	1994: $3.4m (IMET, Narcs)	
	1995: $2.3m (IMET, Narcs)	
$1 = b	1992: 25.4	1993: 25.3
	1994: 25.3	

b = baht

Population: 59,521,000 (Chinese 14%)

	13–17	*18–22*	*23–32*
Men	3,104,600	3,042,500	5,539,000
Women	3,006,600	2,949,500	5,409,000

TOTAL ARMED FORCES:
ACTIVE: 256,000.
Terms of service: conscription, 2 years.
RESERVES: 200,000.

ARMY: 150,000 (80,000 conscripts).
4 Regional Army HQ, 2 Corps HQ.
1 armd div.
1 cav (lt armd) div (2 cav, 1 arty regt).
2 mech inf div.
7 inf div (incl Royal Guard, 5 with 1 tk bn) (1 to be mech, 1 to be lt).

2 SF div.
1 arty div, 1 AD arty div (6 AD arty bn).
19 engr bn.
1 indep cav regt.
8 indep inf bn.
4 recce coy.
Armd air cav regt with 3 air-mobile coy.
Some hel flt.

RESERVES: 3 inf div HQ.

EQUIPMENT:

MBT: 50+ Ch Type-69 (in store), 150 M-48A5, 53 M-60.

LIGHT TANKS: 154 *Scorpion*, 250 M-41, 106 *Stingray*.

RECCE: 32 *Shorland* Mk 3.

APC: 340 M-113, 150 V-150 *Commando*, 450 Ch Type-85 (YW-531H).

TOWED ARTY: 105mm: 200 M-101/-101 mod, 12 M-102, 32 M-618A2 (local manufacture); 130mm: 15 Ch Type-59; 155mm: 56 M-114, 62 M-198, 32 M-71.

MORTARS: 81mm, 107mm.

ATGW: *TOW*, 300 *Dragon*.

RL: M-72 *LAW*.

RCL: 75mm: M-20; 106mm: 150 M-40.

AD GUNS: 20mm: 24 M-163 *Vulcan*, 24 M-167 *Vulcan*; 37mm: 122 Type-74; 40mm: 80 M-1/M-42 SP, 28 L/70; 57mm: 24.

SAM: *Redeye*, some *Aspide*.

AVIATION:

TRANSPORT: 1 Beech 99, 4 C-47, 10 Cessna 208, 1 Short 330, 1 *Beech King Air*.

LIAISON: 62 O-1A, 17 -E, 5 T-41A, 13 U-17A.

TRAINING: 16 T-41D.

HELICOPTERS:

ATTACK: 4 AH-1F.

TRANSPORT: 10 Bell 206, 9 Bell 212, 6 Bell 214, 70 UH-1H.

TRAINING: 36 Hughes 300C, 3 OH-13, 7 TH-55.

SURV: RASIT (veh, arty), AN-TPQ-36 (arty, mor).

NAVY: 63,000 (incl 1,150 Naval Air, 20,000 Marines, Coastal Defence and Coast Guards, and 26,000 conscripts).

3 Fleets:
- 1st: East Thai Gulf.
- 2nd: West Thai Gulf.
- 3rd: Andaman Sea.

2 Naval Air Wings.

BASES: Bangkok, Sattahip (Fleet HQ), Songkhla, Phang Nga, Nakhon Phanom (HQ Mekong River Operating Unit), Trat.

FRIGATES: 9:

FFG: 4:

2 *Chao Phraya* (Ch *Jianghu*-III) with 8 x C-801 SSM, 2 x 2 100mm guns; plus 2 x 5 ASW RL.

2 *Kraburil* (Ch *Jianghu*-IV type) with 8 x C-801 SSM, 1 x 2 100mm guns; plus 2 x 5 ASW RL and *Bell* 212 hel.

FF: 5:

1 *Makut Rajakumarn* with 2 x 3 ASTT (*Sting Ray* LWT); plus 2 x 114mm guns.

2 *Tapi* (US PF-103) with 2 x 3 ASTT (Mk 46 LWT).

2 *Tachin* (US *Tacoma*) with 2 x 3 ASTT (trg).

PATROL AND COASTAL COMBATANTS: 62:

CORVETTES: 5:

2 *Rattanakosin* with 2 x 3 ASTT (*Sting Ray* LWT); plus 2 x 4 *Harpoon* SSM.

3 *Khamronsin* with 2 x 3 ASTT; plus 1 x 76mm gun.

MISSILE CRAFT: 6:

3 *Ratcharit* (It Breda 50-m) with 4 x MM-38 *Exocet* SSM.

3 *Prabparapak* (Ge Lürssen 45-m) with 5 *Gabriel* SSM.

PATROL: 51:

COASTAL: 11:

3 *Chon Buri* PFC, 6 *Sattahip*, 2 *Sarasin* (US PC-461) PCC.

INSHORE: 40: 7 T-11 (US PGM-71), about 33 PCI⟨.

MINE WARFARE: 6:

2 *Bang Rachan* (Ge Lürssen T-48) MCC.

3 *Ladya* (US *'Bluebird'* MSC) MSC.

1 *Thalang* MCM spt with minesweeping capability.

(Plus some 5 MSB.)

AMPHIBIOUS: 9:

2 *Sichang* (Fr PS-700) LST, capacity 14 tk, 300 tps with hel deck (trg).

5 *Angthong* (US LST-511) LST, capacity 16 tk, 200 tps.

2 *Kut* (US LSM-1) LSM, capacity about 4 tk.

Plus about 50 craft: 9 LCU, about 24 LCM, 1 LCG, 2 LSIL, 3 hovercraft, 12 LCVP.

SUPPORT AND MISCELLANEOUS: 11:

1 *Chula* AO, 4 small tankers, 3 survey, 3 trg (incl 1 *Pin Klao* (US *Cannon*) (plus 2 *Tachin* FF and 2 *Sichang* LST listed above).

NAVAL AIR: (1,150); 21 cbt ac; 8 armed hel.

MR/ASW: 3 P-3A *Orion*, 3 Do-228, 3 F-27 MPA, 5 N-24A *Searchmaster* L, 7 S-2F.

ASW HELICOPTERS: 8 Bell 212 ASW.

MR/SAR: 1 sqn with 2 CL-215.

MR/ATTACK: 10 Cessna T-337 *Skymasters*.

SAR: 1 hel sqn with 8 Bell 212, 2 Bell 214, 4 UH-1H.
ASM: AGM-84 *Harpoon* (for F-27MPA).

MARINES: (20,000).
1 div HQ, 6 inf regt, 1 arty regt (3 fd, 1 AA bn); 1 amph aslt bn; recce bn.
EQUIPMENT:
APC: 33 LVTP-7.
TOWED ARTY: 155mm: 18 GC-45.
ATGW: *TOW*, *Dragon*.

AIR FORCE: 43,000; 191 cbt ac, no armed hel.
FGA: 1 sqn with 8 F-5A, 4 -B.
14 F-16A, 4 -B.
FIGHTER: 2 sqn with 37 F-5E, 6 -F.
COIN: 7 sqn:
1 with 15 A-37B.
1 with 7 AC-47.
3 with 24 AU-23A.
2 with 30 OV-10C.
ELINT: 1 sqn with 3 IAI-201.
RECCE: 3 RF-5A, 3RT-33A.
SURVEY: 2 *Learjet* 35A, 3 *Merlin* IVA, 2 *Queen Air*.
TRANSPORT: 4 sqn:
1 with 3 C-130H, 3 C-130H-30, 3 DC-8-62F.
1 with 10 C-123B/-K, 6 BAe-748.
1 with 10 C-47.
1 with 20 N-22B *Missionmaster*.
VIP: Royal flight: 1 Boeing 737-200, 1 *King Air* 200, 3 *Merlin* IV **ac**; 2 Bell 412 **hel**.
TRAINING: 24 CT-4, 31 *Fantrainer*-400, 16 *Fantrainer* -600, 16 SF-260, 10 T-33A, 20 PC-9, 13 T-37B, 6 -C, 11 T-41, 36* L-39ZA/MP.
LIAISON: 3 *Commander*, 2 *King Air* E90, 30 O-1 *Bird Dog*.
HELICOPTERS: 2 sqn:
1 with 18 S-58T.
1 with 21 UH-1H.
AAM: AIM-9B/J *Sidewinder, Python* 3.
AD: *Blowpipe* and *Aspide* SAM. 1 AA arty bty: 4 *Skyguard*, 1 *Flycatcher* radars, each with 4 fire units of 2 x 30mm Mauser guns.

FORCES ABROAD:
UN AND PEACEKEEPING:
IRAQ/KUWAIT (UNIKOM): 6 Observers.

PARAMILITARY:
THAHAN PHRAN ('Hunter Soldiers'): 18,500 volunteer irregular force; 27 regt of some 200 coy.
NATIONAL SECURITY VOLUNTEER CORPS: 50,000.
MARINE POLICE: 2,500; 3 PCO, 3 PCC, 8 PFI, some 110 PCI‹.
POLICE AVIATION: 500; 1 *Airtourer*, 3 AU-23, 1 C-47, 2 Cessna 310, 1 CT-4, 3 DHC-4, 1 Do-28, 4 PC-6, 1 Short 330 **ac**; 27 Bell 205A, 14 Bell 206, 3 Bell 212, 6 UH-12, 5 KH-4, 1 S-62 **hel**.
BORDER PATROL POLICE: 40,000.
PROVINCIAL POLICE: ε50,000, incl Special Action Force (ε500).

VIETNAM

GDP[a]	1992: $16.0bn: per capita $700	
	1993: $17.6bn: per capita $800	
Growth	1992: 8.0%	1993: 7.5%
Inflation	1992: 20.0%	1993: 5.2%
Debt	1992: $16.4bn	1993: $17.8bn
Def exp[a]	1992ε: d 8,020bn ($720.0m)	
Def bdgt[a]	1993: d 3,200bn ($304.8m)	
	1994: d 4,700bn ($435.2m)	
$1 = d	1992: 11,145	1993: 10,500
	1994: 10,800	

d = dong

[a] ppp est.

Population: 72,725,600 (Chinese 3%, Montagnard 1–5%)

	13–17	*18–22*	*23–32*
Men	4,099,600	3,706,800	6,332,200
Women	3,966,000	3,546,300	6,259,000

TOTAL ARMED FORCES:
ACTIVE: 572,000 (referred to as 'Main Force').
Terms of service: 2 years, specialists 3 years, some ethnic minorities 2 years.
RESERVES: 'Strategic Rear Force', some 3–4m manpower potential (see also Paramilitary).

ARMY: 500,000.
8 Military Regions, 2 special areas.
14 Corps HQ.
50 inf div.[a]
3 mech div.
10 armd bde.
15 indep inf regt.
SF incl AB bde, demolition engr regt.
Some 10 fd arty bde.
8 engr div.
10–16 economic construction div; 20 indep engr bde.

EQUIPMENT:
MBT: 1,300: T-34/-54/-55, T-62, Ch Type-59, M-48A3.
LIGHT TANKS: 600 PT-76, Ch Type-62/63.
RECCE: 100 BRDM-1/-2.
AIFV: 300 BMP.
APC: 1,100 BTR-40/-50/-60/-152, YW-531, M-113.
TOWED ARTY: 2,300: 76mm; 85mm; 100mm: M-1944, T-12; 105mm: M-101/-102; 122mm: Type-54, Type-60, M-1938, D-30, D-74; 130mm: M-46; 152mm: D-20; 155mm: M-114.
SP ARTY: 152mm: 30 2S3; 175mm: M-107.
COMBINED GUN/MORTAR: 120mm: 2S9 reported.
ASSAULT GUNS: 100mm: SU-100; 122mm: ISU-122.
MRL: 107mm: 360 Type 63; 122mm: 350 BM-21; 140mm: BM-14-16.
MORTARS: 82mm, 120mm: M-43; 160mm: M-43.
ATGW: AT-3 *Sagger*.
RCL: 75mm: Ch Type-56; 82mm: Ch Type-65, B-10; 87mm: Ch Type-51.
AD GUNS: 12,000: 14.5mm; 23mm: incl ZSU-23-4 SP; 30mm; 37mm; 57mm; 85mm; 100mm.
SAM: SA-7/-16.

[a] Inf div strengths vary from 5,000 to 12,500.

NAVY: ε42,000 (incl 30,000 Naval Infantry).
Four Naval Regions.
BASES: Hanoi (HQ), Cam Ranh Bay, Da Nang, Haiphong, Ha Tou, Ho Chi Minh City, Can Tho, plus several smaller bases.
FRIGATES: 7:
1 *Phan Ngu Lao* (US *Barnegat*) (ASUW), with 2 x SS-N-2 *Styx* SSM, 1 x 127mm gun.
5 Sov *Petya-II* with 4 x ASW RL, 3 x 533mm TT.
1 *Dai Ky* (US *Savage*) with 2 x 3 ASTT (trg).
PATROL AND COASTAL COMBATANTS: 55:
MISSILE CRAFT: 8 Sov *Osa -I I* with 4 x SS-N-2 SSM.
TORPEDO CRAFT: 19:
3 Sov *Turya* PHT with 4 x 533mm TT.
16 Sov *Shershen* PFT with 4 x 533mm TT.
PATROL: 28:
INSHORE: 28:
8 Sov SO-1, 3 US PGM-59/71, 11 *Zhuk*⟨, 4⟨, 2 Sov *Turya* (no TT).
MINE WARFARE: 11:
2 *Yurka* MSC, 4 *Sonya* MSC, 2 Ch *Lienyun* MSC, 1 *Vanya* MSI, 2 *Yevgenya* MSI, plus 5 K-8 boats.
AMPHIBIOUS: 7:
3 US LST-510-511 LST, capacity 200 tps, 16 tk.
3 Sov *Polnocny* LSM, capacity 180 tps, 6 tk.
1 US LSM-1 LSM, capacity about 50 tps, 4 tk.
Plus about 30 craft: 12 LCM, 18 LCU.
SUPPORT AND MISCELLANEOUS: 30+, incl:
1 survey, 4 small tankers, about 12 small tpt, 2 ex-Sov Floating Docks and 3 div spt.
NAVAL INFANTRY: (30,000) (amph, cdo).

AIR FORCE: 15,000; 190 cbt ac, 33 armed hel
(plus many in store). 4 Air Div.
FGA: 1 regt: with 65 Su-22.
FIGHTER: 5 regt with 125 MiG-21bis/PF.
ATTACK HELICOPTERS: 25 Mi-24.
MR: 4 Be-12.
ASW HEL: 8 Ka-25.
SURVEY: 2 An-30.
TRANSPORT: 3 regt: incl 12 An-2, 4 An-24, 30 An-26, 8 Tu-134, 14 Yak-40.
HELICOPTERS: some 70, incl Mi-4, Mi-6, Mi-8.
TRAINING: 3 regt with 53 ac, incl L-39, MiG-21U.
AAM: AA-2 *Atoll*.

AIR DEFENCE FORCE: 15,000.
14 AD div:
SAM: some 66 sites with SA-2/-3/-6.
4 AD arty bde: 37mm, 57mm, 85mm, 100mm, 130mm; plus People's Regional Force: ε1,000 units.
6 radar bde: 100 sites.

PARAMILITARY:
LOCAL FORCES: some 4–5m, incl People's Self-Defence Force (urban units), People's Militia (rural units); comprise: static and mobile cbt units, log spt and village protection pl; some arty, mor and AD guns; acts as reserve.
BORDER DEFENCE CORPS: ε50,000.

FOREIGN FORCES:
RUSSIA: 500: naval base; 1 Tu-142, 8 Tu-16 MR ac on det; AA, SAM, ELINT monitoring system.

Caribbean and Latin America

This year the Caribbean and Latin America section is divided into three regions: Caribbean; Central America; and Latin America.

CARIBBEAN

Political Developments

In Haiti the military regime is still in control and President Jean-Bertrand Aristide remains in the US. In August 1993 one of Aristide's aides was nominated prime minister and the UN Security Council suspended its arms and oil embargo against the country. Violence, however, continued, and in October, following a UN vote, a force comprising US engineers and Canadian Mounted Police was prevented from landing at Haiti. The UN reimposed its arms and oil embargo which was enforced by naval ships from several countries, but smuggling across the Dominican border seriously undermined this effort. International patience is clearly running out. At the Organisation of American States (OAS) annual assembly in June 1994, although several countries argued against military intervention, a number openly supported it. The US call for tighter sanctions was supported, and a commitment to a peaceful solution was noticeably lacking from the final communiqué. The US House of Representatives has voted to withdraw its formal request to President Clinton not to use force. On 31 July 1994 the UN Security Council authorised a multinational force to use 'all necessary means' to facilitate the return of President Aristide.

Military Developments

There have been few military developments in the Caribbean. The Cuban Army is undergoing major reorganisation; manpower strength has been reduced by 60,000 to some 85,000, and is now structured on a brigade as opposed to a divisional basis. No more than 20% of front-line combat aircraft are considered operational. The Defence Budget is said to be being cut by some 50%.

CENTRAL AMERICA

Political Developments

Unrest and guerrilla activity continue to plague the region.

In **El Salvador,** the first election in which the Farabundo Martí National Liberation Front (FMLN) stood as a political party took place in March 1994. The right-wing Arena party failed to win an outright majority at the first ballot, but secured almost 70% of the vote in the second round in April. The FMLN claims that the promise of land for many demobilised soldiers and guerrillas has not yet materialised. Nor has the new civil police force taken over, as had been planned, from the military-controlled police, and there are fears that some 'death squads' could still be intact. The mandate of the UN mission in El Salvador (ONUSAL) has now been extended until November 1994, and a report by the UN into the murder of several senior FMLN officials in late 1993 will not now be presented until the end of July 1994 and is expected to show that 'death squads' do still exist.

In March 1994, the **Guatemalan** government and the opposition coalition, the Unidad Revolucionaria Nacional Guatemalteca (URNG), signed an agreement which may bring an end to the guerrilla conflict. The agreement includes commitments to: demobilisation; setting up a commission to investigate human-rights abuses; and talks leading to a lasting peace settlement by the end of 1994. Since this agreement, violence has re-erupted and, after a number of assassinations – including that of the President of the Constitutional Court – and attacks on foreigners, the Army has been placed in charge of internal security. Government talks with the URNG began again, this time in Oslo, in June 1994. Also in June, the Standing Committee of the Caribbean Community and Common Market (CARICOM) meeting in Belize expressed concern over

Guatemala's renewed territorial claim to Belize. CARICOM urged Guatemala to conclude a treaty recognising Belize's land and sea borders.

In January 1994 there was an uprising in the southern **Mexican** province of Chiapas where the rebel force, Ejército Zapatista de Liberación Nacional (EZLN), claiming to represent the surviving Mayan indians, seized four towns. The government swiftly deployed troops, retook the towns and the Zapatistas withdrew into the jungle. Peace talks began in mid-February and a draft plan covering health, housing, education and community respect was agreed in early March. Later that month the presidential candidate of the ruling Institutional Revolutionary Party (PRI) was assassinated. Peace talks resumed in April, but in June the Zapatistas rejected the draft plan complaining that land reform and indigenous rights were insufficient, and demanding a change in the political system. Interruption of the elections, due on 21 August 1994, has been ruled out, but the rebels are hoping that a provisional government will be formed which will draft a new constitution.

In **Nicaragua**, the last of the Contra rebels agreed to lay down their arms in late February 1994 and were granted an amnesty. In May, President Violeta Chamorro announced that General Ortega would retire from the Army in February 1995.

Military Developments

In **Belize**, the withdrawal of the UK garrison has begun and is due to be completed by the end of 1994. So far 900 of the 1,500 servicemen there have returned home. The Belizean Army has increased its manpower strength by 300 to 900. In **El Salvador**, the Air Force has added six more O-2A COIN aircraft to its inventory. The **Mexican** Navy has commissioned four *Isla Coronada*-class inshore patrol craft with a range of 1,200 miles at 30 knots.

LATIN AMERICA

Political Developments

Colombia is no less violent and unstable, despite, in December 1993, the detection and death in a shoot-out with the police of Pablo Escobar, the leading drug baron. Guerrillas of the Revolutionary Armed Forces of Colombia (FARC) continue their campaign of anti-government violence, and at least ten congressional candidates were murdered during the campaign which elected Ernesto Samper, the ruling Liberal Party's candidate, as President. The drug cartels continue in business and Amnesty International has accused the government and Army of implication in mass murder. The only hopeful sign has been the surrender of weapons by some 600 rebels belonging to three groups who have been granted an amnesty. In May 1994 the US Air Force ended the surveillance in Colombia by AWACS aircraft and ground-based radars which had greatly increased the interception rate of drug-trafficking aircraft over the last four years. One reason given for this closure is that the Colombian authorities have adopted a shoot-down policy in respect of planes without flight plans. US authorities feared they could be liable for damages if US-provided information was deemed responsible for deaths.

The optimism felt in 1993 that violence in **Peru** was coming to an end has not been sustained. The guerrilla war conducted by the *Sendero Luminoso* (Shining Path), revived in September and December 1993, witnessed a number of attacks in Lima. The Army is now mounting what has been described as the final offensive against *Sendero Luminoso* some 300 miles north-east of Lima along the Huallaga River.

Nuclear and Arms-Control Developments

While Argentina, Brazil, Chile and Cuba have yet to accede to the Nuclear Non-Proliferation Treaty (NPT), a number of positive steps have been taken. The Brazilian–Argentine Agency for Accounting and Control of Nuclear Materials (ABACC) was formed in July 1992, and by September 1993 had carried out rather less than half the 60 nuclear-site inspections planned for completion by the end of 1993. In December 1991 an agreement was reached by the two governments, ABACC and the International Atomic Energy Agency (IAEA) providing for full-scope safeguards that bring nuclear materials and plants under both bilateral (ABACC) and international (IAEA) safeguards. Although the Argentinean Congress ratified the agreement in August 1992, it was not until September 1993 that the Brazilian Chamber of Deputies gave its approval, followed by the Senate in February 1994, and the agreement came into force on 4 March 1994.

The Treaty for the Prohibition of Nuclear Weapons in Latin America and the Caribbean, or Treaty of Tlatelolco, was intended to establish a nuclear weapons-free zone stretching from the US–Mexican border to Antarctica. Opened for signature in 1967, it was only on 18 January 1994 that Argentina and Chile signed the Treaty in respect of their territories. Brazil joined the Treaty on 30 May 1994 leaving Cuba the only country still to join, although it has said several times that it will join once all the other states in the region have done so.

Military Developments

The **Argentinean** Air Force has acquired 32 A-4M FGA and four OA-4M FAC aircraft from the US and a further nine IA-58A *Puccara* COIN aircraft from domestic production. In June 1994, President Carlos Menem announced that he would abolish compulsory military service; currently there are some 18,000 conscripts who serve an average of 12 months in the forces. The move is reported to be unpopular with the military leadership who, although they favour an all-volunteer force, wish to introduce this over a four-to-five-year transitional period. The end of conscription will be highly popular in the country. During 1992, the **Bolivian** Army acquired 36 Chinese 122m type-54 towed artillery pieces and the Air Force 18 Chinese 37mm type-65 AD guns. The **Brazilian** Air Force now has ten more AT-26 COIN aircraft, six more AMX FGA aircraft and four more in-flight refuelling tankers (four KC-137). The Navy has commissioned a fourth *Inhauma*-class frigate. There are reports that Brazil will buy a number of Russian shoulder-launched SAM (SA-18). In **Chile**, the Navy has commissioned two more *Micalvi*-class coastal patrol craft with a fourth scheduled to commission in June 1994, and has acquired five P-3 *Orion* maritime reconnaissance aircraft and three more AS-322 ASW helicopters. The Air Force has retired more *Hunter* FGA – only ten are still in service – and has contracted to buy 25 Mirage 5 from Belgium. The Air Force has also received its first in-flight refuelling tankers, two Boeing 707 converted in Israel, as well as a number of *Python* short-range air-to-air missiles from Israel. The **Colombian** Army has formed an additional, thirteenth brigade and a fourth COIN brigade is planned. The **Peruvian** Navy has retired its three *Abtao*-class (US *Mackerel*) submarines and one *Palacios*-class (UK *Daring*) destroyer. **Uruguay** has retired 12 AT-33 and T-33A COIN aircraft. The **Venezuelan** Navy awaits US Congress approval for the lease of two *Knox*-class frigates later this year.

THE CARIBBEAN

THE BAHAMAS

GDP	1992ε: $B 3.5bn ($3.5bn): per capita $10,700	
	1993ε: $B 3.7bn ($3.7bn): per capita $11,100	
Growth	1992: 4.5%	1993: 1.3%
Inflation	1992: 5.8%	1993: 4.0%
Debt	1992: $485.3m	1993: $582.9m
Def exp	1992: $B17.8m ($17.8m)	
Def bdgt	1993: $B18.3m ($18.3m)	
	1994: $B26.4m ($26.4m)	
FMA	1993: $1.3m (Narcs, IMET)	
	1994: $0.7m (Narcs)	
	1995: $0.7m (Narcs)	
$1 = $B	1992–94: 1.0	

$B = Bahamian dollar

Population: 273,400

	13–17	*18–22*	*23–32*
Men	15,200	16,100	27,000
Women	13,900	15,100	27,200

TOTAL SECURITY FORCES:
ACTIVE: 2,550: Police (1,700); Defence Force (850).

NAVY (ROYAL BAHAMIAN DEFENCE FORCE): 830 (incl 50 women).
BASE: Coral Harbour, New Providence Island.
PATROL AND COASTAL COMBATANTS: 12:
INSHORE: 3 *Yellow Elder* PFI, 1 *Marlin*, 3 *Fenrick Sturrup* (ex-USCG *Cape Higgon* Cl) PCI, 5 PCI‹ , plus some ex-fishing vessels and boats.
MISCELLANEOUS: 2: 1 converted LCM (ex-USN), 1 small auxiliary.
AIRCRAFT: 1 Cessna 404, 1 Cessna 421.

CUBA

GDP	1992ε: $13.2bn:	
	per capita $1,200	
	1993ε: $11.37bn:	
	per capita $1,000	
Growth	1992ε: -28%	1993: -16%
Inflation	1992ε: 35%	1993ε: 47%
Debt[a]	1992: $6.8bn	1993ε: $7.0bn
Def bdgt	1992ε: $500m	
	1993ε: $426m	
	1994ε: $266m	
$1 = pC[b]	1993: 0.76	1994: 0.75

pC = Cuban peso

[a] Excl debt to former COMECOM countries, ε$35–40bn.
[b] Official exchange rates. Informal market rates were about pC100 to $1 in 1994.

Population: 11,002,600

	13–17	*18–22*	*23–32*
Men	409,200	510,400	1,113,000
Women	383,300	479,500	1,060,800

TOTAL ARMED FORCES:
ACTIVE: 106,000 (incl Ready Reserves; 74,500 conscripts).
Terms of service: 2 years.
RESERVES: Army: 135,000 Ready Reserves (serve 45 days per year) to fill out Active and Reserve units; see also Paramilitary.

ARMY: ε85,000 (incl Ready Reservists and conscripts).
HQ: 4 Regional Command: 3 Army, 1 Isle of Youth.
4–5 armd bde (Cat A).
ε9 mech inf bde (3 mech inf, 1 armd, 1 arty, 1 AD arty regt) (Cat B).
1 AB bde (Cat A).
14 reserve bde.
1 frontier bde.
AD: AD arty regt and SAM bde (Cat varies: SAM εCat A, AD arty B or C).
Forces combat readiness system: Cat A fully manned by active tps; Cat B: partial manning augmented by reservists on mob; Cat C: active cadre, full manning by reservists on mob.
EQUIPMENT:
MBT: 1,575: 75 T-34 (in store), 1,100 T-54/-55, 400 T-62.
LIGHT TANKS: 50 PT-76.
RECCE: 100 BRDM-1/-2.
AIFV: 400 BMP-1.
APC: 800 BTR-40/-50/-60/-152.
TOWED ARTY: 620: 76mm: M-1942; 122mm: M-1931/37, D-74; 130mm: M-46; 152mm: M-1937, D-20, D-1.
SP ARTY: 40: 122mm: 2S1; 152mm: 2S3.
MRL: 300: 122mm: BM-21; 140mm: BM-14.
MORTARS: 1,000: 82mm: M-41/-43; 120mm: M-38/-43.
STATIC DEFENCE ARTY: some 15 JS-2 (122mm) hy tk, T-34 (85mm), SU-100 (100mm) SP guns.
ATGW: AT-1 *Snapper*, AT-3 *Sagger*.
ATK GUNS: 200: 85mm: D-44; 100mm: SU-100 SP.
AD GUNS: 500 incl 23mm: ZU-23, ZSU-23-4 SP; 30mm: M-53 (twin)/BTR-60P SP; 37mm: M-1939; 57mm: S-60 towed, ZSU-57-2 SP; 85mm: KS-12; 100mm: KS-19.
SAM: ε1,600: SA-6/-7/-8/-9/-13/-14.

NAVY: ε6,000 (ε3,000 conscripts).
2 Naval Districts: Western: HQ Cabanas; Eastern: HQ Holquin. 4 Operational Flotillas.
BASES: Cienfuegos, Cabanas, Havana, Mariel, Punta Movida, Nicaro.
SUBMARINES: some 2 Sov *Foxtrot*† with 533mm and 406mm TT.
FRIGATES: 3 Sov *Koni* with 2 x ASW RL.
PATROL AND COASTAL COMBATANTS: 24:
MISSILE CRAFT: 17:
17 Sov *Osa-I/-II* with 4 x SS-N-2 *Styx* SSM.
TORPEDO CRAFT: some of *Turya* listed below have 4 x 533mm TT.
PATROL: 7:
COASTAL: 1:
1 Sov *Pauk* II PFC with 2 x ASW RL, 4 x ASTT.
INSHORE: some 6 Sov *Turya* PHT.

MINE WARFARE: 15:
3 Sov *Sonya* MSC.
12 Sov *Yevgenya* MSI.
AMPHIBIOUS: 2 Sov *Polnocny* LSM, capacity 6 tk, 180 tps.
SUPPORT AND MISCELLANEOUS: 2:
1 AGI, 1 survey.

NAVAL INFANTRY: (550+).
2 amph aslt bn.

COASTAL DEFENCE:
ARTY: 122mm: M-1931/37; 130mm: M-46; 152mm: M-1937.
SSM: 2 SS-C-3 systems.

AIR FORCE: ε15,000 (incl AD and conscripts);
130† cbt ac, 85 armed hel.
Annual flying hours: less than 50.
FGA: 2 sqn with 10 MiG-23BN.
FIGHTER: 4 sqn:
2 with 30 MiG-21F, 1 with 50 MiG-21bis, 1 with 20 MiG-23MF, 6 MiG-29.
(Probably only some 3 MiG-29, 10 MiG-23, 11 MiG-21bis in operation.)
ATTACK HELICOPTERS: 20 Mi-8, 40 Mi-17, 20 Mi-25.
ASW: 5 Mi-14 hel.
TRANSPORT: 4 sqn: 8 An-2, 3 An-24, 21 An-26, 2 An-32, 4 Yak-40, 2 Il-76 (Air Force ac in civilian markings).
HELICOPTERS: 60 Mi-8/-17.
TRAINING: 25 L-39, 8* MiG-21U, 4* MiG-23U, 2* MiG-29UB, 20 Z-326.
MISSILES:
ASM: AS-7.
AAM: AA-2, AA-7, AA-8, AA-10, AA-11.
SAM: 200+ SAM launchers: SA-2, SA-3.
Civil Airline: 10 Il-62, 7 Tu-154, 12 Yak-42 used as troop tpt.

PARAMILITARY:
YOUTH LABOUR ARMY: 100,000.
CIVIL DEFENCE FORCE: 50,000.
TERRITORIAL MILITIA (R): 1,300,000.
STATE SECURITY (Ministry of Interior): 15,000.
BORDER GUARDS (Ministry of Interior): 4,000; about 27 Sov *Zhuk* and 3 Sov *Stenka* PFI‹, plus boats.

FOREIGN FORCES:
US: 2,240: Navy: 1,900; Marine: 340: 1 reinforced coy at Guantánamo Bay.
RUSSIA: 810: 800 SIGINT personnel; ε10 mil advisers.

DOMINICAN REPUBLIC

GDP	1992:	pRD 99.8bn ($7.8bn): per capita $3,200		
	1993:	pRD 105.5bn ($8.3bn): per capita $3,400		
Growth	1992:	7.7%	1993:	3.8%
Inflation	1992:	6.6%	1993:	3.0%
Debt	1992:	$4.7bn	1993:	$4.7bn
Def bdgt	1993:	pRD 1,371.0m ($108.8m)		
	1994ε:	pRD 1,511.4m ($116.0m)		
FMA	1993:	$0.8m (IMET)		
	1994:	$0.3m (IMET)		
	1995:	$0.2m (IMET)		
$1 = pRD	1992:	12.8	1993:	12.7
	1994:	13.0		

pRD = peso República Dominicana

Population: 7,582,000

	13–17	*18–22*	*23–32*
Men	422,800	390,900	684,400
Women	409,400	379,800	668,400

TOTAL ARMED FORCES:
ACTIVE: 24,500.

ARMY: 15,000.
5 Defence Zones.
5 inf bde (with 9 inf, 7 constabulary bn).
1 armd, 1 Presidential Guard, 1 arty, 1 engr bn.
EQUIPMENT:
LIGHT TANKS: 2 AMX-13 (75mm), 12 M-41A1 (76mm).
RECCE: 8 V-150 *Commando*.
APC: 20 M-2/M-3 half-track.
TOWED ARTY: 105mm: 22 M-101.
MORTARS: 81mm: M-1; 120mm: 24 ECIA.

NAVY: 4,000 (incl marine security unit and 1 SEAL unit).
BASES: Santo Domingo (HQ), Las Calderas.
PATROL AND COASTAL COMBATANTS: 17:
OFFSHORE: 9:
1 *Mella* (Cdn *River*) (comd/trg).
3 *Cambiaso* (US *Cohoes*).
3 armed ocean tugs (ex USCG *Argo*-class).
2 *Prestol* (US *Admirable*).
INSHORE: 8: 1 *Betelgeuse* (US PGM-71), 1 *Capitan Alsina* (trg), some 6 PCI‹. .
AMPHIBIOUS: craft only: 1 LCU.

SUPPORT AND MISCELLANEOUS: 4:
1 AOT (small harbour), 3 ocean tugs.

AIR FORCE: 5,500; 10 cbt ac, no armed hel.
Annual flying hours: probably less than 60.
COIN: 1 sqn with 8 A-37B.
TRANSPORT: 1 sqn with 3 C-47, 1 *Commander* 680, 1 MU-2.
LIAISON: 1 Cessna 210, 4 O-2A, 2 PA-31, 3 *Queen Air* 80, 1 *King Air*.
HELICOPTERS: 8 Bell 205, 1 OH-6A, 2 SA-318C, 1 SA-365 (VIP).
TRAINING: 2* AT-6, 6 T-34B, 3 T-41D.
AB: 1 SF (AB) bn.
AD: 1 bn with 4 20mm guns.

PARAMILITARY:
NATIONAL POLICE: 15,000.

HAITI

GDP	1992ε: G 17.5bn ($2.9bn)	
	per capita $1,100	
	1993ε: G 19.0bn ($2.6bn):	
	per capita $1,000	
Growth	1992ε: -10%	1993ε: -11%
Inflation	1992ε: 20.1%	1993ε: 60.0%
Debt	1991: $804.0m	1993: $866.1m
Def bdgt	1991: G 147m ($29.4m)	
	1992ε: G 328m ($55.0m)	
	1993ε: G 438m ($60.0m)	
$1 = G	1992: 6.0	1993: 11.8
	1994: 12.0	

G = gourde

Population: 7,019,200

	13–17	*18–22*	*23–32*
Men	386,000	343,900	545,200
Women	379,500	339,800	550,800

TOTAL ARMED FORCES:
ACTIVE: 7,300.

ARMY: 7,000 (has police/gendarmerie, fire-fighting, immigration, etc, roles).
1 HQ defence unit (4 inf coy); 1 hy wpn coy.
9 military departments (27 coy).
EQUIPMENT:
APC: 5 M-2, 6 V-150 *Commando*.
TOWED ARTY: 75mm: 5 M-116; 105mm: 4 M-101.
MORTARS: 60mm: 36 M-2; 81mm: M-1.
ATK GUNS: 37mm: 10 M-3A1; 57mm: 10 M-1.
RCL: 57mm: M-18; 106mm: M-40A1.
AD GUNS: 20mm: 6 TCM-20, 4 other; 40mm: 6 M-1.

NAVY: ε150 (Coast Guard).
BASE: Port au Prince.
PATROL CRAFT: boats only.

AIR FORCE: 150; 5 cbt ac, no armed hel.
COIN: 5 Cessna 0-2/337.
TRANSPORT: 1 *Baron*, 1 DHC-6.
TRAINING: 3 Cessna 150, 3 Cessna 172, 5 SF-260TP, 1 *Twin Bonanza*.

JAMAICA

GDP	1992: $J 73.0bn ($3.0bn):	
	per capita $3,800	
	1993: $J 76.4bn ($3.1bn):	
	per capita $4,000	
Growth	1992: 1.2%	1993: 1.2%
Inflation	1992: 41.5%	1993: 30.0%
Debt	1992: $4.3bn	1993: $4.7bn
Def bdgt	1992: $J 590.6m ($25.7m)	
	1993: $J 673.1m ($27.2m)	
	1994: $J 702.3m ($28.4m)	
FMA:	1993: $0.5m (IMET)	
	1994: $0.2m (IMET)	
	1995: $1.4m (Narcs, IMET)	
$1 = $J	1992: 23.0	1993: 24.7
	1994: 29.4	

$J = Jamaican dollar

Population: 2,500,000

	13–17	*18–22*	*23–32*
Men	133,900	134,800	227,800
Women	128,700	129,900	233,800

TOTAL ARMED FORCES (all services form combined Jamaican Defence Force):
ACTIVE: some 3,320.
RESERVES: some 870: Army 800; Coast Guard 50; Air Wing 20.

ARMY: 3,000.
2 inf bn, 1 spt bn.
EQUIPMENT:
APC: 14 V-150 *Commando*.
MORTARS: 81mm: 12 L16A1.
RESERVES: 800: 1 inf bn.

COAST GUARD: ε150.
BASE: Port Royal.
PATROL CRAFT, INSHORE: 4:
1 *Fort Charles* PFI (US 34-m), 3 PFI⟨, plus boats.

AIR WING: 170; no cbt ac, no armed hel.
AIRCRAFT: 2 BN-2A, 1 Cessna 210, 1 Cessna 337, 1 *King Air*.
HELICOPTERS: 3 Bell 205, 1 Bell 205A, 4 Bell 206, 3 Bell 212.

TRINIDAD AND TOBAGO

GDP	1992: $TT 23.1bn ($5.4bn): per capita $8,600	
	1993: $TT 23.5bn ($5.5bn): per capita $8,700	
Growth	1992: -0.6%	1993: -1.0%
Inflation	1992: 8.5%	1993: 17.0%
Debt	1992: $2.3bn	1993: $2.2bn
Def bdgt	1992ε: $TT 314.5m ($74.0m)	
	1993ε: $TT 423.0m ($79.0m)	
	1994: $TT 483.7m ($83.4m)	
FMA	1993: $0.05 (IMET)	
$1 = $TT	1992: 4.3	1993: 5.4
	1994: 5.8	

$TT = Trinidad and Tobago dollar

Population: 1,288,000

	13–17	*18–22*	*23–32*
Men	63,700	56,800	105,300
Women	62,400	56,100	110,300

TOTAL ARMED FORCES (all services are part of the Army):
ACTIVE: 2,600.

ARMY: 2,000.
2 inf bn.
1 spt bn.
EQUIPMENT:
MORTARS: 60mm: ε40; 81mm: 6 L16A1.
RL: 82mm: 13 B-300.
RCL: 84mm: *Carl Gustav*.

COAST GUARD: 600 (incl 50 Air Wing).
BASE: Staubles Bay (HQ), Hart's Cut, Point Fortin, Tobago.
PATROL CRAFT, INSHORE: 9 (some non-op):
2 *Barracuda* PFI (Sw *Karlskrona* 40-m).
7 PCI⟨, plus boats and 3 ex-marine police spt vessels.
AIR WING: 1 Cessna 310, 1 Cessna 402, 1 Cessna 172.

PARAMILITARY:
POLICE: 4,800.

CENTRAL AMERICA

BELIZE

GDP	1992: $BZ 936.1m ($468.1m): per capita $2,300	
	1993: $BZ 994.2m ($497.1m): per capita $2,400	
Growth	1992: 7.6%	1993: 3.5%
Inflation	1992: 2.8%	1993: 2.5%
Debt	1992: $170.1m	1993: $180.0m
Def bdgt	1992ε: $BZ 16m ($8m)	
	1993ε: $BZ 20m ($10m)	
	1994ε: $BZ 22m ($11m)	
FMA[a]	1993: $0.15m (IMET)	
	1994: $0.05m (IMET)	
$1 = $BZ	1992–93: 2.00	1994: 1.99

$BZ = Belize dollar

[a] UK MOD defence expenditure in Belize amounted to $55m in 1992–93 and $51m in 1993–94.

Population: 209,600

	13–17	*18–22*	*23–32*
Men	12,300	12,100	18,000
Women	12,300	12,100	18,000

TOTAL ARMED FORCES:
ACTIVE: 950.
RESERVES: 700 (militia): (400 volunteers).

ARMY: 900.
1 inf bn (3 inf, 1 spt, 1 trg, 3 Reserve coy).
EQUIPMENT:
MORTARS: 81mm: 6.
RCL: 84mm: 8 *Carl Gustav*.
MARITIME WING: 50.
PATROL CRAFT: 1 PCI⟨, plus some 8 armed boats and 3 ramped lighters.

AIR WING: 15: 2 cbt ac, no armed hel.
MR/TRANSPORT: 2 BN-2B *Defender*.

FOREIGN FORCES:

UK: ε600. Army: 1 engr sqn, 1 hel flt (to have withdrawn by December 1994).

COSTA RICA

GDP	1992: C 878bn ($6.5bn):	
	per capita $5,600	
	1993: C 1,007bn ($7.1bn):	
	per capita $6,100	
Growth	1992: 7.3%	1993: 5.7%
Inflation	1992: 18.2%	1993: 11.2%
Debt	1992: $4.0bn	1993: $3.9bn
Sy bdgt[a]	1992ε: C 11.9bn ($88.1m)	
	1993: C 13.6bn ($95.5m)	
	1994: C 14.6bn ($95.7m)	
FMA	1993: $0.2m (IMET)	
	1994: $0.1m (IMET)	
	1995: $0.5m (IMET)	
$1 = C	1992: 134.5	1993: 142.2
	1994: 152.7	

C = colon

[a] No armed forces. Budgetary data are for policing and internal security.

Population: 3,170,800

	13–17	*18–22*	*23–32*
Men	159,700	141,900	268,800
Women	153,500	136,600	259,800

TOTAL SECURITY FORCES:

ACTIVE: 7,500 (Paramilitary).

CIVIL GUARD: 4,300 (incl ε400 Marines).

2 Border Sy Comd (North, South).
2 COIN bn.
Presidential Guard: 1 bn, 11 inf coy.
MARINE: (ε400).
PATROL CRAFT, INSHORE: 7:
1 *Isla del Coco* (US *Swift* 32-m) PFI, 1 *Astronauta Franklin Chang* (US *Cape Higgon*) PCI, 5 PCI⟨; plus about 10 boats.
AIRCRAFT: 4 Cessna 206, 1 *Commander* 680, 3 O-2 (surveillance), 2 PA-23, 3 PA-28, 1 PA-31, 1 PA-34.
HELICOPTERS: 2 Hughes 500E, 1 Hiller FH-1100.

RURAL GUARD (Ministry of Government and Police): 3,200; small arms only.

GUATEMALA

GDP	1992: q 54.3bn ($10.5bn):	
	per capita $3,400	
	1993: q 63.1bn ($11.2bn):	
	per capita $3,700	
Growth	1992: 4.6%	1993: 4.0%
Inflation	1992: 13.7%	1993: 18.9%
Debt	1992: $2.8bn	1993: $3.6bn
Def bdgt	1992: q 565.0m ($109.2m)	
	1993: q 634.2m ($112.6m)	
	1994: q 634.2m ($112.6m)	
FMA	1993: $2.8m (Narcs, IMET)	
	1994: $2.1m (Narcs, IMET)	
	1995: $2.6m (Narcs)	
$1 = q	1992: 5.2	1993: 5.6
	1994: 5.8	

q = quetzal

Population: 10,337,000

	13–17	*18–22*	*23–32*
Men	620,400	517,700	767,000
Women	603,100	504,400	755,100

TOTAL ARMED FORCES (National Armed Forces are combined; the Army provides log spt for Navy and Air Force):

ACTIVE: 44,200 (30,000 conscripts).
Terms of service: conscription; selective, 30 months.
RESERVES: Army ε35,000 (trained), Navy (some), Air Force 200.

ARMY: 42,000 (30,000 conscripts).

19 Military Zones (39 inf, 1 trg bn, 6 armd sqn).
2 strategic bde (6 inf, 1 lt armd bn, 1 recce sqn, 2 arty bty).
1 SF gp (3 coy incl 1 trg).
2 AB bn.
1 inf bn gp (3 inf coy, 1 recce sqn, 1 AA bty).
1 MP bn.
1 Presidential Guard bn.
1 engr bn.
EQUIPMENT:
LIGHT TANKS: 10 M-41A3.
RECCE: 8 M-8, 10 RBY-1.
APC: 9 M-113, 7 V-100 *Commando*, 30 *Armadillo*.
TOWED ARTY: 75mm: 10 M-116; 105mm: 4 M-101, 8 M-102, 56 M-56.
MORTARS: 81mm: 55 M-1; 107mm: 12 M-30; 120mm: 18 ECIA.
RL: 89mm: 3.5-in M-20.

RCL: 57mm: M-20; 105mm: 64 Arg M-1968; 106mm: M-40A1.
AD GUNS: 20mm: 16 M-55, 20 GA1-BO1.
RESERVES: ε19 inf bn.

NAVY: ε1,500 (incl some 650 Marines).
BASES: Santo Tomás de Castilla (Atlantic), Puerto Quetzal (Pacific).
PATROL CRAFT, INSHORE: 9:
1 *Kukulkan* (US *'Broadsword'* 32-m) PFI, 8 PCI‹, plus boats.

MARINES: (some 650); 2 under-strength bn.

AIR FORCE: 700; 14† cbt ac, 7 armed hel. Serviceability of ac is less than 50%.
COIN: 1 sqn with 2 Cessna A-37B, 8 PC-7, 4 IAI-201.
ARMED HELICOPTERS: 6 Bell 212, 1 Bell 412.
TRANSPORT: 1 sqn with 1 C-47, 2 T-67 (mod C-47 *Turbo*), 2 F-27, 1 *Super King Air* (VIP), 1 DC-6B.
LIAISON: 1 sqn with 3 Cessna 206, 1 Cessna 310.
HELICOPTERS: 1 sqn with 9 Bell 206, 5 UH-1D/-H, 3 S-76.
TRAINING: 6 T-41.

PARAMILITARY:
NATIONAL POLICE: 10,000.
TREASURY POLICE: 2,500.
TERRITORIAL MILITIA (R) (CVDC): ε500,000.

OPPOSITION:
UNIDAD REVOLUCIONARIA NACIONAL GUATEMALTECA (URNG): some 800–1,100; coalition of 3 main groups: Ejército Guerrillero de los Pobres (EGP): 300–400; Fuerzas Armadas Rebeldes (FAR): ε300–400; Organización del Pueblo en Armas (ORPA): 200–300.

MEXICO

GDP	1992: Np 1,003.2bn ($323.6bn): per capita $7,600		
	1993: Np 1,034.4bn ($333.7bn): per capita $7,800		
Growth	1992: 2.6%	1993: 0.5%	
Inflation	1992: 11.9%	1993: 8.0%	
Debt	1992: $113.4bn	1993ε: $110.3bn	
Def bdgt	1992: Np 4.7bn ($1.5bn)		
	1993: Np 4.7bn ($1.5bn)		
	1994: Np 4.9bn ($1.6bn)		
FMA	1993: $0.7m (IMET)		
	1995: $0.2m (IMET)		
$1[a] = Np	1992: 3.09	1993: 3.11	
	1994: 3.11		

Np = new peso

[a] The new peso, equal to 1,000 pesos, was introduced on 1 January 1993.

Population: 93,086,800

	13–17	*18–22*	*23–32*
Men	5,265,100	5,137,200	8,312,700
Women	5,082,400	4,996,100	8,269,700

TOTAL ARMED FORCES:
ACTIVE: 175,000 (60,000 conscripts).
Terms of service: 1 year conscription (4 hours per week) by lottery.
RESERVES: 300,000.

ARMY: 130,000 (incl ε60,000 conscripts).
36 Zonal Garrisons: incl 1 armd, 19 mot cav, 1 mech inf, 7 arty regt, plus 3 arty, 80 inf bn. 1 armd bde (3 armd, 1 mech inf regt).
1 Presidential Guard bde (4 inf, 1 arty bn).
1 mot inf bde (3 mot inf regt).
2 inf bde (each 3 inf bn, 1 arty bn).
1 AB bde (3 bn).
AD, engr and spt units.
EQUIPMENT:
RECCE: 50 M-8, 120 ERC-90F *Lynx*, 40 VBL, 70 DN-3/-5 *Caballo*, 30 MOWAG, 40 Mex-1.
APC: 40 HWK-11, 30 M-3 halftrack, 40 VCR/TT.
TOWED ARTY: 75mm: 18 M-116 pack; 105mm: 16 M-2A1/M-3, 60 M-101, 24 M-56.
SP ARTY: 75mm: 5 M-8.
MORTARS: 81mm: 1,500; 120mm: 20 *Brandt*.
ATGW: *Milan* (incl 8 VBL).
ATK GUNS: 37mm: 30 M-3.
AD GUNS: 12.7mm: 40 M-55.

NAVY: 37,000 (incl 1,100 Naval Aviation and 8,000 Marines).
6 Navy regions covering 2 areas:
Gulf: 6 Naval Zones.
Pacific: 11 Naval Zones.
BASES: Gulf: Vera Cruz (HQ), Tampico, Chetumal, Ciudad del Carmen, Yukalpetén, Lerna, Frontera, Coatzacoalcos, Isla Mujéres.
Pacific: Acapulco (HQ), Ensenada, La Paz, San Blas, Guaymas, Mazatlán, Manzanillo, Salina Cruz, Puerto Madero, Lázaro Cárdenas, Puerto Vallarta.

PRINCIPAL AND SURFACE COMBATANTS: 5:
DESTROYERS: 3:
2 *Ilhuicamina* (ex-*Quetzalcoatl*) (US *Gearing*) ASW with 1 x 8 *ASROC*, 2 x 3 ASTT; plus 2 x 2 127mm guns and 1 Bo-105 hel.
1 *Cuitlahuac* (US *Fletcher*) with 5 x 533mm TT, 5 x 127mm guns.
FRIGATES: 2:
2 *H. Galeana* (US *Bronstein*) with 1 x 8 ASROC, 2 x 3 ASTT.
PATROL AND COASTAL COMBATANTS: 104:
PATROL, OFFSHORE: 44:
4 *S.J. Holzinger* (ex *Uxmal*) (imp *Uribe*) with Bo-105 hel.
6 *Cadete Virgilio Uribe* (Sp '*Halcon*') with Bo-105 hel.
1 *Comodoro Manuel Azueta* (US *Edsall*) (trg).
3 *Zacatecas* (US *Lawrence/Crosley*) with 1 x 127mm gun.
17 *Leandro Valle* (US *Auk* MSF).
1 *Guanajuato* with 2 x 102mm gun.
12 D-01 (US *Admirable* MSF), 3 with hel deck.
PATROL, INSHORE: 40:
4 *Isla Coronada* PFI.
31 *Quintana Roo* (UK *Azteca*) PCI.
3 ex-US *Cape Higgon* PCI.
2 ex-US *Point* PCI⟨.
PATROL, RIVER: 20⟨.
AMPHIBIOUS:
2 *Panuco* (US-511) LST.
SUPPORT AND MISCELLANEOUS: 22:
3 AOT, 1 PCI spt, 4 log spt, 6 ocean tugs, 5 survey, 1 *Durango* tpt, plus 2 other tpt.

NAVAL AVIATION: (1,100); 9 cbt ac, no armed hel.
MR: 1 sqn with 9 C-212, 5 HU-16B/D (SAR).
MR HEL: 12 Bo-105 (8 afloat).
TRANSPORT: 1 C-212, 2 Cessna 180, 3 Cessna 310, 1 DHC-5, 1 FH-227, 1 *King Air* 90, 1 *Learjet* 24.
HELICOPTERS: 3 Bell 47, 4 SA-319, 2 UH-1H, 4 MD-500 (trg).
TRAINING: 8 Cessna 152, 2 Cessna 337, 2 Cessna 402, 10 F-33C Bonanza.

MARINES: (8,000).
3 bn (incl 1 Presidential Guard).
15 gp.
EQUIPMENT:
AMPH VEH: 25 VAP-3550.
TOWED ARTY: 105mm: 8 M-56.
MORTARS: 100 incl 60mm, 81mm.
RCL: 106mm: M-40A1.

AIR FORCE: 8,000 (incl 1,500 AB bde); 101 cbt ac, 25 armed hel.
FIGHTER: 1 sqn with 9 F-5E, 2 -F.
COIN: 5 sqn:
3 with 40 PC-7.
1 with 15 AT-33.
1 hel with 5 Bell 205, 5 Bell 206, 15 Bell 212.
RECCE: 1 photo sqn with 10 *Commander* 500S.
SAR: 1 sqn with 5 IAI-201.
TRANSPORT: 5 sqn with 2 BN-2, 12 C-47, 1 C-54, 10 C-118, 9 C-130A, 5 *Commander* 500, 1 -680, 5 DC-6 *Skytrain*, 2 F-27.
HELICOPTERS: 4 Bell-205, 12 Bell-206, 15 Bell-212, 3 SA-330, 2 UH-60.
PRESIDENTIAL TRANSPORT: ac: 7 Boeing 727, 2 Boeing 737, 1 L-188, 3 FH-227, 2 *Merlin*; **hel:** 1 AS-332, 2 SA-330, 2 UH-60.
LIAISON/UTILITY: 2 *King Air*, 1 *Musketeer*, 40 *Beech Bonanza* F-33A, 10 *Beech, Musketeer*.
TRAINING: ac: 20 CAP-10, 20 PC-7, 5 T-39 *Sabreliner*, 35* AT-33; **hel:** 10 MD 530F (SAR/paramilitary/trg).

FORCES ABROAD:
UN AND PEACEKEEPING:
EL SALVADOR (ONUSAL): 39 civ pol.

PARAMILITARY:
RURAL DEFENCE MILITIA (R): 14,000.

NICARAGUA

GDP	1992:	Co 9.2bn ($1.5bn):		
		per capita $2,600		
	1993:	Co 9.4bn ($1.6bn):		
		per capita $2,650		
Growth	1992:	-0.5%	1993:	-0.7%
Inflation	1992:	9.9%	1993:	25.9%
Debt	1992:	$11.1bn	1993:	$10.9bn
Def exp	1992ε:	$214.5m		
	1993ε:	$210.0m		
Def bdgt	1994:	Co 466.3m ($72.9m)		
$1 = Co	1992:	5.5	1993:	6.0
	1994:	6.4		

Co = Cordoba oro

Population: 4,374,600

	13–17	*18–22*	*23–32*
Men	260,600	218,800	331,900
Women	253,100	225,500	336,000

TOTAL ARMED FORCES:

ACTIVE: 15,200.

Terms of service: voluntary, 18–36 months.

RESERVES: ε150,000.

ARMY: ε13,500.

Reorganisation in progress.
7 Regional Commands.
1 mech inf bde (4 mech inf, 1 tk bn).
1 arty bde (3bn).
1 SF bn.
13 inf coy.

EQUIPMENT:

MBT: some 130 T-55 (in store).
LIGHT TANKS: 22 PT-76.
RECCE: 79 BRDM-2.
APC: 20 BTR-60, 102 BTR-152.
TOWED ARTY: 122mm: 36 D-30, 332 *Grad* 1P (single-tube rocket launcher); 152mm: 60 D-20.
MRL: 107mm: 33 Type-63; 122mm: 18 BM-21.
MORTARS: 82mm: 579; 120mm: 24 M-43; 160mm: 4 M-160.
ATGW: AT-3 *Sagger* (12 on BRDM-2).
ATK GUNS: 57mm: 354 ZIS-2; 76mm: 83 Z1S-3.
SAM: 400+ SA-7/-14/-16.

NAVY: ε500.

BASES: Corinto, Puerto Cabezzas, El Bluff.
PATROL AND COASTAL COMBATANTS: 10:
PATROL, INSHORE: 10†:
2 Sov *Zhuk* PFI⟨, 2 N. Korea *Sin Hung* PFI⟨, 6 PCI⟨.
MINE COUNTERMEASURES: 5†:
2 Sov *Yevgenya*, 3 K-8 MSI⟨.

AIR FORCE: 1,200; no cbt ac, 2 armed hel.

ATTACK HELICOPTERS: 2 Mi-25.
TRANSPORT: 8 An-2, 5 An-26.
HELICOPTERS: 19 Mi-8/-17.
UTILITY/TRAINING: ac: 1 Cessna 172, 1 Cessna 185, 1 Cessna 404, 2 *Piper* PA-18, 2 *Piper* PA-28; **hel:** 5 Mi-2.
ASM: AT-2 *Swatter* ATGW.
AD GUNS: 700: 14.5mm: ZEU-1, ZPU-1/-2/-4; 23mm: ZU-23-2; 37mm: M-1939; 57mm: S-60; 100mm: KS-19.

OPPOSITION:

FRENTE NORTE: ε1,200 (former Contra rebels), perhaps 500 armed.

PANAMA

GDP	1992:	B6.0bn ($6.0bn):		
	per capita $5,500			
	1993:	B6.6bn ($6.6bn):		
	per capita $6,000			
Growth	1992:	8.0%	1993:	5.9%
Inflation	1992:	1.8%	1993:	0.5%
Debt	1992:	$6.5bn	1993:	$6.4bn
Def bdgt	1992:	B75.0m ($75.0m)		
	1993:	B79.0m ($79.0m)		
	1994:	B85.8m ($85.8m)		
$1 = B	1992–94:	1.0		
B = balboa				

Population: 2,590,800

	13–17	*18–22*	*23–32*
Men	138,400	133,800	233,200
Women	132,200	128,800	227,500

TOTAL PUBLIC FORCES:

ACTIVE: 11,700.

NATIONAL POLICE FORCE: 11,000.

Presidential Guard bn (-).
1 MP bn plus 8 coys.
18 Police coy.
No hy mil eqpt, small arms only.

NATIONAL MARITIME SERVICE: ε300.

BASES: Amador (HQ), Balboa, Colón.
PATROL CRAFT:
INSHORE: 7:
2 *Panquiaco* (UK Vosper 31.5-m), 1 *Tres de Noviembre* (ex-USCG *Cape Higgon*), 3 ex-US MSB 5-class, 1⟨ (plus about 4 other ex-US patrol/spt craft⟨.
AMPHIBIOUS: craft only: 6 LCM.

NATIONAL AIR SERVICE: 400.

TRANSPORT: 1 CN-235-2A, 1 BN-2B, 1 PA-34, 3 CASA-212M *Aviocar*.
TRAINING: 9 T-35D.
HELICOPTERS: 2 Bell 205, 3 Bell 212, 1 UH-H, 1-N.

FOREIGN FORCES:

US: 7,100. Army: 3,800; 1 inf bde (1 inf bn) and spt elm. Navy: 700. Marines: 200. Air Force: 2,400; 1 air div.

LATIN AMERICA

ARGENTINA

GDP	1992: P 226.6bn ($102.0bn): per capita $5,700	
	1993ε: P 255.0bn ($110.3bn): per capita $6,200	
Growth	1992: 8.6%	1993: 5.4%
Inflation	1992: 24.9%	1993: 7.4%
Debt	1992: $65bn	1993: $68bn
Def exp	1992: P 4.3bn ($2.6bn)	
	1993ε: P 4.4bn ($2.7bn)	
Def bdgt	1993: P 4.1bn ($2.5bn)	
	1994: P 4.7bn ($2.8bn)	
FMA	1993: $0.3m (IMET)	
	1994: $0.1m (IMET)	
	1995: $0.1m (IMET)	
$1 = P[a]	1992: 0.99	1993: 0.99
	1994: 1.00	

P = Argentinean peso

[a] The peso Argentino, equal to 10,000 australes, was introduced on 1 January 1992. The official rate shown above is pegged to the US$. Dollar values are calculated according to the estimated real effective exchange rate. For defence accounts, a defence-specific purchasing-power-parity estimate has been calculated.

Population: 33,735,400

	13–17	*18–22*	*23–32*
Men	1,601,500	1,450,200	2,449,600
Women	1,553,100	1,411,000	2,398,300

TOTAL ARMED FORCES:

ACTIVE: 69,800 (18,400 conscripts).

Terms of service: all services up to 14 months; conscripts may actually serve less than 7 months.

RESERVES: 377,000: Army 250,000 (National Guard 200,000; Territorial Guard 50,000); Navy 77,000; Air 50,000.

ARMY: 40,400 (13,400 conscripts).

3 Corps:
- 1 with 1 armd, 1 mech bde, 1 trg bde.
- 1 with 1 inf, 1 mtn bde.
- 1 with 1 armd, 2 mech, 1 mtn bde.

Corps tps: 1 lt armd cav regt (recce), 1 arty, 1 AD arty, 1 engr bn in each Corps.

Strategic Reserve:

1 AB bde.

1 mech bde (4 mech, 1 armd cav, 2 SP arty bn).

Army tps:

1 mot inf bn (Army HQ Escort Regt).

1 mot cav regt (Presidential Escort).

1 SF coy, 3 avn bn.

1 AD arty bn, 2 engr bn.

EQUIPMENT:

MBT: 266: 96 M-4 *Sherman*, 170 TAM.

LIGHT TANKS: 60 AMX-13, 106 SK-105 *Kuerassier*.

RECCE: 50 AML-90.

AIFV: 30 AMX-VCI, some 160 *TAM* VCTP.

APC: ε75 M-3 half-track, 240 M-113, 80 MOWAG *Grenadier* (mod *Roland*).

TOWED ARTY: 250: 105mm: 150 M-56; 155mm: 100 CITEFA Models 77/-81.

SP ARTY: 50: 155mm: Mk F3, L33.

MRL: 105mm: 30 SLAM *Pampero*; 127mm: 20 SLAM SAPBA-1.

MORTARS: 81mm: 1,000; 120mm: 130 *Brandt* (some SP in VCTM AIFV).

ATGW: 600 SS-11/-12, *Cobra (Mamba)*, 2,100 *Mathogo*.

RCL: 75mm: 75 M-20; 90mm: 100 M-67; 105mm: 150 M-1968.

AD GUNS: 20mm: 130; 30mm: 40; 35mm: 15 GDF-001; 40mm: 80 L/60, 15 L/70; 90mm: 20.

SAM: *Tigercat*, *Blowpipe*, *Roland*, SAM-7.

SURV: RASIT (veh, arty), *Green Archer* (mor).

AIRCRAFT: 5 Cessna 207, 5 *Commander* 690, 2 DHC-6, 3 G-222, 1 *Merlin* IIIA, 4 *Merlin* IV, 3 *Queen Air*, 1 *Sabreliner*, 5 T-41, 12 OV-1D.

HELICOPTERS: 6 A-109, 3 AS-332B, 5 Bell 205, 4 FH-1100, 4 SA-315, 2 SA-330, 9 UH-1H, 8 UH-12.

NAVY: 20,500 (incl 3,000 Naval Aviation, 4,000 Marines and 3,500 conscripts).

3 Naval Areas: Centre: from River Plate to 42° 45' S; South: from 42° 45' S to Cape Horn; and Antarctica.

BASES: Buenos Aires, Ezeiza (naval air), La Plata, Rio Santiago (submarine base), Puerto Belgrano (HQ Centre), Punta Indio (naval air), Mar del Plata (submarine base), Ushuaia (HQ South).

SUBMARINES: 2:

2 *Santa Cruz* (Ge TR-1700) with 533mm TT (SST-4 HWT).

Plus 2 non-op *Salta* (Ge T-209/1200) with 533mm TT (SST-4 HWT) (both in major refit/modernisation).

PRINCIPAL SURFACE COMBATANTS: 13:

DESTROYERS: 6:

2 *Hercules* (UK Type 42) with 1 x 2 *Sea Dart* SAM; plus 1 SA-319 hel (ASW), 2 x 3 ASTT, 4 x MM-38 *Exocet* SSM, 1 x 114mm gun.

4 *Almirante Brown* (Ge *MEKO-360*) ASW with 2 x SA-316 hel, 2 x 3 ASTT; plus 8 x MM-40 *Exocet* SSM, 1 x 127mm gun.

FRIGATES: 7:

4 *Espora* (Ge *MEKO-140*) with 2 x 3 ASTT, hel deck; plus 8 x MM-40 *Exocet*.

3 *Drummond* (Fr A-69) with 2 x 3 ASTT; plus 4 x MM-38 *Exocet*, 1 x 100mm gun.

ADDITIONAL IN STORE: 1 CVS: 1 *Veinticinco de Mayo* (UK *Colossus*).

PATROL AND COASTAL COMBATANTS: 14:

TORPEDO CRAFT: 2 *Intrepida* (Ge Lürssen 45-m) PFT with 2 x 533mm TT (SST-4 HWT).

PATROL CRAFT: 12:

OFFSHORE: 8:

1 *Teniente Olivieri* (ex-US oilfield tug).

3 *Irigoyen* (US *Cherokee* AT).

2 *King* (trg) with 3 x 105mm guns.

2 *Sorbral* (US *Sotoyomo* AT).

INSHORE: 4 *Baradero* PCI〈.

MINE WARFARE: 6:

4 *Neuquen* (UK '*Ton*') MSC.

2 *Chaco* (UK '*Ton*') MHC.

AMPHIBIOUS: 1 *Cabo San Antonio* LST (hel deck), capacity 600 tps, 18 tk.

Plus 20 craft: 4 LCM, 16 LCVP.

SUPPORT AND MISCELLANEOUS: 9:

1 AGOR, 3 tpt, 1 ocean tug, 1 icebreaker, 2 trg, 1 research.

NAVAL AVIATION: (3,000); 42 cbt ac, 13 armed hel.

ATTACK: 1 sqn with 12 *Super Etendard*.

MR/ASW: 1 sqn with 3 L-188, 6 S-2E.

EW: 2 L-188E.

HELICOPTERS: 2 sqn: 1 ASW/tpt with 7 ASH-3H (ASW) and 4 AS-61D (tpt); 1 spt with 6 SA-316/-319 (with SS-11).

TRANSPORT: 1 sqn with 1 BAe-125, 3 F-28-3000, 3 L-188, 4 *Queen Air* 80, 9 *Super King Air*, 4 US-2A.

SURVEY: 3 PC-6B (Antarctic flt).

TRAINING: 2 sqn with 7* EMB-326, 9* MB-326, 5* MB-339A, 10 T-34C.

MISSILES:

ASM: AGM-12 *Bullpup*, AM-39 *Exocet*, AS-12, *Martín Pescador*.

AAM: AIM-9 *Sidewinder*, R-550 *Magic*.

MARINES: (4,000).

Fleet Forces: 2 , each with 2 bn, 1 amph recce coy, 1 fd arty bn, 1 ATK, 1 engr coy.

Amph spt force: 1 marine inf bn.

1 AD arty regt (bn).

2 SF bn.

EQUIPMENT:

RECCE: 12 ERC-90 *Lynx*.

APC: 19 LVTP-7, 6 MOWAG *Grenadier*, 24 Panhard VCR.

TOWED ARTY: 105mm: 15 M-101/M-56; 155mm: 6 M-114.

MORTARS: 81mm: 20.

ATGW: 50 *Bantam*, *Cobra (Mamba)*.

RL: 89mm: 60 3.5-in M-20.

RCL: 105mm: 30 1974 FMK1.

AD GUNS: 30mm: 10 HS-816.

SAM: *Tigercat*.

AIR FORCE: 8,900 (1,200 conscripts); 219 cbt ac, 11 armed hel, 9 air bde, 10 AD arty bty, 1 SF (AB) coy.

AIR OPERATIONS COMMAND (9 bde):

FGA/FIGHTER: 3 sqn:

2 (1 OCU) with 20 *Mirage* IIIC (17 -CJ, 1 -BE, 2 -BJ), 15 *Mirage* IIIEA; 1 with 8 *Mirage* 5P, 23 *Dagger Nesher* (-A: 20; -B :3).

FGA: 4 sqn with 16 A-4B/C, 32 A-4M, 4 OA-4M.

COIN: 3 sqn:

2 with 45 IA-58A, 16 IA-63, 30 MS-760.

1 armed hel with 11 Hughes MD500, 3 UH-1H.

MR: 1 Boeing 707.

SURVEY: 3 *Learjet* 35A, 4 1A-50.

TANKER: 2 Boeing 707, 2 KC-130H.

SAR: 4 SA-315 hel.

TRANSPORT: 5 sqn with: **ac:** 5 Boeing 707, 2 C-130E, 3 C-130B, 5 -H, 1 L-100-30, 6 DHC-6, 10 F-27, 4 F-28, 15 IA-50, 2 *Merlin* IVA. Antarctic spt unit with 1 DHC-6; **hel:** 5 Bell 212, 2 CH-47C, 1 S-61R (*Sea King*).

CALIBRATION: 1 sqn with 2 Boeing 707, 3 IA-50, 2 *Learjet* 35, 1 PA-31.

LIAISON: 1 sqn with 20 Cessna 182, 1 Cessna 320, 7 *Commander*, 1 *Sabreliner*.

AIR TRAINING COMMAND: ac: 28 EMB-312, 10* MS-760, 29 T-34B; **hel:** 3 Hughes 500D.

MISSILES:

ASM: ASM-2 *Martín Pescador*.

AAM: AIM-9B *Sidewinder*, R-530, R-550, *Shafrir*.

FORCES ABROAD:

UN AND PEACEKEEPING:

ANGOLA (UNAVEM II): 2 Observers, 3 civ pol.

CROATIA (UNPROFOR I): 853; 1 inf bn, 5 Observers, plus 23 civ pol.

CYPRUS (UNFICYP): 375; 1 inf bn.

EL SALVADOR (ONUSAL): 4.

IRAQ/KUWAIT (UNIKOM): 49 engr, plus 6

Observers.
MIDDLE EAST (UNTSO): 6 Observers.
MOZAMBIQUE (ONUMOZ): 40, plus 8 Observers.
WESTERN SAHARA (MINURSO): 15 Observers.

PARAMILITARY:

GENDARMERIE (Ministry of Defence): 18,000; 5 Regional Comd.
EQUIPMENT: *Shorland* recce, 40 UR-416; 81mm mor; **ac:** 3 Piper, 5 PC-6; **hel:** 5 SA-315.
PREFECTURA NAVAL (Coast Guard): 13,240; 7 comd.
EQUIPMENT: 6 PCO: 5 *Mantilla*, 1 *Delfin*; 4 PCI, 19 PCI⟨; **ac:** 5 C-212; **hel:** 4 Short *Skyvan*, 3 SA-330, 6 MD-500, 2 Bell-47.

BOLIVIA

GDP	1992:	B 24.3bn ($6.2bn): per capita $2,400		
	1993ε:	B 28.5bn ($6.6bn): per capita $2,300		
Growth	1992:	3.8%	1993:	3.9%
Inflation	1992:	10.5%	1993:	9.4%
Debt	1992:	$4.1bn	1993:	$4.3bn
Def exp	1992:	B 458m ($117m)		
Def bdgt	1992:	B 433m ($111m)		
	1993:	B 538m ($126m)		
	1994ε:	B 538m ($119m)		
FMA	1993:	$36.6m (FMF, Narcs, IMET)		
	1994:	$22.1m (FMF, Narcs, IMET)		
	1995:	$68.0m (Narcs)		
$1 = B	1992:	3.9	1993:	4.3
	1994:	4.5		

B = Boliviano

Population: 7,949,400

	13–17	*18–22*	*23–32*
Men	464,300	386,800	587,300
Women	463,000	391,800	610,700

TOTAL ARMED FORCES:

ACTIVE: 33,500 (some 20,000 conscripts).
Terms of service: 12 months, selective.

ARMY: 25,000 (some 18,000 conscripts).

HQ: 9 Military Regions.
Army HQ direct control:
2 armd bn.
1 mech cav regt.
1 Presidential Guard inf regt.
10 'div'; org, composition varies; comprise:
8 cav gp (5 horsed, 2 mot, 1 aslt); 1 mot inf 'regt' with 2 bn; 22 inf bn (incl 5 inf aslt bn); 1 armd bn; 1 arty 'regt' (bn); 5 arty gp (coy); 1 AB 'regt' (bn); 6 engr bn.
EQUIPMENT:
LIGHT TANKS: 36 SK-105 *Kuerassier*.
RECCE: 24 EE-9 *Cascavel*.
APC: 108: 50 M-113, 10 V-100 *Commando*, 24 MOWAG *Roland*, 24 EE-11 *Urutu*.
TOWED ARTY: 75mm: 70 incl M-116 pack, ε10 Bofors M-1935; 105mm: 30 incl M-101, FH-18. 122mm: 36 Ch Type -54.
MORTARS: 81mm: 50; 107mm: M-30.
RCL: 90mm: 30.
AVIATION: 2 C-212, 1 *King Air* B90, 1 *Super King Air* 200 (VIP).

NAVY: 4,500 (incl Naval Aviation and 2,000 Marines).

6 Naval Districts covering Lake Titicaca and the rivers; each 1 Flotilla.
BASES: Riberalta (HQ), Tiquina (HQ), Puerto Busch, Puerto Guayaramerín (HQ), Puerto Villaroel, Trinidad (HQ), Puerto Suárez (HQ) Cobija (HQ).
RIVER PATROL CRAFT: some 10⟨; plus some 15 US *Boston* whalers.
SUPPORT: some 20 riverine craft/boats.

NAVAL AVIATION:

AIRCRAFT: 1 Cessna 206, 1 Cessna 402.

MARINES: (2,000): 6 bn (1 in each District).

AIR FORCE: 4,000 (perhaps 2,000 conscripts); 52 cbt ac, 10 armed hel.

FIGHTER: 1 sqn with 12 AT-33N, 4 F-86F (ftr/trg).
COIN: 16 PC-7.
SPECIAL OPS: 1 sqn with 10 Hughes 500M hel.
SAR: 1 hel sqn with 4 HB-315B, 2 SA-315B, 1 UH-1.
SURVEY: 1 sqn with 5 Cessna 206, 1 Cessna 210, 1 Cessna 402, 3 *Learjet* 25.
TRANSPORT: 3 sqn:
1 VIP tpt with 1 L-188, 1 *Sabreliner*, 2 *Super King Air*.
2 tpt with 9 C-130, 4 F-27-400, 1 IAI-201, 2 *King Air*, 2 C-47.
LIAISON: ac: 9 Cessna 152, 2 Cessna 185, 13 Cessna 206, 2 Cessna 402; **hel:** 2 Bell 212, 22 UH-1H.
TRAINING: 1 Cessna 152, 2 Cessna 172, 11* PC-7, 4 SF-260CB, 15 T-23, 9* T-33A, 1 Lancair 320.
1 air-base defence regt (Oerlikon twin 20mm, 18 Ch type-65 37mm, some truck-mounted guns).

PARAMILITARY:

NATIONAL POLICE: some 30,000.
NARCOTICS POLICE: some 600.

BRAZIL

GDP	1992:	Cr 1,847bn ($409bn): per capita $5,300		
	1993ε:	Cr 38,984bn ($441bn): per capita $5,700		
Growth	1992:	-1.4%	1993:	5.0%
Inflation	1992:	1,156%	1993:	2,568%
Debt	1992:	$121.1bn	1993:	$120.1bn
Def exp	1992:	Cr 19.3bn ($4.3bn)		
Def bdgt	1993ε:	Cr 389.0bn ($4.4bn)		
	1994ε:	Cr 3,533.0bn ($4.6bn)		
FMA	1993:	$1.8m (Narcs, IMET)		
	1994:	$0.5m (Narcs, IMET)		
	1995:	$1.1m (Narcs, IMET)		
$1 = Cr[a]	1992:	4.5	1993	88.4
	1994:	768.1		

Cr = cruzerio real

[a] The cruzeiro real, equal to 1,000 cruzeiros, was introduced in August 1993.

Population: 161,977,600

	13–17	18–22	23–32
Men	8,311,200	7,554,500	13,621,800
Women	8,254,800	7,564,700	13,687,200

TOTAL ARMED FORCES:

ACTIVE: 336,800 (133,500 conscripts).
Terms of service: 12 months (can be extended by 6 months).
RESERVES: trained first-line: 1,115,000; 400,000 subject to immediate recall. Second-line: 225,000.

ARMY: 219,000 (incl 126,500 conscripts).

HQ: 7 Military Comd, 12 Military Regions.
8 div (3 with Region HQ).
1 armd cav bde (2 mech, 1 armd, 1 arty bn).
3 armd inf bde (each 2 inf, 1 armd, 1 arty bn).
4 mech cav bde (each 3 inf, 1 arty bn).
12 motor inf bde (26 bn).
1 mtn bde.
2 'jungle' bde (7 bn).
1 frontier bde (6 bn).
1 AB bde (3 AB, 1 SF bn).
2 coast and AD arty bde.
3 cav guard regt.
28 arty gp (4 SP, 6 med, 18 fd).
2 engr gp each 4 bn; 10 bn (incl 2 railway) (to be increased to 34 bn).
Avn: hel bde forming, to comprise 50 hel per bn.

EQUIPMENT:
LIGHT TANKS: some 566: some 150 M-3, some 80 X-1A, 40 X-1A2 (M-3 mod); 296 M-41B.
RECCE: 409 EE-9 *Cascavel*, 30 M-8.
APC: 823: 219 EE-11 *Urutu*, 20 M-59, 584 M-113.
TOWED ARTY: 377: 105mm: 285, incl M-101/-102, Model 56 pack; 155mm: 92 M-114.
SP ARTY: 105mm: 72 M-7/-108.
COAST ARTY: some 240 incl 57mm, 75mm, 120mm, 150mm, 152mm, 305mm.
MRL: 108mm: SS-06; 180mm: SS-40; 300mm: SS-60 incl SP; 4 *ASTROS* II.
MORTARS: 81mm; 107mm: 209 M-30; 120mm: 77.
ATGW: 300 *Cobra*.
RCL: 57mm: 240 M-18A1; 75mm: 20 M-20; 105mm; 106mm: M-40A1.
AD GUNS: 20mm; 35mm: 50 GDF-001; 40mm: 60 L-60/-70 (some with BOFI).
SAM: 2 *Roland* II.
HELICOPTERS: 36 SA-365, 20 AS-550 *Fennec*, 21 AS-350 (armed).

NAVY: 58,400 (incl 1,250 Naval Aviation, 15,000 Marines and 2,000 conscripts).

5 Oceanic Naval Districts plus 1 Riverine; 1 Comd.
BASES: Ocean: Rio de Janeiro (HQ I Naval District), Salvador (HQ II District), Natal (HQ III District), Belém (HQ IV District), Rio Grande do Sul (HQ V District).
River: Ladario (HQ VI District), Manaus.
SUBMARINES: 4:
1 *Tupi* (Ge T-209/1400) with 533mm TT (UK *Tigerfish* HWT).
3 *Humaitá* (UK *Oberon*) with 533mm TT (*Tigerfish* HWT).
PRINCIPAL SURFACE COMBATANTS: 21:
CARRIER: 1 *Minas Gerais* (UK *Colossus*) CVS (ASW), capacity 20 ac: typically 6 S-2E ASW ac, 4–6 ASH-3H hel, 3 AS-332 hel and 2 AS-355 hel.
DESTROYERS: 6:
2 *Marcilio Dias* (US *Gearing*) ASW with 1 *Wasp* hel (Mk 46 LWT), 1 x 8 *ASROC*, 2 x 3 ASTT; plus 2 x 2 127mm guns.
4 *Mato Grosso* (US *Sumner*) ASW, 4 with 1 *Wasp* hel, all with 2 x 3 ASTT; plus 3 x 2 127mm guns.
FRIGATES: 14:
4 *Para* (US *Garcia*) with 1 x 8 *ASROC*, 2 x 3 ASTT, 1 x *Lynx* hel; plus 2 x 127mm guns.
4 *Niteroi* ASW with 1 *Lynx* hel, 2 x 3 ASTT, *Ikara* SUGW, 1 x 2 ASW mor; plus 2 x MM-40 *Exocet* SSM, 1 x 114mm gun.

2 *Niteroi* GP; weapons as ASW, except 4 x MM-40 *Exocet*, 2 x 114mm guns, no *Ikara*.
4 *Inhauma*, with 1 *Lynx* hel, 2 x 3 ASTT, plus 4 x MM-40 *Exocet*, 1 x 114mm gun.
PATROL AND COASTAL COMBATANTS: 29:
9 *Imperial Marinheiro* PCO.
1 *Grajaü* PCC.
6 *Piratini* (US PGM) PCI.
3 *Aspirante Nascimento* PCI (trg).
4 *Tracker* PCI⟨.
6 Riverine patrol: 3 *Roraima* and 2 *Pedro Teixeira*, 1 *Parnaiba*.
MINE WARFARE: 6: 6 *Aratü* (Ge *Schütze*) MSI.
AMPHIBIOUS: 3:
2 *Ceara* (US *Thomaston*) LSD capacity 350 tps, 38 tk.
1 *Duque de Caxais* (US *de Soto County* LST), capacity 600 tps, 18 tk.
Plus some 49 craft: 3 LCU, 11 LCM, 35 LCVP.
SUPPORT AND MISCELLANEOUS: 23:
1 *Marajo* AO, 1 *Almirante G. Motta* AO, 1 repair ship, 1 submarine rescue, 4 tpt, 9 survey/oceanography, 1 *Brasil* trg, 5 ocean tugs.

NAVAL AVIATION: (1,250); 29 armed hel.
ASW: 1 hel sqn with 5 ASH-3A (*Sea King*), 4 SH-3D.
ATTACK: 1 with 5 *Lynx* HAS-21.
UTILITY: 2 sqn with 5 AS-332, 7 AS-350B (armed), 8 AS-355 (armed).
TRAINING: 1 hel sqn with 13 TH-57.
ASM: AS-11, AS-12, *Sea Skua*.

MARINES: (15,000).
Fleet Force:
1 amph div (1 comd, 3 inf bn, 1 arty gp).
Reinforcement Comd:
5 bn incl 1 engr, 1 SF.
Internal Security Force:
8+ regional gp.
EQUIPMENT:
RECCE: 6 EE-9 Mk IV *Cascavel*.
AAV: 12 LVTP-7A1.
APC: 26 M-113, 5 EE-11 *Urutu*.
TOWED ARTY: 105mm: 12 M-101, 10 L118; 155mm: 6 M-114.
MORTARS: 81mm: incl 2 SP.
RL: 89mm: 3.5-in M-20.
RCL: 106mm: M-40A1.
AD GUNS: 40mm: 6 L/70 with BOFI.

AIR FORCE: 59,400 (5,000 conscripts); 272 cbt ac, 46 armed hel.
AD COMMAND: 1 gp.
FIGHTER: 2 sqn with 16 F-103E/D (*Mirage* IIIE/DBR).
TACTICAL COMMAND: 10 gp.
FGA: 3 sqn with 48 F-5E, 4 -B, 4 -F, 26 AMX.
COIN: 2 sqn with 58 AT-26 (EMB-326).
RECCE: 2 sqn with 4 RC-95, 10 RT-26, 12 *Learjet* 35 Recce/VIP, 3 RC-130E.
LIAISON/OBSERVATION: 7 sqn: 1 **ac** with 8 T-27; 1 **hel** with 8 UH-1H (armed); 5 ac/hel with 31 U-7 **ac** and 30 UH-1H **hel** (armed).
MARITIME COMMAND: 4 gp.
ASW (afloat): 1 sqn with S-2: 13; -A: 7; - E: 6.
MR/SAR: 3 sqn with 11 EMB-110B, 20 EMB-111.
TRANSPORT COMMAND: 6 gp (6 sqn), plus 7 regional indep sqns:
1 with 12 C-130H, KC-130H.
1 with 4 KC-137 (tpi/tkr).
1 with 12 C-91.
1 with 23 C-95A/B/C.
1 sqn with 17 C-115.
1 sqn (VIP) with **ac:** 1 VC-91, 12 VC/VU-93, 2 VC-96, 5 VC-97, 5 VU-9, 2 Boeing 737-200; **hel:** 3 VH-4.
7 sqn (regional) with 7 C-115, 86 C-95A/B/C, 6 EC-9 (VU-9).
HELICOPTERS: 8 AS-332 (armed), 8 AS-355, 4 Bell 206, 27 HB-350B.
LIAISON: 50 C-42, 3 Cessna 208, 30 U-42.
TRAINING COMMAND: **ac:** 38* AT-26, 97 EMB-110, 25 T-23, 98 T-25, 64* T-27 (*Tucano*), 14* AMX-T; **hel:** 4 OH-6A, 25 OH-13.
CALIBRATION: 1 unit with 2 C-95, 1 EC-93, 4 EC-95, 1 U-93.
AAM: AIM-9B *Sidewinder*, R-530, *Magic* 2.

FORCES ABROAD:
UN AND PEACEKEEPING:
ANGOLA (UNAVEM II): 19, incl 8 Observers, 3 civ pol.
CROATIA (UNPROFOR I): 23 Observers, 10 civ pol.
EL SALVADOR (ONUSAL): 4 Observers, 11 civ pol.
MOZAMBIQUE (ONUMOZ): 27 Observers, 67 civ pol.
UGANDA/RWANDA (UNOMUR): 13 Observers.

PARAMILITARY:
PUBLIC SECURITY FORCES (R): some 385,600 in state military police org (State Militias) under Army control and considered an Army Reserve.

CHILE

GDP	1992: pCh 14,940bn ($41.2bn): per capita $8,000	
	1993: pCh 18,074bn ($44.7bn): per capita $8,700	
Growth	1992: 10.4%	1993: 5.7%
Inflation	1992: 15.6%	1993: 12.7%
Debt	1992: $19.4bn	1993: $19.7bn
Def bdgt[a, b]	1992: pCh 369.0bn ($1.0bn)	
	1993: pCh 405.0bn ($1.0bn)	
	1994: pCh 450.0bn ($1.1bn)	
FMA	1993: $0.3m (IMET)	
	1994: $0.1m (IMET)	
	1995: $0.1m (IMET)	
$1 = pCh	1992: 363	1993: 404
	1994: 430	

pCh = Chilean peso

[a] Incl finance from Codelco (state company) copper fund est to be 10% of earnings ($200m in 1993 and $216m in 1994).
[b] Excl pension costs est to be $629m in 1994.

Population: 13,944,200

	13–17	*18–22*	*23–32*
Men	636,600	618,300	1,225,800
Women	613 ,000	599,800	1,203,600

TOTAL ARMED FORCES:

ACTIVE: 93,000 (31,000 conscripts).
Terms of service: Army 1 year; Navy and Air Force 2 years.
RESERVES: Army 50,000.

ARMY: 54,000 (27,000 conscripts).

7 Military Regions, 2 Corps HQ.
7 div:
- 1 with 3 mot inf, 1 armd cav, 1 arty, 1 engr regt.
- 1 with 1 mot inf, 1 inf, 5 mtn, 1 armd cav, 1 arty, 1 engr regt.
- 1 with 1 inf, 5 mtn, 1 armd cav, 1 mot arty regt.
- 1 with 1 inf, 2 mtn, 3 armd cav, 2 mot arty, 1 engr regt.
- 1 with 2 mtn, 2 armd cav, 1 arty, 1 engr regt.
- 1 with 2 mtn, 1 engr regt.
- 1 with 1 mot inf, 1 cdo regt.

1 bde with 1 armd cav, 1 mtn regt.
Army tps: 1 avn, 1 engr, 1 AB regt (1 AB, 1 SF bn).
EQUIPMENT:
MBT: 136: 117 M-51, 19 AMX-30.
LIGHT TANKS: 81: 21 M-24, 60 M-41.
RECCE: 50 EE-9 *Cascavel.*
AIFV: 20 MOWAG *Piranha* with 90mm gun.
APC: 60 M-113, 80 Cardoen/MOWAG *Piranha*, 30 EE-11 *Urutu,* 50 M-113.
TOWED ARTY: 114: 105mm: 66 M-101, 36 Model 56; 155mm: 12 M-71.
SP ARTY: 155mm: 12 Mk F3.
MORTARS: 81mm: 300 M-29; 107mm: 15; 120mm: 110 ECIA (incl 50 SP).
ATGW: *Milan/Mamba, Mapats.*
RL: 89mm: 3.5-in M-20.
RCL: 150 incl: 57mm: M-18; 75mm; 106mm: M-40A1.
AD GUNS: 20mm: some SP (Cardoen/MOWAG).
SAM: *Blowpipe, Javelin.*
AIRCRAFT:
TRANSPORT: 6 C-212, 1 *Citation* (VIP), 3 CN-235, 4 DHC-6, 3 PA-31, 8 PA-28 Piper *Dakota.*
TRAINING: 16 Cessna R-172.
HELICOPTERS: 2 AB-206, 3 AS-332, 15 Enstrom 280 FX, 5 Hughes 530F (armed trg), 10 SA-315, 9 SA-330.

NAVY: ε25,000 (incl 750 Naval Aviation, ε3,000 Marines, ε1,500 Coast Guard and ε3,000 conscripts).

DEPLOYMENT AND BASES:
3 main commands: Fleet (includes DD and FF), Submarine Flotilla, Transport. Remaining forces allocated to 4 Naval Zones:
1st Naval Zone (26°S – 36°S approx): Valparaiso (HQ), Vina Del Mar.
2nd Naval Zone (36°S – 43°S approx): Talcahuano (HQ), Puerto Montt.
3rd Naval Zone (43°S to Cape Horn): Punta Arenas (HQ), Puerto Williams.
4th Naval Zone (north of 26°S approx): Iquique (HQ).
SUBMARINES: 4:
2 *O'Brien* (UK *Oberon*) with 8 x 533mm TT (Ge HWT).
2 *Thompson* (Ge T-209/1300) with 8 x 533mm TT (HWT).
PRINCIPAL SURFACE COMBATANTS: 10:
DESTROYERS: 6:
2 *Prat* (UK *Norfolk*) DDG with 1 x 2 *Seaslug-2* SAM, 4 x MM-38 *Exocet* SSM, 1 x 2 114mm guns, 1 AB-206B hel plus 2 x 3 ASTT (Mk 44).
2 *Blanco Encalada* (UK *Norfolk*) DDH with 4 x MM-38, 1 x 2 114 mm guns, 2 AS-332F hel; plus 2 x 3 ASTT (Mk 44).
2 *Almirante Riveros* (ASUW) with 4 x MM-38 *Exocet* SSM, 4 x 102mm guns; plus 2 x 3 ASTT (Mk 44 LWT), 2 x 3 ASW mor.
FRIGATES: 4 *Condell* (mod UK *Leander*) 3 with 2 x 3 ASTT (Mk 44), 1 hel; plus 2 x 2 MM-40 (2 with 4 x MM-38) *Exocet*, 1 x 2 114mm guns.

PATROL AND COASTAL COMBATANTS: 19:
MISSILE CRAFT: 4:
2 *Casma* (Is *Reshef*) PFM with 4 *Gabriel* SSM.
2 *Iquique* (Is *Sa'ar*) PFM with 6 *Gabriel* SSM.
TORPEDO CRAFT: 4 *Guacolda* (Ge Lürssen 36-m) with 4 x 533mm TT.
PATROL: 11:
1 PCO (ex-US tug).
3 *Micalvi* PCC.
1 *Papudo* PCC (ex-US PC-1638).
6 *Grumete Diaz* (Is *Dabur*) PCI⟨ .
AMPHIBIOUS: 3:
3 *Maipo* (Fr *BATRAL*) LSM, capacity 140 tps, 7 tk.
Plus craft: 2 *Elicura* LCT.
SUPPORT AND MISCELLANEOUS: 11:
1 *Almirante Jorge Montt* (UK '*Tide*') AO, 1 *Araucano* AO, 1 tpt, 1 survey, 1 *Uribe* trg, 1 Antarctic patrol, 5 tugs/spt.

NAVAL AVIATION: (750); 14 cbt ac, 16 armed hel. 4 sqn.
MR: 1 sqn with 6 EMB-111N, 2 *Falcon* 200, 6 P-3 *Orion* (2 more to be delivered).
ASW HEL: 6 AS-332, 7 Bo-105, 3 AB-206AS.
LIAISON: 1 sqn with 3 C-212A, 3 EMB-110N, 2 IAI-1124.
HELICOPTERS: 1 sqn with 3 AB-206-B, 3 SH-57.
TRAINING: 1 sqn with 10 PC-7.

MARINES: (ε3,000).
4 gp: each 1 inf bn (+), 1 cdo coy, 1 fd arty, 1 AD arty bty.
1 amph bn.
EQUIPMENT:
APC: 40 MOWAG *Roland*, 30 LVTP-5.
TOWED ARTY: 105mm: 16 M-101; 155mm: 36 M-114.
COAST GUNS: 155mm: 16 GPFM-3.
MORTARS: 60mm: 50; 81mm: 50.
RCL: 106mm: ε30 M-40A1.
SAM: *Blowpipe*.

COAST GUARD: (ε1,500).
PATROL CRAFT: 17:
2 PCC (Buoy Tenders), 1 *Castor* PCI, 2 *Alacalufe* PCI, 12 PCI⟨, plus about 12 boats.

AIR FORCE: 14,000 (1,000 conscripts); 98 cbt ac, no armed hel. 5 Air Bde: 5 wings.
FGA: 2 sqn:
1 with 10 *Hunter* (9 F-71, 1 FR-71A).
1 with 16 F-5 (13 -E, 3 -F).
COIN: 2 sqn with 30 A-37B, 24 A-36.
FIGHTER/RECCE: 1 sqn with 15 *Mirage* 50 (8 -FCH, 6 -CH, 1 -DCH).
RECCE: 2 photo units with 1 *Canberra* PR-9, 1 *King Air* A-100, 2 *Learjet* 35A.
AEW: 1 IAI-707 *Phalcon*.
TRANSPORT: 1 sqn with: **ac:** 4 Boeing 707(2 tkr), 2 C-130H, 4 C-130B, 4 C-212, 9 Beech 99 (ELINT, tpt, trg), 14 DHC-6 (5 -100, 9 -300); **hel:** 5 SA-315B.
LIAISON HELICOPTERS: 6 Bo-105CB, 4 UH-1H.
TRAINING: 1 wing, 3 flying schools: **ac:** 16 PA-28, 50 T-35A/B, 20 T-36, 20 T-37B/C, 8 T-41D, 3* Hunters (1 T-67, 2 T-72); **hel:** 10 UH-1H.
MISSILES:
ASM: AS-11/-12.
AAM: AIM-9B *Sidewinder, Shafrir, Python III*.
AD: 1 regt (5 gp) with: 20mm: S-639/-665, GAI-CO1 twin; 35mm: 36, K-63 twin; *Blowpipe*, 12 *Cactus* (*Crotale*), MATRA *Mistral*.

FORCES ABROAD:
UN AND PEACEKEEPING:
EL SALVADOR (ONUSAL): 23 civ pol.
INDIA/PAKISTAN (UNMOGIP): 3 Observers.
MIDDLE EAST (UNTSO): 3 Observers.

PARAMILITARY:
CARABINEROS: 31,000; 8 zones, 38 districts.
EQUIPMENT:
APC: MOWAG *Roland*.
MORTARS: 60mm, 81mm.
AIRCRAFT: 22 Cessna (6-150, 10-182, 6-206), 1 *Metro*.
HELICOPTERS: 2 Bell 206, 12 Bo-105.

OPPOSITION:
FRENTE PATRIOTICO MANUEL RODRIGUEZ/ DISSIDENT (FPMR/D): ε800; leftist.
MOVEMENT OF THE REVOLUTIONARY LEFT (MIR): some 500.

COLOMBIA

GDP	1992:	pC 33,064bn ($43.6bn): per capita $5,800		
	1993:	pC 40,335bn ($46.7bn): per capita $6,200		
Growth	1992:	3.5%	1993:	4.6%
Inflation	1992:	25.2%	1993:	22.5%
Debt	1992:	$17.2bn	1993:	$17.2bn
Def exp	1992:	pC 825.0bn ($1.1bn)		
	1993:	pC 825.0bn ($956.0m)		

Def bdgt	1994:	pC 715.0bn ($768.8m)		
	1995:	pC 858.0bn ($922.6m)		
FMA	1993:	$54.1m (FMF, Narcs, IMET)		
	1994:	$28.6m (FMF, Narcs, IMET)		
	1995:	$68.0m (Narcs)		
$1 = pC	1992:	759	1993:	863
	1994:	930		

pC = Colombian peso

Population: 34,528,200

	13–17	*18–22*	*23–32*
Men	1,913,500	1,786,200	3,230,000
Women	1,828,000	1,721,200	3,183,300

TOTAL ARMED FORCES:

ACTIVE: 146,400 (some 67,300 conscripts).
Terms of service: 1–2 years, varies (all services).
RESERVES: 60,700, incl 2,000 first line: Army 54,700; Navy 4,800; Air Force 1,200.

ARMY: 121,000 (63,800 conscripts).

4 div HQ.
16 inf bde (Regional) each with 3 inf, 1 arty, 1 engr bn, 1 mech gp.
Army Tps:
2 COIN bde (each with 1 cdo unit, 4 COIN bn).
1 Presidential Guard bn.
1 AD arty bn.
EQUIPMENT:
LIGHT TANKS: 12 M-3A1.
RECCE: 4 M-8, 120 EE-9 *Cascavel.*
APC: 80 M-113, 76 EE-11 *Urutu.*
TOWED ARTY: 105mm: 130 M-101.
MORTARS: 81mm: 125 M-1; 120mm: 120 Brandt.
ATGW: *TOW.*
RCL: 106mm: M-40A1.
AD GUNS: 40mm: 30 Bofors.

NAVY (incl Coast Guard): 18,100 (incl 8,900 Marines and 100 Naval Aviation).

BASES: Ocean: Cartagena (main), Buenaventura, Málaga (Pacific).
River: Puerto Leguízamo, Barrancabermeja, Puerto Carreño, Leticia, Puerto Orocue, Puerto Inirida.
SUBMARINES: 2:
2 *Pijao* (Ge T-209/1200) with 8 x 533mm TT (Ge HWT).
Plus 2 *Intrepido* (It SX-506) SSI (SF delivery).
FRIGATES: 5:
4 *Almirante Padilla* with 1 x Bo-105 hel (ASW), 2 x 3 ASTT; plus 8 x MM-40 *Exocet* SSM.
1 *Boyaca* (US *Courtney*) with 2 x 3 324mm TT, 2 x 76mm gun; plus hel deck (to decommission in 1994).
PATROL AND COASTAL COMBATANTS: 39:
PATROL: 39:
OFFSHORE: 3 *Pedro de Heredia* (ex-US tugs).
INSHORE: 11: 6 *Quito Sueno* (US *Asheville*) PFI, 2 *Castillo Y Rada* (Swiftships 32-m) PCI, 3 *Jose Palas* PCI‹.
RIVERINE: 25: 3 *Arauca*, 16 *Juan Lucio*‹, 6 *Capitan* tugs.
AMPHIBIOUS: 8 *Morrosquillo* (ex US) LCUS.
SUPPORT AND MISCELLANEOUS: 4:
1 tpt, 2 research, 1 trg.

MARINES: (8,900); 2 bde (8 bn).

No hy eqpt (to get EE-9 *Cascavel* recce, EE-11 *Urutu* APC).

NAVAL AVIATION: (100).

AIRCRAFT: 2 *Commander*, 2 PA-28, 2 PA-31.
HELICOPTERS: 4 Bo-105.

AIR FORCE: 7,300 (some 3,500 conscripts); 74 cbt ac, 72 armed hel.

AIR COMBAT COMMAND:
FGA: 2 sqn:
1 with 13 *Mirage* 5.
1 with 13 *Kfir* (11 -C2, 2 -TC2).
TACTICAL AIR SUPPORT COMMAND:
COIN: ac: 1 AC-47, 2 AC-47T, 3 IA-58A, 23 A-37B, 6 AT-27, 13 OV-10; **hel:** 5 Bell 212, 12 Bell 205, 2 Bell 412, 26 UH-1H, 2UH-1B, 9 UH-60, 11 MD-500ME, 2 MD-500D, 3 MD-530F.
MILITARY AIR TRANSPORT COMMAND: 1 Boeing 707, 7 C-130B, 2 C-130H, 1 C-117, 2 C-47, 2 CASA 212, 2 *Bandeirante*, 1 F-28.
AIR TRAINING COMMAND: 14 T-27, 6 T-34M, 13 T-37, 8 T-41.
AAM: AIM-9 *Sidewinder*, R-530.

FORCES ABROAD:

UN AND PEACEKEEPING:
CROATIA (UNPROFOR I): 2 Observers, 22 civ pol.
EGYPT (MFO): 500.
EL SALVADOR (ONUSAL): 2 Observers, 28 civ pol.

PARAMILITARY:

NATIONAL POLICE FORCE: 79,000; **ac:** 2 C-47, 9 Cessna (2 -152, 6 -206G, 2 -208), 1 Beech C-99, 5 *Turbo Thrush*; **hel:** 14 Bell (8 -206L, 6 -212), 21 UH-

1H, 3 Hughes 500D.
COAST GUARD: integral part of Navy.

OPPOSITION:

COORDINADORA NACIONAL GUERRILLERA SIMON BOLIVAR (CNGSB): loose coalition of guerrilla gp incl: Revolutionary Armed Forces of Colombia (FARC): ε5,700 active;
National Liberation Army (ELN): ε2,500, pro-Cuban;
People's Liberation Army (EPL): ε500.

ECUADOR

GDP	1992: ES 19,452bn ($12.7bn): per capita $4,400		
	1993: ES 27,902bn ($13.2bn): per capita $4,600		
Growth	1992: 3.5%	1993: 1.7%	
Inflation	1992: 60.2%	1993: 310.0%	
Debt	1992: $12.3bn	1993: $12.8bn	
Def bdgt	1992: ES 614bn ($400m)		
	1993ε: ES 956bn ($503m)		
	1994ε: ES 1,028bn ($531m)		
FMA	1993: $2.3m (Narcs, IMET)		
	1994: $0.9m (Narcs, IMET)		
	1995: $1.3m (Narcs, IMET)		
$1 = ES	1992: 1,534	1993: 1,900	
	1994: 1,935		

ES = Ecuadorean sucre

Population: 11,196,800

	13–17	*18–22*	*23–32*
Men	645,000	579,800	946,600
Women	626,900	565,000	926,600

TOTAL ARMED FORCES:

ACTIVE: 57,500.
Terms of service: conscription 1 year, selective.
RESERVES: 100,000; ages 18–55.

ARMY: 50,000.

4 Defence Zones.
1 div with 2 inf bde.
1 armd bde.
2 inf bde (5 inf, 3 mech inf, 2 arty bn).
3 jungle bde.
Army tps:
1 SF (AB) bde (2 gp).
1 AD arty gp.
1 avn gp.
3 engr bn.

EQUIPMENT:
LIGHT TANKS: 45 M-3, 108 AMX-13.
RECCE: 27 AML-60/-90, 22 EE-9 *Cascavel,* 10 EE-3 *Jararaca.*
APC: 20 M-113, 60 AMX-VCI, 20 EE-11 *Urutu.*
TOWED ARTY: 105mm: 50 M2A2; 155mm: 10 M-198.
SP ARTY: 155mm: 10 Mk F3.
MORTARS: 300: 81mm: M-29; 107mm: 4.2-in M-30; 160mm: 12 Soltam.
RCL: 90mm: 380 M-67; 106mm: 24 M-40A1.
AD GUNS: 20mm: 20 M-1935; 35mm: 30 GDF-002 twin; 40mm: 30 L/70.
SAM: 75 *Blowpipe.*
AIRCRAFT:
SURVEY: 1 Cessna 206, 1 *Learjet* 24D.
TRANSPORT: 1 CN-235, 1 DHC-5, 3 IAI-201, 1 *King Air* 200, 2 PC-6.
LIAISON/TRG/OBS: 1 Cessna 172, 1 -182.
HELICOPTERS:
SURVEY: 3 SA-315B.
TRANSPORT/LIAISON: 10 AS-332, 4 AS-350B, 1 Bell 214B, 3 SA-315B, 3 SA-330, 30 SA-342.

NAVY: 4,500 (incl 250 Naval Aviation and 1,500 Marines).

BASES: Guayaquil (main base), Jaramijo, Galápagos Islands.
SUBMARINES: 2 *Shyri* (Ge T-209/1300) with 533mm TT (Ge SUT HWT).
PRINCIPAL SURFACE COMBATANTS: 2:
FRIGATES: 2 *Presidente Eloy Alfaro* (ex-UK *Leander Batch II*) with 1 206B hel; plus 4 x MM-38 *Exocet* SSM.
PATROL AND COASTAL COMBATANTS: 12:
CORVETTES: 6 *Esmeraldas* with 2 x 3 ASTT, hel deck; plus 2 x 3 MM-40 *Exocet* SSM.
MISSILE CRAFT: 6:
3 *Quito* (Ge Lürssen 45-m) with 4 x MM-38 *Exocet.*
3 *Manta* (Ge Lürssen 36-m) with 4 x *Gabriel* II SSM.
AMPHIBIOUS: 1:
1 *Hualcopo* (US LST-511) LST, capacity 200 tps, 16 tk.
SUPPORT AND MISCELLANEOUS: 8:
1 survey, 1 ex-GDR depot ship, 1 AOT (small), 1 *Calicuchima* (ex UK *Throsk*) armament carrier, 1 water carrier, 2 armed ocean tugs, 1 trg.

NAVAL AVIATION: (250):

LIAISON: 1 *Citation* I, 1 *Super King Air,* 1 CN-235.
TRAINING: 2 Cessna 172, 3 Cessna 337, 3 T-34C.
HELICOPTERS: 5 Bell 206.

MARINES: (1,500); 3 bn: 2 on garrison duties, 1 cdo (no hy weapons/veh).

AIR FORCE: 3,000; 84 cbt ac, no armed hel.
OPERATIONS COMMAND: 2 wings, 5 sqn:
FGA: 2 sqn:
1 with 8 *Jaguar* S (6 -S(E), 2 -B(E)).
1 with 9 *Kfir* C-2, 1 TC-2.
FIGHTER: 1 sqn with 13 *Mirage* F-1JE, 1 F-1JB.
COIN: 1 sqn with 20 A-37B.
COIN/TRAINING: 1 sqn with 2 *Strikemaster* Mk 89, 7 *Strikemaster* Mk 89A.
MILITARY AIR TRANSPORT GROUP:
2 civil/military airlines:
TAME: 6 Boeing 727, 2 BAe-748, 2 C-130H, 3 DHC-6, 1 F-28, 1 L-100-30.
ECUATORIANA: 3 Boeing 707-320, 1 DC-10-30, 2 Airbus A-310.
LIAISON: 1 *King Air* E90, 1 *Sabreliner*.
LIAISON/SAR: hel flt: 2 AS-332, 1 Bell 212, 6 Bell-206B, 6 SA-316B, 1 SA-330, 2 UH-1B, 24 UH-1H.
TRAINING: incl 23* AT-33, 20 Cessna 150, 5 Cessna 172, 19 T-34C, 4 T-41.
AAM: R-550 *Magic*, *Super* 530, *Shafrir*.
1 AB sqn.

FORCES ABROAD:
UN AND PEACEKEEPING:
EL SALVADOR (ONUSAL): 8 Observers.

PARAMILITARY:
COAST GUARD: 400.
PATROL INSHORE: 6 PCI:
2 *25 De Julio* PCI.
2 *5 De Agosto* PCI.
2 *10 De Agosto* PCI⟨, plus some 20 boats.

EL SALVADOR

GDP	1992: C 54.8bn ($6.0bn): per capita $2,300	
	1993: C 56.0bn ($6.4bn): per capita $2,400	
Growth	1992: 4.6%	1993: 5.0%
Inflation	1992: 20.0%	1994: 12.1%
Debt	1992: $2.1bn	1993: $2.2bn
Def exp	1992ε: C 1.6bn ($175.0m)	
Def bdgt	1992: C 917.1m ($100.0m)	
	1993: C 886.5m ($101.9m)	
	1994: C 866.5m ($99.5m)	
FMA	1993: $11.3m (FMF, IMET)	
	1994: $0.4m (IMET)	
$1 = C	1992: 9.2	1993: 8.7
	1994: 8.7	

C = colon

Population: 5,605,000

	13–17	18–22	23–32
Men	362,600	319,800	423,400
Women	350,600	312,200	445,800

TOTAL ARMED FORCES:
ACTIVE: 30,700.
Terms of service: selective conscription, 2 years.
RESERVES: ex-soldiers registered.

ARMY: 28,000 (some conscripts).
3 Military Zones.
6 inf bde (11 inf bn).
1 special sy bde (1 MP, 2 border gd bn).
7 inf det (8 bn).
1 engr comd (1 engr bn).
1 arty bde (3 fd, 1 AD bn).
1 mech cav regt (2 bn).
2 indep bn (1 Presidential Guard, 1 sy).
1 special ops gp (1 para, 1 naval inf, 1 SF coy).
EQUIPMENT:
RECCE: 10 AML-90.
APC: 45 M-37B1 (mod), 14 M-113, 9 UR-416.
TOWED ARTY: 105mm: 36 M-101/102, 14 M-56.
MORTARS: 81mm: incl 300 M-29; 120mm: 60 UB-M52, M-74 (all in store).
RL: *LAW*.
RCL: 90mm: 400 M-67; 106mm: 20+ M-40A1.
AD GUNS: 20mm: 24 Yug M-55, 4 SP.
SAM: some captured SA-7 may be in service.

NAVY: ε700 (incl some 150 Naval Infantry and sp forces).
BASES: La Uníon, La Libertad, Acajutla, El Triunfo.
PATROL AND COASTAL COMBATANTS: 5:
PATROL, INSHORE: 3 Camcraft 30-m, 2 PCI⟨, plus boats.
AMPHIBIOUS: craft only: 2 LCM.

NAVAL INFANTRY (Marines): (some 150).
1 Marine coy (150).

AIR FORCE: 2,000 (incl AD and ε500 conscripts); 27 cbt ac, 18 armed hel.
Annual flying hours for A-37 pilots: less than 50.

COIN: 3 sqn:
1 with 10 A-37B, 2 AC-47, 9 O-2A.
1 with 10 Hughes (armed: 3 MD 500D, 7 -E), 15 UH-1M armed hel.
1 with 35 UH-1H tpt hel.
TRANSPORT: 1 sqn with 4 C-47, 2 C-47 Turbo-67, 1 *Commander*, 1 DC-6B, 3 IAI-201, 1 *Merlin* IIIB, 9 *Rallye*.
LIAISON: 6 Cessna 180, 1 Cessna 182, 1 Cessna 185.
TRAINING: 6* CM-170 (COIN/trg;), 3 T-41C/D.

PARAMILITARY:
NATIONAL CIVILIAN POLICE (Ministry of Interior): some 5,900 (to be 7,000): forming from former FMLN rebels, soldiers and police.

FOREIGN FORCES:
UNITED NATIONS (ONUSAL): 26 Observers, plus 220 civ pol from 14 countries.

GUYANA

GDP	1992: $G 46.9bn ($375.0m): per capita $2,100	
	1993: $G 52.8bn ($416.7m): per capita $2,300	
Growth	1992: 7.8%	1993: 8.3%
Inflation	1992: 15.0%	1993: 7.7%
Debt	1992: $1.9bn	1993: $2.2bn
Def exp	1993: $G 773m ($6.1m)	
Def bdgt	1992: $G 675m ($5.4m)	
	1993: $G 760m ($6.0m)	
	1994: $G 923m ($7.0m)	
$ 1 = $G	1992: 125.0	1993: 126.7
	1994: 131.9	

$G = Guyanese dollar

Population: 814,000

	13–17	*18–22*	*23–32*
Men	43,200	43,400	78,700
Women	41,000	41,500	75,600

TOTAL ARMED FORCES (Combined Guyana Defence Force):
ACTIVE: 1,700.
RESERVES: some 1,500 People's Militia (see Paramilitary).

ARMY: 1,400 (incl 500 Reserves).
1 inf bn, 1 SF, 1 spt wpn, 1 engr coy.

EQUIPMENT:
RECCE: 3 *Shorland*.
TOWED ARTY: 130mm: 6 M-46.
MORTARS: 81mm: 12 L16A1; 82mm: 18 M-43; 120mm: 18 M-43.

NAVY: 200.
BASES: Georgetown, New Amsterdam.
2 boats.

AIR FORCE: 100; no cbt ac, no armed hel.
TRANSPORT: ac: 1 BN-2A, 1 *Skyvan*; **hel:** 1 Bell 206, 1 Bel 412.

FORCES ABROAD:
UN AND PEACEKEEPING:
EL SALVADOR (ONUSAL): 6 civ pol.

PARAMILITARY:
GUYANA PEOPLE'S MILITIA (GPM): some 1,500.

HONDURAS

GDP	1992: L 18.8bn ($3.2bn): per capita $2,000	
	1993: L 21.6bn ($3.4bn): per capita $2,100	
Growth	1992: 5.6%	1993: 3.7%
Inflation	1992: 8.8%	1993: 13.0%
Debt	1992: $3.6bn	1993: $3.6bn
Def exp	1990: L 276.0m ($45.7m)	
Def bdgt	1992: L 247.5m ($42.5m)	
	1993: L 329.0m ($45.3m)	
	1994ε: L 355.0m ($48.9m)	
FMA	1993: $2.9m (FMF, IMET)	
	1994: $0.5m (IMET)	
$1 = L	1992: 5.8	1993: 7.3
	1994: 7.3	

L = lempira

Population: 5,757,800

	13–17	*18–22*	*23–32*
Men	343,600	299,400	448,400
Women	332,400	290,000	440,900

TOTAL ARMED FORCES:
ACTIVE: 16,800 (13,200 conscripts).
Terms of service: conscription, 24 months (to end 1995).
RESERVES: 60,000 ex-servicemen registered.

ARMY: 14,000 (12,000 conscripts).
10 Military Zones.
2 inf bde (each with 3 inf, 1 arty bn).
1 inf bde with 1 inf, 1 arty, 1 engr bn.
1 special tac gp with 1 inf, 1 ranger bn, 2 trg units.
1 territorial force (2 inf, 1 SF, 1 AB bn).
1 armd cav regt (2 bn).
1 arty, 1 engr bn.
RESERVES:
3 inf bde.
EQUIPMENT:
LIGHT TANKS: 12 *Scorpion*.
RECCE: 3 *Scimitar*, 1 *Sultan*, 50 *Saladin*, 12 RBY Mk 1.
TOWED ARTY: 105mm: 24 M-102; 155mm: 4 M-198.
MORTARS: 400 60mm; 81mm; 120mm: 60 Brandt; 160mm: 30 *Soltam*.
RL: 84mm: 120 *Carl Gustav*.
RCL: 106mm: 80 M-40A1.

NAVY: 1,000 (incl 400 Marines and 500 conscripts).
BASES: Puerto Cortés, Puerto Castilla (Atlantic), Amapala (Pacific).
PATROL CRAFT, INSHORE: 11:
3 *Guaymuras* (US Swiftships 31-m) PFI, 2 *Copan* (US Lantana 32-m) PFI⟨, 6 PCI⟨, plus boats.
AMPHIBIOUS: craft only; 1 *Punta Caxinas* LCT; plus some 3 ex-US LCM.

MARINES: (400); 1 bn.

AIR FORCE: some 1,800 (700 conscripts); 38 cbt† ac plus 8 in store, no armed hel.
FGA: 2 sqn:
1 with 13 A-37B.
1 with 10 F-5E, 2 -F.
FIGHTER: 8 *Super Mystère* B2 (in store).
TRANSPORT: 9 C-47, 1 C-123, 4 C-130A, 2 DHC-5, 1 L-188, 2 IAI-201, 1 IAI-1123, 1 -1124.
LIAISON: 1 sqn with 1 *Baron*, 3 Cessna 172, 2 Cessna 180, 2 Cessna 185, 4 *Commander*, 1 PA-31, 1 PA-34.
HELICOPTERS: 9 Bell 412, 4 Hughes 500, 5 TH-55, 8 UH-1B, 7 UH-1H, 1 S-76.
TRAINING: 4* C-101BB, 6 U-17A, 11* EMB-312, 5 T-41A.

FORCES ABROAD:
UN AND PEACEKEEPING:
WESTERN SAHARA (MINURSO): 16, incl 14 Observers.

PARAMILITARY:
PUBLIC SECURITY FORCES (Ministry of Public Security and Defence): 5,500; 11 regional comd.

FOREIGN FORCES:
US: 350: Army: (300); Air: (50).

PARAGUAY

GDP	1992:	Pg 7,545bn ($5.0bn): per capita $3,600		
	1993:	Pg 9,324bn ($5.4bn): per capita $3,800		
Growth	1992:	1.5%	1993:	3.6%
Inflation	1992:	15.1%	1994:	23.8%
Debt	1992:	$1.8bn	1993:	$1.6bn
Def bdgt[a]	1992:	Pg 174bn ($116m)		
	1993:	Pg 150bn ($100m)		
	1994:	Pg 151bn ($87m)		
FMA	1993:	$0.4m (IMET)		
$1 = Pg	1992:	1,500	1993:	1,744
	1994:	1,888		

Pg = Paraguayan guarani

[a] Does not include extra-budgetary funds from military enterprises.

Population: 4,854,000

	13–17	*18–22*	*23–32*
Men	260,900	228,900	392,600
Women	251,700	220,600	377,200

TOTAL ARMED FORCES:
ACTIVE: 16,500 (10,800 conscripts).
Terms of service: 12 months; Navy 2 years.
RESERVES: some 45,000.

ARMY: 12,500 (8,600 conscripts).
3 corps HQ.
9 div HQ (6 inf, 3 cav).
10 inf regt (bn).
2 cav regt (horse).
1 armd cav regt.
2 mech cav regt.
20 frontier det.
4 arty gp (bn).
4 engr bn.
EQUIPMENT:
MBT: 5 M-4A3.
LIGHT TANKS: 18 M-3A1.

RECCE: 8 M-8, 5 M-3, 30 EE-9 *Cascavel*.
APC: 10 EE-11 *Urutu*.
TOWED ARTY: 75mm: 20 Model 1927/1934; 105mm: 15 M-101; 152mm: 6 Mk V 6-in (anti-ship).
MORTARS: 81mm: 80.
RCL: 75mm: M-20.
AD GUNS: 20mm: 20 Bofors; 40mm: 10 M-1A1.

NAVY: 3,000 (incl 500 Marines, 100 Naval Aviation, Harbour and River Guard, and ε1,500 conscripts).
BASES: Asunción (Puerto Sajonia), Bahía Negra, Ciudad Del Este.
PATROL AND COASTAL COMBATANTS: 7:
COASTAL: 5:
2 *Paraguay* with 4 x 120mm guns.
3 *Nanawa* (Arg *Bouchard* MSO).
RIVERINE: 2:
1 *Capitan Cabral* (built 1907).
1 *Itaipu*.
SUPPORT AND MISCELLANEOUS: 6:
1 tpt, 1 *Boqueron* spt (ex-US LSM with hel deck), 1 trg/tpt, 1 survey‹, 2 LCT.

MARINES: (500) (incl 200 conscripts).
2 marine bn.

NAVAL AVIATION: (100); 2 cbt ac, no armed hel.
COIN: 2 AT-6G.
TRANSPORT: 1 C-47.
LIAISON: 3 Cessna 150, 3 Cessna 206, 1 Cessna 210.
HELICOPTERS: 2 HB-350, 1 OH-13, 2 UH-12E.

AIR FORCE: 1,000 (700 conscripts); 17 cbt ac, no armed hel.
COMPOSITE SQN:
COIN: 5 AT-6, 7 EMB-326.
LIAISON: 1 Cessna 185, 2 Cessna 206, 1 Cessna 337, 2 Cessna 402, 2 T-41.
HELICOPTER: 3 HB-350, 1 UH-1B, 4 UH-12, 4 Bell 47G.
TRANSPORT: 1 sqn with 5 C-47, 4 C-212, 3 DC-6B, 1 DHC-6 (VIP).
TRAINING: 5* EMB-312, 6 T-6, 10 T-23, 5 T-25, 10 T-35, 1 T-41.

PARAMILITARY:
SPECIAL POLICE SERVICE: 8,000.

PERU

GDP	1992: NS 56.4bn ($45.0bn): per capita $3,100		
	1993ε: NS 97.2bn ($48.9bn): per capita $3,400		
Growth	1992: -2.8%	1993ε: 6.0%	
Inflation	1992: 73.5%	1993: 39.5%	
Debt	1992: $20.3bn	1993: $20.7bn	
Def bdgt[a]	1992: NS 975m ($782.6m)		
	1993: NS 1,328m ($699.0m)		
	1994ε: NS 1,646m ($748.0m)		
FMA	1993: $17.5m (Narcs)		
	1994: $8.0m (Narcs)		
	1995: $ 42.0m (Narcs)		
$1 = NS	1992: 1.3	1993: 1.9	
	1994: 2.2		

NS = new sol

[a] Does not include some extra-budgetary funds.

Population: 23,633,400

	13–17	*18–22*	*23–32*
Men	1,292,200	1,186,400	1,984,300
Women	1,286,900	1,184,300	1,988,800

TOTAL ARMED FORCES:
ACTIVE: 115,000 (65,500 conscripts).
Terms of service: 2 years, selective.
RESERVES: 188,000 (Army only).

ARMY: 75,000 (50,000 conscripts).
5 Military Regions.
Army Troops:
1 AB 'div' (bde: 3 cdo, 1 para bn, 1 arty gp).
1 Presidential Escort regt.
1 AD arty gp.
Regional Troops:
3 armd div (bde, each 2 tk, 1 armd inf bn,1 arty gp, 1 engr bn).
1 armd gp (3 indep armd cav, 1 fd arty, 1 AD arty, 1 engr bn).
1 cav div (3 mech regt, 1 arty gp).
7 inf div (bde, each 3 inf bn, 1 arty gp).
1 jungle div.
2 med arty gp; 2 fd arty gp.
1 indep inf bn.
1 indep engr bn.
3 hel sqn.
EQUIPMENT:
MBT: 300 T-54/-55 (ε50 serviceable).
LIGHT TANKS: 110 AMX-13 (ε30 serviceable).

RECCE: 60 M-8/-20, 10 M-3A1, 50 M-9A1, 15 Fiat 6616, 30 BRDM-2.
APC: 130 M-113, 12 BTR-60, 130 UR-416, 4 *Repontec*.
TOWED ARTY: 105mm: 20 Model 56 pack, 130 M-101; 122mm: 30 D-30; 130mm: 30 M-46.
SP ARTY: 155mm: 12 M-109A2, 12 Mk F3.
MRL: 122mm: 14 BM-21.
MORTARS: 81mm: incl some SP; 107mm: incl some SP; 120mm: 300 Brandt, ECIA.
RCL: 106mm: M40A1.
AD GUNS: 23mm: 80 ZSU-23-2, 35 ZSU-23-4 SP; 40mm: 45 M-1, 80 L60/70.
SAM: SA-7, 120 SA-14/-16.
AIRCRAFT: 1 Cessna 182, 2 -U206, 1 -337, 1 *Queen Air* 65, 3 U-10, 3 U-17.
HELICOPTERS: 2 Bell 47G, 2 Mi-6, 28 Mi-8, 14 Mi-17, 6 SA-315, 5 SA-316, 3 SA-318, 2 *Agusta* A-109.

NAVY: 25,000 (incl some 700 Naval Aviation, 3,000 Marines and 13,500 conscripts).

3 Naval Force Areas: Pacific, Lake Titicaca, Amazon River.
BASES: **Ocean:** Callao, San Lorenzo Island, Paita, Talara. **Lake:** Puno. **River:** Iquitos, Puerto Maldonado.
SUBMARINES: 6:
6 *Casma* (Ge T-209/1200) with 533mm TT (It A184 HWT).
(Plus 1 *Pedrera* (US *Guppy* I) with 533mm TT (Mk 37 HWT) alongside trg only.)
PRINCIPAL SURFACE COMBATANTS: 11:
CRUISERS: 2:
1 *Almirante Grau* (Nl *De Ruyter*) with 4 x 2 152mm guns, 8 *Otomat* SSM.
1 *Aguirre* (Nl *De 7 Provincien*) with 3 x SH-3D *Sea King* hel (ASW/ASUW) (Mk 46 LWT/AM-39 *Exocet*), 2 x 2 152mm guns.
DESTROYERS: 5:
1 *Palacios* (UK *Daring*) with 4 x 2 MM-38 *Exocet*, 3 x 2 114mm guns, hel deck.
4 *Bolognesi* (Nl *Friesland*) with 4 x 120mm guns, 2 x 4 ASW RL.
FRIGATES: 4 *Carvajal* (mod It *Lupo*) with 1 AB-212 hel (ASW/OTHT), 2 x 3 ASTT; plus 8 *Otomat* Mk 2 SSM, 1 x 127mm gun.
PATROL AND COASTAL COMBATANTS: 7:
MISSILE CRAFT: 6 *Velarde* PFM (Fr PR-72 64-m) with 4 x MM-38 *Exocet*.
PATROL: 1 *Unanue* (ex-US *Sotoyomo*) PCC (Antarctic ops).
AMPHIBIOUS: 4 *Paita* (US *Terrebonne Parish*) LST, capacity 395 tps, 16 tk.
SUPPORT AND MISCELLANEOUS: 9:
3 AO, 2 AOT, 1 tpt, 2 survey, 1 ocean tug (SAR).
RIVER AND LAKE FLOTILLAS: 9:
some 4 gunboats, 5 patrol⟨.

NAVAL AVIATION: (some 700); 7 cbt ac, 14 armed hel.

ASW/MR: 4 sqn with: **ac:** 7* S-2, 6 *Super King Air* B 200T; **hel:** 6 AB-212 ASW, 8 SH-3D (ASW).
TRANSPORT: 2 C-47.
LIAISON: 4 Bell 206B, 6 UH-1D hel, 2 SA-319, 3 Mi-8.
TRAINING: 1 Cessna 150, 5 T-34C.
ASM: *Exocet* AM-39 (on SH-3 hel).

MARINES: (3,000).

1 Marine bde (5 bn, 1 recce, 1 cdo coy).
EQUIPMENT:
RECCE: V-100.
APC: 15 V-200 *Chaimite*, 20 BMR-600.
MORTARS: 81mm; 120mm ε18 .
RCL: 84mm: *Carl Gustav*; 106mm: M-40A1.
AD GUNS: twin 20mm SP.

COAST DEFENCE: 3 bty with 18 155mm how.

AIR FORCE: 15,000 (2,000 conscripts); 94 cbt ac, 15 armed hel.

BOMBERS:
1 gp (2 sqn) with 15 *Canberra* (4 -B(1) 12, 8 -B1(68), 1 T-4, 2 -T54).
FGA: 2 gp: 6 sqn:
3 with 30 Su-22 (incl 4* Su-22U).
3 with 25 Cessna A-37B.
FIGHTER: 3 sqn:
1 with 10 *Mirage* 2000P, 2 -DP.
2 with 10 *Mirage* 5P, 2 -DP.
ATTACK HELICOPTERS: 1 hel sqn with 15 Mi-25.
RECCE: 1 photo-survey unit with 2 *Learjet* 25B, 2 -36A.
TANKER: 1 Boeing KC 707-323C.
TRANSPORT: 3 gp (7 sqn):
AIRCRAFT: 14 An-32, 4 C-130A, 6 -D, 5 L-100-20, 2 DC-8-62F, 12 DHC-5, 8 DHC-6, 1 FH-227, 9 PC-6, 6 Y-12.
PRESIDENTIAL FLT: 1 F-28, 1 *Falcon* 20F.
HELICOPTERS: 3 sqn with 8 Bell 206, 15 Bell 212, 5 Bell 214, 1 Bell 412, 10 Bo-105C, 5 Mi-6, 5 Mi-8, 5 SA-316.
LIAISON: ac: 2 Beech 99, 3 Cessna 185, 1 Cessna 320, 15 *Queen Air* 80, 3 *King Air* 90, 1 PA-31T; **hel:** 8 UH-1D.
TRAINING: ac: 2 Cessna 150, 25 EMB-312, 13 MB-339A, 20 T-37B/C, 15 T-41A/-D; **hel:** 12 Bell 47G.

MISSILES:
ASM: AS-30.
AAM: AA-2 *'Atoll'*, R-550 *Magic*.
AD: 3 SA-2, 6 SA-3 bn with 18 SA-2, 24 SA-3 launchers.

PARAMILITARY:

NATIONAL POLICE: 60,000 (amalgamation of Guardia Civil, Republican Guard and Policia Investigacionara Peruana); MOWAG *Roland* APC.
COAST GUARD: 600; 5 *Rio Nepena* PCC, 3 PCI, 8 riverine PCI‹.
RONDAS CAMPESINAS (peasant self-defence force): perhaps 2,000 *rondas* 'groups', up to pl strength, some with small arms. Deployed mainly in emergency zone.

OPPOSITION:

SENDERO LUMINOSO (Shining Path): some ε3,000; Maoist.
MOVIMIENTO REVOLUCIONARIO TUPAC AMARU (MRTA): ε500; mainly urban gp.

SURINAME

GDP	1992ε: gld 3.4bn ($1.9bn): per capita $3,600	
	1993ε: gld 3.4bn ($1.9bn): per capita $3,600	
Growth	1992: -5%	1993ε: -3.0%
Inflation	1992: 44%	1993ε: 180%
Debt	1992: $162m	1993: $200m
Def bdgt	1991: gld 134.0m ($75.1m)	
	1992: gld 110.0m ($61.6m)	
	1993: gld 110.7m ($61.8m)	
FMA	1993: $0.05m (IMET)	
$1 = gld	1992–94: 1.79	

gld = guilder

Population: 487,800

	13–17	*18–22*	*23–32*
Men	22,600	22,800	46,400
Women	22,100	22,200	46,200

TOTAL ARMED FORCES (all services form part of the Army):

ACTIVE: 1,800.

ARMY: 1,400.

1 inf bn (4 inf coy).
1 mech cav sqn.
1 Military Police 'bde' (bn).
EQUIPMENT:
RECCE: 6 EE-9 *Cascavel*.
APC: 9 YP-408, 15 EE-11 *Urutu*.
MORTARS: 81mm: 6.
RCL: 106mm: M-40A1.

NAVY: 240.

BASE: Paramaribo.
PATROL CRAFT, INSHORE: 5:
3 S-401 (Nl 32-m), 2‹, plus boats.

AIR FORCE: ε150; 5 cbt ac, no armed hel.

COIN: 4 BN-2 *Defender*, 1 PC-7.
LIAISON: 1 Cessna U206.
HELICOPTERS: 2 SA-316, 1 AB-205.

URUGUAY

GDP	1992: pU 34.5bn ($11.4bn): per capita $7,400	
	1993: pU 45.5bn ($11.9bn): per capita $7,700	
Growth	1992: 7.4%	1993: 1.5%
Inflation	1992: 54.3%	1993: 52.8%
Debt	1992: $5.3bn	1993: $5.6bn
Def exp	1992: pU 655m ($216.0m)	
	1993: pU 853m ($223.0m)	
Def bdgt	1994ε: pU 1.0bn ($224.5m)	
FMA	1993: $0.34m (IMET)	
	1995: $0.75m (Narcs, IMET)	
$1 = pU[a]	1992: 3.03	1993: 3.83
	1994: 4.52	

pU = Uruguyan peso

[a] The Uruguayan peso, equal to 1,000 new Uruguayan pesos, was introduced in March 1993.

Population: 3,160,400

	13–17	*18–22*	*23–32*
Men	136,500	132,100	227,600
Women	131,900	127,900	228,600

TOTAL ARMED FORCES:

ACTIVE: 25,600.

ARMY: 17,200.

4 Military Regions/div HQ.
5 inf bde (4 of 3 inf bn, 1 of 1 mech, 1 mot, 1 para bn).

3 cav bde (10 cav bn (4 horsed, 3 mech, 2 mot, 1 armd)).
1 arty bde (2 arty, 1 AD arty bn).
1 engr bde (3 bn).
3 arty, 4 cbt engr bn.
EQUIPMENT:
LIGHT TANKS: 17 M-24, 28 M-3A1, 22 M-41A1.
RECCE: 20 FN-4-RM-62, 25 EE-3 *Jararaca*, 10 EE-9 *Cascavel*.
APC: 15 M-113, 50 *Condor*, 18 EE-11 *Urutu*.
TOWED ARTY: 75mm: 12 Bofors M-1902; 105mm: 50 M-101A/M-102; 155mm: 5 M-114A1.
MORTARS: 81mm: 50 M-1; 107mm: 8 M-30.
ATGW: 5 *Milan*.
RCL: 57mm: 30 M-18; 106mm: 30 M-40A1.
AD GUNS: 20mm: 6 M-167 *Vulcan*; 40mm: 11 L/60.

NAVY: 5,400 (incl 300 Naval Aviation, 400 Naval Infantry, 1,600 Prefectura Naval (Coast Guard)).
BASES: Montevideo (HQ), La Paloma, Fray Bentos.
FRIGATES: 3:
3 *General Artigas* (Fr *Cdt. Rivière*) with 2 x 3 ASTT, 1 x 2 ASW mor, 2 x 100mm guns.
PATROL AND COASTAL COMBATANTS: 10:
INSHORE: 10:
2 *Colonia* PCI (US *Cape*).
3 *15 de Noviembre* PFI (Fr *Vigilante* 42-m).
1 *Salto* PCI, 1 *Paysandu* PCI⟨, and 3 other⟨.
MINE WARFARE: 4:
4 *Temerario* MSC (Ge *Kondor II*).
AMPHIBIOUS: craft only: 2 LCM, 2 LCVP.
SUPPORT AND MISCELLANEOUS: 5:
1 *Presidente Rivera* AOT, 1 *Vanguardia* Salvage, 1 *Campbell* (US *Auk* MSF) PCO (Antarctic patrol/ research), 1 spt (ex GDR *Elbe*-Class), 1 trg.
NAVAL AVIATION: (300); 6 cbt ac, no armed hel.
ASW: 1 flt with 3 S-2A, 3 -G.
MR: 1 *Super King Air* 200T.
TRAINING/LIAISON: 1 *Super Cub*, 2 T-28, 2 T-34B, 2 T-34C, 1 PA-34-200T, 1 C-182 *Skylane*.
HELICOPTERS: 2 Wessex 60, 1 Bell 47G, 1 Bell 222, 2 SH-34J.

NAVAL INFANTRY: (400); 1 bn.

AIR FORCE: 3,000; 24 cbt ac, no armed hel.
COIN: 2 sqn:
1 with 12 A-37B.
1 with 6 IA-58B.
SURVEY: 1 EMB-110B1.
SAR: 1 sqn with: 2 Bell 212, 5 UH-1B, 3 UH-1H hel.
TRANSPORT: 3 sqn with 3 C-212 (tpt/SAR), 3 EMB-110C, 1 F-27, 1 FH-227, 1 C-130B..
LIAISON: 2 Cessna 182, 4 *Queen Air* 80, 4 U-17.
TRAINING: *6 AT-6, 7 T-33, 20 T-34A/B, 6 T-41D.

FORCES ABROAD:
UN AND PEACEKEEPING:
EGYPT (MFO): 64.
INDIA/PAKISTAN (UNMOGIP): 3 Observers.
IRAQ/KUWAIT (UNIKOM): 6 Observers.
LIBERIA (UNOMIL): 20 Observers.
MOZAMBIQUE (ONUMOZ): 820, plus 34 Observers, 10 civ pol.
RWANDA (UNAMIR): 21 Observers.
WESTERN SAHARA (MINURSO): 5 Observers.

PARAMILITARY:
METROPOLITAN GUARD: 700.
REPUBLICAN GUARD: 500.
COAST GUARD: the Prefectura Naval (PNN) is part of the Navy.

VENEZUELA

GDP	1992: Bs 4,132.3bn ($60.4bn): per capita $9,000		
	1993: Bs 5,572.1bn ($61.4bn): per capita $9,100		
Growth	1992: 6.8%	1993: -1.0%	
Inflation	1992: 31.4%	1993: 46.0%	
Debt	1992: $37.2bn	1993: $37.9bn	
Def exp	1992: Bs 104.3bn ($1.5bn)		
Def bdgt	1992: Bs 52.8bn ($772.2m)		
	1993: Bs 93.0bn ($1.0bn)		
	1994: Bs 111.0bn ($984.0m)		
FMA	1993: $0.2m (IMET)		
	1994: $0.2m (IMET)		
	1995: $0.2m (IMET)		
$1 = Bs	1992: 68.4	1993: 90.8	
	1994: 110.3		

Bs = bolivar

Population: 21,634,000

	13–17	*18–22*	*23–32*
Men	1,184,600	1,053,000	1,824,500
Women	1,142,100	1,019,100	1,775,700

TOTAL ARMED FORCES:
ACTIVE: 79,000 (incl National Guard and ε31,000 conscripts).
Terms of service: 30 months selective, varies by region for all services.
RESERVES: Army: ε8,000.

ARMY: 34,000 (incl 27,000 conscripts).
6 inf div.
1 armd bde.
1 cav bde.
7 inf bde (18 inf, 1 mech inf, 4 fd arty bn).
1 AB bde.
1 Ranger bde (6 Ranger bn).
1 avn regt.
RESERVES: ε6 inf, 1 armd, 1 arty bn.
EQUIPMENT:
MBT: 70 AMX-30.
LIGHT TANKS: 75 M-18, 36 AMX-13, ε50 *Scorpion*.
RECCE: 10 AML-60/-90, 30 M-8.
APC: 25 AMX-VCI, 100 V-100, 30 V-150, 100 *Dragoon* (some with 90mm gun), 35 EE-11 *Urutu*.
TOWED ARTY: 105mm: 40 Model 56, 40 M-101; 155mm: 12 M-114.
SP ARTY: 155mm: 5 M-109, 10 Mk F3.
MRL: 160mm: 20 LAR SP.
MORTARS: 81mm: 165; 120mm: 65 Brandt.
ATGW: AT-4, AS-11, 24 *Mapats*.
RCL: 84mm: *Carl Gustav*; 106mm: 175 M-40A1.
AIRCRAFT: 3 IAI-202, 2 Cessna 182, 2 Cessna 206, 2 Cessna 207.
ATTACK HEL: 5 A-109 (ATK).
TRANSPORT HEL: 4 AS-61A, 3 Bell 205, 6 UH-1H.
LIAISON: 2 Bell 206.

NAVY: 15,000 (incl 1,000 Naval Aviation, 5,000 Marines, 1,000 Coast Guard and ε4,000 conscripts).
5 Commands: Fleet, Marines, Naval Avn, Coast guard, Fluvial (River Forces).
5 Fleet sqn: submarine, frigate, patrol, amph, service.
BASES: Caracas (HQ), Puerto Cabello (submarine, frigate, amph and service sqn), Punto Fijo (patrol sqn). Minor bases: Puerto de Hierro, Puerto La Cruz, El Amparo (HQ Arauca River), Maracaibo, La Guaira, Ciudad Bolivar (HQ Fluvial Forces).
SUBMARINES: 2:
2 *Sabalo* (Ge T-209/1300) with 533mm TT (SST-4 HWT) (1 refitting in Germany).
FRIGATES: 6 *Mariscal Sucre* (It *Lupo*) with 1 AB-212 hel (ASW/OTHT), 2 x 3 ASTT (A-244S LWT); plus 8 *Teseo* SSM, 1 x 127mm gun, 1 x 8 *Aspide* SAM. (US has agreed lease of 2 *Knox*-class FF from about mid-1994.)
PATROL AND COASTAL COMBATANTS: 6:
MISSILE CRAFT: 6: 3 *Constitución* PFM (UK Vosper 37-m), with 2 x *Teseo*.
3 *Constitución* PFI with 4 x *Harpoon* SSM.
AMPHIBIOUS: 4:
4 *Capana* LST, capacity 200 tps, 12 tk.
Plus craft: 2 LCU (river comd), 11 LCVP.

SUPPORT AND MISCELLANEOUS: 3:
1 log spt, 1 trg, 1 *Punta Brava* AGHS.

NAVAL AVIATION: (1,000); 4 cbt ac, 8 armed hel.
ASW: 1 hel sqn (afloat) with 8 AB-212.
MR: 1 sqn with 4 C-212.
TRANSPORT: 2 C-212, 1 DHC-7, 1 *Rockwell Commander* 680.
LIAISON: 1 Cessna 310, 1 Cessna 402, 1 *King Air* 90.
HELICOPTERS: 2 Bell 47J.

MARINES: (5,000).
4 inf bn.
1 arty bn (3 fd, 1 AD bty).
1 amph veh bn.
1 river patrol, 1 engr, 2 para/cdo unit.
EQUIPMENT:
AAV: 11 LVTP-7 (to be mod to -7A1).
APC: 25 EE-11 *Urutu*, 10 *Fuchs/Transportpanzer* 1.
TOWED ARTY: 105mm: 18 Model 56.
AD GUNS: 40mm: 6 M-42 twin SP.

COAST GUARD: (1,000).
BASE: La Guaira; operates under Naval Command and Control, but organisationally separate.
PATROL, OFFSHORE: 3:
2 *Almirante Clemente* (It FF type).
1 *Miguel Rodriguez* (ex-US ocean tug).
PATROL, INSHORE: 6: 2 *Petrel* (USCG *Point*-class) PCI‹, 4 riverine PCI‹, plus boats.

AIR FORCE: 7,000 (some conscripts); 119 cbt ac, 27 armed hel.
FIGHTER/FGA: 3 air gp: 1 with 15 CF-5A/B, 15 T-2D; 1 with 2 *Mirage* IIIEV, 5 *Mirage* 50EV; 1 with 18 F-16A, 6 -B.
COIN: 1 air gp with 10 EMB-312, 24 OV-10E, 17 T-2D *Buckeye*.
ARMED HELICOPTERS: 1 air gp with 10 SA-316, 12 UH-1D, 5 UH-1H.
TRANSPORT: ac: 7 C-123, 6 C-130H, 8 G-222, 2 HS-748, 2 B-707 (tkr); **hel:** 3 Bell 214, 4 Bell 412, 5 AS-332B, 2 UH-1N.
PRESIDENTIAL FLT: 1 Boeing 737, 3 *Falcon* 20, 1 *Gulfstream* II, 1 *Gulfstream* III, 1 *Learjet* 24D.
LIAISON: 9 Cessna 182, 1 *Citation* I, 1 *Citation* II, 2 *Queen Air* 65, 5 *Queen Air* 80, 5 *Super King Air* 200, 9 SA-316B *Alouette III*.
TRAINING: 1 air gp: 12 EMB-312, *7 F-5 (1 CF-5D, 6 NF-5B), 20 T-34.
AAM: R-530 *Magic*, AIM-9L *Sidewinder*, AIM-9P *Sidewinder*.

AD GUNS: 110: 20mm: some Panhard M-3 SP; 35mm; 40mm: Bofors L/70 towed, Breda towed.
SAM: 10 *Roland*.

NATIONAL GUARD (Fuerzas Armadas de Cooperación): 23,000 (internal sy, customs).
8 regional commands.
EQUIPMENT: 20 UR-416 AIFV, 24 Fiat-6614 APC, 100 60mm mor, 50 81mm mor.
AIRCRAFT: 1 *Baron*, 1 BN-2A, 2 Cessna 185, 5 -U206, 4 IAI-201, 1 *King Air* 90, 1 *King Air* 200C, 2 *Queen Air* 80.
HELICOPTERS: 4 A-109, 20 Bell 206.
PATROL CRAFT, INSHORE: 22; some 60 boats.

FORCES ABROAD:

UN AND PEACEKEEPING:
CROATIA (UNPROFOR I): 7 Observers.
EL SALVADOR (ONUSAL): 3 Observers.
IRAQ/KUWAIT (UNIKOM): 5 Observers.
WESTERN SAHARA (MINURSO): 9 Observers.

Sub–Saharan Africa

This year the countries of Sub-Saharan Africa have been grouped geographically: Horn of Africa (including Djibouti, Somalia and Sudan, previously listed in *The Military Balance* under the Middle East); East Africa; Central Africa; West Africa; and Southern Africa.

Africa has been the region of the world worst hit by violence over the last 12 months. Of the 30-plus civil wars currently being fought across the world, seven are in Sub-Saharan Africa. The only encouraging news is that few new major weapons systems have been acquired by African states, but when killing is usually accomplished by machine-gun, hand grenade or machete this is little consolation.

Political and Strategic Developments

Horn of Africa

The civil war in northern **Djibouti** rumbles on with neither the government nor the Atar tribesmen of the Front for the Restoration of Unity and Democracy (FRUD) apparently making much effort to win the war. The government and the leader of FRUD, Muhammad Adoyta Youssouf, held talks on 11 and 12 June 1994 amid hopes that the long-standing dispute may yet be settled. To date, no military problems have emerged following **Eritrea's** independence from **Ethiopia**.

While the level of violence in **Somalia** is much reduced, no permanent political solution to the crisis has been found and there is still no central government authority. In the north, Somaliland (controlling the territory of the former British Protectorate) continues as a separate, but unrecognised state without a UN presence, creating a potential problem for Somalia's reconstitution. The composition of the UN peacekeeping force (UNOSOM II) has changed radically over the last 12 months. In July 1993 it included a strong residual US presence and contingents from Belgium, France, Germany and Italy, all of which have now been withdrawn to be replaced by increased numbers of Indian troops and a large Pakistani contingent. The final withdrawal of US troops took place in some disarray. In October 1993, 15 US soldiers were killed and one taken prisoner when some helicopters were forced to land during a Special Forces operation. The small force was not relieved by other UN troops for 15 hours. In the previous two months, 15 other US soldiers had been killed in Mogadishu when newly arrived Rangers had attempted to capture General Aideed. US troops had been given the role of rapid-reaction force for UNOSOM, but remained under US rather than UN control, and by the end of March 1994 the US contingent had completely withdrawn. UN policy towards the warlords, and General Farah Aideed in particular, has changed and the mandate of UNOSOM redefined, no longer allowing the use of force to disarm the factions. UNOSOM's mandate was renewed on 1 June for a further four months, but the warring factions were warned that the mission would end if no progress were made in the peace talks. On 19 June clan leaders agreed to end the fighting in southern Somalia. A number of conferences aimed at producing a political solution have been held, but without positive results.

The civil war in **Sudan** continues, rarely reported in the press and never portrayed on television screens. Slowly but surely government forces are subduing the opposition and taking control of territory. The Sudanese People's Liberation Army (SPLA) remains split between the forces of Colonel Garang, operating in Equitoria province in south-west Sudan, and Riak Machar, operating further to the east. Peace talks were held in Nairobi in March sponsored by Kenya, Uganda, Ethiopia and Eritrea without, as yet, any positive result.

Central Africa

One African problem which has, at long last, been satisfactorily solved is that of the Aouzou strip in northern **Chad**. In February 1994 the International Court of Justice ruled in favour of Chad in its dispute over the strip annexed by Libya in 1973. The Libyan government accepted the ruling and, supervised by the shortest-lived UN mission (UNASOG), withdrew from the Aouzou strip by the end of May 1994. However, Chad still suffers from its own internal dissension caused by rebel movements. These are the Committee of National Revival for Peace and Democracy (CSNPD), which operates in the south of the country; and the National Front of Chad (FNT), which clashed with the Army in January 1994 at the north-eastern town of Abeche.

The dreadful events in Rwanda have tended to cause the massacres that took place earlier in **Burundi** to be forgotten. The assassination on 21 October 1993 of the President of Burundi, along with seven of his cabinet, led first to a wave of attacks on the Tutsi minority population by the Hutu majority. President Melchior Ndadaye, the first Hutu president, had been elected in June 1993. The killing of Tutsis was followed by attacks on Hutus backed by the Tutsi-led Army. Between 100,000 and 200,000 are estimated to have died in late 1993, and some 800,000 people are said to have fled the country to Rwanda, Tanzania and Zaire. Violence has continued virtually unabated throughout 1994. In April 1994, the US found it necessary to deploy marines to Burundi to evacuate US and other foreign nationals.

The violent civil war in **Rwanda** between the mainly Tutsi Rwandan Patriotic Front (RPF) and the Hutu-led government came to a temporary end with the signing of the Arusha Peace Agreement in August 1993. The agreement provided for the establishment of a transitional government and for multi-party elections to be held in October 1995. The UN agreed in June 1993 to establish an observer mission (UNOMUR) on the Ugandan–Rwandan border, and this began to deploy in late August. During September, the OAU military observer group (NMOG) was expanded by troop reinforcements. In October 1993, the UN established the UN Assistance Mission for Rwanda (UNAMIR) which grew to an eventual strength of 2,500, including troops and observers, and the French force which had been sent to Rwanda in February 1993 was withdrawn. Initially UNAMIR was to establish a demilitarised zone in northern Rwanda between the forces of the two warring sides and set up a number of integrated training centres for their troops. However, the civil war re-erupted with unprecedented ferocity after the plane carrying the presidents of Rwanda and Burundi, both Hutus, was shot down over Kigali on 6 April 1994. Within days the RPF had reached the outskirts of Kigali where 11 Belgian UN soldiers were kidnapped and murdered. French and Belgian troops were sent to arrange and protect the evacuation of foreign nationals, but they and the majority of UNAMIR troops had withdrawn by mid-April, leaving only about 250 troops in Kigali to keep the airport open. By mid-May it was clear that strong reinforcements for UNAMIR were needed, but no Western countries and few African states were willing to commit troops. The UN Secretary-General, after obtaining pledges to commit troops from sufficient countries, was able to report to the Security Council at the end of May and his recommendations were approved on 8 June 1994. UNSC 925 authorised the deployment of 5,500 troops, but, at US insistence, only a proportion of these were to deploy immediately. The new mandate directed UNAMIR to protect refugees and other civilians at risk and provide support for humanitarian relief operations. It soon became clear that none of the promised contingents would be available for some weeks, if not months. France decided that unilateral action was essential and mounted *Operation Turquoise*. 2,000 French troops, supported by 300 from Senegal, began deployment into Zaire on 24 June, some crossing into Rwanda to establish protected areas for major concentrations of refugees. The UN had approved the French operation on 22 June, and authorised action under Chapter VII of the UN Charter for a period of two months.

West Africa

A cease-fire, agreed to at the peace talks held in Cotonou, Benin, came into effect in **Liberia** in August 1993. Although there have been frequent violations of the cease-fire, there has been no general resumption of the civil war. A fourth faction, the Liberian Peace Council (LPC), has emerged. The LPC, which is mainly Krahn, claims that the forces of George Taylor had been systematically breaking the cease-fire in their Grand Gedeh region from which they have now evicted Taylor's troops. The United Nations established an Observer Mission in Liberia (UNOMIL) in September 1993 with a mandate to: investigate reports of cease-fire violations; monitor compliance of the Cotonou peace agreement; observe and verify elections; develop a plan for demobilisation; and coordinate with the West African peace-keeping force (ECOMOG). ECOMOG troops and UNOMIL observers have now deployed across the country, except for the area controlled by the LPC which is not a party to the Cotonou agreement and has not yet declared a cease-fire.

Touareg tribal rebels have continued to cause instability in both **Mali** and **Niger**. In Niger the Touaregs are fighting for autonomy and not independence, but the government and the opposition in Niamey are firmly opposed to any change in the country's constitution.

A fresh dispute to develop in 1994 is that between **Nigeria** and **Cameroon** over the Bakassi peninsula, strategically placed at the mouth of Nigeria's Cross river. Nigerian troops moved into the peninsula in February 1994 ostensibly to protect the ethnic Nigerians living there. Both sides have built up their forces in the area, but so far there have been only localised incidents. Cameroon has taken the dispute to the International Court of Justice in the Hague.

President Babangida, who annulled the June 1993 **Nigerian** elections won by Moshood Abiola, bowed to pressure from the armed forces and in August handed over power to Ernest Shonekan (who had headed the Transition Council) with General Sani Abacha, Head of the Armed Forces, as his deputy. In November 1993 General Abacha, who had strengthened his position by dismissing many senior officers who had supported Babangida, took control in a bloodless coup following civil disobedience and a series of strikes which culminated in rioting provoked by sharp fuel price increases. Despite promises of a return to democracy and plans for revising the Constitution, nothing has been achieved. In June 1994 Abiola, who had declared himself president, was arrested by the Army and is to be tried for treason. General Abacha is likely to remain in power so long as he can retain the support of the Army, as there is little likelihood of a coherent national opposition challenging him.

Southern Africa

The civil war in **Angola** has continued unabated over the last 12 months. On 27 June 1994, government and UNITA negotiators agreed an 18-point document on reconciliation. The next step is to agree how the peace plan is to be implemented, and a UN-drafted plan has been submitted as a basis for discussion. One point not yet settled is the status of Jonas Savimbi once reconciliation is achieved.

In **Mozambique**, the process of confinement and demobilisation of both government and the Resistência Nacional Moçambicana (Renamo) is proceeding slowly. It is anticipated that the demobilisation of Renamo troops will be completed by 15 July 1994, and that of government troops by mid-August. The high command of the new joint defence force was created in January 1994 with joint commanders from the government and Renamo. The first infantry battalion of the new army – the Mozambique Democratic Armed Forces (FADM), composed of equal numbers of former government and Renamo soldiers – completed its training at the beginning of June. The British team which has been assisting with the training of FADM units will now stay in Mozambique until October, and a total of 15 battalions are to be formed.

The first multi-racial elections in **South Africa**, held in April 1994, produced what can be said to be a most favourable result. The African National Congress (ANC) received an overwhelming majority, but not as high as the 75% of the vote which would have allowed unilateral changes to be made to the Constitution. The Zulu Inkatha movement, which only joined in the election process at the last minute, secured sufficient votes to be awarded cabinet and government positions. Despite fears to the contrary, the elections took place with virtually no violence and the new government has been welcomed by all sectors of the country. South Africa has rejoined the Commonwealth and been re-admitted to the United Nations, which has lifted the final embargoes still in place against South Africa. South Africa also handed over the Walvis Bay enclave to Namibia on 28 February 1994.

Military Developments

There have been few military developments in those countries not beset by civil war. Any changes either in troop strength or weapons holdings in those countries are obviously of a temporary nature and, in any event, the full extent of such developments is not openly available. *The Military Balance* has been able to revise its entries for a number of Sub-Saharan countries mainly in West and Central Africa, but there have been no dramatic changes either to manpower strengths or weapons holdings. The IISS is unable to give a date for any individual acquisition. While most weapons acquisitions, particularly of naval ships or combat aircraft, receive some publicity in defence journals, there is no similar announcement when elderly and obsolete equipment is retired. No doubt some of the weapons listed in *The Military Balance* Sub-Saharan Africa section are no longer in service.

A number of small increases in weapons holdings were revealed by the UN Register of Conventional Arms to which all members were to report their imports and exports. The following took place, unnoticed by the IISS, during 1992: Sudan received 18 130mm Type 59 from China (the total number of this gun held is 100, *The Military Balance 1993-1994* listed only 27); Zimbabwe received 20 122mm RU-70 MRL from the Czech Republic (the total number held is 55, none were listed in 1993–94); Rwanda received six 122mm howitzer from Egypt; Botswana four ACVs from Israel; Nigeria four 130mm guns and five 122mm MRL from Romania; and Sierra Leone four APCs from Russia.

It is too early to say how the South African Defence Force (SADF) will be reorganised, other than that units integrating SADF troops and men of the ANC military wing, Umkhontowe Sizwe (MK), will be formed. The new force is to be called the South African National Defence Force (SANDF). The SANDF is expected to take in some 30,000 men from other forces including 1,500 from the Azanian People's Liberation Army (APLA), but will return to its current strength in about three years' time.

The Navy is looking to acquire four 2,000-tonne frigates able to embark a medium helicopter, and to have an option for four more around 2005. A large number of bids were submitted and suppliers in Denmark, France, Spain and UK have been short-listed. With the lifting of the UN arms embargo, Armscor is hoping to double the value of its exports, which already go to over 30 countries who have ignored the ban.

HORN OF AFRICA

DJIBOUTI

GDP	1992: frD 81.2bn ($457.0m):	
	per capita $1,100	
	1993ε: frD 82.9bn ($466.0m):	
	per capita $1,100	
Growth	1992: 2.1%	1993: -0.5%
Inflation	1991: 4.0%	1992: 6.0%
Debt	1992: $189.5m	1993: $196.5m
Def exp	1991: frD 6.9bn ($38.9m)	
	1992: frD 6.7bn ($37.9m)	
Def bdgt	1992: frD 4.7bn ($26.6m)	
	1993: frD 5.0bn ($28.2m)	
	1994: frD 4.0bn ($22.5m)	
FMA	1993: $0.2m (IMET)	
	1994: $0.1m (IMET)	
	1995: $0.2m (IMET)	

$1 = frD 1988–94: 177.7
frD = Djibouti franc

Population: 485,400

	13–17	*18–22*	*23–32*
Men	26,200	22,000	36,800
Women	26,100	21,800	32,800

TOTAL ARMED FORCES:

ACTIVE: some 9,600 (incl Gendarmerie).

ARMY: ε8,000.

3 Comd (North, Central, South).
1 inf bn, incl mor, ATK pl.
1 armd sqn.
1 AB coy.
1 arty bty.
1 border cdo bn.
1 spt bn.

EQUIPMENT:

RECCE: 15 M-11 VBL, 4 AML-60, 16 AML-90.

APC: 12 BTR-60 (op status uncertain).

TOWED ARTY: 122mm: 6 D-30.
MORTARS: 81mm: 25; 120mm: 20 *Brandt*.
RL: 73mm; 89mm: LRAC.
RCL: 106mm: 16 M-40A1.
AD GUNS: 20mm: 5 M-693 SP; 23mm: 5 ZU-23; 40mm: L/70.

NAVY: ε200.

BASE: Djibouti.
PATROL CRAFT, INSHORE: 3 PCI⟨†; plus boats.

AIR FORCE: 200; no cbt ac or armed hel.

TRANSPORT: 2 C-212, 2 N-2501F, 2 Cessna U206G, 1 Socata 235GT.
HELICOPTERS: 3 AS-355, 1 AS-350.
(Defected from Ethiopia: Mi-8, Mi-24 hel.)

PARAMILITARY:

GENDARMERIE (Ministry of Defence): 1,200; 1 bn, 1 patrol boat.
NATIONAL SECURITY FORCE (Ministry of Interior): ε3,000.

OPPOSITION:

FRONT FOR THE RESTORATION OF UNITY AND DEMOCRACY: ε4,500.

FOREIGN FORCES:

FRANCE: 3,800; incl 1 inf, 1 Foreign Legion regt, 1 sqn: 10 *Mirage* F-1C, 1 C-160 **ac**, 1 SA-319, 2 AS-355 **hel**.

ERITREA

Population: ε3,000,000

	13–17	*18–22*	*23–32*
Men	167,000	139,000	210,000
Women	161,000	134,000	203,000

Eritrea declared itself independent from Ethiopia on 27 April 1993. Demobilisation of some Eritrean forces began in late 1993. Est strength of these forces is currently about 70,000. A conscription period of 18 months has been authorised to include 6 months mil trg. Registration began in April 1994. No info on division of military assets between Ethiopia and Eritrea is available. Eritrea holds some air and naval assets, however holdings of army assets is unknown. It is likely that close cooperation with Ethiopia will continue to the possible extent of sharing military assets. Numbers given should be treated with caution.

NAVY: strength not known.

BASES: Massawa, Assab, Dahlak.
FRIGATES: 1 *Zerai Deres* (Sov *Petya-II*) with 2 x ASW RL, 10 x 406mm TT.
PATROL AND COASTAL COMBATANTS: 13:
MISSILE CRAFT: 2 Sov *Osa* with 2 x SS-N-2 *Styx* SSM.
TORPEDO CRAFT: 4: 2 Sov *Turya* PHT, 2 *Mol* PFT all with 4 x 533mm TT.
PATROL, INSHORE: 7 PFI: 3 US Swiftships 32-m, 4 Sov Zhuk⟨.
MINE WARFARE: 2: 1 *Natya* MSO, 1 *Sonya* MSC.
AMPHIBIOUS: 2 Sov *Polnocny* LSM, capacity 100 tps, 6 tk.
Plus craft: 3 LCT (1 Fr EDIC and 2 *Chamo* (Ministry of Transport)), 4 LCM.
SUPPORT AND MISCELLANEOUS: 1: 1 AOT.

ETHIOPIA

GDP	1992: EB 13.5bn ($2.7bn): per capita $380	
	1993ε: EB 16.8bn ($3.4bn): per capita $410	
Growth	1992: -0.3%	1993ε: 5.8%
Inflation	1992: 10.3%	1993ε: 10.0%
Debt	1992: $4.4bn	1993: $4.7bn
Def bdgt	1993: EB 1,250m ($250m)	
	1994: EB 700m ($140m)	
FMA	1993: $0.2m (IMET)	
	1994: $0.1m (IMET)	
	1995: $0.3m (IMET)	
$1 = EB	1992: 5.0	1993: 5.0
	1994: 5.0	

EB = birr

Population: ε50,000,000

	13–17	*18–22*	*23–32*
Men	2,783,000	2,309,000	3,489,000
Women	2,674,000	2,221,000	3,386,000

Following the declaration of independence by Eritrea in April 1993, est strength of Ethiopian armed forces is some 120,000. Most are former members of the Tigray People's Liberation Front (TPLF) with maybe 10–15,000 from the Oromo

Liberation Front. No information on division of military assets between Ethiopia and Eritrea is available, although close cooperation is likely between the two countries. All ground and air force assets are listed under Ethiopia and naval assets under Eritrea. Reports indicate that large quantities of equipment are in preservation. Est numbers in service must be treated with caution.

ARMY:†

MBT: ε350 T-54/-55, T-62.
RECCE/AIFV/APC: ε200, incl BRDM, BMP, BTR-60/-152.
TOWED ARTY: 76mm: ZIS-3; 85mm: D-44; 122mm: D-30/M-30; 130mm: M-46.
MRL: BM-21.
MORTARS: 81mm: M-1/M-29; 82mm: M-1937; 120mm: M-1938.
ATGW: AT-3 *Sagger*.
RCL: 82mm: B-10; 107mm: B-11.
AD GUNS: 23mm: ZU-23, ZSU-23-4 SP; 37mm: M-1939; 57mm: S-60.
SAM: 20 SA-2, 30 SA-3, 300 SA-7, SA-9.

AIR FORCE:† 34 cbt ac, 18 armed hel.

Most of the Air Force is grounded. Air Force activity is believed to be limited to reorganisation, some ground-crew training and maintenance. Priority has been given to helicopter and transport aircraft operations. Types and numbers of remaining ac are assessed as follows:
FGA: 16 MiG-21MF, 18 MiG-23BN.
TPT: 4 An-12, 2 DH-6, 1 Yak-40 (VIP), 3 Y-12.
TRG: 14 L-39.
ATTACK HEL: 18 Mi-24.
TPT HEL: 21 Mi-8, 2 UH-1, 2 Mi-14.

SOMALI REPUBLIC

GDP	1992ε: S sh 1,978bn ($755m): per capita $800	
	1993ε: S sh 2,017bn ($770m): per capita $800	
Growth	1992: -16.1%	1993: -0.6%
Inflation	1992: n.k.	1993: n.k.
Debt	1992: $2.5bn	1993: $2.5bn
FMA[a]		
$1 = S sh	1992: 2,620	1993: 2,620
	1994: 2,609	

S sh = Somali shillings

[a] UN reports cite UNOSOM I and II costs for the period May 1992 to February 1994 inclusive as $959m, of which $659m has been appropriated and $300m expenditure has been authorised.

Population: 6,654,000

	13–17	*18–22*	*23–32*
Men	366,800	295,700	449,500
Women	364,500	299,100	466,900

Following the 1991 revolution, no national armed forces have yet been formed. The Somali National Movement has declared northern Somalia as the independent Republic of Somaliland, while in the south, insurgent groups compete for local supremacy. Heavy military equipment which is in a poor state of repair or inoperable is being collected by UNOSOM forces.

CLAN/MOVEMENT GROUPINGS:

'SOMALILAND' (northern Somalia):
UNITED SOMALIA FRONT: sub-clan Issa.
SOMALIA DEMOCRATIC FRONT: sub-clan Gadabursi.
SOMALIA NATIONAL MOVEMENT: clan Isaq, 5–6,000, 3 factions (Tur, Dhegaweyne, Kahin).
UNITED SOMALI PARTY: sub-clan Dolbuhunta, leader Abdi Hasai.
SOMALIA:
SOMALIA SALVATION DEMOCRATIC FRONT: sub-clan Majerteen, 3,000, leaders 'Colonel' Yusuf, Abshir Musa (loose alliance).
UNITED SOMALI CONGRESS: clan Hawije; Aideed Faction: leader Mohammed Farah Aideed, 10,000, Habar Gadir sub-clan.
Ali Mahdi Faction: leader Mohammed Ali Mahdi, 10,000(-), Abgal sub-clan.
SOMALI NATIONAL FRONT: sub-clan Marehan, 2–3,000, leaders Mohamed Said Hersi Morgan, Hashi Ganni, Warsame Hashi.
SOMALI DEMOCRATIC MOVEMENT: clan Dighil and Rahenwein.
SOMALI PATRIOTIC MOVEMENT: sub-clan Ogaden, 2–3,000, leaders Ahmed Omar Jess, Aden Nur Gabiyu.

FOREIGN FORCES:

UN AND PEACEKEEPING:
UNOSOM II: 18,900 tps from 14 countries.

SUDAN

GDP	1992ε: £S 442.8bn ($6.4bn): per capita $1,100	
	1993ε: £S 1,006.8bn ($6.5bn): per capita $1,100	
Growth	1992ε: -11%	1993ε: 0%
Inflation	1992ε: 117.6%	1993ε: 118.7%
Debt	1992: $16.1bn	1993: $16.1bn
Def exp	1992ε: £S 53.1bn ($766.0m)	
Def bdgt	1993ε: £S 116.1bn ($755.0m)	
	1994ε: £S 152.2bn ($700.0m)	
$1 = £S	1992: 69.4	1993: 153.8
	1994: 217.4	

£S = Sudanese pound

Population: 28,259,200

	13–17	*18–22*	*23–32*
Men	1,648,700	1,370,300	2,064,900
Women	1,562,800	1,298,100	1,980,900

TOTAL ARMED FORCES:

ACTIVE: 118,500.

Terms of service: conscription (males 18–30), 3 years.

ARMY: 115,000 (ε30,000 conscripts).

1 armd div.
6 inf div (regional comd).
1 AB div (incl 1 SF bde).
1 mech inf bde.
24 inf bde.
1 recce bde.
7 arty bde.
3 arty regt.
1 engr div.
12 AD arty bde.

EQUIPMENT:

MBT: 250 T-54/-55, 20 M-60A3, 50 Ch Type-59.
LIGHT TANKS: 70 Ch Type-62.
RECCE: 6 AML-90, 90 *Saladin*, 80 *Ferret*, 60 BRDM-1/-2.
APC: 426: 90 BTR-50/-152, 80 OT-62/-64, 36 M-113, 100 V-100/-150, 120 *Walid*.
TOWED ARTY: 489: 105mm: 18 M-101 pack, 24 Model 56 pack; 122mm: 35 D-74, 24 M-1938, 270 Type-54/D-30; 130mm: 100 M-46/Ch Type 59-1; 155mm: 18 M-114A1.
SP ARTY: 155mm: 6 AMX Mk F-3.
MRL: 107mm: 600 Type-63; 122mm: 30 BM-21.
MORTARS: 81mm: 138; 120mm: 12 M-43, 24 AM-49.
ATGW: 4 *Swingfire*.
RCL: 106mm: 72 M-40A1.
ATK GUNS: 76mm: 18 M-1942; 100mm: 40 M-1944.
AD GUNS: 20mm: M-167 towed, M-163 SP; 23mm: ZU-23-2; 37mm: 120 M-1939/Type-63, 200 Type-55; 40mm: 60 L/60; 57mm: 160 Type-59; 85mm: 37 M-1939/1944; 100mm: KS-19 towed.
SAM: SA-7, *Redeye*.
SURV: RASIT (veh, arty).

NAVY: ε500.

BASES: Port Sudan (HQ), Flamingo Bay (Red Sea), Khartoum (Nile).
PATROL CRAFT: 2 *Kadir* PCI⟨; plus 4 riverine PCI⟨ and about 10 armed boats.
AMPHIBIOUS: craft only: some 7 *Sobat* (Yug DTK-221) LCT.

AIR FORCE: 3,000 (incl Air Defence); 63† cbt ac, 2 armed hel.

FGA: 9 F-5 (-E: 7; -F: 2), 10 Ch J-5 (MiG-17), 9 Ch J-6 (MiG-19).
FIGHTER: 8 MiG-21, 3 MiG-23, 6 Ch J-6.
COIN: 1 sqn with 3 BAC-167 Mk 90, 3 *Jet Provost* Mk 55.
MR: 2 C-212.
TRANSPORT: 5 An-24, 5 C-130H, 4 C-212, 3 DHC-5D, 6 EMB-110P, 1 F-27, 2 *Falcon* 20/50.
HELICOPTERS: 1 sqn with 11 AB-412, 8 IAR/SA-330, 4 Mi-4, 5 Mi-8, 2 Mi-24 (armed).
TRAINING: incl 4 MiG-15UTI*, 4 MiG-21U*, 2 JJ-5*, 2 JJ-6*.
AD: 5 bty SA-2 SAM (18 launchers).
AAM: AA-2 *Atoll*.

PARAMILITARY:

POPULAR DEFENCE FORCE: 15,000 active, 60,000 reserve; mil wing of National Islamic Front.

OPPOSITION:

SUDANESE PEOPLE'S LIBERATION ARMY (SPLA): ε30–50,000: four factions, each org in bn; mainly small arms plus 60mm mor, 14.5mm AA, SA-7 SAM; arty reported; operating mainly in southern Sudan.

FOREIGN FORCES:

IRAN: some mil advisers.

EAST AFRICA

KENYA

GDP	1992: sh 258.1bn ($8.0bn):	
	per capita $1,500	
	1993ε: sh 478.0bn ($8.2bn):	
	per capita $1,500	
Growth	1992: 0.4%	1993ε: 0.4%
Inflation	1992: 29.5%	1993: 45.8%
Debt	1992: $6.4bn	1993: $6.5bn
Def exp	1991: sh 5.9bn ($215.0m)	
	1992ε: sh 7.4bn ($230.0m)	
Def bdgt	1993ε: sh 10.4bn ($179.0m)	
	1994ε: sh 10.3bn ($165.0m)	
FMA	1993: $0.7m (IMET)	
	1994: $0.3m (IMET)	
	1995: $0.2m (IMET)	
$1 = sh	1992: 32.2	1993: 58.0
	1994: 62.8	

sh = Kenyan shilling

Population: 27,834,400

	13–17	*18–22*	*23–32*
Men:	1,719,800	1,368,800	1,921,000
Women:	1,721,600	1,376,400	1,944,800

TOTAL ARMED FORCES:

ACTIVE: 24,200.

ARMY: 20,500.

1 armd bde (3 armd bn).
2 inf bde (1 with 2, 1 with 3 inf bn); 1 indep inf bn.
1 arty bde (2 bn). 1 AD arty bn.
1 engr bde. 2 engr bn.
1 AB bn. 1 indep air cav bn.

EQUIPMENT:
MBT: 80 Vickers Mk 3.
RECCE: 52 AML-60/-90, 12 *Ferret*, 8 *Shorland*.
APC: 52 UR-416, 10 Panhard M-3.
TOWED ARTY: 105mm: 40 lt, 8 pack.
MORTARS: 81mm: 50; 120mm: 12 Brandt.
ATGW: 40 *Milan*, 14 *Swingfire*.
RCL: 84mm: 80 *Carl Gustav*.
AD GUNS: 20mm: 50 TCM-20, 11 *Oerlikon*; 40mm: 13 Bofors.

NAVY: 1,200.

BASE: Mombasa.

PATROL AND COASTAL COMBATANTS: 7:
MISSILE CRAFT: 6:
2 *Nyayo* (UK Vosper 57-m) PFM, with 4 *Ottomat* SSM.
1 *Mamba*, 3 *Madaraka* (UK Brooke Marine 37-m/32-m) PFM with 4 x *Gabriel* II SSM.
PATROL, INSHORE: 1: *Simba* (UK Vosper 31-m) PCI.
SUPPORT AND MISCELLANEOUS: 1 tug.

AIR FORCE: 2,500; 32 cbt ac, 34 armed hel.

FGA: 10 F-5 (-E: 8; -F: 2).
COIN: 1 *Strikemaster* Mk 87, 9 *Hawk* Mk 52, 12 *Tucano*.
TRANSPORT: 7 DHC-5D, 7 Do-28D-2, 1 PA-32, 3 DHC-8.
TRAINING: 7 *Bulldog* 103/127.
ATTACK HEL: 11 Hughes 500MD (with TOW), 8 500ME, 15 500M.
TRANSPORT HEL: 9 IAR-330, 12 SA-330, 1 SA-342.
TRAINING: 2 Hughes 500D.
MISSILES:
ASM: AGM-65 *Maverick*, *TOW*.
AAM: AIM-9 *Sidewinder*.

FORCES ABROAD:

UN AND PEACEKEEPING:
CROATIA (UNPROFOR I): 980; 1 inf bn, 46 Observers, 48 civ pol.
IRAQ/KUWAIT (UNIKOM): 7 Observers.
LIBERIA (UNOMIL): 20 Observers.
WESTERN SAHARA (MINURSO): 10 Observers.

PARAMILITARY:

POLICE GENERAL SERVICE UNIT: 5,000.
POLICE AIR WING: 7 Cessna lt **ac**, 3 Bell **hel** (1 206L, 2 47G).
CUSTOMS/POLICE NAVAL SQN: about 5 PCI((2 Lake Victoria), some 12 boats.

MADAGASCAR

GDP	1992: fr 5,584.5bn ($3.0bn):	
	per capita $800	
	1993ε: fr 5,920.7bn ($3.1bn):	
	per capita $810	
Growth	1992: 0.9%	1993ε: 0.5%
Inflation	1992: 14.5%	1993: 10.0%
Debt	1992: $4.4bn	1993: $4.6bn
Def exp	1991: fr 55.8bn ($30.4m)	

Def bdgt	1992ε:	fr 59.2bn ($31.0m)		
	1993ε:	fr 69.3bn ($36.2m)		
	1994ε:	fr 73.9bn ($37.6m)		
FMA	1993:	$0.3m (IMET)		
$1 = fr	1992:	1,864	1993:	1,914
	1994:	1,966		

fr = Malagasy franc

Population: 13,126,600

	13–17	*18–22*	*23–32*
Men	741,100	615,900	948,700
Women	723,800	603,900	939,700

TOTAL ARMED FORCES:

ACTIVE: 21,000.
Terms of service: conscription (incl for civil purposes), 18 months.

ARMY: some 20,000.

2 bn gp.
1 engr regt.
EQUIPMENT:
LIGHT TANKS: 12 PT-76.
RECCE: 8 M-8, ε20 M-3A1, 10 *Ferret*, ε35 BRDM-2.
APC: ε30 M-3A1 half-track.
TOWED ARTY: 76mm: 12 ZIS-3; 105mm: some M-101; 122mm: 12 D-30.
MORTARS: 82mm: M-37; 120mm: 8 M-43.
RL: 89mm: LRAC.
RCL: 106mm: M-40A1.
AD GUNS: 14.5mm: 50 ZPU-4; 37mm: 20 Type 55.

NAVY:† 500 (incl some 100 Marines).

BASES: Diégo-Suarez, Tamatave, Fort Dauphin, Tuléar, Majunga.
PATROL CRAFT: 1 *Malaika* (Fr PR48-m) PCI.
AMPHIBIOUS: 1 *Toky* (Fr *BATRAM*) LSM, with 8 x SS-12 SSM, capacity 30 tps, 4 tk.
Plus craft: 1 LCT (Fr EDIC), 1 LCA, 3 LCVP.
SUPPORT AND MISCELLANEOUS: 1 tpt/trg.

AIR FORCE: 500; 12 cbt ac, no armed hel.

FGA: 1 sqn with 4 MiG-17F, 8 MiG-21FL.
TRANSPORT: 4 An-26, 3 BN-2, 2 C-212, 2 Yak-40 (VIP).
HELICOPTERS: 1 sqn with 6 Mi-8.
LIAISON: 1 Cessna 310, 2 Cessna 337, 1 PA-23.
TRAINING: 4 Cessna 172.

PARAMILITARY:

GENDARMERIE: 7,500, incl maritime police with some 5 PCI⟨.

MAURITIUS

GDP	1992:	R 47.7bn ($3.1bn):		
		per capita $12,400		
	1993:	R 54.9bn ($3.3bn):		
		per capita $13,400		
Growth	1992:	6.3%	1993:	5.4%
Inflation	1992:	4.6%	1993:	10.4%
Debt	1992:	$1.1bn	1993:	$1.0bn
Def exp	1992:	R 175.6m ($11.3m)		
	1993:	R 196.8m ($11.2m)		
Def bdgt	1994ε:	R 207.2m ($11.3m)		
FMA	1993:	$0.07m (IMET)		
$1 = R	1992:	15.6	1993:	17.7
	1994:	18.4		

R = rupee

Population: 1,111,600

	13–17	*18–22*	*23–32*
Men	51,000	52,200	104,500
Women	54,800	51,700	105,400

PARAMILITARY:

SPECIAL MOBILE FORCE: 1,300.
6 rifle, 2 mobile, 1 engr coy, spt tp.
EQUIPMENT:
APC: 10 VAB.
MORTARS: 81mm: 2.
RL: 89mm: 4 LRAC.
COAST GUARD: ε500.
PATROL CRAFT: 4:
1 *Amar* PCI, 1 SDB-3 PFI, 2 Sov *Zhuk* PCI⟨, plus boats.
AIR ARM:
MR: 1 Do-228-101, 1 BN-2T *Defender,* 3 SA-316B.
POLICE AIR WING: 2 *Alouette* III.

SEYCHELLES

GDP	1992:	SR 2,178m ($425m):		
		per capita $4,100		
	1993ε:	SR 2,349m ($453m):		
		per capita $3,900		
Growth	1992:	3.5%	1993ε:	4.0%
Inflation	1992:	3.5%	1993ε:	4.0%
Debt	1992:	$199m	1993:	$201m
Def bdgt	1992ε:	SR 78.0m ($15.2m)		
	1993ε:	SR 82.2m ($15.9m)		
FMA	1993:	$0.1m (IMET)		
$1 = SR	1992:	5.1	1993:	5.2
	1994:	5.2		

SR = Seychelles rupee

Population: 70,400

	13–17	18–22	23–32
Men	4,100	4,000	6,800
Women	4,000	3,600	6,500

TOTAL ARMED FORCES (all services form part of the Army):
ACTIVE: 800.

ARMY: 800 (incl 300 for Presidential sy).
1 inf bn (3 coy). 2 arty tps.
EQUIPMENT:†
RECCE: 6 BRDM-2.
TOWED ARTY: 122mm: 3 D-30.
MORTARS: 82mm: 6 M-43.
RL: RPG-7.
AD GUNS: 57mm: S-60.
SAM: 10 SA-7.

PARAMILITARY:
NATIONAL GUARD: 1,000.
COAST GUARD: ε300, incl 100 Air Wing and ε80 Marines.
BASE: Port Victoria.
PATROL AND COASTAL COMBATANTS: 4:
INSHORE: 4:
1 *Andromache* (It Pichiotti 42-m) PFI.
1 *Zoroaster* (Sov *Turya*, no foils or TT) PCI.
2 *Zhuk* PFI⟨.
AMPHIBIOUS: craft only: 1 LCT.
AIR WING: 100; 1 cbt ac, no armed hel.
MR: 1 BN-2 *Defender*.
HELICOPTERS: 1† *Chetak*.
TRAINING: 1 Cessna 152.

TANZANIA

GDP	1992: sh 807.3bn ($2.7bn): per capita $500	
	1993: sh 1,146.3bn ($2.8bn): per capita $500	
Growth	1992: 3.6%	1993: 2.1%
Inflation	1992: 22.1%	1993: 23.4%
Debt	1992: $6.7bn	1993: $6.9bn
Def bdgt	1992: sh 32.1bn ($107.7m)	
	1993: sh 36.5bn ($90.0m)	
	1994ε: sh 41.7bn ($84.0m)	
FMA	1993: $0.2m (IMET)	
	1994: $0.1m (IMET)	
	1995: $0.1m (IMET)	
$1 = sh	1992: 297.7	1993: 405.3
	1994: 494.4	

sh = Tanzanian shilling

Population: 27,718,600

	13–17	18–22	23–32
Men	1,539,500	1,267,100	1,869,000
Women	1,618,600	1,327,700	2,048,700

TOTAL ARMED FORCES:
ACTIVE: 49,600.
Terms of service: incl civil duties, 2 years.
RESERVE: Citizens' Militia: 85,000.

ARMY: 45,000.
3 div HQ.
8 inf bde. 1 tk bde.
2 arty bn. 2 AD arty bn.
2 mor bn. 2 ATK bn.
1 engr regt (bn).
EQUIPMENT:†
MBT: 30 Ch Type-59, 35 T-54.
LIGHT TANKS: 30 Ch Type-62, 40 *Scorpion*.
RECCE: 40 BRDM-2.
APC: 66 BTR-40/-152, 30 Ch Type-56.
TOWED ARTY: 76mm: 45 ZIS-3; 85mm: 80 Ch Type-56; 122mm: 20 D-30, 100 M-30; 130mm: 40 M-46.
MRL: 122mm: 58 BM-21.
MORTARS: 82mm: 300 M-43; 120mm: 135 M-43.
RCL: 75mm: 540 Ch Type-52.

NAVY:† ε1,000.
BASES: Dar es Salaam, Zanzibar, Mwanza (Lake Victoria – 4 boats).
PATROL AND COASTAL COMBATANTS: 22:
TORPEDO CRAFT: 4 Ch *Huchuan* PHT⟨ with 2 x 533mm TT.
PATROL, INSHORE: 18:
8 Ch *Shanghai* II PFI, some 10 PCI⟨ (4 in Zanzibar), plus boats.

AIR FORCE: 3,600 (incl ε2,600 AD tps); 24 cbt ac†, no armed hel.
FIGHTER: 3 sqn with 3 Ch J-5 (MiG-17), 10 J-6 (MiG-19), 11 J-7 (MiG-21).
TRANSPORT: 1 sqn with 4 DHC-5D, 1 Ch Y-5, 3 HS-748, 2 F-28, 1 HS-125-700.
HELICOPTERS: 4 AB-205.
LIAISON: ac: 7 Cessna 310, 2 Cessna 404, 1 Cessna 206; **hel:** 6 Bell 206B.
TRAINING: 2 MiG-15UTI, 5 PA-28.

AD GUNS: 14.5mm: 40 ZPU-2/-4; 23mm: 40 ZU-23; 37mm: 120 Ch Type-55.
SAM: 20 SA-3, 20 SA-6, 120 SA-7.

FORCES ABROAD:

LIBERIA: ε800 forming part of ECOMOG.

PARAMILITARY:

POLICE FIELD FORCE: 1,400, incl Police Marine Unit.
POLICE AIR WING: **ac:** 1 Cessna U-206; **hel:** 2 AB-206A, 2 -B, 2 Bell 206L, 2 Bell 47G.
POLICE MARINE UNIT: (100); boats only.
CITIZENS' MILITIA: 85,000.

UGANDA

GDP	1992: U sh 3,399bn ($3.0bn): per capita $1,250	
	1993: U sh 3,862bn ($3.2bn): per capita $1,350	
Growth	1992: 7.0%	1993: 5.0%
Inflation	1992: 28.3%	1993: 7.5%
Debt	1992: $3.0bn	1993: $3.2bn
Def bdgt	1992ε: U sh 98.4bn ($86.8m)	
	1993ε: U sh 105.9bn ($88.6m)	
	1994: U sh 105.1bn ($94.4m)	
FMA	1993: $0.2m (IMET)	
	1994: $0.1m (IMET)	
	1995: $0.2m (IMET)	
$1 = U sh	1992: 1,134	1993: 1,195
	1994: 1,113	

U sh = Ugandan shilling

Population: 18,664,400

	13–17	*18–22*	*23–32*
Men	1,089,700	942,000	1,329,400
Women	1,089,500	935,900	1,362,000

TOTAL ARMED FORCES:

ACTIVE: ε50,000 (incl ε400 Marine, 800 Air Wing).

NATIONAL RESISTANCE ARMY (NRA):

4 'div' (closer to weak bde).
EQUIPMENT:†
MBT: 20 T-54/-55.
LIGHT TANKS: 20 PT-76.
APC: 20 BTR-60, 4 OT-64 SKOT.
TOWED ARTY: 76mm: 60 M-1942; 122mm: 20 M-1938.
MRL: 122mm: BM-21; 240mm: BM-24.
MORTARS: 81mm: L 16; 82mm: M-43; 120mm: Soltam.
ATGW: 40 AT-3 *Sagger*.
AD GUNS: 14.5mm: ZPU-1/-2/-4; 23mm: ZU-23; 37mm: M-1939.
SAM: 10 SA-7.
AVIATION: 4 cbt ac†, 5 armed hel.
FGA: 4 MiG-17F.
TRAINING: 3 L-39, 5 SF-260.
HELICOPTERS:
ATTACK: 5 AB-412.
TRANSPORT: 3 Bell 206, 2 Bell 412, 1 Bell 212.
TRANSPORT/LIAISON: 2 AS-202 *Bravo*, 1 L100, 1 *Gulfstream* II.

PARAMILITARY:

POLICE AIR WING:
AIRCRAFT: 1 DHC-2, 1 DHC-4, 1 DHC-6.
HELICOPTERS: 2 Bell 206, 4 Bell 212.
MARINE UNIT: (ε400). 8 riverine patrol craft⟨, plus boats.

OPPOSITION:

HOLY SPIRIT MOVEMENT: ε500.

FOREIGN FORCES:

UNITED NATIONS (UNOMUR): 80 military observers from 8 countries.

CENTRAL AFRICA

BURUNDI

GDP	1992: fr 226.1bn ($1.1bn): per capita $650	
	1993: fr 234.4bn ($1.0bn): per capita $600	
Growth	1992: 2.3%	1993: -7.4%
Inflation	1992: 4.5%	1993: 5.0%
Debt	1992: $1.0bn	1993: $1.1bn
Def bdgt	1991: fr 5.8bn ($28.0m)	
	1992: fr 6.0bn ($29.0m)	
	1993: fr 6.0bn ($25.0m)	
FMA:	1993: $0.4m (IMET)	
$1 = fr	1992: 208	1993: 243
	1994: 260	

fr = Burundi franc

Population: 6,090,400

	13–17	18–22	23–32
Men	334,000	277,700	452,000
Women	330,600	276,000	454,800

TOTAL ARMED FORCES:

ACTIVE: ε14,600 (incl Gendarmerie).

ARMY: ε12,500.

5 inf bn.
2 lt armd bn.
EQUIPMENT:
RECCE: 6 AML-60, 12 -90, 7 *Shorland*.
APC: 29: 9 *Panhard* M-3, 20 BTR-40 and *Walid*.
MORTARS: 82mm: 18 M-43.
RL: 83mm: *Blindicide*.
RCL: 75mm: 15 Ch Type-52.
AD GUNS: 14.5mm: 15 ZPU-4.

AIR: 100; 5 cbt ac, no armed hel.

COIN: 5 SF-260W.
HELICOPTERS: 3 SA-316B, 4 SA-342L.
LIAISON: 2 Reims-Cessna 150, 1 Do-27Q.
TRAINING: 7 SF-260 (3 -C, 4 -TP).

PARAMILITARY:

GENDARMERIE: ε2,000 (incl ε50 Marine Police): Base: Bujumbura; patrol boats, river: ε2.

CAMEROON

GDP	1992: fr 2,835bn ($10.7bn): per capita $2,300	
	1993ε: fr 4,486bn ($10.4bn): per capita $2,210	
Growth	1992: -4.9%	1993ε: -5.9%
Inflation	1992: -3.9%	1993: 12.8%
Debt	1992: $6.6bn	1993: $6.8bn
Def bdgt	1993ε: fr 33bn ($117m)	
	1994ε: fr 29bn ($102m)	
FMA	1993: $0.3m (IMET)	
	1994: $0.1m (IMET)	
$1 = fr	1992: 264.7	1993: 283.2
	1994: 581.4	

fr = CFA franc

Population: 13,190,200

	13–17	18–22	23–32
Men	797,900	609,500	880,700
Women	793,900	610,500	890,800

TOTAL ARMED FORCES:

ACTIVE: 23,600 (incl Gendarmerie).

ARMY: 13,000.

8 Military Regions each 1 inf bn under cmd.
Presidential Guard: 1 guard, 1 armd recce bn, 3 inf coy.
1 AB/cdo bn.
5 inf bn (1 trg).
1 engr bn.
1 arty bn (5 bty).
1 AA bn (6 bty).
EQUIPMENT:
RECCE: 8 M-8, *Ferret*, 8 V-150 *Commando* (20mm gun), 5 VBL.
AIFV: 14 V-150 *Commando* (90mm gun).
APC: 21 V-150 *Commando*, 12 M-3 half-track.
TOWED ARTY: 34: 75mm: 6 M-116 pack; 105mm: 16 M-101; 130mm: 12.
MORTARS: 81mm (some SP); 120mm: 16 *Brandt*.
ATGW: *Milan*.
RL: 89mm: LRAC.
RCL: 57mm: 13 Ch Type-52; 106mm: 40 M-40A2.
AD GUNS: 14.5mm: 18 Ch Type-58; 35mm: 18 GDF-002; 37mm: 18 Ch Type-63.

NAVY: ε1,300.

BASES: Douala (HQ), Limbe, Kribi.
PATROL AND COASTAL COMBATANTS: 2:
MISSILE CRAFT: 1 *Bakassi* (Fr P.48) PFM with 2 x 4 MM-40 *Exocet* SSM.
PATROL, INSHORE: 1 *L'Audacieux* (Fr P.48) PFI.
RIVERINE: boats only, some 30 US Swiftsure-38 (not all op), 6 SM 30/36 types.
AMPHIBIOUS: craft only: 2 LCM.

AIR FORCE: 300; 14 cbt ac, 4 armed hel.

1 composite sqn.
1 Presidential Flt.
FGA/COIN: 4† *Alpha Jet*, 10 CM-170.
MR: 2 Do-128D-6.
ATTACK HEL: 4 SA-342L (with *HOT*).
TRANSPORT: ac: 3 C-130H/-H-30, 1 DHC-4, 4 DHC-5D, 1 IAI-201, 2 PA-23, 1 Boeing 707; **hel:** 3 Bell 206, 3 SE-3130, 1 SA-318, 4 SA-319, 2 AS-332, 1 SA-365.

GENDARMERIE: 9,000; 10 regional groups.

PATROL BOATS: about 10 US Swiftsure-38 (incl in Navy entry).

CAPE VERDE

GDP	1992: CV E 24.0bn ($353.0m): per capita $1,700	
	1993ε: CV E 30.3bn ($376.0m): per capita $1,800	
Growth	1992: 4.1%	1993: 3.9%
Inflation	1992: 3.3%	1993ε: 4.0%
Debt	1992: $159.9m	1993: $174.0m
Def bdgt	1993: CV E 252m ($3.1m)	
	1994: CV E 288m ($3.4m)	
FMA	1993: $0.2m (IMET)	
$1 = CV E	1992: 68.0	1993: 80.4
	1994: 84.6	

CV E = Cape Verde escudo

Population: 421,400

	13–17	*18–22*	*23–32*
Men	23,200	20,100	34,600
Women	23,700	20,600	37,100

TOTAL ARMED FORCES:

ACTIVE: 1,100.

Terms of service: conscription (selective).

ARMY: 1,000.

2 bn.

EQUIPMENT:

RECCE: 10 BRDM-2.

TOWED ARTY: 75mm: 12; 76mm: 12.

MORTARS: 82mm: 12; 120mm: 6 M-1943.

RL: 89mm: 3.5-in.

AD GUNS: 14.5mm: 18 ZPU-1; 23mm: 12 ZU-23.

SAM: 50 SA-7.

COAST GUARD: nucleus of ε50 with 1 PCI⟨.

AIR FORCE: under 100; no cbt ac.

MR: 1 Do-228.

FORCES ABROAD:

UN AND PEACEKEEPING:

MOZAMBIQUE (ONUMOZ): 18 Observers.

CENTRAL AFRICAN REPUBLIC

GDP	1992: fr 354.5bn ($1.3bn): per capita $1,100	
	1993ε: fr 368.4bn ($1.3bn): per capita $1,100	
Growth	1992: -2.4%	1993ε: -3.0%
Inflation	1992: -1.9%	1993: -2.1%
Debt	1992: $901m	1993: $940m
Def bdgt	1992ε: fr 7.4bn ($28.0m)	
	1993ε: fr 8.7bn ($30.6m)	
	1994ε: fr 17.7bn ($30.5m)	
FMA	1993: $0.2m (IMET)	
	1994: $0.2m (IMET)	
$1 = fr	1992: 264.7	1993: 283.2
	1994: 581.4	

fr = CFA franc

Population: 3,362,200

	13–17	*18–22*	*23–32*
Men	176,800	166,200	244,900
Women	180,300	163,600	242,300

TOTAL ARMED FORCES:

ACTIVE: 4,950 (incl Gendarmerie).

Terms of service: conscription (selective), 2 years; reserve obligation thereafter, term unknown.

ARMY: 2,500.

1 Republican Guard regt (2 bn).

1 territorial defence regt (bn).

1 combined arms regt (1 mech, 1 inf bn).

1 spt/HQ regt.

1 Presidential Guard bn.

EQUIPMENT:†

MBT: 4 T-55.

RECCE: 10 *Ferret.*

APC: 4 BTR-152, some 10 VAB, 25+ ACMAT.

MORTARS: 81mm; 120mm: 12 M-1943.

RL: 89mm: LRAC.

RCL: 106mm: 14 M-40.

RIVER PATROL CRAFT: 9⟨.

AIR FORCE: 150; no cbt ac, no armed hel.

TRANSPORT: 1 Cessna 337, 1 *Mystère* 20.

LIAISON: 8 AL-60, 6 MH-1521.

HELICOPTERS: 1 AS-350, 1 SE-3130.

PARAMILITARY:
GENDARMERIE: 2,300;
3 Regional Legions, 8 'bde'.

FOREIGN FORCES:
FRANCE: 1,300; 1 inf bn gp, 1 armd cav sqn, 1 arty bty; 5 *Jaguar*, 3 C-160.

CHAD

GDP	1992:	fr 366bn ($1.4bn):		
		per capita $800		
	1993ε:	fr 387bn ($1.4bn):		
		per capita $750		
Growth	1992:	3.9%	1993:	-3.7%
Inflation	1992:	-5.6%	1993:	2.1%
Debt	1992:	$729m	1993:	$800m
Def bdgt	1992ε:	fr 18.9bn ($71.4m)		
	1993ε:	fr 20.1bn ($71.0m)		
	1994ε:	fr 42.9bn ($73.8m)		
FMA	1993:	$0.4 (IMET)		
	1994:	$0.2 (IMET)		
	1995:	$0.2 (IMET)		
$1 = fr	1992:	264.7	1993:	283.2
	1994:	581.4		

fr = CFA franc

Population: 6,301,600

	13–17	*18–22*	*23–32*
Men:	323,880	275,520	445,080
Women:	325,320	279,400	455,080

TOTAL ARMED FORCES:
ACTIVE: some 30,350 (incl Republican Guard).
Terms of service: conscription authorised.

ARMY: ε25,000 (being re-organised).
7 Military Regions.
EQUIPMENT:
MBT: 60 T-55.
AFV: some 63: 4 Panhard ERC-90, some 50 AML-60/-90, 9 V-150 with 90mm, some EE-9 *Cascavel.*
TOWED ARTY: 105mm: 5 M-101.
MORTARS: 81mm; 120mm: AM-50.
ATGW: *Milan.*
RL: 89mm: LRAC.
RCL: 106mm: M-40A1; 112mm: *APILAS.*
AD GUNS: 20mm, 30mm.

AIR FORCE: 350; 4 cbt ac, no armed hel.
COIN: 2 PC-7, 2 SF-260W.
TPT: 3 C-47, 1 C-130A, 2 -B, 1 -H, 1 C-212, 2 DC-4.
LIAISON: 2 PC-6B, 5 Reims-Cessna FTB 337.

PARAMILITARY:
REPUBLICAN GUARD: 5,000.
GENDARMERIE: 4,500.

OPPOSITION:
WESTERN ARMED FORCES: strength unknown.
MOVEMENT FOR DEVELOPMENT AND DEMOCRACY: strength unknown.

FOREIGN FORCES:
FRANCE: 800; 2 inf coy, AD arty units; 3 C-160 ac.

CONGO

GDP	1992:	fr 748bn ($2.8bn):		
		per capita $2,850		
	1993:	fr 810bn ($2.9bn):		
		per capita $2,850		
Growth	1992:	2.2%	1993:	-1.5%
Inflation	1992:	2.2%	1993ε:	1.6%
Debt	1992:	$4.8bn	1993:	$4.7bn
Def bdgt	1992ε:	fr 33bn ($125m)		
	1993ε:	fr 31bn ($110m)		
FMA	1992:	$0.2m (IMET)		
	1993:	$0.1m (IMET)		
	1995:	$0.2m (IMET)		
$1 = fr	1992:	264.7	1993:	283.2
	1994:	581.4		

fr = CFA franc

Population: 2,595,200

	13–17	*18–22*	*23–32*
Men:	141,800	121,900	189,500
Women:	140,900	121,800	191,800

TOTAL ARMED FORCES:
ACTIVE: 10,000.

ARMY: 8,000.
2 armd bn.
2 inf bn gp (each with lt tk tp, 76mm gun bty).

1 inf bn.
1 arty gp (how, MRL).
1 engr bn.
1 AB/cdo bn.
EQUIPMENT:†
MBT: 25 T-54/-55, 15 Ch Type-59 (some T-34 in store).
LIGHT TANKS: 10 Ch Type-62, 3 PT-76.
RECCE: 25 BRDM-1/-2.
APC: M-3, 50 BTR (30 -60, 20 -152).
TOWED ARTY: 76mm: M-1942; 100mm: 10 M-1944; 122mm:10 D-30; 130mm: 5 M-46; 152mm: some D-20.
MRL: 122mm: 8 BM-21; 140mm: BM-14-16.
MORTARS: 82mm; 120mm: 10 M-43.
RCL: 57mm: M-18.
ATK GUNS: 57mm: 5 M-1943.
AD GUNS: 14.5mm: ZPU-2/-4; 23mm: ZSU-23-4 SP; 37mm: 28 M-1939; 57mm: S-60; 100mm: KS-19.

NAVY:† ε800.
BASE: Pointe Noire.
PATROL AND COASTAL COMBATANTS: 6:
PATROL, INSHORE: 6:
3 *Marien N'gouabi* PFI (Sp *Barcelo* 33-m).
3 Sov *Zhuk* PFI⟨.
RIVERINE: boats only.

AIR FORCE:† 1,200; 22 cbt ac, no armed hel.
FGA: 10 MiG-17, 12 MiG-21.
TPT: 5 An-24, 1 An-26, 1 Boeing 727, 1 N-2501.
TRG: 4 L-39, 1 MiG-15UTI.
HELICOPTERS: 2 SA-316, 2 SA-318, 1 SA-365.

FORCES ABROAD:
UN AND PEACEKEEPING:
ANGOLA (UNAVEM II): 2 Observers.
RWANDA (UNAMIR): 25 Observers.

PARAMILITARY: 6,700:
GENDARMERIE: (2,000); 20 coy.
PEOPLE'S MILITIA: (4,700).

EQUATORIAL GUINEA

GDP	1992: fr 42.2bn ($159.0m): per capita n.k.	
	1993: fr 49.6bn ($175.0m): per capita n.k.	
Growth	1992: 13.0%	1993ε: 7.0%
Inflation	1992: 1.0%	1993: 1.6%
Debt	1992: $148m	1993: $144m
Def bdgt	1992ε: fr 750.0m ($2.9m)	
	1993ε: fr 730.0m ($2.6m)	
	1994ε: fr 1.5bn ($2.5m)	
$1 = fr	1992: 264.7	1993: 283.2
	1994: 581.4	

fr = CFA franc

Population: 376,000

	13–17	*18–22*	*23–32*
Men:	22,160	19,480	32,800
Women:	22,720	20,280	33,240

TOTAL ARMED FORCES:
ACTIVE: 1,320.

ARMY: 1,100; 3 inf bn.
EQUIPMENT:
RECCE: 6 BRDM-2.
APC: 10 BTR-152.

NAVY†: 120.
BASES: Malabo (Santa Isabel), Bata.
PATROL COMBATANTS: 3 PFI⟨, 1 PCI⟨.

AIR FORCE: 100; no cbt ac or armed hel.
TRANSPORT: 1 Yak-40, 3 C-212, 1 Cessna-337.

PARAMILITARY:
GUARDIA CIVIL: 2 coy.

FOREIGN FORCES:
MOROCCO: 360; 1 bn.

GABON

GDP	1992: fr 1,565.2bn ($5.9bn): per capita $5,100	
	1993ε: fr 1,761.9bn ($6.2bn): per capita $5,200	
Growth	1992: -2.4%	1993ε: 2.6%
Inflation	1992: 0.7%	1993ε: 1.2%
Debt	1992: $3.8bn	1993: $3.7bn
Def bdgt	1992ε: fr 40.2bn ($152.0m)	
	1993ε: fr 43.1bn ($154.0m)	
FMA	1993: $0.1m (IMET)	
	$13.3m (France)	
	1994: $12.1m (France)	

$1 = fr	1992: 264.7	1993: 283.2
	1994: 581.4	

fr = CFA franc

Population: 1,269,600

	13–17	*18–22*	*23–32*
Men	58,700	51,500	87,400
Women	60,000	53,400	89,800

TOTAL ARMED FORCES:
ACTIVE: 4,700.

ARMY: 3,200.
Presidential Guard bn gp (1 recce/armd, 3 inf coy, arty, AA bty) (under direct Presidential control).
8 inf, 1 AB/cdo, 1 engr coy.
EQUIPMENT:
RECCE: 14 EE-9 *Cascavel*, 24 AML, 6 ERC-90 *Sagaie*, 12 EE-3 *Jararaca*, 14 VBL.
AIFV: 12 EE-11 *Urutu* with 20mm gun.
APC: 9 V-150 *Commando*, Panhard M-3, 12 VXB-170.
TOWED ARTY: 105mm: 4 M-101.
MRL: 140mm: 8 *Teruel*.
MORTARS: 81mm: 35; 120mm: 4 Brandt.
ATGW: 4 *Milan*.
RL: 89mm: LRAC.
RCL: 106mm: M40A1.
AD GUNS: 20mm: 4 ERC-20 SP; 23mm: 24 ZU-23-2; 37mm: 10 M-1939; 40mm: 3 Bofors.

NAVY: ε500.
BASE: Port Gentil (HQ).
PATROL AND COASTAL COMBATANTS: 3:
MISSILE CRAFT: 1 *General Nazaire Boulingu* PFM (Fr 42-m) with 4 SS-12 SSM.
PATROL COASTAL: 2 *General Ba'Oumar* (Fr P.400 55-m).
AMPHIBIOUS: 1 *President Omar Bongo* (Fr *Batral*) LSM, capacity 140 tps, 7 tk.
Plus craft: 1 LCM.

AIR FORCE: 1,000; 19 cbt ac, 5 armed hel.
FGA: 9 *Mirage* 5 (2 -G, 4 -GII, 3 -DG).
MR: 1 EMB-111.
TRANSPORT: 1 C-130H, 2 L-100-30, 2 EMB-110, 2 YS-11A.
HELICOPTERS:
ATTACK: 5 SA-342.
TRANSPORT: 3 SA-330C/-H.
LIAISON: 3 SA-316/-319.
PRESIDENTIAL GUARD:
COIN: 6 CM-170, 4 T-34.
TRANSPORT: ac: 1 ATR-42F, 1 EMB-110, 1 *Falcon* 900, 1 *Gulfstream* III; **hel:** 1 AS-332.

PARAMILITARY:
COAST GUARD: ε2,800; boats only.
GENDARMERIE: 2,000; 3 'bdes', 11 coy, 2 armd sqn, air unit.

FOREIGN FORCES:
FRANCE: 600; 1 marine inf regt; 1 AS-355 **hel,** 1 C-160, 1 *Atlantic* **ac**.

RWANDA

GDP	1992: fr 217.3bn ($1.6bn): per capita $700	
	1993ε: fr 225.2bn ($1.6bn): per capita $670	
Growth	1992: 0.5%	1993ε: -6.9%
Inflation	1992: 9.6%	1993: 12.3%
Debt	1992: $873m	1993: $891m
Def exp	1991ε: fr 14.7bn ($117.4m)	
	1992ε: fr 15.0bn ($112.5m)	
Def bdgt	1993: fr 16.5bn ($114.0m)	
FMA	1993: $0.2m (IMET)	
	1994: $0.8m (IMET)	
	1995: $0.2m (IMET)	
$1 = fr	1992: 133.4	1993: 144.3
	1994: 147.5	

fr = Rwandan franc

Population: 8,354,000

	13–17	*18–22*	*23–32*
Men	474,500	388,400	562,500
Women	486,700	400,200	586,800

TOTAL ARMED FORCES (all services form part of the Army):
ACTIVE: 5,000.

The information below reflects the situation prior to the outbreak of civil war in 1994. Reliable data in respect of current org and eqpt are not available.

ARMY: 5,000.
1 cdo bn.
1 recce, 8 inf, 1 engr coy.
EQUIPMENT:
RECCE: 12 AML-60, 16 VBL.

APC: 16 M-3.
TOWED ARTY: 122mm: 6 D-30.
MORTARS: 81mm: 8.
RL: 83mm: *Blindicide*.
ATK GUNS: 57mm: 6.
AIRCRAFT: 2 C-47, 1 Do-27Q-4.
HELICOPTERS: 2 SE-316.

AIR FORCE: 200; 2 cbt ac, no armed hel.
COIN: 2 R-235 *Guerrier*.
TRANSPORT: 2 BN-2, 1 N-2501.
LIAISON: 5 SA-316, 6 SA-342L hel.

PARAMILITARY:
GENDARMERIE: 1,200.

OPPOSITION:
RWANDA PATRIOTIC FRONT: 12,000.

FOREIGN FORCES (1 June 1994):
UNITED NATIONS (UNAMIR): some 380 tps, plus 230 military observers and 15 civ pol from 17 countries.

ZAIRE

GDP	1992:	NZ 1.8bn ($8.2bn): per capita $500		
	1993:	NZ 19.5bn ($7.8bn): per capita $450		
Growth	1992:	-8.4%	1993:	-8.2%
Inflation	1992:	4,130%	1993:	12,000%
Debt	1992:	$10.9bn	1993:	$11.1bn
Def bdgt	1992ε:	NZ 53m ($246m)		
	1993ε:	NZ 590m ($235m)		
$1 = NZ[a]	1992:	0.22	1993:	2.51
	1994:	130.00		

NZ = new zaire

[a] Estimating the value of the zaire is difficult due to its rapid devaluation since 1990. The new zaire, equal to 3m old zaires, was introduced in October 1993.

Population: 42,227,200

	13–17	*18–22*	*23–32*
Men:	2,412,000	2,009,600	2,996,400
Women:	2,370,400	1,976,400	3,025,000

TOTAL ARMED FORCES:
ACTIVE: 49,100 (incl Gendarmerie).

ARMY: 25,000.
8 Military Regions.
1 inf div (3 inf bde).
1 Presidential Guard div.
1 para bde (3 para, 1 spt bn) (2nd forming).
1 SF (cdo/COIN) bde.
1 indep armd bde.
2 indep inf bde (each 3 inf bn, 1 spt bn).
EQUIPMENT:
MBT: 20 Ch Type-59, some 40 Ch Type-62.
RECCE:† 60 AML (30 -60, 30 -90).
APC: 12 M-113, 12 YW-531, 60 *Panhard* M-3.
TOWED ARTY: 75mm: 30 M-116 pack; 85mm: 20 Type 56; 122mm: 20 M-1938/D-30, 15 Type 60; 130mm: 8 Type 59.
MRL: 107mm: 20 Type 63; 122mm: 10 BM-21.
MORTARS: 81mm; 107mm: M-30; 120mm: 50 *Brandt*.
RCL: 57mm: M-18; 75mm: M-20; 106mm: M-40A1.
AD GUNS: 14.5mm: ZPU-4; 37mm: 40 M-1939/Type 63; 40mm: L/60.
SAM: SA-7.

NAVY:† ε1,300 (incl 600 Marines).
BASES: Banana (coast), Boma, Matadi, Kinshasa (all river), Kalémié (Lake Tanganyika – 4 boats).
PATROL AND COASTAL COMBATANTS: 4:
INSHORE: 2 Ch *Shanghai* II PFI, about 2 Swiftships⟨, plus about 10 armed boats.
MARINES: (600).

AIR FORCE: 1,800; 22 cbt ac, no armed hel.
FGA/FIGHTER: 1 sqn with 7 *Mirage* 5M, 1 -5DM.
COIN: 1 sqn with 8 MB-326 GB, 6 -K.
TRANSPORT: 1 wing with 1 Boeing 707-320, 1 BN-2, 8 C-47, 5 C-130H, 3 DHC-5.
HELICOPTERS: 1 sqn with 1 AS-332, 4 SA-319, 4 SA-330.
LIAISON: 6 Cessna 310R, 2 Mu-2J (VIP).
TRAINING: incl 12 Cessna 150, 3 Cessna 310, 9 SF-260C **ac;** 6 Bell 47 **hel**.

PARAMILITARY:
GENDARMERIE: 21,000 (to be 27,000); 40 bn.
CIVIL GUARD: 10,000; some *Fahd* APC.

WEST AFRICA

BENIN

GDP	1992: fr 538.2bn ($2.0bn): per capita $1,600	
	1993ε: fr 602.0bn ($2.1bn): per capita $1,700	
Growth	1992: 4.1%	1993: 3.6%
Inflation	1991: 3.6%	1992: 3.5%
Debt	1992: $1.4bn	1993: $1.5bn
Def bdgt	1992ε: fr 7.2bn ($27.2m)	
	1993ε: fr 9.1bn ($32.0m)	
	1994ε: fr 19.2bn ($33.1m)	
FMA	1993: $0.1m (IMET)	
	1994: $0.1m (IMET)	
	1995: $0.1m (IMET)	
$1 = fr	1992: 264.7	1993: 283.2
	1994: 581.4	

fr = CFA franc

Population: 5,346,400

	13–17	*18–22*	*23–32*
Men	305,700	241,400	354,400
Women	319,800	258,500	386,200

TOTAL ARMED FORCES:
ACTIVE: 4,800.
Terms of service: conscription (selective), 18 months.

ARMY 4,500.
3 inf, 1 AB/cdo, 1 engr bn, 1 armd sqn, 1 arty bty.
EQUIPMENT:
LIGHT TANKS: 20 PT-76 (op status uncertain).
RECCE: 9 M-8, 14 BRDM-2, 10 VBL.
TOWED ARTY: 105mm: 4 M-101.
MORTARS: 81mm.
RL: 89mm: LRAC.

NAVY:† ε150.
BASE: Cotonou.
PATROL AND COASTAL COMBATANTS: 1:
PATROL, INSHORE: 1 *Patriote* PFI (Fr 38-m)⟨.
In store: 4 Sov *Zhuk*⟨ PFI†.

AIR FORCE:† 150; no cbt ac.
AIRCRAFT: 3 An-2, 2 An-26, 2 C-47, 1 *Commander* 500B, 2 Do-128.
HELICOPTERS: 2 AS-350B, 1 Ka-26, 1 SE-3130.

PARAMILITARY:
GENDARMERIE: 2,500; 4 mobile coy.

BURKINA FASO

GDP	1992: fr 841bn ($3.2bn): per capita $800	
	1993: fr 934bn ($3.3bn): per capita $850	
Growth	1992: 0.7%	1993: 0.4%
Inflation	1992: 1.8%	1993: 31.2%
Debt	1992: $1.1bn	1993: $1.2bn
Def bdgt	1993: fr 31.3bn ($110.0m)	
	1994: fr 60.2bn ($104.0m)	
FMA	1992: $1.0m (France)	
$1 = fr	1992: 264.7	1993: 283.2
	1994: 581.4	

fr = CFA franc

Population: 10,096,800

	13–17	*18–22*	*23–32*
Men	572,100	466,400	734,400
Women	558,200	471,100	738,800

TOTAL ARMED FORCES:
ACTIVE: 10,000 (incl Gendarmerie).

ARMY: 5,600.
6 Military Regions.
5 inf 'regt': HQ, 3 'bn' (each 1 coy of 5 pl).
1 AB 'regt': HQ, 1 'bn', 2 coy.
1 tk 'bn': 2 pl.
1 arty 'bn': 2 tp.
1 engr 'bn'.
EQUIPMENT:
RECCE: 83: 15 AML-60/-90, 24 EE-9 *Cascavel*, 10 M-8, 4 M-20, 30 *Ferret*.
APC: 13 M-3.
TOWED ARTY: 122mm: 6; 105mm: 8 M-101.
MRL: 107mm: Ch Type-63.
MORTARS: 81mm: Brandt.
RL: 89mm: LRAC, M-20.
RCL: 75mm: Ch Type-52.
AD GUNS: 14.5mm: 30 ZPU.
SAM: SA-7.

AIR FORCE: 200; 10 cbt ac, no armed hel.
COIN: 4 SF-260W, 6 SF-260WP.
TRANSPORT: 2 C-47, 1 *Commander* 500B, 2 HS-748, 2 N-262.

LIAISON: 3 MH-1521M, 1 SA-316B, 2 SA-365N.

PARAMILITARY:

GENDARMERIE: 4,200.
SECURITY COMPANY (CRG): 250.
PEOPLE'S MILITIA (R): 45,000 trained.

CÔTE D'IVOIRE

GDP	1992: fr 2,644bn ($10.0bn): per capita $1,600	
	1993ε: fr 2,871bn ($10.1bn): per capita $1,600	
Growth	1992: 0%	1993: -1.0%
Inflation	1992: 4.2%	1993: 0.8%
Debt	1992: $18.0bn	1993: $19.1bn
Def bdgt	1992ε: fr 37.9bn ($143.3m)	
	1993ε: fr 39.5bn ($139.6m)	
FMA	1993: $0.2m (IMET)	
	1994: $0.2m (IMET)	
	1995: $0.2m (IMET)	
$1 = fr	1992: 264.7	1993: 283.2
	1994: 581.4	

fr = CFA franc

Population: 13,744,400

	13–17	*18–22*	*23–32*
Men	787,900	627,400	964,300
Women	794,900	629,800	928,900

TOTAL ARMED FORCES:

ACTIVE: 13,900 (incl Presidential Guard, Gendarmerie).
Terms of service: conscription (selective), 6 months.
RESERVES: 12,000.

ARMY: 6,800.

4 Military Regions.
1 armd, 3 inf bn, 1 arty gp.
1 AB, 1 AA, 1 engr coy.
EQUIPMENT:
LIGHT TANKS: 5 AMX-13.
RECCE: 7 ERC-90 *Sagaie*, ε16 AML-60/-90.
APC: 16 M-3, 13 VAB.
TOWED ARTY: 105mm: 4 M-1950.
MORTARS: 81mm; 120mm: 16 AM-50.
RL: 89mm: LRAC.
RCL: 106mm: M-40A1.
AD GUNS: 20mm: 16, incl 6 M-3 VDA SP; 40mm: 5 L/60.

NAVY: ε900.

BASE: Locodjo (Abidjan).
PATROL AND COASTAL COMBATANTS: 4:
MISSILE CRAFT: 2 *L'Ardent* (Fr *Auroux* 40-m) with 4 x SS-12 SSM.
PATROL: 2 *Le Vigilant* (Fr SFCN 47-m) PCI.
AMPHIBIOUS: 1 *L'Eléphant* (Fr *Batral*) LSM, capacity 140 tps, 7 tk, hel deck, plus some 8 craft.

AIR FORCE: 700; 5 cbt ac, no armed hel.

FGA: 1 sqn with 5 *Alpha Jet*.
TRANSPORT: 1 hel sqn with 1 SA-318, 1 SA-319, 1 SA-330, 4 SA-365C.
PRESIDENTIAL FLIGHT: ac: 1 F-28, 1 *Gulfstream* IV, 3 Fokker 100; **hel:** 1 SA-330.
TRAINING: 6 Beech F-33C, 2 Reims Cessna 150H.
LIAISON: 1 Cessna 421, 1 *Super King Air* 200.

PARAMILITARY: 7,800:

PRESIDENTIAL GUARD: 1,100.
GENDARMERIE: 4,400; VAB APC, 4 patrol boats.
MILITIA: 1,500.
MILITARY FIRE SERVICE: 800.

FOREIGN FORCES:

FRANCE: 700; 1 marine inf regt; 1 AS-355 hel.

THE GAMBIA

GDP	1992: D 3,117m ($351m): per capita $800	
	1993ε: D 3,434m ($376m): per capita $850	
Growth	1992: 4.0%	1993: 4.5%
Inflation	1992: 11.8%	1993: 5.0%
Debt	1992: $379.2m	1993: $382.0m
Def bdgt	1992ε: D 108.2m ($12.2m)	
	1993ε: D 118.1m ($13.0m)	
	1994: D 132.2m ($13.9m)	
FMA	1993: $0.1m (IMET)	
	1994: $0.1m (IMET)	
	1995: $0.1m (IMET)	
$1 = D	1992: 8.9	1993: 9.1
	1994: 9.7	

D = dalasi

Population: 983,800

	13–17	*18–22*	*23–32*
Men	51,900	42,700	67,600
Women	51,200	43,000	69,600

TOTAL ARMED FORCES:
ACTIVE: 800.

GAMBIAN NATIONAL ARMY (GNA): 800.

1 inf bn (4 coy), engr sqn.
MARINE UNIT: about 70.
BASE: Banjul.
PATROL, INSHORE: 3:
2 *Gonjur* (Ch *Shanghai-II*) PFI, 1 PFI⟨, boats.

FOREIGN FORCES:
NIGERIA: 70+ trg team.

GHANA

GDP	1992: C 3,009bn ($6.9bn): per capita $1,900	
	1993ε: C 4,741bn ($7.5bn): per capita $2,000	
Growth	1992: 3.9%	1993ε: 5.5%
Inflation	1992: 8%	1993: 5%
Debt	1992: $4.3bn	1993: $4.5bn
Def bdgt	1992ε: C 46.0bn ($105.0m)	
	1993: C 68.5bn ($108.0m)	
FMA	1993: $0.3m (IMET)	
	1994: $0.2m (IMET)	
	1995: $0.2m (IMET)	
$1 = C	1992: 437.1	1993: 636.3
	1994: 920.0	

C = cedi

Population: 16,854,800

	13–17	*18–22*	*23–32*
Men	971,300	799,900	1,192,600
Women	964,800	798,500	1,208,000

TOTAL ARMED FORCES:
ACTIVE: 6,850.

ARMY: 5,000.

2 Command HQ.
2 bde (comprising 6 inf bn (incl 1 trg, 1 UNIFIL, 1 ECOMOG), spt units).
1 recce regt (2 sqn).
1 arty 'regt' (mor bn).
1 AB force (incl 1 para coy).
1 fd engr regt (bn).
EQUIPMENT:
RECCE: 3 EE-9 *Cascavel*.
AIFV: 50 MOWAG *Piranha*.
MORTARS: 81mm: 50; 120mm: 28 Tampella.
RCL: 84mm: 50 *Carl Gustav*.
AD GUNS: 14.5mm: ZPU-4; 23mm: ZU-23-2.

NAVY: ε850; Western and Eastern Commands.

BASES: Sekondi (HQ, West); Tema (HQ, East).
PATROL AND COASTAL COMBATANTS: 4:
COASTAL: 2 *Achimota* (Ge Lürssen 57-m) PFC.
INSHORE: 2 *Dzata* (Ge Lürssen 45-m) PCI.

AIR FORCE: 1,000; 18 cbt ac, no armed hel.

COIN: 1 sqn with 4 MB-326K†, 2 MB-339.
TRANSPORT: 3 Fokker (2 F-27, 1 F-28) (VIP); 3 F-27, 1 C-212, 6 *Skyvan*.
HELICOPTERS: 2 Bell 212 (VIP), 2 Mi-2, 4 SA-319.
TRAINING: 1 sqn with 10 *Bulldog* 122†, 12* L-29, 6 MB 326F.

FORCES ABROAD:
LIBERIA: about 1,000 forming part of ECOMOG.

UN AND PEACEKEEPING:
CROATIA (UNPROFOR I): 22 Observers.
IRAQ/KUWAIT (UNIKOM): 6 Observers.
LEBANON (UNIFIL): 787; 1 inf bn.
RWANDA (UNAMIR): 350, incl 24 Observers.
SOMALIA (UNOSOM): 6 civ pol.
WESTERN SAHARA (MINURSO): 1 Observer.

PARAMILITARY:
PEOPLE'S MILITIA: 5,000: part-time force with police duties.
PRESIDENTIAL GUARD: 1 inf bn.

GUINEA

GDP	1992: G fr 2,610.1bn ($3.2bn): per capita $700	
	1993ε: G fr 3,027.0bn ($3.4bn): per capita $750	
Growth	1992: 3.2%	1993ε: 4.5%
Inflation	1991: 12.2%	1992: 17.0%
Debt	1992: $2.7bn	1993: $2.8bn
Def exp	1992ε: G fr 31.7bn ($39.0m)	
	1993ε: G fr 38.0bn ($43.0m)	
	1994ε: G fr 48.8bn ($50.0m)	

FMA	1993: $0.2m (IMET)	
	1994: $0.1m (IMET)	
	1995: $0.2m (IMET)	
$1 = G fr	1992: 813	1993: 883
	1994: 975	

G fr = Guinean franc

Population: 7,503,000

	13–17	*18–22*	*23–32*
Men	359,000	298,100	451,900
Women	368,600	305,200	464,200

TOTAL ARMED FORCES:

ACTIVE: 9,700 (perhaps 7,500 conscripts).
Terms of service: conscription, 2 years.

ARMY: 8,500.

1 armd bn. 1 arty bn.
1 cdo bn. 1 engr bn.
5 inf bn. 1 AD bn.
1 SF bn.

EQUIPMENT:†
MBT: 30 T-34, 8 T-54.
LIGHT TANKS: 20 PT-76.
RECCE: 25 BRDM-1/-2, 2 AML-90.
APC: 40 BTR (16 -40, 10 -50, 8 -60, 6 -152).
TOWED ARTY: 76mm: 8 M-1942; 85mm: 6 D-44; 122mm: 12 M-1931/37.
MORTARS: 82mm: M-43; 120mm: 20 M-1938/43.
RCL: 82mm: B-10.
ATK GUNS: 57mm: M-1943.
AD GUNS: 30mm: twin M-53; 37mm: 8 M-1939; 57mm: 12 S-60, Ch Type-59; 100mm: 4 KS-19.
SAM: SA-7.

NAVY: 400.

BASES: Conakry, Kakanda.
PATROL AND COASTAL COMBATANTS: 8:
PATROL: 8:
Some 3 Sov *Bogomol* PFI.
2 Sov *Zhuk*, 1 US Swiftships-77, 2 other PCI, all‹.

AIR FORCE:† 800; 11 cbt ac, no armed hel.

FGA: 4 MiG-17F, 7 MiG-21.
TRANSPORT: 2 An-12, 4 An-14.
TRAINING: 3 L-29, 2 MiG-15UTI, 6 Yak-18.
HELICOPTERS: 1 IAR-330, 4 Mi-4, 1 SA-316B, 1 SA-330, 1 SA-342K.

FORCES ABROAD:

UN AND PEACEKEEPING:
LIBERIA: some 600, forming part of ECOMOG.
WESTERN SAHARA (MINURSO): 1 Observer.

PARAMILITARY: 9,600:

PEOPLE'S MILITIA: (7,000).
GENDARMERIE: (1,000).
REPUBLICAN GUARD: (1,600).

GUINEA-BISSAU

GDP	1992: pG 1,530bn ($221m): per capita $750	
	1993ε: pG 2,366bn ($235m): per capita $760	
Growth	1992: -9.0%	1993: 3.7%
Inflation	1992: 69.6%	1993: 48.1%
Debt	1992: $634.1m	1993: $662.5m
Def bdgt	1992ε: pG 56.2bn ($8.1m)	
	1993ε: pG 86.7bn ($8.6m)	
	1994ε: pG 106.2bn ($8.6m)	
FMA	1993: $0.2m (IMET)	
	1994: $0.1m (IMET)	
	1995: $0.8m (IMET)	
$1 = pG	1992: 6,934	1993: 10,082
	1994: 12,350	

pG = Guinean peso

Population: 1,058,400

	13–17	*18–22*	*23–32*
Men	60,400	53,400	78,100
Women	56,800	49,300	78,000

TOTAL ARMED FORCES (all services, incl Gendarmerie, are part of the armed forces):

ACTIVE: 9,250.
Terms of service: conscription (selective).

ARMY: 6,800.

1 armd 'bn' (sqn).
5 inf, 1 arty bn, 1 recce, 1 engr coy.

EQUIPMENT:
MBT: 10 T-34.
LIGHT TANKS: 20 PT-76.
RECCE: 10 BRDM-2.
APC: 35 BTR-40/-60/-152, 20 Ch Type-56.
TOWED ARTY: 85mm: 8 D-44; 122mm: 18 M-1938/D-30.
MORTARS: 82mm: M-43; 120mm: 8 M-1943.

RL: 89mm: M-20.
RCL: 75mm: Ch Type-52; 82mm: B-10.
AD GUNS: 23mm: 18 ZU-23; 37mm: 6 M-1939; 57mm: 10 S-60.
SAM: SA-7.

NAVY: ε350.
BASE: Bissau.
PATROL AND COASTAL COMBATANTS: 7:
PATROL, INSHORE: 7:
1 ex-Ge *Kondor-I* PCI, 2 Sov *Bogomol*, 2 Ch *Shantou* PFI, some 2 PCI((incl 1 customs service).

AIR FORCE: 100; 3 cbt ac, no armed hel.
FIGHTER: 3 MiG-17.
HELICOPTERS: 1 SA-318, 2 SA-319.

FORCES ABROAD:
UN AND PEACEKEEPING:
ANGOLA (UNAVEM II): 2 Observers.
LIBERIA (UNOMIL): 20 Observers.
MOZAMBIQUE (ONUMOZ): 37 Observers, 55 civ pol.

PARAMILITARY:
GENDARMERIE: 2,000.

LIBERIA

GDP	1992: $L 1.2bn ($1.2bn):	
	per capita $1,050	
	1993: $L 1.2bn ($1.2bn):	
	per capita $1,050	
Growth	1992: 0.5%	1993ε: 0%
Inflation	1991: ε75%	1992ε: 100%
Debt	1992: $1.95bn	1993: $1.97bn
Def bdgt	1993ε: $L 35.3m ($14.4m)	
$1 = $L[a]	1986–94: 1.0	

$L= Liberian dollar

[a] Exchange rates are based on a fixed relationship with the US dollar. Unofficial rate estimate: $1 = $L30–40.

Population: 2,893,800

	13–17	*18–22*	*23–32*
Men	166,000	138,100	214,400
Women	161,300	134,000	204,700

As a result of civil war the Armed Forces of Liberia (AFL), with a cbt strength of ε3–5,000, are now confined to the capital Monrovia. Eqpt held by the AFL has been destroyed or is unserviceable. The area west of Monrovia, up to the Sierra Leone border, is controlled by the United Liberation Movement for Democracy in Liberia (ULIMO) with a cbt strength of ε5–6,000. Both are opposed by the National Patriotic Forces of Liberia (NPFL) which control most of the country with a cbt strength of ε8–12,000. A four-nation peacekeeping force (ECOMOG) provided by the Economic Community of West African States (ECOWAS) is deployed within the country and is composed of forces from: Ghana (ε1,000); Guinea (ε600); Nigeria (ε10,000); Tanzania (ε800).

The United Nations Observer Mission in Liberia (UNOMIL) has deployed some 390 military observers and spt tps to supervise the disarming of the various factions.

MALI

GDP	1992: fr 748.2bn ($2.8bn):	
	per capita $550	
	1993ε: fr 879.9bn ($3.1bn):	
	per capita $600	
Growth	1992: 6.8%	1993ε: 7.0%
Inflation	1992: 2.0%	1993: 2.4%
Debt	1992: $2.6bn	1993: $2.4bn
Def bdgt	1992ε: fr 17.4bn ($65.6m)	
	1993ε: fr 16.3bn ($60.0m)	
	1994ε: fr 18.6bn ($65.7m)	
FMA	1993: $0.2m (IMET)	
	1994: $0.1m (IMET)	
	1995: $0.1m (IMET)	
$1 = fr	1992: 264.7	1993: 283.2
	1994: 581.4	

fr = CFA franc

Population: 9,504,800

	13–17	*18–22*	*23–32*
Men	547,800	460,800	663,100
Women	545,600	461,300	672,800

TOTAL ARMED FORCES (all services form part of the Army):
ACTIVE: 7,350.
Terms of service: conscription (incl for civil purposes), 2 years (selective).

ARMY: 6,900.
2 tk, 4 inf, 1 AB, 2 arty, 1 engr, 1 SF bn, 2 AD, 1 SAM bty.
EQUIPMENT:†
MBT: 21 T-34.
LIGHT TANKS: 18 Type 62.
RECCE: 20 BRDM-2.
APC: 30 BTR-40, 10 BTR-60, 10 BTR-152.
TOWED ARTY: 85mm: 6 D-44; 100mm: 6 M-1944; 122mm: 8 D-30.
MRL: 122mm: 2 BM-21.
MORTARS: 82mm: M-43; 120mm: 30 M-43.
AD GUNS: 37mm: 6 M-1939; 57mm: 6 S-60.
SAM: 12 SA-3.

NAVY:† about 50.
BASES: Bamako, Mopti, Segou, Timbuktu.
RIVER PATROL CRAFT: 3⟨.

AIR FORCE: 400; 16† cbt ac, no armed hel.
FGA: 5 MiG-17F.
FIGHTER: 11 MiG-21.
TRANSPORT: 2 An-2, 2 An-24, 2 An-26.
TRAINING: 6 L-29, 1 MiG-15UTI, 4 Yak-11, 2 Yak-18.
HELICOPTERS: 2 Mi-4, 1 Mi-8.

FORCES ABROAD:
UN AND PEACEKEEPING:
RWANDA (UNAMIR): 10 Observers, 5 civ pol.

PARAMILITARY:
GENDARMERIE: 1,800; 8 coy.
REPUBLICAN GUARD: 2,000.
MILITIA: 3,000.
NATIONAL POLICE: 1,000.

NIGER

GDP	1992: fr 636.7bn ($2.4bn): per capita $900	
	1993ε: fr 707.1bn ($2.5bn): per capita $950	
Growth	1992: -6.5%	1993ε: 1.4%
Inflation	1992: -1.8%	1993: 0.4%
Debt	1992: $1.7bn	1993: $1.8bn
Def bdgt	1992 fr 8.2bn ($30.9m)	
	1993: fr 9.1bn ($32.0m)	
FMA	1993: $0.4m (IMET)	
	1994: $0.2m (IMET)	
	1995: $0.2m (IMET)	
$1 = fr	1992: 264.7	1993: 283.2
	1994: 581.4	

fr = CFA franc

Population: 8,702,800

	13–17	*18–22*	*23–32*
Men:	480,200	388,300	592,300
Women:	485,600	396,900	608,500

TOTAL ARMED FORCES:
ACTIVE: 5,300.
Terms of service: selective conscription (2 years).

ARMY: 5,200.
3 Military Districts.
4 armd recce sqn.
7 inf, 2 AB, 1 engr coy.
EQUIPMENT:
RECCE: 90 AML-90, 35 AML-60/20, 7 VBL.
APC: 22 M-3.
MORTARS: 81mm: 19 Brandt; 82mm: 17; 120mm: 4 Brandt.
RL: 89mm: 36 LRAC.
RCL: 75mm: 6 M-20; 106mm: 8.
ATK GUNS: 85mm; 90mm.
AD GUNS: 20mm: 39 incl 10 M-3 VDA SP.

AIR FORCE: 100; no cbt ac or armed hel.
TRANSPORT: 2 C-130H, 1 Do-228, 1 Boeing 737-200 (VIP).
LIAISON: 2 Cessna 337D, 1 Do-28D.

PARAMILITARY:
GENDARMERIE: 1,400.
REPUBLICAN GUARD: 2,500.
NATIONAL POLICE: 1,500.

NIGERIA

GDP	1992: N 553.2bn ($32.0bn): per capita $1,300	
	1993ε: N 708.6bn ($32.1bn): per capita $1,250	
Growth	1992: 3.7%	1993ε: -2.4%
Inflation	1992: 44.6%	1993: 57.2%
Debt	1992: $31.0bn	1993: $31.2bn
Def exp[a]	1991: N 2,416m ($244.0m)	
Def bdgt[a]	1992: N 3,060m ($176.9m)	
	1993: N 4,371m ($197.8m)	
	1994: N 4,460m ($202.7m)	

FMA	1993:	$0.2m (IMET)		
$1 = N	1992:	17.3	1993:	22.1
	1994:	22.0		

N = naira

[a] Excl Police, Police Affairs Dept and Internal Affairs Ministry.

Population:[b] 118,700,000

	13–17	*18–22*	*23–32*
Men	5,635,600	4,646,400	6,830,500
Women	5,718,200	4,801,000	7,161,300

[b] The 1991 census indicated a population of 90,500,000. This figure shows a large discrepancy with UN and other projections.

TOTAL ARMED FORCES:

ACTIVE: 76,500.
RESERVES: planned; none organised.

ARMY: 62,000.

1 armd div (2 armd bde).
1 composite div (1 mot inf, 1 amph bde, 1 AB bn).
2 mech div (each 1 mech, 1 mot inf bde).
1 AD bde.
div tps: each div 1 arty, 1 engr bde, 1 recce bn.

EQUIPMENT:
MBT: 178: 60 T-55†, 118 Vickers Mk 3.
LIGHT TANKS: 100 *Scorpion.*
RECCE: 20 *Saladin*, ε120 AML-60, 60 AML-90, 55 *Fox*, 75 EE-9 *Cascavel.*
APC: 10 *Saracen*, 300 *Steyr* 4K-7FA, 70 MOWAG *Piranha.*
TOWED ARTY: 105mm: 200 M-56; 122mm: 200 D-30/-74; 130mm: 4; 155mm: 24 FH-77B.
SP ARTY: 155mm: 25 *Palmaria.*
MRL: 122mm: 5 APR-21.
MORTARS: 81mm: 200; 82mm: 100; 120mm: 30+.
RCL: 84mm: *Carl Gustav*; 106mm: M-40A1.
AD GUNS: 20mm: some 60; 23mm: ZU-23, 30 ZSU-23-4 SP; 40mm: L/60.
SAM: 48 *Blowpipe*, 16 *Roland.*

NAVY: ε5,000 (incl Coast Guard).

BASES: Apapa (Lagos; HQ Western Command), Calabar (HQ Eastern Command), Warri, Port Harcourt.
FRIGATES: 1:
1 *Aradu* (Ge *Meko*-360) with 1 *Lynx* hel, 2 x 3 ASTT; plus 8 x *Otomat* SSM, 1 x 127mm gun.
PATROL AND COASTAL COMBATANTS: 53:
CORVETTES: 2:
2† *Erinomi* (UK Vosper Mk 9) with 1 x 2 ASW mor. (Plus 1 *Otobo* (UK Vosper Mk 3) in Italy since 1988, refitting to PCO.)
MISSILE CRAFT: 6:
3 *Ekpe* (Ge Lürssen 57-m) PFM with 4 x *Otomat* SSM.
3 *Siri* (Fr *Combattante*) PFM with 2 x 2 MM-38 *Exocet* SSM.
PATROL, INSHORE: 45:
4 *Makurdi* (UK Brooke Marine 33-m), some 41 PCI‹.
MINE WARFARE: 2 *Ohue* (mod It *Lerici*) MCC.
AMPHIBIOUS: 2 *Ambe* (Ge) LST, capacity 220 tps, 5 tk.
SUPPORT AND MISCELLANEOUS: 6: 1 *Lana* AGHS, 4 tugs, 1 nav trg.

NAVAL AVIATION:

HELICOPTERS: 2 *Lynx* Mk 89 MR/SAR.

AIR FORCE: 9,500; 92 cbt ac†, 15 armed hel†.

FGA/FIGHTER: 3 sqn:
1 with 20 *Alpha Jet* (FGA/trg).
1 with †6 MiG-21MF, †4 MiG-21U, †12 MiG-21B/FR.
1 with †15 *Jaguar* (12 -SN, 3 -BN).
COIN/TRAINING: 23 L-39MS, 12 MB-339AN.
ARMED HELICOPTERS: †15 Bo-105D.
TRANSPORT: 2 sqn with 5 C-130H, 3 -H-30, 3 Do-228 (VIP), 5 G-222.
PRESIDENTIAL FLT: 1 Boeing 727, 1 *Falcon*, 2 *Gulfstream*, 1 BAe 125-700, 1 BAe 125-1000.
LIGHT TPT: 18 Do-128-6.
HELICOPTERS: 4 AS-332, 2 SA-330.
TRAINING: ac:† 25 *Bulldog*; **hel:** 14 Hughes 300.
MISSILES:
AAM: AA-2 *Atoll.*

FORCES ABROAD:

LIBERIA: some 10,000; 2 inf, 1 arty bde; contingent forms major part of ECOMOG.
THE GAMBIA: 70+ trg team.
SIERRA LEONE: 800; 1 inf bn.
UN AND PEACEKEEPING:
ANGOLA (UNAVEM II): 5 Observers.
CROATIA (UNPROFOR I): 7 Observers, 40 civ pol.
IRAQ/KUWAIT (UNIKOM): 6 Observers.
SOMALIA (UNOSOM II): 745; 1 recce bn, 5 civ pol.
RWANDA (UNAMIR/UNOMUR): 15 Observers.
WESTERN SAHARA (MINURSO): 1 Observer.

PARAMILITARY:
COAST GUARD: incl in Navy entry.
PORT SECURITY POLICE: ε2,000; about 60 boats and some 5 hovercraft.
SECURITY AND CIVIL DEFENCE CORPS (Ministry of Internal Affairs): Police: UR-416, 70 AT-105 *Saxon*† APC; 1 Cessna 500, 3 Piper (2 *Navajo*, 1 *Chieftain*) **ac:** 4 Bell (2 -212, 2 -222) **hel**.

SENEGAL

GDP	1992: fr 1,645.8bn ($6.2bn): per capita $1,900	
	1993: fr 1,793.0bn ($6.3bn): per capita $2,000	
Growth	1992: 2.9%	1993: -0.8%
Inflation	1992: 0%	1993: 0.5%
Debt	1992: $3.6bn	1993: $3.7bn
Def bdgt	1992: fr 33.5bn ($126.7m)	
	1993: fr 37.9bn ($133.8m)	
FMA	1993: $0.8m (IMET)	
	1994: $0.5m (IMET)	
	1995: $0.1m (IMET)	
$1 = fr	1992: 264.7	1993: 283.2
	1994: 581.4	

fr = CFA franc

Population: 8,375,200

	13–17	*18–22*	*23–32*
Men	480,600	394,500	580,700
Women	476,500	396,900	589,500

TOTAL ARMED FORCES:
ACTIVE: 13,350.
Terms of service: conscription, 2 years selective.
RESERVE: exists, no details known.

ARMY: 12,000 (mostly conscripts).
4 Military Zone HQ.
1 armd bn.
6 inf bn.
1 arty bn.
1 cdo bn.
1 engr bn.
1 Presidential Guard (horsed).
3 construction coy.
1 engr bn.
1 Presidential Guard (horsed).
3 construction coy.
1 AB bn.
EQUIPMENT:
RECCE: 10 M-8, 4 M-20, 30 AML-60, 27 AML-90.
APC: some 16 Panhard M-3, 12 M-3 half-track.
TOWED ARTY: 18: 75mm: 6 M-116 pack; 105mm: 6 M-101/HM-2; 155mm: ε6 Fr Model-50.
MORTARS: 81mm: 8 Brandt; 120mm: 8 Brandt.
ATGW: 4 *Milan*.
RL: 89mm: 31 LRAC.
AD GUNS: 20mm: 21 M-693; 40mm: 12 L/60.

NAVY: 700.
BASES: Dakar, Casamance.
PATROL AND COASTAL COMBATANTS: 10:
PATROL, COASTAL: 2:
1 *Fouta* (Dk *Osprey*) PCC.
1 *Njambuur* (Fr SFCN 59-m) PFC.
INSHORE: 8:
3 *Saint Louis* (Fr 48-m) PCI.
3 *Senegal* II PFI⟨.
2 *Challenge* (UK *Tracker*) PCI⟨.
AMPHIBIOUS: craft only: 1 LCT.

AIR FORCE: 650; 8 cbt ac, no armed hel.
COIN: 1 sqn with 4 CM-170, 4 R-235 *Guerrier*.
MR/SAR: 1 EMB-111.
TRANSPORT: 1 sqn with 6 F-27-400M, 2 MH-1521, 1 PA-23 (liaison), 1 Boeing 727-200 (VIP).
HELICOPTERS: 2 SA-318C, 2 SA-330, 1 SA-341H.
TRAINING: 2 *Rallye* 160, 2 R-235A.

FORCES ABROAD:
UN AND PEACEKEEPING:
IRAQ/KUWAIT (UNIKOM): 6 Observers.
RWANDA (UNAMIR): 28 Observers.
UGANDA/RWANDA (UNOMUR): 10 Observers.

PARAMILITARY:
GENDARMERIE: 4,000; 12 VXB-170 APC.
CUSTOMS: 2 PCI⟨, boats.

OPPOSITION:
Casamance Movement of Democratic Forces.

FOREIGN FORCES:
FRANCE: 1,500; 1 marine inf bn, MR *Atlantic* ac. 1 Air tpt unit (1 C-160 **ac**, 1 SA-319 **hel**).

SIERRA LEONE

GDP	1992: Le 259bn ($519m): per capita $700	
	1993ε: Le 307bn ($540m): per capita $750	
Growth	1992: -0.8%	1993: 1.5%

Inflation	1992: 65.5%	1993: 22.2%
Debt	1992: $1.3bn	1993: $1.3bn
Def exp	1990: Le 808.0m ($5.3m)	
	1991ε: Le 3.5bn ($12.0m)	
Def bdgt	1992ε: Le 6.5bn ($13.0m)	
	1993ε: Le 7.7bn ($13.5m)	
FMA	1993: $0.3m (IMET)	
$1 = Le	1992: 499.4	1993: 567.5
	1994: 576.8	

Le = leone

Population: 4,460,600

	13–17	18–22	23–32
Men	237,000	201,800	312,900
Women	235,800	201,900	318,000

TOTAL ARMED FORCES:

ACTIVE: 6,150.

ARMY: ε6,000.

4 inf bn.
2 arty bty.
1 engr sqn.

EQUIPMENT:
APC: 10 MOWAG *Piranha*, 4 *Saracen*, 4 (Russian type nk).
MORTARS: 81mm; 82mm.
RCL: 84mm: *Carl Gustav*.
SAM: SA-7.

NAVY: ε150.

BASE: Freetown.
PATROL AND COASTAL COMBATANTS: 3:
2 Ch *Shanghai-II* PFI, 1 Swiftship 32-m PFI. Plus some 3 modern boats.

PARAMILITARY:

State Security Division: 1 SF bn.

OPPOSITION:

REVOLUTIONARY UNITED FRONT: ε1,000.

FOREIGN FORCES:

NIGERIA: 800; 1 inf bn.

TOGO

GDP	1992: fr 454.8bn ($1.7bn): per capita $1,300	
	1993: fr 482.9bn ($1.7bn): per capita $1,300	
Growth	1992: -4.3%	1993: -3.5%
Inflation	1992: 1.4%	1993: -1.0%
Debt	1992: $1.4bn	1993: $1.4bn
Def bdgt	1992ε: fr 12.4bn ($47.0m)	
	1993ε: fr 13.7bn ($48.2m)	
$1 = fr	1992: 264.7	1993: 283.2
	1994: 581.4	

fr = CFA franc

Population: 4,164,400

	13–17	18–22	23–32
Men:	226,500	183,100	268,500
Women:	237,600	196,800	299,600

TOTAL ARMED FORCES:

ACTIVE: some 6,950.
Terms of service: conscription, 2 years (selective).

ARMY: 6,500.

2 inf regt: 1 with 1 mech bn, 1 mot bn; 1 with 2 armd sqn, 3 inf coy; spt units (trg).
1 Presidential Guard regt: 2 bn (1 cdo), 2 coy.
1 para cdo regt: 3 coy.
1 spt regt: 1 fd arty bty; 2 AD arty bty; 1 log/tpt/engr bn.

EQUIPMENT:
MBT: 2 T-54/-55.
LIGHT TANKS: 9 *Scorpion*.
RECCE: 6 M-8, 3 M-20, 10 AML (3 -60, 7 -90), 36 EE-9 *Cascavel*, 2 VBL.
APC: 4 M-3A1 half-track, 30 UR-416.
TOWED ARTY: 105mm: 4 HM-2.
MORTARS: 82mm: 20 M-43.
RCL: 57mm: 5 ZIS-2; 75mm: 12 Ch Type-52/-56; 82mm: 10 Ch Type-65.
AD GUNS: 14.5mm: 38 ZPU-4; 37mm: 5 M-39.

NAVY: ε200 (incl Marine Infantry unit).

BASE: Lomé.
PATROL AND COASTAL COMBATANTS: 2:
INSHORE: 2 *Kara* (Fr *Esterel*) PFI⟨.

AIR FORCE: 250; 16 cbt ac, no armed hel.

COIN/TRAINING: 5 *Alpha Jet*, 4 CM-170, 4 EMB-

326G, 3 TB-30.
TRANSPORT: 2 *Baron*, 2 DHC-5D, 1 Do-27, 1 F-28-1000 (VIP), 1 Boeing 707 (VIP), 2 Reims-Cessna 337.
HELICOPTERS: 1 AS-332, 2 SA-315, 1 SA-319, 1 SA-330.

FORCES ABROAD:

UN AND PEACEKEEPING:
RWANDA (UNAMIR): 14 Observers, 10 civ pol.
WESTERN SAHARA (MINURSO): 5 civ pol.

PARAMILITARY:

GENDARMERIE (Ministry of Interior): 750; 1 trg school, 2 regional sections, 1 mobile sqn.

SOUTHERN AFRICA

ANGOLA

GDP	1992ε: K 1,839bn ($3.3bn): per capita $1,200	
	1993ε: K 22,100bn ($3.4bn): per capita $1,200	
Growth	1992ε: -1.9%	1993ε: 0%
Inflation	1992ε: 220%	1993ε: 1,840%
Debt	1992: $9.6bn	1993: $10.3bn
Def exp	1992ε: K 362.0bn ($648.0m)	
	1993ε: K 6,825.0bn ($1.1bn)	
Def bdgt	1994ε: K n.k. ($900.0m)	
$1 = K	1992: 558	1993ε: 6,500
	1994ε: 69,500	

K = kwanza

Population: 11,234,400

	13–17	*18–22*	*23–32*
Men	619,100	520,200	784,500
Women	623,100	527,200	806,700

TOTAL ARMED FORCES:

ACTIVE: ε82,000.

ARMY: 75,000.

25 regts (armd, inf, engr, comd – str vary).
EQUIPMENT:†
MBT: 100 T-34†, 100 T-54/-55, some T-62, T-72 reported.
LIGHT TANKS: some 10 PT-76.
AIFV: 50+ BMP.
RECCE: some 40+ BRDM-2.
APC: 100 BTR-60/-152.
TOWED ARTY: 300: incl 76mm: M-1942 (ZIS-3); 85mm: D-44; 122mm: D-30; 130mm: M-46.
ASSAULT GUNS: 100mm: SU-100.
MRL: 122mm: 50 BM-21; 240mm: some BM-24.
MORTARS: 82mm: 250; 120mm: 40+ M-43.
ATGW: AT-3 *Sagger*.
RCL: 500: 82mm: B-10; 107mm: B-11.
AD GUNS: 200+: 14.5mm: ZPU-4; 23mm: ZU-23-2, 20 ZSU-23-4 SP; 37mm: M-1939; 57mm: S-60 towed, 40 ZSU-57-2 SP.
SAM: SA-7/-14.

NAVY: ε1,500–2,000.

BASES: Luanda (HQ), Lobito, Namibe.
PATROL AND COASTAL COMBATANTS:
MISSILE CRAFT: 6 Sov *Osa*-II† with 4 x SS-N-2 *Styx* SSM.
TORPEDO CRAFT: 4 *Shershen*† with 4 x 533mm HWT.
PATROL, INSHORE 7: 2 Sov *Poluchat*†, 1 Sov *Zhuk*⟨†.
4 *Bazan* type 26.5m PCI.
MINE WARFARE: 2 Sov *Yevgenya* MHI.
AMPHIBIOUS: 3 Sov *Polnocny* LSM, capacity 100 tps, 6 tk.
Plus craft: 1 LCT, about 5 LCM.

COASTAL DEFENCE: SS-C-l *Sepal* at Luanda.

AIR FORCE/AIR DEFENCE: †5,500;

79 cbt ac, 40 armed hel.
FGA: 20 MiG-23, 19 Su-22, 10 Su-25.
FIGHTER: 15 MiG-21 MF/bis.
COIN/RECCE: 4 PC-7/-9.
MR: 2 EMB-111, 1 F-27MPA.
ATTACK HELICOPTERS: 28 Mi-25/35, 6 SA-365M (guns), 6 SA-342 (*HOT*).
TRANSPORT: 2 sqn with 9 An-26, 6 BN-2, 6 C-212, 2 L-100-20, 2 Boeing-707.
HELICOPTERS: 2 sqn with 30 IAR-316, 16 SA-316, 16 Mi-8, 7 Mi-17, 5 SA-341, 4 SA-365.
LIAISON: 5 An-2, 5 Do-27.
TRAINING: 3 Cessna 172, 3 MiG-15UTI, 6* MiG-21U, 5* Su-22, 6 Yak-11.
AD: 5 SAM bn†. 10 bty with 40 SA-2, 12 SA-3, 25 SA-6, 15 SA-8, 20 SA-9, 10 SA-13.
MISSILES:
ASM: *HOT*.
AAM: AA-2 *Atoll*.

PARAMILITARY:
INTERNAL SECURITY POLICE: 40,000.

OPPOSITION:
UNITA (Union for the Total Independence of Angola): ε55,000.
EQUIPMENT: captured T-34/-85, 70 T-55 MBT reported, misc APC (not in service); BM-21 122mm MRL; 75mm, 76mm, 122mm, 130mm fd guns; 81mm, 82mm, 120mm mor; 85mm RPG-7 RL; 75mm RCL; 12.7mm hy machine guns; 14.5mm, 20mm, ZU-23-2 23mm AA guns; *Stinger*, SAM-7.
FLEC (Front for the Liberation of the Cabinda Enclave): claims 5,000, actual strength ε600; small arms only.

FOREIGN FORCES:
UNITED NATIONS (UNAVEM II): 51 military observers and 15 civ pol from 16 countries.

BOTSWANA

GDP	1992: P 7.8bn ($3.7bn):	
	per capita $5,000	
	1993ε: P 9.4bn ($3.9bn):	
	per capita $5,200	
Growth	1992: 6.5%	1993ε: 4.6%
Inflation	1992: 16.1%	1993: 14.3%
Debt	1992: $544.8m	1993: $542.2m
Def bdgt	1992ε: P 213.8m ($100.4m)	
	1993ε: P 360.6m ($149.0m)	
	1994ε: P 455.1m ($171.8m)	
FMA	1992: $0.5m (IMET)	
	1993: $0.4m (IMET)	
	1994: $0.10m (IMET)	
$1 = P	1992: 2.13	1993: 2.42
	1994: 2.65	

P = pula

Population: 1,401,200

	13–17	*18–22*	*23–32*
Men	87,500	68,400	99,000
Women	89,400	70,000	108,300

TOTAL ARMED FORCES:
ACTIVE: 7,500+.

ARMY: 7,000.
2 bde: 4 inf bn, 2 fd arty, 2 AD arty, 1 engr regt, 1 cdo unit.

EQUIPMENT:
RECCE: 10 *Shorland*, 12 V-150 *Commando* (11 with 90mm gun), RAM-V.
APC: 30 BTR-60†.
TOWED ARTY: 105mm: 12 lt, 4 Model 56 pack.
MORTARS: 81mm; 120mm: 6 M-43.
ATGW: *TOW* reported.
RCL: 84mm: 30 *Carl Gustav*.
AD GUNS: 20mm: M-167.
SAM: 12 SA-7, 10 SA-16, 5 *Javelin*.

AIR FORCE: 500; 19 cbt ac, no armed hel.
COIN: 1 sqn with 7 BAC-167 Mk 83, 5 BN-2 *Defender*.
TRANSPORT: 1 sqn with 2 *Defender*, 2 CN-235, 2 *Skyvan* 3M, 1 BAe 125-800 (VIP).
LIAISON/TRG: 2 sqn with 2 Cessna 152, 7* PC-7.
HEL: 1 sqn with 2 AS-350L, 5 Bell 412 (VIP).

FORCES ABROAD:
UN AND PEACEKEEPING:
MOZAMBIQUE (ONUMOZ): 768; 1 inf bn(-), 13 Observers, plus 15 civ pol.
SOMALIA (UNOSOM II): 425.
UGANDA/RWANDA (UNOMUR): 9 Observers.

PARAMILITARY:
POLICE MOBILE UNIT: 1,000.

LESOTHO

GDP	1992: M 2,026m ($579m):	
	per capita $2,000	
	1993ε: M 1,937m ($625m):	
	per capita $2,100	
Growth	1992: 0.8%	1993ε: 5.2%
Inflation	1992: 11.7%	1993: 13.9%
Debt	1992: $471.6m	1993: $534.8m
Def exp	1992ε: M 111.4m ($37.8m)	
Def bdgt	1993ε: M 96.1m ($31.0m)	
	1994: M 90.3m ($25.1m)	
FMA	1993: $0.13m (IMET)	
	1995: $0.05m (IMET)	
$1 = M	1992: 3.5	1993: 3.1
	1995: 3.6	

M = maloti

Population: 1,972,000

	13–17	*18–22*	*23–32*
Men	109,400	91,200	139,000
Women	108,700	90,200	141,500

TOTAL ARMED FORCES:
ACTIVE: 2,000.

ARMY: 2,000.
7 inf coy.
1 spt coy (incl recce/AB, 81mm mor).
1 air sqn.
EQUIPMENT:
RECCE: 10 Is RAMTA, 8 *Shorland,* AML-90.
TOWED ARTY: 105mm: 2.
MORTARS: 81mm: some.
RCL: 106mm: M-40.
AIRCRAFT: 2 C-212 *Aviocar* 300, 1 Cessna 182Q.
HELICOPTERS: 2 Bo-105, 1 Bell 47, 3 Bell 412.

MALAWI

GDP	1992:	K 6.7bn ($1.9bn): per capita $650		
	1993:	K 8.9bn ($2.1bn): per capita $750		
Growth	1992:	-7.9%	1993:	11.1%
Inflation	1992:	22.7%	1993:	23.0%
Debt	1992:	$1.7bn	1993:	$1.9bn
Def bdgt	1992ε:	K 70.0m ($19.4m)		
	1993ε:	K 90.8m ($20.4m)		
	1994ε:	K 158.0m ($24.3m)		
FMA	1993:	$0.2m (IMET)		
	1994:	$0.1m (IMET)		
	1995:	$0.1m (IMET)		
$1 = K	1992:	3.6	1993:	4.4
	1994:	6.8		

K = kwacha

Population: 9,745,400

	13–17	*18–22*	*23–32*
Men:	532,000	439,600	660,600
Women:	528,400	449,400	703,300

TOTAL ARMED FORCES (all services form part of the Army):
ACTIVE: 10,400.
RESERVES: Army: 10,000 (militia).

ARMY: 10,000.
3 inf bn; 1 spt bn (incl 1 recce sqn).
EQUIPMENT:
RECCE: 20 *Fox*, 10 *Ferret*, 13 *Eland.*
TOWED ARTY: 105mm: 9 lt.
MORTARS: 81mm: 8 L16.
RL: 89mm: M-20.
RCL: 57mm: M-18.
AD GUNS: 14.5mm: 50 ZPU-4.
SAM: 15 *Blowpipe.*

MARINES: 200.
BASE: Monkey Bay (Lake Nyasa).
PATROL CRAFT: 1 PCI‹, 2 LCVP, some boats.

AIR WING: 200; no cbt ac, 2 armed hel.
TRANSPORT: 1 sqn with 3 Do-228, 2 C-47, 1 HS-125-800 (VIP), 1 *King Air* C90.
HELICOPTERS:
ATTACK: 2 AS-350.
TRANSPORT: 3 SA-319, 3 SA-330, 1 SA-365.

FORCES ABROAD:
UN AND PEACEKEEPING:
RWANDA (UNAMIR): 5 Observers.

PARAMILITARY:
MOBILE POLICE FORCE (MPF): 1,500; 8 Shorland armd car; 3 BN-2T *Defender* (border patrol), 1 *Skyvan* 3M, 4 Cessna **ac**; 2 AS-365 **hel**.

MOZAMBIQUE

GDP	1992:	M 2,764bn ($1.1bn): per capita $600		
	1993:	M 4,022bn ($1.2bn): per capita $650		
Growth	1992:	-3.4%	1993:	6.3%
Inflation	1992:	45.2%	1993:	45.0%
Debt	1992:	$4.9bn	1993:	$5.2bn
Def bdgt[a]	1992ε:	M 256.8bn ($100.7m)		
	1993ε:	M 456.0bn ($117.8m)		
	1994:	M 453.0bn ($84.3m)		
FMA	1993:	$0.2m (IMET)		
	1995:	$0.1m (IMET)		
$1 = M	1992:	2,550	1993:	3,874
	1994:	5,400		

M = meticais

[a] Incl costs of demob programme and new org est at $31m in 1993 and $19m in 1994.

Population: 17,653,400

	13–17	*18–22*	*23–32*
Men	971,000	808,200	1,253,700
Women	986,600	823,800	1,291,000

TOTAL ARMED FORCES:

Under the terms of the 1992 peace accord, government and Renamo forces are to merge forming a new National Army some 30,000 strong. The unified force has a current str of ε2,000 from which the first of 6 inf bn has formed. Weaponry is mainly of Soviet manufacture and of poor serviceability.

ARMY: to be 30,000.

EQUIPMENT:†

MBT: some 80 T-54/-55 (300+ T-34, T-54/-55 non-op).
RECCE: 30 BRDM-1/-2.
AIFV: 40 BMP-1.
APC: 150+ BTR-60, 100 BTR-152.
TOWED ARTY: 100+: 76mm: M-1942; 85mm: 150+: D-44, D-48, Type-56; 100mm: 24 M-1944; 105mm: M-101; 122mm: M-1938, D-30; 130mm: 24 M-46; 152mm: 20 D-1.
MRL: 122mm: 30 BM-21.
MORTARS: 82mm: M-43; 120mm: M-43.
RCL: 75mm; 82mm: B-10; 107mm: B-11.
AD GUNS: 400: 20mm: M-55; 23mm: 90 ZU-23-2; 37mm: 100 M-1939; 57mm: 90: S-60 towed, ZSU-57-2 SP.
SAM: SA-7.
(All eqpt est to be at 10% or less serviceability.)

NAVY†: ε750.

BASES: Maputo (HQ), Beira, Nacala, Pemba, Inhambane, Quelimane (ocean); Metangula (Lake Nyasa) where 3 PCI⟨ (non-op) are based.
PATROL AND COASTAL COMBATANTS: 10:
INSHORE: some 10†:
3 *Zhuk* PFI⟨, some 7 PCI⟨.
MINE WARFARE: 2 Sov *Yevgenya* MSI.
AMPHIBIOUS: craft only: 2 LCU†.

AIR FORCE: 4,000 (incl AD units); 43 cbt ac†, 4 armed hel†.

FGA: 5 sqn with 43 MiG-21.
TRANSPORT: 1 sqn with 5 An-26, 2 C-212, 2 Cessna 152, 1 Cessna 172.
HELICOPTERS:
ATTACK: 4 Mi-24.
TRANSPORT: 5 Mi-8.
TRAINING: 4 PA-32.
AD SAM:† SA-2, 10 SA-3.

FOREIGN FORCES:

UNITED NATIONS (ONUMOZ): 5,100, to be 7,500; 5 inf bn (Bangladesh, Botswana, India, Uruguay, Zambia), 1 engr bn, plus spt units; 327 Observers and 476 civilian police from 27 countries.

NAMIBIA

GDP	1992: $N 7,026m ($2.5bn): per capita $2,500	
	1993ε: $N 8,567m ($2.6bn): per capita $2,600	
Growth	1992: 3.5%	1993: 3.3%
Inflation	1992: 17.8%	1993: 8.6%
Debt	1992: $69.0m	1994: $68.0m
Def exp	1992: $N 191.0m ($67.0m)	
Def bdgt	1993: $N 187.3m ($57.3m)	
	1994: $N 198.1m ($58.3m)	
FMA	1993: $0.3m (IMET)	
	1994: $0.2m (IMET)	
	1995: $0.1m (IMET)	
$ 1 = $N	1992: 2.85	1993: 3.27
	1994: 3.59	

$N= Namibian dollar

Population: 2,011,200

	13–17	*18–22*	*23–32*
Men	115,500	93,900	141,300
Women	115,900	94,400	142,400

TOTAL ARMED FORCES:

ACTIVE: 8,100.

ARMY: 8,000.

1 Presidential Guard bn.
4 mot inf bn.
1 cbt spt bde with 1 arty, 1 AD, 1 ATK regt.
EQUIPMENT:
RECCE: BRDM-2.
APC: some *Casspir, Wolf,* BTR-152.
MRL: 122mm: 5 BM-21.
MORTARS: 81mm; 82mm.
RCL: 82mm: B-10.
ATK GUNS: 57mm; 76mm.
AD GUNS: 14.5mm: ZPU-4; 23mm: 15 ZU-23.
SAM: SA-7.

MARINES: ε100. A Coast Guard is being formed.

BASE: Walvis Bay.
PATROL: 1 PCC plus boats.

SOUTH AFRICA

GDP	1992: R 327.1bn ($114.8bn): per capita $5,700	
	1993: R 365.2bn ($119.0bn): per capita $5,900	
Growth	1992: -2.1%	1993: 1.1%
Inflation	1992: 13.9%	1993: 9.7%
Debt	1992: $16.4bn	1993: $16.4bn
Def exp	1992: R 10.9bn ($3.8bn)	
Def bdgt	1992: R 9.7bn ($3.3bn)	
	1993: R 12.8bn ($3.9bn)	
	1994: R 14.2bn ($4.1bn)	
FMA	1995: $0.3m (IMET)	
$1 = R	1992: 2.85	1993: 3.26
	1994: 3.45	

R = rand

Population: 40,284,600

	13–17	*18–22*	*23–32*
Men:	2,033,200	1,839,600	3,196,400
Women:	2,011,100	1,828,000	3,173,400

TOTAL ARMED FORCES:

ACTIVE: 78,500 (incl 6,000 Medical Services, 35,400 white conscripts; 4,200 women).

Terms of service: conscription ended when the new Constitution became effective in 1994. Voluntary service of 2–6 years is followed by part-time service in Citizen Force (CF), duty not to exceed 60 days trg in any 2-year period.

An estimated 30,000 personnel from other forces, including the ANC and Homelands, are to be absorbed into the new South African National Defence Force. The total Force strength will be reduced over a 3-year period beginning in 1995.

RESERVES:

Citizen Force: 360,000: Active Citizen Force Reserve, 135,000; Commandos, ε140,000.

ARMY: ε58,000 (ε11,000 White; ε45,000 Black and Coloured; ε2,000 women).

10 area comd (area comd consist of HQ and a number of unit HQ, but no tps which are provided when necessary by FT and CF units).

1 AB bde (1 FT, 2 CF AB bn, 1 CF arty bn (FT bty) with 120mm mor).

1 indep mech bde (forms from trg units).

SF: 4 recce coy (3 FT, 1 CF).

7 inf bn (2 coloured, 5 black).

Training/Holding Units (incl armd, inf, arty, engr etc. Cbt role is to provide sub-units either for area comd for internal sy tasks or for mech bde for ops).

RESERVES:

CITIZEN FORCE (CF):

3 div (each 2 armd recce, 2 tk, 2 mech inf, 2 mot inf, 2 arty, 1 MRL, 2 AD, 1 engr bn).

(Corps and div HQ have skeleton FT staff.)

COMMANDOS:

some 250 inf coy home defence units.

EQUIPMENT:

MBT: some 250 *Olifant* 1A/-B.

RECCE: 1,600 *Eland*-60/-90, 100 *Rooikat-76*.

AIFV: 1,500 *Ratel*-20/-60/-90.

APC: 1,500 *Buffel, Casspir*, 160+ *Mamba*.

TOWED ARTY: 350, incl 25-pdr (88mm): 30 G-1 (in store); 5.5-in (140mm): 75 G-2; 155mm: ε75 G-5, some G-4.

SP ARTY: 155mm: ε20 G-6.

MRL: 127mm: 120 *Bataleur* (40 tube), 60 *Valkiri* 22 SP (24 tube); some *Valkiri* 5 towed.

MORTARS: 81mm: 4,000 (incl some SP); 120mm: +120.

ATGW: ZT-3 *Swift* (some SP), *Milan*.

RL: 92mm: FT-5.

RCL: 106mm: M-40A1.

AD GUNS: 600: 20mm: GAI, *Ystervark* SP; 23mm: 18 *Zumlac* (ZU-23-2) SP; 35mm: 150 GDF-002 twin.

SAM: SA-7/-14.

SURV: *Green Archer* (mor).

UAV: RPV-2 *Seeker, Scout*.

NAVY: ε4,500 (ε300 women).

Naval HQ: Pretoria.

Three Flotillas: Submarine; Strike; Mine Warfare.

BASES: Simonstown, Durban (Salisbury Island).

SUBMARINES: 3 *Maria van Riebeek* (Mod Fr *Daphné*) with 550mm TT.

PATROL AND COASTAL COMBATANTS: 12:

MISSILE CRAFT: 9:

9 *Jan Smuts* (Is *Reshef*) with 6–8 *Skerpioen* (Is *Gabriel*) SSM (incl 3 non-op).

INSHORE PATROL: 3 PFI⟨.

MINE WARFARE: 8:

4 *Kimberley* (UK '*Ton*') MSC.

4 *Umzimkulu* MHC.

SUPPORT AND MISCELLANEOUS: 8:

1 *Drakensberg* AO with 2 hel and extempore amph capability (perhaps 60 tps and 2 small landing craft), 1 *Outeniqua* AO with similar capability as

Drakensberg, 1 AGHS, 1 diving spt, 1 Antarctic tpt with 2 hel (operated by Department of Economic Affairs), 3 tugs.

AIR FORCE: 10,000 (ε400 women); 244 cbt ac (plus 11 in store), 14+ armed hel.
1 Territorial Area Comd, AD, Tac Spt, Log, Trg Comd.
FGA: 4 sqn:
2 with 75 *Impala* II.
1 with 29 *Mirage* F-1AZ.
1 with 12 *Cheetah* E.
FTR: 11 *Mirage* F-1 CZ (in store).
TKR/EW: 1 sqn with 4 Boeing 707-320 (EW/tkr).
MR: 1 sqn with 8 C-47TP, 5 C-212.
TRANSPORT: 3 sqn:
1 with 7 C-130B.
1 (VIP) with 3 HS-125 -400B (civil registration), 2 *Super King Air* 200, 1 *Citation*.
1 with 19 C-47 (being modified to C-4 TP).
LIAISON/FAC: 24 Cessna 185.
HELICOPTERS: 4 sqn with 63 SA-316/-319 (some armed), 63 SA-330C/H/L, 10 BK-117.
TRAINING COMMAND (incl OCU): 6 schools: **ac:** 12 C-47, *14 *Cheetah* D, 130 T-6G *Harvard* IIA/III (80 to be updated), *114 *Impala* I, 60 PC-7 (being delivered); **hel:** 37 SA-316/SA-330.
MISSILES:
ASM: AS-11/-20/-30.
AAM: R-530, R-550 *Magic*, AIM-9 *Sidewinder*, V-3C *Darter*, V-3A/B *Kukri*.
GROUND DEFENCE: *Rhino* APC: 1 regt (South African Air Force Regt).
RADAR: 2 Air Control Sectors, 3 fixed and some mobile radars.
SAM: 2 wings (2 sqn each), some *Bofors* 40mm L/70, 20 *Cactus* (*Crotale*), SA-8/-9/-13.

MEDICAL SERVICE: 6,000 (1,500 women).
A separate service within SANDF.

PARAMILITARY:
SOUTH AFRICAN POLICE SERVICE: 110,000; Police Reserves: 37,000.
Air Wing: **ac:** 1 PC-6; **hel:** 1 BK-117, 1 *Hughes* 500, 4 BO-105CBS.

ZAMBIA

GDP	1992: K 568.7bn ($3.6bn): per capita $550		
	1993: K 1,640.8bn ($3.8bn): per capita $470		
Growth	1992: -5.0%	1993: 1.0%	
Inflation	1992: 191%	1993: 187%	
Debt	1992: $7.0bn	1993: $6.6bn	
Def exp	1992: K 9.7bn ($62.1m)		
	1993: K 25.3m ($58.1m)		
	1994: K 26.2bn ($60.2m)		
FMA	1993: $0.2m (IMET)		
	1994: $0.1m (IMET)		
	1995: $0.1m (IMET)		
$1 = K	1992: 156	1993: 435	
	1994: 625		

K = kwacha

Population: 9,230,200

	13–17	*18–22*	*23–32*
Men	535,000	429,100	623,200
Women	528,600	437,100	668,800

TOTAL ARMED FORCES:
ACTIVE: 24,000.

ARMY: 20,000 (incl 3,000 reserves).
3 bde HQ. 1 arty regt.
9 inf bn (3 reserve). 1 engr bn.
1 armd regt (incl 1 armd recce bn).
EQUIPMENT:
MBT: 10 T-54/-55, 20 Ch Type-59.
LIGHT TANKS: 30 PT-76.
RECCE: 88 BRDM-1/-2.
APC: 13 BTR-60.
TOWED ARTY: 76mm: 35 M-1942; 105mm: 18 Model 56 pack; 122mm: 25 D-30; 130mm: 18 M-46.
MRL: 122mm: 50 BM-21.
MORTARS: 81mm: 55; 82mm: 24; 120mm: 14.
ATGW: AT-3 *Sagger*.
RCL: 57mm: 12 M-18; 75mm: M-20; 84mm: *Carl Gustav*.
AD GUNS: 20mm: 50 M-55 triple; 37mm: 40 M-1939; 57mm: 55 S-60; 85mm: 16 KS-12.
SAM: SA-7.

AIR FORCE: 1,600; 60† cbt ac, some armed hel.
FGA: 1 sqn with 12 Ch J-6 (MiG-19)†.

FIGHTER: 1 sqn with 12 MiG-21 MF†.
COIN/TRAINING: 12 *Galeb* G-2, 16 MB-326GB, 8 SF-260MZ.
TRANSPORT: 1 sqn with 4 An-26, 4 C-47, 2 DC-6B, 3 DHC-4, 4 DHC-5D.
VIP: 1 flt with 1 HS-748, 3 Yak-40.
LIAISON: 7 Do-28.
TRAINING: 2-F5T, 2 MiG-21U†.
HELICOPTERS: 1 sqn with 4 AB-205A, 5 AB-212, 12 Mi-8.
LIAISON HELICOPTERS: 12 AB-47G.
MISSILES:
ASM: AT-3 *Sagger*.
SAM: 1 bn; 3 bty: SA-3 *Goa*.

FORCES ABROAD:
UN AND PEACEKEEPING:
MOZAMBIQUE (ONUMOZ): 820; 1 inf bn, plus 8 Observers.

PARAMILITARY:
POLICE MOBILE UNIT (PMU): 700; 1 bn of 4 coy.
POLICE PARAMILITARY UNIT (PPMU): 700; 1 bn of 3 coy.

ZIMBABWE

GDP	1992: $Z 24.5bn ($5.4bn): per capita $1,900	
	1993: $Z 35.3bn ($5.4bn): per capita $1,900	
Growth	1992: -8.4%	1993: -2.6%
Inflation	1992: 46.2%	1993: 27.6%
Debt	1992: $4.0bn	1993: $4.3bn
Def bdgt	1992: $Z 1.15bn ($224.8m)	
	1993: $Z 1.35bn ($208.8m)	
	1994: $Z 1.8bn ($217.7m)	
FMA	1993: $0.4m (IMET)	
	1994: $0.3m (IMET)	
	1995: $0.3m (IMET)	
$1 = $Z	1992: 5.1	1993: 6.5
	1994: 8.0	

$Z = Zimbabwe dollar

Population: 10,916,200

	13–17	*18–22*	*23–32*
Men	647,200	540,800	852,400
Women	645,700	542,700	860,700

TOTAL ARMED FORCES:
ACTIVE: 46,900.

ARMY: 42,900.
7 bde HQ (incl 1 Presidential Guard).
1 armd regt.
24 inf bn (incl 3 guard, 2 mech, 1 cdo, 2 para, 1 mounted).
1 fd arty regt (incl 2 AD bty).
1 engr spt regt.
EQUIPMENT:
MBT: 30 Ch T-59, 10 Ch T-69.
RECCE: 90 EE-9 *Cascavel* (90mm gun).
APC: 8 YW-531, ε40 UR-416, 75 *Crocodile*.
TOWED ARTY: 122mm: 18 Ch Type-60, 12 Ch Type-54.
MRL: 107mm: 18 Ch Type-63; 122mm: 20 RM-70.
MORTARS: 81mm: L16; 82mm; 120mm: 4.
AD GUNS: 14.5mm: ZPU-1/-2/-4; 23mm: ZU-23; 37mm: M-1939.
SAM: SA-7.
SURV: RASIT (veh, arty).

AIR FORCE: 4,000; 46 cbt ac, no armed hel.
FGA/COIN: 2 sqn:
1 with 12 *Hunters* (FGA-9: 10; -F80: 1; -T-81: 1).
1 with 12 *Hawk* Mk 60.
FIGHTER: 1 sqn with 14 Ch J-7 (MiG-21).
COIN/RECCE: 1 sqn with 8 Reims-Cessna 337 *Lynx*.
TRAINING/RECCE/LIAISON: 1 sqn with 13 SF-260C/W *Genet*, 5 SF-260TP.
TRANSPORT: 1 sqn with 6 BN-2, 11 C-212-200 (1 VIP), 10 C-47.
HELICOPTERS: 1 sqn with 2 AB-205, 24 SA-319, 10 AB-412.

FORCES ABROAD:
UN AND PEACEKEEPING:
ANGOLA (UNAVEM II): 5 Observers.
UGANDA/RWANDA (UNAMIR/UNOMUR): 20 Observers.
SOMALIA (UNOSOM II): 1,095; 1 inf bn plus 5 civpol.

PARAMILITARY:
ZIMBABWE REPUBLIC POLICE FORCE: 19,500 (incl Air Wing).
POLICE SUPPORT UNIT: 2,300.
NATIONAL MILITIA: 1,000.

Developments in the Field of Weapons of Mass Destruction

This survey covers international nuclear and chemical weapons, and ballistic-missile developments that have taken place since June 1993. Changes in national nuclear and missile forces are recorded in the text preceding the relevant regional section and are reflected in the relevant national entry.

Strategic Arms Reduction Talks (START)

All five signatories of the May 1992 Lisbon Protocol to the START I Treaty have now ratified both the Protocol and the Treaty. Ukraine, the last to do so, finally ratified the Treaty on 3 February 1994. Belarus acceded to the Nuclear Non-Proliferation Treaty (NPT) in July 1993 and Kazakhstan in February 1994. Although Ukraine, by signing the Lisbon Protocol, committed itself to joining the NPT as a non-nuclear state (a commitment confirmed by President Kravchuk at the 14 January 1994 summit in Moscow and again during US Vice-President Al Gore's visit to Ukraine in May 1994), the Verkhovna Rada has not yet ratified Ukraine's accession. The new Ukrainian Prime Minister, Leonid Kuchma, has pointed out that 'in 1995 the Treaty expires and enters a new stage. We will look at the issue again'. Russian exchange of its ratification of START will not be effected until Ukraine accedes to the NPT and thus the implementation of START and, most importantly, the verification of the elimination process cannot begin.

Nevertheless, considerable numbers of strategic nuclear weapons have been eliminated in four of the five signatory states while a start has been made in the fifth, Belarus, to back-load its mobile SS-25 ICBM to Russia. All nuclear weapons are scheduled to be withdrawn from Belarus and Kazakhstan by the end of 1995. Details of these eliminations and transfers are given in the relevant regional sections.

Elimination of Nuclear Weapons in the Former Soviet Republics

A number of measures have been instituted to assist the four nuclear-armed republics of the former Soviet Union (FSU) with the elimination of nuclear weapons on their soil and with its cost. Other measures will compensate Belarus, Kazakhstan and Ukraine for the loss of nuclear material in the warheads returned to Russia for dismantlement and they will be given security assurances.

In November 1991 the US Congress passed the Soviet Nuclear Threat Reduction Act, more commonly known as 'Nunn–Lugar' legislation and now officially called the Cooperative Threat Reduction (CTR) programme, which authorised $400 million in aid to assist the four republics with the safe and secure dismantlement of their nuclear weapons. Congress authorised a further $400m from the Defense Budget in both FY1993 and FY1994 for the same purpose. By February 1994, $91.4m had been spent, mainly on equipment required should an emergency arise and on protective blankets and storage containers. Projects still in the pipeline are likely to cost over $800m. Much of this will go to fund the destruction of missile silos and the elimination of silo and submarine-launched missiles, missile-armed submarines and rail-mobile launchers. All told the US will provide up to 10,000 containers for the safe transport and long-term storage of nuclear warheads and the plutonium and highly enriched uranium (HEU) taken from dismantled warheads.

In a separate agreement, signed in January 1994, the US agreed to purchase some 500 tons of HEU as this is removed from nuclear warheads and after it has been converted into low-enriched uranium (LEU) from Russia. The contract has a 20-year time frame and Russia will receive around $12 billion. The United States Enrichment Corporation (a government organisation) will be responsible for selling LEU both to US nuclear power stations and to other countries, thus incurring no cost to the US taxpayer. The US has invited a number of other countries to assist it with the cost of nuclear elimination in the former Soviet Union (FSU). The UK, for example, has earmarked £35m for the provision of nuclear weapons containers and transport vehicles, and in May 1994 the first batch of 48 containers was delivered.

On 14 January 1994 a summit meeting was held by Presidents Clinton, Yeltsin and Kravchuk in Moscow. Ukraine agreed to transfer 200 SS-18 and SS-24 nuclear warheads to Russia, and to remove all warheads from its 46 SS-24 ICBM by mid-November 1994. So far, 180 warheads have been transferred. In return Russia will supply Ukraine with fuel assemblies containing 100 tons of LEU for use in its nuclear power stations. The US is to provide Russia with an advance payment of $60m (from the funds due under the HEU contract). The US will also provide Ukraine with a minimum of $175m under the CTR programme.

In respect of security assurances, Presidents Clinton and Yeltsin said that, once the START I Treaty entered into force and Ukraine had become a non-nuclear-state party to the NPT, the US and Russia would:

- Reaffirm their commitment to Ukraine, in accordance with the principles of the Conference on Security and Cooperation in Europe (CSCE) Final Act, to respect the independence and sovereignty and the existing borders of the CSCE member-states and recognise that border changes can be made only by peaceful and consensual means; reaffirm their obligation to refrain from the threat or use of force against the territorial integrity or political independence of any state; and reaffirm that none of their weapons will ever be used except in self-defence or otherwise in accordance with the Charter of the United Nations;
- Reaffirm their commitment to Ukraine, in accordance with the principles of the CSCE Final Act, to refrain from economic coercion designed to subordinate to their own interest the exercise by another CSCE participating state of the rights inherent in its sovereignty and thus to secure advantages of any kind;
- Reaffirm their commitment to seek immediate UN Security Council action to provide assistance to Ukraine as a non-nuclear-weapon-state party to the NPT if Ukraine should become a victim of an act of aggression or the object of a threat of aggression in which nuclear weapons are used; and
- Reaffirm, in the case of Ukraine, their commitment not to use nuclear weapons against any non-nuclear-weapon state party to the NPT, except in the case of an attack on themselves, their territories or dependent territories, their armed forces, or their allies, by such a state in association or alliance with a nuclear weapons state.

The Ukrainian president was told that the UK, the third depositary state of the NPT, would give Ukraine the same security assurances once it had become a non-nuclear-state party to the NPT.

While the problem of disposing, safely and securely, of the HEU content of dismantled nuclear warheads has been satisfactorily solved, the far more substantial problem of disposing of weapons-grade plutonium (W-Pu) has not. It is estimated that the US and Russia will each have at least 50 tons of W-Pu to dispose of when START II is fully implemented. Unlike HEU, which can be readily blended with natural, depleted or (as the Russians are doing) slightly enriched uranium to form LEU, there is no similar solution for W-Pu. Degrading methods exist, but none is simple or cheap and all can be readily reversed by chemical processing. Theoretically it is possible to destroy W-Pu by fission in most conventional reactors, but the cost of fabricating fuel using cost-free W-Pu will be much higher than that fabricated from bought LEU, mainly because of the extra and costly precautions that would be necessary given plutonium's greater radiological toxicity. The resultant reactor-grade Pu would also, like all Pu fuel, have to be guarded lest it be diverted to weapons manufacture. A number of other disposal options have been mooted. The one that has received most attention is that of blending W-Pu with liquid high-level waste prior to vitrification and disposal. This, however, is a costly operation with many technical difficulties. Other less realistic options include: subsea-bed burial; deep bore-hole storage; dilution in the open sea; and even shooting into the sun or solar orbit. All have differing substantial disadvantages such as cost, long-term environmental dangers and, in some cases, the possibility of W-Pu being recovered at a later stage. As the disposal of W-Pu is bound to take many years, or even decades, to complete, safe and secure storage will be the main priority.

A final problem concerning W-Pu disposal will be Russia's unwillingness to dispose of valuable material which could possibly be used or sold to others for use as nuclear fuel.

Nuclear Test Moratorium

President Clinton has extended the moratorium on nuclear testing, instigated originally by President Bush on 1 October 1992, for a further year until the end of September 1995. This leaves a final window of opportunity for testing until the 1992 Energy and Water Development Appropriations Act – which stipulates that after 30 September 1996 no further tests are to take place unless a foreign state conducts a test – comes into force. The US moratorium precludes UK nuclear testing which takes place on US soil.

The situation in France is less clear cut. President Mitterrand has made clear that there will be no more French nuclear testing during his presidency, which ends in May 1995. On the other hand, Prime Minister Edouard Balladur has said 'the government would not subscribe to any definitive test ban as long as it feels that testing is necessary for the technical credibility of its deterrent forces'. Nor did he see any contradiction between France resuming testing while participating in Comprehensive Test Ban Treaty (CTBT) negotiations.

Russia maintains its testing moratorium, and in any event might find it difficult to find a test site now that the Kazakhstan site at Semipalatinsk has been closed and that Novaya Zemlya has become unacceptable to the environmental lobby as well as being opposed by neighbouring states.

China, which never imposed a moratorium on itself, carried out two tests in the last 12 months. It has been assessed that the yield of the weapon exploded on 5 October 1993 was between 10 and 50 kilotons. That on 10 June may also have a yield of between 10 and 50KT. There was speculation after the first test that it was the first in a series of explosions to test a new generation of warheads needed for new missiles believed to be under development.

Targeting

At their Moscow summit on 14 January 1994, Presidents Clinton and Yeltsin announced that, from 30 May 1994, their strategic missiles would no longer be targeted. Targeting data have been removed from US *Trident* C40 and D5 SLBM and *Peacekeeper* ICBM, while, where this is not possible, *Minuteman III* ICBM have been reprogrammed to fall into the open ocean. *Minuteman II* ICBM have already had both their targeting and warhead components removed. It is not known which Russian missiles can be left without target data and which have been re-targetted to sea. On 15 February, UK Prime Minister John Major announced, during his visit to Moscow, that all British SLBM would be re-targetted towards the sea. A UK Ministry of Defence press release stated that 'the guidance computers on UK strategic missiles no longer hold targeting information, and the primary target assignments held in readiness for insertion into the missiles will be points in the open ocean'. Russia's strategic missiles are no longer targeted at the UK or US and vice versa.

This is very much a political gesture as the targeting process can be restored, or the target changed, in a matter of minutes.

Nuclear Non-Proliferation Treaty

Five countries have acceded to the NPT since June 1993, the most important being the currently nuclear-armed states of Belarus and Kazakhstan. Armenia, Guyana and Mauritania have also acceded.

NPT review conferences have been held every five years since the Treaty entered into force in March 1970. At the fifth or 25-year review it should be decided whether the Treaty is to continue in force indefinitely or is to be extended for a further fixed period.

Two meetings have already been held by the Preparatory Committee (PrepCom) and two more are to be held before the review conference starts in New York in mid-May 1995. PrepCom is concentrating on determining procedural issues such as dates, location, agenda and rules for the conference. Some issues not yet agreed concern the choice of conference chairman and whether the decision on extension is to be made by consensus or majority vote (although the Treaty stipulates majority vote).

An important issue many NPT signatories want settled before they address the question of NPT extension is agreement on a Comprehensive Test Ban Treaty. Unsuccessful attempts were made at the 1990 review conference to make NPT extension conditional on the implementation of a CTBT. The issue is bound to be raised in 1995. Non-nuclear states see the lack of a CTBT as allowing declared nuclear states to continue to develop nuclear arsenals while they are denied the ownership of any nuclear weapons. The CTBT process is now under way, but whether it will be completed by 1995 is uncertain. If good progress is made before May 1995, then the lack of a CTBT may not block NPT extension.

Another potentially serious issue for the NPT review is the question of the *de facto* nuclear states: Israel, India and Pakistan. It has been suggested that these states are more in need of a nuclear deterrent than were the two superpowers. None have joined the NPT and it is hard to envisage them acceding to the Treaty at present. India, which exploded a nuclear device in 1974 and is credited with having sufficient W-Pu to make over 50 warheads, believes that the NPT must be radically changed. It requires the Treaty to be universal and non-discriminatory, and to contain a deadline date for global nuclear disarmament. Prime Minister Rao has also ruled out India accepting any regional NPT arrangement. Pakistan has made a number of proposals for preventing the spread of nuclear weapons in South Asia including: the creation of a weapons-free zone; the simultaneous (with India) accession to the NPT; and the simultaneous acceptance of International Atomic Energy Agency (IAEA) safeguards. At the same time several members of the government have made it clear that Pakistan has both the know-how and components to assemble nuclear weapons and that it has no intention of halting its development programme, unless India does so too.

Fissile Material Ban

In September 1993 President Clinton, at the UN General Assembly (UNGA), proposed that an international treaty be negotiated to ban the production of W-Pu and HEU for use in nuclear weapons. The UNGA adopted its annual resolution calling for such a ban, for the first time, by consensus. The UNGA also passed Resolution 48/75L which called for negotiations 'in the most appropriate forum' for a convention banning production. At the first session of the 1994 Geneva Conference on Disarmament (CD), the Canadian Ambassador was mandated to seek members' views and he reported, on 31 March, that while the majority of delegates considered CD to be the most appropriate forum, more discussion would be needed to achieve consensus. He hoped that discussion of the mandate for an *ad hoc* committee on a fissile material production ban could take place at the next session.

President Bush had already announced, in mid-1992, that the US would no longer produce W-Pu or HEU for nuclear explosive purposes. In fact, US production of HEU had ended in 1966 and that of W-Pu in 1988. Russia is to stop production of W-Pu, which is produced by reactors at Krasnoyarsk and Tomsk, in late 1994.

The US and Russia have recently agreed to allow inspection of each other's storage sites where plutonium from dismantled warheads is kept. This is the first time that inspection of fissile material has been allowed and it will permit the progress of warhead dismantlement to be monitored and provide confirmation that W-Pu is stored safely and securely.

Comprehensive Test Ban Treaty

At the end of 1993, the First Committee of the UN General Assembly approved a resolution advocating a global treaty banning all nuclear weapon tests. The resolution was supported by all five recognised nuclear weapons states. Following this, the 1994 CD opened in January and immediately re-established the Nuclear Test Ban Ad Hoc Committee. The Committee's mandate is to 'negotiate intensively a universal and multi-laterally and effectively verifiable comprehensive test ban treaty'. Two working groups have been set up: one to work on legal and institutional matters; the other on verification.

Already a number of treaty drafts have been submitted, notably by Sweden and Australia. The Ad Hoc Committee's chairman, Mexican Ambassador Marin-Bosch, is confident of producing a treaty ready for signature by mid-1995. There are, of course, a number of issues which may prove difficult to resolve. One concerns the definition of what the treaty is setting out to ban; China is keen to see so-called peaceful nuclear explosions (pre-planned explosions designed to assist in civil works projects) permitted, but others consider all explosions should be banned. The Chinese also believe that the treaty should include the commitment to a 'no first-use' policy, an issue not currently included in the nuclear policy of the other four nuclear-armed states. France and the United Kingdom would prefer to see 'safety' tests of nuclear weapons still permitted, albeit at a very low level. Finally there is the problem of verification: what body should be responsible? Who would pay for it? What access would it have to nationally collected data? The US view is that an international regime is necessary with a number of monitoring capabilities, including seismic monitoring stations, atmospheric sampling and on-site inspection. The second round of negotiations resumed on 16 May 1994.

A body of scientific opinion believes that simulation can never totally replace the need to test new weapon designs.

Proliferation: North Korea

Throughout the last 12 months North Korea has continued its policy of promising compliance with the IAEA and then failing to deliver. Talks with South Korea over unification, high-level talks with the US to discuss nuclear issues and US–South Korean joint major exercises, and inspections by the IAEA have been 'on' and 'off' with monotonous repetition. The 'carrot and stick' approach has been tried on several occasions with no success. Unfortunately, there are few carrots or sticks which can be advantageously offered or realistically threatened. The situation was made worse by the North's decision to start the replacement of fuel rods at its 5 megawatt reactor without IAEA supervision. The Director of the IAEA, Hans Blix, reported formally to the UN Secretary-General on 2 June 1994 that he was now unable to give assurances that North Korea had not diverted plutonium to a weapons programme.

The IAEA believe that North Korea is expanding its reprocessing facility which could double production of W-Pu, but full inspection of the site has not been permitted. It had been estimated that with one reprocessing line, the North could produce sufficient W-Pu for four to five weapons by the end of 1994. The other main point of contention is North Korea's refusal to allow the IAEA to visit two waste storage sites whose inspection the IAEA now considers even more important, while the North Korean delegate to the IAEA in Vienna said, on 7 June, that North Korea would never allow their inspection. No new confirmed evidence has been revealed during the year to prove that North Korea is actively pursuing a weapons development programme, although the North's behaviour cannot but lead to that conclusion. A number of senior US officials, including CIA Director James Woolsey and Secretary of Defense William Perry, have clearly stated their belief that North Korea could have already produced a nuclear weapon, and that it has certainly acquired the fissile material necessary to produce between one and five nuclear weapons. As worrying, but this time undeniable, was North Korea's demonstration of its developing missile capability when a *No-Dong* IRBM with an estimated range of 1,000–1,300km was successfully tested in May 1993. It is reliably reported that North Korea is also developing other missiles, sometimes referred to as *Taepo-Dong*, with longer ranges: 1,500–3,500km have been mentioned. The accuracy of any North Korea missile is likely to be poor, with a circular error probable (CEP) of over two kilometres, which points to the advantages that a nuclear warhead would provide.

The UN, pressed by the US and strongly supported by South Korea and Japan (the two countries most threatened by any North Korean nuclear armed missile), is considering imposing sanctions on North Korea. Both the decision to impose sanctions, and the effectiveness of sanctions involving trade embargoes, are dependent on Chinese cooperation.

It was hard to see how the dispute could be satisfactorily resolved, particularly while Kim Il Sung was still alive. Nevertheless, the longer it remained unresolved, the deeper into an inescapable corner North Korea was being pushed, leaving it no option other than a massive climb-down and loss of face or submission to whatever sanctions were imposed. Then it would have had to face up to backing down over its threats to consider sanctions a declaration of war, or be stubborn enough to take some form of military action. It was not an encouraging situation. However, in June 1994 former US President Jimmy Carter visited North Korea and it was announced that there would be a summit meeting between the presidents of North and South Korea and that high-level talks between North Korea and the US on nuclear issues would be resumed. The death of President Kim Il Sung on 8 July has inevitably caused these two events to be postponed.

Chemical Weapons

While the Chemical Weapon Convention (CWC) was signed by 130 states on the day it was opened for signature on 13 January 1993 (157 have now signed), only five have ratified the treaty (and four of these had ratified before July 1993). The treaty cannot come into force before 13 January 1995 at the earliest, but to do so it must have received 65 ratifications before 13 August 1994 (the treaty comes into force 180 days after the 65th ratification instrument is deposited). Governments therefore saw no urgency for early ratification. However, if the 13 January date is to be met, much action will be needed during the summer.

The Organisation for the Prohibition of Chemical Weapons (OPCW) is to be established to ensure implementation of the treaty and to carry out verification. The Preparatory Commission for the OPCW has continued its work throughout the year. Progress has been made in all areas. 16 groups have been set up, five working on issues concerning OPCW internal arrangements and 11 on treaty aspects including: confidentiality; the chemical industry; verification; and challenge inspections.

Ballistic Missiles

The Missile Technology Control Regime (MTCR), established in 1987, is a grouping of nations committed to combatting the proliferation of ballistic missiles by voluntarily imposing export restrictions on equipment and technology that could contribute to missile production. Initially, the MTCR was concerned only with nuclear-armed missiles, but following the Gulf War its provisions were expanded to include any system excluding manned aircraft capable of delivering weapons of mass destruction (currently considered to be nuclear, chemical and biological). The regime covers all systems capable of carrying a 500kg payload over a distance of 300km.

There are now 25 partners in the MTCR and a number of other countries, most recently Brazil and Ukraine, have committed themselves to abide by the criteria and standards of the regime when considering missile-related exports. The commitment by Ukraine is important as a number of former Soviet production plants for ICBM are located in Ukraine. These include the Dnepropetrovsk plant for assembling SS-18 and SS-24 ICBM, as well as satellite launching rockets, and plants producing missile-guidance systems.

The MTCR states hold plenary meetings on an annual basis; the last being from 29 November to 2 December 1993 when a number of amendments regarding equipment and technology, to be implemented by 1 July 1994, were agreed. The next plenary is planned for October 1994.

Other Arms-Control Developments

This section provides a brief up-date on all arms-control matters, other than those concerning weapons of mass destruction (nuclear, chemical, biological and ballistic missiles) for the period June 1993 to July 1994.

Conventional Armed Forces in Europe (CFE) Treaty

The CFE Treaty came into force on 17 July 1992. By 17 November 1993 all signatory states were to have eliminated at least 25% of their reduction liability. Overall the reduction target is judged to have been met, except in the cases of Armenia and Azerbaijan. Some discrepancies were noted, but these have been considered misunderstandings and not deliberate violations. Verification inspections during the past 12 months have revealed no flagrant Treaty violations.

In the months before CFE was signed in November 1990, the Soviet Union transported large numbers of treaty-limited equipment (TLE), including 16,400 tanks, 15,900 ACV and 25,000 pieces of artillery. Many of these were obsolete models. A proportion of this equipment was sent for storage to Kazakhstan and Uzbekistan. In June 1991, the USSR declared its intention to use roughly half the equipment to replace obsolete weapons in its eastern Military Districts (MD) and to store the remainder. Equipment would not be stored in unit mobilisation sets nor in a manner which would allow their rapid return to the Treaty area. Most of the equipment is stored unprotected in the open and its military value now must be doubtful. The Soviet Union also said it would eliminate some 16,000 weapons, mainly those replaced by equipment withdrawn from west of the Urals. By June 1994 formal notification of the destruction of 1,202 TLE had been given and of the planned destruction of 540 more. The IISS has no information on the type of TLE that has been destroyed or where destruction took place.

Russia has raised, at the Joint Consultative Group and elsewhere, the question of altering the limits placed on the numbers of TLE which can be deployed in the flanking zones of the Treaty area on the grounds that, particularly on the southern flank, they are too small to meet Russia's security needs. The other Treaty signatories are opposed to any alteration to the Treaty, considering that allowing even one amendment would start a process which could eventually nullify the aim of the Treaty. In some respects Russian arguments about the changed strategic situation since the CFE Treaty was signed are grounded in genuine concerns. The CFE Treaty zone of application was divided into four overlapping zones, each with its own TLE limits. Article V of the Treaty superimposed a further set of TLE limits in areas considered to be on the flanks of each alliance. For the East, the northern flank purely consisted of the Leningrad MD, while the southern flank area comprised Bulgaria, Romania, the Odessa MD (now in Ukraine) and the Transcaucasus MD (now Georgia, Armenia and Azerbaijan), and all that is left to Russia is the North Caucasus MD. Before the break-up of the USSR, the Soviet Union would, without violating the Treaty, be able to station its troops anywhere in the four MDs. The TLE limits for the USSR on the flanks was 2,850 tanks, 2,600 ACV and 3,675 pieces of artillery. Russia's limit is 1,300 tanks (of which only 700 can be in active units), 1,380 ACV (580 in active units) and 1,680 (1,280 in active units) pieces of artillery. It is, of course, open to Russia under the terms of the Treaty to negotiate exchange TLE quotas within the countries originally forming the Warsaw Pact, but none appear willing to give up any of their quota to Russia. While Russia's main concern must be the unstable region in the Transcaucasus, it would welcome the ability to deploy more troops to the North Caucasus on account of the shortage of suitable accommodation for units withdrawn from Germany in the Moscow and Volga MDs where, for Treaty reasons, they must be located. In an attempt to meet Russian concerns, but without having to amend the Treaty, a number of proposals have been made. For instance, the 600 ACV allowed for internal security purposes could be concentrated in the Caucasus. Troops in the Caucasus could be equipped with the MT-LBT multi-purpose armoured tracked vehicle which is classified as an APC in the Leningrad MD but as 'look-alike' elsewhere. The boundaries of the Military Districts could be altered so that part of the Leningrad MD becomes, with Kaliningrad, the Baltic MD, and so is no longer in the designation flank zone, and transferring part of the North Caucasus MD to the Moscow and Volga MDs. Both Ukraine and Azerbaijan would also like to see the Treaty amended in their defence interests.

During the year Armenia, which had not been able to do so earlier, declared its manpower limit of 32,682 army and air force personnel.

'Open Skies' Treaty

The Treaty on 'Open Skies', which was signed by 27 North Atlantic Treaty Organisation (NATO) and former Warsaw Pact countries in March 1992, allows for a specified number of observation flights to be made over the territory of other signatories. Since June 1993, six further states (France, Georgia, Germany, Kyrgyzstan, Spain and the UK) have ratified the Treaty, but it cannot come into force until a further six do so. Meanwhile, a growing number of practice and training flights have taken place. The US has brought into service three specially equipped planes for 'Open Skies' designated OC-135. The apparent failure to ratify the Treaty by some states is blamed more on lack of parliamentary time than on any reluctance to do so.

United Nations Register of Conventional Arms

The first truly global arms-control transparency measure came into effect in 1993 when UN members were invited to report to the Secretary-General their imports and exports of certain types of military equipment (see *The Military Balance 1993–1994*, p. 248) during the previous calendar year together with details of the exporting and importing states. Reports are due by the end of April each year, but the experience of 1993 when many reports were submitted late (53 by 1 June, 80 by 11 October when the Secretary-General reported to the General Assembly) is being repeated in 1994. Only 69 countries had reported by 5 July. Of these, 21 are countries that did not report in 1993, thus, when the reporting process is closed, a far greater number of reports than in 1993 will have been submitted. The Secretary-General's report for 1993 is not expected to be published until August 1994, too late for analysis in this edition of *The Military Balance*.

Of the 80 countries, out of a total UN membership of 180, who had reported to the UN by 20 October 1993: 20 reported their imports, but had made no exports; seven reported their exports, but had had no imports; 17 reported both imports and exports; while the remaining 36 either reported that they had neither imported nor exported, or provided no information (i.e., did not formally report nil) which in most cases can be counted as a nil report. Of the top 20 arms importers in 1992 (according to the *SIPRI Yearbook 1993*), six (Iran, Saudi Arabia, Syria, ROC (Taipei), Thailand and the UAE) did not report. All of the top 14 arms exporters submitted reports.

States were also invited to provide background information on their weapon inventories, and their procurement from national production. That the provision of background information was more voluntary than that of imports and exports was emphasised by not laying down clear instructions on how background information should be reported, with the inevitable result that the comprehensiveness of some reports is in doubt. (For example, was stored equipment included, or only that with active units?) Far fewer countries provided background information than reported exports and imports. In 1993, 15 countries gave both holdings and national production procurement and nine gave information on holdings only. A further nine countries provided background information which did not include data on either holdings or procurement. So far in 1994, 22 countries have provided background information on military holdings.

In both reports of exports and imports and of background information some countries gave details of the name, designation and model of the equipment concerned, but most purely gave gross figures. There were several discrepancies between what was reported as exported and what was reported as imported.

For the IISS the importance of the reports lies in their ability to verify the accuracy of *The Military Balance*. An analysis of imports and exports showed that 28 movements of military equipment had not previously been noted by the IISS. Of these, one contract was known of, but the date of transfer was not, and two concern the transfer of aircraft probably to and from overhaul and so are not true imports/exports. However, a number of the revealed imports were, for the importing country, significant force improvements. Cameroon was shown to have increased its artillery holdings by 50%; Nepal, its artillery and mortars by 200%; and Moldova its APC by 200% and artillery by nearly 50%. As might be expected those countries which provided the most detailed background information were countries which are traditionally open regarding military data. Of most interest to the IISS was the detailed background information reported by Brazil, Chile and Nicaragua; more or less the same pattern emerged when *The Military Balance* was checked against these. Naval data, including aviation and marines, were virtually 100% correct, air-force data were less accurate, but aircraft numbers were usually within 10% of those reported with *The Military Balance* always giving higher figures. Army equipment holdings were the least accurate, but there are several reasons for this. Far less publicity is given to ground-forces procurement when compared with the launch or commissioning of a naval ship or the introduction of a new type of aircraft. There are, of course, very many more types and numbers of equipments with ground forces then there are for aircraft and ships. On several occasions, *The Military Balance* still listed elderly equipments which had been scrapped without publicity. But caution is required in dealing with the data on some aspects as the reports to the UN may not have been comprehensive.

A UN Group of Experts (comprising mainly diplomats and military officers) has been established to recommend ways to develop and improve the Register. They have received much advice from many sources which advocate: widening the Register by including extra categories of armaments; deepening it by requiring fuller descriptions of the equipments reported; revising it by altering the existing categories of armaments – for example, by lowering the tonnage threshold for naval warships; and clarifying it by desegregating missile launchers from missiles and by identifying the sort of missiles concerned (air-to-air, air-to-ground, surface-to-surface). However, this last may be opposed by several countries on the grounds that it will reveal how few, as opposed to how many, of certain missile types they have obtained. Importance is given to background information on weapon inventories and particularly on reporting procurement through national production. Solely reporting imports and exports is seen as discriminating against those countries which do not have a national production capability. The Group of Experts itself is concentrating, as a first priority, on the more modest goal of simply increasing the number of countries which report.

Multilateral Export Controls

The Coordinating Committee for Multilateral Export Controls (COCOM), which had, since 1949, managed the embargo of exports of military and dual-use equipment, plant and technology primarily to the Warsaw Pact and China, ended on 31 March 1994. Earlier COCOM members (NATO countries less Iceland, plus Japan and Australia) had agreed to establish a successor body with new guidelines more appropriate to the world's changed situation. As yet no agreement has been reached as to: what should be controlled; who would be members of what has come to be known as the New Forum; nor which countries should be proscribed (although some automatically propose themselves). The already postponed target date of October 1994 for establishing the successor regime looks unlikely to be met, although the design for a follow-on organisation has emerged. It is clear that a rather more complicated, but also more flexible rule book will be necessary than was the case for COCOM, where any member could veto another's export of restricted items.

Anti-Ballistic Missile Treaty

The Anti-Ballistic Missile Treaty (ABM), signed by the US and USSR in 1972, prohibited the deployment of nationwide missile defence and restricted ABM to one site only for each side with no more than 100 interceptors protecting either the national capital or an ICBM launch site. A number of agreements made later at the Standing Consultative Commission have been kept secret, but four (plus one concerning the 1971 Agreement on Measures to Reduce the Risk of Outbreak of Nuclear War) were declassified in 1993. Treaty review meetings are held every five years. The latest, in September 1993, was attended by Belarus and Ukraine as well as the US and Russia. While commitment to the Treaty was reaffirmed, no agreement was reached over the issue of successor states to the Soviet Union. ABM-relevant sites, including early-warning radars and missile test sites, are located in five republics of the former Soviet Union. In July 1993, the Clinton Administration announced that it endorsed the traditional, or narrow, interpretation of ABM which recognises that the Treaty prohibits 'the development, testing and deployment of sea-based, air-based, space-based and mobile land-based ABM systems and components without regard to the technology utilised'.

The ABM Treaty was intended to avoid the possibility of a strategic offence–defence arms race and so help the process of limiting offensive missiles. The Strategic Defense Initiative (SDI) would clearly have violated the Treaty, as would the Bush Administration's less ambitious proposal for Global Protection Against Limited Strike. However, Theater Missile Defences (TMD) are not prohibited by ABM so long as they are not given the capabilities to counter strategic ballistic missiles (or anything that has the characteristics of a ballistic-missile flight trajectory). There is no agreed technical definition of an anti-tactical ballistic missile system (ATBM), but it is understood that the US interpreted this as one capable of intercepting an in-coming missile with a speed of not more than 2–4km per second at 40km range. The US Administration includes in its ABM policy the need to specify a dividing line between ABM systems limited by the Treaty and those that are not.

The growing proliferation of non-strategic ballistic missiles, while not threatening US territory, does threaten US allies and US forces overseas. Thus the US has proposed raising the upper limit on ATBM systems to make them capable of intercepting in-coming missiles with a speed of not more than 5km per second (the calculated speed of a missile with about 3,000km range). The Russians accepted the new limit, but only if interceptors were limited to a speed of 3km per second which, it is understood, would not effect THAAD, but might prevent development of the US Navy's Upper Tier system for deployment on *Aegis* ships which would have a speed in excess of 4km per second. In early July, the US proposed a compromise which, while accepting the Russian restriction on land-based missiles and an interim limit on sea-launched tests, would allow a higher interim testing limit of 5km per second for air-launched interceptors. The Clinton Administration is committed to a negotiated agreement which it hopes to sign at the September summit, and will take no unilateral action.

Conference on Security and Cooperation in Europe (CSCE)

The activities of the CSCE now focus increasingly on peacekeeping and preventive diplomacy while confidence-building measures have become a routine, with an additional set of measures adopted on 25 November 1993.

The CSCE established a Permanent Committee which first met in December 1993. It is responsible for the day-to-day operational tasks of the CSCE. The Permanent Committee can take decisions on such matters as increasing the size of missions, approving their budgets, and extending their mandates. It meets on a weekly basis.

In November 1993, the CSCE Forum for Security Cooperation adopted four documents covering future CSCE activity. The 'Programme of Military Contacts and Cooperation' is politically binding and came into force on 1 January 1994. It sets out the various modalities of contacts and cooperation which the CSCE advocates. 'Stabilizing Measures for Localized Crisis

Situations' is a catalogue of measures which could be taken by the parties to a crisis including those requiring support from the CSCE. 'Principles Governing Conventional Arms Transfers' lists principles which CSCE states affirm they will take into account when deciding on arms transfers, and includes a commitment to provide information to the UN Register of Conventional Arms. 'Defence Planning' details the information to be exchanged annually (in addition to that contained in the Vienna Document annual exchange of military information). Additional information is to be provided under the headings: Defence Policy and Doctrine; Force Planning; Information on Previous Expenditure; and Information on Budgets.

The CSCE continues to maintain missions to Estonia, Georgia, Moldova and Skopje and new missions have been established to Latvia in November 1993, and Tajikistan in December 1993. A further mission is to be established in Sarajevo to support the Bosnian Ombudsman and a decision has been taken to establish a mission in Ukraine. The CSCE also provides the CSCE/EU Sanctions Coordinator who overseas the activities of seven Sanctions Assistance Missions which assist their host country with the implementation of UNSC resolutions 713, 757, 787 and 820 concerning embargoes and sanctions imposed on the former Yugoslav republics. The CSCE's Missions of Long Duration, set up in September 1992 in Kosovo, Sanjak and Vojvodina and withdrawn in June 1993 when Yugoslavia declined to extend the Memorandum of Understanding, have not been re-established, although they would undoubtedly play a useful role in these regions of potential instability. A CSCE Parliamentary Assembly Delegation visited Belgrade in June 1994 and was told by the Speaker of the Yugoslav parliament's Chamber of Citizens that the return of the CSCE's missions there as a precondition for Yugoslavia's full participation in the CSCE was not acceptable. A planning group of military officers (Initial Operations Planning Group (IOPG)) has been established in Vienna to prepare the CSCE mission to Nagorno-Karabakh. The mission, which will not deploy until a permanent cease-fire is achieved, is organised on similar lines to UN observer missions. All preparations are complete, bar the assembly of manpower and procurement of stores. The composition of the mission is agreed, as is its requirement for transport, communications and so on, its operating budget and its deployment plan. The role of the IOPG could be seen as a precursor for a future permanent planning and staff cell for any further peacekeeping missions.

The next CSCE Review Conference will be held in Budapest from 10 October to 2 December 1994. Working Groups are to be established to cover matters related to: conflict prevention and crisis management; security cooperation; human rights; and cooperation in the fields of economy, science, technology and the environment.

Conventional Forces in Europe

Manpower and TLE: current holdings and CFE limits of the forces of the CFE signatories
(current holdings are derived from data declared as at 15 December 1993 and so may differ from *The Military Balance* listing)

	Manpower		Tanks[a]		ACV[a]		Arty[a]		Attack Hel		Combat Aircraft[b]	
Country	Holding	Limit	Holding	Limit	Holding	Limit	Holding	Limit	Holding	Limit	Holding	Limit
Budapest/Tashkent Group												
Armenia	32,682	32,682	129	220	346	220	225	285	13	50	6	100
Azerbaijan	56,000	70,000	279	220	736	220	354	285	6	50	53	100
Belarus	92,664	100,000	3,108	1,800	3,414	2,600	1,584	1,615	78	80	260	260
Georgia[c]	–	40,000	41	220	51	220	7	285	1	50	2	100
Moldova	11,123	20,000	0	210	133	210	138	250	0	50	31	50
Russia[e]	1,110,578	1,450,000	7,493	6,400	13,466	11,480	6,069	6,415	954	890	3,921	3,450
Ukraine	495,156	450,000	5,394	4,080	5,803	5,050	3,725	4,040	270	330	1,460	1,090
Bulgaria	98,930	104,000	2,070	1,475	2,133	2,000	2,057	1,750	44	67	296	235
Czech Republic	92,893	93,333	1,525	957	2,254	1,367	1,620	767	36	50	265	230
Hungary	75,294	100,000	1,191	835	1,645	1,700	991	810	39	108	171	180
Poland	269,670	234,000	2,515	1,730	2,232	2,150	2,151	1,610	70	130	446	460
Romania	230,000	230,248	2,568	1,375	2,889	2,100	3,314	1,475	15	120	452	430
Slovakia	54,223	46,667	912	478	1,169	683	931	383	19	25	146	115
North Atlantic Treaty Group												
Belgium	68,688	70,000	339	334	985	1,099	322	320	46	46	200	232
Canada[d]	1,408	10,660	0	77	14	277	6	38	0	13	0	90
Denmark	29,893	39,000	452	353	273	316	553	553	0	12	101	106
France	332,591	325,000	1,309	1,306	3,964	3,820	1,429	1,292	373	352	687	800
Germany	314,688	345,000	5,498	4,166	7,155	3,446	3,504	2,705	250	306	754	900
Greece	163,705	158,621	2,435	1,735	1,421	2,534	2,063	1,878	0	18	494	650
Italy	290,224	315,000	1,354	1,348	3,402	3,339	2,047	1,955	166	142	545	650
Netherlands	66,540	80,000	740	743	1,195	1,080	612	607	31	69	173	230
Norway	26,100	32,000	262	170	196	225	402	527	0	0	80	100
Portugal	42,534	75,000	226	300	369	430	354	450	0	26	109	160
Spain	168,346	300,000	1,044	794	1,310	1,588	1,357	1,310	28	71	174	310
Turkey[e]	575,963	530,000	3,358	2,795	1,964	3,120	3,390	3,523	35	43	428	750
UK	192,547	260,000	958	1,015	2,901	3,176	520	636	361	384	710	900
US	137,271	250,000	2,110	4,006	3,476	5,372	1,502	2,492	302	518	253	784

Notes:
[a] Includes TLE with land-based maritime forces (Marines, Naval Infantry etc.).
[b] Does not include land-based maritime aircraft for which a separate limit has been set.
[c] Did not declare its manpower holding at 15 December 1993.
[d] Canada has now withdrawn all its TLE from the ATTU except for the prepositioned stockpile of 6 arty and 14 ACV in Norway.
[e] Manpower and TLE is for that in ATTU zone only.

Peacekeeping Operations

UNITED NATIONS

It has been a year of mixed results for UN peacekeeping operations. The apparent success of UNTAC in Cambodia, whose mission ended on 26 September 1993, has been marred somewhat by divisions within the government, the continued anti-government operations of the Khmer Rouge and the effective resurgence of the civil war. On 11 October 1993, the UN Mission in Haiti (UNMIH) was prevented from landing and has still not been deployed, leading to the view that a military invasion followed by a very much larger peacekeeping force may be needed to remove the military junta. In Somalia, the withdrawal of US forces was followed by that of all the major European contingents. Pakistan's contribution of a force of 7,150 to UNOSOM is now the largest single national contingent in any UN peacekeeping force. The largest peacekeeping operation remains UNPROFOR in the republics of the former Yugoslavia. At the end of June 1994 UNPROFOR's strength, including civilian staff and police, was 40,000 against an authorised establishment of 50,400. The main events which have affected UNPROFOR's operations are described on pp. 73, 74, 273. Three more UN missions have been established in Georgia, Liberia and Rwanda. The transitions experienced by the last of these, UNAMIR, are described on pp. 224, 225, 272.

In New York, the Department of Peacekeeping Operations (DPKO) has been reorganised and the military element substantially reinforced. The DPKO now has two main offices: Planning and Support; and Operations. Planning and Support comprises two divisions: Planning, which also covers civil police matters, demining and training; and Field Adminstration and Logistics, formerly the Field Operations Division of the Department of Administration and Management and now more correctly placed in the DPKO, which has sections responsible for finance, logistics and communications, and personnel matters. Operations is divided regionally with divisions responsible for peacekeeping missions in: Europe and Latin America; Asia and the Middle East; and Africa. The nearly 100 military officers are deployed throughout the DPKO, mainly in the Situation Centre, the Logistics and Communications Service and as support teams for ONUMOZ, UNAVEM, UNOMIL, UNOSOM and UNPROFOR in the Office of Operations.

There have been a number of developments which will greatly improve the smooth running of peacekeeping operations. The Situation Centre, which has been greatly strengthened, has moved to the UN Secretariat building allowing closer coordination with the departments of Political and Humanitarian Affairs. Its electronic equipment has been upgraded and staff procedures introduced. A separate but co-located UN Crisis Centre is being established to support all UN agencies, not just the DPKO. Two long-standing UN customs have been abandoned. The need for planning is now accepted as essential and a team of ten officers are now employed on planning both in generic terms and for specific potential missions. Intelligence is no longer a UN taboo. As peace operations become more complex it has been realised that information collection on a wide range of topics (terrain, communications, personalities as well as military forces) is essential if, for example, humanitarian relief operations such as in Bosnia and Somalia are to be successful.

The team set up to examine the principles for establishing UN stand-by forces has completed its report. On the basis of this, member-states were invited to inform the Secretary-General of the forces and other capabilities they would have available at an agreed state of readiness should they contribute to a peacekeeping operation. By the end of June 1994, 21 member-states had confirmed their willingness to provide stand-by forces, totalling some 30,000. A further 27 states are expected to make contributions which would raise the numbers potentially available to some 70,000. It is the intention to maintain an up-to-date list of stand-by forces so that the composition of new peacekeeping forces can be agreed at an early stage. Experience has shown that the two main problems facing the establishment of a new peacekeeping force are the provision of technical and specialist units and troops, and the time needed to prepare troops for deployment. The stand-by force principle should ease both these problems.

A number of countries and organisations, including the North Atlantic Treaty Organisation (NATO) and the UK and US Armies, have been studying and developing doctrines for what are variously named peace-support operations, peace operations and wider peacekeeping. All involve military activity beyond what is now considered traditional peacekeeping. A large measure of agreement on the key principles of peace operations is apparent. Impartiality, force level, flexibility and unity of command feature in all three doctrines, while mutual respect, transparency, credibility, freedom of movement, consent, security and legitimacy appear in two of the three. The main difference between them is that the US considers peace enforcement a peace operation while NATO and the UK regard this as beyond the Rubicon and an operation of war, waged with a quite different set of principles.

In May 1994, the US Administration published its policy on 'Reforming Multilateral Peace Operations'. The directive addresses six areas:

• US participation: the operation must advance US interests, the consequences of inaction must be unacceptable, its duration must be anticipated.
• US costs: to reduce the costs to the US, the Administration will work to have its share of costs lowered from 31.7% to 25%. Further reductions can be achieved by reform within the UN.
• Command and control: while the President remains Commander-in-Chief, he may place US forces under the operational control of a foreign commander.
• Reform of UN management: a number of the reforms proposed by the US have already been implemented.
• Improving US management: the Department of Defense is to take the lead in managing any operation involving US combat units or likely to involve combat while the State Department only takes the lead in traditional peacekeeping operations.
• Cooperation between the Executive, the Congress and the American public.

United Nations Truce Supervision Organisation (UNTSO)
Mission: Established in June 1948 to assist the Mediator and the Truce Commission in supervising the observance of the truce in Palestine called for by the Security Council. At present, UNTSO assists and cooperates with UNDOF and UNIFIL in the performance of their tasks; Military Observers are stationed in Beirut, South Lebanon, Sinai, Jordan, Israel and Syria.
Strength: 218. **Cost** 1994: $30m.
Composition: Observers from Argentina, Australia, Austria, Belgium, Canada, Chile, China, Denmark, Finland, France, Ireland, Italy, Netherlands, New Zealand, Norway, Russia, Sweden, Switzerland, the US.

United Nations Military Observer Group in India and Pakistan (UNMOGIP)
Mission: To supervise, in the state of Jammu and Kashmir, the cease-fire between India and Pakistan along the Line of Control.
Strength: 40. **Cost** 1994: $8m.
Composition: Observers from Belgium, Chile, Denmark, Finland, Italy, Norway, Sweden, Uruguay.

United Nations Peacekeeping Force in Cyprus (UNFICYP)
Mission: Established in 1964 to use its best efforts to prevent the recurrence of fighting and, as necessary, to contribute to the maintenance and restoration of law and order and a return to normal conditions. Since the hostilities of 1974, this has included supervising the cease-fire and maintaining a buffer zone between the lines of the Cyprus National Guard and of the Turkish and Turkish-Cypriot forces.
Strength: 1,218. **Cost** 1994: $47m.
Composition: Units from Argentina (inf), Austria (inf), UK (inf, hel, log), Staff Officers from Canada, Denmark, Finland, Hungary and Ireland; civil police detachments from Australia, Ireland.

United Nations Disengagement Observer Force (UNDOF)

Mission: To supervise the cease-fire between Israel and Syria, and to establish an area of separation and verify troop levels, as provided in the Agreement on Disengagement between Israeli and Syrian Forces of 31 May 1974.
Strength: 1,033. **Cost** 1994: $35m.
Composition: Units from Austria (inf), Canada (log), Poland (log).

United Nations Interim Force in Lebanon (UNIFIL)

Mission: Established in 1978 to confirm the withdrawal of Israeli forces from southern Lebanon, to restore international peace and security and to assist the government of Lebanon in ensuring the return of its effective authority in the area.
Strength: 5,231. **Cost** 1994: $138m.
Composition: Units from Fiji (inf), Finland (inf), France (log), Ghana (inf), Ireland (inf, admin), Italy (hel), Nepal (inf), Norway (inf, maint), Poland (medical), Sweden (log).

United Nations Observer Mission in El Salvador (ONUSAL)

Mission: Established in July 1991 to monitor agreements concluded between the government and the Farabundo Martí National Liberation Front (FMLN). A peace agreement was signed between the government and the FMLN in January 1992 under which both sides would report their full strength of troops and weapons to ONUSAL, which would also dispose of FMLN weapons as they were handed over during demobilisation. The UN disbanded ONUCA (the UN Observer Group in Central America) in early 1992 and transferred its manpower and equipment to ONUSAL. ONUSAL is to monitor the cease-fire (military observers), monitor human-rights violations (civilian observers) and establish a police force on democratic lines.
Strength: 30, plus 220 civil police. **Cost** 1994: $24m.
Composition: Observers from Argentina, Brazil, Canada, Colombia, Ireland, Spain, Sweden, Venezuela.

United Nations Iraq/Kuwait Observer Mission (UNIKOM)

Mission: Established in April 1991 following the recapture of Kuwait from Iraq by Coalition Forces. Its mandate is to monitor the Khor Abdullah and a demilitarised zone extending 10km into Iraq and 5km into Kuwait from the agreed boundary between the two. It is to deter violations of the boundary and to observe hostile or potentially hostile actions.
Strength: 1,147. **Cost** 1994: $73m.
Composition: Units from Bangladesh (inf), Denmark (admin), Norway (medical). Observers from Argentina, Austria, Bangladesh, Canada, China, Denmark, Fiji, Finland, France, Ghana, Greece, Hungary, India, Indonesia, Ireland, Italy, Kenya, Malaysia, Nigeria, Norway, Pakistan, Poland, Romania, Russia, Senegal, Singapore, Sweden, Thailand, Turkey, UK, US, Uruguay, Venezuela.

United Nations Mission for the Referendum in Western Sahara (MINURSO)

Mission: Established in April 1991 to supervise a referendum to choose between independence and integration into Morocco. A transitional period would begin with a cease-fire and end when the referendum results were announced. Although a cease-fire came into effect on 6 September 1991, the transitional period did not begin as the UN had been unable to complete its registration of eligible voters. MINURSO is currently restricted to verifying the cease-fire. The referendum is now scheduled for 14 February 1995.
Strength: 310. **Cost** 1994: $40m.
Composition: Units from Canada (movement control), Switzerland (medical). Observers from Argentina, Australia, Austria, Bangladesh, Belgium, Canada, China, Egypt, France, Ghana,

Greece, Guinea, Honduras, Ireland, Italy, Kenya, Malaysia, Nigeria, Pakistan, Poland, Russia, Tunisia, US, Venezuela.

United Nations Angola Verification Mission II (UNAVEM II)
Mission: Established in June 1991 to verify the cease-fire as set out in the Peace Accords agreed to by the government of Angola and the National Union for the Total Independence of Angola (UNITA), and to monitor the Angolan police as set out in the Protocol of Estoril. Plans have been prepared at UN Headquarters, New York, for a major reinforcement of UNAVEM should a new peace agreement be reached.
Strength: 62 military and 15 police observers. **Cost** 1994: $25m.
Composition: Observers from Argentina, Brazil, Congo, Guinea-Bissau, Hungary, India, Jordan, Malaysia, Morocco, Netherlands, New Zealand, Nigeria, Norway, Slovakia, Spain, Sweden, Zimbabwe.

United Nations Operation in Somalia (UNOSOM)
Mission: The UN Security Council adopted Resolution 733 on 23 January 1992 which called on all parties to cease hostilities, and which imposed a general and complete embargo on the delivery of army and military equipment to Somalia. The UN Security Council, by its Resolution 751 on 21 April 1992, established an operation to monitor the cease-fire and to provide protection for relief supply convoys, comprising 50 observers and a Pakistani infantry battalion.
Composition: Observers from Bangladesh, the Czech Republic, Egypt, Fiji, Finland, Indonesia, Jordan, Morocco, Pakistan, Zimbabwe; inf bn from Pakistan.

Unified Task Force (UNITAF)
Mission: In November 1992 the US Administration decided that the tragedy in Somalia, and UNOSOM's apparent failure to carry out its mandate, required urgent action which could only be successful with the large-scale deployment of US troops. On 3 December 1992, the UN Security Council adopted Resolution 794 which authorised, under Chapter VII of the UN Charter, 'member states to use all necessary means to establish a secure environment for humanitarian relief operations'. It also authorised the establishment of a unified command. The US deployment, *Operation Restore Hope*, began with a Marine Corps landing overnight on 8–9 December.

The US had always intended that its command of the operation would be of limited length and on 4 May 1993 handed over command and withdrew the bulk of its troops.
Strength: (at its peak) some 35,000, including 28,000 US.
Composition: US: Elements 1st Marine Division, elements 10th Mountain Division, plus supporting elements including special forces, aviation, military police, engineers, public affairs; all told, elements of over 200 army and marine units and sub-units contributed to the force. Countries contributing infantry battalion plus support: Argentina, Australia, Belgium, Canada, Egypt, France, Italy, Morocco, Nigeria, Pakistan, Saudi Arabia. Other force contributions from 18 other countries.

United Nations Operations in Somalia (UNOSOM II)
Mission: On 26 March 1993 the UN Security Council adopted Resolution 814 which authorised, under Chapter VII of the UN Charter, the expansion of UNOSOM and its mandate, initially until 31 October 1993. The resolution 'emphasised the crucial importance of disarmament'. UNOSOM II assumed control of operations in Somalia on 4 May 1993.
Strength: 18,952. **Cost** 1993: $959m; 1994: $1,000m.
Composition: Australia (66), Bangladesh (975), Botswana (425), Egypt (1,689), Ghana (police, 6), India (4,975), Indonesia (4), Ireland (98), Italy (police, 5), South Korea (8), Malaysia (1,094), Nepal (314), Netherlands (police, 7), New Zealand (50), Nigeria (750), Pakistan (7,152), Romania (231), Sweden (police, 3), Zimbabwe (1,100).

United Nations Operations in Mozambique (ONUMOZ)

Mission: Established on 1 March 1993, ONUMOZ's mandate included: monitoring and verifying the cease-fire, separation and demobilisation of forces; collecting and destroying weapons; providing security for vital national infrastructures and for UN and other international aid activities.
Strength: 5,453, plus 476 civil police. **Cost** 1993: $96m; 1994: $327m.
Composition: Units from: Argentina (medical), Bangladesh (inf bn, engr, medical, log), Botswana (inf bn), India (engr, log), Italy (inf bn, aviation, log), Japan (movement control), Portugal (comms), Uruguay (inf bn), Zambia (inf bn). Observers from: Argentina, Bangladesh, Brazil, Canada, Cape Verde, China, Egypt, Guinea-Bissau, Hungary, Malaysia, Netherlands, New Zealand, Russia, Spain, Sweden, US, Uruguay, Zambia. Civil Police from: Australia, Bangladesh, Botswana, Brazil, Egypt, Finland, Hungary, Ireland, Jordan, Malaysia, Norway, Pakistan, Portugal, Sri Lanka, Spain, Sweden, Switzerland, Uruguay.

United Nations Observer Mission Uganda–Rwanda (UNOMUR)

Mission: On 22 June 1993 the UN Security Council adopted Resolution 846 which authorised the deployment of an observer mission to monitor the Ugandan–Rwandan border to verify that no military assistance reached Rwanda.
Strength: 80. **Cost:** see UNAMIR.
Composition: Observers from Bangladesh, Botswana, Brazil, Hungary, Netherlands, Senegal, Slovak Republic, Zimbabwe.

United Nations Assistance Mission for Rwanda (UNAMIR)

Mandate: Established on 5 October 1993 UNAMIR was to monitor the Arusha agreement reached by the Rwandan government and the Rwanda Patriotic Front (RPF), to establish a demilitarised zone between the two sides in northern Rwanda and to assist in the integration of the two armies. UNAMIR had grown to about 2,500 strong when the civil war re-erupted and the genocidal attacks on the Tutsi minority forced the UN to withdraw, except for the Canadian commander and some 250 troops to keep Kigali airport open for aid flights. On 8 June 1994 the UNSC adopted Resolution 925 approving plans to deploy 5,500 peacekeepers to Rwanda. The new force's mandate is to continue to act as an intermediary between the parties and to achieve a cease-fire agreement. It would also contribute to the protection of refugees and other civilians at risk and provide security and support for the distribution of humanitarian relief.
Strength (1 June 1994): 626. **Cost** 1993: $34m; 1994: $98m.
Composition: Ghana, inf unit (326). Observers from Austria, Bangladesh, Canada, Congo, Egypt, Fiji, Ghana, Malawi, Mali, Nigeria, Poland, Russia, Senegal. In July 1994 UNAMIR was reinforced by a Canadian composite signals/movement control unit and the Ghanaian infantry strength has been increased to 560.

Separate Operations

Operation Turquoise: In June 1994 France decided that, as new UNAMIR deployments would not take place for some weeks, unilateral action was necessary. On 24 June some 2,500 French troops began deployment into Zaire and then Rwanda where they established a number of protected areas. As most refugees north of Lake Kiyu had crossed into Zaire around Goma the French declared the area south-west of a line from Kibuye (on Lake Kiyu) to Butare on the Burundi border a protected area. The UN approved the French operation on 22 June and authorised action under Chapter VII of the UN Charter for a period of two months. The French have been asked to remain after 22 August until UNAMIR is fully established, but are adamant they will not do so. Troops from Senegal and Chad have joined *Operation Turquoise*.

Operation Support Hope: The US decided to deploy troops to support humanitarian aid operations and the first elements reached Zaire on 22 July 1994. The main aims of the US operation were to provide purified water and to assist in cargo handling at a number of African airports. Air Force transport aircraft have joined the aid airlift to Goma and Kigale and an air drop of relief supplies was made on 24 July. The US deployment by 1 August was: Kenya (Entebbe, Mombasa, Nairobi) 866; Rwanda (Kigali) 108; Zaire (Goma) 117; Zimbabwe (Harare) 119.

Humanitarian Support: A number of countries have sent military units to provide support for the civil humanitarian aid organisations working in Rwanda and Zaire. It is not always clear whether these are forming part of UNAMIR or not. Contributions include: Australia (medical unit); Israel; (80, field medical unit) UK (to be about 600, medical, field engineers for road, bridge repairs, mechanical engineeers to maintain UN and other aid transport).

United Nations Observer Mission in Georgia (UNOMIG)

Mission: Established by UNSC Resolution 858 on 24 August 1993. Mandate is to verify compliance with the cease-fire agreement of 27 July 1993 between the Republic of Georgia and forces in Abkhazia; to investigate reports of violations and attempt to resolve; and to report to the Secretary-General on implementation of its mandate including violations of the agreement.
Strength: 21. **Cost** 1994: $5m.
Composition: Observers from: Bangladesh, Denmark, Germany, Hungary, Poland, Sweden, Switzerland.

United Nations Observer Mission in Liberia (UNOMIL)

Mission: Established by UNSC Resolution 866 on 22 September 1993, its mandate is to investigate all reports of violations of the cease-fire agreement and report to the Violations Committee; monitor compliance or other elements of the peace agreement of 25 July 1993 signed by the three Liberian parties in Cotonou; observe and verify the elections process; assist in coordination of humanitarian assistance activities; develop a plan for the demobilisation of combatants; train ECOMOG (Military Observer Group of the Economic Community of West African States) engineers in mine clearance; coordinate with ECOMOG in its separate responsibilities.
Strength: 370 including military observers, medical staff and engineers. **Cost** 1994: $65m.
Composition: Troops from Bangladesh; observers from Austria, Bangladesh, China, Czech Republic, Egypt, Guinea-Bissau, India, Jordan, Kenya, Malaysia, Pakistan, Slovakia, Uruguay.

Former Yugoslavia

United Nations Protection Force (UNPROFOR)

Missions:

Croatia: Established in March 1992, UNPROFOR includes military, police and civilian components. It was originally deployed in three United Nations Protected Areas (UNPAs) (four sectors) in Croatia to create the conditions of peace and security required to permit the negotiations of an overall political settlement of the Yugoslav crisis. UNPROFOR is responsible for ensuring that the UNPAs are demilitarised through the withdrawal or disbandment of all armed forces within them, and that all persons residing in them are protected from fear of armed attack. To this end, UNPROFOR is authorised to control access to the UNPAs, to ensure that they remain demilitarised, and to monitor the functioning of the local police to help ensure non-discrimination and the protection of human rights. Outside the UNPAs, UNPROFOR military observers will verify the withdrawal of all Yugoslav Army (JA) and Serbian forces from Croatia, other than those disbanded and demobilised there.

When the UNSC renewed UNPROFOR's mandate in October 1993 it also adopted Resolution 871 which 'Authorises UNPROFOR, in carrying out its mandate in the Republic of Croatia, acting in self-defence, to take the necessary measures, including the use of force, to ensure its security and freedom of movement'.

Bosnia-Herzegovina: On 29 June 1992 the UN Security Council adopted Resolution 761 which authorised the deployment of additional troops to ensure the security and functioning of Sarajevo airport and the delivery of humanitarian assistance. Initially a Canadian battalion deployed to Sarajevo and was relieved by a small headquarters and three battalions of infantry (from Egypt, France and Ukraine). On 13 August 1992 Security Council Resolution 770 was adopted which called on states to take all measures necessary to facilitate the delivery of humanitarian aid. Following the International Conference in London from 26 to 28 August 1992, NATO offered to provide a force with a headquarters to protect aid convoys. The offer was accepted and authorised by Resolution 776 adopted on 14 September. UNPROFOR II commenced its deployment in October 1992 and four battalion groups were deployed. In November, UN Resolution 781 authorised 75 observers to monitor flights over Bosnia. Observers would be stationed at airfields in Croatia, Bosnia and the Federal Republic of Yugoslavia (39 airfield observers are currently deployed).

Resolution 824 adopted on 6 May 1993, after Serbian attacks in eastern Bosnia had left a number of Muslim towns surrounded, declared that: Sarajevo, Tuzla, Zepa, Gorazde, Bihac and Srebrenica would be treated as safe areas; Bosnian Serb units should cease armed attacks there immediately and withdraw to a distance from where they no longer constituted a menace. The deployment of 50 additional military observers was also authorised. When it was seen that UNPROFOR was not strong enough to deploy sufficient forces to the safe areas, the Security Council adopted Resolution 844 which authorised a reinforcement of 7,600 extra troops for their protection. The Resolution reaffirmed the use of air power to protect UNPROFOR troops should this be necessary.

On 9 February 1994, NATO, after a request from the UN Secretary-General, issued an ultimatum to the Bosnian-Serbs. All heavy weapons had either to be withdrawn 20km from Sarajevo or, if left within the area, placed under UN supervision. Any uncontrolled weapons found in the area after midnight on 20 February or anywhere else which fired on Sarajevo would be subject to air attack. On the same day the UN commander in Bosnia arranged a cease-fire in Sarajevo which also included the withdrawal or control of the heavy weapons of both sides and the interposition of UN troops between the two factions. On 18 March agreement was reached on a cease-fire between the Bosnian government and Bosnian-Croat forces throughout Bosnia-Herzegovina. UN troops were to patrol the cease-fire lines. On 31 March, UNSC Resolution 908 authorised a reinforcement of 3,500 troops for UNPROFOR.

On 10 and 11 April, at the height of Serbian attacks on Goradze, close air support was used to protect UN observers there who were under fire. On 22 April, NATO issued a further ultimatum demanding the immediate end to attacks, the withdrawal of troops and unimpeded movement for UN convoys. Later a cease-fire was agreed to and a heavy weapons exclusion zone, 20 km around Goradze, similar to that around Sarajevo, was agreed to. On 27 April the Security Council authorised further reinforcements of 6,550 troops, 150 military observers and 275 civilian police monitors.

Former Yugoslav Republic of Macedonia: In late 1992, President Gligorov requested a UN presence in Macedonia. A mission from UNPROFOR visited Macedonia from 28 November to 3 December 1992 and its report was accepted. UN Resolution 795 authorised the deployment of an infantry battalion and observers to monitor Macedonia's borders with Albania and the Federal Republic of Yugoslavia, and also to act as a deterrent to attack on Macedonia. On 18 June 1993, the Security Council authorised the reinforcement of the Macedonian Command by the United States.

NATO Operations in Support of the UN

***Operation Provide Promise*:** The airlift of humanitarian aid into Sarajevo airport commenced in July 1992. On 22 March 1994, Tuzla airport was opened to aid flights. During the two years to 3 July 1994, some 119,000 tons of stores had been delivered in 9,880 aircraft sorties. In addition over 900 sick and wounded have been flown out. Some 20 countries have contributed aircraft to the airlift. In February 1993 the operation was extended to include the parachute drop of supplies, originally to the besieged Muslims in the enclaves in eastern Bosnia (Gorazde, Srebenica, Zepa) and later to other towns which road convoys could not reach (Maglaij, Mostar, Tarcin, Tesanj). Aircraft from France, Germany and the US have flown 2,800 sorties dropping some 17,900 tons of stores.

Operation Deny Flight: UN Resolution 781 declared a no-fly zone over Bosnia-Herzegovina in October 1992 which was monitored by NATO early-warning aircraft. UNSC Resolution 816, adopted on 31 March 1993, authorised enforcement of the zone and action in the event of violations. NATO aircraft deployed to Italy and the operation began on 12 April 1993. UNSC Resolution 836 of 10 June 1993 which extended UNPROFOR's mandate to include monitoring cease-fires at the safe areas also gave the authorisation for the use of air power to support UNPROFOR in and around the safe areas. NATO agreed to provide the necessary air support. Land-based and carrier-borne aircraft from France, the Netherlands, Spain, Turkey, the UK and the US, together with aircraft from NATO's multi-national airborne early-warning force, have flown a total of 35,720 aircraft sorties between 12 April 1993 and 28 July 1994 consisting of: 12,570 close air support; 12,280 air defence; 3,330 reconnaissance; 3,190 airborne early-warning; 4,350 in-flight refuelling and other support sorties. The composition of the force is given under Italy on p. 57.

Operation Sharp Guard: UN resolutions established an embargo on the provision of weapons and military equipment to Yugoslavia (713 of 1991) and a general trade embargo, excepting medical and food supplies, on Serbia and Montenegro (757 of 1992). UNSC Resolutions 787 of 1992 and 820 of 1993 authorised implementation and enforcement of the embargo. Until June 1993 two separate naval forces, one under NATO control and one under the Western European Union (WEU), challenged some 12,360 merchant ships and boarded over 1,000 for inspection. Naval ships from 14 nations are operating in the Adriatic as part of Combined Task Force 440 which was formed in June 1993. Since then 24,380 merchant vessels have ben challenged and nearly 2,400 boarded or diverted to port. The forces currently deployed on *Operation Sharp Guard* are shown under Italy on p. 57.

Strengths and Composition (as at 29 June 1994) 40,009 (incl civilians and civil police).
Cost 1993: $1,124m; 1994: $1,900m.
UNPROFOR HQ (responsible for overall UN command and direct command of UN units in Croatia): 1,823, incl Swedish HQ Coy and Finnish Guard Coy. **Sector North:** 3,925, incl inf bn from Denmark, Jordan, Poland and Ukraine: **Sector South:** 4,334, incl inf bn from Canada, Czech Republic, Jordan and Kenya. **Sector East:** 1,842, incl inf bn from Belgium and Russia. **Sector West:** 3,060, incl inf bn from Argentina, Jordan and Nepal, Canadian Coy bn. **UNPROFOR spt units:** 2,909, incl log bn from Canada and France, Slovakian engr bn, Netherlands sigs bn, Norwegian movement control, US Hospital.
Bosnia-Herzegovina Command (BHC): 7,096, incl inf bn from France, Pakistan (two, but neither yet at full strength), Turkey, mixed French/Belgian bn, British Force HQ (incl engr, armd recce and naval hel), Danish HQ Coy, Netherlands tpt bn, Belgian tpt unit, French hel unit. **Sector Sarajevo:** 5,043, incl inf bn from Egypt, France (three), Russia and Ukraine (mainly in Zepa), French spt unit, UK arty radar. **Sector South West:** 5,787, incl inf bn from Canada,

Malaysia, Spain, UK (two). **Sector North East:** 2,873, incl inf bn from Netherlands, Nordic countries, Jordanian radar unit. **Goradze:** 477: elements from UK and Ukraine inf bns, Norwegian med coy.
UNPROFOR (M): 1,107, incl inf bn from Nordic countries and US.

OTHER MISSIONS

Under this heading are listed peacekeeping missions not under UN control. There is still insufficient information available on the mandates, strengths and composition of either ECOMOG in Liberia or the peacekeeping forces deployed by the Commonwealth of Independent States (CIS) to list them here, but known troop contributions are listed in the relevant countries entries.

Conference on Security and Cooperation in Europe (CSCE) Missions

Between August 1992 and February 1994 the CSCE has established seven missions to: Skopje (Former Yugoslav Republic of Macedonia), Georgia, Estonia, Moldova, Latvia, Tajikistan and the Federal Republic of Yugoslavia (FRY). This last, which was deployed to Kosovo, Sanjak and Vojvodina, was withdrawn in July 1993 when the FRY refused to extend the mandate further. Each mission has a specific mandate, but in general they all aim to act as an impartial third-party observer ready to offer advice and to promote stability, dialogue and understanding. Most missions consist of around six to eight members, that to Georgia has 17 members.

CSCE Sanctions Assitance Missions (SAMS)

Mission: Between October 1992 and April 1993, SAMS, consisting of varying numbers of Customs Officers, were established in Albania, Bulgaria, Croatia, Hungary, the Former Yugoslav Republic of Macedonia, Romania and Ukraine. Their function is to provide advice to their host- country authorities on the implementation of sanctions imposed by UNSC Resolutions 713 (arms embargo on all former Yugoslav republics), 757 (trade sanctions against Serbia and Montenegro), 787 and 820 (enforcement of sanctions). 165 customs officers are deployed under the coordination of a CSCE/European Union official whose office is in Brussels.

Multinational Force and Observers (MFO)

Mission: Established in August 1981 following the peace treaty between Israel and Egypt and the subsequent withdrawal of Israeli forces from Sinai. Its task is to verify the level of forces in the zones in which forces are limited by the treaty, and to ensure freedom of navigation through the Strait of Tiran.
Strength: 2,600.
Composition: Units from Australia (HQ unit), Colombia (inf), Fiji (inf), France (fixed-wing aviation), Italy (naval coastal patrol), Netherlands (sigs and military police), New Zealand (trg), Uruguay (engr and tpt), the US (inf and log). Staff Officers from Canada and Norway.

Neutral Nations' Supervisory Commission for Korea (NNSC)

Mission: Established by the Armistice Agreement in July 1953 at the end of the Korean War. The Commission is to supervise, observe, inspect and investigate the Armistice and to report on these activities to the Military Armistice Commission. Today its main role is to maintain and improve relations between both sides and thus keep open a channel of communication.
Composition: Diplomats and military officers from Poland, Sweden, Switzerland.

European Community Monitor Mission (ECMM)

Mission: Established in July 1991 by the CSCE it brings together the 12 EC countries and five CSCE countries (Canada, Sweden, Czech Republic, Slovakia and Poland). Its first task was to

monitor and assist with the withdrawal of the Yugoslav Army (JA) from Slovenia. Its mandate was later extended to Croatia and then to Bosnia-Herzegovina. The mission attempts to achieve preventive diplomacy, mediation and confidence-building between the parties. All ECMM monitors work unarmed. The Head of the Mission and the senior staff are found by the EC Presidency and rotate every six months.
Strength: 200 monitors (mainly serving or retired military officers or diplomats) and 200 support staff. Italy provides three helicopters.

Temporary International Presence in Hebron (TIPH)
Mission: Established in April 1994 following the massacre on 25 February by an Israeli settler of about 40 Palestinians praying at Abraham's Tomb in Hebron. TIPH's aim is to promote security; it is to patrol the city of Hebron but has no military or police powers other than to report possible violations of human rights. While TIPH has immunity from arrest and freedom of access, has found itself subject, on occasion, to the curfews imposed on the civil population. The TIPH mandate was not renewed and the mission was withdrawn in July 1994.
Strength: 120 (160 authorised, 60 observers remainder spt staff) from Denmark, Italy, Norway.

Estimating and Interpreting Defence Economic Data

This note expands on the commentary in the 'Layout and Principles of Compilation' on the methods used by the IISS to estimate and interpret defence economic information for *The Military Balance*.

Economic Data

In the case of the many developed and developing countries which comply with the UN System of National Accounts and report national economic performance on a timely and comprehensive basis, the collation of economic data for *The Military Balance* presents no real problems. Such difficulties that occur typically concern gross domestic product (GDP) and GDP *per capita* valuations, and reflect either the effects of exchange-rate fluctuation and currency devaluation which distort dollar conversions over the short term, or those of multiple exchange rates for currencies which are not fully convertible.

More serious difficulties occur, however, in four distinct cases – late-developing countries, transitional economies, countries in which civil war is taking place, and a small number of states which for political reasons are subject to international isolation.

Late-Developing Economies

The reporting of many late-developing countries in Africa, the Caribbean, Central and South America, and Asia is often not only incomplete and of uncertain reliability, but may also lag several years. Whilst current external debt and consumer price inflation data are generally available, consistent real GDP, GDP growth figures and reliable GDP deflators are more elusive. The IISS valuations are averages derived from several sources. Readers should note that, in providing GDP per capita based on purchasing-power parity (ppp), the IISS is in effect giving two estimates of GDP which establish the effective range in the cases where uncertainty exists. Measuring the size of the informal sectors of these economies presents particular difficulties, notably in the case of the poorest economies in Africa and elsewhere. The ppp estimates tend to diverge the most from exchange-rate conversions in the case of these poorest countries.

Transitional Economies

The data released from many transitional economies – those of former communist countries which were part of the fundamentally autarkic Council for Mutual Economic Assistance (CMEA/COMECON) – currently present severe informational problems. Whilst the economic data provided by former non-Soviet member-states of COMECON are increasingly reliable and the reporting consistent with UN principles, the same does not apply for the Russian Federation and the Newly Independent States (NIS) of the former Soviet Union (FSU), excluding Latvia and Estonia. The effects of economic dislocation remain all too evident. Only to some extent can unreliable statistics be attributed to the teething problems of changeover to the complex UN statistical reporting system. More seriously, they may also reflect an overhang of statistical disinformation formerly practised by communist regimes. A further factor is the relative loss of control of the economy by the governments in question – massive tax evasion being the most evident among several symptoms of government failure. Consequently, an unknown proportion of economic activity is under-reported or completely escapes official recording. Under this heading, for example, might be included domestic barter and transactions conducted with foreign currencies, the output from informal employment and self-employment and, most evident in the case of Russia, export/import trade financed by untaxed Russian capital abroad. In addition to these systemic problems, there are also real technical difficulties in compiling economic statistics because of the rapid rate of price changes across factor, product and services markets. In particular, the effects of price inflation and hyper-inflation on what remain the partially autarkic economies of the FSU make international comparisons difficult and will continue to do so until domestic pricing structures conform more closely to international norms. These factors have prompted a cautious approach towards the official statistics of the Russian Federation and other FSU republics by the International Monetary Fund (IMF), which has modified official statistics in the light of its own observation and analysis.

For the reasons set out above, dollar conversion of nominal and real GDP presents a complex problem in the case of all the FSU economies. The IISS uses a ppp estimate rather than an official or market exchange rate wherever the domestic purchasing power of the national currency differs substantially (particularly in the case of non-tradable goods and services) from that reflected in official or, more often, multiple market exchange rates which are based on prices for internationally traded merchandise and services. The IISS dollar valuation of the GDP of the FSU transitional economies has been influenced by two judgements: first, that the differential effects of economic dislocation have in general been more pronounced at the periphery than at the core of the former Soviet empire; and second, that the changes that have occurred reflect irreversible policy decisions by most of the independent republics to break away from the yoke of Soviet or neo-Soviet autarky. It should be noted that Russian GDP has been calculated at the estimated ppp because this is the most realistic valuation – but it is up to three times greater than a valuation derived from any one of several possible exchange rates. GDP dollar conversions of the other FSU republics are derived from exchange rates, and may understate real GDP. For this reason the IISS also provides a GDP *per capita* measure based on ppp to allow the calculation of an alternative estimate of the GDP of the other former Soviet economies if that derived from multiple exchange rates is construed as misleading.

Civil War

Countries in a state of civil war and those recovering from long civil wars naturally present largely insoluble data problems.

International Isolation

There is a small number of countries which have been placed in international isolation. Obvious examples include Libya, Iraq and North Korea. In such cases, data are often unreliable or else in short supply. External sources can provide at best a rough guide to the economic activity of these countries.

Defence Budgets and Expenditures

The reporting of military expenditure by governments is far less comprehensive than is the case for general economic data. For example, of the 184 countries belonging to the UN, only 33 responded in 1992 to the annual questionnaire on military expenditures sent out by the UN Centre for Disarmament Affairs (UNCDA). Military expenditure entries in the annual IMF *International Finance Yearbook* improve on this record, but are missing or lag several years in many instances. Data collation difficulties can be summarised as follows.

Non-reporting

Although the number of governments which release current defence budgetary information in the public domain is larger than the response rate to the UN and IMF suggests, a large minority of UN member-states formally report neither defence budgets nor expenditures. Such practice is usually due to the perception of national security interests and the associated sensitivity of military-related information. Several developing countries in the Middle East, Africa, Latin America and Asia fall into this category, as do more recently some of the former Soviet Union republics.

Under-reporting

Although there exist ready definitions of military expenditure (North Atlantic Treaty Organisation – NATO) and standardised formats for the presentation of disaggregated military expenditure (NATO, UNCDA), many governments only release an aggregate figure. In such cases, it is impossible to be certain what military activities are subsumed under the budgetary heading. The practice identifies those governments which may not be concealing military expenditure, but whose perception of national-security interests causes them to limit transparency to the bare minimum. In addition, where falsification is also present, failure to release disaggregated data prevents verification.

Falsification

Some governments deliberately seek to conceal both the scale and scope of military expenditure. From a strategic perspective, analysis of this category poses the greatest challenge. Where cases of falsification are suspected, the IISS cites both official defence budgets and estimated real military expenditure where there is a material variance. The case studies of Russian and Chinese military accounting are intended to illustrate the problems arising from falsification.

It is also worth noting that differences in budgetary allocation and actual out-turn do not necessarily reflect falsification. For example, the accounting practices of some defence ministries (notably the US Department of Defense and the Japanese Self-Defence Agency) depart from the annualised norm to allow rolling expenditure to be carried over into the next financial year and beyond, in which case outlay may exceed budget. Exceptional circumstances also arise where unforeseen expenditure causes out-turn to rise above budget (e.g., the Gulf War, UN peacekeeping missions, contingency weapons procurement).

The overall effect of these problems is in many instances to set a limit on precise measurement of military expenditure. Where lack of transparency and falsification are also accompanied by economic raw data inadequacies (as is often the case), the statistical manipulation of what raw data exist is subject to a set of additional factors.

Causes of Variance in Military Expenditure Estimates

The shortcomings in raw data account for much of the variance in military expenditure estimates by government agencies and independent research analysts. Thereafter, there are four factors which most affect the estimating process.

Definition of Military Expenditure

Definitions of military expenditure vary. For example, accounting practices in respect of military pensions, paramilitary forces, civil defence and foreign military aid may or may not be included in the defence budget. The IISS method is to cite official defence budgets, and to adjust where necessary military expenditure to include all other military-related spending. The only exception occurs in the case of North Atlantic Treaty Organisation (NATO) countries, where the IISS uses the figures released by governments, and for comparison also cites the NATO-defined expenditures.

Interpretation of Falsification

The most significant factor in causing variance is the interpretation of falsification and the ensuing estimation of concealed expenditure. Here government agencies normally have an informational advantage over other analysts by virtue of their intelligence capability.

Deflating Prices to Constant Values

Differences in the methodology for adjusting current prices to constant prices in the national currency also help to explain material levels of variance. Reliable GDP deflators and sector-specific constant price indices are not available in the case of transitional and many developing economies. Defence-specific deflators have to be estimated from what statistical evidence is available on the macro-economic level and on economy-wide price inflation. Some information may be available on specific economic sectors, but invariably not on the defence sector. Under these conditions variations are bound to arise in the deflating of current prices to constant values.

Purchasing-power Parity and Dollar Conversion

Dollar conversion values are extremely sensitive to assumptions made about purchasing-power parity. Very different pricing structures for capital, equipment and services compared to world levels persist in the defence sectors of transitional and some developing economies. In the latter case, economy-wide price differences extending to the defence sector reflect the level of economic development, a relatively low level of external trade, a reliance on a small number of commodities for export revenue, and the mechanisms of the informal economy. The case of transitional economies subsumes all of these factors and is yet more complex. First, because of pervasive price distortion: under communist central planning, prices were determined by the state rather than markets. Real costs could be disguised through price subsidies to priority supply-side interests (notably defence research and industry). Second, because of the extent of Soviet autarky (extending to COMECON members): external trade to non-communist countries and China accounted for a very small proportion of total COMECON trade, the large part being intra-CMEA trade. In the case of the USSR, total external trade inclusive of COMECON represented only a small proportion of indigenous economic activity. One consequence of this self-sufficiency was that Soviet prices often bore little resemblance to international prices – a situation equally applicable to the defence sector.

The significance of incompatible pricing structures in accounting for dollar conversion variance becomes all the more apparent when taking into account the different methods of estimating purchasing-power parity in defence-specific sectors. Various methods give rise to a range of estimates. High dollar estimates arise when US prices (capital, equipment and services) are used as the measure of value. Low dollar estimates occur when the domestic prices of the country in question are used. In between these high–low estimates come purchasing-power-parity estimates which use international prices as the benchmark. In principle, the purchasing-power-parity method offers the most rigorous solution for determining the relative cost-structure of military expenditure. Some methodological flexibility in the case of countries in transition and some developing economies remains desirable, however, given the raw data limitations in general and those of the defence sector in particular.

Russia's Military Expenditure

Russian military expenditure remains nearly as resistant to precise measurement as that of the USSR. It seems possible that official military expenditure by the USSR and the Russian Federation has declined by over 40% in real terms over the period 1989–94. Although Russia accounted for over 60% of Soviet gross national product (GNP) according to official figures, it is not clear what the Russian share of Soviet military expenditure was, nor what proportion of funds was levied in Russia itself; estimates of Russia's share of Soviet military expenditure range from 60–84%. Allowing for this uncertainty, it seems likely that some part, possibly most, but certainly not all, of the reduction can be attributed to the loss of fiscal revenue from the new republics following the dissolution of the USSR. By comparison, cuts in the defence budgets of some NATO member-states were delayed by the Gulf War and, whilst real defence spending reductions into the late 1990s are typically set to increase to 20–30% against 1989 levels, actual reductions in expenditure to 1994 have generally been restricted to about one-third of this range. There is, however, a significant contrast in the two complementary processes of demilitarisation. Whereas NATO defence spending cuts have been planned and generally transparent, those in the USSR and Russia can only be attributed in part to a coherent policy and cannot be described as transparent. The probability is that they were and remain in part involuntary and, moreover, reversible if a reaction to political and economic reform occurs.

The last commentary on Soviet military expenditure to appear in *The Military Balance* is to be found in the 1991–92 edition. As a rule the IISS chose not to provide independent assessments of Soviet military expenditure, citing data inadequacies and methodological problems as reasons constraining precise measurement, and instead provided a range of estimates supplied to the public domain by governments and independent analysts. Notwithstanding some improvements in transparency initiated by the Gorbachev regime and continued by the Russian government, independent measurement of Russian military expenditure continues to be constrained by uncertainties, largely because official Russian military accounting remains shrouded in secrecy. In addition, there is the new problem of hyper-inflation to reckon with.

Beginning in 1989, the Soviet government released figures on what were claimed to be the real defence budgets of the USSR (rouble 77bn in 1989, or 8.5% of GNP). Previously the Soviets had claimed to be spending about 3% on defence or an annual r17–20 bn during the 1980s. Regarding the earlier official figures, there existed a consensus among NATO intelligence agencies and independent research institutions that actual military expenditure levels were 2–3 times higher than admitted. There are similar doubts to this day about the reliability of Russian military accounting, although it has to be said that the scope for falsification by the Russian Ministry of Defence is reduced by the cooperation between the Russian Ministry of Finance and the IMF.

The official defence budgets of the USSR and Russia for the period 1989–94 are shown in Table 1. Taken at face value, the figures invite two conclusions. First, the effects of high and hyper-inflation in the period 1991–94 have raised the nominal values of defence budgets several fold and have wreacked havoc on the budgetary planning process. Indeed, quarterly budgets were introduced for the period 1992–94 to enable adjustment for inflation. The annual allocation for defence in early 1993 was some r3.5 trillion for the year growing to r6.4tr by mid-year with the allocation for the last quarter alone some r4.5tr. As a consequence of uncontrolled inflation, the Russian government has been unable to calculate and publish a price deflator to establish whether these figures represent real growth or decline. Second, the only trend that is apparent from official data relates to the proportion of GNP/GDP accounted for by the defence budget. Assuming the Russian proportion of Soviet GNP and defence expenditure to be equal (which is not necessarily the case), the official defence budget has declined as a proportion from some 8.5% of GNP in 1989 to a predicted 6% of GDP in 1994, according to the Russian government. Whether this represents a real fall depends, of course, on the size of the difference between the Russian share of Soviet GNP and Russian GDP.

Table 1: Official Defence Budgets of the USSR and Russia (billions of current roubles)

	USSR	Russia	% Growth	% Defence Budget GNP	% Defence Budget GDP
1989	77	-	0	8.5	-
1990	71	-	-8	7.8	-
1991	97	-	-14	6.7	-
1992	-	985	n.k.	-	6.5
1993	-	10,795	n.k.	-	5.5
1994	-	40,626	n.k.	-	6.0

Despite the February 1992 Minsk agreement calling for a common CIS defence budget, it seems likely that Russia has borne the brunt of the costs of the Russian military presence in the newly independent states of the FSU. Confronted with the reality of dissolution of the USSR into independent republics, the Ministry of Defence made an effort early in 1992 to impose a joint defence budget for the first quarter (r50.4bn) on other CIS members of which Russia would pay r42.4bn (84%) and the remaining CIS states the balance of r8bn (16%). Thereafter, as the CIS failed to gain acceptance as a political institution, Russia appeared to abandon the effort to generate a common CIS defence budget. It has also solicited UN funding for peacekeeping operations in the FSU, albeit unsuccessfully to date.

Some effort has also been made to release official disaggregated expenditures by function (Table 2). It should be emphasised that these contain the bare minimum of information, and cannot be verified by cross-checking with other official statistics such as real salary levels and weapon and equipment procurement quantities. However, one important conclusion may be drawn from the official data which is supported by other evidence. These figures suggest that there has been a significant increase in expenditure on Personnel, Operations and Maintenance (PO&M) – from 26% in 1989 to 54% in 1994 – on Infrastructure (from 6% to 12%) relative to Procurement (down from 42% to 21%) and on Research and Development (R&D) (down from 20% to 6%). If the evidence of reductions in Russian defence budgets over those of the USSR is accepted, a plausible deduction would be that the brunt of the real cuts have been in procurement (which is supported by other evidence) and R&D (for which there is less evidence). The PO&M figures are also compatible with the increasing use of short-contract volunteers (160,000–200,000 by the end of 1993) in the Armed Forces to counteract the effects of severe manpower shortages caused by deferment from, and evasion of, compulsory military service.

Table 2: Official Defence Budgets by Expenditure Function (billions of current roubles)

	1989	%	1991	%	1994	%
PO&M	20.2	26	30.3	31	22,105	54
Procurement	32.6	42	38.8	40	8,442	21
R&D	15.3	20	12.7	13	2,433	6
Infrastructure	4.6	6	5.9	6	4,778	12
Pensions	2.3	3	3.9	4	1,994	5
Demilitarisation	-	-	-	-	874	2
Other	2.3	3	4.9	5	-	-
Total	77.3	100	96.5	100	40,626	100

Numbers may not add up because of rounding.

Soviet defence budgets did not include all military expenditure as defined by NATO. For example, the budgets of the Ministry of Internal Affairs (MVD) – r5.6bn – and the Committee for State Security (KGB) – r4.9bn – were released for the first time in 1991, confirming that funding for these organisations had hitherto not been part of the official defence budget. Two other major sources of funds for the military which were contained in the budget for 'Appropriations of Financing the Development of the National Economy' subsumed price supports for both defence R&D and industry. These and similar instances of concealed Soviet military expenditure in central government budgets and extra-budgetary accounts had long been identified in principle by NATO agencies and independent analysts and the limited efforts at transparency during the last years of the USSR merely confirmed previous assessments.

To make official figures realistic, therefore, it is necessary to add estimations of concealed spending to the budgetary allocations. This provides an enlarged rouble figure to which two adjustments have to be made. First, there has to be adjustment for inflation to enable assessments of real growth and decline. The IISS uses IMF statistics for industrial producer and labour price inflation together with an estimate of defence-specific price escalation across capital (i.e., human, technological and land resources), equipment and labour-market sectors. Second, inflation together with an estimate of defence-specific price escalation across capital (i.e., human, technological and land resources), equipment and labour-market sectors. Second, conversion to a convertible currency (typically the US dollar) is required to enable international comparisons of the real level of military spending. Dollar conversion of official defence budgets and independent assessments of real expenditures is a perennial problem. These problems remain in the Russian case due to the continuing existence of substantial differentials between domestic Russian and world price. In the period 1992–94, the existence of multiple exchange rates signified the continuing non-convertibility of the Russian rouble, although there were signs by 1994 that the gap between Russian and world prices is closing.

For illustrative purposes, estimates of real Soviet expenditures for selected years from 1985–91 by the US Arms Control and Disarmament Agency (ACDA) are shown in Table 3. These estimates represent the high end of non-communist calculations of real Soviet military expenditure (about three times the official budgetary figures at the prevailing official exchange rate) and also of real Soviet GNP (estimated at nearly two-thirds of the USA's in 1985 and just under half in 1991 compared to official estimates of between one-quarter and one-fifth). ACDA adds the qualification that its estimates are based on what it would cost the US in dollars to generate a military effort equivalent to that of the USSR, noting that estimates of this type may overstate the relative scale of Soviet expenditures because US prices and wage rates are assumed.

Table 3: ACDA Estimates of USSR Military Expenditure (in constant 1993 $ billion)

	Military Expenditure ($bn)	GNP ($bn)	% ME/GNP
1985	364	2,778	13
1989	346	3,018	11
1990	319	2,911	11
1991	273	2,662	10

Source: ACDA, *World Military Expenditures and Arms Transfers 1991–1992* (Washington DC: USGPO, 1993).

The IISS dollar estimates (Table 4) of Soviet and Russian defence budgets have been calculated from official and IMF economy-wide and sectoral price inflation indices with adjustments for defence-specific price levels. Some important conclusions may be drawn about the funding priorities in contemporary Russian defence budgets.

Table 4: IISS Dollar Valuation of USSR and Russian Defence Budgets (in constant 1993 $ billion)

	1989	%	1991	%	1994	%
PO&M	35	26	33	31	41	54
Procurement	57	42	43	40	16	21
R&D	27	20	14	13	5	6
Infrastructure	8	6	7	6	9	12
Pensions	5	3	5	4	3	5
Demilitarisation	-	-	-	-	2	2
Other	4	3	6	5	-	-
Total	136	100	107	100	77	100

Numbers may not add up because of rounding.

First, the 1994 Russian defence budget has declined in real terms by over 40% compared to the 1989 Soviet budget. The IISS believes that the largest effective cut may have occurred as a result of the political and economic dislocation of 1991–92 and may have been to some extent involuntary, as neither the Ministry of Finance nor the Ministry of Defence were able to adjust to the loss of fiscal and monetary control over the former Soviet republics and, indeed, Russia itself. Since 1992, the IISS believes that Russian defence budgets have been effectively static in real terms with perhaps a small increase in 1994. This assumption contradicts assessments of real decline in defence budgets based on the evidence of GDP decline in official statistics and cautiously supported by the IMF. Since defence budgets officially account for 5–6% of GDP in 1993–94, after successive annual GDP declines of 11.5% in 1993 and a projected 10–12% in 1994, it follows, according to the official line, that defence budgets must also have fallen as GDP has shrunk. The IISS purchasing-power-parity estimates for the 1992 and 1993 defence budgets ($77bn) constitute very different values from those derived from market exchange rates ($40bn in 1992 and $29bn in 1993) cited in the two previous editions of *The Military Balance*. Since the defence budget does not cover all military-related activities, this estimate represents the low end of a range of possible expenditures.

Second, funding priority has switched from procurement to personnel, operations and maintenance. PO&M funding may have increased by as much as 75% since 1989. Third, procurement expenditure has more than halved. This assessment is consistent with other evidence of greatly reduced levels in output of weaponry and military equipment in the Russian defence industry compared to the Soviet era. Russian arms sales have also greatly declined from Soviet levels, although much of the fall can be attributed to the emphasis on hard-currency earnings initiated under the Gorbachev regime. In 1992, according to official figures, arms deliveries were worth $1.5bn, increasing to $1.9bn in 1993. There is also evidence of a substantial cut in real expenditure on R&D which appears less plausible, given the stated policy of the Ministry of Defence to modernise weapons and equipment in the light of experience drawn from the performance of Soviet weaponry in the 1991 Gulf War. It is therefore conceivable that additional R&D funding may be contained in other parts of the State budget and extra-budgetary accounts. Finally, the official Border Guard budget, which is not part of the defence budget, amounts to r2.2tr in 1994. Questions remain about other military expenditure not apparently accounted for in the defence allocation, including that on space, the intelligence services, and R&D and defence industry subsidies.

In summary, the IISS estimate of a $78bn (in constant 1993 US$) defence budget for Russia in 1994 has to be qualified by the reminder that official military accounting by the Ministry of Defence remains far from transparent even before the technical problems of hyper-inflation and purchasing-power parity are addressed, and that this figure probably understates actual military expenditure. It represents the low end of a range of possible expenditure. Defence cuts in the USSR and Russia appear to have been relatively more substantial than those in NATO member-states over the period 1989–90, as much the result of involuntary as planned policy, and are more easily reversible given that democracy has yet to take root in Russia. Finally, in any global comparison Russian military expenditure remains in real terms substantially higher than that of any country apart from the USA, even at the low estimate derived from official budgets. There should also be caution about attributing too much significance to apparently low current spending levels. A balance sheet of Russian military assets would reveal what is also evident from the scale and scope of Russia's military establishment – namely, that Russia remains a formidable and unpredictable military power.

Reader Reaction Questionnaire

A Reader Reaction Questionnaire was enclosed in copies of *The Military Balance 1993–1994* sent to IISS Members and publications subscribers. In all, some 6,000 questionnaires were sent out. To date, some 220 have been returned, not an encouragingly high proportion. What was encouraging, however, was the tenor of the replies which were generally very favourable to the present format. Completed questionnaires were received from 41 countries and from a wide range of people: the military; diplomats; academics; and journalists.

On the whole, the response was positive; the majority wanted little changed. While a number of proposals for added improvements were welcomed, there were no suggestions as to what could be dropped that is currently included. The page length of *The Military Balance* is restricted by the publisher's contract, and for some years now the book has been overlength, a cost borne by the IISS. However, under the proposed contract with the new publisher, page length will be increased from 240 to 320 pages. Although it is not intended to expand to the full length immediately, most of the suggested improvements can be introduced in the next two to three years.

Respondents found the introductory prose to each regional section helpful: most praised the practice of highlighting the major changes in organisation and weapons holdings noted in the previous 12 months. It remains important for *The Military Balance* clearly to distinguish between genuinely new developments, and those that have only been revealed by improved information although they occurred some time earlier. The majority favoured including more information on strategic events and potential problems, a practice introduced rather tentatively in 1993 and continued in this edition.

Encouragement was given to continue to include, as in past years, tables comparing the characteristics of major weapons systems, such as attack aircraft, artillery and tanks. The increased page length should mean that a number of comparative tables, not just one, can be included every year. The effort involved in up-dating an annual table is, of course, far less than creating it, more or less from scratch, every five or so years. More information was requested on nuclear and chemical weapons, although there is a distinct possibility, bar certain notable exceptions, that their utility is being increasingly questioned and their numbers are being significantly reduced. More information was also asked for on ballistic missiles and on the emerging new 'exotic', and in some cases non-lethal, weapons.

Over 30 responses supported more information on peacekeeping operations, and an attempt will be made to expand the data given on each mission and provide, where relevant, a short commentary on its success or otherwise over the previous 12 months. While obtaining basic information on UN operations is relatively straightforward, it is more difficult to obtain information on those mounted by other organisations, such as the Economic Community of West African States (in Liberia) and the Commonwealth of Independent States in regions of the former Soviet Union, such as Abkhazia/Georgia, Dniestr/Moldova and Tajikistan. Details of multinational operations, such as the air exclusion zones over Bosnia, and sanctions enforcement, for example in the Adriatic, have been included in the Peacekeeping section.

A very large number of suggestions was made regarding maps. The idea of including a map of each regional section was popular, and this will shortly be achieved. Of the nine regional sections in *The Military Balance*, four normally have a dedicated map, although the whole of the East Asia and Australasia region cannot be usefully portrayed on a single page, and a fifth covers Europe, thus serving both the NATO and Non-NATO Europe sections (although with the development of NACC, Partnership for Peace and the European Stability Pact this distinction becomes increasingly blurred). No maps have been included this year because of page length overrun, but they will be reinstated in 1995–96.

Some 80 suggestions for improving the detail provided by the regional maps and for including those depicting other strategic topics were made. Unfortunately, *The Military Balance* page size very much restricts the amount of detail that can be clearly shown, particularly as colour cannot be used. It is appreciated that maps that only show political boundaries are not adequate (this realisation was the motivation behind the Institute's efforts to publish a strategic atlas which over 75% of respondents said they would buy. The project is currently in abeyance as no publisher can be found to take on the project and guarantee a realistic copy price). The loose wall map was also considered useful and over 50 suggestions for future topics were made. There is undoubtedly a great interest in maps and many readers would like to see significant statistics presented graphically rather than laboriously hunting through the relevant pages of text.

More information on the defence industry was requested and over 70 suggestions for the sort of information to be included were put forward. *The Military Balance* does not intend to compete with the wealth of detailed data and statistics provided by the *Stockholm International Peace Research Institute Yearbook*. It intends purely to cover, once the relevant information has been collected, industrial capability. This means what each country can manufacture and, equally, or possibly more important, what it must import. This section will consider not only major weapons and equipments, but also important components, be they aero-engines or silicon chips. It may, however, be a year or two before this development can be introduced.

Economic and demographic improvements were suggested in some 50 responses. Information on the break-down of defence expenditure into categories such as Research and Development, Procurement, Operations and Maintenance, is even more difficult to obtain than accurate data on total defence spending – and this is not easy. The IISS Defence Economist will continue to gather as much detailed data as possible from as many countries as possible, but the data are unlikely to be published as they will be so incomplete. However, enquiries can always be made to the Institute's Information Section regarding specific countries. A major problem lies in the true comparison of defence expenditure between states where difficulties over exchange rates exist. This topic is covered more fully on pp. 278–85 of this edition. More data regarding significant ethnic minority populations are being published in the book.

The questionnaire also asked whether significant equipments other than weapon systems should be included. Some suggestions were made as to what these might be and, from this year, two new systems have been included: mortar/artillery-locating radar; and unmanned aerial vehicles (UAV) used for reconnaissance and intelligence-gathering. It was also asked whether other Air Force information was required and many more suggestions, over 40, were received. While most suggestions were eminently sensible, acquiring the necessary data would be difficult, indeed virtually impossible. As a start, where available, the average annual hours flown by air crew is being published.

Finally, some 70% of respondents supported the idea of including an annual chronology of military events. This would cover international treaties, significant operational events (invasions, cease-fires) and major equipment introductions. The idea needs to be developed further and will not be introduced until it is clear how much of the additional page length will be taken up by the other proposals which are being introduced.

While the IISS is most grateful for the replies to the questionnaire received and for the excellent suggestions made, the level of response was disappointing. Copies of the questionnaire are still available for anyone who would like to comment in full on the contents of *The Military Balance*. Individual comments and suggestions for improvements are welcome at any time, as are comments and criticisms as to the accuracy of the data portrayed.

ABBREVIATIONS

<	under 100 tons
–	part of unit is detached/less than
+	unit reinforced/more than
*	training aircraft considered as combat capable
†	serviceability in doubt
ε	estimated
‘ ’	unit with overstated title/ ship class nickname
AA(A)	anti-aircraft (arty)
AAM	air-to-air missile
AAV	amphibious armoured vehicle
AAW	anti-air warfare
AB	airborne
ABD	airborne division
ABM	anti-ballistic missile
about	the total could be higher
ac	aircraft
ACM	advanced cruise missile
ACV	air cushion vehicle/vessel/ armoured combat vehicle
AD	air defence
adj	adjusted
AE	auxiliary, ammunition carrier
AEF	auxiliary, explosives and stores
AEW	airborne early warning
AF	stores ship with RAS capability
AFB/S	Air Force Base/Station
AGHS	hydrographic survey vessel
AGI	intelligence collection vessel
AGM	air-to-ground missile
AGOR	oceanographic research vessel
AGOS	ocean surveillance vessel
AH	hospital ship
A(I)FV	armoured (infantry) fighting vehicle
AIP	air-independent propulsion
AK	cargo ship
ALCM	air-launched cruise missile
amph	amphibious/amphibian
AMRAAM	advanced medium-range air-to-air missile
AO	tanker(s) with RAS capability
AOE	auxiliary, fuel and ammunition, RAS capability
AOT	tanker without RAS capability
AP	passenger ship
APC	armoured personnel carrier
Arg	Argentina
ARM	anti-radiation (anti-radar) missile
armd	armoured
arty	artillery
AS	submarine depot ship
aslt	assault
ASM	air-to-surface missile
ASTT	anti-submarine TT
ASUW	anti-surface-unit warfare
ASW	anti-submarine warfare
AT	tug
ATACMS	army tactical missile system
ATBM	anti-tactical ballistic missile
ATGW	anti-tank guided weapon
ATK	anti-tank
Aust	Australia
avn	aviation
AWACS	airborne warning and control system
BB	battleship
bbr	bomber
bde	brigade
bdgt	budget
Be	Belgium
BMD	ballistic missile defence
bn	battalion/billion
bty	battery
Bu	Bulgaria
cal	calibration
CAS	close air support
casevac	casualty evacuation
Cat	Category
cav	cavalry
cbt	combat
CBU	cluster bomb unit
CC	cruiser
Cdn	Canada
cdo	command
CFE	Conventional Armed Forces in Europe Treaty
CG	SAM cruiser
CGH	CG with helicopters
CGN	nuclear-fuelled CG
cgo	freight aircraft
Ch	China (PRC)
civ pol	civilian police
COIN	counter-insurgency
comb	combined/combination
comd	command
comms	communications
CONUS	Continental United States
coy	company
CV	aircraft carrier
CVBG	carrier battle group
CVN	nuclear-fuelled CV
CVV	V/STOL and hel CV
CW	chemical warfare/weapons
Cz	The Czech Republic
DD	destroyer
DDG	destroyer with area SAM
DDH	destroyer with hel
DDS	dry dock shelter
def	defence
defn	definition
det	detachment
div	division
Dk	Denmark
ECM	electronic countermeasures
ECR	electronic combat and reconnaissance
ELINT	electronic intelligence
elm	element
engr	engineer
EOD	explosive ordnance disposal
eqpt	equipment
ESM	electronic support measures
est	estimate(d)
EW	electronic warfare
excl	excludes/excluding
exp	expenditure
FAC	forward air control
fd	field
FF	frigate
FFG	frigate with area SAM
FFH	frigate with helicopter
FGA	fighter, ground-attack
flt	flight
FMA	foreign military assistance
FMF	foreign military financing
Fr	France
FRY	Federal Republic of Yugoslavia
FSU	former Soviet Union
ftr	fighter (aircraft)
FW	fixed-wing
FY	fiscal year
GDP	gross domestic product
Ge	Germany
GNP	gross national product
gp	group
Gr	Greece
GS	General Service (UK)
GW	guided weapon
HARM	high-speed anti-radiation missile
hel	helicopter
HMMWV	high mobility multipurpose wheeled vehicle
HS	Home Service (UK)
HWT	heavy-weight torpedo
Hu	Hungary
hy	heavy
ICBM	intercontinental ballistic missile
IMET	international military education and training
imp	improved
incl	includes/including
indep	independent
Indon	Indonesia
inf	infantry
IRBM	intermediate-range ballistic missile
Is	Israel
It	Italy
JSTARS	joint strategic airborne reconnaissance system
KT	kiloton
LAMPS	light airborne multi-purpose system
LANTIRN	low altitude navigation and targeting infra-red system night
LCA	landing craft, assault
LCAC	landing craft, air cushion
LCM	landing craft, mechanised

LCT	landing craft, tank
LCU	landing craft, utility
LCVP	landing craft, vehicles and personnel
LGB	laser-guided bomb
LHA	landing ship, assault
LKA	assault cargo ship
log	logistic
LPD	landing platform, dock
LPH	landing platform, helicopter
LSD	landing ship, dock
LSM	landing ship, medium
LST	landing ship, tank
lt	light
LWT	light-weight torpedo
maint	maintenance
MBT	main battle tank
MCC/I/O	mine countermeasures vessel, coastal/inshore/ offshore
MCMV	mine countermeasures vessel
MD	Military District
mech	mechanised
med	medium
MG	machine gun
MHC/I/O	minehunter, coastal/inshore/ offshore
MICV	mechanised infantry combat vehicle
mil	military
MIRV	multiple independently-targetable re-entry vehicle
misc	miscellaneous
Mk	mark (model number)
ML	minelayer
mob	mobilisation/mobile
mod	modified/modification
mor	mortar
mot	motorised/motor
MLRS	multiple-launch rocket system
MPA	maritime patrol aircraft
MPS	marine prepositioning squadron
MR	maritime reconnaissance/ motor rifle
MRBM	medium-range ballistic missile
MRD	motor rifle division
MRL	multiple rocket launcher
MRR	motor rifle regiment
MRV	multiple re-entry vehicle
MSC/I/O	minesweeper, coastal/ inshore/offshore
msl	missile
MT	megaton
mtn	mountain
n.a.	not applicable
NBC	nuclear, biological and chemical
NCO	non-commissioned officer
n.k.	not known
Nl	Netherlands
nm	nautical mile
NMP	net material product
No	Norway
nuc	nuclear
obs	observation
OCU	operational conversion unit(s)
off	official
OOA	out of area
OOV	objects of verification
op/ops	operational/operations
org	organised/organisation
OTH	over-the-horizon
OTH-B	over-the-horizon backscatter (radar)
OTHR	over-the-horizon radar
OTHT	over-the-horizon targeting
para	parachute
pax	passenger/passenger transport aircraft
PCC/I/O	patrol craft, coastal/ inshore/offshore
pdr	pounder
PFC/I/O	fast patrol craft, coastal/ inshore/offshore
PFM	fast patrol craft, SSM
PFT	fast patrol craft, torpedo
PHM/T	hydrofoil, SSM/torpedo
pl	platoon
Pol	Poland
POMCUS	prepositioning of materiel configured to unit sets
Port	Portugal
ppp	purchasing-power parity
publ	public
RAS	replenishment at sea
RCL	recoilless launcher
R&D	research and development
recce	reconnaissance
regt	regiment
RL	rocket launcher
Ro	Romania
ROC	Republic of China (Taipei)
ro-ro	roll-on, roll-off
RPV	remotely piloted vehicle
Rus	Russia
RV	re-entry vehicle
SAM	surface-to-air missile
SAR	search and rescue
SEAL	Sea–Air–Land
SES	surface-effect ship
SEWS	satellite early-warning system
SF	Special Forces
SIGINT	signals intelligence
sigs	signals
SLBM	submarine-launched ballistic missile
SLCM	sea-launched cruise missile
SLEP	service life extension programme
some	up to
Sov	Soviet
Sp	Spain
SP	self-propelled
spt	support
sqn	squadron
SRAM	short-range attack missile
SRBM	short-range ballistic missile
SS(C/I)	submarine (coastal/inshore)
SSB	ballistic-missile submarine
SSBN	nuclear-fuelled SSB
SSGN	SSN with dedicated non-ballistic missile launchers
SSM	surface-to-surface missile
SSN	nuclear-fuelled submarine
START	Strategic Arms Reduction Talks
STOL	short take-off and landing
STOVL	short take-off, vertical landing
SUGW	surface-to-underwater GW
Sw	Sweden
SWATH	small waterplane area twin hulled (vessel)
Switz	Switzerland
sy	security
t	tonnes
TA	Territorial Army (UK)
tac	tactical
TASM	tactical air-to-surface missile
TD	tank division
tempy	temporary
tk	tank
tkr	tanker
TLE	treaty-limited equipment (CFE)
TMD	theater missile defense
tps	troops
tpt	transport
tr	trillion
trg	training
TT	torpedo tube
Tu	Turkey
UAV	unmanned aerial vehicle
UN	United Nations (see pp. 268–77 for peacekeeping forces)
URG	underway replenishment group
USGW	underwater-to-surface GW
UUGW	underwater-to-underwater GW
veh	vehicle
VIP	very important person
VLS	vertical launch system
V(/S)TOL	vertical(/short) take-off and landing
wg	wing
wpn	weapon
Yug	Yugoslavia